INTELLECTUAL PROPERTY AND THE COMMON LAW

In this volume, leading scholars of intellectual property and information policy examine what the common law – understood broadly as a method of reasoning, an approach to rulemaking, and a body of substantive law – can contribute to discussions about intellectual property. Drawing on a range of interdisciplinary ideas and principles that are embedded within the working of the common law, the volume shows that answers to many of modern intellectual property law's most puzzling questions may be found in the versatility and adaptability of the common law in all of its wisdom. The various chapters argue that, despite the degree of interdisciplinary specialization that the field sees today, intellectual property is fundamentally a creation of the law; and that the basic building blocks of the law can shed important light on the working of our various intellectual property regimes.

Shyamkrishna Balganesh is an Assistant Professor of Law at the University of Pennsylvania Law School. His scholarship focuses on understanding how intellectual property and innovation policy can benefit from the use of ideas, concepts, and structures from different areas of private law. He obtained his J.D. from Yale Law School, where he was an Articles & Essays Editor at the *Yale Law Journal* and a Student Fellow at the Information Society Project.

Intellectual Property and the Common Law

Edited by

SHYAMKRISHNA BALGANESH

University of Pennsylvania Law School

CAMBRIDGE
UNIVERSITY PRESS

CAMBRIDGE
UNIVERSITY PRESS

32 Avenue of the Americas, New York, NY 10013-2473, USA

Cambridge University Press is part of the University of Cambridge.

It furthers the University's mission by disseminating knowledge in the pursuit of education, learning, and research at the highest international levels of excellence.

www.cambridge.org
Information on this title: www.cambridge.org/9781107014152

First published 2013

Printed in the United States of America

A catalog record for this publication is available from the British Library.

Library of Congress Cataloging in Publication Data
Intellectual property and the common law / edited by Shyamkrishna Balganesh, University of Pennsylvania Law School.
pages cm
Includes bibliographical references and index.
ISBN 978-1-107-01415-2 (hardback)
1. Intellectual property. 2. Common law. I. Balganesh, Shyamkrishna, editor of compilation.
K1401.I5524 2013
346.04'8–dc23 2013011076

ISBN 978-1-107-01415-2 Hardback

Contents

Contributors

Shyamkrishna Balganesh is an Assistant Professor of Law at the University of Pennsylvania Law School.

Dan L. Burk is the Chancellor's Professor of Law at the University of California-Irvine School of Law.

Eric R. Claeys is a Professor of Law at the George Mason University School of Law.

Thomas F. Cotter is the Briggs and Morgan Professor of Law at the University of Minnesota Law School.

Hanoch Dagan is the Stewart and Judy Colton Professor of Law at the Tel-Aviv University Faculty of Law.

Richard A. Epstein is the Laurence A. Tisch Professor of Law at the New York University School of Law. He is also the Peter and Kirsten Bedford Senior Fellow at the Hoover Institution and the James Parker Hall Distinguished Service Professor of Laws (Emeritus) and Senior Lecturer at the University of Chicago.

Jeanne C. Fromer is a Professor of Law at the New York University School of Law.

Wendy J. Gordon is a William Fairfield Warren Distinguished Professor and Professor of Law at Boston University School of Law.

Paul J. Heald is a Professor of Law at the University of Illinois College of Law.

Steven Hetcher is visiting scholar at the University of Tennessee, Knoxville, School of Law.

David Lametti is an Associate Professor of Law at the McGill University Faculty of Law.

Mark A. Lemley is the William H. Neukom Professor of Law at the Stanford Law School.

Margaret H. Lemos is a Professor of Law at the Duke University School of Law.

Mark P. McKenna is a Professor of Law at the Notre Dame University Law School.

Peter S. Menell is the Koret Professor of Law at the University of California Berkeley Law School.

Gideon Parchomovsky is the Robert G. Fuller, Jr., Professor of Law at the University of Pennsylvania Law School.

Lee Petherbridge is a Professor of Law and the Richard A. Vachon, S.J. Fellow at Loyola Law School, Los Angeles.

Michael Risch is a Professor of Law at the Villanova University School of Law.

Jennifer E. Rothman is a Professor of Law and the Joseph Scott Fellow at Loyola Law School, Los Angeles.

Emily Sherwin is a Professor of Law at the Cornell University Law School.

Henry E. Smith is the Fessenden Professor of Law at the Harvard Law School.

Madhavi Sunder is a Professor of Law at the University of California Davis School of Law.

Molly Shaffer Van Houweling is a Professor of Law at the University of California Berkeley School of Law.

R. Polk Wagner is a Professor of Law at the University of Pennsylvania Law School.

Christopher S. Yoo is the John H. Chestnut Professor of Law, Communication, and Computer & Information Science and the Founding Director of the Center for Technology, Innovation and Competition at the University of Pennsylvania.

Acknowledgments

This volume originated at a symposium on the connection between intellectual property and the common law, held at the University of Pennsylvania Law School on May 6–7, 2011. The symposium was sponsored by the law school's Center for Technology, Innovation and Competition (CTIC), and it brought together a wonderful group of scholars working in the areas of intellectual property law, common law, and legal philosophy. Most of the chapters in this volume were presented in draft form at the symposium and formed the basis for discussion there. I am especially grateful to my colleague Christopher S. Yoo for encouraging me to explore the connection between intellectual property and the common law, which is the dominant theme in my own work, as part of a full symposium and volume (his idea that I should look for a theme that "really pops" resonated well with me). I would also like to thank my other colleagues on the Penn Law faculty who work on intellectual property issues – David Abrams, Gideon Parchomovsky, and R. Polk Wagner – for their encouragement, and Dean Michael Fitts for his unfailing support and help in making the symposium happen.

Working with the authors of the chapters in this volume has been a genuine pleasure, and I am grateful to them for the readiness with which they all embraced the broad theme, even when it did not fully fit with their prior research, and for sharing in my general sentiment that there was indeed something meaningful to explore in the connection between intellectual property and the common law. I owe each of them a debt of gratitude for their creative contributions to the volume and, above all, for their patience and cooperation during the editing process. At the law school, Anna Gavin played a pivotal role in helping with the logistics of the symposium from which this volume arose. I also owe special thanks to my research assistant at the law school, Eric Hague, who did a masterful job editing the various chapters, and to John Berger at Cambridge University Press for facilitating the endeavor.

Introduction

Exploring an Unlikely Connection

*Shyamkrishna Balganesh**

I. BACKGROUND: WHAT IS THE COMMON LAW?

On the face of things, the areas of intellectual property and the common law may seem to have very little in common. The common law is often viewed as an archaic body of rules and principles with little direct relevance to contemporary issues and debates. Intellectual property law, by contrast, is in large measure a modern subject, dealing with the regulation of culture, technology, and informational goods. What then might a body of law that had its origins in the twelfth century contribute to discussions about a subject that is about regulating innovation and creativity – and thus, the future? As it turns out, quite a lot indeed.

As a preliminary, appreciating the depth and pervasiveness of this connection necessitates an understanding of what indeed it is that the "common law" connotes. The common law is ordinarily thought to consist of legal rules that are almost entirely the creation of judges. Indeed, this institutional aspect – the equation of the common law with its "judge-made" status – is today the dominant way of defining what the common law is. As one noted scholar of the common law thus defines it, "[t]he common is that part of the law that is not based on [authoritative] texts, but instead is within the province of the courts themselves to establish."[1] Yet, hidden underneath this salient institutional dimension are other equally important facets to the common law, and it is hard to determine the extent to which these facets were influenced by (and not themselves influences on) the common law's judge-made nature. As Roscoe Pound put it more broadly, the common law "is essentially a mode of judicial and juristic thinking, [and] a mode of treating legal problems rather than a fixed body of definite rules."[2] The common law was, to Pound, synonymous with "our Anglo-American legal tradition."[3]

* Assistant Professor of Law, University of Pennsylvania Law School.

[1] Melvin Aron Eisenberg, The Nature of the Common Law vii (1988).

[2] Roscoe Pound, The Spirit of the Common Law 1 (1921).

[3] *Id.*

Pound's observations are telling, because they echo the idea that the common law is at base a way of thinking about rules and institutions and the deployment of an "arsenal of sound common sense principles" during the process.[4] This idea no doubt revolves around the concept of heightened judicial involvement in the lawmaking process, but it certainly entails more. In its broadest sense then, the "common law" in the United States today implicates *five* possible ideas about the law and lawmaking, and most uses of the phrase – both in this volume and elsewhere – invoke some or all of them.

1. *As judge-made law*. This is the standard and indeed most common use of the phrase. Used in this sense, the phrase ordinarily entails an allusion to the question of separation of powers and the institution that is most appropriately suited to the task of lawmaking in an area.[5] Situations where judges actively *make* the law, rather than just interpret and apply it, are taken to be covered by the idea.
2. *As a mode of legal reasoning*. Judge-made law ordinarily follows a form of reasoning that is fairly distinctive, given its attempt to develop a forward-looking rule while at the same time focusing on the dispute at hand and relying on precedent for support. When used in this sense, scholars associate the common law with a form of practical reasoning that relies heavily on analogy, coherence, and incremental modification over time. It is in this sense that some use the phrase "the common law method."[6]
3. *As state rather than federal law*. This dimension of the common law is unique to the United States. With the Supreme Court's famous observation in *Erie* that "there is no federal general common law" in the country, in areas where Congress does not actively delegate lawmaking to federal courts or other narrowly circumscribed domains, federal courts are routinely seen as incapable of making law.[7] State courts were, as a result, to be the primary creators of the common law, which was thus state law. When used in this context the common law is synonymous with state law, even in situations where such law is not entirely uncodified.
4. *As an evolving and pluralistic body of law*. One of the features of legal rules that originate in judicial decisions is their intrinsic malleability in order to accommodate new situations. This dynamism imbues such rules with a fallibility that is rarely seen in relation to statutory law or indeed in judicial interpretations

4 Mogul Steamship Co. v. McGregor, 23 Q.B.D. 598, 611 (1889).
5 *See generally* NEIL K. KOMESAR, IMPERFECT ALTERNATIVES: CHOOSING INSTITUTIONS IN LAW, ECONOMICS, AND PUBLIC POLICY (1997).
6 *See* RICHARD B. CAPPALLI, THE AMERICAN COMMON LAW METHOD (1997); Frederick Schauer, *Is the Common Law Law?*, 77 CAL. L. REV. 455 (1989).
7 Erie R.R. Co. v. Tompkins, 304 U.S. 64, 78 (1938).

of statutes (i.e., "statutory precedents").[8] It also allows the law and lawmaking exercise to consider a variety of normative ideas and values in the formulation of the rule, given the intertemporal nature of any rule and its development. Consequently, it is not uncommon to use the term "common law" to connote bodies of rules that are developed inductively, from individual situations, and that accommodate a variety of normative goals in their functioning.

5. *As certain foundational subject areas*. The "common law" is also routinely used to reference the law's basic substantive areas of tort, property, contracts, and crimes (and in other common law countries, unjust enrichment), which form the building blocks of most other subject areas and were developed entirely by courts incrementally.[9] This is not to suggest that there aren't other – more advanced – areas that would fit this description just as well (e.g., antitrust law), just that ordinary usage routinely looks to these subjects, all of which constitute the standard first-year curriculum in most U.S. law schools.

II. OVERVIEW

Every one of these understandings of the common law has something important to contribute to discussions of intellectual property, and the chapters in this volume seek to illuminate the extent, significance, and likely implications of this interaction. Using this classification, these five understandings might thus be categorized into five broad themes, depending on the specific aspect of the common law that forms their focus.

A. *Judge-Made Intellectual Property Law*

Most intellectual property law today is statutory. Patent, copyright, and trademark law in the United States are today codified at the federal level.[10] Nonetheless, an unappreciated reality of U.S. intellectual property, across different regimes, is the fact that, despite this codification, courts continue to play an extremely important role in developing the law gradually. This process is seen in a variety of contexts: when the statute is silent and consciously delegates the development of a rule to courts, when the statute is ambiguous and necessitates judicial creativity to give it meaning and purpose, when the statute does not cover all of the doctrine in an area, or indeed when a regime is developed by state courts, completely independent of

[8] *See* William N. Eskridge, Jr., *Overruling Statutory Precedents*, 76 Geo. L.J. 1361, 1362 (1988) (outlining the hierarchy involved in courts' presumptions on the correctness of decisions).

[9] As an illustration, these were the standard subjects covered by Holmes in his classic book on the subject. *See* Oliver Wendell Holmes, Jr., The Common Law (1897).

[10] *See* 35 U.S.C. §101 *et seq.* (2005) (federal patent law); 17 U.S.C. §101 *et seq.* (2005) (federal copyright law); 15 U.S.C. §§1051–1141 (2005) (federal trademark law).

both federal and state legislative enactments. Each of these realities gives the lie to the idea that intellectual property (IP) lawmaking is within the exclusive purview of legislatures, and several chapters in this volume explore different dimensions of "judge-made" IP law.

In his contribution to the volume, Hanoch Dagan argues that there is nothing distinctive (or "exceptional") about property institutions that necessitates a heightened passivity among judges in relation to lawmaking.[11] Indeed there might – and indeed are – situations where courts have distinct institutional advantages over legislatures and ought to exercise their lawmaking abilities within these contexts. Although he does not suggest that judicial lawmaking is to be preferred in the context of property, he remains equally skeptical of "property exceptionalism," which asks judges to refrain from lawmaking in the areas of property and intellectual property. In Chapter 2, Henry Smith explores one such distinct context in which judicial lawmaking is often criticized: the judge-made IP doctrine of misappropriation.[12] Smith argues that those skeptical of misappropriation and its utility routinely fail to appreciate the fact that its origins were in "equity" rather than the traditional common law, a form of judge-made law that originated to mitigate the rigors of the common law. Equity works to control opportunistic behavior made possible by the common law, which Smith illustrates by offering a reconstruction of the misappropriation doctrine.[13]

Peter Menell and Margaret Lemos, in their respective contributions, offer various analytical and interpretive lessons that flow from recognizing the role that judges play in IP lawmaking. In Chapter 3, Menell systematically traces the symbiotic role that Congress and the courts have played in developing federal patent and copyright law, something that their facial statutory nature does not fully capture; he argues that this "mixed heritage" requires courts to trace the origins of a doctrine or proposition of law more fully before they choose an appropriate interpretive framework to use in molding and applying it.[14] Lemos asks a more general question: is the category of "common law statutes," which are treated as delegations of lawmaking power by Congress to courts, an analytically coherent category? She answers the question in the negative, arguing that the label obscures a variety of important institutional and normative questions that ought to be openly discussed, even (and perhaps, especially) in subject areas where courts might indeed be better than legislatures at law- and policy making.[15]

11 Hanoch Dagan, *Judges and Property*, *in* INTELLECTUAL PROPERTY AND THE COMMON LAW, in this volume.

12 Henry E. Smith, *Equitable Intellectual Property: What's Wrong with Misappropriation?*, in this volume.

13 *Id.*

14 Peter Menell, *The Mixed Heritage of Federal Intellectual Property Law and Ramifications for Statutory Interpretation*, in this volume.

15 Margaret H. Lemos, *Interpretive Methodology and Delegations to Courts: Are "Common-Law Statutes" Different?*, in this volume.

A few other contributions examine the role of judicial lawmaking within specific areas of IP law. Two chapters do so within the context of patent law's claim construction exercise. In Chapter 5, Dan Burk examines what the claim construction process might learn from the process of statutory interpretation, a task that courts at all levels routinely employ.[16] Noting that the jurisprudence of claim construction is entirely judge-made, Burk argues that courts would stand to benefit from an approach that eschews formalism in favor of one that he describes as "dynamic claim interpretation," which builds on the idea of dynamic statutory interpretation and modifies it to the context of patent law.[17] In the following chapter Polk Wagner and Lee Petherbridge undertake an empirical examination of the impact that one landmark en banc common law decision of the Federal Circuit, on the question of claim construction, actually has had on the jurisprudence in the area.[18] In *Phillips* v. *AWH*[19] the Federal Circuit, which sees itself as tasked with managing patent law jurisprudence, sought to clarify its rules on claim construction in an effort to provide lower courts (and presumably, parties) with clear guidance. Examining later opinions on claim construction, the authors conclude that the *Phillips* opinion was largely unsuccessful in its efforts at clarifying the law, which continues to remain in a state of disarray and inconsistency.

Michael Risch examines the effect that codification has had on the law of trade secrets.[20] Unlike the dominant forms of IP law, trade secret law was originally entirely judge-made, being a creation of state common law courts. After decades of common law development by state courts, the Uniform Trade Secrets Act (UTSA) was passed, which has since been adopted by forty-six states. Risch's chapter explores, using empirical methods, the impact that this codification has had on the substantive law; he shows that a majority of courts continue to rely on traditional common law rules and precedents even in the face of the statute and examines the conditions under which they do so. In his contribution to the volume, Christopher Yoo asks a similar question in relation to copyright law and the comprehensive codification of the subject that Congress undertook in 1976.[21] Arguing that courts have continued to develop copyright law in common law fashion, Chapter 8 examines the propriety of this reality, concluding that the debate about the appropriate institutional role in copyright law needs to be more "context-specific," with courts avoiding broad generalization in favor of a more granular and provision-specific approach.

16 Dan L. Burk, *Dynamic Claim Interpretation*, in this volume.

17 *See* William N. Eskridge, Jr., Dynamic Statutory Interpretation (1994).

18 R. Polk Wagner & Lee Petherbridge, *Did* Phillips *Change Anything? Empirical Analysis of the Federal Circuit's Claim Construction Jurisprudence*, in this volume.

19 Phillips v. AWH Corp., 415 F.3d 1303 (Fed. Cir. 2005).

20 Michael Risch, *An Empirical Look at Trade Secret Law's Shift from Common to Statutory Law*, in this volume.

21 Christopher S. Yoo, *The Impact of Codification on the Judicial Development of Copyright*, in this volume.

B. *The Common Law Method in Intellectual Property*

In developing the law through individual cases on an incremental basis, common law courts have long been known to employ a host of distinctive methods and techniques, which together comprise the common law method. These methods include the use of "analogical reasoning" in relying on prior decisions as precedent to formulate new rules,[22] the process of incremental (or gradual, context-specific) rule development,[23] and the reliance on customary practices in developing the law.[24] Courts involved in IP disputes too routinely deploy several of these techniques, with mixed results, and three chapters in this volume examine their pros and cons, offering different prescriptions for courts engaged in the process.

Tom Cotter in Chapter 9 explores what "legal pragmatism," long known to be the preferred method of rule development in the common law, can bring to lawmaking in intellectual property. Identifying the contextualization of thought, a rejection of foundationalism, an emphasis on consequences, situation sensitivity, and the use of practical reason as legal pragmatism's key attributes, Cotter argues that when applied to IP lawmaking, legal pragmatism has both strengths and weaknesses. He concludes that courts relying on it ought to do so in a nondogmatic and open-minded manner, recognizing that it is not likely to be a panacea for all hard questions and that it too – like most methods of legal reasoning – has important limitations when applied within certain contexts.[25]

In her chapter, Jennifer Rothman cautions against the unthinking use of custom in deciding IP cases. Noting that hallmarks of the common law method of reasoning have been its use of custom and its attempt to generalize a rule of conduct from the actual practices of parties, Rothman argues that IP law needs to adopt a more nuanced process of examining customary practices before treating them as sources of law. Examining how courts have used custom in the context of copyright's fair use defense, Rothman concludes that the utility of custom as a source of law depends on a variety of context-specific considerations, which courts ought to pay close attention to before converting custom into law.[26]

Analogical reasoning – the process of developing a rule of decision from prior opinions – is commonly taken to be the "classical" form of common law reasoning, and some scholars have argued that as a form of legal reasoning it is both autonomous

[22] *See* Cass R. Sunstein, *On Analogical Reasoning*, 106 Harv. L. Rev. 741 (1993); Melvin A. Eisenberg, *The Principles of Legal Reasoning in the Common Law*, *in* Common Law Theory 81, 96–101 (Douglas Edlin ed. 2007).

[23] *See* Richard A. Epstein, *Cybertrespass*, 70 U. Chi. L. Rev. 73, 73 (2003).

[24] *See* N. Neilson, *Custom and the Common Law in Kent*, 38 Harv. L. Rev. 482 (1925); A.W.B. Simpson, *The Common Law and Legal Theory*, *in* 1 Folk Law: Essays in the Theory and Practice of *Lex Non Scripta* 119 (Alison Dundes Renteln & Alan Dundes eds. 1994).

[25] Thomas F. Cotter, *Legal Pragmatism and Intellectual Property Law*, in this volume.

[26] Jennifer E. Rothman, *Copyright, Custom, and Lessons from the Common Law*, in this volume.

and distinctive.[27] In her contribution to the volume, Emily Sherwin argues that, at least within the context of making laws for the Internet and information distribution therein, analogical reasoning is fraught with problems. Examining the doctrine of cybertrespass that courts developed to deal with information misuse on the Internet, Sherwin argues that reasoning by analogy is largely illusory as a stand-alone method. She notes that, in reality, judges purporting to reason from analogy are either engaged in a process of natural reasoning to what John Rawls described as a "reflective equilibrium" or in a rule-based decision-making process and shows how these methods might have been at play in cybertrespass.[28]

C. *State Intellectual Property Law*

The federal nature of the U.S. legal system has meant that both federal and state regimes of intellectual property have existed side-by-side for a long time. Although patent law and copyright law are today principally federal, other regimes of intellectual property such as trademark law, the law of trade secrets, publicity rights, and misappropriation operate either at both federal and state levels (e.g., trademark law) or exclusively at the state level. This has in turn prompted the development of a set of second-order rules to determine when and under what circumstances the presence of federal law has displaced state law on an issue: this is the question of federal preemption.[29] Whereas federal patent and copyright law seek to preempt most forms of analogous state law, federal trademark law is less restrictive and only preempts "interference[s]" from state law,[30] which has in turn allowed state trademark law to coexist with federal trademark law. Two contributions to this volume examine the interaction between federal and state intellectual property laws.

In Chapter 12, Jeanne Fromer seeks to make sense of the Supreme Court's somewhat confusing jurisprudence relating to the federal preemption of state IP laws. She argues that this jurisprudence is best understood against the backdrop of the Intellectual Property Clause of the U.S. Constitution (contained in Article I, Section 8, Clause 8), which informs Congress's purpose and intent behind the federal patent and copyright laws. Although it is not preemptive on its own, she nonetheless concludes that this clause adds content to the Court's preemption jurisprudence and suggests that state laws are preempted whenever they fall within the clause's "preemptive scope" and attempt to undermine the "balance" that Congress sought to give effect to in its federal laws.[31]

[27] *See* Gerald J. Postema, A Similibus ad Similia: *Analogical Thinking in Law, in* COMMON LAW THEORY 102, 103–08 (Douglas Edlin ed. 2007).

[28] Emily Sherwin, *Common Law Reasoning and Cybertrespass*, in this volume.

[29] *See generally* Viet D. Dinh, *Reassessing the Law of Preemption*, 88 GEO. L.J. 2085 (2000).

[30] *See* 15 U.S.C. §1127 (2005) ("The intent of this chapter is to . . . protect registered marks used in such commerce from interference by State, or territorial legislation.").

[31] Jeanne C. Fromer, *The Intellectual Property Clause's Preemptive Effect*, in this volume.

Whereas Fromer's chapter focuses on patent and copyright law – given that trademark law is not covered by the Intellectual Property Clause of the Constitution – Mark McKenna's contribution does just the opposite: it examines the interaction between federal and state trademark laws. The concurrent existence of federal and state trademark laws has often led to the observation that state trademark law continues to play an important (and independent) role in the area. McKenna argues that this belief is mistaken: state trademark law, both as a historical matter and in the present, has played a fairly insignificant "substantive" role in the area, which has seen an extensive amount of federalization over the years. He concludes by arguing that, given this reality, scholars would do well to examine and understand the reasons for this federalization and engage with it directly – to see if trademark law ought to move in the direction of patent and copyright law in this respect.[32]

D. *Plural Values in Intellectual Property*

Utilitarianism, often couched in economic terms, is today the dominant way of thinking about (and justifying) intellectual property. This dominance has in many ways undervalued the possibility of additional normative values and considerations working within various IP regimes and interfacing with their broad utilitarian mandate. One of the enduring features of the common law has remained its value pluralism: its ability to accommodate a multiplicity of considerations – both deontological and consequentialist – within its functioning through a variety of structural and functional mechanisms. Three chapters argue that IP law can, ought to, and perhaps already does build on the common law to internalize some of these methods and ideas.

In my own chapter, I focus on the role that the "normative structure" of a regime can play in informing its goals and ideals. I argue that the economic account of copyright law, which is today the dominant approach to understanding the institution, originated as an explanatory and positive account rather than as a justificatory and openly prescriptive one. In contrast, copyright's core architecture has remained constant over time, and its reliance on the idea of "exclusion" and "liability" reflects a deeper commitment to the ideal of outcome responsibility. Although these ideas are in the end perfectly compatible with the institution's overall functioning in utilitarian terms, they nonetheless remain distinct and independently valuable.[33]

Madhavi Sunder's contribution argues that this pluralism – originating in the common law – is indeed at work in the law of trade secrets, which contemporary analyses of the subject all too often ignore in focusing on its role as a mechanism of incentives in promoting the goal of economic efficiency. Examining the historical evolution of trade secret law and its connection to the employment market and

[32] Mark P. McKenna, *Trademark Law's Faux Federalism*, in this volume.
[33] Shyamkrishna Balganesh, *The Normative Structure of Copyright Law*, in this volume.

conditions therein, she concludes that the values of human freedom, development, and democracy have played an important role in the development and functioning of the law of trade secrets and that they are in many ways compatible with the idea of economic efficiency on which modern accounts of the law seem to focus. Remembering trade secret law's origins in the common law, she argues, will ensure that we neither forget nor reject these "broad-ranging values."[34]

In Chapter 16 David Lametti argues that various areas of intellectual property all reflect an "ethical teleology" that is all too easily glossed over when we discuss the system in individualistic, rights-based terms. Drawing on "virtue ethics," a branch of philosophy that traces itself back to Aristotle and that has begun to gain some prominence in the world of property theory, Lametti argues that an "ethical thread" might indeed be constructed that encapsulates the interconnected areas of private law, property, and intellectual property. Central to this ethical thread is a commitment to enlightened, self-reflective, and self-critical judgment and to the deployment of practical reason to realize a balanced decision-making process. Scholars have routinely noted how these ideals are a central feature of the common law process, and Lametti's chapter makes a persuasive argument for their instantiation in both property and intellectual property.[35]

E. *Parallels between the Substantive Common Law and Intellectual Property*

Beyond its origins in judicial opinions, the "common law" also routinely connotes a set of basic subject areas, all of which are today the staple of the first-year law school curriculum: torts, contracts, property, and criminal law. In innumerable ways, the basic edifices of intellectual property – whether patent, copyright, trademark law, or various other state regimes – are built on these foundational common law areas, a reality that has produced its own set of debates about how best to use, extend, or indeed minimize the functional salience of this provenance. Property law has clearly been the most visible area of influence in these debates, and more recently tort law has emerged as an entrant into the fray. Several chapters in this volume examine different aspects of this parallelism or provenance, suggesting a variety of prescriptive solutions. They may be usefully grouped into three categories based on the substantive area of the common law in which they seek their parallels.

Two chapters focus on the relationship between IP law and the common law rules of real property. In Chapter 17, Molly Van Houweling examines the lessons that the real property rules relating to servitudes might hold for intellectual property, specifically in relation to information costs. She focuses on one type of information cost that is of special importance to intangible rights such as intellectual property – "tracing costs" – the costs associated with identifying and locating the

34 Madhavi Sunder, *Trade Secret and Human Freedom*, in this volume.

35 David Lametti, *Laying Bare an Ethical Thread: From IP to Property to Private Law?*, in this volume.

owner of a right. She concludes that intellectual property might usefully incorporate several strategies seen in the law of servitudes, including modifications to the current law relating to exhaustion.[36] Eric Claeys' chapter focuses on a conceptual confusion, which he argues has obscured IP scholars' engagement with the institution of property over the years. Whereas most scholars have focused on property as the right to exclude in discussing its application to intellectual property, Claeys argues that some intellectual property rights such as trade secrets and misappropriation are better understood as usufructuary rights, which he defines as "a proprietor's right to use an asset, to continue using it, and to be free from attempts to divert his efforts to extract benefits from it." Claeys concludes that this conceptual confusion about property and its different manifestations have together produced an anti-property turn in IP scholarship, which is worthy of reexamination.[37]

Two chapters in the volume examine the relationship between intellectual property and the law of torts, an interface that has begun to assume some importance in recent scholarship.[38] Both chapters, somewhat interestingly, examine this interaction within the context of copyright law. In his contribution, Steven Hetcher argues that the common description of liability for copyright infringement as strict is inaccurate; as a descriptive – rather than normative – matter, copyright law today already incorporates a "fault standard" into its functioning, in the nature of the fair use doctrine. He argues that the fair use doctrine ought to be understood as a component of the plaintiff's prima facie case, as a result of which the plaintiff would bear the burden of proving that the defendant's copying constituted an "unfair use" (in addition to the other elements that the plaintiff needs to establish) and suggests that a variety of important structural and practical considerations are likely to flow from this understanding.[39] In Chapter 20, Wendy Gordon unpacks the nature of the copyright tort. She argues that the ideas of "harm" and "fault" already play a role in its functioning and that an ideally reformulated version of the tort should perhaps give a more significant role to the concept of "harm." The chapter examines what "harm" can or should mean by reviewing four plausible candidates for cognizable harm in copyright law (rivalry-based losses, foregone fees, loss of exclusivity, and subjective distress) and canvassing three philosophical conceptions of "harm" (counterfactual, historical-worsening, and noncomparative), and discusses the appropriateness of using each in the copyright context. While Gordon argues that there remain too many issues that need to be resolved before harm becomes a formal pre-requisite for liability in copyright, her chapter takes steps toward resolving

36 Molly Shaffer Van Houweling, *Technology and Tracing Costs: Lessons from Real Property*, in this volume.

37 Eric R. Claeys, *Intellectual Usufructs: Trade Secrets, Hot News, and the Usufructuary Paradigm at Common Law*, in this volume.

38 *See, e.g.*, Avihay Dorfman & Assaf Jacob, *Copyright as Tort*, 12 THEORETICAL INQ. IN LAW 59 (2011); Shyamkrishna Balganesh, *The Obligatory Structure of Copyright Law: Unbundling the Wrong of Copying*, 125 HARV. L. REV. 1664 (2012).

39 Steven Hetcher, *The Fault Liability Standard in Copyright*, in this volume.

some of these open issues, and suggests that copyright law and theory would benefit from a more nuanced engagement with the idea.[40]

The next two chapters look to the common law for substantive comparisons, but without limiting themselves to one or more (or indeed any) specific areas of law for the analysis. Analyzing the role of "unfair competition" in the common law, Gideon Parchomovsky and I examine how the concept has played an underappreciated yet important role in shaping different common law actions, several of which relate to intellectual property. In this chapter, we argue that unfair competition has played a dual role in the common law – as a structural principle and as a normative ideal – and that the interaction between these roles has allowed it to be employed to frame, broaden, or cabin different IP rights in various contexts.[41] In Chapter 22 Mark Lemley examines the structure of modern patent law to argue that we have moved from a "holistic" approach to patent adjudication, which involved comparing the plaintiff's product against the defendant's, to a "fractioned" approach that parses the infringement inquiry into a host of smaller questions, with the patentee required to win on all of these questions to succeed on the overall claim. The older, flexible system was a product of equity and functionally favored patentees. Although Lemley is agnostic on the question of which system is preferable overall, he concludes that recognizing this evolution in approach as a contributing factor is important in discussions about patent reform.[42]

The last two chapters in this category move from the varied rights structures in different common law areas to the remedies that the common law – or more specifically, the law of equity – affords IP rights-holders and the lessons one might draw about these remedies based on their origins in equity. Both chapters discuss the use of injunctions in patent cases, but focus on different forms that this relief takes and the effects that it has on the system's overall functioning. Paul Heald's chapter focuses on permanent injunctions in patent disputes and the ways in which such injunctions operate as punitive measures in actual practice. It examines how permanent injunctions routinely operate as the equivalent of punitive damages in practice, explores the economic rationale and idea behind punitive damages in the common law, and suggests that courts awarding permanent injunctions learn from the common law and its shaping of punitive damages to avoid the unintended consequence of imbuing such remedies with a punitive dimension when completely unnecessary.[43] In Chapter 24, Richard Epstein examines a different aspect of injunctive relief in patent cases: situations of "sequential injunctions," where a plaintiff is granted an injunction for a second (or later) time after the defendant attempted

[40] Wendy J. Gordon, *The Concept of "Harm" in Copyright*, in this volume.

[41] Shyamkrishna Balganesh & Gideon Parchomovsky, *The Role of Unfair Competition in the Common Law*, in this volume.

[42] Mark A. Lemley, *The Fractioning of Patent Law*, in this volume.

[43] Paul J. Heald, *Permanent Injunctions as Punitive Damages in Patent Infringement Cases*, in this volume.

to design around the patent that it was initially found to be infringing. The chapter focuses on a seminal case that discussed this very issue and adopted a new standard – *TiVo* v. *Echostar*[44] – in which Epstein filed an amicus brief on behalf of the plaintiff. The chapter argues that the old standard was preferable to the new one for a variety of functional and conceptual reasons; Epstein concludes that the lower court's "pro-property approach" is favorable to the Federal Circuit's "pro-defendant" one.[45]

CONCLUSION: A COMMON THEME

Given the diversity of methodologies, substantive areas, normative positions, and indeed conceptions of the common law adopted by these chapters, it might seem as though they lack a common theme. Despite their superficial incoherence, the various contributions to this volume do indeed come together to advance a simple, yet fundamentally important idea. In the last few decades, especially with the advent of the Internet, IP law scholarship has been characterized by a growing degree of specialization. Scholars within one area of intellectual property, or adopting one methodological orientation within the field, only rarely look to other areas of IP law (let alone to other areas of the law more generally) or methodologies for analogies, parallels, and guidance, which has produced a somewhat fragmented scholarly community. In spite of their specialized area and subject matter, each of the chapters in this volume stands for the common idea that looking to the common law for guidance – through analogies, structural principles, doctrinal affinities, and historical lessons – can indeed be a fruitful exercise, not because the past matters in some dispositive way, but rather because the common law embodies a wide variety of ideas and concepts that form the building blocks for the more advanced, specialized areas of law that are the mainstay of the legal system today, such as intellectual property. They thus stand for the ultimate realization that, despite the degree of interdisciplinary specialization that the field today sees, intellectual property is fundamentally a creation of the law, and this being the case, the basic building blocks of the law can indeed shed important light on what intellectual property can, should, and was perhaps meant to be.

At first blush, this idea may seem somewhat elementary. Yet, it is far too easy to lose sight of it, given the numerous invaluable contributions that the disciplines of economics, philosophy, political science, cultural theory, and history have made to intellectual property. It is through the law as a melting pot and in legal analyses that these various disciplines find their means of contributing to the subject of intellectual property. Indeed, it falls to the law to translate these disciplines' insights and contributions into meaningful normative outcomes and positions, all in the quest

44 TiVo, Inc. v. Echostar Corp., 646 F.3d 869 (Fed. Cir. 2011).

45 Richard A. Epstein, *Sequential Injunctions in Patent Litigation: The Gratuitous Novelty of TiVo* v. *EchoStar*, in this volume.

of welfare and justice. And to do so, the law looks to its timeworn concepts, ideas, devices, and techniques, employing what is commonly described as the process of "thinking like a lawyer."[46] It is precisely this exercise – of thinking like a common lawyer and using the common law's accumulated wisdom – that this volume collectively seeks to bring to bear on some of the most pressing questions of intellectual property and information regulation. In setting the stage for a common law approach to IP questions, its objective is hardly to develop a new way of thinking about the subject; it is instead to offer "a new name for some old ways of thinking,"[47] in the hope that these old ways do not fall into complete desuetude.

46 *See, e.g.*, FREDERICK SCHAUER, THINKING LIKE A LAWYER: A NEW INTRODUCTION TO LEGAL REASONING (2012).

47 *See generally* WILLIAM JAMES, PRAGMATISM: A NEW NAME FOR SOME OLD WAYS OF THINKING (1907).

PART I

Judge-Made Intellectual Property Law

1

Judges and Property

*Hanoch Dagan**

INTRODUCTION

Much of private law in the common law tradition is judge-made law. Both the significant impact that judges have had in the past on the laws of contracts, torts, and restitution and the continuous active role of adjudication in private law's normative development – at times as interpreters of legislated statutes – are taken as obvious features of these fields.[1] Property law may seem different. Many years ago, the English legal historian W. S. Holdsworth noted that "the Legislature has had a larger share in shaping the land law than it has had in shaping any other branch of private law."[2] Recently, the dominance of legislation seems as apparent regarding property's frontiers: the law of intellectual property.[3] As Shyamkrishna Balganesh – a friend of common law – observes, "the frequency with which Congress amends the patent and copyright statutes seems to leave little doubt that it alone determines intellectual property's precise content and coverage."[4]

These descriptive propositions should be treated cautiously,[5] but may nonetheless seem conceptually tempting. They may invite a claim regarding the deep

* Stewart and Judy Colton Professor of Law, Tel-Aviv University Faculty of Law. Thanks to Lisa Austin, Shyam Balganesh, Eyal Benvenisti, Michael Birnhack, Avihay Dorfman, Ron Harris, Shelly Kreiczer-Levy, Roy Kreitner, David Lametti, Daphna Lewinsohn-Zamir, David Schorr, Henry Smith, Molly Van Houweling, Christopher Yoo, and Ben Zipursky for their helpful comments.

1 *See, e.g.*, Melvin A. Eisenberg, *Principles of Legal Reasoning in the Common Law*, *in* COMMON LAW THEORY 81, 82 (Douglas E. Edlin ed. 2007).

2 W.S. HOLDSWORTH, AN HISTORICAL INTRODUCTION TO THE LAND LAW 325 (1927).

3 Some scholars resist this classification of copyright. I address this concern infra, text accompanying notes 41–42.

4 Shyamkrishna Balganesh, *The Pragmatic Incrementalism of Common Law Intellectual Property*, 63 VAND. L. REV. 1543, 1544 (2010).

5 Reliance on Holdsworth's statement must be of limited value in this context given that his book was published shortly after the massive statutory revision of land law in England. Nor is it at all clear that legislation dominated American property law (particularly in comparison to contract law, given the predominant status of the Uniform Commercial Code). *See, e.g.*, GREGORY S. ALEXANDER,

foundations of property law, which makes property conceptually distinct from other areas of private law. Property, in this view, is by essence less amenable to judge-made law than the rest of private law. An even more important lesson that might be learned is that judges should altogether avoid the business of affecting – creating, modifying, or abolishing – property rights, leaving this task entirely to legislatures. This temptation of property exceptionalism seems to be validated by the *numerus clausus* principle, which prescribes that, at any given time, property law offers only a limited number of standardized forms of property. As a principle of "judicial conservatism regarding innovation in the system of property rights," which is a typical feature of many (and perhaps most) modern legal systems,[6] *numerus clausus* may be interpreted as the doctrinal manifestation of such property exceptionalism.

I begin this chapter with the claim that the temptation of property exceptionalism should be resisted. I recognize that, in certain property law contexts, the appropriate judicial strategy is indeed passivity and deference. This is the case, for example, when the property right in question has been crafted only recently by the legislature or where a property innovation can best be implemented via a regulatory structure, such as a formal registration of rights. These examples are quite obvious because they represent particular cases with close analogies outside property law, which specifically tilt considerations of democratic legitimacy or expected performance in favor of judicial conservatism. Because the sense in which these important considerations call for judicial conservatism in these cases applies also to parallel cases in other areas of private law (and of law at large), they cannot support the position of property exceptionalism.

Although I dispute the exceptionalists' presentation of property's uniqueness and therefore reject their blueprint for a priori judicial conservatism, I do not deny that property has typical characteristics. The character of property – its role in creating and sustaining important default frameworks of interpersonal interaction with respect to resources that consolidate people's expectations and express the law's normative ideals for such core types of human relationships – both explains and justifies *numerus clausus* as a principle of *legal* conservatism. But this understanding

COMMODITY & PROPRIETY: COMPETING VISIONS OF PROPERTY IN AMERICAN LEGAL THOUGHT 1776–1970, at ch. 4 (1997) (discussing the limited success of the New York legislature's attempt to launch a comprehensive revision of land law); STUART BANNER, AMERICAN PROPERTY: A HISTORY OF HOW, WHY, AND WHAT WE OWN (2011) (surveying the evolution of American property law and property rights, for which the judiciary had a significant contribution). On courts' continued activity in developing intellectual property law notwithstanding the significant expansion of statutory law, see Balganesh, *supra* note 4; Mark McKenna, *Trademark Law's Faux Federalism* Section II.A (in this volume); Peter Menell, *The Mixed Heritage of Federal Intellectual Property Law and Ramifications for Statutory Interpretation* Pt. II (in this volume).

6 Thomas W. Merrill & Henry E. Smith, *Optimal Standardization in the Law of Property: The Numerus Clausus Principle*, 110 YALE L.J. 1, 59 (2000). Merrill and Smith overstate this point by presenting the *numerus clausus* principle as universal, but in fact, some modern legal systems "have opted for an 'open-list' principle of property rights." Daphna Lewinsohn-Zamir, *The Objectivity of Well-Being and the Objectives of Property Law*, 78 N.Y.U. L. REV. 1669, 1733 (2003).

of property, which I call "property as institutions," does not make the required conservatism of the judiciary conceptually or qualitatively different from that of the legislature. Indeed, given the virtues of what Karl Llewellyn described as the "Grand Style" of the common law tradition,[7] the conception of property as institutions may occasionally support some degree of judicial activism and innovation.

The key to understanding, evaluating, and guiding the proper judicial strategy regarding property law does not lie in the grand categorical proposition of property exceptionalism. Rather, given the character of property as institutions, crafting the proper strategy requires a careful comparative analysis of the relevant features of the judiciary vis-à-vis those of the legislature in terms of democratic legitimacy and expected performance. This chapter seeks to provide a preliminary outline for such an analysis.

I. REJECTING PROPERTY EXCEPTIONALISM

Property exceptionalism crystallized in property discourse as part of the attempt to account for the *numerus clausus* principle. The most prominent of these accounts is the one by Thomas Merrill and Henry Smith,[8] making them the most influential supporters of property exceptionalism. Merrill and Smith argue that the regulation of property as a fixed menu of options reduces the communication costs of third parties who need to determine the attributes of these rights, both to avoid violating them and to acquire them from present owners. Law, they claim, should be reluctant to recognize new types of property rights because parties who create such rights are unlikely to take into account the full magnitude of costs incurred by such strangers in determining the attributes of these rights. This account finds the distinctive features of property in its effects on "classes of individuals who fall outside the zone of privity."

Conceptualizing the focus on the communication costs of third parties as the core concern of property justifies, according to Merrill and Smith, rendering the judiciary an "inhospitable forum" for creating or modifying property rights. The comparative advantage of legislation over adjudication in communicating information to third

[7] Karl L. Llewellyn, The Common Law Tradition: Deciding Appeals 37–38 (1960). My reliance on this account to present an attractive ideal of adjudication does not imply involvement in the historical debate about the original nature of common law adjudication. For competing views on this matter, see David Lobban, The Common Law and English Jurisprudence 1760–1850 at 12–16 (1991); William Cornish, *Sources of Law*, in 11 The Oxford History of the Laws of England 41, 45 (2010); Gerald J. Postema, *Classical Common Law Jurisprudence (Part I)*, 2 Oxford U. Commonwealth L.J. 155 (2002); Gerald J. Postema, *Classical Common Law Jurisprudence (Part II)*, 3 Oxford U. Commonwealth L.J. 1 (2003); A. W. B. Simpson, *The Common Law and Legal Theory*, in 1 Folk Law: Essays in the Theory and Practice of *Lex Non Scripta* 119 (Alison Renteln & Alan Dundes eds., 1994).

[8] *See* Merrill & Smith, *supra* note 6, at 26–34, 56–68. *See also* Carol M. Rose, *What Government Can Do for Property (and Vice Versa), in* The Fundamental Interrelationships Between Government and Property 209, 213–15 (Nicholas Mercuro & Warren J. Samuels eds., 1999); Henry E. Smith, *The Language of Property: Form, Context, and Audience*, 55 Stan. L. Rev. 1105 (2003).

parties, they argue, justifies channeling parties interested in such changes to the legislature. The reason for this comparative advantage is twofold.[9] First, whereas common law rules need to be extracted from a complex body of case law, legislated rules "are set forth in a canonical text which is easy to identify and usually terse," rendering them clearer and thus cheaper to be identified and grasped. Second, whereas decisional rules evolve incrementally – resolving questions regarding issues such as their scope and precise effects as they arise in the adjudicated cases – legislation tends to deal comprehensively and less frequently with the multiple questions evoked by any innovation, again economizing on the gathering of needed information. These comparative advantages of legislation over adjudication, conclude Merrill and Smith, are significant enough to override the public choice problems of "the legislative process emphasized by supporters of common-law courts," which they find to be less significant "in the context of reforming property regimes [than] elsewhere."

Contrary to Merrill and Smith's functional account of property exceptionalism, Avihay Dorfman's argument rests on ideas of political legitimation.[10] Dorfman's starting point is that the *numerus clausus* is "a purely formalistic device," because parties can achieve new goals by tinkering with property's existing forms.[11] Dorfman then argues – in line with what I have claimed elsewhere[12] and elaborate later – that the various forms of property (what I call property institutions) "represent society's *shared acknowledgement* of the basic terms of interactions for private individuals seeking to trade property rights." In sharp contrast with my position, however, Dorfman further claims that this understanding of the forms of property suggests that *only* the legislature should be authorized to create or modify new forms.

Investing this authority in the democratic process, Dorfman argues, expresses the fundamental democratic tenet that political authority must be grounded in the citizens' co-authorship of the laws governing their interactions. Property forms, he claims, should "embody the shared understandings and commitment characteristic of the collective undertaking facilitated (only) through democracy," which explains "why the legislature is the only possible entity (in a representative democracy)" to

9 Merrill and Smith mention six reasons, but I note two for these reasons: (1) The ambiguity resulting from the limited binding effect of decisional rules of intermediate courts of appeal and the lack of a federal common law jurisdiction are of limited significance, because they do not argue against decisional rules prescribed by a State Supreme Court. (2) Their discussion of the stability of legislation adds little to that of comprehensiveness, and therefore, I combine both into one category. (3) The features of prospectivity and implicit compensation are, as Merrill and Smith admit, far less relevant to information costs. More significantly, the possible disruption of the common law traditional retroactive application and the ability of legislatures to provide implicit compensation as part of a comprehensive statute are by no means, even on their face, peculiar to property. I thus discuss these features in Section IV.A.

10 *See* Avihay Dorfman, *Property and Collective Undertaking: The Principle of Numerus Clausus* 61 U. Toronto L.J. 467, 510–13 (2011).

11 *Contra* Lewinsohn-Zamir, *supra* note 6, at 1733 (insisting that the justification of the *numerus clausus* principle is to assure "some predefined 'core' of minimal content" for each property right).

12 *See* Hanoch Dagan, *The Craft of Property*, 91 Cal. L. Rev. 1517, 1558–70 (2003).

legitimately create or modify property forms. Courts, he insists, are not qualified for this purpose, because decisional law "is neither co-authored" (as it involves only the particular parties to the dispute, excluding all other citizens from the process) "nor self-given (as the final decision is made by an unelected judge)." Except for cases where the legislative process not only underperforms due to interest groups and the like but is also "incapable of performing at all," the mere fact that "the ordinary democratic process falls short of an ideal one" does not justify bypassing it.

Both these statements of property exceptionalism fail, although, as shown later, their inadequacy will help develop a more nuanced analysis of the proper role of judicial activity in property.[13]

Merrill and Smith's account of property exceptionalism does not hold because the *numerus clausus* principle is not fully explained by the concern of communication costs. In their critique of Merrill and Smith's theory, Henry Hansmann and Reinier Kraakman argue that limiting the forms of property does not reduce communication costs, given the parties' ability to tinker with the specific content of each property form. On these grounds, Hansmann and Kraakman maintain that the standardization of property is unjustified and that the only concern of third parties that property law should facilitate is the verification of ownership of rights. Accordingly, the distinguishing feature of property law for Hansmann and Kraakman must be the regulation of notice: providing mechanisms for giving effective notice about the partitioning of property rights in a given asset among several people.[14]

In response, Merrill and Smith correctly indicate that the dismissal of standardization as a means for economizing on communication costs is overstated, because the way information is structured affects the costs of processing it.[15] Yet, the gist of Hansmann and Kraakman's critique is still correct: the relevant concern of third parties is verification, and it is indeed hard to see how this concern can justify the onerous *numerus clausus* principle.[16] Accordingly, insofar as this principle captures something unique about property, as Merrill and Smith argue, communication costs cannot justify a sharp preference for legislative rulemaking in property as opposed to other branches of private law.[17]

13 To be sure, the comparison to other branches of private law is only suggestive because (1) judicial activism in these fields may be premised on justifications that are inapplicable to property or (2) activist practice in these branches may be misguided. Because such comparisons cannot do the real work of assessing judicial activism in property, I turn in Part IV to an examination of it in terms of legitimacy and expected performance.

14 Henry Hansmann & Reinier Kraakman, *Property, Contract, and Verification: The Numerus Clausus Problem and the Divisibility of Rights*, 31 J. LEGAL STUD. 373, 374–75, 380–84, 416–17, 419 (2002). *See also, e.g.*, Glen O. Robinson, *Personal Property Servitudes*, 71 U. CHI. L. REV. 1449, 1484–88 (2004).

15 Merrill & Smith, *supra* note 6, at 33, 43–45.

16 *See also* Sarah Worthington, *The Disappearing Divide Between Property and Obligation: The Impact of Aligning Legal Analysis and Commercial Expectations*, 42 TEXAS INT'L L. REV. 917, 926 (2007).

17 It is thus not surprising that Merrill's general position regarding statutory interpretation recommends minimizing normative reasoning. *See* Thomas W. Merrill, *Faithful Agent, Integrative, and Welfarist Interpretation*, 14 LEWIS & CLARK L. REV. 1565 (2011).

Dorfman's account is no more successful. Why should legislatures enjoy a strict monopoly regarding the creation and modification of property forms? Why exclude judges from engaging in these matters while allowing them to actively develop the common law of contracts, torts, and unjust enrichment, as well as to interpret and develop existing property forms, either legislated or judge-made? Dorfman may respond to the challenge of property exceptionalism by emphasizing that only property rights affect the obligations of third parties.[18] But this response, as noted, only means that property law should ensure that no such external effects are validated without proper notice.[19] Dorfman would be right to insist that, given the role that property law plays in structuring people's interpersonal relationships, notice can help only if we want to *publicly* acknowledge the relevant form of property.[20] Because property law is not the only private law field that structures our daily interactions, however, this response does not explain why only the legislature can legitimately provide such a public acknowledgment, assuming that the judiciary is in principle a proper agent of private law rulemaking.

The challenge of the courts' significant role in interpreting existing property forms is not easily answered either. The evolution of common law is largely characterized as a series of cautious, incremental changes resulting from the interpretation of the existing legal landscape, which eventually generate new and at times innovative doctrines.[21] Such interpretive leeway is indeed always available. Despite the wide acceptance of H. L. A. Hart's claim that the indeterminacy of any given legal norm is limited to "hard cases,"[22] Legal Realists have convincingly demonstrated that the indeterminacy of doctrine as a whole is primarily premised on the availability of multiple potentially applicable sources. Because legal rules never exist in solitude and are always part of the legal system in which they are embedded,[23] doctrine as such, including a doctrine enshrined in a statute, always "speaks with a forked tongue" so that, at least potentially, the judicial task is never one of sheer application.[24]

Furthermore, even on its own terms, it is hard to accept Dorfman's binary split between legislation as a process of collective co-authorship versus adjudication as lacking that democratic virtue. Unless this dichotomy is simply stipulated (thus

18 He may also add that, insofar as tort law is indeed analogous, it too is – or should be – subject to *numerus clausus*. *See* Dorfman, *supra* note 10, at 512 n.137. My reply in the text addresses this response as well.

19 This is taken care of by the law of legal accidents, which deals with conflicts between original owners and third parties and takes into account issues of verification and of notice, as well as other normative concerns pertinent to such conflicts. *See generally* Dagan, *supra* note 12, at 1544–47.

20 *See* Dorfman, *supra* note 10, at 495–96.

21 *Cf.* Don Herzog, Poisoning the Minds of the Lower Orders 18 (1998).

22 H. L. A. Hart, The Concept of Law 123, 141–42, 144 (1961).

23 *See* Hans Kelsen, General Theory of Law and State 3, 110–23 (Anders Wedberg Trans., 1946).

24 Karl L. Llewellyn, *Some Realism about Realism, in* Jurisprudence: Realism in Theory and in Practice 42, 70 (1962). *See generally* Hanoch Dagan, Reconstructing American Legal Realism & Rethinking Private Law Theory 19–22 (2013).

begging the needed justification), the issue of collective co-authorship must be carefully and contextually examined. One need not reject the significance of public deliberation in the pursuit of the common good, as highlighted by the supporters of deliberative democracy,[25] to appreciate that such deliberation is both impossible and undesirable across the (broad) board of public decisions;[26] even if we are content with the deliberations of elected representatives, their intensity and quality are not uniform across the board. Similarly, if the *numerus clausus* is supposed to ensure the participation of that subset of citizens likely to be affected by a given property form in its creation and modification, examining the property exceptionalist thesis requires a comparison between the characteristic forms of participation in these issues in legislation and in adjudication. Given the public choice difficulties mentioned earlier on the one hand, and the possibility, however limited, that courts function in property matters as public fora of grassroots democracy on the other, an a priori preference for legislation seems questionable.

Although unsuccessful in their attempt to defend property exceptionalism, these accounts yield important lessons. First, they represent an increasing sense among property theorists that the *numerus clausus* principle is a doctrinal manifestation of an important characteristic of property. Second, they point to the two main – and interrelated – considerations that should guide the division of labor between legislatures and courts once the character of property is properly identified: democratic legitimacy and expected performance. These two lessons guide the discussion that follows. Part II offers a conception of property as institutions that takes its cue from the *numerus clausus* principle, Part III presents a charitable account of adjudication as a forum for rulemaking, and Part IV uses the lessons of the previous two parts to sketch a comparative analysis of the democratic legitimacy and expected performance of courts and legislatures in property matters.

II. THE CHARACTER OF PROPERTY

The *numerus clausus* principle, which limits property to some set of identifiable and standardized forms, goes well beyond what can be justified by reference to third parties' interests. This seems to be a devastating conclusion to scholars who hold that the core idea of property lies in the relationships of owners and non-owners. In line with the Blackstonian conception of property as "sole and despotic dominion,"[27] these scholars understand this "external dimension" of property (as I call it) in radically one-sided terms as exhausted by the obligations that property imposes on

[25] *See, e.g.*, Amy Gutman & Dennis F. Thompson, Democracy and Disagreement (1996); Henry S. Richardson, Democratic Autonomy: Public Reasoning about the Ends of Policy (2002).

[26] *See, e.g.*, Richard A. Posner, Law, Pragmatism, and Democracy 108–09, 132–43 (2003).

[27] 2 William Blackstone, Commentaries on the Laws of England 2 (Univ. of Chi. ed. 1979) (1765–69).

non-owners. Thus, for example, if "the differentiating feature of a system of property [is] the right of the owner to act as the exclusive gatekeeper of the owned thing,"[28] then, as Hansmann and Kraakman maintain, notice is crucial, but standardization, as they indeed insist, is unjustified.

However, before we dismiss the *numerus clausus* principle, some caution seems warranted given that it is such a pervasive characteristic of property law in postfeudal property systems. The *numerus clausus* can be read more charitably and the character of property better understood if we question the Blackstonian presupposition underlying the claims of both sides to this debate. Indeed, notwithstanding its recent impressive resurrection, the Blackstonian understanding of property[29] is profoundly mistaken. Property requires attention not only to the external dimension addressing third parties' interests but also to the internal dimension, which focuses on property governance, namely, on the relationship among stakeholders. Furthermore, even regarding third parties, property is not just about exclusion. In fact, limitations on the right of owners to exclude are quite prevalent, and non-owners are at times even entitled to be included – to buy, rent, use, or physically enter. A better understanding of property that accommodates these two corrections to the Blackstonian model can justify the *numerus clausus* principle. This conception, of "property as institutions," can also explain why I believe that the various forms of intellectual property – which are the focus of this volume – should be analyzed as property institutions; finally it can helpfully guide our inquiry as to the proper role of judicial rulemaking in property.

The conception of property as an exclusive right erroneously looks only at property's external dimension, ignoring the significant role that the governance of property's internal life plays in our understanding of property. I do not question that in some property institutions the name of the game is indeed external, and that part of the drama of property law is the productive struggle between autonomous excluders, with each individual cloaked in the Blackstonian armor of sole and despotic dominion. But the property institutions constituted in this way – atomistic, competitive, and vindicating negative liberty[30] – by no means exhaust property law. Property institutions provide structures for various types of interpersonal relationships: from strangers and market transactors, through landlords and tenants, members of a local community, neighbors, co-owners, and partners, up to intimate relationships among family members. Accordingly, people experience property both as a locus of competition and as an arena for cooperation. In other words, governance – the

[28] Thomas W. Merrill & Henry E. Smith, *The Morality of Property*, 48 Wm. & Mary L. Rev. 1849, 1850 (2007).

[29] In addition to Merrill and Smith's work, see also, e.g., J. E. Penner, The Idea of Property in Law (1997); Larissa Katz, *Exclusion and Exclusivity in Property Law*, 58 U. Toronto L. J. 275 (2008).

[30] For a provocative account of these institutions as intrinsically social, see Avihay Dorfman, Property, Trespass, and the Form/Function Gap (unpublished manuscript).

ongoing management of cooperative relationships – typifies property as much as exclusion.

Property law supports a wide range of institutions that facilitate the economic and social gains made possible by cooperation. Some of these institutions, such as a publicly held corporation, are mainly about the economic gains of securing the efficiencies of economies of scale and of risk spreading, with social benefits merely an occasionally pleasant side effect. Other institutions, such as marriage, are more about the intrinsic good of being part of a plural subject, where the *raison d'être* of the property institution refers more to one's identity and relationships, and the attendant economic benefits are usually perceived as helpful byproducts rather than the primary premise of cooperation. In between, there are many other property institutions such as close corporations, partnerships, common-interest communities, and co-ownerships, where both the economic and the social aspects are significant. The underlying character of these divergent relationships is legally significant because it proves to be the key for explaining the particular property configuration that serves as the default for the property institution at hand.[31] Indeed, alongside its support of more market-oriented types of interaction, property law appropriately provides governance mechanisms that facilitate other, equally valuable spheres of human interaction and human flourishing, in which cooperation looms large.

Like its marginalization of property's internal dimension, the Blackstonian definition of property's external dimension as strictly limited to outsiders' obligations is also mistaken and misleading. As Felix Cohen demonstrated long ago, every property right certainly involves *some* power to exclude others from doing something. But as Cohen further emphasized, this is a rather modest truism that hardly yields any practical implications. Owners' right to exclude is often subject to limitations and obligations, and "the real problems we have to deal with are problems of degree, problems too infinitely intricate for simple panacea solutions."[32] Limits on the right of individual or group property owners to exclude, whether by refusing to sell or lease or by insisting that non-owners refrain from physically entering their land, are indeed quite prevalent in property law.[33] Furthermore, in certain circumstances, such as the law of public accommodations, the copyright doctrine of fair use, and the law of fair housing, notably in the contexts of common-interest communities law and landlord-tenant law, the right of non-owners to be included is also quite typical of property. And, as I show elsewhere, although they are less typical of property, these rights to entry or access and the limitations of exclusion on which they rely are just as intrinsic to it. Like owners' rights to exclude, they too are grounded in

[31] *See* Hanoch Dagan, Property: Values and Institutions ch. 10 (2011).

[32] Felix S. Cohen, *Dialogue on Private Property*, 9 Rutgers L. Rev. 357, 362, 370–74, 379 (1954).

[33] *See* Kevin Gray & Susan Francis Gray, *Civil Rights, Civil Wrongs and Quasi-Public Space*, 1 Eur. Hum. Rights L. Rev. 46 (1999); Joseph W. Singer, *No Right to Exclude: Public Accommodations and Private Property*, 90 Nw. U. L. Rev. 1283, 1303, 1466 (1996). *See also, e.g.*, James Gordley, Foundations of Private Law: Property, Tort, Contract, Unjust Enrichment 130–39 (2006), discussing the doctrine of necessity.

the very reasons, the very same property values, that justify the law's support for the pertinent property institution in the first place.[34]

Implicit in these comments is a different conception of property, one that is both loyal to the practice of property and more normatively attractive than its Blackstonian counterpart. In this conception, which I defend in my book *Property: Values and Institutions*, property is understood as an umbrella for a set of institutions bearing family resemblances. Each such property institution entails a specific composition of entitlements that constitute the contents of an owner's rights vis-à-vis others (co-owners or other stakeholders, as well as various types of non-owners) with respect to a given resource. The particular configuration of these entitlements is, or at least should be, determined by its character, namely, by the particular balance of property values characterizing the institution at issue. At least ideally, these values both construct and reflect the ideal ways in which people interact with one another in a given category of social contexts – such as market, community, and family – and with respect to a given category of resources, such as land, chattels, copyright, and patents. The ongoing process of reshaping property as institutions, and thus facilitating various forms of human interaction and human flourishing, is often rule-based and is usually addressed with an appropriate degree of caution. But the possibility of repackaging makes it (at least potentially) an exercise in legal optimism, in which lawmakers explicate and develop existing property institutions by accentuating their normative desirability while remaining attuned to their social context. In appropriate cases, they may also divide up a property institution, minimize its scope of application or outright eliminate it, or create new property institutions for new types of resources or emerging categories of interpersonal interaction.[35]

In this framework of property as institutions, limiting property to some set of identifiable and standardized forms as the *numerus clausus* principle prescribes is understood as a means of facilitating stable (and thus necessarily a limited number of) categories of human interaction. More precisely, the institutions of property consolidate people's expectations so that they know what they are getting into when entering, for example, a joint tenancy, a common-interest community, or, for that matter, a marriage. Thus, a set of fairly precise rules and informative standards must govern each property institution to enable people to predict the consequences of various future contingencies and to plan and structure their lives accordingly.[36]

[34] *See* DAGAN, *supra* note 31, at ch. 2.

[35] DAGAN, *supra* note 31, at chs. 1–4.

[36] As the text implies, nothing in the conception of property as institutions suggests that property law should adopt the form of vague standards as opposed to bright-line rules. Quite the contrary: the ways in which the various property values are embedded in these institutions are or at least can and should be based on clear rules or informative standards, rather than affected by the equities of each particular case. Moreover, only some legal actors, notably judges of appellate courts, should occasionally use new cases as triggers for an ongoing refinement of existing doctrine, based on a contextual application of normative judgment rather than on their subjective preferences. This allows property as institutions

Furthermore, the institutions of property may also affect people's ideals and therefore their preferences with respect to these categories of relationships. In this latter role, property institutions perform a significant expressive and cultural function. Both roles – consolidating expectations and expressing ideal forms of relationships – require some measure of stability. To form effective frameworks of social interaction and cooperation, property law can recognize a necessarily limited number of categories of relationships and resources. This prescription of standardization is particularly acute with regard to the expressive role, which mandates limiting the number of property institutions because law can effectively express only so many ideal categories of interpersonal relationships.

Indeed, the best justification for the standardization of property lies exactly in the aspects of property that the Blackstonian conception obscures. Limiting the number of property forms and standardizing their content facilitate the role of property in consolidating expectations and expressing ideal forms of interpersonal interaction, both within the privity zone and as per the various types of external relationships that property constitutes. Both the understanding of property as a "laundry list" of limitless permutations ("bundle of rights") and its conception as a monistic bulwark of exclusion, even if combined with broad contractual freedom with regard to property's internal affairs, fail to sustain the normative integrity of the institutions of property. Thus, they undermine the role of property law in consolidating expectations, as well as its function in expressing such normative ideals for core types of human relationships.

Admittedly, my reconstruction of the *numerus clausus* principle, just like other interpretations of it that also do not purport to expose the original intent of its promulgation, does not perfectly fit its operation in practice. Thinking about *numerus clausus* through the prism offered here may imply, for instance, that some forms are overly broad because they cut through types of resources or categories of relationships that are too heterogeneous. Rather than as a pitfall, however, I see these gaps between the justification of the *numerus clausus* principle and its actual manifestation as a helpful product of my proposed reconstruction because they help push the evolution of property institutions in felicitous directions.

One important implication of this account of the *numerus clausus* principle is that, in contrast with Merrill and Smith's theory, *numerus clausus* can peacefully coexist with a liberal take on the possibility of contracting around property rules. If the *numerus clausus* principle focuses on policing the externalization of verification costs to third parties, contractual freedom in property is justifiably curtailed as long as the contracting parties' frustration costs are lower than the third parties' verification costs.[37] By contrast, the understanding of the institutions of property as

to respect property's stability and predictability. For a skeptical view, see Henry E. Smith, *Property Is Not Just a Bundle of Rights*, 8 ECON. J. WATCH 279, 287 (2011). For my response, see DAGAN, *supra* note 24, at ch. 9.

37 *Cf.* Merrill & Smith, *supra* note 6, at 38.

unifying normative ideals for core categories of interpersonal relationships coexists comfortably with a much broader realm of freedom of contract. In most cases, allowing people to opt out and tailor their property arrangements in accordance with the way they prefer to shape their interpersonal relationships does not undermine law's functions of consolidating expectations and expressing ideals for core types of human interaction. People may legitimately want to accommodate their property arrangements to their particular needs and circumstances. Furthermore, in a liberal society, citizens should be free to reject many of law's messages and repudiate at least some of the values recommended by the state. Thus, the conception of property as institutions welcomes the trend in property law that is most significantly manifest in the traditionally immutable areas of marital property and of servitudes.[38] Except for cases of illegitimate external effects,[39] proscribing contractual opting out in property is justifiable only in extreme cases, when the social or cultural role of a property institution is both overwhelming and likely to be particularly facilitated by immutability.[40] In all other cases, as long as opting out does not generate such externalities, the particular configurations of the various property institutions should be understood as defaults.

A second implication of understanding property as institutions refers to intellectual property. Appreciating the multiple faces of property should lessen the resistance of guardians of the public domain to the understanding of intellectual property as property.[41] Property as institutions undermines the view, which these scholars take seriously, that once products of creative activity are classified as property the public domain is necessarily threatened. Because the institutions of property are as diverse in their normative underpinnings and in their doctrinal detail as the categories of human interaction, the idea that the entitlements that owners typically have in one type of property institution (governing, for example, the home) necessarily apply with respect to others (such as those dealing with creative activity) is both foreign to property law and dramatically distant from the daily experience of property on the ground. Therefore, instead of agonizing over the propertization of creativity, property as institutions suggests that friends of the public domain should work toward a redefinition of the incidents of property rights in creative products, so that they properly respond to the normative concerns pertinent to the assignment of rights in information. As I show elsewhere, this should be a happy exercise for these scholars because the rich intellectual resources offered by the institutions, values, and doctrines of property actually support a robust public domain.[42]

38 *See* American Law Institute, Principles of the Law of Family Dissolution: Analysis and Recommendations ch. 7 (2002); Restatement (Third) of Servitudes §§2.1, 2.4, 2.6, 3.2 (2000).

39 Shelley v. Kraemer, 334 U.S. 1 (1948) is a case in point.

40 Defaults, and not only immutable rules, may also have some expressive effect that may entail other significant real-life consequences. In particular, prescribing the baseline from which deviations require active contracting imposes burdens of disclosure on parties who want to deviate from these normative baselines.

41 This paragraph relies on Dagan, *supra* note 31, at ch. 4.

42 Dagan, *supra* note 31, at 50–52, 77–84.

The final significant implication of my account regarding the character of property deals directly with the key question of this chapter[43]: the scope of legitimate judicial rulemaking in property law. I elaborate on this issue in Part IV after providing a rough account of judicial rulemaking at its best. One preliminary comment in this respect is nonetheless in order, because it naturally follows my previous point. As indicated at the outset, intellectual property is an important context for the question of judicial involvement in property rulemaking. One tempting strategy for common law supporters in this context is to justify the robust activism of state courts in developing common law intellectual property by emphasizing the limited exclusion that these types of rights typically entail.[44] These common law supporters thereby imply that their legitimacy is unthreatened by the implicitly justified strong association between "full-blown" property rights, for which exclusion is the name of the game, and the legislative monopoly of rulemaking. Should the earlier analysis of the character of property prove persuasive, this strategy is doomed to fail because exclusion is not the core of property and because the various types of intellectual property, be they legislated or judge-made, are no less members of the family of property institutions than is the fee simple absolute. Fortunately, as shown later, this failure is inconsequential because the legitimate scope of judicial activity *throughout property law* covering the various property institutions assembled under the umbrella of property is in fact rather broad.

III. GRAND STYLE ADJUDICATION

An analysis of the division of labor concerning rulemaking between the legislature and the judiciary, in property or indeed in any other legal field, requires a careful comparison of their respective expected performances in developing the doctrines under consideration and the democratic legitimacy of their doing so. Because this exploratory chapter examines the position that judges should not participate in the creation and modification of property rights, my focus here is on the judiciary. Relying on what I take to be the core contribution of Legal Realism to this topic,[45] the following discussion outlines some of the virtues of adjudication that, together with the understanding of the character of property outlined earlier, can help articulate a proper domain for judicial property activism.

Legal Realists are always wary of romanticizing law and its carriers. They take to heart Oliver Wendell Holmes's statement that "in societies like ours the command of the public force is entrusted by judges in certain cases, and the whole power of the state will be put forth, if necessary, to carry out their judgments and decrees."[46] They further realize that certain built-in features of law – notably, the institutional

43 As the text hints, the issue of contractual freedom in property is also relevant to the scope of legitimate judicial rulemaking in property. *See infra* text accompanying note 90.

44 *See* Balganesh, *supra* note 4, at 1553–54, 1570.

45 This part draws on Dagan, *supra* note 24, at ch. 2.

46 Oliver W. Holmes, *The Path of the Law*, in Collected Legal Papers 167, 167 (1920).

division of labor between "interpretation specialists" and the actual executors of their judgments, and our tendency as lawyers, and even as citizens, to "thingify" legal constructs and accord them an aura of obviousness and acceptability – render the danger of obscuring law's coerciveness particularly troubling.[47]

Alongside their wariness of romanticism, Realists are also careful not to fall into the trap of cynicism. They reject as equally reductive the mirror image of adjudication, which portrays it as sheer power (or interest, or politics). Realists insist that legal discourse is also a forum of reason and that reason poses real, albeit elusive, constraints on the choices of law's carriers. Furthermore, because so much is at stake in reasoning about law, legal reasoning becomes particularly urgent and rich, attentive, careful, and serious. Legal actors understand that reasons can justify law's coercion only if they are properly, even if implicitly, grounded in human values.[48] Realists reject cynicism about law because the need to justify is a fruitful source of social and moral progress that forces, at the minimum, a respectable façade – an idealized picture of law that can often challenge conventional opinions and practices.[49]

The task of articulating an account of legitimate adjudication is formidable for Legal Realists because, as noted,[50] they reject the formalist reliance on doctrine per se as the sole constraining feature of judicial discretion. Because law is always dynamic, at least potentially, Realists consider hopeless the legal positivist attempt to understand law statically by sheer reference to verifiable facts, such as the authoritative commands of a political superior or the rules identified by a rule of recognition.[51] Nevertheless, Legal Realists insist that judge-made law is quite predictable and largely legitimate, even salutary. They celebrate common law's Grand Style, described by Llewellyn as "a functioning harmonization of vision with tradition, of continuity with growth, of machinery with purpose, of measure with need," mediating between "the seeming commands of the authorities and the felt demands of justice."[52]

47 *See* Felix S. Cohen, *Transcendental Nonsense and the Functional Approach*, 35 Colum. L. Rev. 809, 811–12, 820–21, 827–29 (1935); John Dewey, *Logical Method and Law*, in American Legal Realism 185, 191, 193 (William W. Fisher III et al. eds., 1993); Oliver W. Holmes, *Law in Science and Science in Law*, *in* Collected Legal Papers, *supra* note 46, at 210, 230, 232, 238–39. *See also* Robert Cover, *Violence and the Word*, in Narrative, Violence, and the Law 203 (Martha Minow et al. eds., 1992).

48 *See* K. N. Llewellyn, *The Normative, the Legal, and the Law-Jobs: The Problem of Juristic Method*, 49 Yale L.J. 1355, 1362–65, 1367–68, 1370, 1381–83, 1387 (1940). *See also, e.g.*, Thomas W. Bechtler, *American Legal Realism Revaluated*, in Law in Social Context: Liber Amicorum Honouring Professor Lon L. Fuller 3, 20–21 (Thomas W. Bechtler ed., 1978); Harry W. Jones, *Law and Morality in the Perspective of Legal Realism*, 61 Colum. L. Rev. 799, 801, 809 (1961); Hessel E. Yntema, *The Rational Basis of Legal Science*, 31 Colum. L. Rev. 295, 255 (1931).

49 *See* Dagan, *supra* note 24, at 158.

50 *See supra* text accompanying note 24.

51 *See* John Dewey, *My Philosophy of Law*, in My Philosophy of Law 73, 77 (1941); Karl L. Llewellyn, *My Philosophy of Law*, *id.*, 183, 183–84; Max Radin, *My Philosophy of Law*, *id.*, at 285, 295.

52 Llewellyn, *supra* note 7, at 37–38. *See also Ronald Dworkin, Law's Empire* (1986). I discuss the relationship between the realist conception of law and Dworkin's conception of law as integrity in Dagan, *supra* note 24, at 65–67.

Llewellyn thus argued that, although adjudication is necessarily creative, it is invariably constrained by legal tradition. More specifically, he observed that cases are decided with "a desire to move in accordance with the material as well as within it . . . to reveal the latent rather than to impose new form, much less to obtrude an outside will." The case law *system* imposes "a demand for moderate consistency, for reasonable regularity, for on-going conscientious effort at integration." The instant outcome and rule must "fit the flavor of the whole;" it must "think with the feel of the body of our law" and "go with the grain rather than across or against it." Legal Realists begin with the existing doctrinal landscape because it may and often does incorporate valuable normative choices, even if implicitly and sometimes imperfectly executed. They nonetheless recognize that the existing legal environment always leaves considerable interpretive leeway and, furthermore, believe that law's potential dynamism is laudable because it represents law's perennial quest for justice. Adjudication is thus "the constant questing for better and best law" – a relentless "re-examination and reworking of the heritage." And judges have the "duty to justice and adjustment," which means an "on-going production and improvement of rules."[53]

This forward-looking aspect of legal reasoning in its realist rendition relies on both science and craft. Realists recognize the profound differences between, on the one hand, lawyers as social engineers who dispassionately combine empirical knowledge with normative insights, and, on the other hand, lawyers as practical reasoners who employ contextual judgment as part of a process of dialogic adjudication. They nonetheless insist that, at least at its best, common law adjudication accommodates science and craft.

Realists place a high premium on studying two types of social facts pertinent to the development of legal doctrine. They follow Roscoe Pound's prescription for looking at "the actual social effects of legal institutions and legal doctrines," both in law reform and in the application and interpretation of existing law.[54] Moreover, they believe with Benjamin Cardozo that judges must also rely on "the life of the community" and that, to further stabilize the objectivity and legitimacy of law, judges should generally respond "to the accepted standards of the community, the *mores* of the time," namely, the actual normative preferences of law's constituents.[55] But Legal Realism, at least at its best, rejects any pretense that knowledge of all these important social facts can be a substitute for political morality. Realists realize that value judgments are indispensable not only when evaluating empirical research but also when simply choosing the facts to be investigated. Moreover, they are careful not to accept existing normative preferences uncritically. They thus insist that neither science nor an ethics that ignores the data of science offers a

[53] LLEWELLYN, *supra* note 7, at 36, 38, 190–91, 217, 222–23; Llewellyn, *supra* note 48, at 1385.

[54] Roscoe Pound, *The Scope and Purpose of Sociological Jurisprudence*, 25 HARV. L. REV. 489, 513 (1912).

[55] BENJAMIN N. CARDOZO, THE NATURE OF THE JUDICIAL PROCESS 105–06, 108 (1921).

valid test of law's merits. Legal analysis needs both empirical data and normative judgments.[56]

Because law affects people's lives dramatically, these social facts and human values must always inform the direction of legal evolution. Legal reasoning necessarily shares this feature with other forms of practical reasoning, but Realists also emphasize that legal reasoning is, to some extent, a distinct mode of argumentation and analysis. Hence, they pay attention to the distinctive institutional characteristics of adjudication and study their potential virtues, while still being aware of their possible abuse. The procedural characteristics of the adversary process – as well as the professional norms that bind judicial opinions, notably the requirement of a universalizable justification – provide a unique social setting for adjudication. These procedural characteristics encourage judges to develop what Cohen terms "a many-perspectived view of the world" that "can relieve us of the endless anarchy of one-eyed vision," a "synoptic vision" that is "a distinguishing mark of liberal civilization."[57] Moreover, because the judicial drama is always situated in a specific human context, lawyers have constant and unmediated access to human situations and to actual problems of contemporary life. This contextuality of legal judgments ensures that lawyers have a unique skill in capturing the subtleties of various types of cases and in adjusting legal treatment to the distinct characteristics of each category.[58]

IV. LEGISLATURES AND COURTS

Having (briefly) introduced both the character of property and the idealized view of common law adjudication, we are finally in a position to consider the comparative democratic legitimacy and expected performance of legislatures and courts in property matters. Two remarks are still in order before taking on this task (in reverse order, for the convenience of exposition):

1. On its face, by revealing the breadth of potential judicial choice, the radical doctrinal indeterminacy noted by Realists[59] makes our inquiry redundant. But the fact that judges can use such potential does not mean that they always do

[56] *See* Felix S. Cohen, *Modern Ethics and the Law*, 4 Brook. L. Rev. 33, 45 (1934); Cohen, *supra* note 47, at 848–49; William Twining, *The Idea of Juristic Method: A Tribute to Karl Llewellyn*, 48 U. Miami L. Rev. 119, 151–52 (1993).

[57] Felix S. Cohen, *Field Theory and Judicial Logic*, *in* The Legal Conscience: Selected Papers of Felix S. Cohen 121, 125–26 (Lucy Kramer Cohen ed., 1960). *See also, e.g.*, Llewellyn, *supra* note 7, at 46–47, 132; Llewellyn, *American Common Law Tradition and American Democracy*, *in* Jurisprudence, *supra* note 24, at 282, 308–10.

[58] Herman Oliphant, *A Return to Stare Decisis*, 14 A.B.A. J. 71, 73–74, 159 (1928). *See also, e.g.*, Llewellyn, *A Realistic Jurisprudence: The Next Step*, *in* Jurisprudence, *supra* note 24, at 3, 27–28, 32; Walter Wheeler Cook, *Scientific Method and the Law*, *in* American Legal Realism, *supra* note 47, at 242, 246.

[59] *See supra* text accompanying note 24.

or that they should, insofar as property is concerned. Doctrinal indeterminacy does not rule out the position that judges should abstain from property rule-making and limit their role to applying the existing understandings of property law (within the relevant legal community) to the cases before them. Although doctrinal indeterminacy implies that new cases *can* serve as opportunities to rethink, it does not exclude the possibility that these opportunities are (and should be) used only infrequently and only by *certain* legal actors – notably, judges of appellate courts – who are responsible for the ongoing refinement of the existing private law rules qua rules.[60]

2. The realist celebration of common law does not purport to provide a real-life description of adjudication. Rather, parallel to the understanding of legislation as an exercise of co-authorship that Dorfman endorses, or to the more conventional reason for the authority of legislation based on legislators' political accountability (to which I also refer later), it provides an account of the ideal of adjudication that should serve as a benchmark for evaluating its daily operation. A comparison between legislatures and courts regarding property lawmaking should consider both these idealized pictures of rulemaking and the likely failures of their actual manifestations.[61]

A. *Performance*

The core claim of Merrill and Smith's functionalist case against judicial activism in property law, as noted, is that the comparative legislative advantages in terms of clarity and comprehensiveness are particularly significant in property because of its strong connection to the economization of communication costs. Although I reject this characterization of property, in this section I follow their insight that the character of property revealed by looking at the underlying rationale of the *numerus clausus* principle is the key to a functionalist analysis of judicial rulemaking in property. Given the earlier discussion of the character of property as institutions, the task is therefore to evaluate the relative performance of the legislature and the judiciary in shaping the core default legal regimes governing interpersonal relationships dealing with resources so as to stabilize people's expectations and express our normative ideals.

The character of property explains and justifies its relative stability and conservatism vis-à-vis other segments of our private law. Although property lawyers should

60 *See* DAGAN, *supra* note 24, at 55.

61 *But see* ADRIAN VERMEULE, JUDGING UNDER UNCERTAINTY: AN INSTITUTIONAL THEORY OF LEGAL INTERPRETATION (2006), in which Vermeule argues that an institutional inquiry must be thoroughly empirical, studying "the actual capacities and interactions of judges, legislatures, and agencies." *Id.*, at 10. Empirical inquiries regarding judicial capacity are surely important. But they cannot be plausibly answered without reference to the ideals of adjudication, which enter judges' utility function both directly and via the impact of the social and professional groups that judges seek to please. *See* DAGAN, *supra* note 24, at 76–77. *See also infra* text accompanying notes 87–88.

be cautious not to engage in a "blind imitation of the past" by upholding doctrines whose "grounds have vanished,"[62] they should appreciate the added value of adherence to tradition in property matters, in addition to the more general value of following legal tradition. The restraint imposed by the virtues of stable expectations and effective transmission of normative ideals, however, is by no means unique to judges. Rather, to the extent that the character of property justifies an attitude of forbearance and temperateness, this approach should guide judges and legislators alike.[63]

But restraint is not synonymous with stagnation. Expectations can be stable even if rules are not frozen in time, as long as they are not revisited too frequently.[64] The proper frequency must surely also be affected by the pace of other developments, for instance in technology, pertinent to the property institution. Equally, and to avoid the risk of romanticizing the law, we must not be overly deferential to its existing doctrine. Both law's normative ideals and its means for promoting them should therefore be challenged and properly reexamined. Property law has indeed evolved throughout its history: new types of property institutions have emerged (consider equitable servitudes, common-interest communities, and various types of intellectual property); old types have been marginalized and at times vanished (such as the fee tail[65]); and many others have been modified. In some cases, the reform of a given property institution has been relatively radical (as was the case with leaseholds[66] and marital property[67]). Sometimes, more moderate options seemed in order, such as restating the doctrine pertaining to a property institution in a way that brings its rules closer to its underlying commitments, in the process removing indefensible rules (one example here is the *Restatement of Servitudes*[68]).

As these examples demonstrate, both legislatures and courts were involved in these developments. If property is about consolidating expectations and expressing normative ideals with respect to core types of human relationships regarding resources, it is indeed hard to justify excluding judges from lawmaking. The reason is that, in this conception of property, the creation and modification of property institutions

62 HOLMES, *supra* note 46, at 187.

63 In fact, this attitude seems particularly amenable to common law judges given their incrementalist disposition. *See* Balganesh, *supra* note 4.

64 *See* TIMOTHY A. O. ENDICOTT, *The Impossibility of the Rule of Law*, *in* VAGUENESS IN LAW 185, 193 (2000).

65 *See, e.g.*, DUKEMINIER ET AL., PROPERTY 200–01 (7th ed. 2010).

66 For significant developments in landlord-tenant law, see, for example, the Fair Housing Act, 42 U.S.C. 3601–3619, 3631 (2002) (limiting landlords' discretion in selecting tenants); Myers v. E. Ohio Gas Co., 464 N.E.2d 1369, 1373 (Ohio 1977) (loosening the rigid forms of leasehold estates); Hilder v. St. Peter, 478 A.2d 202 (Vt. 1984) (implying an unwaivable warranty of habitability). *See generally* Edward H. Rabin, *The Revolution in Residential Landlord-Tenant Law: Causes and Consequences*, 69 Cornell L. Rev. 517 (1984).

67 The most important developments here are the rise of no-fault divorce, the entrenchment of the norm of equal division, and the expansion of the scope of the marital property estate. *See generally* DAGAN, *supra* note 31, at ch. 9.

68 *See* RESTATEMENT (THIRD) OF SERVITUDES (2000).

are, or at least should be, triggered by challenges bearing on the desirability of the normative underpinnings of property institutions, their responsiveness to their social context, or their effectiveness in promoting their contextually examined normative goals. Challenging property law to live up to the ideals embedded in its institutions, or to shape these or new institutions in a way that promotes other worthy ideals, can definitely come from the legislature. But why discount the possibility or the desirability that such challenges might come about via the adjudicatory process? At least in its Grand Style discussed earlier, adjudication is a perfectly appropriate forum for developing property law along these lines.

The last feature of adjudication mentioned in Part III merits emphasis partly because it is the flip side of the legislative comprehensiveness celebrated by Merrill and Smith. A judicial drama is not a dialog about principles of abstract justice, but is situated in a given human context, which is significant because, as Herman Oliphant observed, it holds judges close to "the actual transactions before them." This daily and unmediated access to actual human situations and problems in contemporary life serves as an "alert sense of actuality" that "checks our reveries in theory." It provides judges with "the illumination which only immediacy affords and the judiciousness which reality alone can induce," and it encourages them to shape law "close and contemporary" to the human problems with which they deal.[69]

To clarify: as Llewellyn explained, the claim is *not* that "the equities or sense of the particular case or the particular parties" is determinative.[70] Rather, the idea is that judges develop the law while "testing it against life-wisdom," benefiting from "the sense and reason of some significantly seen *type* of life-situation."[71] Therefore, if the development of property law indeed is (as I claim it should be) an ongoing dialog regarding our property institutions, aimed at their reconstruction along the lines mentioned earlier, this unique feature of adjudication must count as a significant comparative advantage.[72]

69 Oliphant, *supra* note 58.

70 Frederick Schauer has argued that rather than being illuminating, the concrete examples that judges face distort their judgment by systematically triggering certain cognitive biases. *See* Frederick Schauer, *Do Cases Make Bad Law?* 73 U. Chi. L. Rev. 883 (2006); *see also* Larry Alexander & Emily Sherwin, Demystifying Legal Reasoning 111–14 (2008). But as Jeffrey Rachlinski shows, alongside the cognitive weaknesses of adjudication, courts have several cognitive advantages over legislatures that might facilitate superior lawmaking. *See* Jeffrey J. Rachlinski, *Bottom-Up Versus Top-Down Lawmaking*, 73 U. Chi. L. Rev. 933, 950–61 (2006).

71 Llewellyn, *The Current Recapture of the Grand Tradition*, *in* Jurisprudence, *supra* note 24, at 215, 217, 219–220. *See also* Postema, Part I, *supra* note 7, at 167, 175, 177–80. Joseph Raz's analysis of the phenomenon of distinguishing cases brings home a similar point. *See* Joseph Raz, The Authority of Law 183–97 (1979). For a careful account of the process by which a given case is taken as an example, see Gerald J. Postema, A Similibus ad Similia *Analogical Thinking in Law*, *in* Common Law Theory, *supra* note 1, at 122–24.

72 Thus, Balganesh welcomes the development of common law intellectual property as centered on such ideas as "proceeding with caution, balancing multiple values or interests, looking to the context and necessities of an area to tailor a rule, and paying close attention to the actual practical consequences that flow from a rule so as to reformulate it, when needed." Balganesh, *supra* note 4, at

None of this implies that there are no functional difficulties with judicial property lawmaking or that there are no limitations to its proper domain. But these problems are not unique to property or particularly acute in property matters, nor do they apply across the board of property law. Without attempting to be exhaustive, it seems safe to mention three significant types of cases limited to particular subsets of property doctrines in which judicial caution is in place. They are premised on three familiar and general limitations of judicial competence:

1. At least in its conventional rendition, adjudication does not involve the creation of complex and elaborate regulatory schemes as may at times be required to create or modify a property institution (as, for example, in the formal registration of property rights).[73]
2. Contexts requiring specialized knowledge and expertise, such as innovative technologies or complex market ramifications, may justify judicial deference to governmental agencies equipped with such technical expertise.[74] The Israeli doctrine that in principle allows unjust enrichment claims for imitations of nonpatentable designs if an additional unspecified element is present seems to violate this prescription.[75]
3. Finally, some modifications, such as the annulment of an existing property institution, generate widespread excessive[76] redistribution so that their retroactive application, as the common law usually applies, is inappropriate.[77] Certain cases are obviously exceptions, as when people's reliance on the preexisting distribution was illegitimate (think of slave owners) and thus unworthy of legal

1549. He mentions in this context the option of relying on customary practices for guidance, but prudently observes that they may distort the law when they "systematically undervalue the interests of less powerful participants." *Id.* at 1584. Another and even more obvious potential difficulty with the heavy reliance on custom is the temptation of participants to externalize costs on outsiders (e.g., customers). *See, e.g.*, Jennifer Rothman, *Copyright, Custom, and Lessons from the Common Law* (in this volume).

73 *See, e.g*, Merrill, supra note 17, at 1578; *but see* Owen Fiss, *The Forms of Justice*, *in* THE LAW AS IT COULD BE 1 (2003).

74 *See, e.g.*, NEIL K. KOMESAR, IMPERFECT ALTERNATIVES: CHOOSING INSTITUTIONS IN LAW, ECONOMICS, AND PUBLIC POLICY 139–40 (1991); Margaret H. Lemos, *Interpretive Methodology and Delegation to Courts: Are "Common Law Statues" Different?* (in this volume).

75 *See* HANOCH DAGAN, PROPERTY AT A CROSSROADS 90–96 (2005) [in Hebrew]. For similar reasons, I find it hard to celebrate Int'l News Services v. Associated Press, 248 U.S. 215 (1918), and I tend to prefer Judge Learned Hand's more cautious attitude in Cheney Bros. v. Doris Silk Corp., 279, 280 (2d Cir. 1929). *See* HANOCH DAGAN, THE LAW AND ETHICS OF RESTITUTION 137–38 (2004). For a careful, narrow reading of *INS*, which may well be acceptable, see Shyamkrishna Balganesh, *"Hot News": The Enduring Myth of Property in News*, 111 Colum. L. Rev. 419 (2011).

76 The question of when such changes are excessive is indeed one of the most serious and complicated issues in property law and theory. For my answer, see DAGAN, *supra* note 31, at Pt. II.

77 Recall that Merrill and Smith mention this feature when making their case for property exceptionalism. *See supra* note 9. As the text implies, however, not only is this feature not unique to property, but it does not even apply across the board of property law. *Cf.* Stop the Beach Renourishment v. Fla. Dep't of Envtl. Prot., 130 S.Ct. 2592 (2010).

protection.[78] In others, however, the fact that legislatures can and typically do apply their norms prospectively, and can moreover provide explicit or implicit compensation or set up other ameliorating means for the transition period, such as grandfather clauses, may count as a significant reason for judicial caution.

B. *Legitimacy*

When judged from the viewpoint of comparative performance, then, property – understood as an umbrella for a set of institutions governing core types of interpersonal relations regarding resources – seems quite amenable to judicial development, subject to its general conservative tilt and to the three local qualifications just mentioned. But this answer is not enough to justify judicial engagement in the shaping of our property institutions. Although Dorfman's attempt to provide a strong a priori case against judicial activism in property fails, he must be correct in insisting that the topic of judges and property should be approached as one of legitimacy and not as one – or, rather, not only as one[79] – of expected performance. The following discussion addresses this aspect. As in the previous section, I understand the development of property law as directed to refine our repertoire of default frameworks for interpersonal relations so that they live up better to their ideals, or shape them or create new ones in a way that promotes other worthy ideals.

I obviously do not challenge the legitimacy of legislatures taking part in such an exercise. As elected institutions, they are or, in a democracy, are at least presumed to be "well suited to represent the multiple interests involved in [] property law, and to reach compromises when necessary."[80] This simple proposition requires, for

[78] *See* Hanoch Dagan, *Restitution and Slavery: On Incomplete Commodification, Intergenerational Justice, and Legal Transitions*, 84 B.U. L. REV. 1139 (2004).

[79] Following Darwall's critique of Raz's service conception of authority, one may wonder (as Dorfman does) whether expected performance should have *any* significance, because grounding a right to rule or an obligation to obey in superior knowledge is difficult in a democracy. *See* Stephen Darwall, *Authority and Reasons: Exclusionary and Second-Personal*, 120 ETHICS 257 (2010). But as Scott Hershovitz correctly claims, it is nonetheless important to notice that there are practices in which "the role of authority is, as Raz says, to help subjects conform to reason, and one may not have authority in that kind of practice unless one can play that role." As Hershovitz further claims, this means that (1) like coaches or physicians, who participate in practices aimed at helping subjects to better conform to reason, judges too need to ground their authority in tools such as "expertise, freedom from bias, [or] an ability to solve coordination problems." (2) As in other such practices, judge-made law – the practice in which judges' role of normative authority plays a part – needs to be justified in a way that will not collapse to the service conception of authority. *See* Scott Hershovitz, *The Role of Authority*, 11 PHILOSOPHERS' IMPRINT art. 7 (2011). Thus, whereas Raz's service conception of authority implies legitimacy's collapse to expected performance, and whereas Darwall's critique dismisses expected performance as a basis for authority, I believe (with Hershovitz) that both expected performance and legitimacy are significant.

[80] *See* Balganesh, *supra* note 4, at 1592.

example, significant judicial deference in contexts of newly enacted legislation,[81] and renders legislative responses to judicial activism in other contexts obviously legitimate.

As with expected performance, however, the legitimacy of judicial activism in property must be addressed in comparative terms and without assuming that the legislature's authority necessarily implies the exclusion of the judiciary. Rather, to figure out the proper domain of judicial creation and modification of property institutions, if any, we need to examine potential bases of democratic legitimacy of judicial rulemaking in property matters given the character of property. Though I could not possibly hope to provide here an adequate account of democratic legitimacy, the following remarks should suffice to support the claim that the legitimate scope for judicial rulemaking in property is in fact rather broad.[82]

Consider the view endorsed by Dorfman that democratic legitimacy turns on co-authorship. To be meaningful, as noted, the ideal of co-authoring the shared commitments manifest in property law must not be axiomatically attached only to the legislative process. Rather, a commitment to co-authorship requires a more careful comparative account of meaningful participation and deliberation in legislation and in adjudication. This account can either look at the participation of the citizens directly or via elected representatives, or focus on the participation of the subset of citizens who are likely to be affected by the property law development at hand.

In general, participation and deliberation will more likely be found in legislation than in adjudication because lawmaking is legislation's only task, whereas in adjudication it emerges as part of the resolution of discrete disputes.[83] But the broad or representative participation that might significantly foster collective co-authorship does not seem typical in legislation on property matters. Quite the contrary. Some property doctrines, such as the law of co-ownership or of common interest communities, may seem too mundane as a subject for real democratic deliberation.[84] By contrast, where the creation or modification of property institutions provides significant opportunities for rent seeking, as in the repeated extensions of the term and scope of copyright, the legislative process is dominated by interest groups promoting narrow distributive goals[85] and thus cannot meaningfully count as collective co-authorship.

81 See Andrei Marmor, *Legislative Intent and the Authority of Law*, *in* Interpretation and Legal Theory 155 (1992). *See also* William N. Eskridge Jr., Dynamic Statutory Interpretation (1994).

82 Note that I do not claim for judicial supremacy, as in judicial review. My sole focus is on the legitimacy of judicial rulemaking where legislatures are silent.

83 Another reason relates to comparative costs: voters "often face a far less expensive road [than litigants] to registering their needs . . . in the political process." *See* Komesar, *supra* note 73, at 127.

84 *Cf.* Merrill & Smith, *supra* note 6, at 67. To preempt a possible objection, I may add that the notion that judicial passivity can upset the marginality of these topics within our public discourse does not seem particularly plausible.

85 *See generally* Jessica Litman, Digital Copyright (2001). *But cf.* Jonathan M. Barnett, *What's So Bad About Stealing?*, 4 J. Tort L. 1 (2011) (emphasizing the de facto reduction in copyright protection given the widespread disobedience of copyright law).

The ideal of participation by parties affected by the proposed development of property law is a more realistic expectation. But insofar as this participatory ideal is concerned, adjudication fares quite well and in some contexts probably better than legislation. The adjudicatory adversarial process fares well because, as hinted in Part III, it invites disagreements on questions of facts, opinion, and law, thus creating a forum where judges' normative and empirical horizons are constantly challenged by conflicting perspectives.[86] As Neil Komesar shows regarding tort law, at times adjudication seems to provide a qualitatively better forum for the participation of affected parties. One instance are cases where there is a sharp "distinction between ex ante and ex post stakes," so that the low ex ante probability of harm may obscure an important perspective rendered vivid in the ex post litigation triggered by the unfortunate realization of such harm.[87] Certain important developments of property institutions such as marital property, cohabitation, and leaseholds by the judiciary may also fit well into this category.

But perhaps democratic legitimacy should require only accountability of decision makers rather than the participation of citizens. Accountability is a more modest standard: it does not require active participation or deliberation, but merely insists that decision makers be responsive to citizens' values and preferences. As with participation, the accountability requirement may in the abstract appear as a trump in favor of elected legislators vis-à-vis unelected judges, given that re-election is a rather potent guarantee of responsiveness. But my previous observations regarding skewed participation in property matters immediately and detrimentally affect legislators' responsiveness as well. If most or many property matters are either politically marginal or dominated by interest groups, the legislators' expected responsiveness is likely to be rather limited. Likewise, an outright dismissal of judges' responsiveness seems exaggerated. As Llewellyn insisted, in their opinions judges need to "account to the public, to the general law-consumer" on a regular basis and in detail; they must persuade not only their brethren but also the legal community, including losing counsel, "that outcome, underpinning, and workmanship are worthy" and that their judgment was formed "in terms of the Whole, *seen whole*."[88] Although real-life adjudication surely falls short of these ideals, having these standards in place is nonetheless significant because it affects judges' utility function and thus informs judicial behavior, as even the tough-minded portrayals of judges as maximizers of their utility function admit.[89]

86 *Cf.* Alon Harel & Tsvi Kahana, *The Easy Core Case for Judicial Review*, 2 J. LEGAL ANALYSIS 1 (2010). Unlike Harel and Kahana, I do not claim that this feature of adjudication can justify judicial review.

87 *See* KOMESAR, *supra* note 73, at 135–36.

88 LLEWELLYN, THE COMMON LAW TRADITION, *supra* note 7, at 48, 132; LLEWELLYN, *American Common Law Tradition*, *supra* note 57, at 309–10.

89 *See* RICHARD A. POSNER, HOW JUDGES THINK 11–12, 60–61, 371 (2008). *See also* LAWRENCE BAUM, JUDGES AND THEIR AUDIENCES: A PERSPECTIVE ON JUDICIAL BEHAVIOR 16–21, 90, 106 (2006); Frederick Schauer, *Incentives, Reputation, and the Inglorious Determinants of Judicial Behavior*, 68 U. CIN. L. REV. 615, 615–17, 619–21 (2000).

Finally, consider again my critique of the conception of property as an exclusive right for its excessive focus on property's external dimension and its exaggerated emphasis on outsiders' obligations. Consider also my endorsement of a competing conception that perceives property as an umbrella for a set of property institutions, offered as default frameworks of interpersonal interactions embodying diverse ideals of human flourishing. The former conception, which imagines the development of property law as involving mandatory rules generating additional obligations on people, raises a significant requirement of legitimacy throughout the entire domain of property law possibly analogous to that of tort law. As noted, I obviously do not claim that property is not about others' obligations as well, and the earlier discussion is aimed at addressing the legitimacy challenge posed by property law developments that carry such an effect.[90] Yet, both the fact that the new or modified property institutions are often more about governance than about exclusion or that they weaken third-party obligations vis-à-vis the status quo, and the role that freedom of contract plays in property matters, as it indeed should, render judicial activism in property quite innocuous. The development of property law often generates additional frameworks of interpersonal interaction that enrich the repertoire of available options open to tailor-made adjustments. Insofar as this is the case or, in other words, insofar as the more power-conferring (as most contract law is) rather than the duty-imposing (á-la tort law)[91] aspects of property law are at stake, it is particularly difficult to justify the insistence on the exclusivity of legislatures in the creation and modification of property institutions.[92]

CONCLUDING REMARKS

Property is a complex and heterogeneous area of law, best thought of as a loose coalition of property institutions. The creation of new property institutions and the modification of existing ones are major events in the development of our social frameworks of interpersonal interaction. They shape and reshape our social order, adjusting it to new circumstances, challenges, and opportunities (think about the environment, the information revolution, or gender equality). In a democracy, legislatures have an important role to play in such developments. In certain contexts – as where a property innovation requires a regulatory structure, depends on specialized knowledge available elsewhere, or involves excessive widespread redistribution – judges should generally avoid taking part in this drama. They should likewise be

90 Consider, for example, cases in which the plaintiffs argue for some degree of protection against appropriation of a resource they hold, where the preexisting law perceives this type of resource as part of the public domain.

91 *See* Hanoch Dagan & Michael A. Heller, *Freedom of Contracts* § I.C.1 (unpublished manuscript).

92 A subset of these types of property development may, however, involve significant redistributive effects, which then may serve as an independent justification for judicial passivity. *See supra* text accompanying notes 75–77.

significantly deferential regarding newly enacted property legislation. But these qualifications of judicial authority are not unique to property, and other than them (or parallel ones I may have failed to mention), there seem to be no good reasons, either from expected performance or from legitimacy, for a particularly heightened degree of judicial passivity in property matters. Judges must respect property's stability and the conservatism entrenched in the *numerus clausus* principle, but so must legislators. Still, when appropriate, both legislators and judges should use their distinct comparative advantages to create new property institutions and modify existing ones so as to enrich and refine our repertoire of default frameworks of interpersonal relations.

2

Equitable Intellectual Property

What's Wrong with Misappropriation?

*Henry E. Smith**

INTRODUCTION

Misappropriation makes people nervous. Seen as a judge-made intellectual property regime it poses a cluster of related dangers. If it is a potential generator of property rights in information, it threatens free access to knowledge and the public domain.[1] Because the generators of those property rights are judges, it raises the specter of judicial overreach and activism.[2] If it is an open-ended source of property rights, it potentially imposes information costs widely on third parties and undermines the standardization of property.[3] And in its intermittent reliance on custom, it reinforces the sum of all these fears. All of these negative reactions are on display in the mixed reception to the landmark case of *International News Service* v. *Associated Press*.[4] The majority's decision to allow a claim for misappropriating hot news as "quasi-property" in the news business has raised objections from proponents of the public domain, legislative supremacists, property standardizers, and skeptics of custom – all of whom prefer Justice Brandeis's clarion call that information should be "free as the air to common use,"[5] and who find relief in efforts by subsequent courts,

* Fessenden Professor of Law, Harvard Law School. Email: hesmith@law.harvard.edu. For their helpful comments, I would like to thank Eric Claeys, Hanoch Dagan, Emily Sherwin, and the participants at the University of Pennsylvania symposium on Intellectual Property and the Common Law. All errors are mine.

1 *See, e.g.*, Peter S. Mennell, *Regulating "Spyware": The Limitations of State "Laboratories" and the Case for Federal Preemption of State Unfair Competition Laws*, 20 BERKELEY TECH. L.J. 1363 (2005).

2 *See, e.g.*, Ely-Norris Safe Co. v. Mosler Safe Co., 7 F.2d 603, 604 (2d Cir. 1925), *rev'd on other grounds*, 273 U.S. 132 (1927) ("Yet there is no part of the law which is more plastic than unfair competition, and what was not reckoned an actionable wrong 25 years ago may have become such today.... As we view it, the question is, as it always is in such cases, one of fact.").

3 *Cf.* Thomas W. Merrill & Henry E. Smith, *Optimal Standardization in the Law of Property: The Numerus Clausus Principle*, 110 YALE L.J. 1, 19–20 (2000).

4 248 U.S. 215 (1918).

5 *Id.* at 250 (1918) (Brandeis, J., dissenting); *see also* Cheney Brothers v. Doris Silk Corp., 35 F.2d 279 (2d Cir. 1929) (Hand, J.).

most notably Learned Hand and the mid-century Second Circuit, to put the genie of misappropriation back in its bottle.[6] Now that companies in the news business, including the Associated Press, are trying with limited success to push a misappropriation theory to hamper efforts by news aggregators and websites using facts from news stories,[7] the problems with misappropriation are as acute and as timely as ever.

At first blush, an invocation of traditional principles of equity would only exacerbate the fears of the critics of misappropriation. To them, equity looks like unconstrained and potentially out-of-control judicial innovation that can draw on custom and a judge's sense of amorphous "fairness" to reach any result imaginable and enshrine it as a property right binding on others who might use the classic nonrival resource – information. That Justice Pitney and the majority in *INS* v. *AP* were well aware that they were acting as a "court of equity," that the main remedy in equity was an injunction, and that much of the entire body of misappropriation law traces back to equity in its role of implementing some version of "commercial morality" all only reinforce this suspicion.[8] To the fears of the intellectual property skeptics can now be added the longstanding suspicion of courts of equity.

6 *See, e.g.*, Cheney Brothers v. Doris Silk Corp., 35 F.2d 279 (2d Cir. 1929) (Hand, J.). Douglas Baird recounts the concerted efforts of Judge Hand and the Second Circuit to constrict the reach of *INS* v. *AP*: "Learned Hand told other members of the panel in *Cheney* privately that although *INS* 'is somewhat of a stumbling block,' and although 'on principle it is hard to distinguish, and . . . the language applies, I cannot suppose that any principle of such far-reaching consequence was intended.'" Douglas G. Baird, *Common Law Intellectual Property and the Legacy of* International News Service v. Associated Press, 50 U. CHI. L. REV. 411, 419 (1983) (quoting Memorandum from Learned Hand to Martin T. Manton & Thomas W. Swann 2 (Oct. 8, 1929) (Learned Hand Papers, Harvard Law School Library)). Baird further notes that "[i]n his later opinions, Hand did not elaborate; he simply cited *Cheney* for the proposition that *INS* was to be narrowly construed and repeated his basic belief that artists had no 'natural right' to their efforts, but only those rights given them by the legislature." *Id.* (citing RCA Mfg. Co. v. Whiteman, 114 F.2d 86 (2d Cir.), *cert. denied*, 311 U.S. 712 (1940)). As for the rest of the court, Baird observes that the judges freely admitted to each other that they were reluctant to apply *INS*; he cites Judge Clark's quip during deliberations over the merits of *RCA Manufacturing Co. v. Whiteman* to Hand that "[i]n principle, this case is entirely indistinguishable from *International News Service v. A.P.* . . . and we might as well admit it. But we have conquered the News case before; it can be done again.'" *Id.* (citing Memorandum from Charles E. Clark to Learned Hand & Robert P. Patterson 3 (June 21, 1940) (Learned Hand Papers, Harvard Law School Library)).

7 *See, e.g.*, Barclays Capital Inc. v. Theflyonthewall.com, Inc., 650 F.3d 876 (2d Cir. 2011) (overruling anti-misappropriation injunction granted in Barclays Capital Inc. v. Theflyonthewall.com, 700 F. Supp. 2d 310 (S.D.N.Y. 2010)); Associated Press v. All Headline News Corp., 608 F. Supp. 2d 454 (S.D.N.Y. 2009) (holding inter alia that New York hot-news misappropriation law governs the claim).

8 R. Heinisch's Sons Co. v. Boker, 86 F. 765, 768 (C.C.S.D.N.Y. 1898) ("A court of equity keeps pace with the rapid strides of the sharp competitors for the prize of public favor, and insists that it shall be won only by fair trade."); *see also* Grafton Dulany Cushing, *On Certain Cases Analogous to Trade-Marks*, 4 HARV. L. REV. 321, 321 (1891) ("The underlying principle of the law of trade-marks is that of preventing one man from acquiring the reputation of another by fraudulent means, and of preventing fraud upon the public; in other words, the application of the broad principles of equity."); *id.* at 332 ("In cases analogous to trade-marks fraud is the gist of the action, and where fraud is found the court is able to give equitable relief, whether there is a breach of a technical right or not; and the relief may extend to whatever acts cause the damage complained of, whether or not the acts would be a breach of the plaintiff's right in the case of a trade-mark proper. [¶]The decision of the courts, in cases of this sort, have a far-reaching effect on commercial morality. It is not simply a question of expediency

This chapter challenges this skepticism.[9] The suspicion that equity would make misappropriation worse can be put down to a misunderstanding of equity. Rightly understood, the role for equity in private law, and in misappropriation in particular, is not to create property rights but to counteract the opportunistic misuse of the existing framework of property rights.[10] When it comes to private law, the common law and statutes set up simple structures such as basic entitlements and frameworks for parties to coordinate with each other. Simple structures are open to manipulation by those with too much information. For example, the common law provides for exceptions to the law of trespass for wandering cattle in open range,[11] for certain building encroachments,[12] and for those who mix their labor with others' materials.[13] In all these situations, bad faith is disqualifying,[14] because of the invitation for opportunistic invocation of these doctrines by those who are well aware of the boundaries and seek to take more than the intended advantage of the law's indulgence of low-level trespasses. Rather than use a bright-line cut-off based on the amount or type of use, the law makes an ex post inquiry keyed to opportunism. A system that reserves ex post harsh treatment for a limited domain of behavior that is highly likely to be opportunistic can be better than a system with either all law-style or all equity-style decision making.[15] Equity as a safety valve on the law raises issues of ex ante spelling out versus ex post discretionary decision making – rules versus standards[16] – but it also consists of a number of other features

which they are called upon to try, but how best to mould the opinion of the community that right may prevail rather than wrong.").

9 This chapter tries to answer some of the questions I raised in Henry E. Smith, *Does Equity Pass the Laugh Test?: A Response to Oliar and Sprigman*, 95 VIRGINIA LAW REVIEW IN BRIEF 9 (2009), http://www.virginialawreview.org/inbrief/2009/04/20/smith.pdf.

10 Henry E. Smith, An Economic Analysis of Law versus Equity (draft May 30, 2011), available at http://www.law.northwestern.edu/colloquium/law_economics/documents/2011_SmithLawVersusEquity.pdf.

11 *See, e.g.*, ROBERT C. ELLICKSON ORDER WITHOUT LAW: HOW NEIGHBORS SETTLE DISPUTES 42–43 (1991); Kenneth R. Vogel, *The Coase Theorem and California's Animal Trespass Law*, 16 J. LEGAL STUD. 149 (1987).

12 *See* Golden Press, Inc. v. Rylands, 235 P.2d 592 (Colo. 1951); Raab v. Casper, 124 Cal.Rptr. 590 (Cal. Ct. App. 1975) (California Good Faith Improver Act); Kelvin H. Dickinson, *Mistaken Improvers of Real Estate*, 64 N.C. L. REV. 37, 42–49 (1985).

13 Wetherbee v. Green, 22 Mich. 311 (1871); Richard A. Epstein, *Possession as the Root of Title*, 13 GA. L. REV. 1221 (1979); Thomas W. Merrill, *Accession and Original Ownership*, 1 J. LEGAL ANALYSIS 459 (2009); Henry E. Smith, *Intellectual Property as Property: Delineating Entitlements in Information*, 116 YALE L.J. 1742, 1766–77 (2007).

14 *See* Light v. United States, 220 U.S. 523, 537 (1911) (noting that fencing out rules "are intended to condone trespasses by straying cattle; they have no application to cases where they are driven upon unfenced land in order that they may feed there"). On bad faith in accession, *see, e.g.*, Union Naval Stores Co. v. United States, 240 U.S. 284, 291 (1916); Betts v. Lee, 5 Johns. 348, 349–50 (N.Y. Sup. Ct. 1810); *see also* Jay L. Koh, *From Hoops to Hard Drives: An Accession Law Approach to the Inevitable Misappropriation of Trade Secrets*, 48 AM. U. L. REV. 271, 333–34 (1998).

15 Smith, *supra* note 10, at 39–55; see also Kenneth Ayotte, Ezra Friedman, & Henry E. Smith, A Safety Valve Model of Equity as Anti-Opportunism (March 30, 2013), available at SSRN: http://ssrn.com/abstract=2245098.

16 *See, e.g.*, FREDERICK SCHAUER, PLAYING BY THE RULES: A PHILOSOPHICAL EXAMINATION OF RULE-BASED DECISION-MAKING IN LAW AND IN LIFE 7–8 (1991); Louis Kaplow, *Rules Versus Standards: An*

that work together, including in personam and not in rem effect, the emphasis on good faith and notice, the employment of moral standards, and its often inherent vagueness. These features work together to counteract party opportunism.

The law of misappropriation shows both the strengths and the limits of equity. These limits are better known than the potential advantages of equity. In this chapter, I set forth a number of features of traditional equity and show how they target opportunistic behavior and so potentially cabin the excesses of the equitable approach to misappropriation that worry so many today. Certain areas of intellectual property that are ambiguous in terms of how open-ended they are – trade secret, publicity rights, misappropriation, and unfair competition in general – both show the historical traces of equity and are the parts of intellectual property that could – if any can – most benefit from a limited equitable safety valve that would respond to the open-endedness of opportunistic behavior.

This chapter focuses on those proxies used by equity to target opportunism: in personam (or less than fully in rem) application, disproportionate harm, bad faith, and deception. Equity is not an invitation to sail free on an ocean of "commercial morality," nor is it even close to being a cost-benefit test or an all-things-considered judicial discretionary fiat. The account of equity as a targeted judicial intervention against party opportunism suggests that it has a limited but ongoing role as a backstop to more central laws of intellectual property such as patent, copyright, and trademark and, in a more modest way, industry custom. Areas such as trade secret and publicity rights that are related to unfair competition can draw in a limited way on the constrained safety valve provided by equity.

Part I examines misappropriation and the hot-news doctrine from the point of view of its roots in equity and its continuing equitable nature at the time of *INS v. AP*. In Part II, I set forth a functional theory of equity as a safety valve aimed at discouraging the opportunism made possible by the ex ante structures of the private law. Equity is not free-floating judicial discretion based on personal notions of morality. Rather it filters very basic common sense morality through a structure of proxies for opportunism and shifting burdens of justification. Part III then applies this theory of equity as a limited safety valve to offer a reconstruction of misappropriation. I also offer a few tentative thoughts on the influence that Legal Realism and its aftermath have had on equity and its role in misappropriation in particular. Part IV concludes.

I. MISAPPROPRIATION

Misappropriation is the unwanted stepchild of intellectual property. It grew out of unfair competition, an area that traces back to the limited efforts of equity courts to

Economic Analysis, 42 DUKE L.J. 557 (1992); Amnon Lehavi, *The Dynamic Law of Property: Theorizing the Role of Legal Standards*, 42 RUTGERS L.J. 81 (2010); Kathleen Sullivan, *The Justices of Rules and Standards*, 106 HARV. L. REV. 22, 56–67 (1992).

enforce commercial morality.[17] In our era, commentators from across the spectrum are skeptical of efforts of judges to apply notions of commercial morality directly, which to cynical ears sounds oxymoronic. This part sets forth the contours of misappropriation, especially in its application to hot news, and notes the features that raise red flags for a wide variety of intellectual property (IP) commentators.

Consider hot news. In the early twentieth century courts were sometimes called on to restrict the unauthorized use of information by another business. The landmark in this area is the much-noted case of *International News* v. *Associated Press*.[18] The INS and AP were both consortia of newspapers that cooperated in gathering news. The AP accused the INS of using its news stories in three ways: by bribing employees to divulge the news before it had been disseminated by AP papers, by inducing AP newspapers to breach their agreement with the AP not to spread news other than through their newspapers, and finally and most controversially by copying or using (with rewrite) uncopyrighted news reports from the AP's newspapers for its own newspapers. Copyright was not available because of the formalities required at the time, and in any event it would only protect against lifting expression – not against use of the hot news qua information. The bribery and inducement are relatively uncontroversial applications of trade secret – itself an outgrowth of misappropriation and unfair competition. But the lifting of the news and the repackaging of it are the tough problem.

The majority per Justice Pitney held that the lifting of the hot news was misappropriation and enjoinable. Often overlooked, but as we will see quite importantly, the Supreme Court emphasizes at the outset that it was operating as an equity court, and in holding for the AP it drew on this source of power in saying that the complained-of behavior should not be beyond a court of equity to enjoin: "The transaction speaks for itself and a court of equity ought not to hesitate long in characterizing it as unfair competition in business."[19] Indeed the Court repeatedly makes reference to the case as one sounding in equity and its role as an equity court in such a case.[20]

The majority opinion itself weaves together – or at least collocates – a number of strands that along with the stirring dissent by Justice Brandeis help explain its enduring fascination. The majority notes that the INS was trying "to reap where it has not sown,"[21] suggesting a Lockean natural rights grounding for the rights against misappropriation. Because Lockean labor-desert theory is one major justification often offered for IP and for property more generally, some have seen *INS* v. *AP*, rightly or wrongly, as standing for the generative power of Lockean natural rights

[17] *See* Zechariah Chafee, Jr., *Unfair Competition*, 53 HARV. L. REV. 1289 (1940). Chafee identifies the first use of the term "unfair competition" in Lord Eldon's opinion in Hogg v. Kirby, 8 Ves. 215 (1803). *Id.* at 1296 n.15.

[18] 248 U.S. 215 (1918).

[19] 248 U.S. at 240.

[20] *Id.* at 237–38; *id.* at 240 (twice).

[21] *Id.* at 239.

theory for property rights in information.[22] Relatedly, without protection, the gatherer of the news would have less incentive to gather it and the business might collapse altogether.

A full-blown Lockean property theory would be highly generative in another sense: it might affect a wide and disparate set of duty bearers. To head off this objection the Court holds that the right avails only against those in direct competition with the gatherer of the hot news: to capture this limitation on the circle of duty bearers, the Court terms the entitlement that the AP holds as "quasi-property" – the "quasi" to reflect that it is not fully in rem. Thus, people are as free as ever to discuss the news around the water cooler even if the news still has news value (making it gossip-worthy). If, however, the right expands outward to more duty bearers and to new subject matters, it is in potential conflict with the principle of standardization in property – the *numerus clausus*.[23] According to the *numerus clausus* courts are supposed to leave the creation of new in rem property rights to the legislature. Otherwise the information costs and general imposition on others – here others who would like to make use of what would be in the public domain – would be severe.

The famous dissent of Justice Brandeis hits these cautionary themes. Perhaps most famously he argues that the default for information should be that it is in the public domain – that it should be "free as the air to common use."[24] For a nonrival resource such as information there is no allocation problem to be solved via property rights: more than one person can "use" the news without interfering with others' use. He admitted that a solution to the problem of incentives for news gatherers who cannot appropriate a sufficient return might be required, but Congress, which has better access to all the relevant information on the size and effect of the problem and the various solutions, is in a better position to furnish such a solution and to balance it against concerns about free speech. As an aside, he notes that the INS was shut out from news channels including transatlantic cables because the Allied authorities in Britain and France did not like the coverage of the war provided in the Hearst newspapers that formed a large part of the INS. Justice Brandeis sees even quasi-property as imposing on third parties. Legislatures, by contrast, would be in a better position to ration property treatment. In the years after *INS*, other industries tried to secure protection against misappropriation – notably, the clothing industry wanted protection for fashions. The Second Circuit and Judge Learned Hand in particular nipped this further development in the bud.[25] Indeed Judge Hand behind

22 *See, e.g.*, Justin Hughes, *The Philosophy of Intellectual Property*, 77 Geo. L.J. 287, 305–06 (1988) (discussing *INS* v. *AP* as example of "value added" version of Lockean labor theory); *see also* Baird, *supra* note 6, at 413 (criticizing Lockean basis for *INS* v. *AP*). For a Lockean justification of usufructuary IP rights, see Eric R. Claeys, *Intellectual Usufructs: Trade Secrets, Hot News, and the Usufructuary Paradigm at Common Law* (in this volume).

23 Merrill & Smith, *supra* note 3, at 19–20.

24 248 U.S. at 250.

25 *See, e.g.*, Cheney Brothers v. Doris Silk Corp., 35 F.2d 279 (2d Cir. 1929) (Hand, J.). *See supra* note 6.

the scenes was a determined opponent of an expansive version of *INS* v. *AP* and even thought that the Supreme Court could not really have meant what it said about protecting time-sensitive information.[26]

To these themes of potential expansiveness, institutional competence, and third-party information costs can be added the role of custom. Richard Epstein seeks to put *INS* v. *AP* on a firmer footing by explaining it as the adoption of a custom among news organizations not to reproduce news from rivals while it still had news value but to use rivals' stories as the source of tips – in a form of "reverse engineering."[27] The cost advantage of a free-rider is not implicated when a news organization does go to the trouble of tracking down the news for itself. This equilibrium would be stable if the competitors' long-term benefits from mutual forbearance outweighed the short-term gain they could achieve by defecting. The one caveat in Epstein's endorsement of the majority opinion is that he argues that the custom may have been subject to a necessity exception or defense.[28] The INS could not reverse engineer the AP's stories because it was shut off from the news by the Allied authorities. To evaluate the INS's possible necessity defense under the custom we would want to know if the INS was appropriating any stories other than those about the war in Europe to which it did not have direct access.

Resting *INS* v. *AP* on custom leads to some of the same objections that have been raised against hot-news misappropriation itself. The custom might be good for those who devise and enforce it, but it may impose externalities on those who would like to enjoy the public domain.[29] Custom also may present third-party information costs for others,[30] and it is open to question whether limiting misappropriation rights to quasi-property will be enough to cabin the third-party information costs sufficiently to make misappropriation rights worthwhile.

An alternative to this Lockean property version of misappropriation emphasizes unfair competition. In an insightful recent article, Shyam Balganesh argues that *INS* v. *AP* does not create property rights, but represents the intersection of unfair competition and unjust enrichment.[31] On his account the hot-news doctrine is a common law response to the problem of free-riders in an industry characterized by shared news gathering. The free-rider is simply liable for the costs saved of news gathering, on a restitution theory. This account has the virtue of cabining the *INS* v. *AP*–style misappropriation and, like the equitable account I offer later, emphasizes

26 *See supra* note 6.

27 Richard A. Epstein, International News Service v. Associated Press: *Custom and Law as Sources of Property Rights in News*, 78 Va. L. Rev. 85 (1992).

28 *Id.* at 117–18.

29 *See* Jennifer E. Rothman, *The Questionable Use of Custom in Intellectual Property*, 93 Va. L. Rev. 1899 (2007); *cf.* Ellickson, *supra* note 11, at 169–70.

30 *See* Henry E. Smith, *Community and Custom in Property*, 10 Theoretical Inquiries L. 6, 35–36 (2009).

31 Shyamkrishna Balganesh, *"Hot News": The Enduring Myth of Property in News*, 111 Colum. L. Rev. 419 (2011).

the non-in rem character of quasi-property – preventing it from being the generator of property rights in news in a promiscuous fashion. The problem is that the remedy in *INS* v. *AP* and other misappropriation cases is an injunction, not an award of restitution damages for unjust enrichment.[32] Nor does the Court invoke restitution in its opinion. Perhaps most importantly, unjust enrichment makes people nervous for some of the same reasons that misappropriation does: on a common view, it is hardly less expansive, discretionary, and potentially arbitrary than misappropriation itself.[33] I argue later that Balganesh's basic picture has a lot going for it, but that being too exclusively focused on the common law,[34] it could still benefit from the role that traditional equity has played as a safety valve to the common law.

Although Epstein's invocation of custom and Balganesh's emphasis on unfair competition and the "quasi" in quasi-property are helpful in narrowing in on what is – and should be – going on in misappropriation, they do not go far enough. It is time to return to equity.

II. EQUITY AS A SOLUTION TO OPPORTUNISM

At first blush, equity would seem to exacerbate these problems rather than form their solution. Equity is sometimes thought to be unconstrained, ex post fairness-based decision making according to an individual judge's unconstrained discretion informed by his or her moral views – the "Chancellor's foot."[35]

32 Balganesh regards this as a mistake. *Id.* at 480–86. For an expansive approach to misappropriation based on unjust enrichment, see Rudolf Callmann, *He Who Reaps Where He Has Not Sown: Unjust Enrichment in the Law of Unfair Competition*, 55 HARV. L. REV. 595, 600 (1942) ("It is not the purpose of this article to lay down a developed law of unfair competition, but only to advocate the extension of that law as it exists today to include a concept of unjust enrichment."). For a recent proposal to use restitution remedies to protect the framework of competition rules in situations similar to that in *INS* v. *AP*, see Ofer Grosskopf, *Protection of Competition Rules via the Law of Restitution*, 79 TEX. L. REV. 1981 (2001).

33 Indeed the literature on restitution struggles constantly with this problem, as does the new Restatement. *See, e.g.*, RESTATEMENT (THIRD) ON RESTITUTION AND UNJUST ENRICHMENT § 2; *see also, e.g.*, Andrew Kull, *Rationalizing Restitution*, 83 CAL. L. REV. 1191 (1995); Emily Sherwin, *Restitution and Equity: An Analysis of the Principle of Unjust Enrichment*, 79 TEX. L. REV. 2083 (2001). The new Restatement's solution is to emphasize sources of liability in other areas of law and then to invoke the civilian-style notion of unjustified enrichment – enrichment without an adequate legal basis – as the predicate for liability in restitution. I would claim that the approach to equity I am arguing for would help define the contours of unjust enrichment, but that is an issue best left for another day.

34 Balganesh, *supra* note 31, at 495–97; *see also* Shyamkrishna Balganesh, *The Pragmatic Incrementalism of Common Law Intellectual Property*, 63 VAND. L. REV. 1543, 1560–62 (2010).

35 The phrase encapsulates Selden's famous critique of equity: "Equity is a Roguish thing: for law we have a measure, know what to trust to; Equity is according to the Conscience of him that is Chancellor, and as that is larger or narrower, so is Equity. 'Tis all one as if they should make the Standard for the measure we call a Foot, a Chancellor's Foot; what an uncertain Measure would be this. One Chancellor has a long Foot, another a short Foot, a Third an indifferent Foot: 'Tis the same thing in the Chancellor's Conscience." John Selden, *Equity*, *in* TABLE-TALK: BEING THE DISCOURSES OF JOHN SELDEN, ESQ. 43, 43–44 (London, J.M. Dent & Co. 2d ed. 1689).

Traditional equity was more than this, and in related work, I argue that a major theme of equity in private law is anti-opportunism.[36] Misappropriation grew out of equity. This history is suggestive and not random, but my main purpose here is to apply a functional theory of the role of equity to the problem of misappropriation and to show how it has the potential of solving some of the concerns with misappropriation. Briefly put, equity serves as a limited safety valve to discourage opportunism that might arise from people taking hard-to-foresee advantage of the inevitable inadequacies of the ex ante structures of the common and statutory law.

One might think that the inherent vagueness of the notion of opportunism causes the equitable approach to be yet another recapitulation of the vagueness and expansiveness of *INS*-style misappropriation. Because I argue that equity used a system of proxies for opportunism and shifting presumptions triggered by the proxies, providing an exact definition of opportunism turns out not to be necessary. Indeed, the inability to define opportunism with exactitude ex ante is the whole point of invoking equity in the first place. Nonetheless, opportunism has been an important notion in law and economics, and to have proxies for opportunism we need to know something about what those proxies are proxies of.

So, what is opportunism? Here is a working definition: the use of the system in hard-to-foresee ways by better informed parties even at the expense of shrinking total surplus.[37] Opportunism is a moral notion, but it presents a special problem because of transaction costs. If opportunism were easy to define and detect ex ante, it could be handled by rules, and parties in personal contact with each other, including competitors not restrained by antitrust, would contract such behavior away. But ex ante measures are not costless, and opportunists, in their search for overlooked mismatches between a rule and its purpose, present high costs of deterrence through rules. This is familiar from tax law, where the announcement of a bright-line rule invites a search for loopholes and efforts at manipulation.[38] "Walking the line" – or dancing around it – is the result.[39]

This account of equity is functional rather than historical, but it is traditional, in the sense that proponents and practitioners of equity can be interpreted as more or less consciously battling opportunism. And they have been fairly direct about it – something that is lost in our post-fusion caricature of equity as freely contextualized

36 Smith, *supra* note 10.

37 For discussions of opportunism in economics, see, e.g., OLIVER E. WILLIAMSON, THE ECONOMIC INSTITUTIONS OF CAPITALISM 47 (1985) (defining "opportunism" as "self-interest seeking with guile."); Margaret F. Brinig & Steven M. Crafton, *Opportunism in Marriage*, 22 J. LEGAL STUD. 869 (1994); Timothy J. Muris, *Opportunistic Behavior and the Law of Contracts*, 65 MINN. L. REV. 521 (1981); Oliver E. Williamson, *Opportunism and its Critics*, 14 MANAGERIAL & DECISION ECON. 97 (1993).

38 *See* David A. Weisbach, *Formalism in the Tax Law*, 66 U. CHI. L. REV. 860 (1999); *see also* Stanley S. Surrey, *Complexity and the Internal Revenue Code: The Problem of the Management of Tax Detail*, 34 L. & CONTEMP. PROBS. 673, 707 n.31 (1969).

39 *Cf.* Duncan Kennedy, *Form and Substance in Private Law Adjudication*, 89 HARV. L. REV. 1685, 1695–96 (1976) (noting tendency of rules to encourage people to "walk the line" in order to comply with the letter but not the spirit of a rule).

discretionary decision making. The equitable tradition traces back to Aristotle, who held that equity must intervene when law is imperfect owing to its generality,[40] and judges have invoked the Aristotelian tradition of equity explicitly.[41] One reason that law is imperfect from its generality is that the generality causes an imperfect fit between means and ends, which in turn gives opportunists an opening to exploit the gap. Even more strikingly, in the nineteenth century, equity courts employed a system of presumptions based on notions of "near fraud," in which a highly unequal exchange or "disproportionate hardship" is a proxy raising a presumption of fraud, even though it might not be full-blown fraud provable through conventional means.[42]

The question that a hybrid decision-making system raises is what proxies courts should use to identify opportunism. There are two problems. Not only is opportunism inherently difficult to specify ex ante, at least without producing more opportunism, but there is also the problem of opportunists' ability to adjust to nominally ex post decision making. If ex post decision making is purely predictable and parties can adjust to it, it is no different from ex ante decision making from the point of view of the opportunist. What the equitable decision-making mode requires are proxies that are either robust enough or adjustable enough not to fall into this trap.

Several themes of equity can be seen as isolating such robust high-level proxies. First is good faith. Good faith in equity turns on notice. If someone acts with notice, a strong, sometimes conclusive presumption of opportunism is warranted. If an actor knows the exact location of the line that the law draws and takes an unexpected, self-serving action with respect to it, this shifts the presumption to the actor to justify the action. Thus, a bad faith purchaser cannot take advantage of rules that protect buyers of goods entrusted to merchants who are dealing in the kind of good in question.[43]

40 Courts of equity have often quoted Aristotle's distinction between law and equity in which equity corrects "law where law is defective because of its generality." ARISTOTLE, NICOMACHEAN ETHICS 317 (G.P. Goold ed., H. Rackham trans., 1982). One problem of generality is its invitation to opportunism.

41 *See, e.g.*, Riggs v. Palmer, 22 N.E. 188, 189 (N.Y. 1889) (quoting Aristotle on equity); see also Christopher St. German, DOCTOR AND STUDENT 94–107 (T.F.T. Plucknett & J.L. Barton, eds. 1974); Eric G. Zahnd, *The Application of Universal Laws to Particular Cases: A Defense of Equity in Aristotelianism and Anglo-American Law*, 59 LAW & CONTEMP. PROBS. 263, 270–75 (Winter 1996) (documenting influence of Aristotelian equity on Anglo-American law); *but cf.* Darien Shanske, *Four Theses: Preliminary to an Appeal to Equity*, 57 STAN. L. REV. 2053 (2005) (arguing that Aristotle's equity was not primarily legal).

42 Richard Epstein's theory of unconscionability as a presumption against deals that raise the specter of fraud without the full evidence for it ("near-fraud") is a perhaps slightly narrowed-down version of this vision. Richard A. Epstein, *Unconscionability: A Critical Reappraisal*, 18 J.L. & ECON. 293, 293, 293–301 (1975). On the nineteenth century view that unconscionability referred to fraud that could not readily be proved, *see, e.g.*, Seymour v. Delancey, 3 Cow. 445, 521–22, 15 Am.Dec. 270 (N.Y. Sup. 1824) ("Inadequacy of price, unless it amount to conclusive evidence of fraud, is not itself a sufficient ground for refusing a specific performance of an agreement") (citing cases); James Gordley, *Equality in Exchange*, 69 CAL. L. REV. 1587, 1639 (1981).

43 *See generally* Saul Levmore, *Variety and Uniformity in the Treatment of the Good-Faith Purchaser*, 16 J. LEGAL STUD. 43 (1987).

Another proxy for opportunism that I concentrate on in the following is disproportionate hardship.[44] This concept is most familiar in the standard for injunctions as a safety valve: if someone is otherwise entitled to an injunction but the harm to the defendant is greatly disproportionate to the benefit to the plaintiff, then there is a reason not to grant the injunction. Some see this as ex post second-guessing but note – as is sometimes forgotten – that this is not a simple ex post balancing test in the sense of looking for which side's hardship outweighs the other's.[45] Nor is it an invitation to do a cost-benefit analysis. Rather the question for the court is gross disparity in burden and benefit. This issue can be eyeballed, without drawing the court into valuation difficulties. Importantly, gross disparity also can be an invitation to or result of opportunistic behavior.

Interestingly, the gross disparity test has a parallel in Harold Demsetz's standard for regulating the competitive process. Because competition is presumptively good and courts are not equipped to evaluate the benefits and costs of various competitive practices, we should only make illegal those devices in which the harm clearly outweighs the benefit.[46] In other words, if the standard were equipoise, Type I errors would likely outnumber Type II errors and outweigh them in severity, requiring an adjustment in favor of allowing the competition (or granting the injunction for an established rights violation). Adding opportunism to the picture only reinforces the relative weight of the two kinds of error and therefore strengthens the conclusion that only competitive practices that are clearly bad should be dealt with. For opportunism, this evaluation often needs to be made ex post and somewhat vaguely, triggered by proxies such a good faith, and notice, as well as disproportionate hardship.

Take trespass to land as an illustration of the structure of proxies and presumptions in traditional equity. The basic rule is that equity will not enjoin a mere trespass.[47] But for continuing and repeated trespasses, the legal remedy is inadequate – because of valuation problems, a multiplicity of suits, and the inability to exercise the power of an owner without answering to a damages-measuring court. So equity will afford an injunction for continued or repeated trespasses.[48] But in the case of building

44 Smith, *supra* note 10, at 14–16, 34–36, 38–39, 50.

45 *See* Mark R. Gergen, John M. Golden, & Henry E. Smith, *The Supreme Court's Accidental Revolution? The Test for Permanent Injunctions*, 112 COLUM. L. REV. 203, 226–30, 246–49 (2012). Related is the notion of a forfeiture, which also shifts the burden of justification.

46 Harold Demsetz, *Wealth Distribution and the Ownership of Rights*, 1 J. LEGAL STUD. 223, 231–32 (1972).

47 *See, e.g.*, Justices of Pike Cnty. v. Griffin & W. Point Plank Rd. Co., 11 Ga. 246, 250 (1852) ("It is well understood that Equity will not interfere in a case of a mere trespass.").

48 *See, e.g.*, Lucy Webb Hayes Nat'l Training Sch. for Deaconesses & Missionaries v. Geoghegan, 281 F. Supp. 116, 117 (D.D.C. 1967) ("It has been established for a great many years that equity will enjoin a continuing trespass or a series of repeated trespasses where an action for damages would not be an adequate remedy."); Doody v. Spurr, 51 N.E.2d 981, 984 (Mass. 1943) ("An injunction is an appropriate remedy to enjoin repeated trespasses, even though no substantial damage is thereby incurred by the landowner.").

encroachments, which are continuing trespasses,[49] the injunction can be a severe remedy. The traditional rule was to enjoin encroaching structures anyway,[50] but the tendency has been to soften this rule and allow a damages remedy instead.[51] Sometimes this response is taken as evidence of ex post aversion to waste. But disproportionate hardship can be regarded more generally as a proxy for opportunism and a trigger to reverse the burden to justify the result. Here disproportionate hardship flips the presumption against an injunction. However, if the encroacher is in bad faith – in the sense of the encroacher's knowledge of the boundary and the violation of right – the accommodation for undue hardship does not apply and the presumption shifts decisively back to the injunction.[52] This is a highly structured decision-making procedure, and it is quite tailored to a problem – the problem of opportunism.

To discourage opportunism, equity's safety valve goes beyond the use of standards, although use of ex post decision making is certainly part of the picture.[53] Equity exhibits a wide range of features that work together as a safety valve and serve to minimize the destabilizing and chilling effect it can cause. Start with ex post decision making: opportunism by its nature may be punished more cost effectively ex post than defined and forbidden by trying to close off every loophole ex ante.[54] Closing nine loopholes is no better than not closing any if all the sophisticated parties will rush through the tenth one that remains open.

The downside to ex post standards that leave content to be filled in by a decision maker ex post at the point of application is that they can chill legitimate behavior by those who worry about whether the ex post judgment may fall on them; this effect

49 Restatement (Second) of Torts § 158 ("One is subject to liability to another for trespass . . . if he intentionally . . . (c) fails to remove from the land a thing which he is under a duty to remove"); id. § 161(1) ("A trespass may be committed by the continued presence on the land of a structure . . . which the actor tortiously placed there whether or not the actor has the ability to remove it").

50 *See, e.g.*, Pile v. Pedrick, 31 A. 646 (Pa. 1895); Restatement (First) of Restitution § 42(1) (1937).

51 *See* Golden Press, Inc. v. Rylands, 235 P.2d 592 (Colo. 1951); Raab v. Casper, 124 Cal.Rptr. 590 (Cal. Ct. App. 1975) (California Good Faith Improver Act); Restatement (Third) of Restitution and Unjust Enrichment § 10 (2011); Dickinson, *supra* note 12, at 42–49.

52 Golden Press, 235 P.2d at 595 (citing cases). For an extreme example in which a court punished an apparently originally good faith improver who demolished the building after fruitless negotiations with the encroached-on landowner, see Producers Lumber & Supply Co. v. Olney Building Co., 333 S.W.2d 619 (Tex. Ct. Civ. App. 1960).

53 *See, e.g.*, Schauer, *supra* note 16, at 7–8; Kaplow, *supra* note 16, at 557; Lehavi, *supra* note 16; Sullivan, *supra* note 16, at 56–67

54 The civilians seem to have something like this in mind when they speak of "abuse of right." *See, e.g.*, Anna di Robilant, *Abuse of Rights: The Continental Drug and the Common Law*, 61 Hastings L.J. 687 (2010); Antonio Gambaro, *Abuse of Rights in Civil Law Tradition*, 4 Eur. Rev. Priv. L. 561 (1995); Larissa M. Katz, A Jurisdictional Principle of Abuse of Right (Draft, February 8, 2010), available at SSRN: http://ssrn.com/abstract=1417955; Lehavi, *supra* note 16; Joseph M. Perillo, *Abuse of Rights: A Pervasive Legal Concept*, 27 Pac. L.J. 37 (1995); A. N. Yiannopoulos, *Civil Liability for Abuse of Right: Something Old, Something New . . .*, 54 La. L. Rev. 1173, 1192–93 (1994) (noting similarities and differences between abuse of right and equity).

stems from the vagueness of the legal directive.[55] At first this downside might seem to be equity's downfall, but some of the features of equity potentially lessen these impacts. First, equity only acts in personam, not in rem,[56] and protects property rights, but is supposed to avoid declaring property rights.[57] It was this limit that the Court in *INS* v. *AP* was invoking when it emphasized that misappropriation did not give rise to in rem rights but only quasi-property whose duty holders were those in direct competition. Further, equity's irreparable injury requirement, which used to be jurisdictional and is sill a threshold inquiry for injunctions, makes of equity an exception, a safety valve.[58] As we have seen, equity in all its manifestations is keyed to notice (good faith), which limits the class of people on whom the hammer can fall, somewhat along the lines of the scienter requirements in criminal law.

Finally, although one might think that invocations of commercial morality are inherently vague, this is not always true. The customs of an industry may be very clear, especially in their broad outlines, and more generally, simple everyday morality is

[55] *See, e.g.*, John E. Calfee & Richard Craswell, *Some Effects of Uncertainty on Compliance with Legal Standards*, 70 VA. L. REV. 965 (1984).

[56] *See* HAROLD GREVILLE HANBURY & RONALD HARLING MAUDSLEY, MODERN EQUITY 15 (10th ed. 1976) ("The key to understanding the nature of equitable remedies is the appreciation of the importance of the maxim that 'Equity acts in personam.' This has been the basis of the jurisdiction from the earliest days; and is so today"); 2 JOSEPH STORY, COMMENTARIES ON EQUITY JURISPRUDENCE AS ADMINISTERED IN ENGLAND AND AMERICA §§ 743–44 (Melville M. Bigelow ed. 13th ed., 1988, 2d print 1999) (1853); James Barr Ames, *Law and Morals*, *in* LECTURES ON LEGAL HISTORY 435, 443–44 (1913) ("Blackstone has asserted that the common-law judges, by a liberal interpretation of the Statute of Westminster, by means of the action on the case, might have done the work of a court of equity. Such an opinion betrays a singular failure to appreciate the fundamental difference between law and equity, namely, that the law acts in rem, while equity acts in personam. The difference between the judgment at law and the decree in equity goes to the root of the whole matter."); Charles E. Rounds, Jr., *Relief for IP Rights Infringement Is Primarily Equitable: How American Legal Education Is Short-Changing the 21st Century Corporate Litigator*, 26 SANTA CLARA COMPUTER & HIGH TECH. L.J. 313, 322 (2010) ("Whereas a judgment at law declared the plaintiff's rights, a decree in Equity imposed duties on the defendant. In other words, equity acted and still acts in personam."); Roger Young & Stephen Spitz, *SUEM-Spitz's Ultimate Equitable Maxim: In Equity, Good Guys Should Win and Bad Guys Should Lose*, 55 S.C. L. REV. 175, 177, 182–84 (2003) (exploring nine equitable principles, including "[e]quity acts in personam, not in rem"). As Lord Campbell memorably put it, "I have the most sincere deference for the Court of Chancery, acting within its jurisdiction. I believe there never was a tribunal established in any country which is more entitled to respect, but still there are limits to its jurisdiction, it cannot do every thing. The Lord Chancellor, I presume, would not grant an injunction against the French Republic marching an army across the Rhine or the Alps. The Court of Chancery must be kept within its jurisdiction, and then I am sure it confers the highest benefits upon the community." Duke of Brunswick v. King of Hanover, (1848) 9 Eng. Rep. 993, 1003, 2 H.L.C. 1, 27; *see also* JOHN MCGHEE, SNELL'S EQUITY (13th ed. 2000) § 3–27 (discussing maxim "[e]quity acts *in personam*," setting out statutory extension of equity jurisdiction and noting persisting limits by quoting Lord Campbell in Duke of Brunswick v. King of Hanover (1848) 9 Eng. Rep. 993, 2 H.L.C. 1 at 27, per Lord Campbell).

[57] *See, e.g.*, Charles M. Gray, *The Boundaries of the Equitable Function*, 20 AM. J. LEGAL HIST. 192, 202–06 (1976) (illustrating how courts of equity were prevented from judging title).

[58] Douglas Laycock has argued that this requirement no longer binds, see, e.g., DOUGLAS LAYCOCK, THE DEATH OF THE IRREPARABLE INJURY RULE (1991); Douglas Laycock, *The Death of the Irreparable Injury Rule*, 103 HARV. L. REV. 687, 688–701 (1990), but I would argue that it is not a "rule" and serves as a loose proxy. *See* Smith, *supra* note 10.

accessible to all people and can serve as a coordinating device – akin to *malum in se* in criminal law. Of course, a direct and unconstrained appeal to morality by itself might be vague in too many of its applications, but recall that the moral notions only come into play when the threshold test of irreparable harm is met and moral notions themselves are filtered through the set of proxies and presumptions that give equity its structure.

III. JUDICIAL REGULATION OF THE COMPETITIVE PROCESS

In this part, I argue that the safety valve theory of equity provides a potential way out of the dilemmas of misappropriation. The question to ask is whether equity in its protection of existing law and custom, filtered though the proxies and presumptions, would condemn what the INS did. Equity provides a very qualified endorsement of the result in *INS* v. *AP*, but it does not countenance the more expansive theories of misappropriation advanced in its aftermath and also very recently.

First, although courts and commentators did not use the term "opportunism," many of them held such a notion to be central to equity and to equity's approach to unfair competition.[59] Interestingly, the connection to fraud and the inability to define it ex ante figure in the following comment by Edward S. Rogers about the notion of unfair competition:

> It is as unwise to attempt to define unfair competition as to define fraud. Definitions limit. Once several years ago, after a course on the subject, a student who, with an endurance which did him credit, had attended throughout, came up to speak to me. I said, "What is your idea of this subject?" and received the answer, "Well, it seems to me that the courts try to stop people from playing dirty tricks." One might spend weeks reading cases and find many definitions less satisfactory than this.[60]

59 *See, e.g.*, R. Heinisch's Sons Co. v. Boker, 86 Fed. 765, 768 (S.D.N.Y. 1898) ("A court of equity keeps pace with the rapid strides of the sharp competitors for the prize of public favor, and insists that it shall be won only by fair trade."); Note, *Unfair Competition: Necessity for Actual Competition*, 38 HARV. L. REV. 370, 373 (1925) ("The principles in this particular branch of the law should be sufficiently general and elastic to cope with the constantly developing ingenuity of the trade parasite."); *see also*, *e.g.*, Cushing, *supra* note 8, at 332 ("Whether trade rivalry shall be open and fair, so that each may be stimulated to his best endeavor in the knowledge that his exertions will bring him in to the full the honor and profit which are his due, or whether fraud, which knows how to evade definite rules, shall reap the fruits of honest labor and hardly-won reputation, is within the discretion of the court."); Edward S. Rogers, *The Ingenuity of the Infringer and the Courts*, 11 MICH. L. REV. 358, 362–63 (1913) ("As a general thing the infringer has always been a little ahead of the courts. By the time the judicial machinery arrives at a place where the pirate was yesterday, ready to deal with him, that elusive person has moved forward and is still a little ahead, – at a place the courts will not reach until tomorrow – and is there engaged in doing something which will enable him to advantage himself at some one else's expense in some manner hitherto unthought of. The various methods briefly outlined of stealing a man's business and good will were very effectively and adequately dealt with by the courts *when they got to them*, but one has only to study the reported cases during even the last twenty years to be convinced that as the judicial conscience has expanded, the ingenuity of the infringer has been correspondingly stimulated.").

60 Edward S. Rogers, *Book Review: The Law of Unfair Competition and Trade Marks, by Harry D. Nims*, 39 YALE L.J. 297, 300–01 (1929).

This characterization of unfair competition is reminiscent of Justice Story's observation in his equity treatise that equity must be ex post because "[f]raud is infinite" given the "fertility of man's invention,"[61] and that equity protects the law from "crafty evasions."[62] This need to keep up with inventive opportunism was a theme during the development of equitable interventions in unfair competition.[63] Zechariah Chafee, another expert on equity, noted that a lot of dirty tricks are not prohibited under unfair competition and that courts are cautious when their interventions are likely to generalize, as opposed to the occasional case-specific intervention that might not recur for a long time.[64]

Equity was not supposed to be a generator of property rights,[65] and unfair competition should be no exception. The Court in *INS* was thus correct in its characterization as far as it goes:

> In order to sustain the jurisdiction of equity over the controversy, we need not affirm any general and absolute property in the news as such. The rule that a court of equity concerns itself only in the protection of property rights treats any civil right of a pecuniary nature as a property right; and the right to acquire property by honest labor or the conduct of a lawful business is as much entitled to protection as

[61] 1 J. Story, Commentaries on Equity Jurisprudence, as Administered in England and America 184 n.1 (9th ed. 1866) (quoting a Letter from Lord Hardwicke to Lord Kaims (June 30, 1759)). Or, as Chancellor Ellesmere put the point: "The Cause why there is a Chancery is, for that Mens Actions are so divers and infinite, That it is impossible to make any general Law which may aptly meet with every particular Act, and not fail in some Circumstances." The Earl of Oxford's Case, 21 Eng. Rep. 485, 486 (Ch. 1615).

[62] Or, as one court quoted by Story put it: "Now equity is no part of the law, but a moral virtue, which qualifies, moderates, and reforms the rigour, hardness, and edge of the law, and is an universal truth; it does also assist the law where it is defective and weak in the constitution (which is the life of the law) and defends the law from crafty evasions, delusions, and new subtilties, invented and contrived to evade and delude the common law, whereby such as have undoubted right are made remediless; and this is the office of equity, to support and protect the common law from shifts and crafty contrivances against the justice of the law. Equity therefore does not destroy the law, nor create it, but assist it." Dudley v. Dudley, (1705) 24 Eng. Rep. 118, 119 (Ch.) (U.K.), quoted in 1 Joseph Story, Commentaries on Equity Jurisprudence 18–19 (reprint ed. 1972) (1836).

[63] For example in a case that fell just outside of trademark the court, in disapproving of the "wicked contrivances" used to deceive customers to come to the defendant's store, stated, "[T]he fact that the question comes to us in an entirely new guise, and that the schemer had concocted a kind of deception heretofore unheard of in legal jurisprudence, is no reason why equity is either unable or unwilling to deal with him. It has been said by some judge or law-writer that 'no fixed rules can be established upon which to deal with fraud, for, were courts of equity to once declare rules prescribing the limitations of their power in dealing with it, the jurisdiction would be perpetually cramped and eluded by new schemes which the fertility of man's invention would contrive.' By device defendant is defrauding plaintiff of its business. He is stealing its goodwill, a most valuable property, only secured after years of honest dealing and large expenditures of money; and equity would be impotent, indeed, if it could contrive no remedy for such a wrong." Weinstock, Lubin & Co. v. Marks, 42 P. 142, 145 (Cal. 1895).

[64] Chafee, *supra* note 17, at 1316–17.

[65] For an excellent historical account, see Gray, *supra* note 57.

> the right to guard property already acquired. It is this right that furnishes the basis of the jurisdiction in the ordinary case of unfair competition.[66]

But the Court only sowed confusion with its invocation of the reap-sow principle,[67] and we need some more specific source of the entitlement that can be given non-in-rem effect in equity. Where an independent tort such as interference with contract or trespass has occurred, that would furnish the interference with property rights needed as a predicate for liability in equity. What is the predicate for liability in hot-news misappropriation?

I suggest that custom could furnish the baseline entitlement here.[68] Equity has had a special role in enforcing customary rights.[69] First, for a variety of reasons, custom might be hard to prove in a court of law, and equity would step up to afford a remedy. The notion that equity would intervene to avoid the need for a "multiplicity of suits" has its origin in part in the enforcement of custom in courts of equity in the seventeenth to nineteenth centuries. Especially intermediate-sized (one might say "quasi-in-rem") groups, such as common pool resource users and parishioners, would enforce customary rights (which has been vastly expanded into the current class action).[70] Moreover, equity courts were sensitive to how enforcement of custom could veer off into declaring in rem rights, especially through the notion of a "general right."[71] The point is that the custom should not be the equivalent of an in rem property right, but should hold in a more close-knit context. In the case of hot news this would be the set of competitors in the news industry, on the assumption that there is such competition.[72]

66 248 U.S. at 236–37. The problem is that traditionally equity would intervene only to protect property rights, and the Court here is declining to follow the somewhat more freewheeling approach of the "ticker case." National Teleg. News Co. v. Western Union Teleg. Co., 119 F. 294, 300 (7th Cir. 1902) ("Here, as elsewhere, the eye of equity jurisdiction seeks out results, and though the immediate thing to be acted upon by the injunction is not itself, alone considered, property, it is enough that the act complained of will result, even though somewhat remotely, in injury to property.").

67 Baird, *supra* note 6.

68 I use the term "entitlement" because the baseline here need not be a full-blown property right. Whether any rule forming the competitive framework could be a predicate for equity, I leave open. *Cf.* Grosskopf, *supra* note 32, at 1983–89, 1996–2018 (sharply distinguishing the rules for "allocation by entitlement" and "allocation by competition" and arguing that restitution remedies are most appropriate for the latter).

69 *See* Robert G. Bone, *Personal and Impersonal Litigative Forms: Reconciling the History of Adjudicative Representation*, 70 B.U. L. Rev. 213 (1990).

70 Stephen C. Yeazell, *Group Litigation and Social Context: Toward a History of the Class Action*, 77 Colum. L. Rev. 866 (1977).

71 Mayor of York v. Pilkington, 26 Eng. Rep. 180, 181 (Ch. 1737); *see also* 2 J. Story, Commentaries on Equity Jurisprudence as Administered in England and America §§ 855–856 (1835).

72 Douglas Baird has argued that the news business was not competitive and that the copying by the INS was beside the main point: the cartel arrangements that the AP had with foreign news services that put it in a unique competitive position. Douglas G. Baird, *The Story of INS v. AP: Property, Natural Monopoly, and the Uneasy Legacy of a Concocted Controversy*, *in* Intellectual Property Stories 9 (Jane C. Ginsburg & Rochelle Cooper Dreyfuss eds., 2006). I address this issue later.

What is the custom? Here we suffer from the Court's relative indifference to the custom, as opposed to what a truly traditional court of equity might have emphasized. The custom might be the one argued halfheartedly in the case of not taking news except as tips to be independently investigated, which Epstein argues for (subject to a necessity defense).[73] Indeed, Epstein's discussion of necessity highlights the connection between the notion of necessity and that of disproportionate hardship: the holder of a property right would inflict much greater harm on the one in peril than the benefits thereby secured.[74] Or the custom might be the arrangement of pooled news gathering, as Balganesh suggests,[75] which might have included a norm of not taking without paying. Either way, the problem is that the INS is allegedly taking opportunistic advantage of the custom.[76] If custom can be a limited source of baseline entitlement here, then appropriation in violation of the custom becomes a form of "profiting from one's own wrong."[77] And much of equitable enforcement of custom came in the form of showing that a violation of custom evidenced bad faith.[78] It would not constitute a property right or have any kind of in rem effect.

The point is that the deception coupled with some evidence of the custom would shift the burden of justification to the (mis)appropriator, here the INS. There are hints in the opinion that the Court in *INS* v. *AP* considered the burden to have shifted to INS.[79] The Court also obliquely invokes the equitable notion of estoppel in structuring the kind of justification that will be allowed.[80] What then? Perhaps there was a necessity exception, although given that the news business was not so competitive, the case was hardly about the custom or necessity.[81]

73 Epstein, *supra* note 27.

74 *Id.* at 118 ("The basic intuition behind these necessity cases is a sound one. In necessity cases, a system of absolute and exclusive property rights that normally promotes industry and trade imposes incredible bargaining and holdout problems in situations where the (next best) value in use of the land to an owner is a tiny fraction of the value of the use of that land to a person in peril of his life.").

75 Balganesh, *supra* note 31.

76 Interestingly, Epstein mentions opportunism in passing, but in the sense of general defection from the norm and without noting the connection to equity: "More generally, decentralized customs may be generated without legal interference and control, but legal force may be necessary to maintain them against systematic defection. Indeed, the entire debate over whether some level of coercion is required first to form, and then to maintain, the state rests in part upon the common (dare one say customary) perception that purely private agreements will break down in the face of opportunistic behavior. That argument is not overcome by showing that customs in particular trades or industries have proved stable without government support. In many instances, these customs were able to form only because the government had supplied industry with the essential protection against external aggression that it needed to survive and flourish." Epstein, *supra* note 27, at 127–28.

77 *See, e.g.*, Riggs v. Palmer, 22 N.E. 188 (N.Y. 1889).

78 Emily Kadens, *The Myth of the Customary Law Merchant*, 90 Texas L. Rev. 1153, 1193–94 (2012).

79 248 U.S. at 239 ("which is what defendant has done and seeks to justify").

80 The Court blocked one argument this way: "But in a court of equity, where the question is one of unfair competition, if that which complainant has acquired fairly at substantial cost may be sold fairly at substantial profit, a competitor who is misappropriating it for the purpose of disposing of it to his own profit and to the disadvantage of complainant cannot be heard to say that it is too fugitive or evanescent to be regarded as property." 248 U.S. at 240. Again "property" here is not in rem property.

81 Baird, *supra* note 72.

More intriguingly, there might well have been some scope for the equitable defense of unclean hands.[82] As Douglas Baird points out, the INS could have argued that the AP's bylaws protecting the markets of individual AP members and its cartel arrangements with foreign news sources were an illegal restraint of trade or should have been subject to common carrier duties; a court of equity could have refused an injunction as long as the AP refused to provide the news to anyone who would pay or to share government documents it had obtained through a cartel arrangement.[83] Baird is correct to mention equity in this regard, because such problems – even though William Randolph Hearst and the INS were not in a position to invoke them[84] – would fit squarely under the rubric of unclean hands,[85] as well as the requirement for one seeking equity to do equity.[86]

An interesting point of comparison to the theory of equity as a safety valve is the tort-based theories of unfair competition of Holmes and Wigmore. Both defined torts in terms of a presumption from harm: intentional infliction of harm raises a presumption of injury that the defendant then has to justify.[87] When applied to unfair competition, this leads to a theory of "unjustified competition." It is much broader than the traditional equitable approach because it uses intentional harm (of any kind), whereas equity uses narrower proxies such as disproportionate hardship (in a situation of knowing harm) and deception, and it measures opportunism against the framework of entitlements from law and, to a much lesser extent, custom.[88]

The real problem with *INS* v. *AP* and misappropriation law is that it is not sufficiently connected to the traditions of equity. Yes, the Court did invoke "equity," but did not follow through on the use of triggering proxies and presumptions that courts before the era of classical jurisprudence in the late nineteenth century would

82 The unclean hands defense was argued in the case in connection with INS's allegation that AP itself was copying, and AP's response that it was only using others' news stories as a source of tips. Judge Augustus Hand considered this defense at length and rejected it, because the use of stories as a source of tips was generally accepted. Associated Press v. International News Service, 240 F. 983, 995 (S.D.N.Y.), *modified*, 245 F. 244 (2d Cir. 1917), *aff'd*, 248 U.S. 215 (1918). It is mentioned briefly in Justice Pitney's opinion. 248 U.S. at 242–43.

83 *Id.* at 24–25, 28.

84 Hearst had no interest in making the news business more competitive in general, and he knew he could get away with the kind of copying he was mostly engaged in. Baird, *supra* note 72, at 28.

85 *See, e.g.*, Carmen v. Fox Film Corp., 269 F. 928 (2d Cir. 1920).

86 *See, e.g.*, *Ingram v. Kasey's Associates*, 531 S.E.2d 287 (S.C. 2000); Young & Spitz, *supra* note 56, at 175, 186.

87 Oliver Wendell Holmes, Jr., *Privilege, Malice, and Intent*, 8 HARV. L. REV. 1 (1894); John H. Wigmore, *The Tripartite Division of Torts*, 8 HARV. L. REV. 200 (1894); John H. Wigmore, *A General Analysis of Tort Relations*, 8 HARV. L. REV. 377 (1895); *see also* Aikens v. Wisconsin, 195 U.S. 194, 204 (1904) (Holmes, J.) ("It has been considered that, *prima facie*, the intentional infliction of temporal damage is a cause of action, which, as a matter of substantive law, whatever may be the form of pleading, requires a justification if the defendant is to escape."). For a discussion, see Chafee, *supra* note 17, at 1303–04.

88 Equity also used "spite" as a triggering proxy, but spite in this context means wholly malevolent and without any motivation of other benefit to the defendant. As many have noted this is a very narrow notion.

have found quite natural – and I argue would have been quite practical and sensible. The older traditions of equity were only half-alive in 1918 and have been further obscured by the completion of the fusion of law and equity – and even more so by Legal Realism and its aftermath.

How might the Legal Realist approach to equity have affected the law of misappropriation? There are quite a few candidates for channels of influence, some more general than others.[89] The Realists generally promoted contextualized decision making across the board, and the Realists can be thought of as embracing equity without its built-in limits.[90] The dispute now tends to be polarized, with the post-Realists embracing an unconstrained version of "equity" and neo-formalists trying to minimize it.[91] Recent years have also seen the misinterpretation of equity, especially in the context of awarding injunctions.[92]

The theory of the equitable safety valve helps explain how misappropriation has been recast in more recent times. As is well known, the Second Circuit has provided an influential restatement of the law of misappropriation, in Judge Winter's opinion in *National Basketball Association* v. *Motorola*[93] – whether this remains the Second Circuit's definitive statement of the doctrine or, as the Second Circuit suggested recently, is a set of "sophisticated observations in aid" of an analysis of preemption.[94] The opinion makes misappropriation turn on a five-factor test:

> (i) a plaintiff generates or collects information at some cost or expense; (ii) the value of the information is highly time-sensitive; (iii) the defendant's use of the

89 For example, as hinted in *INS* v. *AP* itself, injunctions in the First Amendment and labor contexts were quite controversial, and it may well be that use of injunctions in unfair competition was less favored because of these other connections.

90 *See* Sidney Post Simpson, *Fifty Years of American Equity*, 50 Harv. L. Rev. 171, 185–86 (1936); *see also* Callmann, *supra* note 32 (proposing expansive tort-like theory of unfair competition); Chafee, *supra* note 17, at 1302–21 (noting expansive tendency in unfair competition especially in light of New Deal legislation and proposing middle way of "exploration" between "conservatism" and "conquest"); James F. Oates, Jr., *Relief In Equity Against Unfair Trade Practice of Non-Competitors*, 25 Ill. L. Rev. 643, 652 672 (1931) (applauding expansion of unfair competition outside traditional equitable lines, including Holmes's concurrence in *INS* v. *AP*); Edward S. Rogers, *New Directions In The Law of Unfair Competition*, 74 N.Y. L. Rev. 317, 339–41 (1940) (arguing against need to find a property right in unfair competition cases and advocating a flexible inquiry into "fact"); Note, *Unfair Competition – Necessity for Actual Competition*, 38 Harv. L. Rev. 370 (1925) (criticizing traditional equity cases for not going far enough and advocating greater flexibility in dealing with the "trade parasite").

91 *See* Smith, *supra* note 10. For a classic example, see *Grupo Mexicano de Desarrollo, S.A. v. Alliance Bond Fund, Inc.*, 527 U.S. 308 (1999).

92 Gergen, Golden, & Smith, *supra* note 45.

93 105 F.3d 841 (2d Cir. 1997). For an endorsement of *NBA v. Motorola* as a way station in needed common law development of misappropriation in an era of rapid change, see Dale P. Olson, *Common Law Misappropriation in the Digital Era*, 64 Mo. L. Rev. 837 (1999).

94 Barclays Capital Inc. v. Theflyonthewall.com, Inc., 650 F.3d 876, 901 (2d Cir. 2011); *but see id.* at 911 (Raggi, J., concurring) (arguing that the five-part test was necessary to the result in *NBA*). It is not clear why the elements of the test or the doctrine' survival was relevant to the court's preemption analysis in the *Barclays Capital* case, and it appears that the court was trying to cut back on the doctrine. *See* Shyamkrishna Balganesh, *The Uncertain Future of "Hot News" Misappropriation After* Barclays Capital v. theflyonthewall.com, 112 Colum. L. Rev. Sidebar 134 (2012).

> information constitutes free-riding on the plaintiff's costly efforts to generate or collect it; (iv) the defendant's use of the information is in direct competition with a product or service offered by the plaintiff; (v) the ability of other parties to free-ride on the efforts of the plaintiff or others would so reduce the incentive to produce the product or service that its existence or quality would be substantially threatened.[95]

Not surprisingly, courts have tried to put some structure back into what was an equitable test through multifactor tests;[96] this approach is understandable now that the traditional approach has been partially forgotten. The structure of a multifactor test is different from the one characteristic of traditional equity. On the account of equity as a safety valve aimed at opportunism, misappropriation is about ethics, in a fashion that is consistent with promoting efficiency.[97]

Finally, the equitable approach is potentially quite constraining. Absent a custom or other baseline entitlements that are being manipulated opportunistically, equity should not intervene. Thus, the recent case of *Barclays Capital Inc.* v. *Theflyonthewall.com*,[98] where the trial court granted an injunction (later overturned) against disseminating plaintiff's stock recommendations until the later of either one half-hour after the opening of the New York Stock Exchange or 10:00 a.m., went far beyond the equitable safety valve theory. Unless there is some provable custom against posting stock recommendations without the authorization of the originating financial services firm – and there appears to be no evidence of such a custom – equity should not intervene under the banner of misappropriation. "Sweat of the brow" is not nearly enough.[99] Moreover, where equity does intervene it is not in the business of declaring in rem rights. Fashion imitators, news gatherers, and the like are not enjoinable absent triggering by one of the traditional equitable proxies for

95 105 F.3d at 852 (citations omitted).

96 The ahistorical and misleading four-factor test for injunctions recently adopted by the Supreme Court is the most recent example. eBay v. MercExchange, 547 U.S. 388, 390 (2006). *See* Gergen, Golden, & Smith, *supra* note 45.

97 The *NBA* opinion appears to sound in property and to disavow equity: "*INS* is not about ethics; it is about the protection of property rights in time-sensitive information so that the information will be made available to the public by profit seeking entrepreneurs." 105 F.3d at 853. "Property rights" may be meant here in an economic sense. I am arguing that misappropriation is not property in the in rem sense and is about "ethics" in the highly structured form that it takes in traditional equity.

98 Barclays Capital Inc. v. Theflyonthewall.com, 700 F. Supp. 2d 310, 332 (S.D.N.Y. 2010) ("Thus, in *INS*, misappropriation doctrine was developed to protect costly efforts to gather commercially valuable, time-sensitive information that would otherwise be unprotected by law."), overruled in Barclays Capital Inc. v. Theflyonthewall.com, Inc., 650 F.3d 876 (2d Cir. 2011).

99 *See* Agora Financial, LLC v. Samler, 725 F. Supp. 2d 491 (D. Md. 2010) (holding plaintiff publisher of financial newsletter's hot-news claim to be preempted by Copyright Act and casting doubt on *Barclays Capital* as relflecting too robust a version of the "sweat of the brow" doctrine); *see also* Feist Publ'ns, Inc. v. Rural Tel. Serv. Co., Inc., 499 U.S. 340, 354 (1991) ("Without a doubt, the 'sweat of the brow' doctrine flouted basic copyright principles.... 'Protection for the fruits of such research... may in certain circumstances be available under a theory of unfair competition. But to accord copyright protection on this basis alone distorts basic copyright principles in that it creates a monopoly in public domain materials without the necessary justification of protecting and encouraging the creation of 'writings' by 'authors'" (quoting Nimmer § 3.04, p. 3–23 (footnote omitted)).

opportunistic abuse of the framework of entitlements and an inability to justify the practice or employ an equitable defense such as unclean hands.

IV. CONCLUSION

Equity points to the importance of custom and commercial morality, but traditional equity used proxies such as good faith and disproportionate hardship to trigger a shift in the burden of justification of the practices in question. Equity is a safety valve. It protects entitlements from custom, the common law, and statutes against opportunistic misuse. Rather than being the problem, equity can be a source of the solution when it comes to misappropriation.

3

The Mixed Heritage of Federal Intellectual Property Law and Ramifications for Statutory Interpretation

*Peter S. Menell**

At first blush, there would not appear to be much role for the judiciary in the development and evolution of patent and copyright law. The United States Constitution grants Congress authority to enact patent and copyright laws, leaving to courts the more limited role of interpreting the laws.[1] And Congress has acted on that authority, enacting lengthy federal patent and copyright statutes that preclude and largely preempt state statutory and common law protections for inventions and creative expression.[2] But first impressions can be deceiving.

When we examine the substance of modern federal intellectual property (IP) law, the judiciary's imprint and evolving role are unmistakable and profound. Many critical features of patent and copyright law – such as the limitations on patentable subject matter, the standards for patent infringement (doctrine of equivalents), the standards for copyright infringement, the scope of indirect copyright liability, and many other doctrines (inequitable conduct, copyright misuse) – cannot be found in the United States Code. They exist only in judicial decisions. And several essential

* Koret Professor of Law and Director, Berkeley Center for Law & Technology. I would like to thank Shyam Balganesh for organizing the May 2011 symposium on Intellectual Property and the Common Law and the exceptional group of scholars assembled for this event for their comments.

1 *See* U.S CONST. art 1, § 8, cl. 8; *cf.* Shyamkrishna Balganesh, *The Pragmatic Incrementalism of Common Law Intellectual Property*, 63 VAND. L. REV. 1543 (2010) (observing that "[i]ntellectual property is today thought to be principally of statutory origin. Discussions of the subject invariably revolve around a close scrutiny of the federal statutes involved. Indeed, the frequency with which Congress amends the patent and copyright statutes seems to leave little doubt that it alone determines intellectual property's precise content and coverage."); Edward Walterscheid, *Understanding the Copyright Act of 1790: The Issue of Common Law Copyright in America and the Modern Interpretation of the Copyright Power*, 53 J. COPYRIGHT SOC'Y 313 (2006) (explaining that there has never been a federal common law of copyright); Wheaton v. Peters, 33 U.S. 591, 661 (1834) (holding that federal copyright protection "originated, if at all, under the acts of Congress"). Prior to 1978, *state* common law copyright protected unpublished works.

2 *See* 17 U.S.C. § 301 (preempting state common law copyright protection as of January 1, 1978); Bonito Boats, Inc. v. Thunder Craft Boats, Inc., 489 U.S. 141 (1989); Sears, Roebuck & Co. v. Stiffel Co., 376 U.S. 225 (1964).

statutory provisions – such as patent law's nonobviousness requirement and copyright law's fair use doctrine – were created by the courts and later codified in ways that perpetuate judicial crafting of these doctrines.

The reality of modern IP law thus diverges from the conventional constitutional allocation of lawmaking authority: Congress passes statutes, the executive branch implements them, and the federal judiciary interprets them in adjudicating cases and controversies. By contrast, intellectual property reflects a mixed heritage in which courts, operating in what can most aptly be characterized as a common law mode, came to play a principal role in fleshing out and evolving terse early legislative enactments. Although Congress has partially codified several of these judicial doctrines, the courts continue to play a central, although contextually variable, role in the evolution of IP law. As newer aspects of patent and copyright law have taken on greater legislative specificity, the mix between common law and statutory interpretation has shifted. Nonetheless, it would be a mistake to presume that legislative directive has supplanted the judiciary's "common law" role in many important areas of federal IP law.

This chapter traces the development and evolution of federal IP law. The history can usefully be broken out into three principal, although somewhat overlapping, phases: (I) the formative period, during which the courts fleshed out the early formulations with relatively broad and deep strokes; (II) the codification period, in which Congress integrated jurisprudence into statutory text while leaving more limited room for judicial innovation; and (III) the modern period, in which interest group politics has generated some highly detailed provisions. The final section of this chapter sketches some of the ramifications of this history for statutory interpretation.

I. THE FORMATIVE PERIOD

Article I, Section 8, Clause 8 of the U.S. Constitution, ratified in 1787, authorized Congress "To promote the Progress of Science and useful Arts, by securing for limited Times to Authors and Inventors the exclusive Right to their respective Writings and Discoveries." In the nation's first State of the Union address, President Washington urged the Congress to exercise this power:

> The advancement of agriculture, commerce and manufactures, by all proper means, will not, I trust, need recommendation. But I cannot forbear intimating to you the expediency of giving effectual encouragement as well to the introduction of new and useful inventions from abroad, as to the exertions of skill and genius in producing them at home....
>
> Nor am I less persuaded, that you will agree with me in opinion, that there is nothing which can better deserve your patronage, than the promotion of Science and Literature. Knowledge is in every country the surest basis of publick happiness.[3]

[3] George Washington, State of the Union Address, Journal of the Senate, 1st Cong., 2d Sess. 5 to 8 (Jan. 8, 1790).

Congress soon thereafter established federal protection for "any map, chart, [or] book"[4] and "any useful art, manufacture, engine, machine, or device."[5] Both of the laws set forth concise general standards for protection, duration, rights, and remedies, but few details. They each totaled fewer than 1,400 words. By comparison, the modern Copyright and Patent Acts span 100,000 and 45,000 words, respectively,[6] although both track many of the original formulations regarding protection standards, rights, and remedies. To a large extent, the first Congress left many of the operational details open, and the courts filled them in using their perception of the constitutional and statutory purposes underlying these laws, experience from protecting other interests, and common law reasoning.

A. *Copyright Law*

Modeled on England's Statute of Anne,[7] the Copyright Act of 1790 granted to authors of maps, books, and charts the "sole right and liberty of printing, reprinting, publishing and vending" their works for fourteen years (which could be renewed for an additional fourteen-year term).[8] The Act required that, to enforce such rights, the author must deposit a print copy of such work with the district court in the judicial district in which the author resided and notify the public by posting a notice for four weeks in one or more of the newspapers printed in the United States.[9] The Act did not specify the threshold for protection nor standards for determining infringement.

Judges inquired into the general scope and object of Congress as well as English case law to flesh out the Copyright Act.[10] Eaton Drone, author of the leading nineteenth-century copyright treatise, observed,

> While, then, the legislature has passed laws for the protection of literary property in books without specifying more definitely the kinds of compositions intended to be included the courts have construed those laws so as to embrace within their protection the entire field of honest literary labor. Hence the literary productions in which valid copyright will subsist are almost if not quite as unlimited in variety as are the productions themselves. Books entitled to the protection of copyright embrace the profoundest work on the universe and the simplest rhyme for the nursery; the most fascinating production of the imagination and the dryest catalogue of names.[11]

4 Copyright Act of 1790, 1st Cong., 2d Sess., 1 Stat. 124 May 21, 1790.
5 Patent Act of 1790, Ch. 7, 1 Stat. 109–112 (April 10, 1790).
6 *See* 17 U.S.C. § 1, et seq.; 35 U.S.C. § 1 et seq.
7 Statute of Anne Ch. 19 (1710).
8 Copyright Act of 1790, § 1.
9 Copyright Act of 1790, § 3.
10 *See generally* Eaton Sylvester Drone, A Treatise on the Law of Property in Intellectual Productions in Great Britain and the United States (1879); Atwill v. Ferrett, 2 Blatchf. 39, 2 F.Cas. 195, 197–98 (C.C.N.Y. 1846) (reasoning that "a just construction of both [the U.S. copyright statute and the Statute of Anne] will render their provisions concurrent").
11 *See id.* at 144.

In explaining the scope of protection in the parts of a work, Drone wrote,

> The copyright protects the whole and all the parts and contents of a book. When the book comprises a number of independent compositions, each of the latter is as fully protected as the whole. And so the copyright protects not only the text, but also any engravings, illustrations, figures, &c., contained in the book. The copyright will not extend to any part which is not a proper subject of copyright. But the fact that a part may not be entitled to protection does not affect the copyright in the rest. The copyright is valid to the extent of the matter which will stand all the tests of the law. "The courts of justice," said Lord Kenyon, "have been long laboring under an error, if an author have no copyright in any part of a work unless he have an exclusive right to the whole book."[12]

Drawing on his extensive experience with intellectual property cases, knowledge of English case law, common law orientation, and philosophical bent, Justice Joseph Story took a relatively free hand in crafting copyright (and patent) law. Nowhere is this more evident than in his 1841 decision laying the foundation for copyright law's fair use doctrine:

> This is one of those intricate and embarrassing questions, arising in the administration of civil justice, in which it is not, from the peculiar nature and character of the controversy, easy to arrive at any satisfactory conclusion, or to lay down any general principles applicable to all cases. Patents and copyrights approach, nearer than any other class of cases belonging to forensic discussions, to what may be called the metaphysics of the law, where the distinctions are, or at least may be, very subtile and refined, and, sometimes, almost evanescent. In many cases, indeed, what constitutes an infringement of a patented invention, is sufficiently clear and obvious, and stands upon broad and general agreements and differences; but, in other cases, the lines approach very near to each other, and, sometimes, become almost evanescent, or melt into each other. So, in cases of copyright, it is often exceedingly obvious, that the whole substance of one work has been copied from another, with slight omissions and formal differences only, which can be treated in no other way than as studied evasions; whereas, in other cases, the identity of the two works in substance, and the question of piracy, often depend upon a nice balance of the comparative use made in one of the materials of the other; the nature, extent, and value of the materials thus used; the objects of each work; and the degree to which each writer may be fairly presumed to have resorted to the same common sources of information, or to have exercised the same common diligence in the selection and arrangement of the materials. . . . But, then, what constitutes a *fair* and bona fide abridgment, in the sense of the law, is one of the most difficult points, under particular circumstances, which can well arise for judicial discussion.[13]

12 *See id.* (citing English law cases).

13 *See* Folsom v. Marsh, 9 F. Cas. 342, 344–45 (C.C.Mass. 1841) (Justice Story was sitting as a circuit judge). The decision refers liberally to English precedents under the Statute of Anne.

Throughout the nineteenth and twentieth centuries, courts built the copyright liability regime through common law development. As stated in 1869, "[r]ights secured by copyright are property within the meaning of the law of copyright, and whoever invades that property beyond the privilege conceded to subsequent authors commits a tort. . . ."[14] Lacking specific statutory guidance,[15] the courts developed and evolved infringement standards using the general purpose of copyright law ("the encouragement of learning"),[16] common law experimentation, and pragmatism. Early English cases recognized the importance of protecting pioneering authors while not choking off cumulative creativity – those who build on the knowledge base.[17] George Ticknor Curtis, author of an influential early copyright treatise (as well as an even more influential early patent treatise[18]), explained that

> the principles on which this kind of [literary] property depends and the doctrines which are already well established in English and American jurisprudence will be found hereafter when fully carried out to extend an adequate and just protection to literature even if such protection is not now administered with all the success that could be desired. In endeavoring to trace the just scope of these principles

14 Lawrence v. Dana, 2 Am. Law T. Rep. (N.S.) 402 (C.C.Mass. 1869); see also Ted Brown Music Co. v. Fowler, 290 F. 751, 754 (2d Cir. 1923) (observed that "[c]opyright infringement is a tort"); Underhill v. Schenck, 238 N.Y. 7, 14, 143 N.E. 773 (1924) (Judge Benjamin Cardozo) ("The author who suffers infringement of his copyright . . . may count upon the infringement as a tort, and seek redress under the statute by action in the federal courts."). Early tort treatises featured a separate chapter on copyright protection. *See, e.g.*, J. F. Clerk & W. H. B. Lindell, The Law of Torts 587 (2d ed. 1896).

15 *See* George Ticknor Curtis, A Treatise on the Law of Copyright 240 (1847) ("The statutes which secure the exclusive rights of authors, do not define, in any terms, what shall constitute an infringement of copyright. It is left to the tribunals to decide."); Drone, *supra* note 10, at 383 ("The legislature has not defined piracy, or indicated how far a person may lawfully go in appropriating the results of another's labors."). Neither the Copyright Act of 1790 nor the 1831, 1870, and 1909 general revisions provided a formal definition of copyright infringement. *See* H. Committee Print, 89th Cong., 1st Sess., Copyright Law Revision Part 6, Supplementary Report of the Register of Copyrights on the General Revision of the U.S. Copyright Law; 1965 Revision Bill (May 1965), at 131 ("It seems strange, though not very serious, that the present law lacks any statement or definition of what constitutes an infringement."). The Copyright Act of 1976, which was the first to include an express infringement provision, states tautologically that "[a]nyone who violates any of the exclusive rights of the copyright owner as provided by sections 106 through 118, or who imports copies or phonorecords into the United States in violation of section 602, is an infringer of the copyright." 17 U.S.C. § 501(a).

16 The Statute of Anne sought to "encourag[e] learning, by vesting the copies of printed books in the authors or purchasers of such copies." Statute of Anne Ch. 19 (1710). The Copyright Act of 1790 mirrored that purpose in proclaiming in its preamble "[a]n Act for the encouragement of learning, by securing the copies of maps, Charts, And books, to the authors and proprietors of such copies, during the times therein mentioned."

17 *See, e.g.*, Cary v. Kearsley, 4 Esp. 168, 170–71 (1803) ("while I shall think myself bound to secure every man in the enjoyment of his copyright, one must not put manacles on science"); Sayre v. Moore, 1 East 361 n. (b), 102 Eng.Rep. 139, 140 n. (b) (K.B.1785) ("[W]e must take care to guard against two extremes equally prejudicial; the one, that men of ability, who have employed their time for the service of the community, may not be deprived of their just merits, and the reward of their ingenuity and labour; the other, that the world may not be deprived of improvements, nor the progress of the arts be retarded.").

18 *See infra* note 65.

> and doctrines we must bear in mind that while the primary object of the law of copyright is protection to the product of all literary labor the interests of knowledge demand a reasonable freedom in the use of all antecedent literature. To administer the law in such a manner as not to curtail the fair use of existing materials in any department of letters is one of the great tasks of jurisprudence. It proposes to itself first the vindication of rights acquired by genius, discovery, invention, and labor in the productions of the mind; secondly the acknowledgment upon motives of public policy of the right to a fair use by any writer of all that has been recorded by previous authors.[19]

Decades later, Judge Learned Hand would weave the various strands of copyright protection law and policy in formulating an infringement standard that continues to guide courts today.[20]

Courts drew on the emerging tort doctrines of *respondeat superior*,[21] contributory liability,[22] and vicarious liability[23] in fleshing out the scope of copyright liability and standards of proof. They developed standards for originality[24] and the distinction between unprotectable ideas and protectable expression[25] in a common law fashion. Courts established and fashioned what came to be known as copyright's work made for hire doctrine based on the rise of the corporation and changes in employment contracting, exposure to a greater range of authorship, the changing nature of copyrightable works and authorship in the industrializing economy (e.g., the emergence of collective works), and evolution in contract default rules.[26] They also

19 *See* CURTIS, *supra* note 15, at 236–37.

20 *See* Nichols v. Universal Pictures Corporation, 45 F.2d 119 (2d Cir. 1930).

21 *See* Fishel v. Luekel, 53 F. 499 (S.D.N.Y. 1892); American Code Co. v. Bensigner, 282 F. 829, 834 (2d Cir. 1922) ("The joinder of these parties [publisher, binder, and seller of book] as defendants proceeds upon the theory that infringement of a copyright is a tort, and that all persons concerned therein are jointly and severally liable."); *see generally* Peter S. Menell & David Nimmer, *Unwinding Sony*, 95 CAL. L. REV. 941, 996–1005 (2007) ("Over the course of nearly a century, courts had drawn on the principles of tort liability and the policies of the copyright system to weave a sophisticated web of indirect liability doctrines to address the distinctive challenges of enforcing copyright law.").

22 *See* Harper v. Shoppell, 28 F. 613 (C.C. S.D.N.Y. Sept. 8, 1886); 26 F. 519 (C.C. S.D.N.Y. Feb. 6, 1886).

23 *See* Kalem Co. v. Harper Brothers, 222 U.S. 55, 62 63 (1911); Scribner v. Straus, 210 U. S. 352 (1908); Buck v. Jewell-La Salle Realty Co., 283 U.S. 191 (1931); Dreamland Ball Room v. Shapiro, Bernstein & Co., 36 F.2d 354 (7th Cir. 1929).

24 *See* Bleistein v. Donaldson Lithographing Co., 188 U.S. 239 (1903); Henderson v. Tompkins, 60 F. 758, 764 (C.C.D. Mass. 1894) (requiring "moderate degree of literary merit" for a dramatic composition); CURTIS, *supra* note 15, at 169 n.1, 172 (tracing originality to use of the term "Author" in the Copyright Act and observing that originality must be based on "some substantial product of original thought or labor").

25 *See* Baker v. Selden, 101 U.S. 99 (1879); Perris v. Hexamer, 99 U.S. 675 (1879); Emerson v. Davies, 8 F. Cas. 615 (C.C. D. Mass. 1845).

26 *See generally* Catherine L. Fisk, *Authors at Work: The Origins of the Work-for-Hire Doctrine*, 15 YALE J.L. & HUMAN 1 (2003) (providing a rich contextual account of how the courts shifted from an author-centric conception of initial copyright ownership to recognition of employer and commissioning party *ab initio* rights based on contract principles); *compare* Atwill v. Ferrett, 2 F. Cas. 195 (C.C.S.D.N.Y.

embroidered various limitations such as the exhaustion principle[27] into the fabric of copyright law.

B. *Patent Law*

Although also tracing to 1790, the patent system took an early detour before getting settled on its track. The 1790 Patent Act authorized the granting of a patent for a term not exceeding fourteen years to any person who "invented or discovered any useful art, manufacture, engine, machine, or device, or any improvement therein not before known or used [deemed by the Secretary of State, the Secretary for the Department of War, and the Attorney General, or any two of them] sufficiently useful and important."[28] This original formulation of the patent system was, however, short-lived for several reasons. It called on Secretary of State (Thomas Jefferson), the Secretary for the Department of War, and the Attorney General to personally examine patents, which, in light of their other responsibilities, proved untenable.[29] Second, inventors were displeased with the high and vague threshold for protection: that inventions be deemed "sufficiently useful and important."[30]

As a result, in 1793 Congress struck the requirement that inventions be "sufficiently useful and important" and replaced the examination process with a registration system,[31] leaving the evaluation of patentability entirely to the courts. The Patent Act of 1793 retained a terse standard for patentability: an inventor could patent "any new and useful art, machine, manufacture or composition of matter, or any new and useful improvement on any art, machine, manufacture or composition of matter, not known or used before the application."[32] The inventor was still required to provide a written description of the invention and the manner of use "in such full, clear and exact terms, as to distinguish the same from all other things before known, and to enable any person skilled in the art or science, of which it is a branch, or with which it is most nearly connected, to make, compound, and use the same."[33]

1846) (holding "to constitute one an author, he must, by his own intellectual labor applied to the materials of his composition, produce an arrangement or compilation new") *with* Keene v. Wheatley, 14 F. Cas. 180 (C.C.Pa. 1861) (articulating a default rule of employer ownership) and Lawrence v. Dana, 15 F. Cas. 26 (C.C.D. Mass. 1869) (same).

27 *See* Bobbs-Merrill Co. v. Straus, 210 U.S. 339 (1908) (interpreting the copyright statutes to prevent restraints on alienation following the sale of a copyrighted work); Zechariah Chafee, *Equitable Servitudes on Chattels*, 41 HARV. L. REV. 945 (1928) (tracing roots of first sale doctrine to English common law rule against restraints on the alienation of property).

28 Patent Act of 1790, § 1.

29 *See* Letter from Thomas Jefferson to Hugh Williamson (Apr. 1, 1792), *in* 6 THE WORKS OF THOMAS JEFFERSON 458, 459 (Paul Leicester Ford ed., Fed. ed. 1904).

30 Steven Lubar, *The Transformation of Antebellum Patent Law*, 32 TECH. & CULTURE (Special Issue) 932, 936 (1991).

31 Patent Act of Feb. 21, 1793, ch.11, 1 Stat. 318.

32 *See id.* at § 1.

33 *See id.* at § 3.

The courts gave content to and filled in the gaps in this lean statute,[34] drawing heavily on English case law in the early years. In 1818, Justice Story, who would write forty patent law opinions between 1813 and 1845, issued a paper stating,

> The patent acts of the United States are, in a great degree, founded on the principles and usages which have grown out of the English statute on the same subject. It may be useful, therefore, to collect together the cases which have been adjudged in England, with a view to illustrate the corresponding provisions of our own laws; and then bring in review the adjudications in the courts of the United States.[35]

In his first patent law opinion, Justice Story, sitting as a Circuit Justice, distinguished between unpatentable elements of motion and "the modus operandi, the peculiar device or manner of producing any given effect"[36] and recognized an experimental use defense based on the inference that "it could never have been the intention of the legislature to punish a man, who constructed such a machine merely for philosophical experiments, or for the purpose of ascertaining the sufficiency of the machine to produce its described effects."[37] In 1817, he fleshed out the meaning of "useful invention"[38] and novelty.[39] In 1829, Justice Story interpreted the novelty requirement of "not known or used before the application" to pertain only to knowledge or use "*by the public*."[40]

The courts also established standards for disclosure, requiring that the patent document identify the patented invention with specificity and distinguish it from the prior art.[41] In the absence of an ex ante examination system, the patent bar developed the patent claim as a means of reducing the risk of an invalidity ruling and of more easily establishing infringement.[42]

Nonetheless, the lack of an examination system eroded faith in the patent system because it led to the proliferation of "unrestrained and promiscuous grants of patent

34 *See generally* Craig Allen Nard, *Legal Forms and the Common Law of Patents*, 90 B.U. L. Rev. 51 (2010).

35 *See* On the Patent Laws, 16 U.S. (3 Wheat.) App. 13–29 (1818) (quoted in Edward C. Walterscheid, *To Promote the Progress of Useful Arts: American Patent Law and Administration, 1787–1836 (Part 1)*, 79 J. Pat. & Trademark Off. Soc'y 61 (1997)); Frank D. Prager, *The Influence of Mr. Justice Story on American Patent Law*, 5 Am. J. Leg. Hist. 254 n.1 (1961).

36 Whittemore v. Cutter, 29 F. Cas. 1123, 1124 (C.C.Mass. 1813).

37 *See id.* at 1121.

38 *See* Bedford v. Hunt, 3 F. Cas. 37, No. 1217 (C.C.D. Mass. 1817) (a useful invention need not "supersede all other inventions now in practice to accomplish the same purpose").

39 *See id.* at 37–38 (holding that a patentee must have been the first to invent, which entails reduction to practice); *see also* Reed v. Cutter, 20 F. Cas. 435 (C.C.D. Mass. 1841).

40 *See* Pennock v. Dialogue, 27 U.S. 1, 19 (1829) (emphasis added).

41 *See* Lowell v. Lewis, 15 F. Cas. 1018, No. 8568 (C.C.D. Mass. 1817); Evans v. Eaton, 20 U.S. 356, 434–35 (1822).

42 *See* Joshua D. Sarnoff, *The Historic and Modern Doctrines of Equivalents and Claiming the Future, Part I (1790–1870)*, 87 J. Pat. & Trademark Off. Soc'y 371, 384 (2005) ("In response to [Justice Story's decisions in *Lowell v. Lewis* and *Evans v. Eaton*], patent applicants began to include summary language at the end of their specifications that more specifically identified what they regarded as and claimed to be their inventions and what distinguished them from the prior art.").

privileges."[43] The Senate Report Accompanying the Patent Act of 1836 lamented that "[a] considerable portion of all the patents granted are worthless and void, as conflicting with, and infringing upon one another;" the country had become "flooded with patent monopolies, embarrassing to bona fide patentees, whose rights are thus invaded on all sides;" and the "interference and collision of patents and privileges" had produced ruinous vexatious litigation.[44] In response, the Patent Act of 1836 instituted examination in a newly constituted Patent Office, codified claiming conventions that grew out of jurisprudence,[45] and introduced other procedural and institutional reforms, but perpetuated the standards of the 1793 Act as interpreted by the courts.

In the century following the 1836 Act, the Supreme Court and lower federal courts established and fleshed out many of the key patent law doctrines: nonobviousness,[46] limitations on patentable subject matter,[47] written description,[48] the doctrine of equivalents,[49] the doctrine of abandonment, suppression, or concealment as a limitation on prior art,[50] the best mode requirement,[51] contributory infringement,[52] experimental use exception to the statutory bar,[53] and accidental anticipation doctrine.[54]

As their experience with the patent system and its effects on competition developed, and as concerns about economic concentration grew (and became manifest in the form of antitrust law[55]), the courts became more skeptical of patent protection. Professor Lawrence Friedman observes that, toward the end of the nineteenth century, the courts seemed "to become keenly aware that a patent could be used to stifle competition [and] they became stingy with preliminary injunctions against infringement."[56] In 1883, Justice Bradley observed that, although inventors of substantial discoveries "are worthy of all favor,"

> [i]t was never the object of those laws to grant a monopoly for every trifling device, every shadow of a shade of an idea, which would naturally and spontaneously occur to any skilled mechanic or operator in the ordinary progress of manufactures. Such

43 *See* John Ruggles, Select Committee Report on the State and Condition of the Patent Office, S. Doc. No. 24–338, at 4 (1836).

44 *See* Senate Report Accompanying Senate Bill No. 239, 24th Cong., 1st Sess. (Apr. 28, 1836).

45 *See* N.J. Brumbaugh, *History and Purpose of Claims in United States Patent Law*, 14 J. Pat. Off. Soc'y 273, 276 (1932) (commenting that the 1836 Act requirement that inventors "particularly specify and point out" their invention "merely endorsed and positively required what inventors had been doing voluntarily for years").

46 Hotchkiss v. Greenwood, 52 U.S. 248 (1850).

47 Le Roy v. Tatham, 55 U.S. (14 How.) 156, 156 (1853); O'Reilly v. Morse, 56 U.S. 62 (1853).

48 1 O'Reilly v. Morse, 56 U.S. 62 (1853).

49 *See* Winans v. Denmead, 56 U.S. 330 (1854).

50 *See* Kendall v. Winsor, 62 U.S. 322, 328 (1858).

51 *See* Magic Ruffle Co. v. Douglas, 16 F. Cas. 394, 396–97, No. 8948 (C.C.S.D.N.Y. 1863).

52 *See* Wallace v. Holmes, 29 F. Cas. 74, No. 17,100 (C.C. Conn. 1871); Thomson-Houston Elec. Co. v. Ohio Brass Co., 80 F. 712 (6th Cir. 1897).

53 *See* Elizabeth v. Pavement Company, 97 U.S. 126 (1877).

54 *See* Tilghman v. Proctor, 102 U.S. 707 (1880).

55 *See* Sherman Act, July 2, 1890, ch. 647, 26 Stat. 209.

56 *See* Lawrence M. Friedman, A History of American Law 380 (1973).

> an indiscriminate creation of exclusive privileges tends rather to obstruct than to stimulate invention. It creates a class of speculative schemers who make it their business to watch the advancing wave of improvement, and gather its foam in the form of patented monopolies, which enable them to lay a heavy tax upon the industry of the country, without contributing anything to the real advancement of the art. It embarrasses the honest pursuit of business with fears and apprehensions of concealed liens and unknown liabilities to lawsuits and vexatious accountings for profits made in good faith.[57]

These concerns no doubt contributed to judicial development of the exhaustion doctrine,[58] the enablement doctrine,[59] the patent misuse doctrine,[60] the reverse doctrine of equivalents,[61] and laches.[62]

Throughout the nineteenth century and into the twentieth century, courts fleshed out the skeletal, inchoate early copyright and patent statutes by filling in statutory gaps; integrating constitutional, antitrust, and pragmatic limitations; and drawing on tort and equity principles to effectuate the enforcement of rights. Reflecting the jurisprudential style of those eras and the influence of their common law roots, character, and responsibilities,[63] the most influential intellectual property jurists – including Justice Joseph Story,[64] Justice Benjamin Robbins Curtis,[65] and later Judge

57 Atlantic Works v. Brady, 107 U.S. (17 Otto) 192, 200 (1883); *see also* Densmore v. Scofield, 102 U.S. 375, 378 (1880) ("Patents rightfully issued are property, and are surrounded by the same rights and sanctions which attend all other property. Patentees as a class are public benefactors, and their rights should be protected. But the public has rights also. The rights of both should be upheld and enforced by an equally firm hand, wherever they come under judicial consideration.").

58 *See* Adams v. Burke, 84 U.S. 453 (1873).

59 *See* The Incandescent Lamp Patent, 159 U.S. 465 (1895).

60 *See* Motion Picture Patents Co. v. Universal Film Mfg. Co., 243 U.S. 502 (1917).

61 *See* Westinghouse v. Boyden Power Brake Co., 170 U.S. 537 (1898).

62 *See* Woodbridge v. United States, 263 U.S. 50 (1923); Webster Electric Co. v. Splitdorf Electrical Co., 264 U.S. 463 (1924).

63 *See generally* Harlan Fiske Stone, *The Common Law in the United States*, 50 HARV. L. REV. 4 (1936) (describing the tensions between common law and statutory interpretation at the dawn of the New Deal).

64 *See generally* Prager, *supra* note 35, *at* 254.

65 Justice Curtis was part of a small circle that took a deep interest and had particular influence on the development of patent law. *See* Andrew P. Morriss & Craig Allen Nard, *Institutional Choice & Interest Groups in the Development of American Patent Law: 1790–1870*, 19 SUP. CT. ECON. REV. 143 (2011) (observing that "[d]uring most of the nineteenth century, patent law developed in the courts, and instrumental to this development were a relatively small patent bar, a subset of the judiciary, and several repeat parties who played a role in a significant proportion of patent cases."). Justice Curtis brought the doctrine of equivalents into patent law, *see* Winans v. Denmead, 56 U.S. 330 (1854), and would likely have had further direct influence had he not left the Court in bitterness over the *Dred Scott* decision. It is perhaps no coincidence that Benjamin Curtis practiced patent law before his appointment to the Supreme Court. *See, e.g.*, Le Roy v. Tatham, 55 U.S. 156, 156 (1852) ("Mr. Justice Curtis, having been of counsel for the defendants in error, upon the letters-patent drawn in question in this case, did not sit at the hearing"); O'Reilly v. Morse, 56 U.S. 62, 63 (1853) ("(Mr. Justice Curtis) having been of counsel [to Samuel F.B. Morse], did not sit in this cause."). His brother, George

Learned Hand[66] – operated in a less formal, common law–oriented mode.[67] They perceived their responsibility to bring logic, consistency, and balance to the patent and copyright systems.[68] As a consequence, they did not typically tie their interpretation tightly to statutory text. Through a pragmatic process drawing on statutory, constitutional, and experiential sources as well as common sense, they evolved copyright and patent law into workable, dynamic systems.

Ticknor Curtis, authored influential IP treatises of the era. *See* GEORGE TICKNOR CURTIS, A TREATISE ON THE LAW OF PATENTS FOR USEFUL INVENTIONS, AS ENACTED AND ADMINISTERED IN THE UNITES STATES OF AMERICA (1st ed. 1849; 2nd ed. 1854; 3rd ed. 1867; 4th ed. 1873); GEORGE TICKNOR CURTIS, A TREATISE ON THE LAW OF COPYRIGHT 240 (1847). The Curtis brothers were closely connected with Justice Story through professional contact. For George, there was also a family connection; he married Justice Story's daughter. *See* R. KENT NEWMYER, SUPREME COURT JUSTICE JOSEPH STORY: STATESMAN OF THE OLD REPUBLIC 321 (1985).

66 *See, e.g.*, Royal Typewriter Co. v. Remington Rand, Inc., 168 F.2d 691, 692 (2d Cir. 1948) (explaining that "after all aids to interpretation have been exhausted, and the scope of the claims has been enlarged as far as the words can be stretched, on proper occasions courts make them cover more than their meaning will bear"). Judge Learned Hand's integrated interpretive approach – using common law reasoning and pragmatic insight to explicate terse statutory formulations – established key components of the modern IP system. *See, e.g.*, Sheldon v. Metro-Goldwyn Pictures Corp., 81 F.2d 49 (2d Cir. 1936) (explaining the originality standard in copyright law); Nichols v. Universal Pictures, 45 F.2d 119 (2d Cir. 1930) (articulating a framework for copyright infringement analysis). Judge Learned Hand was renowned for his common law jurisprudence. *See, e.g.*, United States v. Carroll Towing Co. 159 F.2d 169 (2d. Cir. 1947) (establishing what has come to be known as the Hand balancing test for determining negligence).

67 *See* WILLIAM C. ROBINSON, THE LAW OF PATENTS FOR USEFUL INVENTIONS 15 n.3 (1890) ("Our patent acts have always depended upon common-law principles for their construction and until recently have been uniformly treated as a part of that great body of theoretical and practical jurisprudence. Patent law is as truly though not so extensively a matter of historical development as the law of real property, and can no more be beneficially administered as a mere statutory system inoperative except where verbally declared, than any other of those ancient branches of the law which we have inherited from our Anglo Saxon ancestors.").

68 Justice Oliver Wendell Holmes, who brought this reasoning into development of copyright's originality standard, *see* Bleistein v. Donaldson Lithographic Co., 188 U.S. 239 (1903), wrote eloquently about the common law method. *See* O. W. HOLMES, JR., THE COMMON LAW 5 (1881) ("The customs, beliefs, or needs of a primitive time establish a new rule or a formula. In the course of centuries the custom, belief, or necessity disappears, but the rule remains. The reason that gave rise to the rule has been forgotten, and ingenious minds set themselves to inquire how it is to be accounted for. Some ground of policy is thought of, which seems to explain it and to reconcile it with the present state of things; and then the rule adapts itself to the new reasons that have been found for it, and enters on a new career. The old form receives a new content, and in time even the form modifies itself to fit the meaning which it has received."). Justice Benjamin Cardozo played a role in developing copyright's infringement standards, *see* Underhill v. Schenck, 143 N.E. 773, 775 (1924) ("The author who suffers infringement of his copyright commits a tort . . . "), as well as modern tort law, *see, e.g.*, MacPherson v. Buick Motor Co., 111 N.E. 1050 (1916) (developing the concept of enterprise liability); he took a broad view of the judicial role and the malleability of the common law. *See* BENJAMIN N. CARDOZO, THE GROWTH OF THE LAW 117–20 (1924) ("Sooner or later, if the demands of social utility are sufficiently urgent, if the operation of an existing rule is sufficiently productive of hardship or inconvenience, utility will tend to triumph."); BENJAMIN N. CARDOZO, THE NATURE OF THE JUDICIAL PROCESS 112 (1921) ("My analysis of the judicial process comes then to this, and little more: logic, and history, and custom, and utility, and the accepted standards of right conduct, are the forces which singly or in combination shape the progress of the law.").

II. STATUTORY CONSOLIDATION, CODIFICATION, AND REVISION

The patent and copyright statutes underwent relatively modest changes during the middle and latter parts of the nineteenth century. In conjunction with general efforts to codify the laws of the United States,[69] Congress consolidated, codified, and revised copyright law in 1909 and patent law in 1952. Congress extensively codified and revised copyright law in 1976. These statutes brought some of the judicial doctrines into the statutory law – sometimes with but often times without modification and with an intention for courts to perpetuate common law evolution of doctrines that they had developed.

A. *Copyright Law*

Congress made numerous incremental additions to the Copyright Act throughout the nineteenth and early twentieth centuries. These changes fell into two general categories: (1) expansions and amendments to address new subject matters, requirements, rights, and remedies[70] and (2) general revisions in 1831,[71] 1870,[72] and 1909. Congress enacted an omnibus reform of copyright law in 1976, which both codified some judicial doctrines (such as fair use) and left many judicially crafted doctrines, such as the originality threshold and infringement standards, with the courts.

The Copyright Act of 1909 began the process of integrating judicial doctrines into the copyright statute.[73] The most notable changes to copyright protection were to expand the subject matter of copyright to encompass "all writings" of an author, to extend the renewal term to twenty-eight years, and to create a compulsory license for musical compositions. Congress expressly codified the Supreme Court's 1908 decision[74] recognizing the exhaustion of rights following sale of a copyrighted work.[75]

69 *See generally* Charles Cook, American Codification Movement (1981); Ralph H. Dwan & Ernest R. Feidler, *The Federal Statutes – Their History and Use*, 22 Minn. L. Rev. 1008 (1938).

70 *See, e.g.*, Act of Apr. 29, 1802, 7th Cong., 1st Sess., 2 Stat. 171 (adding "historical and other prints" and requiring notice on every copy of a work distributed to the public).

71 *See* Act of Feb. 3, 1831, 21st Cong., 2d Sess., 4 Stat. 436. Among the principal changes were express protection for musical compositions (but without a performance right) and all types of cuts and engravings and extension of the original term of copyright from fourteen to twenty-eight years.

72 Act of July 8, 1870, §§ 85–111, 41st Cong., 2d Sess., 16 Stat. 198, 212 to 16. The major changes were to expand copyright protection to paintings, drawings, chromolithographs, statues, and "models or designs intended to be perfected as works of fine art" and to transfer copyright administration to the Library of Congress.

73 *See* Act of Mar. 4, 1909, Pub. L. No. 60–349, 60th Cong., 2d Sess., 35 Stat. 1075.

74 *See* Bobbs-Merrill Co. v. Straus, 210 U.S. 339 (1908).

75 *See* Copyright Act of 1909 § 41 (later renumbered as § 27). The House Report states that "Section 41 is not intended to change in any way existing law, but simply to recognize the distinction, long established, between the material object and the right to produce copies thereof." H.R. Rep. No. 2222, 60th Cong., 2d Sess. (1909).

In 1947, Congress codified the Copyright Act of 1909, as amended, as Title 17 of the United States Code.[76]

In 1955, Congress set in motion the process that would eventually yield the Copyright Act of 1976 when it appropriated funds to the Librarian of Congress to study the development and operation of the copyright law.[77] These studies, prepared by Copyright Office staff, scholars, and practitioners, would provide the backdrop for updating, harmonizing, and rationalizing copyright protection in light of the significant developments in technology and communications since 1909.

Several of the background studies explicated the substantial role that courts had played in fleshing out and evolving the copyright law.[78] The legislative history leading up to the 1976 Act took note of the judicial role in developing the fair use doctrine and infringement standards.[79] The final legislation, which was substantially completed by 1965, but which was stalled by discord over how to handle cable television,[80] combines terse statutory standards and codifications of judicial doctrines with highly detailed statutory compromises – particularly the compulsory license provisions. The legislative history expressly instructs courts to perpetuate common law type development of the fair use doctrine.[81] In other areas, legislative intention for courts to evolve copyright standards can be inferred.[82] More generally, Congress drafted the

[76] *See* Act of July 30, 1947, Pub. L. No. 80–281, 80th Cong., 1st Sess., 61 Stat. 652.

[77] *See* Copyright Law Revision, H.R. Rep. No. 94–1476, at 47 (1976) (hereinafter cited as "1976 Act House Report").

[78] *See, e.g.*, Alan Latman & William S. Tager, Study No. 25: Liability of Innocent Infringers of Copyrights (Jan. 1958) (tracing the development of indirect infringement doctrines); Alan Latman, Study No. 14: Fair Use of Copyrighted Works (Mar. 1958) (tracing development of the fair use doctrine); Borge Barmer, Study No. 13: Works Made for Hire and On Commission, (Apr. 1958); Abraham L. Kaminstein, Study No. 11: Divisibility of Copyrights (Jun. 1957); George D. Cary, Study No. 12: Joint Ownership of Copyrights (Aug. 1958); Walter J. Derenberg (and members of the New York Law Review), The Meaning of "Writings" in the Copyright Clause of the Constitution, Study No. 3, 83–84 (Nov. 1956) ("Largely unnoticed and unquestioned, the courts have interpreted the copyright provision of the Constitution – far beyond its literal wording.... *Writings, thus, are defined not in terms of concrete, tangible forms, but in terms of principles and standards.* " (emphasis in original)).

[79] *See, e.g.*, Copyright Law Revision Part 6: Supplementary Report of the Register of Copyrights on the General Revision of the U.S. Copyright Law: 1965 Revision Bill IX–XVI (House Comm. on the Judiciary Print) 25, 131 (May 1965).

[80] The stalemate over how to address cable television resulted in Congress passing the Sound Recording Amendments Act of 1971 as a stopgap measure to provide federal protection against the growing problem of record piracy. *See* Act of October 15, 1971, Pub. L. No. 92–140, 92d Cong., 1st Sess., 85 Stat. 391. Protection for sound recordings would be folded into the omnibus legislation passed in 1976.

[81] *See* 1976 Act House Report, *supra* note 79, at 66 (1976) ("The bill endorses the purpose and general scope of the judicial doctrine of fair use, but there is no disposition to freeze the doctrine in the statute, especially during a period of rapid technological change. Beyond a very broad statutory explanation of what fair use is and some of the criteria applicable to it, the courts must be free to adapt the doctrine to particular situations on a case-by-case basis.").

[82] *See id.* at 51 (1976) ("The phrase 'original works of authorship,' which is purposely left undefined, is intended to incorporate without change the standard of originality established by the courts under the present [1909] copyright statute."); *id.* at 61 ("The exclusive rights accorded to a copyright owner under section 106 are 'to do and to authorize' any of the activities specified in the five numbered clauses. Use of the phrase 'to authorize' is intended to avoid any questions as to the liability of contributory

bill in general terms so as to provide courts with some flexibility to address inevitable waves of technological change.[83]

B. *Patent Law*

After reinstituting patent examination in 1836, Congress added procedural improvements (such as judicial review of Patent Office decisions) and the novelty grace period in 1839.[84] Congress did not tinker with patent law again until 1870[85] when it consolidated and largely recodified the prior legislation.[86] The 1870 Act clarified the requirement that inventors "particularly point out and distinctly claim" their inventions and codified the judicially developed best mode requirement.[87]

infringers."); *id.* at 121 ("There is also no need for a specific statutory provision concerning the rights and duties of the coowners of a work; court-made law on this point is left undisturbed. Under the bill, as under the present law, coowners of a copyright would be treated generally as tenants in common, with each coowner having an independent right to use of license the use of a work, subject to a duty of accounting to the other coowners for any profits.").

83 The Supplementary Report of the Register of Copyrights from 1965 presciently observed: "Obviously no one can foresee accurately and in detail the evolving patterns in the ways author's works will reach the public 10, 20, or 50 years from now. Lacking that kind of foresight, the bill should, we believe, adopt a general approach aimed at providing compensation to the author for future as well as present uses of his work that materially affect the value of his copyright. . . . A real danger to be guarded against is that of confining the scope of an author's rights on the basis of the present technology so that, as the years go by, his copyright loses much of its value because of unforeseen technical advances.

For these reasons, we believe that the author's rights should be stated in the statute in broad terms, and that the specific limitations on them should not go any further than is shown to be necessary in the public interest. . . .

[I]t it is becoming increasingly apparent that the transmission of works by nonprofit broadcasting, linked computers, and other new media of communication, may soon be among the most important means of disseminating them, and will be capable of reaching vast audiences." *See* Copyright Law Revision Part 6, *supra* note 77 at 13–14.

With regard to copyrightable subject matter, the House Report accompanying the 1976 Act states: "Authors are continually finding new ways of expressing themselves, but it is impossible to foresee the forms that these new expressive methods will take. The bill does not intend either to freeze the scope of copyrightable subject matter at the present stage of communications technology or to allow unlimited expansion into areas completely outside the present congressional intent. Section 102 implies neither that that subject matter is unlimited nor that new forms of expression within that general area of subject matter would necessarily be unprotected.

The historic expansion of copyright has also applied to forms of expression which, although in existence for generations or centuries, have only gradually come to be recognized as creative and worthy of protection. The first copyright statute in this country, enacted in 1790, designated only "maps, charts, and books"; major forms of expression such as music, drama, and works of art achieved specific statutory recognition only in later enactments. Although the coverage of the present statute is very broad, and would be broadened further by the explicit recognition of all forms of choreography, there are unquestionably other areas of existing subject matter that this bill does not propose to protect but that future Congresses may want to." 1976 Act House Report, *supra* note 77, at 51–52 (1976).

84 *See* Patent Act of 1839, 5 Stat. 353.

85 Patent Act of 1870, 16 Stat. 198.

86 *See generally* Dwan & Fiedler, *supra* note 69.

87 *See* Patent Act of 1870 § 26.

Congress did not return to patent lawmaking until 1952 when it codified patent law in Title 35 of the U.S. Code[88] and responded to pressure to correct court decisions from the prior two decades that had substantially raised the inventiveness bar.[89] The House Report characterized codification as the "principal purpose" of the bill.[90] One leading treatise observes that "[v]ery ancient statutory language was thus carried over, in a conscious effort to preserve existing statutory interpretations."[91]

Much of the 1952 Act restated provisions from prior law while integrating, codifying, and in a few instances altering judicial doctrines. It retained the 1793 Act's text governing patentable subject matter virtually verbatim. The only pertinent difference between the 1793 and 1952 provisions is the substitution of the word "process" for "art." This alteration was not intended to effect any substantive change or to supplant more than a century of jurisprudence interpreting "art," but rather to avoid confusion with other uses of the word "art."[92] Congress carried over the language of § 102(a) from the prior statute, "recognizing that the interpretation excludes various kinds of private knowledge not known to the public."[93] In explaining § 102(e), the drafters comment that this provision "is another well-recognized condition imposed by a decision of the Supreme Court which was not expressed in the existing law."[94]

The House Report noted two "major" substantive changes to the substantive patent law: "incorporating a requirement for invention in § 103 and the judicial doctrine of contributory infringement in § 271."[95] During the 1930s and 1940s, the Supreme Court substantially tightened the judicially developed nonobviousness standard to require a "flash of genius."[96] In response, Congress formally codified the nonobviousness requirement while lowering the bar to what had previously been recognized by the courts before the 1930s as the appropriate level: whether "the differences between the subject matter sought to be patented and the prior art are such that the subject matter as a whole would have been obvious at the time the invention was made to a person having ordinary skill in the art to which said subject matter pertains."[97]

88 Patent Act of 1952, Pub. L. No. 82-593, ch. 950, 82nd Cong., 2nd Sess., 66 Stat. 792 (July 19, 1952).

89 *See* P.J. Federico, *Origins of Section 103*, 5 AIPLA Q.J. 87 (1977).

90 *See* H.R. Rep. No. 82-1923, at 5 (1952).

91 *See* R. Carl Moy, Moy's Walker on Patents §1:23 (4th ed. 2010).

92 *See* Peter S. Menell, *Forty Years of Wondering in the Wilderness and No Closer to the Promised Land: Bilski's Superficial Textualism and the Missed Opportunity to Return Patent Law to its Technology Mooring*, 63 Stan. L. Rev. 1289, 1296–97 (2011).

93 *See id.* at 6, 17.

94 *See id.* at 6–7; *see also id.* at 17 (observing that paragraph (e) enacts the rule of Alexander Milburn Co. v. Davis-Bournonville Co., 270 U.S. 390 (1926)).

95 *See id.* at 5.

96 *See* Cuno Eng'g Corp. v. Automatic Devices Corp., 314 U.S. 84, 91 (1941); see also Great Atl. & Pac. Tea Co. v. Supermarket Equip. Corp., 340 U.S. 147, 152 (1950) (holding that courts "should scrutinize combination patent claims with a care proportioned to the difficulty and improbability of finding invention in an assembly of old elements").

97 *See* 35 U.S.C. § 103. The statute expressly notes that "[p]atentability shall not be negatived by the manner in which the invention was made." The legislative history notes that the statutory standard

Congress also codified judicially developed indirect liability doctrines, although with some adjustment to partially blunt recent expansion in the judicially developed patent misuse doctrine. The legislative history notes that "[t]he doctrine of contributory infringement has been part of our law for about 80 years,"[98] but that "[c]onsiderable doubt and confusion as to [its] scope" have resulted from recent patent misuse cases.[99] In response, Congress expressly recognized the contributory infringement cause of action while codifying an express exclusion for the sale of staple articles of commerce suitable for non-infringing use.[100] The 1952 Act also changed to equitable conditions on reissue[101] and expressly authorized the use of means plus function claims, although with limitations on their scope.[102]

Although the Patent Act of 1952 simplified and fleshed out the patent law, it left many important doctrines free floating in the ether. Even after this codification, the formal patent law still contained no mention of limitations on patentable subject matter, the experimental use exception to the statutory bar, the accidental anticipation doctrine, the doctrine of equivalents, the reverse doctrine of equivalents, the experimental use defense, the exhaustion doctrine, the patent misuse doctrine, the inequitable conduct doctrine, laches, or equitable estoppel.

Thus, although the Copyright of 1976 and the Patent Act of 1952 – the statutory foundations of the current patent and copyright systems – integrated several judicially developed doctrines into statutory law (in some cases with modification), Congress did not intend these enactments to freeze these provisions as enacted, but rather envisioned that courts would continue to evolve aspects of these doctrines. Furthermore, the statutes left many significant doctrines entirely outside of the formal law.

III. THE MODERN ERA

The patent and copyright systems entered a new era in the 1970s, partly as a reflection of larger general changes taking place in legislation, delegation, and judicial interpretive philosophy.[103] Other factors – advances in digital technology and the decision

"paraphrases language which has often been used in the decisions of the courts." *See* H.R. Rep. No. 82–1923, at 7(1952); *see also id.* at 18.

98 *See* H.R. Rep. No. 82–1923, at 9 (1952).

99 *See id.* (referring principally to Mercoid Corp. v. Mid-Continent Inv. Co., 320 U.S. 661 (1944)).

100 *See id.*; 35 U.S.C. § 271(c).

101 *See* 35 U.S.C. §§ 252–53; H.R. Rep. No. 82–1923, at 8, 26–27 (1952).

102 *See* §112, – 3, 66 Stat. at 798 (now codified at 35 U.S.C. §112, – 6) (overturning Halliburton Oil Well Cementing Co. v. Walker, 329 U.S. 1, 12 (1946), which barred functional claiming).

103 *See generally* Sidney A. Shapiro and Robert L. Glicksman, *Congress, the Supreme Court, and the Quiet Revolution in Administrative Law*, 1988 Duke L.J. 819, 819 (1988) ("In the last decade, the relationship between legislative and judicial control of federal administrative discretion has changed dramatically. In the 1960s and 1970s, Congress continued its long tradition of transferring authority to administrative agencies in broad and relatively standardless delegations. . . . In the 1980s, however, the Supreme Court has adopted a more restrained approach to the review of administrative decisions, restricting or eliminating almost all of the activist techniques previously employed to police agency

to centralize patent law appeals – exerted even greater force on the development of federal IP law.

A. *Copyright Law*

More than anything else, advances in digital technology have driven copyright law's modernization. Even before the ink from the Copyright Act of 1976 was dry, the rapid development of a marketplace for computer software, followed in the 1990s by the widespread deployment of digital distribution platforms, thrust the copyright system into the digital age. Congress extended copyright protection to computer software, with the courts mediating that expansion in a manner that addressed the growing piracy concern without bestowing protection on software's functional features.[104] Whereas the first few decades of computer technology had relatively little impact on markets for copyrighted works, cumulative and rapid advances in computer speed, storage capacity, and network technology caused a sea change in the distribution of copyrighted works beginning in the 1990s.[105] During that decade, Congress added more text to the Copyright Act than in the entire prior 200 years of the republic. Nonetheless, new controversies would push courts to improvise solutions and fill gaps.

At the outset of the process for revising copyright law in the late 1950s, computer technology was still on the distant horizon. The computer industry was a hardware business in which software typically came with or was custom produced for particular machines and users. Congress was focused on many other issues, such as shifting to a unified term of protection, protecting sound recordings, and dealing with broadcasting. Because of the long gestation of the copyright reform effort, however, legal protection for computer software was a concern for copyright policy makers as the legislation came to fruition. Rather than risk delaying enactment of copyright reform to tackle this new set of challenges, Congress established the National Commission on New Technological Uses of Copyrighted Works (CONTU) in 1974[106] for the purpose of recommending "a national policy for both protecting the rights of copyright owners and ensuring public access to copyrighted works when they are used in computer and machine duplication systems."[107]

discretion. At the same time, Congress has increasingly resorted to narrow and specific legislative grants of authority.") (footnotes omitted)); William Eskridge, Jr., *Politics Without Romance: Implications of Public Choice Theory for Statutory Interpretation*, 74 VA. L. REV. 275 (1988).

104 *See* Peter S. Menell, *An Epitaph for Traditional Copyright Protection of Network Features of Computer Software*, 43 ANTITRUST BULL. 651 (1998).

105 *See* Peter S. Menell, *Envisioning Copyright Law's Digital Future*, 46 N.Y. L. SCH. L. REV. 63 (2002).

106 Pub. L. 93-573 (1974).

107 *See* Final Report of the National Commission on New Technology Uses of Copyrighted Works 3 (1978) (hereinafter cited at "CONTU Final Report"). The Copyright Act of 1976 provided an interim solution. The legislative history states that the term "literary works" "includes computer data bases, and computer programs to the extent that they incorporate authorship in the programmer's expression of original ideas, as distinguished from the ideas themselves." H.R. Rep. 94-1476, 52–53 (1976).

In 1978, CONTU recommended modest changes to the 1976 Copyright Act to accommodate legal protection computer software: (1) to make explicit that computer programs, to the extent that they embody an author's original creation, are proper subject matter of copyright and (2) to authorize rightful possessors of copies of computer programs to use or adapt these copies.[108] The CONTU Report emphasized the importance of applying the judicially developed idea-expression doctrine to ensure that copyright protection did not interfere with technological progress in computer programming.[109] Congress implemented these changes, with some textual adjustments, in the Computer Software Copyright Act of 1980.[110]

That put courts in the critical role of adapting copyright law's traditional, judicially developed standards – originality, idea-expression dichotomy, fair use – to the rapidly developing medium of computer software.[111] Over the course of the next two decades, the courts successfully surmounted the challenge. After some initial missteps that threatened to provide undue legal protection for the first entity to develop computer software for a particular purpose (such as managing a dental laboratory's records),[112] courts came to apply the idea-expression doctrine and other critical limiting doctrines with greater appreciation of the purposes underlying copyright protection.[113] Courts also interpreted the scope of the fair use doctrine to permit reverse engineering of copyrighted software for purposes of developing interoperable products.[114]

The federal courts' success in adapting copyright law to computer software successfully discouraged piracy of software products without unduly hindering innovation and competition.[115] As a result, there has not been any substantial effort to seek major legislative reform of this aspect of copyright law.[116] The same cannot

[108] *See* CONTU Final Report, *supra* note 107, at 1.

[109] *See id.* at 20.

[110] Pub. L. No. 96-517, 94 Stat. 3007, 3028 (codified at 17 U.S.C. §§ 101, 117).

[111] *See* Peter S. Menell, *An Analysis of the Scope of Copyright Protection for Application Programs*, 41 STAN. L. REV. 1045 (1989); Peter S. Menell, *Tailoring Legal Protection for Computer Software*, 39 STAN. L. REV. 1329 (1987).

[112] *See* Whelan Associates, Inc. v. Jaslow Dental Laboratory, Inc., 797 F.2d 1222 (3d Cir. 1986), *cert. denied* 479 U.S. 1031 (1987); Apple Computer v. Franklin Computer Co., 545 F.Supp. 812 (E.D. Pa. 1982), *aff'd* 714 F.2d 1240 (3d Cir. 1983), *cert. dismissed*, 464 U.S. 1033 (1984).

[113] *See* Computer Assocs. Int'l v. Altai, Inc., 982 F.2d 693 (2d Cir. 1992); 17 U.S.C. §102(b); Bateman v. Mnemonics, Inc., 79 F.3d 1532, 1543–45 (11th Cir. 1996); Apple Computer v. Microsoft Corp., 35 F.3d 1435 (9th Cir. 1994); Engineering Dynamics, Inc. v. Structural Software, Inc., 26 F.3d 1335 (5th Cir. 1994); Gates Rubber Co. v. Bando Chemical Indus., 9 F.3d 823 (10th Cir. 1993); Atari Games Corp. v. Nintendo, 975 F.2d 832 (Fed. Cir. 1992); Mark A. Lemley, *Convergence in the Law of Software Copyright?*, 10 HIGH TECH. L.J. 1 (1995); *see also* Lotus Dev. Corp. v. Borland Int'l, Inc., 49 F.3d 807 (1st Cir. 1995), *aff'd by equally divided court*, 516 U.S. 233 (1996); Dennis S. Karjala & Peter S. Menell, *Applying Fundamental Copyright Principles to Lotus* Development Corp. v. Borland Int'l, Inc., 10 HIGH TECH. L.J. 177 (1995).

[114] *See* Sega Enterprises Ltd. v. Accolade, Inc., 977 F.2d 1510 (9th Cir. 1993).

[115] *See* Menell, *supra* note 104.

[116] Congress did expand the scope of Section 117 to clarify that the creation of copies of a program in the course of maintenance or repair of a computer did not infringe copyright in the program. *See* 17 U.S.C. §117(c). See Digital Millennium Copyright Act of 1998, Pub.L. 105–304, Title III, § 302(3).

be said for the challenge posed by digital technology to markets for conventional copyrighted works – movies, sound recordings, and books.

The controversy over the digital distribution of copyrighted works was foreshadowed in the early 1980s by the battle over the video cassette recorder (VCR) that unfolded primarily in the courts. Hollywood motion picture studios brought suit alleging that Sony's Betamax contributed to infringement by enabling households to record television broadcasts. Borrowing from patent law, the Supreme Court ultimately held that Sony could not be held contributorily liable because its device was capable of substantially non-infringing use. The basis for the decision misapprehended the tort law roots of indirect copyright liability, the relationship of patent and copyright law, the text of the statute, and the legislative history of the 1976 Act, although it reached the proper outcome for this particular technology.[117] These interpretive weaknesses would result in further common law evolution distinguishing and limiting the Sony "staple article of commerce" safe harbor.[118] All the while, Congress has stayed on the sidelines on this particular issue.

Congress sought to craft a digital copyright regime in anticipation of technological change in the early 1990s, although its efforts would miss the target. But even here, litigation provided the spark. As occurred with the introduction of video cassette recording technology in the early 1980s, copyright owners sued the principal manufacturer of digital recording technology, the Sony Corporation, as it brought the first commercial digital audio tape (DAT) device into the marketplace.[119] In the shadow of costly and uncertain litigation (and following Sony's acquisition of CBS Records, one of the major record labels, in 1987), the various interests resolved their differences through negotiations that culminated in Congress's passage of the Audio Home Recording Rights Act of 1992.[120] For the first time in the history of copyright, the government imposed technological design constraints on the manufacture of copying devices. This legislation also established a royalty on the sale of devices and blank recording media and afforded immunity for noncommercial use of analog or qualifying digital devices for making copies. This legislation would prove irrelevant as computers and portable computing devices (MP3 players) displaced DAT devices in the marketplace.[121]

The emergence of the Internet as a widespread communication and commercial medium in the mid-1990s presented the next and perhaps greatest challenge for copyright law. The courts once again were at the forefront. In *Religious Technology Center* v. *Netcom On-Line Communication Services, Inc.*,[122] a copyright owner sued

[117] *See* Menell & Nimmer, *supra* note 21.

[118] *See* Peter S. Menell & David Nimmer, *Legal Realism in Action: Indirect Copyright Liability's Continuing Tort Framework and Sony's De Facto Demise*, 55 UCLA L. Rev. 143 (2007).

[119] *See* Cahn v. Sony Corp., 90 Civ. 4537 (S.D.N.Y. Jul. 9, 1990).

[120] Pub. L. No. 102–563, 106 Stat. 4237 (1992) (codified at 17 U.S.C. §§ 1001–10 (2002)).

[121] *See* Recording Industry Ass'n of America v. Diamond Multimedia Systems, 180 F.3d 1072 (9th Cir. 1999) (holding that the AHRA does not apply to MP3 devices).

[122] 907 F. Supp. 1361 (N.D. Cal. 1995).

an Internet access provider (Netcom) and its subscriber, a computer bulletin board service (BBS) hosting a Usenet newsgroup, for direct and indirect copyright liability on the basis of material posted to the newsgroup. Netcom employed an automated system for relaying messages on Usenet groups without any monitoring or control of content. Judge Ronald Whyte determined that "[a]lthough copyright is a strict liability statute, there should still be some element of volition or causation which is lacking where a defendant's system is merely used to create a copy by a third party."[123] To hold otherwise would "result in liability for every single Usenet server in the worldwide link of computers transmitting [the poster's infringing] message to every other computer."[124] With regard to contributory liability, the court held that when a BBS cannot reasonably verify a claim of infringement – because of "the copyright holder's failure to provide the necessary documentation to show that there is a likely infringement" or otherwise – then the knowledge element of contributory infringement should be deemed lacking.[125] As to participation, the court concluded that "it is fair, assuming Netcom is able to take simple measures to prevent further damage to plaintiffs' copyrighted works, to hold Netcom liable for contributory infringement where Netcom has knowledge of [the poster's] infringing postings yet continues to aid in the accomplishment of [the infringer's] purpose of publicly distributing the postings."[126] In so doing, the court established a limited immunity for online service providers (OSPs).[127]

Controversy over the scope of liability of OSPs fed directly into legislative negotiations over what would become the Digital Millennium Copyright Act of 1998 (DMCA).[128] This legislation establishes a series of safe harbors insulating OSPs from liability for various acts, such as transmitting, storing, or linking to unauthorized content, modeled in part on the *Netcom* decision.[129] It perpetuates the judicial role through its incorporation of judicially developed indirect liability standards. Unfortunately, legislative history is ambiguous on aspects of this role, as reflected in the following language from the Senate Report accompanying the DMCA:

> Rather than embarking upon a wholesale clarification of [judicially developed doctrines of contributory and vicarious liability], the Committee decided to leave current law in its evolving state and, instead, to create a series of "safe harbors," for certain common activities of service providers. A service provider which qualifies for a safe harbor, receives the benefit of limited liability.[130]

[123] *See id.* at 1370.
[124] *See id.* at 1369.
[125] *See id.* at 1374.
[126] *See id.* at 1375.
[127] Other courts adopted the *Netcom* approach. *See* ALS Scan, Inc. v. RemarQ Cmtys., Inc., 239 F.3d 619 (4th Cir. 2001); Marobie-Fl, Inc. v. National Ass'n of Fire and Equipment Distributors, 983 F. Supp. 1167 (N.D. Ill. 1997).
[128] Pub. L. 105–304, 112 Stat. 2860.
[129] *See* R. Anthony Reese, *The Relationship Between ISP Safe Harbors and Ordinary Rules of Copyright Liability*, 32 Colum. J.L. & Arts 427, 429 (2009).
[130] Senate Judiciary Committee Report on the DMCA, S. Rep. 105-190 at 19.

While clearly articulating an intention to leave the evolution of the doctrines of contributory and vicarious liability to the courts, the report fails to clarify how specific exceptions to the DMCA's safe harbors that use language derived from vicarious liability case law[131] should be interpreted.[132]

The DMCA also established a wholly new regime of anti-circumvention prohibitions designed to assist copyright owners in protecting their works.[133] As an exception to these restrictions, Congress largely incorporated the judicially developed fair use ruling authorizing reverse engineering of computer programs for the "sole purpose of identifying and analyzing those elements of the program that are necessary to achieve interoperability of an independently created computer program."[134] The anti-circumvention regime does not, however, generally exempt circumvention for fair use purposes.[135]

Technological advance has continued apace, placing courts in the position of interpreting creaky statutory provisions and evolving judicially developed doctrines. The emergence of peer-to-peer file sharing technology barely a year after the DMCA's enactment confronted courts with a host of challenging questions involving the scope of the DMCA's OSP safe harbors, the Audio Home Recording Act's noncommercial use immunity, and the *Sony* staple article of commerce doctrine.[136] The hosting of user-generated content confronted courts with another set of challenges,[137] as have efforts to impose liability on those making copyrighted works available without authorization on peer-to-peer networks.[138] Congress has remained on the sidelines during the past decade as the courts have weathered the digital distribution onslaught.

[131] *See* 17 U.S.C. §§ 512(c)(1)(B), (d)(2).

[132] *See* Reese, *supra* note 129.

[133] *See* 17 U.S.C. §§ 1201–04.

[134] *See* 17 U.S.C. § 1201(f).

[135] *See* Universal City Studios, Inc. v. Corley, 273 F.3d 429, 452–53 (2d Cir. 2001) (holding that distribution of DVD copying software, even if used to enable owners to play DVDs on Linux computers, is prohibited by the DMCA); 321 Studios v. Metro-Goldwyn-Mayer, Inc., 307 F. Supp. 2d 1085, 1101–03 (N.D. Cal. 2004) (holding liable a provider of software that decrypted a DVD but allowed owners of a DVD only to make a single backup copy).

[136] *See* A&M Records v. Napster, 114 F. Supp. 2d 896 (N.D. Cal. 2000), *aff'd* 239 F.3d 1004 (9th Cir. 2001); *see also* MGM Studios, Inc. v. Grokster, Ltd. 545 U.S. 913 (2005); *In re* Aimster Copyright Litig., 334 F.3d 643 (7th Cir. 2003); *cf.* Perfect 10, Inc. v. Amazon.com, Inc., 508 F.3d 1146 (9th Cir. 2007); Perfect 10, Inc. v. CCBill LLC, 488 F.3d 1102 (9th Cir. 2007); Columbia Pictures Industries, Inc. v. Fung, 96 U.S.P.Q.2d 1620 (C.D. Cal. 2009).

[137] *See, e.g.*, Viacom Intern. Inc. v. YouTube, Inc., 676 F.3d 19 (2d Cir. 2012); Peter S. Menell, Judicial Regulation of Digital Copyright Windfalls: Making Interpretive and Policy Sense of Viacom *v. YouTube and UMG Recordings v. Shelter Capital Partners* (2012), http://papers.ssrn.com/sol3/papers.cfm?abstract_id=2059445.

[138] *See, e.g.*, Sony BMG Music Entertainment v. Tenenbaum, 721 F. Supp. 2d 85 (D. Mass. 2010); Capitol Records Inc. v. Thomas-Rasset, 680 F. Supp. 2d 1045 (D. Minn. 2010); Capitol Records, Inc. v. Thomas, 579 F. Supp. 2d 1210 (D. Minn. 2008); Atlantic Recording Corp. v. Howell, 554 F. Supp. 2d 976 (D. Ariz. 2008); *see generally* Peter S. Menell, *In Search of Copyright's Lost Ark: Interpreting the Right to Distribute in the Internet Age*, 59 J. COPYRIGHT SOCIETY 1 (2011).

B. *Patent Law*

Although advances in digital technology also affected the patent system – particularly with regard to the scope of patentable subject matter – Congress's establishment of the Court of Appeals for the Federal Circuit appears to have had the most profound effects on the patent system.[139] Congress sought to provide greater doctrinal consistency and stability by creating a unified, specialized appellate court.[140] This new institution has significantly increased the rate at which patents have been upheld[141] and expanded the scope of patentable subject matter.[142] Perhaps more importantly, it has greatly increased the velocity of patent jurisprudence, heightening the responsiveness of the patent system to perceived problems.[143] It also awakened the Supreme Court to problems in the patent system, which has significantly increased its role in steering the patent law.[144]

The vast expansion of patenting in the 1990s generated significant concerns about patent quality, anticompetitive patent thickets, and patent "trolls."[145] Comprehensive studies by the Federal Trade Commission and the National Academies of Sciences recommended comprehensive reforms – from tightening the nonobviousness standard to raising the bar for obtaining injunctive relief, clarifying (and tightening) the willfulness standard, and rationalizing the determination of patent damages.[146]

Beginning in 2005, Congress took up these and other recommendations (such as expanding postgrant review, moving to a first-to-file system) but struggled to find common ground amidst the cacophony of competing interest groups.[147]

[139] *See* Federal Court Improvements Act of 1982, Pub. L. No. 97–164, 96 Stat. 25.

[140] *See* Rochelle Dreyfuss, *The Federal Circuit: A Case Study in Specialized Courts*, 64 N.Y.U. L. REV. 1 (1989).

[141] *See* William M. Landes & Richard A. Posner, *An Empirical Analysis of the Patent Court*, 71 U. CHI. L. REV. 111, 112 (2004).

[142] *See* State Street Bank and Trust Company v. Signature Financial Group, Inc., 149 F.3d 1368 (Fed. Cir. 1998); AT&T Corp. v. Excel Commc'ns, Inc., 172 F.3d 1352 (Fed. Cir. 1999); *In re* Alappat, 33 F.3d 1526 (Fed. Cir. 1994) (en banc).

[143] *See* Ryan Vacca, *Acting Like an Administrative Agency: The Federal Circuit En Banc*, 76 MISSOURI L. REV. 733 (2011) (showing that the Federal Circuit has had the highest rate of en banc rulings across all federal appellate courts between 2000 and 2009 and suggesting that the Federal Circuit is using en banc review as a form of rulemaking akin to that conducted by administrative agencies); *see also* Tony Dutra, *Lawyers, Judges at "Bench & Bar" Conference Explore Mutual Role in Spurring Innovation*, BNA'S PATENT, TRADEMARK, & COPYRIGHT JOURNAL No. 128 (July 5, 2011) (reporting that Chief Judge Randall R. Rader, in his "state of the court address," commented that the U.S. Court of Appeals for the Federal Circuit was committed to taking important cases en banc to provide more consistent decisions "beyond the next panel").

[144] The Supreme Court reviewed seven patent cases between 1990 and 2000. The Supreme Court doubled that number between 2001 and 2012 (even as its total number of certiorari grants declined).

[145] *See* ADAM B. JAFFE & JOSH LERNER, INNOVATION AND ITS DISCONTENTS (2004).

[146] *See* A PATENT SYSTEM FOR THE 21ST CENTURY (Stephen A. Merrill, Richard C. Levin & Mark B. Myers eds., 2004); Fed. Trade Comm'n, To Promote Innovation: The Proper Balance of Competition and Patent Law and Policy (2003).

[147] *See* DAN L. BURK & MARK A. LEMLEY, THE PATENT CRISIS AND HOW THE COURTS CAN SOLVE IT 100–02 (2009).

Meanwhile, the Supreme Court and the Federal Circuit have addressed much of the reform agenda through statutory interpretation and the crafting of judicially created doctrines. The Supreme Court tightened the nonobviousness requirement[148] and the standard for obtaining injunctive relief.[149] The Federal Circuit raised the bars for proving willful infringement[150] and reasonable royalty.[151] Only after the courts had resolved the most controversial issues dividing interest groups did Congress pass the America Invents Act (AIA) in September 2011.[152] Although touted as the most significant change in patent legislation since the 1952 Act,[153] the AIA principally addressed administrative changes in the patent system: a shift to a modified first-to-file system (retaining a grace period for inventor disclosure) and implementation of postgrant review. Congress did not disturb judicial resolution of the most divisive issues – tightening of the nonobviousness standard, a higher threshold for equitable relief, and reining in of reasonable royalty determinations.

IV. THE RAMIFICATIONS OF THE MIXED HERITAGE OF COPYRIGHT AND PATENT LAW FOR THE CONTINUED EVOLUTION OF INTELLECTUAL PROPERTY LAW

As the foregoing has traced, copyright and patent protection emerged in terse formulations during the early republic and has evolved through symbiotic processes of judicial common law–type development, legislative codification and correction, and legislative additions. The rapidity and unpredictability of technological change have buffeted courts with new challenges, and in response they have employed common law tools and functional reasoning to evolve the intellectual property system. This institutional mechanism in the face of Congress's inability to act expeditiously and lack of sustained focus has enhanced the courts' substantive imprint on federal intellectual property law.

148 *See* KSR Intern. Co. v. Teleflex Inc., 550 U.S. 398 (2007).

149 *See* eBay Inc. v. MercExchange, L.L.C., 547 U.S. 388 (2006).

150 *See* In re Seagate Tech., LLC, 497 F.3d 1360 (Fed. Cir. 2007) (en banc).

151 *See* Uniloc USA, Inc. v. Microsoft Corp., 632 F.3d (Fed. Cir. 2011); Lucent Technologies, Inc. v. Gateway, Inc., 580 F.3d 1301 (Fed. Cir. 2009); IP Innovation L.L.C. v. Red Hat, Inc., 705 F. Supp. 2d 687 (E.D. Tex. 2010) (Federal Circuit Judge Rader, sitting by designation); Cornell University v. Hewlett-Packard Co., 2008 WL 2222189 (N.D.N.Y. 2008) (Federal Circuit Judge Rader, sitting by designation).

152 *See* Pub. L. No. 112–29, 125 Stat. 284 (2011).

153 *See* U.S Department of Commerce, President Obama Signs America Invents Act and Announces New Steps to Help Entrepreneurs Create Jobs (Set. 16, 2011), *available at* http://www.commerce.gov/news/press-releases/2011/09/16/president-obama-signs-america-invents-act-and-announces-new-steps-hel (press release touting the AIA as "the most significant reform of the Patent Act since 1952"); The White House, President Obama Signs America Invents Act, Overhauling the Patent System to Stimulate Economic Growth, and Announces New Steps to Help Entrepreneurs Create Jobs (Sept. 16, 2011), *available at* http://www.whitehouse.gov/the-press-office/2011/09/16/president-obama-signs-america-invents-act-overhauling-patent-system-stim (same).

The evolution of copyright law's fair use doctrine and of patent law's nonobviousness requirement illustrates important symbiotic pathways by which IP law has developed and evolved from its terse original formulation. Justice Story crafted copyright's fair use defense from the general purposes of the copyright system and English case law. Courts evolved this doctrine over more than a century before Congress brought it into the statute – but with the expressed intention that courts would continue to evolve the doctrine.[154] Although the early U.S. patent statutes required only that an invention be novel and useful to be patentable,[155] the Supreme Court in 1850 read such a separate inventiveness limitation into the statute based on the intuition that the mere substitution of porcelain for wood or metal in the design of a doorknob, even if novel, lacked the requisite "skill and ingenuity which constitute essential elements of every invention."[156] The courts evolved this doctrine over the course of a century.[157] The source of the requirement – whether constitutional, statutory, jurisprudential, or some combination – remained somewhat murky.[158] After the Supreme Court elevated the nonobviousness threshold to a "flash of creative genius,"[159] Congress stepped in and integrated a nonobviousness standard into the statute, but specifically removed the reference to "creative" or "inventive genius."[160] Courts today focus on the statutory text, but they also reference the historical development of the nonobviousness doctrine.[161]

[154] *See*, *supra* notes 79, 81.

[155] *See* Edmund W. Kitch, Graham v. John Deere Co.: *New Standards for Patents*, 1966 SUP. CT. REV. 293, 303–04 (1966).

[156] *See* Hotchkiss v. Greenwood, 52 U.S. 248, 266–67 (1850) ("[U]nless more ingenuity and skill . . . were required . . . than were possessed by an ordinary mechanic acquainted with the business, there was an absence of that degree of skill and ingenuity which constitute essential elements of every invention. In other words, the improvement is the work of the skilful mechanic, not that of the inventor.").

[157] *See* Graham v. John Deere Co. of Kansas City, 383 U.S. 1, 11–12 (1966) (noting that *Hotchkiss* "gave birth to 'invention' as a word of legal art signifying patentable inventions. . . . The *Hotchkiss* formulation, however, lies not in any label, but in its functional approach to questions of patentability.").

[158] *Compare* Great Atlantic & Pac. Tea Co. v. Supermarket Equipment Corp., 340 U.S. 147, 155 (1950) (Douglas J., concurring) (stating that "[t]he standard of patentability is a constitutional standard"); Cuno Engineering Corp. v. Automatic Devices Corp., 314 U.S. 84, 91 (1941) (invalidating a patent on the ground that "[w]e cannot conclude that [the patentee's] skill in making this contribution reached the level of inventive genius which the Constitution, Art. I, § 8, authorizes Congress to reward"); Thompson v. Boisselier, 114 U.S. 1, 11 (1885) (same) *with* Graham v. John Deere Co. of Kansas City, 383 U.S. 1, 15 (1966) (upholding the 1952 Patent Act's formulation of the nonobviousness requirement, which abolished the "flash of creative genius" standard).

[159] *See* Great Atlantic & Pac. Tea Co. v. Supermarket Equip. Corp., 340 U.S. 147, 156 (1950) (invalidating a patent on a commercially successful mechanical device as "wanting in any unusual or surprising consequences"); Cuno Engineering Corp. v. Automatic Devices Corp., 314 U.S. 84, 91 (1941) ("the flash of creative genius, not merely the skill of the calling").

[160] *See* H.R. REP. No. 1923, 82d Cong., 2d Sess. 18 (1952) ("The second sentence states that patentability as to this requirement is not to be negatived by the manner in which the invention was made, that is, it is immaterial whether it resulted from long toil and experimentation or from a flash of genius.")

[161] *See* KSR Int'l Co. v. Teleflex, Inc., 550 U.S. 398 (2007); Graham v. John Deere Co. of Kansas City, 383 U.S. 1 (1966).

The courts continue to play a central role in developing these "statutory" regimes. And although the modern statutes have become bloated with detailed and often technical provisions,[162] fundamental aspects of the copyright and patent regimes trace back to the original statutory enactments, remain relatively terse, and reflect the judicial gloss and fine-tuning that ensued.[163]

The mixed heritage of IP law has important ramifications for statutory interpretation. In applying IP law, courts should trace the origin of statutory text or doctrine to determine the proper judicial lens – whether to use a common law approach or to focus narrowly on statutory text. In assessing the provenance of statutory provisions, courts should be open to examining legislative history, especially with regard to codification statutes and other amendments intended to explain the nature and purpose of judicially developed doctrines. This use of legislative history does not force courts to follow any particular mode of statutory interpretation, but rather guides them in determining their own role in applying the law. That use largely sidesteps the more controversial issues surrounding legislative history.[164] There is very little reason to suspect that lobbyists in the period from 1950 to 1952 (with respect to the modern Patent Act) or from 1955 to 1976 (with respect to the modern Copyright Act) were distorting the role of judicial doctrine in the evolution of these systems. There is extensive historical and jurisprudential evidence to corroborate those accounts.[165] The copyright studies that formed the basis for omnibus reform were thoughtfully prepared, widely vetted, and thoroughly discussed in open sessions. The patent codification and reform processes were carefully conducted and documented.

The development of copyright and patent law also informs the growing debate over the treatment of so-called common law statutes.[166] It lends support to Professor

162 *See* David Nimmer, *Codifying Copyright Comprehensibly*, 51 UCLA L. REV. 1233 (2004).

163 *See* Nard, *supra* note 34; WILLIAM F. PATRY, PATRY ON COPYRIGHT, §2:1 (2006) ("[D]espite the bulk of the Copyright Act, and despite some of the detailed regulatory provisions, critical components of copyright law are judge-made. These components include (1) the nature of originality; (2) the scope of copyright; (3) the nature of the contribution necessary to qualify one as an author; and (4) the elements of and standards for an infringement claim. Fair use, while statutorily recognized in Section 107, remains a creature of common law. The case law that has developed around all these issues is centuries old. Thus, when one refers to "interpreting" the Copyright Act, it is well to keep in mind that the Act is a mixture of statutory and common-law features." (footnote omitted)); MOY, *supra* note 91, at §1:17 ("[T]o a degree remarkable in comparison to other statutory areas of the law, patent law has shown a tendency over the last two centuries to develop by case-law decision. Much of this has occurred when the courts have ostensibly been engaged in statutory interpretation. But the courts have shown an unusually large propensity to create new rules of patent law according to their own sense of what fairness requires. In this sense, then, patent law is controlled to a much larger extent by common law and common law principles that are other areas of federal substantive law." (footnotes omitted)).

164 *See* John F. Manning, *Second-Generation Textualism*, 98 CAL. L. REV. 1287 (2010); Philip P. Frickey, *Interpretive-Regime Change*, 38 LOY. L.A. L. REV. 1971 (2005).

165 *See* OMNIBUS COPYRIGHT REVISION LEGISLATIVE HISTORY (George S. Grossman ed., 2001); H.R. Rep. No. 82–1923 (1952); Frederico, *supra* n.89.

166 *See* Frank H. Easterbrook, *Statutes' Domains*, 50 U. CHI. L. REV. 533, 544 (1983) ("The statute books are full of laws, of which the Sherman Act is a good example, that effectively authorize courts to create

Margaret Lemos's skepticism (see Chapter 4) about labeling statutes as "common law" or "ordinary."[167] Rather than distinguishing between two caricatured buckets, courts should recognize that there can be a spectrum of statutory/common law regimes even within the same statute. The patent and copyright regimes are particularly distinctive in their mixed heritage – tracing back to the founding of this nation when courts played a greater role in fleshing out statutes and evolving through various stages of judicial embellishment and tweaking, legislative codification, and transformative technological change. The analogy to the Sherman Act may be apt for particular judicially developed and legislatively delegated features, but does not make sense for some of the highly specified legislative compromises passed within the past few decades. Courts should be mindful of the provenance and distinctive context by which statutes emerge and develop.

As this chapter has illustrated, the modern copyright and patent regimes can best be understood as rich mosaics – each comprising detailed and specific statutory provisions, open-ended statutory standards authorizing judicial common law development, and important elements still existing entirely outside of the statutory text. Over more than two centuries of statutory accretion, the source and character of the statutory strata have evolved. As a result, tracing the contextual background of particular provisions is essential to interpreting and applying the copyright and patent laws faithfully. Furthermore, a robust, contextually grounded judicial role is critical to maintaining the vitality of the IP system. For these reasons, courts should be especially careful to trace the provenance of copyright and patent provisions and doctrines to determine the proper interpretive lens in applying these laws.

new lines of common law."); Shyamkrishna Balganesh, *Debunking Blackstonian Copyright*, 118 YALE L.J. 1126, 1167 (2008) (describing the Copyright Act as a "common law statute"); Nard, *supra* note 34, at 53 (2010) (describing the Patent Act as a "common law enabling statute").

[167] *See* Margaret H. Lemos, *Interpretive Methodology and Delegations to Courts: Are "Common-Law Statutes" Different?* (in this volume).

4

Interpretive Methodology and Delegations to Courts

Are "Common Law Statutes" Different?

*Margaret H. Lemos**

INTRODUCTION

It is hard to find consensus on questions of statutory interpretation. Debates rage on about the appropriate goals of interpretation and the best means of achieving those ends. Yet there is widespread agreement, even among traditional combatants on the statutory interpretation field, when it comes to so-called common law statutes. Textualists concede that text is not controlling;[1] originalists admit that judicial construction of common law statutes need not be keyed to the specific intent of the enacting Congress;[2] and staunch defenders of strict statutory stare decisis allow frequent departures from precedent.[3]

So what *are* common law statutes? It is easy enough to name a few, and courts and commentators often do. The list always begins with the Sherman Act[4] and typically

* Professor, Duke University School of Law. Much of the work on this chapter was completed while I was on the faculty at the Benjamin N. Cardozo School of Law, and I thank colleagues and staff there for their support. Special thanks for helpful comments and suggestions are due to the participants at the May 2011 symposium, Intellectual Property and the Common Law, as well as to Rick Bierschbach, Michael Herz, Max Minzner, Alex Reinert, Kevin Stack, Stewart Sterk, and participants at the Legislation Roundtable held at Columbia Law School on April 8, 2011. Michael Silverstein provided excellent research assistance.

1 *See* Miranda McGowan, *Do as I Do, Not as I Say: An Empirical Investigation of Justice Scalia's Ordinary Meaning Method of Statutory Interpretation*, 78 Miss. L.J. 129, 134 (2008) ("Justice Scalia entirely suspends textualism in about a quarter of the cases in the study's sample because he believes that he is interpreting a statute that has granted common law authority to the courts.").

2 *See* Frank Easterbrook, *Statutes' Domains*, 50 U. Chi. L. Rev. 533, 544 (1983) (arguing that "the domain of the statute should be restricted to cases anticipated by its framers and expressly resolved in the legislative process" except in the case of the Sherman Act and like statutes "that effectively authorize courts to create new lines of common law").

3 *See* Guardians Assoc. v. Civil Serv. Comm'n, 463 U.S. 582, 641 & n.12 (1982) (Stevens, J., dissenting) (arguing that "when the Court unequivocally rejects one reading of a statute, its action should be respected in future litigation," but making an exception for common law statutes such as the Sherman Act and § 1983).

4 *See* Leegin Creative Leather Prods., Inc. v. PSKS, Inc., 551 U.S. 877, 899–900 (2007) ("From the beginning the Court has treated the Sherman Act as a common-law statute."); Easterbrook, *supra*

includes § 1983,[5] the Taft-Hartley Act, and statutory provisions on securities fraud.[6] In the realm of intellectual property, scholars have argued that many of the major enactments make the cut.[7]

What is missing is any clear conception of what defines this special category, uniting common law statutes and distinguishing them from the rest. The relevant case law and commentary reveal two features that are thought to qualify statutes like the Sherman Act for special treatment: such statutes are written in broad terms[8] and build on a tradition of common lawmaking.[9] In this chapter, I argue that neither of the proposed distinctions is persuasive, because the relevant features are shared by many other statutes that do not appear on the privileged list. Any differences are in degree, not in kind.

Of course, it is hardly uncommon for the law to mistake points on a continuum for separate categories, and the "common law" label may serve as an easy – if mildly inaccurate – shorthand for the group of statutes that actively embrace lawmaking by courts. I hope to show, however, that the label is not so benign. Instead, the continuing fiction that there is a categorical difference between common law statutes and "normal" statutes like, say, Title VII of the Civil Rights Act of 1964,[10] works to obscure the difficult line-drawing problems that interpreters otherwise would have to confront. If statutes like the Sherman Act and Title VII coexist on a scale of statutory vagueness,[11] it is a mistake to suggest that questions of interpretive methodology switch on and off in an automatic fashion depending on whether the statute at hand is a common law statute.

An additional problem with the "common law" label is that it diverts attention away from significant questions concerning delegations of lawmaking power to the judiciary. How should the legal system identify such delegations? When are they

note 2, at 544 ("The statute books are full of laws, of which the Sherman Act is a good example, that effectively authorize courts to create new lines of common law.").

5 *See* Cass Sunstein, *Interpreting Statutes in the Regulatory State*, 103 HARV. L. REV. 405, 421–22 (1989) (arguing that, because § 1983 "is silent on many important questions, including available defenses, burdens of pleading and persuasion, and exhaustion requirements[,] . . . the statute delegates power to make common law").

6 *See* William N. Eskridge, Jr., *Public Values in Statutory Interpretation*, 137 U. PA. L. REV. 1007, 1052 (1989) (describing § 301 of the Taft-Hartley Act and the anti-fraud provisions of the securities laws as "common law statutes"); *see also* Blue Chip Stamps v. Manor Drug Stores, 421 U.S. 723, 737 (1975) ("When we deal with private [securities fraud] actions under Rule 10b-5, we deal with a judicial oak which has grown from little more than a legislative acorn.").

7 *See* Shyamkrishna Balganesh, *Debunking Blackstonian Copyright*, 118 YALE L.J. 1126, 1167 (2008) (describing the Copyright Act as a "common law statute"); Pierre N. Leval, *Trademark: Champion of Free Speech*, 27 COLUM. J.L. & ARTS 187, 198–99 (2004) (describing the Lanham Act and the Federal Trademark Dilution Act as "delegating" statutes); Craig Allen Nard, *Legal Forms and the Common Law of Patents*, 90 B.U. L. REV. 51, 53 (2010) (describing the Patent Act as a "common law enabling statute").

8 *See infra* Part II.

9 *See infra* Part III.

10 42 U.S.C. §§ 2000e-1 to 2000e-17.

11 For ease of exposition, I use the Sherman Act and Title VII throughout this chapter as examples of "common law" and "normal" (i.e., *not* common law) statutes, respectively.

a good idea, and when should Congress rely on agencies instead? The notion that delegations to courts can be identified and justified simply by drawing an analogy to the Sherman Act conceals those issues from view. But once the label is peeled back, it becomes clear that our current treatment of common law statutes raises more questions than it answers about delegations to courts.

I. COMMON LAW STATUTES AND CONGRESSIONAL DELEGATIONS

To see what common law statutes are and are not, it helps to begin with how they are treated. Most everyone agrees that common law statutes represent delegations to courts.[12] (The harder question is *why*, and I turn to that later.) Thus, common law statutes are "enabling" statutes: they authorize courts to make law.[13]

Understanding common law statutes as enabling acts helps explain why interpreters of different stripes have been able to agree on a common methodology. Simply put, delegations to courts take many of the familiar arguments about statutory interpretation off the table. Consider the question whether courts should give effect to the intentions of the enacting legislators or interpret the statute dynamically in light of evolving norms. Whatever may be true in other circumstances, it makes little sense to insist on fidelity to original legislative intent where the only discernible intent on the issue was to leave it to the courts.[14]

More fundamentally, much of statutory interpretation theory is focused on controlling or justifying a judicial role in the project of law creation and development. For example, textualists reject common law approaches to statutory interpretation on the ground that "[i]t is simply not compatible with democratic theory that laws mean whatever they ought to mean, and unelected judges decide what it is."[15] The argument assumes that judges have a choice: they can "stick . . . close to the surface of statutory texts," thereby leaving policy making in the hands of Congress, or they can embrace a policy-making role of their own.[16] But that choice evaporates when Congress delegates broad lawmaking power to the courts. The Sherman Act – the

[12] *See, e.g.*, Ethan J. Leib & Michael Serota, *The Costs of Consensus in Statutory Construction*, 120 Yale L.J. Online 47, 53 (2010) ("In the world of what are sometimes known as common law statutes, broad delegation to the judiciary is uncontroversial, and the legislature expects judges to develop the law over time by utilizing a free-form common law method."). For a discussion of delegations to courts generally, see Margaret H. Lemos, *The Other Delegate: Judicially Administered Statutes and the Nondelegation Doctrine*, 81 S. Cal. L. Rev. 405 (2008).

[13] Herbert Hovenkamp, Economics and Federal Antitrust Law 52 (student ed. 1985) ("[T]he Sherman Act can be regarded as 'enabling' legislation – an invitation to the federal courts to learn how businesses and markets work and formulate a set of rules that will make them work in socially efficient ways.").

[14] *See* Thomas W. Merrill, *The Common Law Powers of Federal Courts*, 52 U. Chi. L. Rev. 1, 46 (1985) (explaining how delegations to courts can coexist peacefully with an intentionalist approach to statutory interpretation).

[15] Antonin Scalia, A Matter of Interpretation: Federal Courts and the Law 22 (1997).

[16] Cass R. Sunstein & Adrian Vermeule, *Interpretation and Institutions*, 101 Mich. L. Rev. 885, 908 (2002).

prototypical common law statute – illustrates the point. Although the Act prohibits all contracts, conspiracies, and combinations "in restraint of trade,"[17] the Supreme Court long has held that the operative question is whether the conduct at issue restrained trade *unreasonably*.[18] A "reasonableness" standard plainly invites judicial policy making. The standard requires further elaboration to clarify its contents, and even the Court's most committed textualists recognize that the text of the statute plays a minimal role in that process.[19]

Similar reasons explain the Court's relaxation of statutory stare decisis in the context of common law statutes. Federal courts normally purport to apply a super-strong version of stare decisis to statutory precedents, on the view that once a court authoritatively interprets a statute, any change should come from Congress.[20] That view rests in part on the notion that the "functional consequences" of overrulings are "legislative rather than judicial."[21] And it rests in part on an assumption that Congress "approves" of any interpretations it leaves in place.[22] Finally, super-strong statutory stare decisis reflects a sense that Congress is the appropriate body to weigh the advantages of updating the law against the likely disruption of public and private reliance interests.[23]

Each strand of reasoning suggests a discomfort with judicial lawmaking and a preference for congressional action. But such reasoning seems out of place in contexts like antitrust, where the Court has been thrust headlong into a lawmaking role. Why insist that Congress make *this* decision, when courts have made so many others? Recognizing as much, the Court has treated the Sherman Act and other common law statutes as exceptions to statutory stare decisis.[24] Because common law

[17] 15 U.S.C. § 1.

[18] Leegin Creative Leather Prods., Inc. v. PSKS, Inc., 551 U.S. 877, 885 (2007) ("While § 1 could be interpreted to proscribe all contracts, the Court has never taken a literal approach to its language. Rather, the Court has repeated time and time again that § 1 outlaw[s] only unreasonable restraints." (internal quotation marks omitted)).

[19] *See* Daniel A. Farber & Brett H. McDonnell, *"Is There a Text in this Class?" The Conflict Between Textualism and Antitrust*, 14 J. Contemp. Legal Issues 619, 621 (2004) ("[A]lthough textualists have sometimes been described as striving with missionary zeal to narrow the focus of consideration to the statutory text and its 'plain meaning,' this is hardly true in antitrust law." (internal quotation marks omitted)).

[20] *See* Amy Coney Barrett, *Statutory Stare Decisis in the Courts of Appeals*, 73 Geo. Wash. L. Rev. 317, 348 (2004) ("[C]ourts most often assert simply that if a prior judicial interpretation does not capture the statute's meaning, Congress can – and therefore should – be the one to fix it."); William N. Eskridge, Jr., *Overruling Statutory Precedents*, 76 Geo. L.J. 1361, 1366–68 (1987) (describing the rationale for statutory stare decisis). *Cf.* Lawrence C. Marshall, *"Let Congress Do It": The Case for an Absolute Rule of Statutory Stare Decisis*, 88 Mich. L. Rev. 177, 200–19 (1989) (arguing that any judicial policy making is countermajoritarian and should be avoided, and proposing that the Supreme Court shift policy-making responsibility back to Congress by applying an absolute rule of statutory stare decisis).

[21] Eskridge, *supra* note 20, at 1366 (quoting Frank E. Horack, Jr., *Congressional Silence: A Tool of Judicial Supremacy*, 25 Tex. L. Rev. 247, 250–51 (1947)).

[22] Alex Hosiery Co. v. Leader, 310 U.S. 469, 488–89 (1940).

[23] Eskridge, *supra* note 20, at 1367.

[24] *Id.* at 1377–81.

courts would not apply an especially strict version of stare decisis when developing the law, the Court assumes that the same should be true of common lawmaking pursuant to statute.

All of this makes sense if common law statutes are viewed in isolation from the rest of statutory law. But a puzzle emerges if we consider such statutes alongside their cousins in the administrative sphere – statutes that delegate to agencies. The comparison reveals that, although the methodological consequences of a delegation are similar in the judicial and administrative contexts, the means of identifying delegations are significantly different.

At first blush, delegations to agencies seem to support the methodological approach courts have taken to common law statutes. We do not expect agencies to adhere to the specific intentions of the enacting Congress, because we recognize that Congress may have chosen open-textured commands over specific directives so that the agency could work out the details. We do not expect agencies to "stick . . . to the surface of the text" of the statutes they implement, because we recognize that the text is often vague or incomplete. And we do not expect agencies to set their statutory interpretations in stone, because we recognize that the relative flexibility of administrative decision making is one of its primary advantages over legislation.

These views are captured in the Court's seminal decision in *Chevron U.S.A., Inc.* v. *Natural Resources Defense Council, Inc.*,[25] in which it acknowledged that an agency's resolution of statutory ambiguity inevitably entails an exercise of discretion. The agency's job, the Court explained, "necessarily requires the formulation of policy and the making of rules to fill any gap left . . . by Congress."[26] When Congress's intent is unclear, the agency has no choice but to make "policy choices – resolving the competing interests which Congress itself either inadvertently did not resolve, or intentionally left to be resolved by the agency."[27]

The prevailing approach to common law statutes effectively empowers courts to act like agencies do. Courts develop the law in the context of specific cases and controversies[28] rather than via generally applicable regulations,[29] and judge-made law may differ in important respects from agency-made law.[30] Nevertheless, the notion that congressional delegations call for an interpretive approach that is both flexible and sensitive to policy unites the worlds of agency-administered and common law statutes.

[25] 467 U.S. 837 (1984).

[26] *Id.* at 843.

[27] *Id.* at 865.

[28] U.S. Const'n, Art. III.

[29] *See* Administrative Procedure Act, 5 U.S.C. § 553 (detailing the procedural requirements for agency rulemaking).

[30] *See* Margaret H. Lemos, *The Consequences of Congress's Choice of Delegate: Judicial and Agency Interpretations of Title VII*, 63 VAND. L. REV. 363, 387–433 (2010) (discussing differences between the Supreme Court's and the EEOC's interpretations of Title VII).

The difference lies in how courts identify the triggers for judicial and agency lawmaking. Some agency statutes make the authorization explicit, directing agencies to enact regulations implementing the terms of the statute and in some cases making clear that the statute will have no legal effect until the agency acts.[31] Explicit delegations of substantive lawmaking power to courts are rare,[32] but courts long have recognized that delegations may be implicit as well as explicit.[33] Under *Chevron*'s famous test, if "the statute is silent or ambiguous with respect to the specific issue," the court must defer to the agency's answer so long as it is "reasonable."[34] Thus, statutory ambiguity is "agency-liberating" in the sense that it converts the administrative inquiry from a search for what the statute means to a determination of what it ought to mean.[35] Provided that Congress has vested the relevant agency with the authority to act with the force of law,[36] the only question of law for the reviewing court is whether the agency "acted within the scope of its discretion."[37]

Matters look very different in the judicial context. Although statutory ambiguity may open the door to nontextual sources of statutory meaning, it is hardly the case that all judges take ambiguity as an implicit authorization for them to make law in the freewheeling manner permitted agencies and associated with common law statutes. Textualist judges see ambiguity as a challenge that can be surmounted by reference to statutory context and the canons of construction. For intentionalist judges, textual ambiguity simply means that other indications of congressional intent must be consulted. The goal remains the same, however: identify what the statute

[31] *See* Edward L. Rubin, *Law and Legislation in the Administrative State*, 89 COLUM. L. REV. 369, 381 (1989) (discussing agency statutes that are intransitive in application).

[32] Congress sometimes explicitly empowers the federal courts to create procedural law. *See, e.g.*, 28 U.S.C. § 2072 (authorizing the Supreme Court to prescribe general rules of practice and procedure and rules of evidence for federal cases); FED. R. EVID. 501 (providing that in federal question cases, "the privilege of a witness, person, government, State, or political subdivision thereof shall be governed by the principles of the common law as they may be interpreted by the courts of the United States in light of reason and experience"). On the substantive side, the best example is § 301(a) of the Labor Management Relations Act, which provides for federal court jurisdiction over "[s]uits for violation of contracts between an employer and a labor organization . . . in an industry affecting commerce." 29 U.S.C. § 185(a). On its face, that provision is simply a grant of jurisdiction and not a delegation of lawmaking power at all. Nevertheless, the Court has interpreted § 301(a) as an authorization to the federal courts to "fashion a body of federal law for the enforcement of these collective bargaining agreements." Textile Workers Union v. Lincoln Mills, 353 U.S. 448, 452 (1957); *cf.* Michael Rosensaft, *The Role of Purposivism in the Delegation of Rulemaking Power to the Courts*, 29 VT. L. REV. 611, 614, n.9 (2005) (citing "liberal construction" clauses as a species of explicit delegation).

[33] U.S. v. Mead Corp., 533 U.S. 218, 229 (2001) ("'[S]ometimes the legislative delegation to an agency on a particular question is implicit'" (quoting *Chevron*, 467 U.S. at 844)).

[34] *Chevron*, 467 U.S. at 843–44.

[35] Antonin Scalia, *Judicial Deference to Administrative Interpretations of Law*, 1989 DUKE L.J. 511, at 521.

[36] *Mead*, 533 U.S. at 226–27 (limiting *Chevron* deference to instances where Congress delegated authority to the agency generally to make rules carrying the force of law, and the agency exercised that authority when adopting the interpretation at issue).

[37] Scalia, *supra* note 35, at 516.

means and give effect to that meaning.[38] Moreover, although agencies are free to change their interpretations of ambiguous statutes, courts are not.[39] It is only in the realm of common law statutes that these constraints on judicial decision making can be avoided without controversy. The location of the dividing line is far from clear, but it is clearly not the line that courts have drawn in the administrative sphere.

Courts' treatment of common law statutes therefore begs the important question why the agency-liberating line is different from the court-liberating line. And where, exactly, *is* the court-liberating line? As noted earlier, two possibilities emerge from the relevant case law and commentary. One is that common law statutes are defined by the nature of their texts: although mere ambiguity is not enough to signal a delegation to the judiciary, truly open-textured language is. The second possibility is that common law statutes are defined by the fact that they were enacted against a backdrop of common law. In the remainder of this chapter, I seek to show that neither of the proposed definitions supports a sharp distinction between common law statutes and other judicially administered acts. If statutory ambiguity is a poor proxy for identifying delegations to courts, we have yet to find a better one.

II. "SWEEPING, GENERAL TERMS"

Perhaps the most conventional way of describing common law statutes is by reference to how they are written. Common law statutes, we are told, are "phrased in sweeping, general terms."[40] Congress did not define the precise content of common law statutes, but instead "expect[ed] the federal courts to interpret them by developing legal rules on a case-by-case basis in the common law tradition."[41]

As a description of statutes like the Sherman Act, that characterization is uncontroversial. It does not work, however, to define a self-contained category of statutes. So-called common law statutes represent a subset of the larger class of statutes for which courts have primary interpretive authority. It is no secret that many statutes in that larger class contain gaps and ambiguities.[42] In the hands of agencies, such statutes would be taken as implicit delegations of policy-making authority. But with no agency to fill in the blanks, the job is entrusted to judges. How and why are such judicially administered statutes different from common law statutes?

38 *See* Lisa Schultz Bressman, *Chevron's Mistake*, 58 Duke L.J. 549, 559 (2008) ("Although the dominant theories of statutory interpretation differ in many ways, they share an important feature; they invite courts to construe statutory text as if Congress intended that text to have a relatively specific meaning.").

39 *See* Neal v. United States, 516 U.S. 284, 295 (1996) (explaining that, although an agency "[e]ntrusted within its sphere to make policy judgments" may change its interpretations, courts "do not have the same latitude to forsake prior interpretations of a statute").

40 Guardians Assoc. v. Civil Serv. Comm'n, 463 U.S. 582, 641 & n.12 (1982) (Stevens, J., dissenting).

41 *Id.*

42 *See* Lemos, *supra* note 12, at 429–34.

Consider a statute like Title VII – a "normal" statute that most would agree lies outside the privileged common law category. Title VII bars employment discrimination on the basis of race, sex, religion, and national origin, but leaves many key issues to be resolved by courts in the course of case-by-case adjudication. For example, the statute does not define the term "discrimination," and it says nothing about whether or to what extent "employer[s]" are liable for the actions of supervisors or other employees. In short, it is "silent or ambiguous"[43] in significant respects. And, because the relevant agency does not have the authority to create binding substantive regulations interpreting and implementing Title VII, as a practical matter courts are responsible for elaborating the meaning of the statute.[44] Thus, even if it is not a common law statute, Title VII constitutes a delegation to courts.[45]

To be sure, the delegation is more limited than the Sherman Act's, and the commands of Title VII are specified in more detail than those of federal antitrust law. But the differences are not *categorical* differences; they are differences in degree. It should come as no surprise, then, that proponents of purposive, dynamic statutory interpretation advocate a purposive, dynamic approach to interpreting Title VII.[46] Yet, although such arguments are widely accepted in the narrow context of common law statutes, they are met with stiff resistance when applied to most other judicially administered statutes, including Title VII.[47]

If statutes like Title VII and the Sherman Act represent different degrees of delegation rather than distinct conceptual categories, it becomes harder to explain why the appropriate interpretive methodology changes as courts move from one to the other. That is not to say that an explanation is unavailable, but merely that one is needed. Perhaps a textualist, for example, would answer that the more comprehensive text of Title VII enables a textual approach that is not possible in Sherman Act cases. On that view, the textualist concession for common law statutes is akin to an impossibility defense, and the difference between statutory ambiguity and "sweeping . . . general[ity]" matters because it marks the line where textualism becomes infeasible.

My own view is that the proposed textualist distinction is unpersuasive. First, it is not obviously true that a textualist approach is not feasible in the context of the

43 Chevron U.S.A., Inc. v. Natural Resources Defense Council, Inc., 467 U.S. 837, 843 (1984).

44 *See* Lemos, *supra* note 30, at 384–87 (describing Title VII's institutional arrangements).

45 *See id.*

46 *See* William N. Eskridge, Jr., *Dynamic Statutory Interpretation*, 135 U. PA. L. REV. 1479, 1488–96 (1986) (pressing a dynamic approach to interpreting Title VII); *id.* at 1517–18 (arguing that the reasons for interpreting statutes dynamically rather than "with strict regard to original legislative intent" "apply not only to common law statutes such as § 1983 and the Sherman Act, but also to more detailed statutes such as Title VII").

47 *See, e.g.*, Johnson v. Transp. Agency, Santa Clara Cty., 480 U.S. 616, 671 (1987) (Scalia, J., dissenting) (bemoaning the majority's infidelity to "what the law as enacted meant"); *cf. id.* at 644 (Stevens, J., concurring) (accepting a construction of Title VII "that is at odds with my understanding of the actual intent of the authors of the legislation" on the basis of stare decisis).

Sherman Act.[48] Not only does the Sherman Act itself contain clues that textualism ordinarily would attend to, but Congress also has enacted several other statutes in the antitrust field that speak in far more specific terms.[49] Moreover, the Sherman Act incorporates the common law concept of "restraint of trade." Although that concept may be "dynamic,"[50] a textualist approach would focus on the evolving content of the common law, whereas the Court has treated the common law as a jumping-off point for independent policy analysis.[51] Indeed, what is striking about the prevailing judicial approach to antitrust law is that courts do not even *try* to find guidance in the relevant statutory texts and other textualism-approved sources of meaning.

Second, it is not clear that textualism is capable of achieving its normative goals in the context of statutes that delegate less broadly than the Sherman Act. I do not rehearse here the many arguments that have been levied against textualism, but it is worth mentioning at least one problem with a textualist approach to Title VII and similar statutes: deliberate ambiguity. Even within a relatively comprehensive statute, legislators may use ambiguity to secure majority support for provisions that could not be enacted if they were explicit.[52] Title VII itself contains provisions that reflect a legislative agreement to disagree,[53] as do other more detailed statutes.[54]

48 *Cf.* Bilski v. Kappos, 130 S.Ct. 3210 (2010) (taking a textualist approach to interpreting the Patent Act). Although *Bilski*'s "textualist turn" is certainly open to criticism, *see generally* Peter S. Menell, *Forty Years of Wondering in the Wilderness and No Closer to the Promised Land: Bilski's Superficial Textualism and the Missed Opportunity to Ground Patent Law Interpretation and Return Patent Law to its Technology Mooring*, 63 Stan. L. Rev. 1289 (2011), the majority's opinion illustrates that a textualist approach is *possible* even for broadly worded statutes. Indeed, the *Bilski* majority drew a textualist inference from the very breadth of the statute's text, emphasizing the "ordinary meaning" of the "broad terms" governing patentable subject matter and reasoning that Congress's choice of "expansive terms . . . modified by the comprehensive 'any'" weighs against recognizing judicially crafted exceptions. 130 S.Ct. at 3225–26.

49 *See* Farber & McDonnell, *supra* note 19, at 644–54 (discussing the Clayton and FTC Acts); *cf.* Peter L. Strauss, *The Common Law and Statutes*, 70 U. Colo. L. Rev. 225, 244 (1999) ("What the Court has made of the Sherman Act competes with what the text of the Act seems to say and what more recent enactments have been generally understood to accomplish.").

50 Bus. Elec. Corp. v. Sharp Elec. Corp., 485 U.S. 717, 731 (1988).

51 *See* Farber & McDonnell, *supra* note 19, at 632–39 (discussing several ways that the common law could guide and constrain antitrust jurisprudence).

52 Victoria F. Nourse & Jane S. Schacter, *The Politics of Legislative Drafting: A Congressional Case Study*, 77 N.Y.U. L. Rev. 575, 595–97 (2002) (discussing statutory drafters' use of deliberate ambiguity).

53 *See* Rebecca Hanner White, *The EEOC, the Courts, and Employment Discrimination Policy: Recognizing the Agency's Leading Role in Statutory Interpretation*, 1995 Utah L. Rev. 51, 52 ("[I]n enacting the Civil Rights Act of 1991, which amends Title VII . . . in many important respects, Congress was often purposefully ambiguous, essentially choosing not to decide polarizing issues in order to pass a bill the President would sign."); Civil Rights Act of 1991, Pub. L. No. 102–166, § 105(b), 105 Stat. 1071, 1075 (1992) (limiting courts' consideration of legislative history regarding the term "business necessity" to an interpretive memorandum stating that the term is "intended to reflect the concepts enunciated by the Supreme Court" in cases "prior to" *Wards Cove Packing Co. v. Atonio*, 490 U.S. 642 (1989)).

54 *See* Joseph A. Grundfest & A. C. Pritchard, *Statutes with Multiple Personality Disorders: The Value of Ambiguity in Statutory Design and Interpretation*, 54 Stan. L. Rev. 627, 665–66 (2002) (discussing Congress's agreement to disagree on the pleading standard set out in the Private Securities Litigation Reform Act of 1995).

Although it would be possible for a textualist interpreter to construct a meaning for such provisions, it is hard to see such behavior as an exercise of judicial restraint.[55] Nor can such construction be defended on "democracy-forcing" grounds,[56] because it does nothing to deter future legislative coalitions from dodging contentious questions while "both side[s] . . . hope that the Supreme Court w[ill] eventually rule in their favor."[57]

Finally, the proposed distinction entails an extremely stingy view of delegations to courts, suggesting that courts should decline congressional invitations to policy making if they possibly can. As I suggest later, there is a respectable argument that Congress is less likely to delegate to courts than to agencies, given concerns about courts' comparative institutional competence and their political insulation. Yet it is one thing to say that delegations to courts should not be lightly presumed and quite another to suggest that that they must be rebuffed. Absent a claim that delegations to courts are invalid (rather than merely a bad idea), a refusal to recognize statutes like Title VII as at least partial delegations would seem to reflect precisely the sort of contested policy judgment that textualism insists be left to Congress.

The important point for present purposes, however, is not that textualist distinctions between Title VII and the Sherman Act are wrongheaded, but that they ought to be brought out into the open. As others have observed, the reasons textualists have offered for exempting antitrust law from the methodological strictures of textualism "are remarkably cursory."[58] The fiction that the Sherman Act is different in kind from other judicially administered statutes perpetuates this state of affairs, allowing textualists to finesse some of the hardest cases for their preferred approach without articulating why textualism gives way in contexts like antitrust, and where exactly it kicks back in.[59]

III. COMMON LAW HISTORY

If the "sweeping . . . terms" of common law statutes do not differentiate them categorically from other judicially administered statutes, perhaps their common law

55 *Cf.* Nourse & Schacter, *supra* note 52, at 618 ("If the expectation in a particular circumstance among those responsible for drafting a bill is that a court will resolve the meaning of a particular provision, is it activist or restrained for a court to insist that Congress answered that question and to attribute responsibility for its reading of the language to Congress?").

56 Adrian Vermeule, *Interpretive Choice*, 75 N.Y.U. L. Rev. 74, 103 (2000) ("A central argument for textualism is that it has a democracy-forcing effect: Judicial refusal to remake enacted text forces Congress to legislate more responsibly *ex ante*.").

57 Grundfest & Pritchard, *supra* note 54, at 658.

58 Farber & McDonnell, *supra* note 19, at 622.

59 The argument in the text has focused on textualism for the sake of brevity, but the same points hold for the other methodological exceptions allowed for so-called common-law statutes. That is, it may be possible for intentionalist interpreters, or proponents of strict statutory stare decisis, to explain why Title VII and the Sherman Act should be treated differently. But the convenient "common law" label masks both the need for such explanations and the thorny problems of line drawing they inevitably would confront.

heritage does. Most of the statutes that appear regularly on the "common law" list codify legal principles that had been developed by the courts as common law.[60] Arguably, that feature might signal an implicit delegation to courts, taking the place of ambiguity as the relevant proxy.[61]

The argument that a common law history serves as a trigger for ongoing judicial lawmaking finds oblique support in the literature on why Congress delegates to agencies. Although that literature is agency-focused, even a brief review reveals that delegations to courts are hard to explain in the conventional terms. For example, one of the principal justifications for agency delegations, particularly in complex policy areas, is that agencies have expertise that Congress lacks.[62] Delegations to courts are a mystery on this view, because generalist judges are unlikely to possess any special expertise.[63] Moreover, Congress has political and procedural tools for steering agency policy making before it becomes final, thereby minimizing the principal-agent problem inherent in any delegation of power.[64] But Congress lacks equivalent mechanisms for influencing judicial decision making. The only way to correct "bad" judicial decisions is via override legislation, a significantly less attractive option for legislators.[65]

These considerations suggest that Congress may have fewer reasons to delegate to courts than to agencies. Perhaps it follows that treating statutory ambiguity as

60 *See, e.g.*, Bus. Elec. Corp. v. Sharp Elec. Corp., 485 U.S. 717, 731–32 (1988) (explaining that the Sherman Act "invokes the common law itself"); Dura Pharm., Inc. v. Broudo, 544 U.S. 336, 341 (2005) (explaining that the private right of action under § 10(b) of the Securities Exchange Act and SEC Rule 10b-5 "resembles, but is not identical to, common-law tort actions for deceit and misrepresentation"); Balganesh, *supra* note 7, at 1167–68 (explaining that the fair use doctrine and the idea-expression dichotomy in the Copyright Act "merely codify rules developed independently by courts in the past"); Menell, *supra* note 48, at 1294–96 (detailing the common law background of the Patent Act).

61 *See* Leval, *supra* note 7, at 197 ("Regardless . . . of whether the text is detailed or consists of only a vague generalized reference to the body of doctrine, if the intention of the statute was not to make law but to give recognition in statutory form to a previously developed body of court-made law, proper interpretation of the statute demands that it be so understood."); Merrill, *supra* note 14, at 44 ("[A]n inference of delegation arises when . . . Congress adopts a legal standard that is borrowed from (or 'codifies') the common law."); Richard A. Posner, *Statutory Interpretation – in the Classroom and in the Courtroom*, 50 U. Chi. L. Rev. 800, 818 (1983) ("If the legislature enacts into statute law a common law concept, . . . that is a clue that the courts are to interpret the statute with the freedom with which they would construe and apply a common law principle – in which event the values of the framers may not be controlling after all."); *cf.* Farber & McDonnell, *supra* note 19, at 658 ("One of the main arguments for the delegation theory is that the Sherman Act uses common law terms, and must therefore contemplate a common-law process of law development."); Menell, *supra* note 48, at 1311 (arguing that the common law history of the Patent Act demands that courts "perpetuate the common law-type jurisprudential tradition").

62 *See* David Epstein & Sharyn O'Halloran, *The Nondelegation Doctrine and the Separation of Powers: A Political Science Approach*, 20 Cardozo L. Rev. 947, 967 (1998).

63 Chevron U.S.A., Inc. v. Natural Resources Defense Council, Inc., 467 U.S. 837, 865 (1984) ("Judges are not experts in the field.").

64 For a useful overview, see Bressman, *supra* note 38, at 569–71.

65 *See* Lemos, *supra* note 30, at 420–23.

evidence of a "legislative intent to confer discretion"[66] – as courts do in the administrative context – would overestimate Congress's desire to authorize judicial policy making. And, perhaps, a history of common law authority offers a more accurate proxy for an intent to delegate. Notions of judicial expertise may have more traction in areas that have traditionally been the province of the common law, where courts have substantial experience. Similarly, the incrementalism of common law decision making, and the related idea that the common law will "work[] itself pure" over time,[67] may reduce the risk that judge-made law will veer sharply away from congressional expectations. In short, courts may seem like better delegates when the job consists of building on a body of law that they themselves constructed.

Again, this view may work as a description of many statutes that enjoy the "common law" label, but it does not work as a means of demarcating a separate category of such statutes. Many, perhaps most, judicially administered statutes build on common law concepts, yet do not trigger the methodological concessions that courts have made for the Sherman Act and its peers.[68] Here, too, any difference between common law statutes and "normal" statutes is one of degree rather than kind.

Common law concepts enjoy pride of place in many statutes that no one has ever categorized as common law statutes.[69] For example, the Employee Retirement Income Security Act (ERISA) – a statute the Court has described as "comprehensive and reticulated"[70] – incorporates the general jurisprudence of trusts.[71] Title VII and other statutes that forbid discrimination against "employees" incorporate the common law of agency in defining that term.[72] Federal courts draw from common law principles developed at the state level when interpreting such statutes,[73] but they do not feel free to elaborate the law in the policy-driven manner associated with antitrust law.

66 Scalia, *supra* note 35, at 516.

67 Lon L. Fuller, The Law in Quest of Itself 140 (1940) ("The common law works itself pure and adapts itself to the needs of a new day.").

68 *See, e.g.*, Northwest Airlines, Inc. v. Transport Workers Union of America, 451 U.S. 77, 95 n.34 (1981) ("[O]nce Congress addresses a subject, even a subject previously governed by federal common law, the justification for lawmaking by the federal courts is greatly diminished. . . . [T]he task of the federal courts is to interpret and apply statutory law, not to create common law.").

69 Although my focus here is on civil statutes, common law concepts are legion in federal criminal law. For an illuminating discussion of the role federal courts play in elaborating federal criminal law, notwithstanding the rule of lenity and the longstanding rule barring federal "common law" crimes, United States v. Hudson & Goodwin, 11 U.S. (7 Cranch.) 32 (1812), see Dan M. Kahan, *Three Conceptions of Federal Criminal-Lawmaking*, 1 Buff. Crim. L. Rev. 5, 6–9 (1997).

70 Mertens v. Hewett & Assocs., 508 U.S. 248, 251 (1993).

71 *See, e.g.*, Varity Corp. v. Howe, 516 U.S. 489, 496–97 (1996) (noting that fiduciary duties under ERISA "draw much of their content from the common law of trusts"); Firestone Tire & Rubber Co. v. Bruch, 489 U.S. 101, 110–11 (1989) (invoking the *Restatement (Second) of Trusts* to identify the standards that courts should use in reviewing benefit determinations made by ERISA plan administrators).

72 Caleb Nelson, *The Persistence of General Law*, 106 Colum. L. Rev. 503, 521–22 (2006) (discussing courts' treatment of the Americans with Disabilities Act, the Age Discrimination in Employment Act, and Title VII).

73 *Id.*

With respect to statutes that come closer to the "sweeping . . . general[ity]" of the Sherman Act, the Court's approach has been at best inconsistent.[74] Consider the Federal Employers' Liability Act (FELA), which created a federal tort remedy for railroad workers injured by their employers' negligence. The statute "does not define negligence, leaving that question to be determined . . . 'by the common law principles as established and applied in the federal courts.'"[75] As Peter Strauss has detailed, early courts "accepted [FELA] as a remedy to 'be developed and enlarged to meet changing conditions and changing concepts of the industry's duty toward its workers.'"[76] But the Supreme Court has shifted course in more recent years, grounding its interpretations of FELA in the common law as it existed when the statute was enacted in 1908 and disclaiming any authority to adjust the statutory remedy in light of modern demands.[77] Although the Court does not deny that the statute's meaning may evolve over time as the common law of negligence evolves, it sees state – not federal – courts as the appropriate drivers of such change.[78]

The Court's treatment of the Sherman Act provides a sharp contrast. The Court has rejected a static view of the Sherman Act under which the statute's meaning would be determined by "the contours of the common law of 1890."[79] Writing for the Court in *Business Electronics Corp.* v. *Sharp Electronics Corp.*, Justice Scalia explained that the Sherman Act "adopted the term 'restraint of trade' along with its dynamic potential. It invokes the common law itself, and not merely the static content that the common law had assigned to the term in 1890."[80] Yet the Court has not linked its decisions to contemporary common law either. Instead it has treated the Sherman Act as "an exercise in applied economics," pursuing the statute's

[74] *Compare* Eskridge, *supra* note 46, at 1485–88 (critiquing cases in which the Court took a static approach to § 1983 rather than drawing guidance from "[t]he modern common law of tort remedies and immunities" and "the Court's ongoing policy-balancing"), *with id.* at 1540 & n.247 (citing cases in which the Court "relied mainly on current policy and common law doctrine" in interpreting § 1983); *compare* Menell, *supra* note 48, at 1299–1304 (criticizing *Bilski* majority for focusing on the ordinary meaning of the words in § 101 of the Patent Act rather than their common law meaning), *with* J.E.M. Ag. Supply, Inc. v. Pioneer Hi-Bred Int'l, Inc., 534 U.S. 124, 135 (2001) (explaining that § 101 is a "dynamic provision designed to encompass new and unforeseen inventions").

[75] Urie v. Thompson, 337 U.S. 163, 174 (1949) (quoting Urie v. Thompson, 175 S.W.2d 471, 474 (Mo. 1943)).

[76] Peter L. Strauss, *On Resegregating the Worlds of Statute and Common Law*, 1994 Sup. Ct. Rev. 429, 431 (quoting Kernan v. American Dredging Co., 355 U.S. 426, 432 (1958)).

[77] *Id.* at 421–34 (discussing *Gottshall v. Conrail*, 512 U.S. 532 (1994)); *cf.* Monessen Southwestern R. Co. v. Morgan, 486 U.S. 330 (1998) (holding that FELA does not permit the recovery of prejudgment interest, in part because such interest was generally barred in common law actions in 1908).

[78] Strauss, *supra* note 76, at 436 ("It is as if Congress's delegation to the federal courts to develop common law remedies for railroad worker injuries conveyed or recognized far less judicial authority than a state common law court would have – an authority necessarily dependent on what state courts were doing.").

[79] Farber & McDonnell, *supra* note 19, at 636 (outlining the "substantial argument" for such a static view).

[80] 485 U.S. 717, 731 (1988).

presumed goal of preserving competition "without regard to the strictures of the common law."[81]

This contrast undermines any claim that the freewheeling policy making associated with common law statutes (or at least some of them, some of the time) can be explained and justified by a tradition of common lawmaking. Something is amiss here. If a common law tradition is persuasive evidence of a congressional intent to delegate broad authority to the judiciary, courts are ignoring many delegations by focusing on the short list of common law statutes. If, in contrast, a common law tradition signals at most that courts may continue to rely on common law developments in interpreting the statute over time, then the Court has overstepped its bounds in the Sherman Act and perhaps elsewhere.[82] I suspect the answer lies somewhere in the middle and that the appropriate approach to common law concepts turns on contextual factors, including the purpose of the statute, the importance of stability and predictability in the relevant area, courts' relative institutional competence to craft policy on the subject, and other evidence of a congressional desire to leave the resolution of the issue to the judiciary. But rather than engaging with those or other explanatory factors, the Court proceeds as if certain methodological consequences follow inevitably from Congress's incorporation of common law concepts – ignoring the fact that in one case the common law is constraining and, in another, liberating.

IV. DELEGATIONS TO COURTS TODAY

In sum, the label of "common law statute" obscures more than it illuminates. It is difficult, if not impossible, to define a category of common law statutes in a way that differentiates statutes like the Sherman Act from the many other statutes that judges must interpret and implement. If there are salient differences between the Sherman Act and Title VII, for example, they are differences in emphasis. The difficult questions are when, whether, and why those more subtle differences justify a shift in methodology – that is, why textualism, intentionalism, and super-strong statutory stare decisis are appropriate for some statutes but not others. The fiction that there is a naturally occurring category of common law statutes deflects much-needed attention from those questions.

But the problem with the "common law" label goes beyond the interpretive questions on which I have focused so far. The label also serves to mask an important set of institutional questions about when, whether, and why delegations to courts make sense today. By tethering such delegations to the venerated tradition of the common law, the label makes judicial policy making seem familiar, uncontroversial,

[81] Farber & McDonnell, *supra* note 19, at 639.

[82] *See id.* at 659 ("When Congress contemplates common-law decisions by the courts, there is no reason to suppose that it had this kind of blatantly result-oriented decisionmaking in mind. There is particularly little reason to ascribe this view to Congresses that acted in the era of *Swift v. Tyson*, when it was thought that judges 'found' rather than 'made' common law.").

inevitable. In so doing, it assumes away the many differences between common lawmaking of yesteryear and common law making today.

Consider, first, the divergence between *how* courts make law today and how they made law when many of the so-called common law statutes were enacted. For example, the traditional conception of common lawmaking was passive, "a corollary of the [courts'] obligation to decide . . . any matters that parties put before them."[83] That ceased to be true, at least for the Supreme Court, with the advent of discretionary jurisdiction. The modern Court's certiorari power enables the Justices to pick and choose opportunities for lawmaking, "encourages them to speak more broadly than the particular facts before them require," and "permits them to defend themselves against the inconvenience of facts that might appear to compel movement opposite to the direction they prefer."[84] Moreover, given the Court's shrinking docket, a great deal of time may elapse before the Court considers an issue, allowing a consensus to develop in the lower courts. Historically, "[t]hat trend would itself operate as a signal to a common law court – a reason if not precedent for reaching a similar conclusion."[85] But the Court seems to grant little deference to the legal conclusions of the lower courts.[86] As a result, its interventions into statutory law may be far more disruptive than the common law tradition would suggest. The ever-growing ratio of cases to courts places additional strain on the analogy to traditional common law practices and on the notion that a common law background can function as a substitute for specialized expertise. Courts cannot develop familiarity with statutes when they confront them so rarely. Although the problem is most stark at the Supreme Court level, it extends all the way down the federal judicial hierarchy.[87]

A backward-looking conception of common law statutes ignores these and other changes in the procedures for judicial lawmaking. Perhaps more importantly, a focus on common law history conceals how much the relevant subject areas have changed since the statutes were enacted. The Patent Act illustrates the problem. The first Patent Act was enacted in 1790.[88] At that time, technology was mostly uniform: "if you put technology in a bag and shook it, it would make some noise."[89] Patent law was understood as a subset of property law, and analogies to land were common.[90] Moreover, the administrative state was still in the gestational stage. The

83 Peter L. Strauss, *Courts or Tribunals? Federal Courts and the Common Law*, 53 Ala. L. Rev. 891, 895 (2001).

84 *Id.*

85 Strauss, *supra* note 49, at 246.

86 *See* Lemos, *supra* note 30, at 429 (discussing the relationship between Supreme Court and lower court decision making in the context of Title VII).

87 For example, the average district judge sees only a few patent cases a year and handles a patent trial once every seven years. *See* Peter Lee, *Patent Law and the Two Cultures*, 120 Yale L.J. 2, 16 (2010).

88 Act of April 10, 1790, 1 Stat. 109.

89 Robert P. Merges, *As Many as Six Impossible Patents Before Breakfast: Property Rights for Business Concepts and Patent System Reform*, 14 Berkeley Tech. L.J. 577, 585 (1999).

90 *See* Michael J. Burstein, *Rules for Patents*, 52 Wm. & Mary L. Rev. 1747, 1764–66 (2011) (describing early understandings and applications of patent law).

institutional choice for Congress at the time was between legislating with specificity or leaving matters largely to the courts; the option of delegating lawmaking authority to a regulatory agency had yet to become conventional.[91]

Fast forward to today. Innovation is becoming increasingly technologically and economically diverse. Patent scholars now recognize that harnessing the innovation-promoting potential of patent requires distinguishing among industries and inventions – a task that demands a sophisticated understanding of both technology and economics.[92] Meanwhile, there is good reason to believe that clarity and predictability are particularly valuable in the patent field, because "setting ex ante expectations is critical to well performing property systems."[93] Yet courts' lack of expertise and the sporadic nature of their encounters with patent law limit their ability to craft bright-line rules that serve those goals without sacrificing accuracy in individual cases.[94] Commentators have urged courts to focus instead on elaborating the law case by case in the incremental common law fashion.[95] The advantage of the common law method, at least in theory, is that it enables judges to apply the law with sensitivity to the circumstances of each case. But to translate that advantage from theory to practice, judges must be able to understand the circumstances of each case. That may not be true in most patent cases.[96]

All of this has prompted claims that the "patent system is in crisis."[97] Nevertheless, most scholars have focused their attention on tweaking the current system of judicial administration, without seriously considering whether that system is up to the modern task.[98] Only a few have suggested moving primary authority for law elaboration from the federal courts to an expert agency.[99]

91 *See* Jonathan S. Masur, *Regulating Patents*, 2010 Sup. Ct. Rev. 275.

92 *See generally* Dan L. Burk & Mark A. Lemley, The Patent Crisis and How the Courts Can Solve It (2009).

93 Burstein, *supra* note 90, at 36.

94 *See generally* Arti K. Rai, *Engaging Facts and Policy: A Multi-Institutional Approach to Patent System Reform*, 103 Colum. L. Rev. 1035 (2003).

95 *See, e.g.*, John F. Duffy, *Rules and Standards on the Forefront of Patentability*, 51 Wm. & Mary L. Rev. 609, 614 (2009) (arguing that standards for patentable subject matter perform better than rules in the long run); Rai, *supra* note 94, at 1101–02 (advocating standard- rather than rule-driven patent doctrine that is sensitive to facts and policy).

96 Not only is the law of patent "rather arcane," Lee, *supra* note 87, at 12, but applying the law to the facts of each case requires a great deal of technological sophistication. *See* Arti K. Rai, *Specialized Trial Courts: Concentrating Expertise on Fact*, 17 Berkeley Tech. L.J. 877, 878 (2002) ("[D]ifficult questions of scientific fact are likely to arise more routinely in patent law than in virtually any other field of law.")

97 Merges, *supra* note 89 at 591; *see also* Burk & Lemley, *supra* note 92.

98 *See generally, e.g.*, Jeanne C. Fromer, *Patentography*, 85 N.Y.U. L. Rev. 1444 (2010) (arguing that venue rules should be adjusted so as to concentrate patent cases by industry in select district courts); Craig Allen Nard & John F. Duffy, *Rethinking Patent Law's Uniformity Principle*, 101 Nw. U. L. Rev. 1619 (2007) (arguing that, in addition to the Federal Circuit, at least one generalist circuit court should be authorized to hear patent appeals); Rai, *supra* note 96 (urging the creation of specialized trial courts).

99 *See generally* Burstein, *supra* note 90; Masur, *supra* note 91.

Similar problems are evident in the antitrust field.[100] Antitrust law today implicates complicated and contested questions of economic theory. As such, it poses serious challenges for generalist judges and juries. If anything, those challenges have intensified in recent years, as the Court has moved away from per se rules and toward more flexible standards that allow judges to consider the challenged conduct in context to determine whether it appears to be an unreasonable restraint of trade. But the more nuanced and complex antitrust law becomes, the farther it drifts from the ken of the average federal judge. As in patent, although flexible standards hold the promise of improving the fit between the law and the facts of each case, courts' limited expertise sharply reduces the accuracy of case-by-case adjudication.

Considerations of institutional competence therefore call into question whether a robust judicial role in policy making is in fact a good idea within the supposed category of common law statutes. The point is not that courts should revert to a more formalist methodology in interpreting the Patent or Sherman Acts. Unless and until Congress adjusts the prevailing institutional arrangements, courts have little choice but to continue to muddle along; pretending that the statutes answer questions they clearly do not answer is not an attractive alternative. But neither does it make sense to pretend that the delegation can be justified by the common law tradition that existed when the statutes were enacted.

The argument here works both ways. If, as I have suggested, the "common law" label is unhelpful insofar as it connects modern delegations to historical common lawmaking, the problem is one of exclusion as well as inclusion. That is, reliance on the label may suggest – perhaps improperly – that statutes outside the special category do not confer discretion on the courts. Yet courts may be much better suited to develop the law of employment discrimination, for example, than the law of antitrust. Not only do courts have experience enforcing the antidiscrimination provisions of the Constitution, but their remove from majoritarian politics also may make them particularly valuable delegates on the statutory side of antidiscrimination law.[101] And, with no agency presently empowered to play a strong role in interpretation and implementation of Title VII, the practical need for judicial policy making is at least as strong as in the fields of patent and antitrust.

This chapter is not the place to make a comprehensive case for beefing up the judicial role in elaborating antidiscrimination law or for rolling back judicial involvement in patent and antitrust. My goal is more modest. I have sought to show that our existing practice with respect to delegations to courts is, at best, half correct. On the one hand, courts' treatment of the so-called common law statutes reflects a healthy recognition that delegations matter and that the appropriate approach to statutory interpretation depends on the role courts must play in developing the law. On the other hand, neither courts nor commentators have devoted much effort

[100] *See generally* Daniel Crane, *Rules Versus Standards in Antitrust Adjudication*, 64 WASH. & LEE L. REV. 49 (2007).

[101] *See* Lemos, *supra* note 12, at 470.

to identifying court-liberating statutes or assessing when and why such liberation is normatively attractive. The prevailing rhetoric on delegations obscures those important issues by perpetuating the fiction that delegations to courts occupy an easily identifiable, self-enclosed category of common law statutes. The fiction is counterproductive, and we should abandon it.

5

Dynamic Claim Interpretation

Dan L. Burk[*]

INTRODUCTION

Common law doctrinal development is intimately bound up in the exercise of judicial interpretation. At times courts may develop doctrine from whole cloth, out of their own reasoning and authority. But more often in the modern state, doctrine accretes around islands of text: statutory or constitutional or regulatory texts that require interpretation in order to function as legal imperatives.[1] The meanings attributed to these texts are the product of judicial reasoning and authority. Additionally, the rules by which courts interpret such texts are themselves the product of common law development, typically developed ex nihilo by the courts themselves. Such rules are routinely applied across substantive doctrinal areas; the tools developed to build common law structures in one area are frequently carried over to do similar work elsewhere.

This is true not only across substantive areas, but across different types of legal texts: the judicial tools that render meaning from statutes render meaning from contracts, from deeds, from wills as well. Such common law processes are directly implicated in the construction of patents as legal documents. Textual claims are the heart of the patent document and the core of patent law itself. Much of patent practice and policy revolves around determining the scope granted to patent claims, and modern patent scholarship has shown how claim scope is central to the purposes of the patent system. The process of interpreting, or construing, patent claims is grounded in practices of judicial reasoning and authority, much as is interpretation for other legal texts.

* Chancellor's Professor of Law, University of California at Irvine.

[1] *See* Margaret Lemos, *Interpretive Methodology and Delegations to Courts: Are "Common Law Statutes" Different?* (in this volume) (discussing development of common law from certain statutes); *see also* Craig Allen Nard, *Legal Forms and the Common Law of Patents*, 90 B.U. L. Rev. 51 (2011) (arguing that the U.S. patent statutes are properly a starting point for common law development).

And, as with other judicial interpretation, the development of interpretive rules for patent claims is itself a common law process. To the extent that a jurisprudence of claim construction exists, it is a creation of the courts. Patent claim construction is not dictated by Congress. No portion of the patent statutes prescribes the standards or methodologies that are to be used in parsing the text of claims; such "meta-rules" regarding the process of interpretation are wholly the creatures of the judges who apply them.

Not surprisingly, the process of claim interpretation, and the rules that claim interpretation is said to follow, closely parallel those for other interpreted documents. Claim interpretation often encompasses familiar statutory or constitutional methodologies, such as the application of competing canons of construction, reliance on dictionary definitions, and searching the documentary history for clues as to its original meaning. The process of claims interpretation draws heavily on the common law interpretive tool kit. Indeed, the United States Court of Appeals for the Federal Circuit (CAFC), which has been criticized for its highly formalistic approach to statutory interpretation, including "plain meaning" methodologies and lexical constructs, has applied essentially the same approaches to claim interpretation.[2] The interpretive tools that construct common law meaning have been re-deployed to construct claim meaning.

Statutory and constitutional interpretation has generated a vast literature analyzing, critiquing, and advocating different modes of judicial interpretation. But, despite the obvious parallels, surprisingly little of this vast literature has been brought to bear on patent claim interpretation.[3] In this chapter, I offer a modest down payment on such an approach to patent claim interpretation, using some of the tools that have been developed for analyzing the common law interpretive process. Specifically, I look to the interpretive principles laid out in William Eskridge's landmark work *Dynamic Statutory Interpretation* for guidance in approaching claim construction.[4] I critique the noted tendency of the U.S. Court of Appeals for the Federal Circuit to adopt formalist approaches to textual interpretation; as Eskridge noted more than a decade ago, such approaches tend to conceal more than they disclose. However, because the parallels between patent claims and other legal texts are not perfect, and Eskridge's approach was developed for statutory interpretation, I offer some thoughts on how his insights might be modified to develop a school of dynamic claim interpretation.

[2] *See* Timothy R. Holbrook, *Substantive Versus Process-Based Formalism at the Federal Circuit*, 9 Lewis & Clark L. Rev. 123 (2005); John R. Thomas, *Formalism at the Federal Circuit*, 52 Am. U.L. Rev. 771 (2003).

[3] Dan L. Burk & Mark A. Lemley, *Quantum Patent Mechanics*, 9 Lewis & Clark L. Rev. 29, 49 (2005). Notable exceptions to this absence include Craig Allen Nard, *A Theory of Claim Interpretation*, 14 Harv. J. L. & Tech. 1 (2000); Kristen Osenga, *Linguistics and Patent Claim Construction*, 38 Rutgers L.J. 61 (2006); Kelly Casey Mullally, *Patent Hermeneutics: Form and Substance in Claim Construction*, 59 Fla. L. Rev. 333 (2007).

[4] William N. Eskridge, Jr., Dynamic Statutory Interpretation (1994).

I. PATENTS AND CLAIMS

Patent law hinges on the interpretation of a legal text to determine questions of scope, of infringement, and of validity, all of which are assessed in reference to the textually claimed invention. The patent document concludes with one or more numbered sentences stating the characteristics and parameters of the technology over which the inventor claims exclusive rights: these sentences are termed the patent claims.[5] Claims are drafted in a combination of technological and legal language that may be almost incomprehensible to those unfamiliar with it. The syntax of claims follows a very particular and unusual structure that communicates important features of their scope and meaning to those who are familiar with their compositional peculiarities.[6]

The ultimate form of a patent's claims is developed in an epistolary dialog between a patent applicant and one or more examiners at the Patent Office. Inventors submit draft claims as part of their patent application; the examiner assigned to review the application responds with a document in which he or she may reject claims that do not meet statutory criteria or may require that the claims be amended for compliance with the requirements of the statute before the patent may issue.[7] Applicants respond in kind; they may add, delete, or amend claims in various ways in answer to the demands of the Patent Office.[8] This process may be repeated several times in a back-and-forth exchange termed the "prosecution" of the patent.[9] The resulting documentary prosecution history reflects the evolution and origins of the final text.

The provision of claims in the patent system – and indeed, the provision of the patent document itself – sets patents apart from other modes of intellectual property protection. Only in patent law do the exclusive rights of the creator proceed from a textual description of those rights.[10] In the case of copyright protection, we work from an artifact – a painting, a sculpture, a text, a series of sounds – that is both an object of the exclusive rights and the template for defining the extent of those exclusive rights.[11] We look at the image or statue or poem or song itself in order to determine what the parameters of the copyright in that creation may be, or to determine whether some other artifact infringes on that copyright. Similarly, in trademark law, the extent of the rights in the mark are determined by looking to an artifact, by considering the depiction of the mark itself, to determine the scope of protection and the incidence of infringement. There are no copyright claims or

5 35 U.S.C. § 112 (2008).

6 Janice M. Mueller, Patent Law 78 (3d ed. 2009).

7 Irah H. Donner, Patent Prosecution: Law, Practice, and Procedure 218 (5th ed. 2007).

8 *Id.*

9 *Id.*

10 *See* Dan L. Burk & Mark A. Lemley, *Fence Posts or Sign Posts? Rethinking Patent Claim Construction*, 157 U. Penn. L. Rev. 1743, 1774–75 (2009).

11 Jeanne Fromer, *Claiming Intellectual Property*, 76 U. Chi. L. Rev. 719, 744 (2009).

trademark claims describing the rights of the copyright or trademark owner – only the subject matter of the right itself.[12]

But in patent law, an embodiment of the invention itself is not used as the basis for determining the inventor's exclusive rights; at least, this has not been the case since working models are no longer required to be submitted to the patent office as part of a patent application. Rather, in patent law, we look to a text – to the claims – to determine the scope of the patentee's rights, and to decide whether infringement has occurred.[13] Indeed, because the current patent regime is one of "peripheral" claiming, in which the inventor seeks to describe the outermost boundaries of the patent claim, we do not even look to a text that describes the inventor's actual invention.[14] The scope of the claims is certainly related to the actual invention – patent law does require that the scope of the inventor's claims be commensurate with the disclosure of the invention in the specification.[15] But the claims are not descriptions of the invention – they are descriptions of the inventor's exclusive rights couched in terms of the technology covered by those rights.[16]

As a rule, claims are used in comparative determinations, although the class of objects of comparison may differ somewhat depending on the legal question under consideration. Legal determinations in patent law are generally questions of validity or of infringement. Both these questions entail determinations of patent scope. However, the artifacts under consideration may differ in these different determinations. In determining the scope and validity of a patent, we typically rely on a comparison of textual claims with previous texts, in the form of prior art references.[17] Most often prior art references are printed publications, and even though in some cases the prior art can constitute uses of technology or activities, as a practical matter these must also be codified, reduced to an affidavit or other textual description, before comparison with the claims.[18]

Infringement determinations pose a rather different scenario. In determining infringement, the court is generally comparing the text of claims with an infringing device or process; that is, comparing the description in a text to something nontextual.[19] Black-letter patent law requires that a court must find every element of the claims in the accused device, either literally or by equivalents, in order to reach a finding of infringement.[20] Courts must map the terms of the claim onto the

[12] *See* Burk & Lemley, *supra* note 10.

[13] *See* Burk & Lemley, *supra* note 3, at 36.

[14] MUELLER, *supra* note 6, at 333.

[15] In re Hyatt, 708 F.2d 712, 714 (Fed. Cir. 1983).

[16] *See* Janice Mueller, *A Rich Legacy*, 81 J. PAT. & TRADEMARK OFF. SOC'Y. 755, 758–59 (1999) (quoting remarks of Federal Circuit Judge Giles Rich).

[17] *See* Burk & Lemley, *supra* note 10, at 1759.

[18] Dan L. Burk, *The Role of Patent Law in Knowledge Codification*, 23 BERKELEY TECH. L.J. 1009, 1031 (2008).

[19] Markman v. Westview Instr., Inc., 52F.3d 967, 980–81 (Fed. Cir. 1985) *aff'd* 517 U.S. 370 (1996).

[20] *Id.* at 976.

features of an object or process, the accused device – in essence comparing the mental image conjured up by the text to a tangible artifact, comparing the ideal with the real. As I have observed elsewhere, a parallel mapping exercise may sometimes arise in other areas of intellectual property – say, in copyright determining the substantial similarity of sculpture to a character described in a literary work – but this exercise is uniquely endemic to patent law.[21]

II. CLAIM CONSTRUCTION

Each of these legal determinations must begin with an assessment of the meaning of the claims, in order to compare the claims to the prior art or to an accused device. This process necessarily involves an exercise in textual interpretation, ascribing meaning both to the words of the claims and to the relationships between individual terms of the claims. Courts routinely employ heuristics that appear to have been drawn from other types of textual interpretation or that parallel other interpretive exercises in the law.

For example, claim construction is frequently guided by canons of interpretation that dictate particular outcomes in certain repeated interpretive situations. One patent canon holds that courts generally should not adopt a claim interpretation that would exclude the preferred embodiment of the invention.[22] Courts similarly apply a canon of claim differentiation, under which the use of a limiting term in a dependent claim of a patent is assumed not to limit the independent claim to which it refers – the logic here being that the language in the narrower claim ought not to be read as redundant.[23] Courts also favor interpretations that do not read terms out of the claim or make them superfluous.[24]

Judges construing claims may also look to related documents for guidance on the meaning to be ascribed to the claims.[25] The patent's prosecution history, recording the exchanges between the patent examiner and the inventor (or inventor's representative), as well as the evolution of the claims in response to office actions, may yield clues as to what the inventor and the examiner thought the claims meant.[26] Aside from explicit statements about the meaning that the patent applicant was attempting to infuse into the claim terminology, the prosecution history may allow the court to pursue certain textual forensics – looking at textual additions, deletions, and amendments during the course of the patent prosecution. A court might draw inferences regarding a particular change subsequent to a particular office action.

21 Burk & Lemley, *supra* note 10, at 1759.
22 Elektra Instrument S.A. v O.U.R. Scientific Int'l, Inc., 214 F.3d 1302 (Fed. Cir. 2000).
23 SRI Int'l v. Matsushita Elec. Corp., 775 F.2d 1107, 1122 (Fed. Cir. 1985) (en banc).
24 August Technology Corp. v. CamTek, Ltd., (Fed. Cir. 2011).
25 Phillips v. AHW Corp., 415 F.3d 1303 (Fed. Cir. 2005).
26 Southwall Techs., Inc. v. Cardinal IG Co., 54F.3d 1570, 1579 (Fed. Cir. 1995).

Claims interpretation is also affected by substantive patent doctrines that dictate certain readings of the claims. As noted above, modern claims in the United States are understood to be "peripheral" claims; that is, they are intended to be read as a description of the outermost permissible boundary of the technology to which the patent owner claims exclusive rights.[27] Under past versions of the U.S. statute, and in other jurisdictions, claiming has at times constituted "central" claiming; that is, intended to describe the heart or gist of what the inventor actually created.[28] Peripheral claiming, it is hoped, gives better notice of the extent of the patent right; it demarcates the edge of the patent claim, rather than its center.

In theory then, patent claims are intended to give public notice of the boundaries of the exclusive rights in the claimed technology, to alert the public to what activities would constitute infringement and what is safely beyond the inventor's purview. Yet "public notice" here is something of a term of art; the claims are typically drafted in such a specialized syntax and are so densely laden with legal and technical jargon as to be incomprehensible to the general reader. Realistically, the general public could not possibly comprehend the meaning of most claims. Indeed, given the peculiar syntax and format of the claims, sophisticated technological experts would have trouble understanding most patent claims. It falls to a relatively small group of specialized lawyers to give meaning to the mixture of legal and technical terminology peculiar to their community.

In fact, peripheral claiming, by whomever interpreted, does not and cannot demarcate the edge of exclusive rights. Due to the inherent ambiguity of language, the boundary remains necessarily indeterminate, and a patent owner has every incentive to take advantage of every indeterminacy to expand the ambit of exclusivity a little farther.[29] Under the peripheral claiming system, inventors, or more likely their lawyers, draft claims out to the limit of what the patent disclosure will bear and then later argue for even more expansive interpretations of the claims. Thus the conceit of a precise boundary, coupled with the intrinsic imprecision of the text, inevitably leads to a reading that is even broader than the patent drafter might originally have expected.

III. READING LEGAL TEXTS

The net result of these characteristics I have described is that the text of the claims has far more to do with lawyerly drafting than it has to do with innovative inventing.[30] Thus, claims are quintessentially *legal* texts, and take on the attributes of legal interpretation. Courts are well known to work through an interpretive process with other legal texts: with contracts, constitutions, and statutes. There is a vast literature

[27] MUELLER, *supra* note 6, at 65–66.
[28] TOSHIKO TAKENAKA, INTERPRETING PATENT CLAIMS: THE UNITED STATES, GERMANY AND JAPAN (1995).
[29] *See* Burk & Lemley *supra* note 10, at 1752–53.
[30] *Id.* at 1762.

discussing, analyzing, and critiquing the interpretive process for such texts. Theories on the proper methods for interpretation abound. Certainly this body of theory and practice holds some insight for claim interpretation, although deciding what kinds of parallels are appropriate has itself been a matter of some controversy.

Some scholars have suggested that patents resemble contracts in certain dimensions and that patent interpretation might draw from past literature and experience in contract interpretation.[31] This analogy draws salience from particular parallels between patents and contracts. Patents have often been cast in terms of a bargain between the inventor and the public, a quid pro quo by which the inventor trades public disclosure of a detailed description of the inventions in exchange for a limited period of exclusive rights.[32] Additionally, the patent claims are the result of an iterative negotiation between the inventor and the patent examiner. There are in a sense two parties to the patent bargain, especially if the patent examiner is taken to be the representative of the public, or at least of the government. And similar to contracts, patents are left to private enforcement; the patent owner, not a prosecutor or other government official, determines when to bring an infringement suit.

Yet, unlike contracts, where the primary interpretive question is determining the intent of the parties to the bargain, patents cannot simply be treated as an enforceable agreement between those negotiating the final text of the document. Patents have a clear public dimension that will affect others who were never parties to the bargain, except in the most tenuous sense of being part of the "public" that constitutes the examiner's fictional principal. The language of patent claims, defining a property right, is not simply efficacious as between the parties: it is intended to be efficacious against the world. It is not that the federal government, in the form of the Patent Office, is consenting to bind itself by means of the claim language; it is rather that the federal government employs its regulatory authority to establish certain legal rights and responsibilities, as it would in the case of a statute or administrative regulation. Patents are therefore texts that have the force of law in the sense that a statute, rather than a contract, has the force of law. The patent is good against the world, although promulgated for the benefit of an individual – the patent holder. The patent claim in this sense resembles a private statute or perhaps private rulemaking more than anything else.

At the same time, John Thomas cautions that patent claims have their own character, not as statutes per se, but as the product of statutes, and the point is worth remembering.[33] Claims are a step or two removed from the seat of legislative authority. They do not reflect the intent of the legislature – if indeed there is such a thing – except in the most general and abstract sense that the legislature authorized

[31] Robert Patrick Merges & John Fitzgerald Duffy, Patent Law and Policy: Cases and Materials 906–07 (3d ed. 2002).

[32] J.E.M. Ag Supply, Inc. v. Pioneer Hi-Bred Int'l, Inc. 534 U.S. 124, 142 (2001).

[33] *See* John R. Thomas, *On Preparatory Texts and Proprietary Technologies: The Place of Prosecution Histories in Patent Claim Interpretation*, 47 UCLA L. Rev. 183, 210 (1999).

the administration of patent claims as part of a broad policy of innovation. Claims may reflect the intent of the inventor, who is not a public official, or perhaps reflect the intent of the patent examiner, who is a public official, but who is a ministerial functionary following a statutory mandate rather than any republican imperative.[34] The language of a claim cannot be treated quite the same as that of a statute.

Nonetheless, given the close parallels between patent claims and statutes, it should not be surprising to find interpretive strategies common to both.[35] The process of examining the prosecution history in claim construction also closely parallels the common practice of examining legislative histories in statutory interpretation[36] – albeit the prosecution history is conceptually simpler, because it reflects the views of only two, or at most a handful of participants, and not the dozens or hundreds that might have a say in legislative enactments.

Similarly, the canons of claims construction described above closely track classic textual canons of statutory and constitutional interpretation; for example, the *expressio unius* rule, that expression of one thing suggests the exclusion of others. Or, to take another example, the *ejustdem generis* rule, that one should interpret a general term to include the class of items suggested by more specific terms following it. Courts have determined that, to borrow the patent vernacular, Congress is its own lexicographer – that is, that terms are given their ordinary meaning unless Congress specifies a specialized or technical meaning. Similarly, the canons that statutory provisions should be read "holistically" in light of the whole enactment or that a court should avoid interpretations that render other provisions of a statute superfluous or redundant are well established in the jurisprudence of statutory interpretation.[37]

IV. ORDINARY CLAIM MEANING

It may indeed be the canon of "plain meaning" that provides the strongest point of contact between patent claim construction and statutory interpretation. The membership of the Federal Circuit appears to be dominated by judges who lean toward strong forms of textualism. Some commentators examining the court's claim construction methodology have dubbed these judges as "proceduralist,"[38] whereas other commentators have characterized them as "hypertextualist"[39] or "literalist;"[40] however, with minor variations in definition, this school of judges holds that, absent

34 As noted by Judge Mayer of the Federal Circuit. *Markman*, 52 F.3d at 998, n. 8 (Mayer, J., concurring).

35 *See* D. Chisum, Chisum on Patents §18.03[2][a] at 18–212 (3d ed. 2011).

36 *See id.* at §18.03[2][d][i] at 18–510.

37 William Eskridge, Jr., & Philip Frickey, *The Supreme Court, 1993 Term – Foreword: Law at Equilibrium*, 108 Harv. L. Rev. 26, 97–108 (1994) (collecting interpretive canons from the Rehnquist Court).

38 *See* R. Polk Wagner & Lee Petherbridge, *Is the Federal Circuit Succeeding? An Empirical Assessment of Judicial Performance*, 152 U. Pa L. Rev. 1105, 1111 (2004).

39 *See* Nard, *supra* note 3, at 4.

40 *See* D. Chisum, *supra* note 35, at 18–189.

some manifest ambiguity, the proper interpretation of claim text can be determined from an examination of the text itself, with little or no resort to other sources.

These judges rely in the first resort on a canon of "plain meaning" or "ordinary meaning" of the text. Perhaps somewhat counterintuitively, such hypertextualists are inclined to consult dictionaries – which would seem to be external authorities outside the claim text, but which are characterized as illuminating "intrinsic" interpretation – in order to determine the ordinary meanings of claim terms.[41] Examination of extrinsic interpretive sources is on this approach disfavored and permissible only as an extraordinary measure. Similarly, adherents of this approach are willing to depart from the ordinary dictionary definition of a term when it is demonstrated that the patentee has acted as his or her "own lexicographer;" that is, when the patentee has explicitly defined terms differently than their ordinary usage.[42]

Other members of the court, whom various commentators have referred to as either "pragmatic textualists"[43] or "holists"[44] or "contextualists,"[45] appear to be more open to the examination of sources outside the claim text, including the prosecution history, technical documents, and expert testimony in the relevant art. As the labels assigned to them suggest, these jurists seek to understand the claims by considering the facts and circumstances surrounding the patent prosecution. The differences between these two methodological camps loom large in patent claim jurisprudence, where much of the discussion has centered on the proper use of 'intrinsic" or "extrinsic" evidence. The distinction drawn between so-called hypertextualist and pragmatic textualist judges turns largely on the treatment of these sources: on the allowance as to whether and when to go beyond intrinsic sources, and on the philosophical openness to extrinsic sources.[46]

Not every judge adopts one or the other approach all of the time, although empirical investigation suggests fairly clear trends in the methodological orientation of the CAFC judges.[47] And, there may be far less to this nominal distinction than there might seem to be. However strident the rhetoric in some CAFC opinions regarding intrinsic and extrinsic sources, each of the approaches observed is essentially originalist in orientation, meaning that each is looking for a fixed and determined "correct" meaning to a given claim term.[48] Neither approach adopts any of the panoply of non-originalist interpretive approaches found in scholarly literature or debated with regard to the meaning of other legal texts. Hermeneutics, deconstructionism, and

[41] *See* Vitronics Corp. v. Conceptronic, Inc., 90 F.3d 1576, 1584 n.6 (1996).

[42] *See* Canaan Prod., Inc. v. Edward Don & Co. 388 F.3d 540, 544, (7th Cir. 1968); Lear Siegler, Inc. v. Aeroquip Corp. 733 F.2d 881, 889 (Fed. Cir. 1984).

[43] *See* Nard, *supra* note 3, at 4.

[44] *See* Wagner & Petherbridge, *supra* note 38.

[45] *See* D. Chisum, *supra* note 35, at 18–19.

[46] *See* Nard, *supra* note 3, at 6–7.

[47] *See* Wagner & Petherbridge, *supra* note 38.

[48] *See* Eskridge, *supra* note 4, at 10 (defining "originalist" approaches to legal texts).

other critical or literary theories of interpretation are certainly nowhere to be seen in the judicial approaches to claim meaning.

The intended audience of patent claims also poses something of a problem for a plain meaning rule. The plain meaning rule sets the definitional default of claim terms as their common or ordinary meaning.[49] This makes some sense in the case of general statutes that govern the public at large – attempting to determine a meaning most likely to be understood by the general population and that is perhaps most likely to have been intended by the statutory drafters. Indeed, black-letter patent law purports that claims, too, are intended to give public notice of the boundaries of exclusivity surrounding the patented technology.[50] Yet patent doctrine also holds that claims are oriented to the understanding of one having skill in the art – a technically sophisticated reader.[51] And the claims are construed by a judge, a legally sophisticated reader, but usually not a technically sophisticated reader. Thus, even on its own terms, it is not clear that the ordinary meaning rule functions in its usual role when applied to patent claims.

The gaps in such textualist approaches become very stark when claim construction by trial judges is reviewed by the Federal Circuit. Some studies of the Federal Circuit's reversal rate for trial court claim construction indicate that the Federal Circuit finds the trial judge's interpretation wrong in a significant number of appeals, ranging from 30 percent to nearly half the time.[52] Indeed, by some accounts the trial court judge's most meticulous reading of the claims is not much better than a coin toss.[53] Even more surprising, some studies indicate that the reversal rate for district court judges does not improve with experience[54]: the reversal rate for judges who are experienced at claim construction, having overseen multiple patent cases, seems to be about the same as that for judges who have not had previous claim construction experience.[55]

This dichotomy between the construction of claims in the trial courts and the reconstruction of claims in the Federal Circuit belies the certainty of plain meaning rules. It is surely not the case that the trial judge cannot read the text or lacks access to a dictionary. If this were all that were required to reach the plain, ordinary meaning

[49] W.E. Hall Co., Inc.v. Atlanta Corrug., LLC, 370 F.3d 1343, 1353 (Fed. Cir. 2004).

[50] *See* Festo Corp. v. Shokestsu Kinzoku Kogyo Kabushiki Co., 535 U.S. 722, 731 (2002).

[51] Eolas Tech. Inc. v. Microsoft Corp., 399 F.3d 1325, 1336 (Fed. Cir. 2005).

[52] Kimberly A. Moore, *Are District Court Judges Equipped to Resolve Patent Cases?*, 15 HARV. J.L. & TECH. 2 (2001); Andrew T. Zidel, *Patent Claim Construction in Trial Courts: A Study Showing the Need for Clear Guidance From the Federal Circuit*, 33 SETON HALL L. REV. 711 (2003); Kimberley A. Moore, *Markman Eight Years Later: Is Claim Construction More Predictable?*, 9 LEWIS & CLARK L. REV. 231 (2005).

[53] *See* Zidel, *supra* note 52, at 747.

[54] David L. Schwartz, *Practice Makes Perfect? An Empirical Study of Claim Construction Reversal Rates in Patent Cases*, 107 MICH L. REV. 223 (2008); David L. Schwartz, *Courting Specialization: An Empirical Study of Claim Construction Comparing Patent Litigation Before Federal District Courts and the International Trade Commission*, 50 WILLIAM & MARY L. REV. 1699 (2009).

[55] *See* Schwartz, *Practice Makes Perfect?*, *supra* note 54.

of claims, then one might expect trial court claim construction to be upheld with the same frequency that they are in fact overruled. What is clear is that plain meaning is not so plain.

V. DYNAMIC STATUTORY INTERPRETATION

At one level it is perhaps no surprise that the interpretive approaches found among Federal Circuit judges parallel originalist approaches to statutes. Originalism has certainly been in ascendancy in the federal judiciary for some time, and the current rhetorical fad for loudly berating judicial activism would make any judge anxious to shift responsibility for the outcomes of decisions from him- or herself to the text. In an age when Supreme Court nominees who are well aware that appellate judges make law engage in extended denunciations of judicial authority,[56] no jurist wants to be labeled an activist judge.

But in addition to constituting a reflection of the current judicial zeitgeist – and perhaps constituting a source of the current judicial zeitgeist – originalist approaches promise certainty of meaning, untainted by judicial predilections or ideologies. The appeal of originalism, whether to the Federal Circuit or to other courts, is the appeal of assurance, of freedom from ambiguity. Originalism in effect treats text as fact, approaching the meaning of terms in a statute as predetermined rather than as a matter of judgment. This is how Western society commonly treats matters of fact, as inevitable outcomes of the logic of science: as certain, as objectively determined, as matters to be discovered rather than interpreted.[57] Courts have far less discretion where "fact" is concerned; the discretion they have is related to the determination of fact, not to the facts themselves.

This yearning for certainty is consistent with the general jurisprudential leanings of the Federal Circuit. The Federal Circuit has a history of favoring bright-line legal rules in its patent jurisprudence.[58] In a wide range of doctrines, it has tended over the past two decades to eschew wherever possible more flexible or nuanced analyses in favor of simpler binary tests. This tendency toward ostensibly clear rules has been repeatedly rejected when Federal Circuit doctrines are reviewed by the Supreme Court.[59] And indeed, in another context, that of evaluating non-obviousness, the Supreme Court has – perhaps ironically[60] – chided the Federal Circuit for its obsession with textual determinism, instructing the lower court to consider unwritten

56 Peter Baker & Neil A. Lewis, *Sotomayor Vows "Fidelity to the Law" as Hearings Start*, N.Y. TIMES (July 13, 2009).

57 *See* Jacob Bronowski, *The Laws of Nature and the Nature of Laws*, in THE ORIGINS OF KNOWLEDGE AND IMAGINATION 65, 80 (1978).

58 *See* Timothy Holbrook, *Substance vs. Process Based Formalism in Claim Construction*, 9 LEWIS & CLARK L. REV. 123 (2005), Thomas, *supra* note 2.

59 *See* Peter Lee, *Patent Law and the Two Cultures*, 120 YALE L.J. 2, 46 (2010).

60 *See* Jonathan Siegel, *Naive Textualism in Patent Law*, 76 BROOK. L. REV. 1019–32 (2011) (arguing that the Supreme Court has engaged in "naïve textualism" in its recent patent decisions).

facts and circumstances, such as the "common sense" of the practitioners in the art, when deciding the question of non-obviousness.[61]

Yet, as close critiques of scientific epistemology have long pointed out, facts are not the determined entities popularly supposed: they are themselves value-laden judgments.[62] In the same vein, texts do not read themselves. Reading requires a reader, and the reader is never divorced from the act of reading, as originalist approaches seem to promise. Originalist theories are on this view especially pernicious, because they promise a determined meaning that they cannot deliver.

Indeed, the supposed clarity and certainty of originalism may serve to cloak judicial activism or at least judicial preference. The facade of originalism deflects attention away from the judge's ideology and preferences toward a supposedly neutral reading of the text, or toward the imagined corporate purpose of a past legislature, or toward the external authority of a lexical definition. Reliance on dictionaries and other seemingly objective authorities particularly heightens the sense of detachment and impartiality in interpretation; the author of the judicial opinion did not write the dictionary definition, and the common perception of most readers, since grade school, is that dictionaries are the final authority on the definition of words. But in fact the choice of lexical authority, and of definitions promulgated by that authority, can be manipulated to a preferred outcome.

Such potential for originalist mischief is the starting point for William Eskridge's classic critique of originalism.[63] Eskridge is of course not the first to point out that the originalist emperor has no clothes, but he offers perhaps the most comprehensive critique, and the most comprehensible alternative, to originalist thinking. Eskridge argues that, because the values of the interpreter will inevitably shade the meaning assigned to the text, the antidote is to be aware of such bias and indeed to embrace it.[64] The cure for hidden biases and assumptions in interpretation, so far as there can be one, is to be transparent about the range of possible meanings suggested by the primary text and other associated texts, and transparent about the choice made among those meanings.

Eskridge advocates what he terms "dynamic statutory interpretations." Rather than confining itself to a single interpretive methodology or to a constrained universe of permissible interpretive factors, dynamic statutory interpretation combines the tools of various interpretive schools, recognizing that different interpretive tasks require different interpretive considerations.[65] These considerations are bound together by a unifying element of "critical pragmatism," under which the interpreter actively and openly contemplates and assesses the potential outcomes from different readings

[61] KSR Int'l Co. v. Teleflex Inc., 550 U.S. 398, 421 (2007).

[62] *See, e.g.*, Jacob Bronowski, *The Abacus and the Rose: A New Dialogue on Two World Systems*, *in* SCIENCE AND HUMAN VALUES 77, 88–91 (Harper & Row rev. ed. 1965).

[63] *See* ESKRIDGE, *supra* note 4.

[64] *Id.* at 175–76.

[65] *Id.* at 200.

of the text.[66] The text remains central to this approach, as does the intent of the textual authors, as indicated through legislative histories or other related paratexts.[67] Dictionaries and the like might be taken into account as well. According to Eskridge, the dynamic statutory interpreter will take into account all of these potential sources of meaning, but will not necessarily grant any of them primacy.[68]

If dynamic statutory interpretation seems to cede interpretive latitude to judges, it does – or rather, it recognizes the latitude judges have, which originalism serves to conceal. But it is hardly a recipe for judicial activism, if activism is understood as the judiciary arrogating to itself the mandate of the legislature. Rather, Eskridge argues that for dynamic statutory interpreters, the preferences and values of the current legislature should be as important, and perhaps more important, than those of the legislature that initially enacted the statute under consideration.[69] The analogy he draws is to an agent who is given instructions by a principal; although the circumstances may change over time, the agent remains empowered to carry out the objectives as initially instructed, but would surely take into account the current wishes and expectations of the principal in executing them.[70] Similarly, the courts, as agents empowered by statute to carry out certain objectives, should be aware not only of the intent of past legislatures but also of the needs and expectations of current legislatures.

Overall, Eskridge's dynamic statutory interpreter is one who is guided in his or her reading of the text by the best potential outcome.[71] The many possible inputs to interpretation must be given an overall coherence according to contemporary values – but these values would inevitably color the reading of the text anyway. Among these values, civic or republican values are given primacy. In particular, Eskridge argues that the best outcomes are those that are guided by a sense of justice: readings that empower or protect the underprivileged are to be preferred, as are those that correct dysfunctions of the political process.[72] Interpretation is colored by value judgments; Eskridge argues that better interpretations and better values will come to the fore if we admit what is occurring in the interpretive process.

VI. CONSTRUCTING CLAIMS DYNAMICALLY

Although originalism offers only a false hope of certainty, dynamic interpretation demands the juridical maturity to accept and master ambiguity. Instead of reciting rote ideological mantras, dynamic interpretation unpacks the unruly process

66 *Id.* at 176.

67 *See* Dan L. Burk, *Copyright and Paratext in On-Line Gaming* in EMERGING ETHICAL ISSUES OF LIFE IN VIRTUAL WORLDS 33 (Charles Wankel & Sean Malleck eds., 2010) (describing the concept of paratexts, texts that mediate the interpretation of other primary texts).

68 *Id.* at 200.

69 *Id.* at 11.

70 *Id.* at 125.

71 *Id.* at 149.

72 *Id.* at 294.

by which meaning is determined. Dynamic interpretation is tailored to the circumstance, rather than insisting every circumstance conform to a single approach. Consequently, rather than a ready-made interpretive theory out of the box, dynamic interpretation requires effort to assemble a coherent theory of texts on a case-by-case basis.

Translating Eskridge's theory of dynamic statutory interpretation to the context of claim interpretation likely requires some additional work, because the nature of the texts under consideration is somewhat different than those Eskridge originally considered. Certain aspects of the theory likely carry straight across between texts. Adopting a posture of critical pragmatism, by which the interpreter considers the best potential outcome of a given interpretation, seems as feasible for patent claims as for statutes, even if the outcomes for patent claim interpretations may be particular to the patent system. In the case of patent claims, a dynamic interpreter might consider whether a particular construction of the claim will grant broad or narrow coverage to the patentee and what such coverage might mean to competitors and to the industry in which the patent is situated.

But other aspects of the theory seem either not to apply to claims interpretation or to require application in a modified form. As the controversy over analogies between claims and contracts, and between claims and statutes suggests, patent claims differ somewhat from the statutory texts that are Eskridge's focus. Claims are not legislative enactments; as we have seen they are rather the product of legislative enactments and issue from an administrative agency rather than from the legislature. The statute requires claims, but does not dictate their particular content, nor even their particular form.

Thus, it is not altogether clear that the deference that one might want to accord to the originators of a statute – the legislature – properly belongs to the originator of the patent claims – the Patent Office. Or at least, deference might not lie in quite the same way. Republican values such as deference to the plenary power of an elected body are not necessarily furthered by deferring to an unelected ministerial employee. Patent examiners are no more the elected representatives of the populace than are federal judges; examiners are at best the executors of statutory instructions from such elected representatives.

Here Eskridge's conception of judicial agency may be useful, although perhaps not quite as he intended. Under dynamic statutory interpretation, it may be that courts are the agents of the legislature, charged with fulfilling the current needs of the "principal" in the relationship. But in a democratic system, the legislature is itself an institutional agent, representing the electorate – suggesting that it is in fact the public, not merely their agents once removed, whose interests a dynamically interpretive court ultimately serves. A court dynamically interpreting claims may be required to look past the official who certifies the text, holding the public interest in mind, and not merely the expectation of the public's legislative or executive agents.

At the same time, looking to the goals of the patent statute may often be an exercise of relatively little assistance in guiding the dynamic claim interpreter. The generalized outcome mandated by the statute is, of course, to promote innovation, but that broad objective by itself will not necessarily indicate how particular claim terms ought to be read. Certainly they ought to be read in such a way as to promote innovation, but whether giving them a broad scope or a narrow scope, or whether adopting a dictionary definition or a definition inferred from the prosecution history will do so may not be immediately apparent in a given case.

Eskridge is deeply concerned with interpreting statutes in ways that construe close cases against the politically powerful or in ways that foster the rights of the subordinated or disadvantaged.[73] However one views the incorporation of such concerns into statutory interpretation, they seem largely inapposite or extrinsic to the project of claim interpretation. Patents are by no means untouched by racial, gender, or other social bias.[74] Certainly one could attempt to read claims so that close cases benefit the disempowered or discomfit the powerful. But the circumstances that should prompt such a reading are exceptionally difficult to assess: it is difficult to know whether the smaller and seemingly less powerful party in a case is in fact a patent "troll" seeking to block innovation or whether a monopolistic entity armed with a patent might distribute a product that might ultimately improve the lives or social positions of the least privileged.

Eskridge's suggestion that courts adopt interpretations that cure dysfunctions in the political process may have greater traction in claims interpretation. Courts might sometimes decide close cases by interpreting claims in a way that takes into account biases or mistakes that occurred in the legislative development of the patent statute. This might include ameliorating errors or absurdities that entered the statute due to the misunderstanding or oversight of a technically unsophisticated legislature. More boldly, this approach might include ameliorating political favoritism that entered the statute through lobbying or other types of rent seeking – perhaps, for example, countering statutory trends originally intended to benefit politically favored industries that have since reached obsolescence in the ferment of technological change.

Such opportunities for legislative cure may be rare, because, as I have noted, it is the claims that are interpreted, not the statute itself, and the claims are more than a few steps removed from the legislative foundations of the patent system. It may be more likely that the dynamic interpreter should focus on repairing the biases of the governmental institution that actually promulgated the claims, which is to say curing dysfunctions of the Patent Office. It does not seem to be stretching the role of interpretive actors at all to argue that courts should in close cases adopt

73 *See* ESKRIDGE, *supra* note 4, at 294.

74 *See* Dan L. Burk, *Do Patents Have Gender?*, 19 AM. U. J. GENDER SOC. POL'Y & L. 881 (2011); Kara Swanson, *Getting a Grip on the Corset: Gender, Sexuality and Patent Law*, 23 YALE J.L. & FEMINISM 57 (2011).

interpretations that correct systemic problems in the Patent Office. This is certainly not to argue that a court construing claims should usurp the job of the Patent Office in issuing claims, or preempt processes such as reexamination or reissue by which clearly defective claims can be corrected.[75] But where multiple readings of issued claims exist, as they inevitably will, a corrective focus guide the court toward the construction that preserves the integrity of the claims granting system as a whole.

CONCLUSION

Dynamic claim interpretation, like dynamic statutory interpretation, is not a call to abandon the text under consideration, but it is a call to recognize that meaning is not manifest, immutable, or hermetic. Although there is some superficial appeal to the certainty promised by originalism, reliance on the "plain" or "ordinary" or otherwise purportedly self-evident meanings of claims is more apt to deter innovation than is transparent, dynamic interpretation. Real uncertainty is the product of rules that purport to offer a determined outcome, but are in fact a facade for subjective, ad hoc decision making. Businesses are accustomed to dealing with uncertainty so long as the uncertainties are apparent and not hidden. Once innovators know the rules of the game, even if these are "muddy" or subjective rules, they can begin to adapt their choices to the likely risks and outcomes. It is when the rules are clandestine or obscure that investment suffers. Patent jurisprudence could likely use a healthy dose of legal realism.

[75] *See* 35 U.S.C § 302 (2008) (reexamination); 35 U.S.C. § 251 (2008) (reissue).

6

Did *Phillips* Change Anything?

Empirical Analysis of the Federal Circuit's Claim Construction Jurisprudence

*R. Polk Wagner** *and Lee Petherbridge*†

INTRODUCTION: THE DESIGN OF THE FEDERAL CIRCUIT

As we move past the twenty-fifth anniversary of the establishment of the United States Court of Appeals for the Federal Circuit (CAFC),[1] that court has become, by far, the most powerful and influential force in the U.S. patent system. The significance of this development is impossible to overstate: even as the patent system has grown in economic importance, technological complexity, and public awareness, the administration of the entire enterprise increasingly depends on the twelve active judges of the Federal Circuit.[2]

Conferring such dominating power on the Federal Circuit has long been justified by the premise that this centralization of legal authority would yield a clearer, more coherent, more predictable legal infrastructure for the patent system. Indeed, as a response to widespread dissatisfaction caused by confusion and uncertainty under the decentralized administration of the patent law, the Federal Circuit was created to play this very role.[3] And since its inception, the court – with some assistance from the Supreme Court[4] – has moved aggressively in support of its widely perceived mandate.

* Professor of Law at the University of Pennsylvania Law School.

† Professor of Law and the Richard A. Vachon, S.J. Fellow at Loyola Law School, Los Angeles.

1 The Federal Circuit was created by the *Federal Courts Improvement Act of 1982*. *See* Pub. L. No. 97–164, 96 Stat. 25 (relevant provisions codified as amended in scattered sections of 28 U.S.C.).

2 *See* Pub. L. No. 97-164, 96 Stat. 25 (authorizing up to twelve judges).

3 *See* Commission on Revision of the Federal Court Appellate System, Structure and Internal Procedures: Recommendations for Change 15, reprinted in 67 F.R.D. 195, 220 (1975); S. Rep. No. 275, 97th Cong., 2d Sess. 17 (1981), reprinted in 1982 U.S. Code Cong. & Admin. News 11, 14–15 [hereinafter S. Rep. No. 275] (merger of Court of Claims and Court of Customs and Patent Appeals (CCPA) provides more efficient administration of patent claims). Perhaps the seminal work considering the formation of the Federal Circuit and its theoretical basis is Rochelle Cooper Dreyfuss, *The Federal Circuit: A Case Study in Specialized Courts*, 64 N.Y.U. L. Rev. 1 (1989).

4 Note in particular the Supreme Court's decision in *Markman* v. *Westview Instruments, Inc.*, 517 U.S. 370 (1996) [hereinafter *Markman II*], allocating the authority to interpret patent claims to judges. *Markman II*, of course, is central to the project described in this chapter.

This chapter – and the broader project of which it is a part[5] – investigates the obvious (and yet surprisingly ephemeral) question concerning the Federal Circuit's role in the patent system: *is it succeeding?* Has its mandate been fulfilled? Has this grand experiment in allocating judicial authority resulted in clearer, more consistent, more coherent rules surrounding patents? Utilizing a novel ten-year empirical study of judicial performance, we hope to provide some insights into these questions.

In earlier related studies, we found that the Federal Circuit was a court in a period of significant transition – one driven by an ongoing effort to meet the requirements of its special mandate and important changes in court personnel.[6] In this aspect of the project, we offer a more detailed look at the court's recent efforts, via the en banc decision of *Phillips* v. *AWH*[7], to revise its jurisprudence in the area of claim construction.

The balance of this chapter moves in four parts. In Part I, we offer a brief overview of the concept of claim construction – the interpretation of patent claims – and sketch the recent history of claim construction jurisprudence at the Federal Circuit, noting how the *Phillips* v. *AWH* en banc decision was a response to the significant divisions concerning the methodological approach to claim construction highlighted by our first publication, *Is the Federal Circuit Succeeding?*[8] In Part II, we outline the design and techniques used in the empirical study reported here. Part III presents the results and offers some analysis. Part IV places these results in a normative context.

I. THE PRELUDE TO *PHILLIPS*: A RECAP OF RECENT CLAIM CONSTRUCTION HISTORY

A. *An Introduction to Claim Construction*

By law, every patent must contain "claims particularly pointing out and distinctly claiming the subject matter which the applicant regards as his invention."[9] Claims are thus the touchstone of the patent grant, both establishing the boundaries of the patentee's statutory right to exclude[10] and defining the scope of the invention for evaluation under the requirements of the Patent Act.[11] As Judge Giles Rich once famously noted, in patent law, "the name of the game is the claim."[12]

5 *See* The FedCir Project [http://www.fedcir.org/], which is an umbrella project incorporating this project – The Claim Construction Project, http://www.claimconstruction.com.

6 *See generally* R. Polk Wagner & Lee Petherbridge, *Is the Federal Circuit Succeeding? An Empirical Assessment of Judicial Performance*, 152 U. Pa. L. Rev. 1105 (2004).

7 415 F.3d 1303 (Fed. Cir. 2005) (en banc).

8 *See supra* note 6.

9 *See* 35 U.S.C. § 112 (2006).

10 *See* 35 U.S.C. § 271 (2006) (defining infringement).

11 *See, e.g.*, 35 U.S.C. § 101 (subject matter requirement); § 102 (novelty requirement); § 103 (nonobvious requirement); § 112 (disclosure requirements).

12 *See* Giles Sutherland Rich, *Extent of Protection and Interpretation of Claims – American Perspectives*, 21 Int'l Rev. Indus. Prop. & Copyright L. 497, 499 (1990) ("The U.S. is strictly an examination

Claim "construction," then, is the process whereby the language found in the claims is, in essence, translated into a meaningful context – either to determine whether infringement has occurred (i.e., "Does the term 'coupled' allow for an electrical, rather than a physical connection?"[13]) or whether the patent claim itself is valid (i.e., "Is the 'approximately round' structure *obvious* in light of the prior art?").

The straightforward, simple structure of the claim construction inquiry is deceptive, however. Claim construction is inherently one of the most difficult aspects of the patent law, fundamentally requiring that technological ideas – inventions – be captured (precisely!) by language, and later "de-translated" back into their technological essence by those other than the inventors. In an ideal world, patent claims might function approximately like the title documents to the real property they weakly resemble and thus have a clear and specific analytic framework. But in the real world, this is simply unachievable. Patents cover intangible concepts rather than physical locations or objects; the precision of real-space descriptions cannot be replicated for the products of human creativity. Further, patents often deal with technologies at the leading edge of human knowledge, where the vocabulary is necessarily less developed. Therefore, it would be difficult to overstate the inherent complexity – and difficulty – of patent claim construction.

In addition to its inherent difficulty, there are at least two other aspects of claim construction that make it notable (and worthy of extensive study):

1. *Everyone is a consumer of claim construction.* Claim construction is conducted by all players in the patent system: the U.S. Patent and Trademark Office must evaluate the claims in patent applications to determine patentability; private parties construe claims to evaluate potential infringement risk or as part of an investment decision; and of course, the various courts construe claims to resolve disputes surrounding infringement and validity.
2. *Claim construction is overwhelmingly the most critical patent issue in litigation.* Claim construction is a key issue in virtually every patent case and likely is the dispositive issue in a majority of cases. Because virtually everything in a patent case turns on claim construction – whether infringement has occurred, whether the patent meets the disclosure requirements or runs afoul of prior art – claim construction is often the single most important issue.

country and the main purpose of the examination, to which every application is subjected, is to try to make sure that what each claim defines is patentable. To coin a phrase, the name of the game is the claim.").

[13] Yes. At least in U.S. Patent No. 5,202,835 (issued Apr. 13, 1993), entitled "Trolling Motor With Heading Lock." *See* Johnson Worldwide Assocs. v. Zebco Corp., 175 F.3d 985 (Fed. Cir. 1999).

B. *Claim Construction and Institutional Design*

Even beyond its inherent complexity and clear centrality, perhaps the most important aspect of the modern practice of claim construction is how it enforces – and, indeed, extends – the particular institutional design of the patent system. As noted briefly earlier, this institutional design locates the Federal Circuit as the arbiter of virtually every important patent case: the sole appellate body for appeals from district courts related to patent cases and for challenging the decisions of the U.S. Patent and Trademark Office. And although the statutory framework plays a significant formal role in establishing the Federal Circuit's dominance,[14] the role of claim construction cannot be overlooked.

As we have analyzed extensively elsewhere,[15] the Supreme Court in *Markman* v. *Westview Instruments* (*Markman II*) established that the question of patent claim construction (unlike the question of infringement) was *not* subject to the Seventh Amendment's jury trial right and, further, that pragmatic reasons required that this analysis be conducted by judges, rather than juries.[16] These "functional considerations" took two forms. The first was the Court's expectation that judges – by virtue of their special skills and experience, as well as the "highly technical" nature of patent claim construction and the "special doctrines" developed by the courts for their interpretation – were simply more likely to be better at the task than "jurors unburdened by training in exegesis."[17] Second, the allocation of interpretive authority to judges was, the Court suggested, likely to promote the goals of intrajurisdictional certainty and uniformity.[18] From an institutional design perspective, *Markman II* placed the judges at the forefront of the patent system.

Significantly, the Federal Circuit has amplified the effect of *Markman II* and effectively taken full control over the claim construction issue. In *Cybor* v. *FAS Technologies, Inc.*, the Federal Circuit declared the question of claim construction to be "purely legal," and thus reviewed de novo on appeal.[19] And although the *Cybor* decision has been among the most controversial in the Federal Circuit's history,

[14] *See, e.g.*, Federal Courts Improvement Act of 1982, Pub. L. 97-164, 96 Stat. 25 (April 2, 1982).

[15] *See generally*, Wagner & Petherbridge, *supra* note 6.

[16] Markman v. Westview Instruments, Inc., 517 U.S. 370 (1996).

[17] *Id.* at 388.

[18] The Court's discussion noted that it was especially concerned with uniformity of treatment concerning a particular patent – one that presumably might be litigated nearly contemporaneously in multiple jurisdictions. By designating the interpretive issue as a matter of law, *Markman II* suggested that principles of stare decisis might serve to maintain intrajurisdictional uniformity prior to appellate review. *See id.* at 391 (noting that issue preclusion would be unavailable against new and independent infringement defendants). On this ground, however, the Court's concerns seem overstated; the district courts have used their discretionary case management tools to largely avoid any potential intrajurisdictional conflicts concerning the same patent.

[19] Cybor Corp., 138 F.3d at 1456 ("[W]e therefore reaffirm that, as a purely legal question, we review claim construction de novo on appeal . . .").

both within[20] and without[21] the court, the Federal Circuit has adhered to it, despite repeated opportunities to amend or overrule.[22]

The Federal Circuit's current claim construction doctrine thus combines the rule of *Markman II* (judicial interpretation of patent claims) with the rule of *Cybor* (no deference to district court determinations on claim construction). Therefore, because claim construction is likely the single most important issue in patent litigation, and because the *Markman-Cybor* framework effectively delivers to the Federal Circuit the sole source of authority to determine claim construction, the Federal Circuit becomes virtually the sole arbiter of a significant fraction of patent disputes (albeit an arbiter that can take years and millions of dollars in trial costs to engage).

Therefore, irrespective of one's view on the wisdom of the current institutional regime, there can be little dispute that the *Markman-Cybor* framework places the question of claim construction – more particularly, the Federal Circuit's success in developing the jurisprudence of claim construction – at center stage in any discussions of the institutional design of the patent system. Put another way, it may well be that the Federal Circuit's success (or lack thereof) in using its dominant role in developing the law of claim construction is an important signal for its success or failure as an institutional player.

C. *Earlier Related Studies and Their Findings*

In *Is the Federal Circuit Succeeding? An Empirical Assessment of Judicial Performance*, we undertook an empirically based analysis of the Federal Circuit's claim

20 Judge Mayer in particular has been consistently biting in his opposition to de novo review of claim construction and its effect on the institutional design of the patent system:

> This court was created for the purpose of bringing consistency to the patent field. Instead, we have taken this noble mandate, to reinvigorate the patent and introduce predictability to the field, and focused inappropriate power in this court. In our quest to elevate our importance, we have, however, disregarded our role as an appellate court; the resulting mayhem has seriously undermined the legitimacy of the process, if not the integrity of the institution.

Phillips v. AWH Corp., 415 F.3d 1303, 1330 (Fed. Cir. 2005) (Mayer, J., dissenting) (citations omitted). Judge Mayer was a vigorous opponent of *Cybor* from the outset. *See, e.g.*, Cybor v. FAS Techs., 138 F.3d at 1464–67 (Fed. Cir. 1998) (Mayer, CJ, dissenting).

21 For a strong argument that the *Cybor* approach is both inconsistent with *Markman II* and normatively undesirable, *see* William H. Burgess, *Simplicity at the Cost of Clarity: Appellate Review of Claim Construction and the Failed Promise of* Cybor, 153 U. PENN L. REV. 763 (2004). *See also, e.g.*, John F. Duffy, On *Improving the Legal Process of Claim Interpretation: Administrative Alternatives*, 2 WASH. U. J.L. & POL'Y 109 (2000); Craig Allen Nard, *Process Considerations in the Age of* Markman *and Mantras*, 2001 U. ILL. L. REV. 355 (2001); Christian A. Chu, *Empirical Analysis of the Federal Circuit's Claim Construction Trends*, 16 BERKELEY TECH. L.J. 1075 (2001).

22 *See, e.g.*, Phillips, 415 F.3d at 1328 (declining to address the question the Court ordered to be briefed that presented the Cybor issue); *see also* Amgen Inc. v. Hoechst Marion Roussel, Inc., 469 F.3d 1039 (Fed. Cir. 2006) (order denying en banc review of *Cybor* question).

construction jurisprudence from *Markman II* (April 1995) through November 1, 2002.[23] The core strategy for this analysis was developed as follows:

1. Gathering all of that court's opinions with a discernible analysis of claim construction;
2. Developing a coding scheme that was drawn from an analysis of the jurisprudence, the experiences of practicing lawyers, and the academic literature;
3. Categorizing (coding) each analysis according to that scheme; and,
4. Statistically analyzing the results to determine what patterns, if any existed.

The coding scheme developed for this project has as its core the distinction between two forms of claim construction methodology extant[24] in the jurisprudence:

1. The ***procedural*** approach, which gives primary weight to the claim language (and the ordinary meaning thereof, often derived from dictionaries); and,
2. The ***holistic*** approach, which interprets patent claims via an all-encompassing, open-ended reading of the claim language, patent disclosure, prosecution history, relevant dictionaries, and on-point expert testimony.

The choice of methodological approach to claim construction directly affects the results of litigation. The importance of the dichotomy was confirmed by an array of robustness analyses; for example, differences in methodological approach are present in 95 percent of claim construction disputes among Federal Circuit judges[25] and in 75 percent of that court's reversals of district courts' claim construction analyses.[26]

To systematically analyze the Federal Circuit's claim construction jurisprudence, we developed a method for scoring opinions according to the choice of methodological approach.[27] This categorization scheme captured both general methodology and the strength of its form; broadly speaking, each of the two methodological approaches noted earlier had three possible strengths of analysis (strong, intermediate, and weak).[28] Thus there were six possible coding categories, depicted in Figure 6.1. The table in Appendix A offers additional details and some specific examples.

Coding all opinions in the dataset yielded a variety of empirical insights and results. Perhaps the most important finding was the confirmation of what many patent lawyers and scholars had been noting for years – that the Federal Circuit had developed two distinct approaches to claim construction and utilized those interchangeably. The results in the initial project suggested that the procedural approach was used in more than 63 percent of the court's opinions, with the holistic approach being used about 37 percent of the time.[29] The trend, moreover, favored

[23] Wagner & Petherbridge, *supra* note 6, at 1145.
[24] *Id.* at 1133–45.
[25] *Id.* at 1144.
[26] *Id.* at 1145.
[27] *Id.* at 1133–45.
[28] *Id.*
[29] *See* Wagner & Petherbridge, *supra* note 6, at 1148 (Table 2).

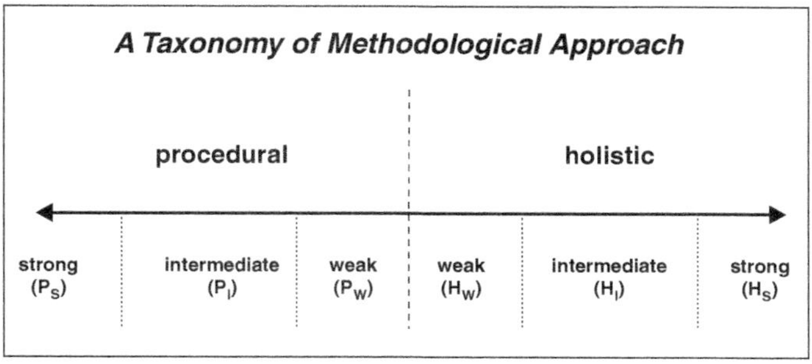

FIGURE 6.1. Coding Scheme

the procedural approach.[30] In addition, we found that, in many cases, the choice of methodological approach could be empirically associated with individual judges,[31] groups of judges,[32] and even judicially assigned panels.[33] (Indeed, in some cases, the likely methodological approach could be predicted with great certainty.[34]) In sum, the results in *Is the Federal Circuit Succeeding?* described a court that had yet to develop a fully coherent, consistent jurisprudence of claim construction[35] – as well as one with significant splits among the judges themselves.

D. *The* Phillips *v.* AWH *Response*

The July 12, 2005, *Phillips* v. *AWH* en banc opinion, by its terms, was an effort by the Federal Circuit to "clarif[y]" its jurisprudence with respect to claim construction methodologies[36] – in particular to discuss the relationship among the claim language, the specification, and dictionaries. In broad terms, the Court decided to "return" to the claim construction doctrine embodied (the court suggested) by the *Vitronics*[37] line of cases, and in particular to deprecate the more recent reliance in some cases on dictionaries for evidence of an ordinary meaning. Thus, the *Phillips* case clearly addresses the basic methodological split identified in *Is the Federal Circuit Succeeding?* – the procedural versus holistic approaches.[38]

As between these two methodological approaches, the en banc *Phillips* opinion clearly suggests that the holistic approach is likely to be the better one, because of its close focus on the context of the claim language rather than the generalizable

30 *Id.* at 1150–56.
31 *Id.* at 1156–62.
32 *Id.*
33 *Id.* at 1162–70.
34 *See* http://predictor.claimconstruction.com/.
35 *See* Wagner & Petherbridge, *supra* note 6, at 1171–79.
36 415 F.3d 1303, 1312.
37 90 F.3d 1576 (Fed. Cir. 1996).
38 415 F.3d at 1310.

meaning of the terms used. The court criticizes the procedural approach (which it refers to by a notable case in that genre, *Texas Digital*[39]) as error prone and disconnected from the technological inquiry at the core of claim construction.

Although the *Phillips* majority makes clear its preference for the open-ended holistic analysis, it does not, interestingly, declare *Texas Digital* (or any other case) to be overruled or otherwise in error. Instead, the opinion takes pains to clarify the "anything goes" nature of claim construction:

> [T]here is no magic formula or catechism for conducting claim construction. Nor is the court barred from considering any particular sources or required to analyze sources in any specific sequence, as long as those sources are not used to contradict claim meaning that is unambiguous in light of the intrinsic evidence. . . . The sequence of steps used by the judge in consulting various sources is not important; what matters is for the court to attach the appropriate weight to be assigned to those sources in light of the statutes and policies that inform patent law. In [prior case law], we did not attempt to provide a rigid algorithm for claim construction, but simply attempted to explain why, in general, certain types of evidence are more valuable than others.[40]

Despite the lack of clear guidelines, the *Phillips* court was confident that its new-old approach was an improvement, in part because the court seemed to downplay the complexities inherent in claim construction:

> The line between construing terms and importing limitations can be discerned with reasonable certainty and predictability if the court's focus remains on understanding how a person of ordinary skill in the art would understand the claim terms.
>
> Much of the time, upon reading the specification in that context, it will become clear whether the patentee is setting out specific examples of the invention to accomplish those [disclosure] goals, or whether the patentee instead intends for the claims and the embodiments in the specification to be strictly coextensive. The manner in which the patentee uses a term within the specification and claims usually will make the distinction apparent.[41]

Thus, the *Phillips* en banc decision, by attempting to clarify the divergent methodological approaches, provides an excellent opportunity to observe the success – or lack thereof – of this effort. Indeed, during the two years since *Phillips* issued, the Federal Circuit has issued more than 134 opinions with an observable claim construction analysis,[42] which offers the possibility of conducting a pre-*Phillips* versus post-*Phillips* comparison of the jurisprudence.

[39] 415 F.3d at 1319–24. *Texas Digital* is available at 308 F.3d 1193 (Fed. Cir. 2002).

[40] 415 F.3d at 1324.

[41] 415 F.3d at 1323.

[42] This is near the average of about seventy-one opinions per year during the period of the overall dataset (from May 15, 1996 to April 15, 2007).

II. STUDY DESIGN AND METHODOLOGY

As noted briefly earlier, the basic strategy of this study is to systematically categorize (or "code") judicial opinions falling within a defined range and to use the data that result from the coding to empirically analyze the nature of the jurisprudence. This is both a widely accepted technique (generally falling under the description of "content analysis"), as well as one with which the authors are familiar. The following sections briefly describe the study design and methodology.

A. *About Content Analysis*

Content analysis[43] refers to the systematic reading and analysis of texts.[44] As such, it differs from more traditional forms of legal scholarship in that it seeks an objective understanding of a body of law, rather than an interpretation of judicial opinions that are viewed as symbolic or important. According to Hall and Wright, "[s]ystematic content analysis allows scholars to verify, analyze, or refute the empirical claims about caselaw that are implicit or explicit in all branches of legal scholarship."[45]

Although there are a variety of ways to approach content analysis, the genre typically includes the basic strategy used here: selecting cases, coding cases, counting case contents, and analyzing case coding.[46] The range of possible analyses include examining connections between case outcome and external influences, examining relationships among the factors present in a case that might show order or be predictive of a particular outcome, or, as reported in this chapter, testing empirical claims concerning the nature and effect of doctrine.[47]

There are, to be sure, important caveats to choosing judicial opinions as a dataset, the most important of which affect not only content analysis but also more traditional interpretive forms of legal scholarship. These include unobserved reasoning, selection bias, and strategic behavior.[48] Analyzing the content of judicial opinions relies on the assumption that facts and reasoning that appear in an opinion accurately reflect those from the underlying case. This situation may not always be true given that opinion authors are generally concerned with justifying their conclusion "by showing that it proceeds from accepted sources by legitimate, properly argued steps."[49] Judicial opinions are also subject to selection bias at several levels. Some types of disputes may be less likely to reach trial; others that reach trial may be

43 For a more detailed description of content analysis and its techniques, *see* Lee Petherbridge & R. Polk Wagner, *The Federal Circuit and Patentability: An Empirical Assessment of the Law of Obviousness*, 85 TEX. L. REV 2051 (2007), at 20–22.

44 *See* Mark A. Hall & Ronald F. Wright, *Systematic Content Analysis of Judicial Opinions*, SSRN.

45 *Id.* at 10.

46 *Id.*

47 *Id.*

48 *See* Wagner & Petherbridge, *supra* note 6, at 1128–30.

49 Edward L. Rubin, *The Concept of Law and the New Public Scholarship*, 89 MICH. L. REV. 792, 801 (1991).

less likely to generate opinions. Of those that are tried, some will not be appealed, but even when appealed some cases may not generate an opinion.[50] Others may generate only an unpublished opinion,[51] which may affect the scope or depth of analysis that the court will provide. And even when opinions are published, they are subject to strategic behavior. The litigation choices of the parties can affect the facts that make it into a case; litigants, having different expectations for the outcome, may contend that the same governing doctrinal principle controls a case, making it more likely that the court will address that principle in any opinion it might author.

There is little question that these potential limitations exist to some degree in the study underlying this chapter. We believe, however, that given the methodologies used, the benefits outweigh the limitations, and the insights gained are worth exploring – although the study's inherent limitations must be kept in mind.

B. *Database Construction*

The dataset used in this study includes all observable Federal Circuit claim construction analyses during the time period from May 15, 1996, to April 15, 2007.[52] Potential cases were collected via the use of various searches in the Lexis Federal Circuit database (CAFC). We analyzed each case during the coding process to determine whether it met the inclusion criteria: an observable claim construction analysis. A total of 785 opinions met these criteria; of these, 712 opinions were opinions for the court.[53]

Each opinion meeting the inclusion criteria was coded for twenty-two fields, a complete listing of which is provided in Appendix B. All fields except for the "Methodology" field (which contained the procedural-versus-holistic coding noted earlier) were coded by custom computer software developed for this purpose. The Methodology field was human-coded.

C. *Testing for Reliability*

All human coding was done by multiple independent coders. Because of the need to use as many coders as possible, a web-based coding system was built for this application.[54] The system allows coders to log in via a unique username and password, whereupon they are presented with a list of cases to code, via pull-down

[50] *See, e.g.*, Fed. Cir. R. 36 (summary affirmance).

[51] *See, e.g.*, Fed. Cir. R. 47.6 (Nonprecedential Opinion or Order).

[52] May 15, 1996, was chosen because it is the date that the first Federal Circuit claim construction analysis was issued after the *Markman II* case on April 23, 1996. April 15, 2007, was chosen because the data collection for this segment of the project needed to be finished in time to conduct an analysis.

[53] Note that we use *opinions* as the basic unit of analysis rather than *cases*, although we distinguish in the analysis between opinions for the court (*i.e.*, sole or majority opinions) and alternative opinions (concurrences or dissents). Therefore, multiple opinions in a case can meet the inclusion criteria.

[54] *See* http://staff.claimconstruction.com/.

TABLE 6.1. *Frequency of methodologies (all court opinions, binomial, n = 712)*

	Procedural	Holistic
N	467	245
%	65.6%	34.4%

menus. After multiple coders code a case, the project manager can review all codes entered for each case, determine the final coding, and submit the case into the public database. Because the dataset was built (and coded) in stages since mid-2002, the number of coders has ranged from a minimum of two to a maximum of seven.[55]

All discrepancies among coders were identified, tracked, tabulated, and corrected. In general, we found the reliability of the coding system to be good, with inter-rater agreement (on the broad procedural/holistic distinction) ranging from 93 percent (during pre-*Phillips* time periods) to 90 percent (during the post-*Phillips* time period). The agreement among coders for the more fine-grained coding was somewhat less good: 72 percent in pre-*Phillips* jurisprudence and less than 60 percent in post-*Phillips* jurisprudence. This last number – about 60 percent of inter-rater agreement – suggests that the post-*Phillips* coding on the fine-grained categories is relatively unreliable – though the coding on the broader distinction remains reasonably consistent with the earlier dataset.

III. RESULTS

A. *The Phillips Effect, Part 1: Aggregate Results*

Table 6.1 describes the overall frequency distribution of the Federal Circuit's claim construction methodologies (including all opinions for the court since May 15, 1996, where the methodological approach is expressed in binomial form – that is, where the strong/intermediate/weak categories are collapsed).[56]

Table 6.1 shows that the procedural approach remains predominant, though not overwhelmingly so. This is consistent with our earlier results and reveals that the Federal Circuit opinions authored after November 1, 2002,[57] have not changed the overall frequency distribution of the competing methodologies. Although this is a significant observation, it may be masking the impact of the *Phillips* opinion. For example, if the *Phillips* opinion selected a particular claim interpretation methodology, it might not be revealed by the overall frequency distribution due to the

55 The coders in this study were all attorneys with significant exposure to Federal Circuit doctrine, most with technical backgrounds and admitted to practice before the U.S. Patent Office.

56 Unless otherwise specified, the results in the following section reflect opinions written *for the court only*; alternative opinions (dissents, concurrences) otherwise in the dataset were omitted.

57 *See* Wagner & Petherbridge, *supra* note 6, at 1145, 1148.

TABLE 6.2. *Frequency of methodologies, pre- and post-*Phillips *(court opinions, binomial)*

		Procedural	Holistic
Pre-Phillips	N	393	203
	%	65.9%	34.1%
Post-Phillips	N	74	42
	%	63.8%	36.2%

large number of data points in the dataset that derive from pre-*Phillips* opinions. In effect, the weight of the earlier data points might be operating to mask the impact of *Phillips*.

To obtain a better view of whether the *Phillips* opinion affected the court's claim interpretation methodology, we compared the rate of each methodological approach across two segments of the entire dataset, using the date of the *Phillips* decision (July 12, 2005) as a dividing line (see Table 6.2).[58]

Table 6.2 appears to confirm that there was little significant pro-holistic change in the frequency distribution of the different claim construction methodologies between November 2002 and July 12, 2005.[59] What is particularly remarkable in Table 6.2, however, is the frequency distribution post-*Phillips*. As can be seen, the difference in rate of application of the methodological approach was very small: about 2 percent.[60] Given that the procedural approach to claim interpretation was largely disparaged in the *Phillips* opinion, this result is quite interesting.

Because the post-*Phillips* database (116 opinions for the court) is much smaller – in both time covered and quantity – than the pre-*Phillips* database (682 opinions for the court), it is possible that its small size is masking what would otherwise be significant differences. To investigate this possibility, we compared the methodological approach in two segments of the dataset using a symmetric subset of the data,[61] with the *Phillips* opinion again serving as the dividing point (and, here, the center) of the analysis. Table 6.3 shows the comparative frequency of methodologies.

Table 6.3 is supportive of the observation that Federal Circuit opinions did not become significantly more holistic between the end of the period studied in *Is the Federal Circuit Succeeding?* and the *Phillips* opinion. Like Table 6.2, Table 6.3

58 As noted in Wagner & Petherbridge, *supra* note 6, the federal circuit issued 134 opinions with an observable claim interpretation analysis during the period following *Phillips* and ending on April 15, 2007. Of these, 116 were opinions for the court.

59 *Compare* Wagner & Petherbridge, *supra* note 6, at 1148 (63.1 percent Procedural/36.9 percent Holistic) *with* Table 2 "Pre-*Phillips*" (65.9 percent Procedural/34.1 percent Holistic).

60 And statistically insignificant. That is, using the χ^2 test, we cannot reject the null hypothesis ($p = .683$) that the post-*Phillips* results were independent of the *Phillips* decision. *Compare also* Wagner & Petherbridge, *supra* note 6, at 1148 (63.1 percent Procedural/36.9 percent Holistic) *with* Table 3 "Post-*Phillips*" (63.8 percent Procedural/36.2 percent Holistic).

61 As shown in Table 6.3, the symmetric subset included the 116 opinions of the court leading up to *Phillips* and the 116 opinions of the court that followed (until April 15, 2007).

TABLE 6.3. *Frequency of methodologies, symmetric about* Phillips *(court opinions, binomial)*

		Procedural	Holistic
Pre-Phillips	N	79	37
	%	68.1%	31.9%
Post-Phillips	N	74	42
	%	63.8%	36.2%

shows that the observed frequency distributions leading up to the *Phillips* opinion and those following the *Phillips* opinion are quite similar. That is, the observed differences are small and statistically insignificant.[62]

Tables 6.2 and 6.3 thus present something of a puzzle: why would there be virtually no change in the way that the court used the methodological approach to claim construction, even after the en banc treatment of the issue in *Phillips*? We discuss this issue further in Part IV.C.

B. *The Phillips Effect, Part 2: Methodological Trends*

The next area of inquiry is the effect, if any, that *Phillips* has had on the *trends* of the methodological approach to claim construction. Note that because of the lack of temporality of court opinions – they do not issue on a regular or systematic schedule related to the calendar – we use lagged averages as the method of analysis. A lagged average looks backward at the court's jurisprudence for a specified number of opinions by the court (here, we use a twenty-case lagged average), thus providing a means of determining the recent-average methodological approach at any given point in the dataset. Because the opinions are distributed over time in the dataset (though, as noted, they are not evenly distributed), changes in the lagged average thus reflect changes in the jurisprudence over time.

Figure 6.2 provides an overall view of the dataset, expressed in terms of a twenty-case lagged average of methodological approach. The vertical axis describes the percentage of court opinions coded *Procedural*; that is, the higher the data point, the more procedural the jurisprudence. A linear trend line is provided.

Figure 6.2 shows several trends in the court's claim construction jurisprudence. First, the long-run overall trend remains directed toward the procedural approach, consistent with our earlier findings.[63] Second, note the wide variance over time; the twenty-case lagged average ranges from more than 90 percent procedural to less than 25 percent procedural. Finally, as might have been expected, something

[62] Using the χ^2 test, we cannot reject the null hypothesis ($p = .683$) that the post-*Phillips* results were independent of the *Phillips* decision.

[63] *See* Wagner & Petherbridge, *supra* note 6, at 1148–56.

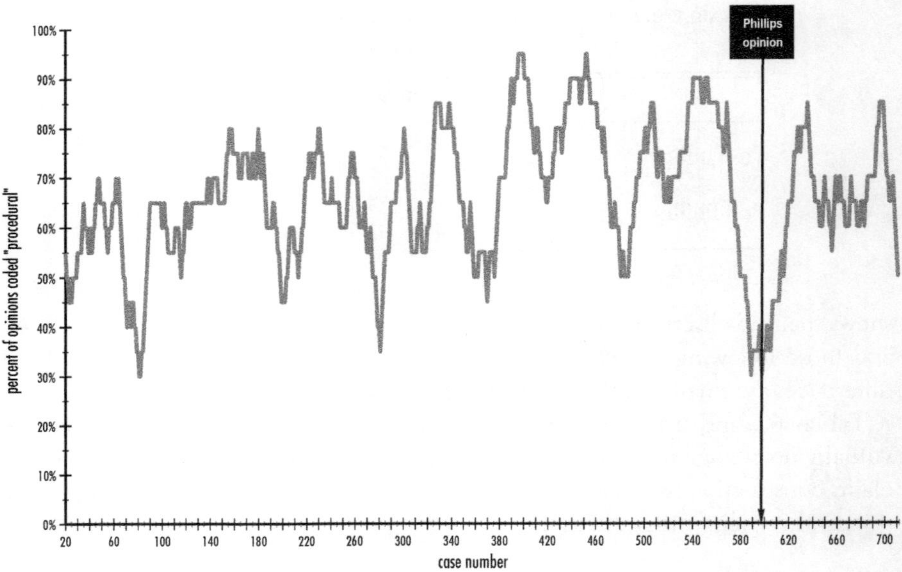

FIGURE 6.2. Trends of Claim Construction Jurisprudence at the Federal Circuit, 1995–2007 (court opinions, 20-case lagged average, n = 712)[64]

jurisprudentially significant appears to happen to the jurisprudence at or near the *Phillips* en banc opinion in July 2005.

As shown in Figure 6.2, there is a dramatic reduction in procedural opinions around the time of the *Phillips* en banc opinion. This suggests at least two avenues for additional inquiry:

1. Whether the overall trend line depicted in Figure 6.2 might be masking a shorter-term trend in claim construction jurisprudence around the time of the *Phillips* en banc opinion;[65] and
2. Whether the apparent changes in methodological approach surrounding the publication of the opinion suggested that something interesting happened around that time that deserves a closer look.

To better understand the trends in methodological approach surrounding the *Phillips* en banc opinion, we examined the twenty-case lagged average of the same symmetric subset of opinions described in Table 6.2.[66] Figure 6.3 shows the methodological trends in a more focused view, reporting the location in the dataset of important dates with respect to *Phillips*: the date that the order granting en banc

64 The trends in methodological approach reported in Figure 6.2 are based on binomial characterization.

65 As before, of particular concern is the impact that the large number of pre-*Phillips* opinions may have on this trend.

66 *See* Section III.A.

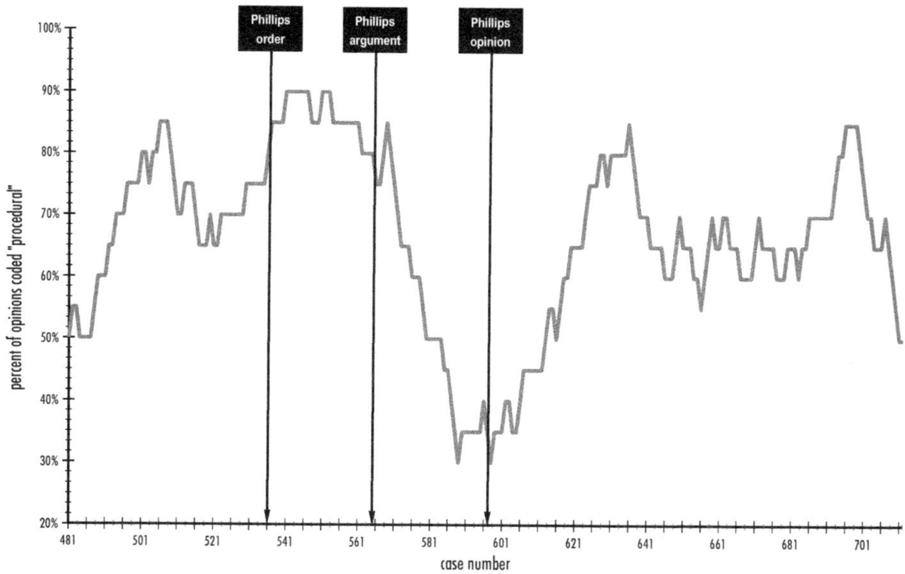

FIGURE 6.3. Claim Construction Jurisprudence at the Federal Circuit, Pre- and Post-*Phillips* (court opinions, symmetric about *Phillips*, 20-case lagged average, n = 231)[67]

treatment was issued (July 21, 2004), the date of the oral argument (February 8, 2005), and the date of the opinion (July 12, 2005).

Figure 6.3 offers a very different picture from Figure 6.2. First, the overall trend in claim construction methodology has been redirected (albeit slightly) in favor of the holistic approach, as shown in Figure 6.3 by the reversed (compared to Fig. 6.2) trend line. This move in favor of the holistic methodology during this time frame is consistent with what one would have expected, given the pro-Holistic *Phillips* opinion.[68]

Importantly, Figure 6.3 shows a very substantial change in average methodological approach between the oral argument and the publishing of the *Phillips* en banc opinion. This is of course consistent with the hypothesis that the en banc opinion in *Phillips* was meant to deprecate the procedural approach, in favor of the holistic approach. Yet somewhat remarkably, the graph also shows a return in average claim construction methodology to nearly the pre-*Phillips* equilibrium of about 60–70 percent procedural. Moreover, although it is likely too soon to say definitively, the average claim construction methodology appears to be stabilizing at or near the pre-*Phillips* average.[69] (This observation is consistent with the overall numbers reported in Tables 6.2 and 6.3.) This circumstance challenges the conclusion that *Phillips* has changed the law. That is, the graphs confirm and illuminate what the

[67] The trends in methodological approach reported in Figure 6.3 are based on binomial characterization.
[68] *See* Section I.D.
[69] Roughly 65 percent procedural. *See* Figure 6.3.

TABLE 6.4. *Alternative opinions (concurrences/dissents) on claim construction*

	Alternative opinions	Rate of alternative opinions (percent of total)
All cases, 1995–2007	73	9.5%
Pre-*Phillips*	55	8.4%
Post-*Phillips*	18	13.4%

simple aggregate numbers showed inTables 6.3 and 6.4: *Phillips* has, at least on this measure, had relatively little effect on the case law. More specifically, and in view of Figures 6.2 and 6.3, it appears that Phillips *did in fact correspond with a significant change in the jurisprudence, but that the change was relatively short-lived.* Finally, it appears that the change occurred *before* the *Phillips* opinion was issued[70] and that, after the opinion was issued, there was a return to the pre-*Phillips* equilibrium.

C. *Why Did* Phillips *Not Change the Law?*

Taken together, the results reported in Parts III.A and III.B are puzzling. Why was there so little change in the jurisprudence, when *Phillips* clearly attempted to favor one methodological approach over the other? Why do we see a significant, but temporary, change in the case law? Why is the timing of the case at odds with what one would expect? As a set of brief, preliminary answers, we think there are at least six possible explanations for these results, as follows.

1. The Nonbinding Nature of the *Phillips* Opinion

One possibility is that these results reflect the open-ended nature of the *Phillips* en banc opinion itself, which allows both methodological approaches to exist.[71] As one of us has written before, "the new rule is that there are no rules."[72] Thus, judges with existing views on the correct methodological approach are not required, under the terms of *Phillips*, to deviate from them. This explanation is consistent with the similarity between pre- and post-*Phillips* results. However, there is reason to think this explanation is not complete: Another way to understand the consequences of the open-ended nature of the *Phillips* opinion is that judges no longer feel

[70] *See* Figure 6.3.

[71] For example, in addition to holding that there "is no magic formula or catechism for conducting claim construction," 415 F.3d at 1324, the court states that "we do not intend to preclude the appropriate use of dictionaries. Dictionaries or comparable sources are often useful to assist in understanding the commonly understood meaning of words and have been used both by our court and the Supreme Court in claim interpretation [citations omitted]," *id.* at 1322.

[72] See R. Polk Wagner, Phillips *Analysis, Part 1: The New Rule is There are No Rules*, PolkWagner.com (July 15, 2005), at http://www.law.upenn.edu/blogs/polk/archives/2005/07/phillips_analys.html.

constrained when authoring opinions to rely[73] on a particular approach or, perhaps more practically, to reveal or appear to emphasize a particular approach.

2. The Federal Circuit's Decision-Making Process

The results might reflect the way that the *Phillips* decision was made by the Federal Circuit. That is, one might assume that the legal result of *Phillips* (the choice of the holistic approach over the procedural approach) was made at or slightly before the oral argument: that is, when the judges of the court began to focus on the question. There is then a significant (here, about six-months) time lag before that result is announced. But the judges (and their clerks) already know the result and begin issuing opinions reflecting the new legal framework – much more holistic, much less procedural. Yet the *Phillips* en banc opinion – the actual prose – turns out to be less substantial than expected. That is, it leaves open the availability of even the strongest of procedural approaches and pointedly eschews any strict guidance concerning methodologies. (Given the voting patterns in the en banc majority, it would not be surprising if the opinion were written explicitly to try to capture unanimity.) Thus, once the opinion issues and the new framework applies, the judges and parties find that *Phillips* does not mark much of a change from earlier case law.

3. A Results-Oriented Court

These results may expose a view at the Federal Circuit that the jurisprudence of claim construction is, in essence, meaningless. Under this hypothesis, the post-*Phillips* rebound to at or near the pre-*Phillips* average methodological distribution may reflect either (1) the views of the persons who actually drafted the opinion, which is not going to be much altered because the court sees it as irrelevant; (2) the ease or convenience of conveying a particular claim construction in a particular set of circumstances;[74] or (3) a decision on claim construction masking (or avoiding) a more difficult decision according to some other doctrine, such as invalidity or the doctrine of equivalents. That is, the Federal Circuit may use claim construction as a general-purpose tool for reaching the "right" results in each case; the flexibility and discretion provided by

73 Or, perhaps, to show reliance.

74 In view of the signaling prospect discussed in number 4, this might mean that once you start with the claims you are more likely to not move too far from their plain import in an analysis. The further one gets from the meaning of the claim language, the more likely it might be that one could make a technical or factual mistake. Also, the more one relies on the written description or the file wrapper, the more information external to the claims must be mastered and applied. In cases where the written description and file history are confused, ambiguous, or otherwise of poor quality, the court may not feel comfortable relying on them. For safety and efficiency purposes then, staying nearer to the ordinary art established meaning of the words of a claim may be more a more satisfying and reproducible intellectual exercise for the court.

the post-*Phillips* claim construction regime make this approach particularly useful. In our view this is a troubling interpretation of *Phillips*, not the least because it renders claim construction methodology even more (intentionally?) opaque.

4. Patent Drafting Drives the Results

The post-*Phillips* rebound to at or near the pre-*Phillips* average methodological distribution may reflect less about the law and more about the way patents are drafted. In other words, perhaps about two-thirds of patents[75] are drafted in a way that is amenable to interpretation from a careful analysis of the claim language, whereas about one-third require a broader, more open-ended inquiry. Thus the court adapts its methodological approach to the patent at hand. This may mean that, absent a change in the law mandating a particular methodological approach, the rate of each methodological approach is relatively immune to change.

5. Jurisprudential Time Lag

The results reflect the cases appealed to the Federal Circuit. That is, most cases in our post-*Phillips* dataset were litigated at district courts under the pre-*Phillips* regime, so aspects of that jurisprudence are embedded in the cases. Thus, the similarity with pre-*Phillips* cases.

6. Failure of the Study

The results may reflect problems with the design of the study itself. Perhaps it is simply too early to discern any patterns, and more data are needed. Perhaps, too, the coding scheme is missing the essential post-*Phillips* change.[76]

In reality, of course, the true answer is probably some combination of these six possibilities. Hypothesis 2, we believe, is the one analysis that can explain virtually all of the current data patterns. But Hypothesis 6 is almost certainly partially correct – more data would allow the patterns, if any, to become clearer.

In any event, the most important aspect of our results is this: *at least to date, the Phillips en banc opinion has not yielded any significant observable effects on the claim construction jurisprudence of the Federal Circuit.*

D. *If Phillips Did Not Change the Law, What Did It Do?*

Even if the *Phillips* en banc opinion did not change the law, it may well have had an important impact in clarifying or stabilizing the jurisprudence. Although the measurement of jurisprudential stability or clarity is an uncertain business at best, we

75 Appealed patents – and by logical extrapolation all patents.

76 If for example, *Phillips* is encouraging "procedural appearing" opinions, that are by the current design of the study undetectably not.

offer here an analysis of two potentially useful measures of jurisprudential stability – the rate of disagreements among panel members concerning claim construction analysis and the rate at which questions of claim construction are being appealed.

1. Reduce Disputes among Federal Circuit Judges?

One measure of jurisprudential clarity is whether judges can apply the doctrine in a way that is relatively undisputed by their colleagues on the court. Under this theory, the rate of concurrences or dissents (what we designate as "alternative opinions") should be inversely correlated with the clarity and coherence of the doctrine.

Table 6.4 shows the rate of alternative opinions for three groupings of the data: all cases, the pre-*Phillips* cases, and the post-*Phillips* cases. According to our results, *Phillips* has not reduced the rate of disputes concerning claim construction by the judges of the Federal Circuit. If anything, it may have increased it. Figure 6.4 shows how this rate of alternative opinions has varied across time, using a twenty-case lagged average.

2. Reduce Appeals on Claim Construction?

Another possible measure of stability and clarity is the rate at which issues of claim construction get appealed to the Federal Circuit, with the theory being that the rate

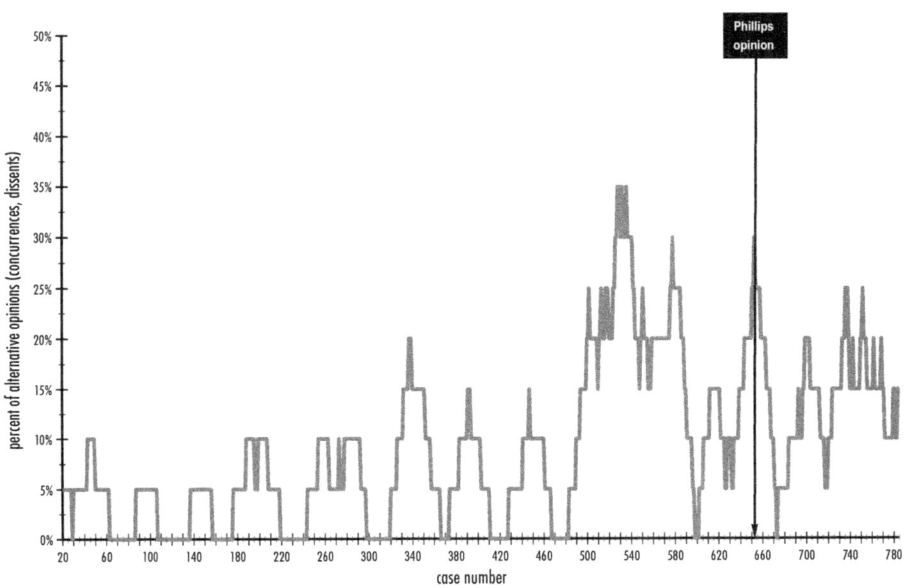

FIGURE 6.4. Rate of Alternative Opinions on Claim Construction (20-case lagged average, n = 785)

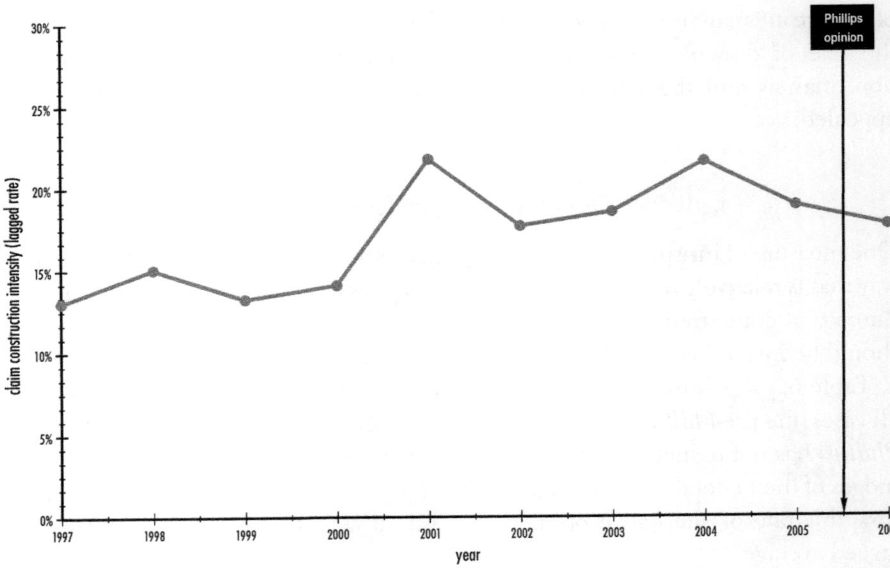

FIGURE 6.5. Claim Construction Intensity (lagged rate of claim construction decisions per patent appeal)[77]

of appeals is – as with the rate of disagreements – inversely related to the clarity, stability, and predictability of the doctrine.[78] The data (Fig. 6.5) show that the intensity (or share) of claim construction among patent appeals has been generally rising in our dataset. Given the data available at this time, we cannot draw any clear conclusions about the effect of *Phillips*, if any.

On balance, then, we are unable to confirm – at least on these measures, and with the data available – that *Phillips* has had a significant impact on the stability and predictability of the Federal Circuit's claim construction jurisprudence.

IV. *IS THE FEDERAL CIRCUIT SUCCEEDING?* REVISITED: THE LESSONS OF *PHILLIPS*

The empirical analysis presented here suggests – strongly – that the *Phillips* decision has to date not had any significant measurable effect on either the jurisprudence of

[77] In this figure, *claim construction intensity* is defined as the number of Federal Circuit cases with claim construction decisions, divided by the one-year lagged patent appeals filed. The one-year lag is intended to account for the pendency of appeals at the Federal Circuit. Note that the intensity number likely significantly understates the importance of claim construction jurisprudence, because the number of appeals filed is much higher than the number of decisions issued by the Court. The numbers of patent appeals are provided by the Federal Circuit and are available at http://www.fedcir.gov/pdf/Patent%20filings%20historical.pdf.

[78] *See generally* BRUCE L. HAY & KATHRYN E. SPIER, *Settlement of Litigation*, in 3 NEW PALGRAVE DICTIONARY OF ECONOMICS AND THE LAW 442, 443 (Peter Newman ed., 1998); George L. Priest & Benjamin Klein, *The Selection of Disputes for Litigation*, 13 J. LEGAL STUD. 1, 16 (1984).

claim construction at the Federal Circuit or on our (admittedly imperfect) measures of stability and predictability of the doctrine. The question of why this appears to be the case is unclear, as we discussed earlier, though we offered several hypotheses.[79] Beyond the need for a satisfactory explanation for these empirical observations, however, the Federal Circuit's en banc opinion in *Phillips* also has important normative implications, both for the course of the patent law and for the future of the court. In our view, the Federal Circuit's decision in *Phillips*, and its explanation of the decision, was deeply unfortunate – likely the worst possible option available to the court – and will have ongoing negative consequences for the law of claim construction, the patent system, and the court itself.

A. *Wrong Choice Number One: Embracing the Holistic Methodological Approach*

As we have argued elsewhere, the procedural approach to claim construction analysis clearly dominates the alternative, holistic approach – because it is the procedural approach that best supports the public notice function of patent claims.[80] This function, at its most basic, requires that the claim language convey clear and useful information about the scope of the patent grant. This aspect of patent claims – as the ultimate definition of the metes and bounds of a patentee's rights – is a fundamental tenet of the modern patent system and must be respected.[81] In economic terms, patent claims seek to resolve an information cost problem with respect to publicly conferred rights to exclude others from the marketplace: by delineating the borders between protected and unprotected subject matter, claim language addresses what would otherwise be a paralyzing information-cost problem, namely, uncertainty and unpredictability about the scope and location of patent rights.[82] Put more simply, absent clarity and predictability, the public notice function of patent claims cannot be achieved.

79 *See supra* Section III.C.

80 *See, e.g.*, Wagner & Petherbridge, supra note 6, at 1176. *See also Brief of Amicus Curiae Patent Law Professors R. Polk Wagner & Joseph Scott Miller, Phillips v. AWH*, No. 03-1269 (Fed. Cir. Sept. 20, 2004).

81 Giles S. Rich, *Extent of Protection and Interpretation of Claims – American Perspectives*, 21 Int'l Rev. Indus. Prop. & Copyright L. 497, 499 (1990) ("To coin a phrase, the name of the game is the claim.").

82 *See generally* R. Coase, *The Problem of Social Cost*, 3 J. Law & Econ. 1 (1960) (discussing uncertainty about the boundaries of rights as an impediment to socially desirable transactions). *See also* R. Polk Wagner, *Reconsidering Estoppel: Prosecution History and the Failure of* Festo, 151 U. Pa. L. Rev. 159, 222–25 (discussing information-cost problems in patent law); R. Polk Wagner, *Of Patents and Path-Dependency: A Comment on Burk and Lemley*, 18 Berkeley Tech. L. J. 1, 18–20 (noting the benefits of clarity in patent rights); Kimberly A. Moore, *Forum Shopping in Patent Cases: Does Geographic Choice Affect Innovation*, 79 N.C. L. Rev. 889, 928 (2001) (discussing costs attending unpredictability and uncertainty about patent claim scope).

There can be little dispute that the public notice function of claims is best served when the meaning of claim language is readily apparent to patent readers. Conversely, the public notice function is worst served when litigation is required to interpret even the most banal of claim terms. The question, then, is how to construct a methodological approach that yields the former at the expense of the latter.

An approach to patent claim construction that firmly embraces the commonly understood meaning of words and places the burden on the patent applicant to clearly explain any deviations from the ordinary meaning is the most likely to yield claim language and thus claim construction decisions that comport well with the public notice function of claims. The procedural approach, which presumptively applies the ordinary meaning – perhaps from relevant technical, scientific, or general-purpose dictionaries or perhaps via experts in the field – to disputed claim language, and yet fully embraces any clear, specific, and objective reasons to deviate from the ordinary meaning, makes transparent the analytic process underlying claim construction. By contrast, the holistic approach embraced by the Federal Circuit in *Phillips,* which suggests that "what matters is for the court to attach the appropriate weight to be assigned to those sources [or claim meaning] *in light of the statutes and policies that inform patent law,*" offers nothing concerning guidance, and results in a standardless, ad hoc determination of claim meaning.[83]

We also think that the procedural approach best aligns the incentives of patentees and the public. That is, under a procedural claim construction regime, a patent applicant would understand with reasonable certainty the meaning that the courts were likely to attach to claim terms – the ordinary meaning, unless the patentee clearly provided some other definition. Thus the patent applicant would bear the burden (and have the knowledge of this burden) of affirmatively providing a clear definition of the claim language, or accepting the presumptive ordinary meaning. Thus, the incentives would prompt patent applicants to say *more* about their inventions and to clarify, as much as possible, the meaning of claim terms. By contrast, the *Phillips* holistic approach, which contemplates an open-ended search for "contextual" meaning in the patent document and prosecution history, encourages patent applicants to either (a) say as little as possible about their inventions, for fear that descriptive matter would be "discovered" as providing a contextual meaning altering the scope of the claims, or (b) obfuscate the meaning of the claim language as much as possible, by offering multiple, contradictory "contexts" in which claim language could be understood, thus leaving the scope of the claim uncertain (until at least millions of dollars of have been spent on litigation).

Third, the procedural approach best utilizes the skills of both the technologists (PHOSITAs: persons having ordinary skill in the art) and the nontechnologist decision makers (such as judges). Patent documents are written for a technical audience,

[83] *See* 415 F.3d at 1324.

and as such the focus must remain on what the relevant technologists would understand the language to mean. *Phillips*' methodological approach, the drawing of subjective inferences by parsing the often complex language of a patent specification, for example, is a task that – although uniquely lawyerly in nature – seems a relatively poor fit for judges in the modern patent environment.[84] By contrast, the procedural approach leverages the skills of courts in implementing and enunciating clear rules based on the available clear, specific, and objective evidence of the meaning of language. Under the procedural approach, the knowledge of technologists determines the meaning (presumptively, the "ordinary meaning"), while the lawyers and judges implement and execute the interpretive procedure. Under *Phillips*, the judges play the role of technologists and operate without any meaningful legal restrictions.

We do not suggest that the procedural approach is free from flaws or is, as the *Phillips* opinion derided, a "magic formula or catechism for conducting claim construction."[85] Far from it: claim construction is inherently a difficult process, and no methodological approach can eliminate that difficulty. And certainly the procedural approach has problematic aspects. An "ordinary meaning" is not synonymous with a "undisputed meaning," of course. Even the most precise of technical dictionaries often have an array of definitions for key terms. Used improperly, the procedural approach might indeed allow for claim constructions that are wholly divorced from the invention-at-issue. But these problems, although real, pale in comparison to the damage wrought by the pervasive uncertainty, perverse incentives, and technological amateurishness created by the *Phillips* embrace of the holistic approach.

B. *Wrong Choice Number Two: The "Anything Goes"* Phillips *Opinion*

Although we have little doubt that the court chose unwisely in embracing a holistic approach in *Phillips*, it compounded this mistake by issuing an opinion in the case that, while firmly embracing the holistic methodological approach, fails to provide any meaningful legal framework whatsoever. In Section I.D we noted the pervasive "anything goes" nature of the *Phillips* approach to claim construction analysis, wherein judicial decision makers are commanded to attach "appropriate weight" to the complex and contradictory information offered as part of modern claim construction analysis.

The results presented in Part III demonstrate the largely content-free nature of the *Phillips* opinion: notwithstanding the clear choice in favor of a more holistic approach, we find no measurable difference in the court's overall jurisprudence.[86]

[84] In this context, the *Phillips* opinion's statement that judges can conduct this process "with reasonable certainty and predictability if the court's focus remains on understanding how a person of ordinary skill in the art would understand the claim terms" seems plainly unreasonable. *See* 415 F.3d at 1323.

[85] *See* 415 F.3d at 1323.

[86] *See* Section III.A. and Section III.B.

Furthermore, it seems clear that the *Phillips* opinion did not resolve disputes among the members of the Federal Circuit concerning claim construction analysis: Table 6.4 and Figure 6.4 reveal that, if anything, the rate of disagreement has risen.

Taken together, the open-ended nature of the *Phillips* language, the data showing no measurable jurisprudential effect, and the failure to resolve disagreements among the judges make reasonably clear that the *Phillips* opinion – perhaps written to secure as many votes as possible – has utterly failed in advancing the Federal Circuit's management of claim construction doctrine and has most likely made it worse.

C. *Wrong Choice Number Three:* Phillips *Cannot Be Squared with* Cybor

In *Is the Federal Circuit Succeeding?* we argued that the Federal Circuit's approach in *Cybor* was not only defensible but was also likely the correct approach. In broad strokes, we argued that the *Markman II* decision by the Supreme Court, which allocates interpretive authority to judges on the basis of "functional considerations," in essence creates a mandate for the Federal Circuit to develop the law of claim construction in a way that enhances uniformity and certainty.[87] Under this view, the *Cybor* decision is correct on institutional design grounds: by taking control of the law of claim construction, the Federal Circuit could best manage the development of "rules and tools" that would lead to *Markman II*'s mandate for uniformity and certainty. That is, by enabling the Federal Circuit to act in claim construction cases without deference to the district courts, we suggested the following:

> Instead of viewing de novo review as an invasive mechanism by which the appellate court can put its stamp of approval on every decision, it can be viewed as a means to an end: a tool with which to develop and enforce rules governing claim construction. That is, if the de novo review process allows the Federal Circuit to establish clear guidelines for the interpretation of patent claims, certainty and efficiency would be enhanced, not diminished. Clear rules would allow district court judges to implement claim constructions with greater confidence, allow the parties to better evaluate their chances of success (both post-judgment and pre-litigation), and, perhaps most significantly, result in patentees drafting clearer claims even prior to a patent's issue.[88]

87 *See* Wagner & Petherbridge, supra note 6, at 1122–24. For example, in suggesting that judges were likely to be better at construing claims, the Court cited "special doctrines" relating to construction embedded in the law. *See Markman II*, at 389. Further, *stare decisis* – that is, the existence (and development) of legal rules – anchored the Court's argument that judicial decision making in this context would enhance uniformity and certainty. *See id.* at 391. Thus, *Markman II*'s functionalist approach was largely based on the theory that allocating the interpretive task to judges would extend and enhance the development of legal rules guiding the construction of patent claims.

88 *See id.* at 1124 n.80. This point – that patent rules are best considered as ex ante incentive-based mechanisms is a point one of us has made elsewhere. *See generally* Wagner, *supra* note 79, at 159.

However, our embrace of the *Markman-Cybor* framework was conditional – contingent on the Federal Circuit actually developing a reasonably coherent, clear, and predictable doctrine of claim construction. Absent this active management, the premise of the *Markman II* mandate, and thus the premise of *Cybor*, falls away.[89]

As of 2002, when our earlier dataset closed, we were reasonably upbeat about the Federal Circuit's progress on this front, concluding that

> many findings [in this study] are unquestionably encouraging, suggesting that the court's effort to meet its mandate is both well underway and moving in the right direction. The picture of the Federal Circuit that emerges, we submit, is of a court in broad transition. Driven in part by new appointments and an effort to respond to its special mandate, a new Federal Circuit is emerging – one that appears to be more rules-driven and more consistent than before. It is too early to be sure, but the findings here, perhaps bolstered by the procedural and jurisprudential reforms we derive from the results, suggest that the Federal Circuit's unique position in the judiciary may yet be vindicated.[90]

Unfortunately, our interpretation of the results of this study is not nearly so encouraging. Given what we have found, we view *Phillips*, both normatively and in fact, as a large step backward for the Federal Circuit (and, by extension, the patent law). That is, we find a law of claim construction that is virtually unchanged in some important respects, but simultaneously less transparent and predictable. The debates within the Court continue, as does the very substantial split in methodological approach.

More troubling, however, is the damage that *Phillips* has done to the goal of *Markman II* (and, indeed, the Federal Circuit itself). When it defined for itself a role as the ultimate decision maker on claim construction, the Federal Circuit, in our view, also embraced the need to develop clear and coherent legal rules for claim construction. By failing to do so – and, in *Philips*, actually embracing an "anything goes" approach to claim construction – the court has betrayed the premise of *Cybor*: that claim construction was a legally defined process, subject to coherent legal limits. This, we think, is untenable. Either claim construction is a deeply fact-based technological question ("How would a person of skill in the art understand the scope of this patent, given all the information available?"), or it is a carefully delineated legal framework. If it is the latter, then we think that the Federal Circuit is best suited to establish and maintain that structure, on a de novo basis. But if it is the former, then there is little justification for failing to give deference to district courts. Thus, in *Phillips*, we fear that the Federal Circuit sounded the death knell for the promise of *Markman II* – a clearer, more coherent, and more predictable law of claim construction.

89 *See* Wagner & Petherbridge, supra note 6, at 1124 (making this point).
90 *Id.* at 1179.

CONCLUSION

Phillips v. *AWH* lies at the center of the debate concerning the intuitional structure of the patent system and the role the Federal Circuit should play. In the post-*Markman* era, claim construction represents that court's most important example of what might be best understood as the "muscular" theory of the Federal Circuit: a court that stands astride the U.S. patent law, managing the jurisprudence in a way that builds confidence in the coherence, stability, and predictability of a complex regime that is increasingly under political scrutiny.

Unfortunately, *Phillips* does not – at least to date – represent the Federal Circuit's finest hour. We find little here to suggest that the avowed goal of *Phillips* – to resolve the court's methodological disputes over claim construction – has been met in any measurable way. We also find that the open-ended nature of the *Phillips* opinion and its failure to resolve the longstanding split in claim construction jurisprudence have undermined the Federal Circuit's efforts to develop a coherent and predictable jurisprudence.

APPENDIX A: CODING DETAIL

Binomial Categories	Procedural			Holistic		
Detailed Categories	Strong (Ps)	Intermediate (Pi)	Weak (Pw)	Weak (Hw)	Intermediate (Hi)	Strong (Hs)
Textual Description & Coding Instrument	Expresses rigid process. Ordinary meaning controls, absent express definitions, etc.	Framework of formal process established. Departure along some dimension: no talk of presumption, extensive discussion of specification.	Difficult to discern the form of analysis. Some discussion / hint of process.	Difficult to discern the form of analysis. Little or no discussion of process or ordinary meaning.	Acknowledgment of process, but not used. Specification/ prosecution history is clearly dispositive.	No discussion of process. Immediate use of specification or prosecution history.
Example Cases	*Johnson Worldwide Assocs.* v. *Zebco Corp.*, 175 F.3d 985 (*Fed. Cir.* 1999) *Neomagic Corp.* v. *Trident Microsystems Inc.*, 87 F.3d 1062 (*Fed. Cir.* 2002) *CCS Fitness Inc.* v. *Brunswick Corp.*, 309 F.3d 1373 (*Fed Cir.* 2002)	*Insituform Techs.* v. *Cat Contr.*, 99 F.3d 1098 (*Fed. Cir.* 1996) *Micro Chem. Inc.* v. *Great Plains Chem. Co.*, 194 F.3d 1250 (*Fed. Cir.* 1999) 3M v. *Chemque Inc.*, 303 F.3d 1294 (*Fed. Cir.* 2002)	*Ethicon Endo-Surgery* v. *United States Surgical Corp.*, 93 F.3d 1572 (*Fed. Cir.* 1996) *Key Pharms.* v. *Hercon Lab. Corp.*, 161 F.3d 709 (*Fed. Cir.* 1998) *Brassica Protection Products LLC* v. *Sunrise Farms*, 301 F.3d 1343 (*Fed. Cir.* 2002)	*Litton Sys.* v. *Honeywell Inc.*, 87 F.3d 1559 (*Fed. Cir.* 1996) *DSC Communs. Corp.* v. *Pulse Communs. Inc.*, 170 F.3d 1354 (*Fed. Cir.* 1999) *Viskase Corp.* v. *American Nat'l Can Co.*, 261 F.3d 1316 (*Fed. Cir.* 2001)	*Harris Corp.* v. *IXYS Corp.*, 114 F.3d 1149 (*Fed. Cir.* 1997) *Aqua-Aerobic Sys.* v. *Aerators Inc.*, 211 F.3d 1241 (*Fed. Cir.* 2000) *Smith & Nephew Inc.* v. *Ethicon Inc.*, 276 F.3d 1304 (*Fed. Cir.* 2002)	*O.I. Corp.* v. *Tekmar Co.*, 115 F.3d 1576 (*Fed. Cir.* 1997) *Wang Lab. Inc.* v. *America Online Inc.*, 197 F.3d 1377 (*Fed. Cir.* 1999). *Cultor Corp.* v. *A.E. Staley Manufacturing Co.*, 224 F.3d 1328 (*Fed. Cir.* 2000)

APPENDIX B: DATABASE FIELDS

#	Field ID	Description	Form	Coding	Notes
1	Serial	serial number	[integer]	Machine	*unique record identifier*
2	Title	case title	Text	Machine	
3	Docket	case docket numbers	[xx-xxxx]	Machine	*may have multiple dockets*
4	Citation	full citations	text, citation format	Machine	
5	LEXIS_Cite	LEXIS Citation	[xxxx U.S. App. LEXIS xxxxxx]	Machine	
6	Date	date issued	[date]	Machine	
7	Published	publication status	[yes | no]	Machine	
8	Cert_Denied	was certiorari denied	[yes | no]	Machine	
9	Case_Below	title & court below	Text	Machine	*incomplete, especially before 2002*
10	LEXIS_Cite_ Below	LEXIS Citation Below	[xxxx U.S. Dist. LEXIS xxxxxx]	Machine	*incomplete, especially before 2002*
11	Disposition	case outcome	[affirmed | reversed | vacated | mixed]	Machine	
12	Judge1	Judge assigned	Text	Machine	
13	Judge2	Judge assigned	Text	Machine	
14	Judge3	Judge assigned	Text	Machine	
15	Author	author of court's opinion	Text	Machine	
16	Opinion_Type	type of opinion	[sole | majority]	Machine	
17	Author	author of alternative opinion	Text	Machine	*may not be present*
18	Opinion_Type	type of opinion	[concur | dissent]	Machine	*may not be present*
19	Author	author of alternative opinion	Text	Machine	*may not be present*
20	Opinion_Type	type of opinion	[concur | dissent]	Machine	*may not be present*
21	Methodology	Methodological approach used	[Ps, Pi, Pw, Hw, Hi, Hs]	Human	

7

An Empirical Look at Trade Secret Law's Shift from Common to Statutory Law

*Michael Risch**

INTRODUCTION

Like many of its unfair competition brethren, trade secret law developed in the courts of England and the United States. Until 1979, the elements of trade secret misappropriation were exclusively defined by the common law developed by U.S. state and federal courts. Like its intellectual property brethren, trade secret law is now governed by statute. In 1979, the Uniform Trade Secrets Act, affectionately known as the UTSA, was introduced. The UTSA has since become widely adopted – forty-seven states now follow it.

The UTSA did not represent a complete break from the common law. The comments make clear that it was intended to codify the common law where the two did not conflict. Whereas the common law used to define the core definition of trade secrets, it is now relegated to the penumbra of statutory interpretation. Thus, as used throughout this chapter, "common law" generally refers to the historical, nonstatutory definition of trade secrets and misappropriation, rather than the more general concept of all judicial opinions.

Even so, there is a lingering influence of the common law over core aspects of trade secret law, even when that law conflicts with newer statutory provisions. For example, courts might use old definitions of trade secrets or old rules about ex-employees despite new statutory language to the contrary. Anecdotal studies have considered the continuing influence of the common law,[1] but, to date no study has

* © 2011 Michael Risch, Professor, Villanova University School of Law. The author thanks Suzanne Clain for assistance with empirical analysis; he also thanks David Abrams, R. Polk Wagner, and participants in the symposium, Intellectual Property and the Common Law, held at the University of Pennsylvania, and in the Villanova Junior Faculty Workshop for their helpful comments. Dustin Bednarz, Huan "Brian" Duong, Simran Kaur, Jonathan Lombardo, Priya Narahari, and Megan Wood provided valuable research assistance.

[1] *See, e.g.*, Sarah Gettings, Note, *Burbank Grease Services, LLC v. Sokolowski: Frustrating Uniformity in Trade Secret Law*, 22 BERKELEY TECH. L.J. 423 (2007).

comprehensively or empirically tested whether and how courts rely on the common law in spite of the shift to a uniform statute.

This chapter presents an empirically driven attempt to understand the continuing role of common law definitions and rules after adoption of the UTSA. Its methodology was straightforward: gather observable data about the statutory and case law that courts rely on to decide trade secret cases. The goals were to study how the old rules are being applied in the context of the new statute and to understand what factors might affect whether an old common law rule will be cited in a new statute-based court decision.

Fortunately, the role of the common law in trade secrecy may be more immediately observable than in other IP areas because it is relatively new. Trade secret law did not develop under the common law until long after trademark, patent, and copyright law developed. Also, trade secret law is the most recently codified intellectual property law: the statute is only about thirty years old.

Further, the federalist nature of trade secret law allows for richer data. First, each state might adopt the law at different times, allowing for observation of behavior both with respect to when the UTSA was passed in the state and also with respect to a common reference point. Second, states adopting the law might rely on older case law in different ways. Third, both federal and state courts apply the law, allowing for observation based on the type of venue.

Fourth, uniform laws such as the UTSA allow state legislators to adopt sister-state statutory interpretations when they enact the law, and states may do so in different ways.[2] Each state's UTSA case law could theoretically apply in every other state adopting it, an important benefit for small states that do not have enough litigation activity to generate substantial trade secret case law of their own.[3] Reliance on other state law, too, can be observed by looking at the type and source of precedent cited by courts.

Results of a preliminary study imply that common law trade secret rules continue to dominate even in the face of the uniform act.[4] For example, federal courts in West Virginia, a state with no common law or UTSA trade secret precedent of its

[2] *See, e.g.*, W. Va. Code § 47-22-8 (2010) (stating that the West Virginia Trade Secrets Act "shall be applied and construed to effectuate its general purpose to make uniform the law with respect to the subject of this act among states enacting it"). *But see, e.g.*, Ark. Code. Ann. §§ 4-75-601 to -607 (2011) *and* 765 Ill. Comp. Stat. 1065/1-9 (2011) (omitting the UTSA uniformity of application and construction provision in its Trade Secrets Act). Additionally, the Alabama, Hawaii, Idaho, Indiana, Maine, Minnesota, Nebraska, New Mexico, Nevada, North Carolina, North Dakota, and Virginia trade secret acts do not include the UTSA uniformity of application and construction provision. Linda B. Samuels & Bryan K. Johnson, *The Uniform Trade Secrets: The States' Response*, 24 CREIGHTON L. REV. 49, 91–92 (1990).

[3] Such uniform laws are not without their costs. To the extent that different states implement their laws differently, each state might need to consider additional information to sort out how it will enforce the law.

[4] Michael Risch, Essay, *A Failure of Uniform Laws?*, 159 U. Pa. L. Rev. PENNumbra 1 (2010), *available at* http://www.pennumbra.com/essays/10-2010/Risch.pdf.

own, routinely failed to cite case law precedent that applied the UTSA and instead relied on cases that applied old common law rules.

This chapter expands that preliminary study nationwide. It examines both federal and state opinions to test whether the common law of trade secrets continues to reign despite widespread adoption of the UTSA. The end result is a positive account of the common law's influence on courts applying the UTSA. Although this study is normatively agnostic, the potential normative implications are apparent. If the UTSA is considered the better policy, and courts follow the common law rather than the UTSA, then courts are not implementing better policy.[5] Of course, the opposite may be true, depending on one's normative position on any of the legal issues studied.

This chapter begins by briefly describing the shift from a common law definition of trade secret misappropriation to a statutory one, including some of the differences between the two. The remainder of the chapter develops a model to describe and test some descriptive questions that arise from the shift: Do courts follow the UTSA? When are they more likely to do so? Which courts are more likely to follow it? What factors affect whether a court will cite cases that follow the UTSA rather than the common law?

I. BACKGROUND

A. A *Brief History of Trade Secret Law*[6]

The history of trade secret law is an interesting study in how certain IP rights have developed. Whereas copyright and patent law in the United States find legal justification in the Constitution[7] and implementing federal statutes, trade secret law grew out of the common law and has now been codified separately in most states.

Although trade secrets originated in the early 1800s in England,[8] the development of a cause of action for misappropriation in the United States took a bit longer. In *Vickery* v. *Welch*,[9] the Massachusetts Supreme Court held that a secret manufacturing process was an asset that could be transferred to another[10] and that it was not a restraint of trade to include a covenant barring the seller from disclosing the

[5] *See generally*, Sharon K. Sandeen, *The Evolution of Trade Secret Law and Why Courts Commit Error When They Do Not Follow the Uniform Trade Secrets Act*, 33 HAMLINE L. REV. 493 (2010).

[6] A prior version of this subsection originally appeared in Michael Risch, *Why Do We Have Trade Secrets?*, 11 MARQ. INTELL. PROP. L. REV. 1 (2007). For a thorough discussion of the common law evolution of trade secret law, *see* Catherine Fisk, *Working Knowledge: Trade Secrets, Restrictive Covenants in Employment, and the Rise of Corporate Intellectual Property*, 1800–1920, 52 HASTINGS L.J. 441 (2001).

[7] U.S. Const. art. I, § 8, cl. 8.

[8] RESTATEMENT (THIRD) OF UNFAIR COMPETITION § 39 cmt. a (1995), Fisk, *supra* note 6.

[9] 19 Pick. 523 (Mass. 1837).

[10] Fisk, *supra* note 6, at 463 (Vickery is an "unwitting precursor[] of the modern notion that trade secrets are a species of property in ideas.").

secret.[11] The path to a developed trade secret remedy was not linear, however. In *Demming* v. *Chapman*,[12] for example, the New York Supreme Court recognized that misuse of secret information might give rise to damages, but that secrecy could not be enforced by injunction. Just a few years later, however, in *Hammer* v. *Barnes*,[13] the Supreme Court of New York allowed a complaint for damages and an injunction go forward against a party not in contractual privity with the plaintiff.

In *Peabody* v. *Norfolk*, the Massachusetts Supreme Court may have been the first court in the United States to describe a complete view of trade secrets[14]:

> If [a person] invents or discovers, and keeps secret, a process of manufacture, whether a proper subject for a patent or not, he has not indeed an exclusive right to it as against the public, or against those who in good faith acquire knowledge of it; but he has a property in it, which a court of chancery will protect against one who in violation of contract and breach of confidence undertakes to apply it to his own use, or to disclose it to third persons.[15]

This formulation is Lockean in nature;[16] the court noted both the right to an injunction for breach of trust and the inclusion of secret methods as part of the goodwill of a business that can be sold.[17] It discussed at length the fact that protection of secret information should go beyond simple breach of contract; the court also discussed both implied and express contracts and implied and express duties.[18]

By 1907, trade secret misappropriation was well embedded in the common law, and the California Supreme Court declared "[t]hat equity will always protect against the unwarranted disclosure of trade secrets and confidential communications and the like is, of course, settled beyond peradventure."[19]

At some point, courts and scholars shifted focus away from the strict property view. Professor Bone attributes this move to a shift to Legal Positivism and Realism, which rejected the "natural law" view of trade secrets as property in favor of social goals.[20] Justice Holmes's 1917 Supreme Court opinion in the *E.I. duPont deNemours Powder*

[11] 19 Pick. 523. *See also*, Jarvis & Lobdell v. Peck, 10 Paige. Ch. 118 (NY Chancery Ct. 1843); *Hard v. Seeley*, 47 Barb. 428 (NY Sup. Ct. 1865); 2 JOSEPH STORY, COMMENTARIES ON EQUITY JURISPRUDENCE § 952 (1839) (injunctions may issue to protect secrets learned by employees).

[12] 11 How. Pr. 382 (NY Sup. Ct. 1854).

[13] 26 How. Pr. 174 (NY Sup. Ct. 1863).

[14] *See* Kewanee Oil Co. v. Bicron Corp., 416 U.S. 470, 493 n.23 (1974); Warner-Lambert Co. v. Execuquest Corp., 691 N.E.2d 545, 547 (Mass. 1998).

[15] Peabody v. Norfolk, 98 Mass. 452, 458 (1868).

[16] The influence of Locke is clearer in an earlier quote in the opinion: "If a man establishes a business and makes it valuable by his skill and attention, the good will of that business is recognized by the law as property." *Id.* at 457.

[17] *Id.* at 458–59.

[18] *Id.* at 459.

[19] Empire Steam Laundry v. Lozier, 130 P. 1180, 1182 (Cal. 1913) (*citing Peabody*, 98 *Mass.* 452).

[20] Robert G. Bone, *A New Look at Trade Secret Law: Doctrine in Search of Justification*, 86 CAL. L. REV. 241, 259–60 (1998).

Co. v. *Masland*[21] case certainly had an effect on conventional thinking about trade secrets:

> The case has been considered as presenting a conflict between a right of property and a right to make a full defence.... We approach the question somewhat differently. The word property as applied to trade-marks and trade secrets is an unanalyzed expression of certain secondary consequences of the primary fact that the law makes some rudimentary requirements of good faith. Whether the plaintiffs have any valuable secret or not the defendant knows the facts, whatever they are, through a special confidence that he accepted. The property may be denied but the confidence cannot be. Therefore the starting point for the present matter is not property or due process of law, but that the defendant stood in confidential relations with the plaintiffs, or one of them.[22]

This resulted in the formulation of trade secrets in the *Restatement (First) of Torts* in which the theory of property is expressly rejected.[23] It is telling that trade secrets are in the section titled "Interference with Advantageous Economic Relations" – trade secrets were now clearly considered part of unfair competition law, and even today trade secrets are covered in the *Restatement (Third) of Unfair Competition*. The unfair competition and breach of confidence view of trade secrets continued and, to a large extent, still continues as the modern view of trade secrets.[24]

In 1979, the National Conference of Commissioners on Uniform State Laws recommended the UTSA.[25] The model law takes no position on whether or not trade secrets are property, but it does set forth a broader and more protective version of trade secret law than was present in the *Restatement*.[26] As mentioned earlier, the UTSA has been adopted in forty-seven states[27] over its thirty-year existence.[28]

B. *The Shift from Common Law to Statutory Law*

What happens, however, after a state moves from the common law to a uniform statute? The answer likely depends on a variety of factors, such as how long the statute has been in effect, how different the statute is from the common law, and whether the statute claims to preempt the common law.

21 E.I. duPont deNemours Powder Co. v. Masland, 244 U.S. 100 (1917).

22 *Id.* at 102.

23 Restatement (First) of Torts § 757 cmt. a (1939) ("The suggestion that one has a right to exclude others from the use of his trade secret because he has a right of property in the idea has been frequently advanced and rejected. The theory that has prevailed is that the protection is afforded only by a general duty of good faith and that the liability rests upon breach of this duty.").

24 Pamela Samuelson, *Information as Property: Do Ruckelshaus and Carpenter Signal a Changing Direction in Intellectual Property Law?*, 38 Cath. U. L. Rev. 365, 396 (1989).

25 Unif. Trade Secrets Act (amended 1985).

26 Some of these differences are discussed *supra* Part I.

27 1 Melvin F. Jager, Trade Secrets Law §3:29 (2010).

28 For further reading about the development of trade secrets law, *see*, Henry H. Perritt, Trade Secrets: A Practitioner's Guide § 1:7 (2nd ed. 2005); Sandeen, *supra* note 5; Fisk, *supra* note 6.

The UTSA presents an interesting conflict with respect to these factors. On the one hand, the drafters made clear that the statute was intended – in general, at least – to codify the existing common law of trade secrets.[29] On the other hand, there are marked differences between the common law and the UTSA. For example, with respect to the definition of trade secrets, some of the key differences are (i) the exception for "single use" information (such as a short-term marketing plan) in the *Restatement*, where such information can be trade secret under the UTSA; (ii) the requirement of continuous use in business in the *Restatement*, which is not required under the UTSA; and (iii) less emphasis on efforts to maintain secrecy in the *Restatement* than under the UTSA. With respect to misappropriation, the *Restatement* and the UTSA are similar, except the UTSA introduces the notions of "threatened" misappropriation and misappropriation by acquisition (even if unused), whereas the *Restatement* typically required the actual use of information.

This conflict is exacerbated by an explicit preemption clause in the UTSA.[30] In theory, any common law rules that differ from the statute are preempted. To complicate matters further, the American Law Institute has since withdrawn trade secrets from the *Restatement (Second) of Torts* in favor of their inclusion in the newer *Restatement (Third) of Unfair Competition*, which leads to two different restatements covering the same law. A few states (and federal and state agencies that deal with trade secrets) continue to use the *Restatement (Second) of Torts* definition. Although the *Restatement (Third) of Unfair Competition* is cited periodically, no state appears to use it as its primary source of trade secret law. It is unclear why a restatement of the law is necessary where a uniform statute covers the same acts, especially where the statute preempts any common law.[31] The notion of a *Restatement of Patents or Copyrights* seems silly in light of preemptive governing statutes.

The conflict between the application of codified common law and new/preemptive statutory law both raises questions and provides some possible answers. It raises the primary question of this chapter – how and when are the various courts in states that have adopted the UTSA applying the common law as opposed to the statute? One possible answer is that the application depends on the type of issue. One would expect that statutory provisions unique to the UTSA would apply UTSA reasoning, whereas rules that existed in common law would be governed by common law or UTSA reasoning.[32]

29 UNIF. TRADE SECRETS ACT prefatory note ("The Uniform Act codifies the basic principles of common law trade secret protection, preserving its essential distinctions from patent law.").

30 UNIF. TRADE SECRETS ACT § 7.

31 In fact, the *Restatement* may not follow the UTSA; for example, the *Restatement (Third) of Unfair Competition* defines trade secrets as "information that can be used in the operation of a business or other enterprise and that is sufficiently valuable and secret to afford an actual or potential economic advantage over others." RESTATEMENT (THIRD) OF UNFAIR COMPETITION § 39 (1995). This definition is decidedly different from that of the UTSA, even though the comments to section 39 of the *Restatement (Third) of Unfair Competition* state that the definition is intended to track the definitions set forth in the UTSA *Id.* cmt. a–f.

32 *See* Sandeen, *supra* note 5, for a normative perspective on this question.

II. THE UNIQUE DATASET

To study the law's transition, we[33] selected a sample of Federal District Court and State Appellate Court opinions from states that have adopted the UTSA. This is an important terminology of the study – we read primary "opinions." Those opinions cited to other judicial decisions, which are called "precedents" here. This framework is designed to determine whether any case precedent cited by an opinion applied UTSA principles or common law.[34] We also recorded whether the case cited to the UTSA itself, as well as to other authorities, such as the *Restatement*.

The primary opinions were selected to match those selected in an earlier randomized study of trade secret cases in the United States. Almeling et al. undertook extensive efforts to identify and randomly choose federal[35] and state[36] opinions relating to trade secrets. Almeling's data were preferable to new opinion selection for several reasons. First, it was comprehensive, representing a large and random sample of trade secret decisions. Second, in light of its comprehensive nature, it was expedient. Third, it allowed for direct comparison between this study and Almeling's study. For example, Almeling measured the number of times the *Restatement* was cited; this finding may conflict with findings of this study based on differing methodology. It may be that the *Restatement* was not cited by an observed court opinion, but precedential cases citing the *Restatement* were relied on by that same opinion. Use of the same dataset allows for apples-to-apples comparison of study results.

We studied a subset of the opinions selected by Almeling, most notably those that were issued in UTSA jurisdictions after the UTSA was in force there.[37] Because the superset of all opinions is random, the subset of UTSA opinions represents a random sample as well, although the sample is obviously self-selected – and purposely so – for those states that have adopted the UTSA. The result was 241 federal district court opinions and 279 state appellate court opinions for a total of 520 primary opinions.

Most of the opinions directly related to a trade secret misappropriation claim, but some related to other areas where trade secrets might play a role, such as litigation discovery or the enforcement of noncompetition agreements. These are called

33 "We" implies the author and his research assistants/coders, although the author made all final determinations if necessary.

34 Understandably, some of the opinions might also be precedents in other opinions; this endogeneity should not affect the analysis for two reasons. First, each opinion might have one or more legal issues, such that precedents that are also opinions will only affect the issues for which they are cited. Second, the application of UTSA or common law has a web-like character that the model should capture. If it turned out that UTSA law was always cited by opinions because those opinions were also precedents in other cases, then that still answers the question about the role and growth of common law in the observed opinions. In any event, time-based factors help capture any covariation by correcting for the timing of opinions in relation to precedents that are also studied opinions.

35 *See* David S. Almeling et al., A *Statistical Analysis of Trade Secret Litigation in Federal Courts*, 45 Gonz. L. Rev. 291, 298–99 (2010) (describing the federal case selection criteria).

36 *See* David S. Almeling et al., *A Statistical Analysis of Trade Secret Litigation in State Courts*, 46 GONZ. L. REV. 57, 62–63 (2011) (describing the state case selection criteria).

37 This excluded Massachusetts, New Jersey, New York, and Massachusetts.

"collateral" cases.[38] This study did exclude a few opinions that were so collateral that they did not mention any of the studied trade secret issues.

It should also be noted that there is some asymmetry between the state and federal data. The federal cases are district court opinions. These trial court rulings are the most likely to deal with the widest range of issues, but may also have less analysis than a circuit court opinion. The state cases are appellate court cases. Although state trial court opinions might have been preferred, it is unlikely that they would have provided the detail available in federal opinions. Anecdotally, at least, federal district courts write more detailed opinions than state trial courts. More practically, state trial opinions were too difficult to find, as discussed by Almeling. Thus, the state opinions may be different in kind from federal opinions. The analysis throughout this chapter distinguishes between state/federal opinions both to minimize any bias and to test whether the UTSA is applied differently by different courts.

Each opinion might have involved a variety of legal issues associated with trade secrets, such as the definition of trade secrets or the definition of misappropriation. Some of these issues, such as whether a claim is preempted by the statute, are uniquely associated with the UTSA. Other issues, such as whether there is irreparable harm supporting an injunction, would be relevant under the UTSA or the common law.

For each case and each issue, we identified the authorities, if any, relied on by the court's opinion. Those authorities were other judicial decisions (precedents), the UTSA statute, the *Restatement*, or no authorities. We excluded authorities that were cited but not relied on by the court; for example, if a court noted that a party had urged its acceptance of a precedent, but the court refused to do so, then we did not include that precedent in the study. For each case precedent cited by the opinion, we determined some "bibliographic" information, such as year of the precedent, whether the precedent was from the same state as the primary opinion, and whether the precedent was issued by a federal or state court.

We also coded for the key question whether the precedent relied on the UTSA as its governing law. A precedent's treatment was recorded for the legal issue for which it is cited: some precedents might apply the UTSA to analyze some issues but not others.

Some precedents were easy to categorize. For example, an opinion might have cited a precedent from before the UTSA was written; this precedent would not rely on the UTSA. A case might also cite a precedent from one of the non-UTSA states; this, too, would be a non-UTSA precedent. Other cases quite clearly applied UTSA principles.

Some cases, however, were more difficult to code; a case might cite a precedent that gave "lip service" to the UTSA, but then applied common law principles.[39] Lip

38 Risch, *supra* note 3, at 4–5.

39 This is where this study differs most from Almeling, *supra* note 35. Almeling recorded whether the UTSA was cited by a case. However, Almeling did not look at the judicial precedents cited by each case. Further, Almeling did not consider whether the UTSA was cited but then ignored by the case.

service occurred most often with respect to the definition of trade secrets. Typically, a precedent would cite the UTSA definition of trade secrets and then would analyze the information using the six-factor test set forth in the *Restatement (Second) of Torts*. Where the precedent failed to explain why or how the *Restatement* analysis was consistent with the UTSA definition, it was considered to be applying the common law principles of the *Restatement*, rather than the statutory definition of the UTSA.[40]

For example, *Learning Curve Toys, Inc.* v. *Play-Wood Toys, Inc.*,[41] discusses the *Restatement*'s factors, but includes the following passage: "[W]e interpret the common law factors as instructive guidelines for ascertaining whether a trade secret exists under the Act. The language of the Act itself makes no reference to these factors as independent requirements for trade secret status." We coded this case as following UTSA principles. In contrast, in *Electro-Craft Corp.* v. *Controlled Motion, Inc.*,[42] the court cited the UTSA and then explicitly adopted a definition of trade secrets that required "novelty," a rule created before passage of the UTSA and not present in the UTSA.[43] We coded this case as not following the UTSA, despite the lip service to the contrary.

Following the common law did not always require variance with the UTSA – the results and even the analysis may have been identical. The question was the source of precedential authority. Further, following the UTSA did not necessarily mean the "right" result. There are cases that reach conclusions most would agree are contrary to UTSA principles, but the analysis used to achieve each "wrong" ruling was still an interpretation of the statute rather than a reliance on the common law. For example, Gettings[44] argued that a Wisconsin court misapplied the UTSA on the issue of preemption of common law claims for misappropriation of confidential information. This study determined the same case to have applied UTSA principles on that issue, without regard to whether the ruling was "correct."

III. SUMMARY OF RESULTS

The results of the study are listed in the following tables by issue and by state/federal jurisdiction. The following two tables list each of the issues coded for the study – more than 3,500 observed citations from 520 opinions. The first table presents the data for core trade secret issues – definition and misappropriation. The second table addresses more tangential issues such as attorneys fees, injunctions, and preemption. Others,

40 At least two and, in some cases, five coders gave independent input on whether a particular case precedent applied the UTSA. The author made all final decisions.

41 342 F.3d 714, 722 (7th Cir. 2003).

42 332 N.W.2d 890, 898 (Minn. 1983).

43 *Id.* at 899.

44 *Supra* note 1.

such as the definition of trade secrets, are different in the UTSA, but not unique to it.

As expected, the two injunction-related legal issues – those least related to the UTSA and most related to the common law – resulted in the lowest UTSA law citation percentage. Further, preemption – a legal issue that would not exist but for the UTSA – resulted in the highest percentage of citation to the statute and UTSA-based cases. Other legal issues are a bit more mixed, although the trend appears to be that at least some UTSA law is primarily relied on by about 75–80 percent of the opinions and is at least cited in nearly 90 percent of the cases.

The percentage of cases citing primarily or even some UTSA law does not tell the whole story, however. First, the percentage of cases citing *only* UTSA law drops off precipitously – between 10 and 20 percent for core issues. For example, only 54 percent of the cases cite only UTSA case precedents or the statute. Furthermore, where opinions cite non-UTSA law, they do so in force. Depending on the issue, 46–65 percent of the cases cited followed the UTSA, with higher percentages for UTSA unique issues.

The differences are more pronounced with respect to federal courts. In general, federal courts appear to rely less on the UTSA. For noncore issues, the differences are large. For example, with respect to determining whether attorneys' fees should be paid, 76 percent of state opinions cited only to UTSA law, whereas only 42 percent of federal opinions cited only UTSA law. Even so, there were some significant differences among the core issues as well, albeit at much lower confidence thresholds. Fisher's exact tests showed statistically significant distribution differences for the following issues: definition of trade secret ($p < .1$), not readily ascertainable, ($p < .1$), definition of misappropriation ($p < .05$), irreparable harm ($p < .001$), and attorneys' fees ($p < .05$).

Examination of the source of citations partially explains the differences between federal and state courts. The following table shows the source of cited precedent for each of the studied legal issues. Some of the legal issues are unique to the UTSA's statutory provisions; these issues are marked with an asterisk. On the left are citations to state court case precedents, and on the right are citations to federal court case precedents. Each precedent is further categorized by the state of source. Thus, on the left are citations to a state court case from the same state as the court issuing the opinion (California court citing California state court case) as well as state courts outside the state (California court citing Illinois state court case). On the right are citations to federal court cases from the same state as the court issuing the opinion (California court citing N.D. Cal. court case), as well as to federal court cases from the federal district and appellate courts of other states and the Supreme Court (California court citing 7th Cir. court case). For each of these possibilities, the number of citations was tallied by state or federal opinion (California state court citing California state court case versus N.D. Cal. court citing California state court case).

Issue	Definition of trade secret		Not readily ascertainable*		Reasonable precautions*		Independent economic value*		Definition of misappropriate		Inevitable disclosure/ threatened misappropriation	
	State	Fed	State	Fed	State	Fed	State	Fed	State	Fed	State	Fed
Cases citing statute and UTSA case law	60	45	25	7	35	16	16	8	16	25	5	4
%	28.44%	23.08%	20.66%	15.56%	28.69%	18.18%	22.54%	18.60%	10.96%	18.80%	12.20%	8.70%
Cases citing statute only	51	56	48	14	47	35	32	25	74	63	18	21
%	24.17%	28.72%	39.67%	31.11%	38.52%	39.77%	45.07%	58.14%	50.68%	47.37%	43.90%	45.65%
Cases citing UTSA case law only	4	5	10	6	7	7	3	3	7	6	3	5
%	1.90%	2.56%	8.26%	13.33%	5.74%	7.95%	4.23%	6.98%	4.79%	4.51%	7.32%	10.87%
Cases citing statue, UTSA, and non-UTSA case law	41	44	15	3	14	11	7	0	12	7	9	5
%	19.43%	22.56%	12.40%	6.67%	11.48%	12.50%	9.86%	0.00%	8.22%	5.26%	21.95%	10.87%
Cases citing UTSA and non-UTSA case law	3	8	3	2	2	2	0	1	2	2	2	2
%	1.42%	4.10%	2.48%	4.44%	1.64%	2.27%	0.00%	2.33%	1.37%	1.50%	4.88%	4.35%
Cases citing statute and non-UTSA case law	42	22	7	10	9	6	6	1	8	15	3	3
%	19.91%	11.28%	5.79%	22.22%	7.38%	6.82%	8.45%	2.33%	5.48%	11.28%	7.32%	6.52%
Cases citing non-UTSA case law only	5	10	7	3	3	5	3	3	12	12	0	3
%	2.37%	5.13%	5.79%	6.67%	2.46%	5.68%	4.23%	6.98%	8.22%	9.02%	0.00%	6.52%
Cases citing no law	5	5	6	0	5	6	4	2	15	3	1	3
%	2.37%	2.56%	4.96%	0.00%	4.10%	6.82%	5.63%	4.65%	10.27%	2.26%	2.44%	6.52%
Total cases	211	195	121	45	122	88	71	43	146	133	41	46
% citing to some UTSA	95.26%	92.31%	89.26%	93.33%	93.44%	87.50%	90.14%	88.37%	81.51%	88.72%	97.56%	86.96%
% citing primarily UTSA law	75.36%	81.03%	83.47%	71.11%	86.07%	80.68%	81.69%	86.05%	76.03%	77.44%	90.24%	80.43%
% citing only UTSA law	54.50%	54.36%	68.60%	60.00%	72.95%	65.91%	71.83%	83.72%	66.44%	70.68%	63.41%	65.22%
% of all cases cited that follow UTSA	52.74%	42.37%	65.68%	51.67%	66.42%	50.00%	58.73%	61.54%	46.72%	47.83%	59.26%	43.14%

An asterisk (*) marks those issues that are unique to the UTSA.

Issue	Attorneys' fees*		Injunction public interest		Irreparable harm for injunction		Preemption*		Statute of limitations*	
	State	Fed	State	Fed	State	Fed	State	Fed	State	Fed
Cases citing statute and UTSA case law	5	1	0	0	1	0	12	21	0	3
%	13.16%	3.85%	0.00%	0.00%	2.78%	0.00%	41.38%	61.76%	0.00%	21.43%
Cases citing statute only	24	10	1	2	1	0	10	6	5	8
%	63.16%	38.46%	16.67%	3.92%	2.78%	0.00%	34.48%	17.65%	55.56%	57.14%
Cases citing UTSA case law only	0	0	0	0	4	0	1	3	0	0
%	0.00%	0.00%	0.00%	0.00%	11.11%	0.00%	3.45%	8.82%	0.00%	0.00%
Cases citing statue, UTSA, and non-UTSA case law	2	1	0	0	0	0	3	3	1	1
%	5.26%	3.85%	0.00%	0.00%	0.00%	0.00%	10.34%	8.82%	11.11%	7.14%
Cases citing UTSA and non-UTSA case law	0	0	0	1	1	8	0	0	0	0
%	0.00%	0.00%	0.00%	1.96%	2.78%	12.12%	0.00%	0.00%	0.00%	0.00%
Cases citing statute and non-UTSA case law	2	1	1	2	3	0	3	0	3	2
%	5.26%	3.85%	16.67%	3.92%	8.33%	0.00%	10.34%	0.00%	33.33%	14.29%
Cases citing non-UTSA case law only	2	6	2	21	24	40	0	0	0	0
%	5.26%	23.08%	33.33%	41.18%	66.67%	60.61%	0.00%	0.00%	0.00%	0.00%
Cases citing no law	3	7	2	25	2	18	0	1	0	0
%	7.89%	26.92%	33.33%	49.02%	5.56%	27.27%	0.00%	2.94%	0.00%	0.00%
Total cases	38	26	6	51	36	66	29	34	9	14
% citing to some UTSA	86.84%	50.00%	33.33%	9.80%	27.78%	12.12%	100.00%	97.06%	100.00%	100.00%
% primarily citing UTSA law	81.58%	46.15%	16.67%	5.88%	19.44%	12.12%	89.66%	97.06%	66.67%	85.71%
% citing only UTSA law	76.32%	42.31%	16.67%	3.92%	16.67%	0.00%	79.31%	88.24%	55.56%	78.57%
% of all cases cited that follow UTSA	44.44%	14.29%	0.00%	2.13%	9.68%	5.17%	88.89%	88.73%	38.39%	70.00%

An asterisk (*) marks those issues that are unique to the UTSA.

The results show clear differences in citation patterns. For example, state courts cite almost exclusively to the cases issuing from their own state courts (270), and rarely to federal cases, whether from their own state (29) or otherwise (39). Federal courts, in contrast, tend to cite the opinions of local state courts (186), local federal courts (118), and other federal courts (112) about equally.

Surprisingly, for many legal issues state court precedent from other states trailed the other categories by a wide margin in both state and federal opinions. These differences were accompanied by large differences in the percentage of cases that applied UTSA law. This seems to contradict one purpose of the UTSA, which is that interpretations in one state can guide another. It is unclear why judges rarely cite state courts outside their own. One intuition is that courts prefer to cite their own cases, but this does not explain federal cases, where courts cited cases from remote federal courts more than three times as often as they cited cases from remote state courts.[45]

The source of citation data is an important factor in the citation (or lack thereof) to UTSA-based precedent. Federal courts overwhelmingly cite cases from other federal jurisdictions, which overwhelmingly fail to apply UTSA principles. However, although a summary of the sources of precedent provides an interesting and helpful look into the role of common law in trade secret cases, summaries do not tell enough of the story because they do not reveal the conditions under which each source of citation will apply UTSA principles, nor can the table correct for preferences based on type of legal issue. Other factors may play a more important role in the decision to cite UTSA-based precedents.

As a result, these summary tables do not fully explain what factors might affect the citation of UTSA law. For example, although the type of issue appears to be important, it is unclear whether other factors have a greater effect that might be masked by the type of issue. Further, the tables show little about how long after passage of the UTSA the opinion issued or the court's experience with trade secret law.

Thus, a more detailed model may provide additional insight into the role of the common law in statutory trade secret jurisprudence.

IV. TESTING THE ROLE OF THE COMMON LAW

Several questions emerge from the background and summary data discussed in the previous part. The primary question is the extent to which the UTSA displaced the common law of trade secrets. A secondary question is whether application of the common law was appropriate – that is, confined to those legal issues where the UTSA merely codified the common law without change. Federal/state differences in UTSA law reliance and citation sources lead to two more questions. Are state courts more likely to rely on UTSA principles? Are state courts more likely to cite other

45 It is possible, though improbable, that federal courts did not have access to state court opinions from other states. That said, they likely had easier access to local precedent.

Jurisdiction of Precedent	State court precedents				Federal court precedents					
Source of Precedent	Same state		Other state		Same state		Other states		Sup. court	
Jurisdiction Citing Precedent	State	Fed.	State	Fed.	State	Fed.	State	Fed.	State	Fed.
% of all cases applying UTSA	54%	46%	56%	26%	67%	55%	50%	27%	0%	0%
Definition of trade secret	270	186	36	38	29	118	39	112	4	5
Reasonable Precautions*	83	32	14	21	16	29	23	48	1	4
Not Readily Ascertainable*	84	22	11	8	16	17	29	11	4	2
Ind. Econ. Value*	40	13	6	2	6	8	10	3	1	0
Definition of Misappropriate	77	36	23	7	9	42	12	25	1	2
Inevitable Disclosure/ Threatened Misappropriation	19	12	4	7	10	16	21	16	0	0
Attorneys' Fees*	18	7	0	0	0	4	0	4	0	1
Irreparable Harm for injunction	56	16	2	5	3	60	1	88	0	5
Injunction public interest	2	9	1	0	0	22	0	12	0	3
Statute of Limitations*	9	3	2	0	6	4	1	3	0	0
Preemption*	11	8	16	5	6	35	30	23	0	0
Grand Total	669	344	115	93	101	355	166	345	11	22

state courts? Finally, several questions relate to the factors correlated with whether a citation is based on the UTSA. Do only local citations follow the UTSA? Does court experience with trade secrecy law affect citations? Are courts more likely to cite UTSA case law as time passes?

These questions lead to four testable hypotheses:

H_0: *Opinions issued in UTSA jurisdictions cite cases that apply the UTSA rather than the common law of trade secrets.*

This may be the most difficult hypothesis to test with a model estimation. At most, any regression will loosely predict whether a court will cite a UTSA case under a particular set of conditions.

H_1: *Where opinions apply common law precedent, such cases were associated with legal issues not specific to the UTSA.*

Here, we would expect the likelihood of citation to the UTSA to increase when the legal issue is unique to the UTSA.

H_2: *State court opinions are more likely to cite UTSA-based case precedent than federal court opinions.*

Testing this hypothesis should be straightforward – state courts should be more likely to cite case precedents that apply UTSA principles.

H_3: *State court case precedent is more likely to follow UTSA principles than federal case precedents.*

Like the previous hypothesis, this one can be tested by examining whether state court precedents are more likely to follow the UTSA, all other variables being equal.

These hypotheses, as well as the other correlations, can be tested using the same model.

A. *The Model*

The role of the common law can be represented by the propensity of a judge to apply a common law precedent, as opposed to UTSA-based precedent. Determining this propensity presents a definitional challenge, because many might consider case law applying and interpreting a statute to be a common law penumbra around the statute. Although that may be true, the model here need not consider this definitional imprecision. Testing the continuing role of common law among case precedents differs slightly from the question presented in the earlier tables, which present overall citation patterns, including to the statute; conclusions about the shift from common law to the UTSA will depend on one's view of both whether citation to just the statute is enough to consider a case UTSA-based and what percentage of citation is sufficient.

However, because courts often pay lip service to the statute by citing and then disregarding it, the more appropriate model looks only at the conscious choice by the court to cite precedential case law to support its analysis. The case citation model, therefore, asks a different question. If a court is inclined to cite case precedent to support, interpret, or otherwise decide a legal issue, what is the likelihood that the court will select precedent that applies the UTSA? This question is an alternative, though not necessarily better, way to look at the continuing role of the common law. Given that the common law must necessarily rely on case precedent, then looking at its continuing role, if any, requires an apples-to-apples comparison of citation to UTSA and non-UTSA–based case law. Of course, that comparison should consider whether the court has also cited to the statute itself, because doing so should have an effect on whether common law case is cited.

Thus, in this model, common law means a precedent that applies the principles of the *Restatement* or any other common law of trade secrets as it existed before the UTSA.[46] Statutory-based case law – UTSA-based precedents – means a case precedent that interprets or applies the principles of the UTSA.

Mathematically, this might look like

$$\overline{Y} = \sum_n W_n F_n$$

where $\overline{Y}$ is the propensity of a court to apply UTSA law in any given opinion, F_n are a series of factors that affect that propensity, and W_n are the weights associated with each factor. Where $\overline{Y} > 0$, the court applies UTSA law, and where $\overline{Y} \leq 0$ the court applies the common law. The factors that might affect the court's propensity include at least those discussed earlier: the type of legal issue, the timing of the state's adoption of the UTSA, the amount of available in-state law, and the source of any out-of-state citations.

Of course, $\overline{Y}$ cannot be directly observed. Instead, past revealed preferences of courts deciding cases in UTSA states must serve as a proxy. Those preferences are revealed in a variety of cases, and the data points are the courts' own citations of common and UTSA case law.

Using these data points, the estimated equation looks like this:

$$y = \sum_n w_n f_n + \varepsilon$$

where y is the estimated dependent variable, whether a particular case precedent cited by a court opinion applies UTSA law. In turn, f_n is each independent factor measured by the study as described later, whereas w_n represents the estimated coefficient for each factor. The error term, ε, may be either normally or logistically distributed.[47]

46 It turns out that the *Restatement* itself is rarely cited; instead courts cite to other cases, which may have, in turn, relied on the *Restatement*. Almeling et al., *supra* note 36, at 57, 78–79.

47 Each assumption was tested using the appropriate estimation technique.

B. *Factors in the Model*

The dependent variable was coded as follows: UTSACase (y) is 1 where the precedent case applies UTSA principles and 0 where the precedent applies only common principles with respect to the issue for which it is cited.

The data allowed for coefficient estimates for several factors, as follows:

Federal is 1 where the citing opinion was issued by a federal court and 0 where the case was issued by a state court. Federal courts might differentially cite precedents that rely on the UTSA.

UTSAIssue is 1 where the issue is unique to the UTSA and 0 where the issue might apply in the common law as well. One would expect UTSA-based legal issues to cite UTSA precedents.

Collateral is 1 where the citing opinion is not a trade secret misappropriation case and 0 where the opinion is a typical misappropriation action. As discussed in *A Failure of Uniform Laws?*, one would expect collateral opinions to worry less about applying statutory principles.

SameState (state court precedent from the same state as the opinion), OtherState, SameFed (federal precedent from the same state as the opinion), OtherFed, Supreme Court are 1 if the precedent fits into the appropriate category and 0 if it does not. Federal appellate courts were coded by the lower court that heard the case, so that appeals to the same circuit, but from other states in the circuit, were considered OtherFed. These factors allow modeling of the influence of proximity and jurisdiction on statutory application.

NumUTSA is the count of other UTSA precedents in the same opinion *for the same legal issue*. This factor serves two purposes. First, it allows for estimation of the judge's individual propensity to cite UTSA law. In theory, the more UTSA cases are cited, the more likely that the marginal case will also be UTSA. Second, it allows for some proportionality/self-selection correction. Otherwise, one case with many cites could drown out the results of other cases. Clustering was also used in the regression to account for high covariance within any given opinion.

NumNoCites is the total number of issues in the same opinion that are discussed without statutory or precedential authority. In theory, the more issues discussed without citation, the more likely that any precedent cited will be based on the common law. Thus, one would expect this coefficient to be negative.

IssueStatute is 1 if the opinion also cites to the UTSA *for the same legal issue* and 0 if the opinion does not cite to the statute for that issue. This factor tests whether citation to the statute increases the propensity of the court to cite precedential cases that also apply on the UTSA.

NumStatute is the total number of times in the same opinion that the statute is cited *for all legal issues*. In theory, the more issues that involve citation of the statute, the more likely any precedent cited will be based on the UTSA. This factor captures issues in the case for which no case precedent is cited, because the dependent variable UTSACase will not be observed for issues where only the statute was cited without any supporting case precedent.

ActivityGroup is a number from 1 to 8 that represents the state's "experience" with trade secret law.[48] It is based on the number of *state court* (not federal) decisions relating to trade secrets. The intuition is that state court precedents should guide local federal courts,[49] and the more state court experience there is, the more likely the statute will be followed by both state and federal courts. The groupings are nonlinear,[50] and some groups have only a single state.

UTSAYear is the difference between the year of the case and the year the UTSA became effective in a state. It is another way to estimate a state's "experience" with the UTSA. In theory, the longer the UTSA has been in force in the state, the more likely any cited precedent will apply UTSA principles.[51]

The following table presents some summary statistics about the variables in the model.

	Categorical		Continuous			
N = 2221	N (0)	N (1)	Mean	Std. Dev.	Min	Max
Utsacase	1166	1055				
Isfederal	1062	1159				
isutsaissue	1461	760				
Collateral	2149	72				
Samestate	1208	1013				
Otherstate	2013	208				
Samefed	1765	456				
Otherfed	1710	511				
Numutsa			1.99	2.932	0	23
numstatute			3.12	1.872	0	7
issuestatute	611	1610				
numnocites			0.16	0.433	0	3
activitygroup						
1	1781	440				
2	1902	319				
3	1324	827				
4	2135	86				
5	2116	105				
6	0	0				
7	1869	352				
Utsayear			15.253	6.234	0	28

48 Population and population density were tested as proxies for a state's litigation experience, but the results were not significant. This is not surprising, because there is little reason to believe that population affects citation patterns.

49 Erie R.R. v. Tompkins, 304 U.S. 64 (1938).

50 The breakdowns were as follows: 1–5 cases (group 1), 6–10 (2), 11–15 (3), 16–25 (4), 26–35 (5), 36–45 (6), 46+ (7). Group 6 was empty – no states had between 36 and 45 cases.

51 We tested an alternative model including the absolute passage of time since 1979, rather than the time since the UTSA was enacted in the state. In contrast to UTSAYear, this factor is absolute. The factor was highly correlated with UTSAYear (.66) and dropped from the model.

C. *Model Estimation*

The Appendix presents results of the probit model estimation with marginal effects and diagnostic information.[52] The estimation was performed by clustering the data by primary opinion, because the propensity of a given judge to cite a UTSA-based case in a given opinion will not necessarily be independent from the propensity with respect to the other citations in the opinion. In other words, clustering helps account for individual preferences of the opinion's author. The model is statistically significant, with a p value of 0.000. Goodness-of-fit tests show a 75 percent prediction probability when the data are run through the estimation.

1. Testing H_0: Do Courts Apply UTSA law?

Testing the null hypothesis is not straightforward; the obvious choice would be to test the probability that any given cited case applies UTSA law. That probability is .47, which is no surprise given that it is the mean of the dependent variable UTSACase. It is also not surprising given the percentage of all cited cases that apply the UTSA listed on the bottom row in the tables.

A more nuanced test considers the marginal probability that a court *today* in a typical case will cite UTSA-based case precedents. The base case deals directly with trade secret misappropriation (Collateral = 0) and cites to some law (NumNoCites = 0). Because the hypothesis is tested today, UTSAYear is arbitrarily large (say, twenty years, to represent UTSA passage in 1991).[53] Because it is marginal, the assumption is that no other UTSA-based cases have been cited (NumUTSA = 0). Finally, because most opinions at least cite to the statute, the base case assumes that IssueStatute is 1 and that NumStatutes is 1.

Given these assumptions, the estimated probability is .49 ($p < .001$), barely more than the mean. This implies that, across all issues, courts will cite to a UTSA case only about half the time, even if they have already cited to the statute. This result is certainly not enough to reject the hypothesis that UTSA-based precedent has replaced common law precedent.

However, not all legal issues present the same need to apply UTSA case law, so it may be helpful to further differentiate between those cases that are uniquely based on the UTSA and those that are not (UTSAIssue). As noted later, the hypothesis that these two types of issues are the same can be rejected. When UTSAIssue is assumed equal to 1, the marginal probability that a court will cite a case applying UTSA principles is .61 ($p < .001$). When UTSAIssue is assumed equal to 0, the marginal probability that a court will cite a UTSA case is .42 ($p < .001$). In other

[52] A logit model yielded similar results. The supremecourt independent variable was dropped from the estimation. It was 0 in most cases and thus perfectly predicted the independent variable. Further, it was perfectly collinear with the other source dummies (samestate, otherstate, samefed, and otherfed), such that it would have been dropped anyway.

[53] Every year change adjusts the probability about one percent.

words, even where a court is confronted with a legal issue introduced by the UTSA, even where it has cited the statute, and even where twenty years have passed since the enactment of the UTSA, it is still only 61 percent likely to cite a case that applies UTSA principles. This is not enough to conclude that UTSA-based case analysis has superseded common law analysis. The results are mathematically consistent with the opinion-by-opinion tabulation showing reliance on the UTSA because many of the cases in the table cited only to the statute; the implications of the apparent differences between the estimation and the summary tables are discussed in the conclusion.

2. Testing H_1: Do Issues Unique to the UTSA Increase the Propensity to Cite UTSA-Based Cases?

As expected, the coefficient on IsUTSAissue is both positive and statistically significant. This implies that legal issues unique to UTSA have a positive effect on whether a cited precedent applies UTSA law. The marginal effect appears to increase the likelihood that any given case cited applies UTSA principles about 20 percent.

3. Testing H_2: Are State Courts More Likely to Cite UTSA-Based Case Precedents than Federal Courts?

The clear preference for federal courts to cite federal court precedents rather than state court precedents implies that state courts are more likely to cite cases applying UTSA principles, but surprisingly the null hypothesis cannot be rejected.

The coefficient associated with IsFederal is not statistically significant and does not affect the model when removed.[54] Further, its marginal magnitude (though negative) is only .05, such that it would not affect the dependent variable much even if it were significant.

The Appendix further tests this hypothesis by calculating the marginal effects of a change from state to federal court for any given source of citation. The marginal effect is insignificant, both statistically and practically.

The reason for this result can probably be explained by examining the marginal effects of precedent citations from state and federal courts. Although state courts favor citation of state court precedents, and federal courts favor citation of federal court precedents, the propensity for any citation to be UTSA-based is actually higher for federal citations from the same state. This offsets the fact that federal citations from other states are markedly lower – and that federal courts almost exclusively used such citations.

54 It also does not become significant when citation source dummies are removed from the estimation, as discussed further with respect to alternative models tested.

4. Testing H_3: Are State Court Precedents More Likely to Apply the UTSA?

The coefficients on the source of the citation (state/federal, in-state/out-of-state) are all statistically significant, each with a z-score more than 30. Interestingly, the marginal effect is positive for all of them, seemingly implying that any citation is likely to be a UTSA precedent. Of course, this cannot be true, because UTSA is often 0. This effect is probably caused by the omitted variable supremecourt, which *never* applied UTSA law. Thus, where each of the included dummies is 0, then the dependent variable UTSACase must necessarily be 0. As a result, if the citation comes from a source other than the U.S. Supreme Court (meaning every source dummy in the model), then it must necessarily increase the chances that UTSACase will be 1.[55] Indeed, the marginal effect of each hovers near the mean of the dependent variable UTSACase (.47); because one of the dummies must be present in virtually every case, the practical marginal effect is only slightly positive (about .08 for SameFed) and at worst slightly negative (about –.03 for OtherFed).

This means that these variables do not add much explanatory power to the overall model, which is reported as Alternative 2 in the Appendix. Removing these dummy variables leads to little decrease in fit. The coefficients and marginal effects stay roughly the same,[56] and the prediction rate remains at 74 percent, though the pseudo R^2 drops to .20. Although the Wald chi-squared score drops by nearly 1,000, both models are significant at $p < .001$.

However, leaving the variables in the model does provide some useful information; the best way to consider the role of source is to compare the differing magnitude of their marginal effects rather than of their absolute effects. This comparison allows for testing of H_3, to determine whether state court precedents are more likely to apply UTSA principles.

It appears that citations from federal case precedents from other states are less likely to apply UTSA principles. Citation to in-state law adds approximately 10 percent to the probability that the citation will be UTSA-based case law. This might imply a bias against the UTSA by federal courts (and a rejection of the null hypothesis). However, the highest likelihood of UTSA law is associated with federal cases from the same state. Further, H_2 cannot be rejected, which implies a lack of bias by federal courts doing the *citing*; by extension, the federal courts that are being *cited to* are likely not biased. Together with the effects associated with state court case law,[57] the results imply that federal courts do a good job of applying UTSA law if that law

55 Note that the constant is both negative and of great magnitude (−6.7 in a model where the dependent variable never exceeds 1). Given that one of the source dummies is set in virtually every observation, it combines with the constant to make a sort of "hybrid" constant based on citation source.

56 The primary difference is that the constant increases from −6.7 to −1.44, which further supports the "hybrid constant" theory discussed in note 55.

57 There is a 5 percent differential effect on probabilities between state court law cited from the same state versus other states.

comes from its own state (from either state or federal courts), but that out-of-state citations (whether state or federal) are based more on helpful fact patterns than on close ties to the UTSA. Locally based citation is consistent with citation studies in other areas.[58]

D. *Analysis of Other Factors*

Other factors in the model yield some interesting results. As expected, IssueStatute is both significant and practically important with a marginal effect of .175. One would expect that, if an opinion cites the statute with respect to a particular legal issue, any case law associated with that issue is more likely to apply UTSA principles. Surprisingly, the coefficient on NumStatute is both statistically significant and negative in magnitude. This is counter to the expectation. Perhaps it means that courts that cite the statute once will cite UTSA law, but if they cite it for multiple legal issues, they find little need to cite UTSA cases for each issue as well.[59] This theory is consistent with the expectedly negative coefficient on NumNoCites, the number of issues that had no citation at all. However, NumNoCites is not statistically significant.

The number of times an opinion cites other UTSA cases with respect to the same legal issue (NumUTSA), although statistically significant, has less than half the marginal effect (.069) than citation to the statute itself. However, this is a continuous variable rather than a dummy, which means that citation to two other UTSA cases would increase this likelihood that another case citation would apply UTSA law by 14 percent.

Finally, it appears that experience with the UTSA does have some positive correlation with the citation of UTSA law. Although the marginal effect is small (.01), it adds up as years pass. The probability that a given case citation will apply the UTSA increases by nearly 23 percent between UTSAYear 1 and 20.

However, a state's volume of trade secret cases is not statistically significant for any ActivityGroup. Furthermore, the signs alternate between positive and negative with no seeming pattern, and the marginal effects are small as well. Alternative tests for activity levels are discussed later.

The combination of results relating to UTSAYear and ActivityGroup is curious. One would expect that both more trade secret litigation and more years under the UTSA would lead to more UTSA-based case law for opinions to cite. However, it appears that only time makes a significant difference. Perhaps this is because time

58 *See, e.g.*, Adam B. Jaffe, *et al.*, *Geographic Localization of Knowledge Spillovers as Evidenced by Patent Citations*, 108 Q. J. ECON. 577 (1993).

59 An unreported estimation drops IssueStatute. In that estimation, the coefficient on NumStatute remains negative, but gets smaller and is no longer statistically significant. This implies that the effect of citing the statute for a legal issue is different from the effect of citing the statute multiple times.

increases the number of citations available in other states as well, whereas the volume of litigation in a state only affects in-state precedent.

E. *Alternative Models and Sensitivity Analysis*

Also reported are three alternative models. The first alternative drops the IsFederal variable because it was partially correlated with the source dummies, as shown in the earlier table. The results had virtually no effect on the model's other estimations, either in terms of magnitude or significance. This reinforces the finding that H_2 cannot be rejected. The jurisdiction of the court issuing the opinion does not appear to make a difference beyond any difference once the source of the citation is determined.

The second alternative estimation drops the source citations, but keeps IsFederal. The theory was that, if the source of citation is caused by federal/state distinctions, then IsFederal would become significant in the absence of source citations. This was not the case; whereas the two variables are correlated, they are not so strongly correlated to be endogenous. Inclusion of both IsFederal and the source citations is important to testing whether state or federal courts are more likely to cite to UTSA-based case precedent.

The third alternative drops the ActivityGroup variable to test for sensitivity of the model to this statistically insignificant measurement. The results appear similar to the primary model. Another unreported alternative tested each state to ensure that activitygroup is not rendered insignificant due to the grouping of states in groups 1–3 as compared to sparse representation in more active groups. The results yielded only a single state with a statistically significant impact on the dependent variable.

Finally, an unreported Heckman selection probit model was tested on all 3,546 data points. Because the estimation only models the observed citations – that is, where a case precedent was actually cited – it might lose information associated with the unestimated data: those where only a statute was cited (or nothing was cited at all). The Heckman model allows for a two-step estimation that includes the likelihood that any case will be cited at all. The results of this estimation yielded similar results as the reported model, both in magnitude and significance of coefficients. Inclusion of the numstatute and NumNoCites variables in the primary model may have assisted in reconciling the two estimations by factoring in "unobserved" but related information.

CONCLUSION AND IMPLICATIONS

With respect to the core question – whether the UTSA has displaced the common law – the results of this study are ambiguous. The tabular data imply that courts rely on UTSA principles much of the time. They cite to the statute alone, and they cite to the statute and UTSA-based cases (sometimes along with common law cases). But they also cite to the statute and non-UTSA cases without any citation to UTSA cases, and they sometimes cite only common law cases with no mention of the UTSA at all.

On margin, even when courts have cited the statute, they are about as likely to also cite to non-UTSA cases. However, they are slightly more likely to rely on UTSA-based case precedents with those issues that are unique to the UTSA, such as preemption.

These apparently contradictory conclusions may be reconciled. Where the court cites only to the statute, the statutory interpretation or factual pattern may be self-revealing. This means that courts do, in fact, recognize that they are in states that follow the UTSA and cite the statute for it. Where, however, there is a need for any kind of interpretation, guidance, or other gloss on the statute, courts are more willing to look to the common law for help. This results in a pattern where many of the opinions rely only on UTSA principled precedent, but also where many of the opinions look to the common law or to both.

The reasons for this phenomenon may vary. A qualitative analysis of the opinions shows a variety of reasons that common law cases continue to be cited. In the rare case, the court simply disregards the statute by failing to mention it, instead discussing some older case for general propositions that are surely false under the UTSA (e.g., "marketing plans cannot be trade secrets"). In many cases, courts cite the common law for general propositions that are also true under a UTSA analysis (e.g., "customer lists can be trade secrets"). This type of citation does not always lead to UTSA-based analysis (e.g., "the common law provided that customer lists must be printed to be trade secrets, and therefore they must be printed now"). Finally, some courts cite to similar fact patterns associated with older cases (e.g., "not requiring employees to sign confidentiality agreements voids trade secrecy").

In sum, the common law has a continuing influence in UTSA states, though not necessarily in bad ways. After all, the model confirmed several factors that were expected to positively influence the propensity to cite UTSA precedents, including the passage of time. Further, factors that were supposed to have negative effects on that propensity, such as the federal/state court divide and the number of issues without any citation, were statistically insignificant. Although the UTSA does not appear to fulfill the goal of providing neighboring states with statute-based case precedents to apply, it does provide a rich history that courts draw on depending on the circumstances.

APPENDIX I

Utsacase	Primary model Coef. (Std. Err.)	Primary model Marginal Effect[60]	Alternate 1 Coef. (Std. Err.)	Alternate 2 Coef. (Std. Err.)	Alternate 3 Coef. (Std. Err.)
Isfederal	−.134 (.109)	−.041		−.118 (.106)	−.162 (.115)
Isutsaissue	.505 (.075)***	.158	.523 (.077)***	.477 (.078)***	.519 (.073)***
Collateral	−.093 (.224)	−.028	−.042 (.223)	−.173 (.232)	−.108 (.209)
Samestate	5.466 (.174)***	.533	5.465 (.164)***		5.405 (.137)***
Otherstate	5.142 (.245)***	.505	5.134 (.241)***		5.022 (.209)***
Samefed	5.759 (.205)***	.552	5.714 (.187)***		5.673 (.167)***
Otherfed	4.99 (.212)***	.441	4.961 (.202)***		4.938 (.174)***
Numutsa	.228 (.074)**	.069	.228 (.075)**	.220 (.071)**	.224 (.074)**
Numstatute	−.063 (.027)*	−.019	−.059 (.028)**	−.080 (0.029)**	−.074 (.029)**
Issuestatute	.567 (.100)***	.175	.583 (.098)***	.564 (.102)***	.581 (.100)***
Numnocites	−.002 (.103)	−.001	−.005 (.102)	.038 (.099)	−.036 (.105)
activitygroup					
1	−.111 (0.248)	−.034	−.051 (.250)	−.0915 (0.244)	
2	−.078 (.269)	−.024	−.017 (.271)	.068 (.268)	
3	−.235 (.249)	−.072	−.181 (.242)	−.030 (.246)	
4	.450 (.360)	.136	.542 (.361)	.609 (.366)	
5	−.142 (.293)	−.043	−.039 (.293)	.019 (.299)	
7	.124 (.258)	.038	.189 (.254)	.296 (.251)	
Utsayear	.039 (.008)***	.011	0.041 (.009)***	.042 (.009)***	.040 (.007)***
Constant	−6.702 (.319)***		−6.869 (0.322)***	−1.44 (.309)***	−6.688 (.213)***

Numbers in parenthesis indicate robust standard errors, clustered on primary opinion.
* $p < .05$; ** $p < .01$; *** $p < .001$

Diagnostics for primary model:

Number of obs = 2,221, Number of covariate patterns = 1,132

(Std. Err. adjusted for 425 clusters in caseid)

Wald chi2(18) = 1405.47, Prob > chi2 = 0.0000

Pearson chi2(1113) = 186070.61, Prob > chi2 = 0.0000

D(2201): 2332.789, LR(18): 740.621, Prob > LR: 0.000

McFadden's R2: 0.241, McFadden's Adj R2: 0.228

Correct prediction rate: 75.51%, Percent reduction in error: 48.44%

Log-Likelihood Intercept Only: −1536.705, Log-Likelihood Full Model: −1166.395

Variance of y*: 2.387, Variance of error: 1.000

60 Marginal effects were calculated using –margins- command in stata, with dummy variables treated as factors. The resulting marginal effects are the discrete differences from moving the dummy from 0 to 1.

Marginal effects testing on federal v. state court opinions for fixed source of precedent:

dy/dx w.r.t. : isfederal	dy/dx	Std. Err.	P>|z|
At *samestate* = 1	−.0208	.017	.220
At *otherstate* = 1	−.004	.003	.212
At *samefed* = 1	−.009	.008	.223
At *otherfed* = 1	−.009	.007	.220

8

The Impact of Codification on the Judicial Development of Copyright

*Christopher S. Yoo**

INTRODUCTION

Ever since *Wheaton* v. *Peters* rejected the idea of a robust vision of common law copyright,[1] modern copyright has been widely acknowledged to be statutory in nature. At the same time, before 1976, the copyright statutes employed general language that left most of the key interpretive issues to the courts. Over time, courts embraced this role, fashioning a wide variety of doctrines that gave content to the broad directives contained in the statute and developing new law where necessary to govern important situations that Congress did not address.[2]

The Copyright Act of 1976 took a different approach. Congress replaced much of the general language with more detailed and specific statutory provisions. A key question is what effect, if any, did this reform legislation have on the role of courts in the development of copyright. As a general matter, "[w]hen the legislature enters the field, the courts operate under a narrower delegation."[3] Under some theories of legisprudence, codification displaces judicial development altogether. Under other theories, judicial lawmaking can continue, but subject to greater constraints.

Since the enactment of the 1976 Act, courts have continued to engage in common law development in many important areas of copyright law. The question is

* John H. Chestnut Professor of Law, Communication, and Computer & Information Science and Founding Director, Center for Technology, Innovation and Competition at the University of Pennsylvania. I would like to thank John Woo for his outstanding research assistance.

[1] 33 U.S. (8 Pet.) 591, 658–62 (1834).

[2] *See, e.g.*, Pierre N. Leval, *An Assembly of Idiots?*, 34 CONN. L. REV. 1049, 1050, 1061–62 (2002); Joseph P. Liu, *Regulatory Copyright*, 83 N.C. L. REV. 88, 101 (2004); Peter S. Menell & David Nimmer, *Unwinding Sony*, 95 CAL. L. REV. 941, 996, 998 (2007).

[3] Samuel Estreicher, *Judicial Nullification: Guido Calabresi's Uncommon Common Law for a Statutory Age*, 57 N.Y.U. L. REV. 1126, 1164 (1982).

whether and how this practice can be squared with the dominant understanding that recognizes the supremacy of the legislature in determining the scope of the law. Some of the innovations raise unique issues, in that they take place in areas where Congress has been silent with respect to copyright, but has enacted specific provisions with respect to patent. It is an open question whether the patent provisions establish broad policies that should be applied to copyright law or whether the failure to enact parallel provisions with respect to copyright gives rise to a negative inference that renders such importation illegitimate.

Arguments raised in the Supreme Court during the briefing and oral argument for *Kirtsaeng* v. *John Wiley & Sons* have heightened the importance of determining the impact of codification on the continued judicial development of copyright. The brief filed by the United States as amicus curiae argued that, even though Congress had twice codified the first sale doctrine, the Supreme Court retained considerable authority to adjust its contours.[4] In so arguing, the government implicitly took the position, largely accepted by the Court, that codification did not necessarily deprive precodification decisions of vitality or foreclose courts from continuing to shape and reshape copyright law.

The propriety of courts continuing to play an active role in articulating and extending copyright depends on the theory one adopts regarding the proper relationship between courts and legislatures. From some viewpoints, courts' ongoing willingness to develop the law is altogether proper and appropriate. From other perspectives, it is potentially problematic.

This chapter offers an assessment of the propriety of these courts' actions. Part I describes four areas in which courts have continued to develop copyright law since 1976: fair use, copyright misuse, third-party liability, and the first sale doctrine. Part II reviews the leading theories of legisprudence, examining those that accord courts wide latitude, no latitude, and limited authority to develop the law. Part III applies these theories to the four substantive areas described in Part I, while offering some reflections on the judiciary's authority in areas where Congress has not yet acted.

I. FOUR EXAMPLES OF POSTCODIFICATION JUDICIAL DEVELOPMENT OF COPYRIGHT LAW

The enactment of more specific provisions in the Copyright Act of 1976 might have been expected to attenuate the judicial development of copyright. In a number of areas, however, courts have continued to play an active role in shaping and reshaping the contours of copyright law. Four of the most active areas are fair use, copyright misuse, third-party liability, and the first sale doctrine.

4 Brief for the United States as Amicus Curiae Supporting Respondent at 27–29, 133 S. Ct. 1351 (2013) (mem.) (No. 11-697).

A. *Fair Use*

The roots of the fair use doctrine are typically traced to *Folsom* v. *Marsh*, in which Justice Story held that a two-volume work of George Washington's letters and papers that copied 388 pages of material from a previous twelve-volume set of Washington's papers infringed the original work's copyright.[5] Story noted, however, that access to Washington's papers might be justifiable depending on "the nature and objects of the selections made, the quantity and value or the materials used, and the degree in which the use may prejudice the sale, or diminish the profits, or supersede the objects, of the original work."[6]

Subsequent courts expanded on Justice Story's suggestion and began to develop the doctrine of fair use.[7] The resulting doctrine was so variegated that courts criticized it as "the most troublesome in the whole area of copyright"[8] and "so flexible as virtually to defy definition."[9] The two fair use cases that reached the Supreme Court provided little guidance, because both were affirmed without opinion by an equally divided Court, a resolution that carries no precedential value.[10] The major copyright reform legislation enacted in 1909 did not include a provision on fair use.[11]

Congress finally codified fair use in 1976. The statute is striking in its level of detail, specifically providing that "the fair use of a copyrighted work . . . for purposes such as criticism, comment, news reporting, teaching (including multiple copies for classroom use), scholarship, or research, is not an infringement of copyright."[12] The stature further provides,

> In determining whether the use made of a work in any particular case is a fair use the factors to be considered shall include –
>
> (1) the purpose and character of the use, including whether such use is of a commercial nature or is for nonprofit educational purposes;
> (2) the nature of the copyrighted work;
> (3) the amount and substantiality of the portion used in relation to the copyrighted work as a whole; and
> (4) the effect of the use upon the potential market for or value of the copyrighted work.[13]

[5] 9 F. Cas. 342, 348 (C.C.D. Mass. 1841) (Story, J.).
[6] *Id.*
[7] For a review of the early judicial development of the fair use doctrine, see WILLIAM F. PATRY, THE FAIR USE IN COPYRIGHT LAW (2d ed. 1995).
[8] Dellar v. Samuel Goldwyn, Inc. 104 F.2d 661, 662 (2d Cir. 1939).
[9] Time, Inc. v. Bernard Geis Assocs., 293 F. Supp. 130, 144 (S.D.N.Y. 1968).
[10] *See* Benny v. Loew's Inc., 239 F.2d 532 (9th Cir. 1956), *aff'd by an equally divided court sub nom.* CBS, Inc. v. Loew's Inc., 356 U.S. 43 (1958); Williams & Wilkins Co. v. United States, 487 F.2d 1345, 1362 (Ct. Cl. 1973), *aff'd by an equally divided court*, 420 U.S. 376 (1975).
[11] *See* Sony Corp. of Am. v. Universal City Studios, Inc., 464 U.S. 417, 447 n.29 (1984) ("The Copyright Act of 1909 . . . did not have a 'fair use' provision" (citation omitted)).
[12] 17 U.S.C. § 107.
[13] *Id.*

Moreover, "[t]he fact that a work is unpublished shall not itself bar a finding of fair use if such finding is made upon consideration of all the above factors."[14]

Although most courts have organized their discussions of fair use around these four factors, some courts have continued to incorporate others into their analysis.[15] These include such considerations as bad faith,[16] the public interest,[17] and privacy implications.[18]

B. *Copyright Misuse*

Another area of copyright law in which courts have continued to innovate since the enactment of the 1976 Act is copyright misuse. The doctrine was first recognized in the Fourth Circuit's 1990 decision in *Lasercomb America, Inc.* v. *Reynolds*, which held that "a misuse of copyright defense is inherent in the law of copyright just as a misuse of patent defense is inherent in patent law."[19] The court based its decision on the clear establishment of a patent misuse defense by statute, the parallels between patent and copyright under early English law, and "the similarity of the policies underlying patent and copyright."[20]

Since the Fourth Circuit's *Lasercomb* decision, three additional circuits have recognized copyright misuse as a defense,[21] whereas three other circuits have declined to adopt it.[22] In so doing, some courts have begun to express some discomfort with the lack of statutory authorization. For example, in *Atari Games Corp.* v. *Nintendo of America Inc.*, the Federal Circuit noted that the Supreme Court had given its tacit approval of the copyright misuse defense in *Loew's*, subject to the reservation that "[i]n the absence of any statutory entitlement to a copyright misuse defense, however, the defense is solely an equitable doctrine."[23]

Interestingly, some differences in the application of copyright misuse and patent. misuse have begun to emerge. For example, a 1988 amendment to the patent

14 *Id.*

15 *See* 4 Melville B. Nimmer & David Nimmer, Nimmer on Copyright § 13.05[A][5][b] (2005).

16 *See* Roy Export Co. Establishment v. CBS, Inc., 503 F. Supp. 1137, 1146 (S.D.N.Y. 1980), *aff'd*, 672 F.2d 1095 (2d Cir. 1982).

17 *See* Castle Rock Enter. v. Carol Pub. Group, Inc., 150 F.3d 132, 146 (2d Cir. 1998).

18 *See* New Era Pubc'ns Int'l v. Henry Holt & Co., 695 F. Supp. 2d 1493, 1504–05 (S.D.N.Y. 1988), *aff'd*, 873 F.2d 576 (2d Cir. 1989).

19 911 F.2d 970, 973 (4th Cir. 1990).

20 *Id.*

21 *See* DSC Commc'ns Corp. v. DGI Tech., Inc., 81 F.3d 597, 601–02 (5th Cir. 1996); Practice Mgmt. Info. Cor. v. Am. Med. Ass'n, 121 F.3d 516, 521 (9th Cir. 1997), *amended*, 133 F.3d 1140 (9th Cir. 1998); Video Pipeline, Inc. v. Buena Vista Home Entmt., Inc., 342 F.3d 191, 206 (3d Cir. 2003).

22 *See* BellSouth Advertising & Publ'g Corp. v. Donnelley Info. Publ'g, Inc., 933 F.2d 952, 961 (11th Cir. 1991), *rev'd on other grounds on reh'g*, 999 F.2d 1436, 1446 (1993); Assessment Techs. of Wis., LLC v. WIREdata, Inc., 350 F.3d 640, 647 (7th Cir. 2003); Garcia-Goyko v. Law Envt'l Consultants, Inc., 428 F.3d 14, 21 n.7 (1st Cir. 2005).

23 975 F.2d. 832, 846 (Fed. Cir. 1992).

statute established that refusal to license does not constitute patent misuse.[24] Copyright courts, however, have continued to rule that refusal to license may constitute copyright misuse.[25] In cases where refusals to license are alleged to violate the antitrust laws, a context that courts have long recognized is closely related to copyright misuse,[26] courts have concluded that the fact that Congress amended the patent statute to exempt refusals to license from misuse while declining to enact a similar amendment to the copyright laws suggests that different policies should apply.[27]

C. *Third-Party Liability*

Although earlier precedents exist,[28] third-part liability under copyright law is traditionally traced to Justice Holmes's opinion in *Kalem Co.* v. *Harper Bros.*, which held a filmmaker liable for creating and distributing unauthorized films based on the copyrighted book, *Ben Hur*.[29] The fact that the filmmaker did not exhibit the films itself meant that it was not a direct infringer. This did not absolve it from liability, however, because the filmmaker both expected and encouraged others to use the film in an infringing manner, which was both "the most conspicuous purpose for which [the films] could be used, and the one for which especially they were made."[30] The Court observed that liability for those who did not take part in the final act, but nonetheless contributed to it, is "recognized in every part of the law."[31] Although the Court recognized that "nice questions may arise" when "an ordinary article of commerce" is used for infringement, the filmmaker's complicity was so flagrant that "no such niceties are involved here."[32] Subsequent lower court decisions developed the doctrine still further.[33]

When revising the patent statute in 1952, Congress included a specific provision to govern third-party liability. The statute imposed vicarious liability on those who

[24] 35 U.S.C. § 271(d)(4).

[25] *See* A&M Records, Inc. v. Napster, Inc., 239 F.3d 1004, 1027 n.8 (9th Cir. 2001) (noting that "a unilateral refusal to license a copyright may constitute wrongful exclusionary conduct giving rise to a claim of misuse, but assume that the 'desire to exclude others . . . is a presumptively valid business justification for any immediate harm to consumers'" (quoting Image Tech. Servs. v. Eastman Kodak Co., 125 F.3d 1195, 1218 (9th Cir. 1997)); *accord In re* Indep. Serv. Orgs. Antitrust Litig., 964 F. Supp. 1454, 1461 (D. Kan. 1997).

[26] *Lasercomb*, 911 F.2d at 977–78.

[27] Data Gen. Corp. v. Grumman Sys. Support Corp., 36 F.3d 1147, 1187 (1st Cir. 1994).

[28] *See* Fishel v. Lueckel, 53 F. 499 (S.D.N.Y. 1892); Scribner v. Straus, 210 U.S. 352 (1908). For a useful review of the early history of third-party liability doctrine, see Menell & Nimmer, *supra* note 2, at 996–1005.

[29] 222 U.S. 55, 60–61 (1911).

[30] *Id.* at 62–63.

[31] *Id.* at 63.

[32] *Id.* at 62.

[33] *See, e.g.*, Gershwin Publ'g Corp. v. Columbia Artists Management, Inc., 443 F.2d 1159, 1162 (2d Cir. 1971); Shapiro, Bernstein & Co. v. H. L. Green Co., 316 F.2d 304, 307 (2d Cir. 1963); M. Witmark & Sons v. Calloway, 22 F.2d 412, 414 (E.D. Tenn. 1927).

knowingly "actively induce[] infringement of a patent."[34] It also classified as a contributory infringer anyone who sells "a component of a patented machine . . . or a material or apparatus for use in practicing a patented process, constituting a material part of the invention, knowing the same to be especially made or especially adapted for use in an infringement of such patent, and not a staple article or commodity of commerce suitable for substantial noninfringing use."[35]

Congress did not include a similar provision when overhauling the copyright laws in 1976. The Supreme Court did not find the failure to do so of any particular import, concluding in *Sony Corp. of America* v. *Universal Studios, Inc.* that "[t]he absence of such express language in the copyright statute does not preclude the imposition of [third-party] liability for copyright infringements."[36] Instead, the Court regarded third-party liability as a widely acknowledged background principle, reasoning that "vicarious liability is imposed in virtually all areas of the law, and the concept of contributory infringement is merely a species of a broader problem of identifying the circumstances in which it is just to hold one individual accountable for the actions of another."[37] In addition to analogizing to *Kalem*, the *Sony* Court drew parallels between patent and copyright, explicitly importing the exception for a "staple article or commodity of commerce suitable for substantial noninfringing use."[38] Although the Court acknowledged that differences between these two bodies of law existed, neither was relevant to the area of third-party liability.[39]

The Court reaffirmed this conclusion in *Metro-Goldwyn-Mayer Studios Inc.* v. *Grokster, Ltd.*, holding that "[a]lthough '[t]he Copyright Act does not expressly render anyone liable for infringement committed by another,' these doctrines of secondary liability emerged from common law principles and are well established in the law."[40] The immateriality of the copyright statute was further underscored by the fact that the Court's principal authority for the doctrine of contributory infringement was a lower court case decided before the enactment of the 1976 Act.[41] Similarly, the Court held that its prior decision in *Sony* "was never meant to foreclose rules of fault-based liability derived from the common law."[42] Rather than develop the common law analysis, the Court followed *Sony*'s lead by analogizing to patent, concluding that the same reasons that led to the *Sony* Court to adopt the patent law standard for determining when to impute the intent to

34 35 U.S.C. § 271(b).

35 35 U.S.C. § 271(c).

36 464 U.S. 417, 435 (1984).

37 *Id.*

38 *Id.* at 435–41.

39 *Id.* at 439 n.19, 442.

40 Metro-Goldwyn-Mayer Studios Inc. v. Grokster, Ltd., 545 U.S. 913, 930 (2005) (citations omitted) (quoting *Sony*, 464 U.S. at 434; and citing *Kalem*, 222 U.S. at 62–63; *Gershwin*, 443 F.2d at 1162; 3 NIMMER & NIMMER, *supra* note 15, § 12.04[A]).

41 *See id.* at 930 (citing *Gershwin*, 443 F.2d at 1162).

42 *Id.* at 934–35.

infringe to a third party based on circumstantial evidence also justified adopting the patent law standard for assessing direct evidence of an unlawful purpose.[43] With the exception of *Kalem*, the Court built its argument on the authority of lower court patent precedents, citing those decided before the enactment of the Patent Act of 1952 interchangeably with those decided after.[44] Although the Court noted that third-party liability had been codified with respect to patent law,[45] the failure to include a similar provision in the copyright statute did not have any effect on its analysis.

D. *First Sale Doctrine*

The first sale doctrine originated in the Supreme Court's 1908 decision in *Bobbs-Merrill C. v. Straus*, which arose when retailer R.H. Macy & Co. purchased books from a publisher that were sold subject to the condition that no dealer was licensed to sell the book for less than one dollar, yet nonetheless resold them for eighty-nine cents.[46] The publisher disclaimed any relief under contract and relied exclusively on the argument that Macy's actions violated copyright law.[47] The Court held that, although copyright holders' exclusive right of "vending" their works[48] permitted the publisher to determine the price at which it sold its books to Macy's, it did not give the publisher the right "to qualify the title of a future purchaser."[49] Indeed, "[t]o add to the right of exclusive sale the authority to control all future retail sales . . . would give a right not included in the terms of the statute, and, in our view, extend its operation, by construction, beyond its meaning."[50] The Court framed its decision as "purely a question of statutory construction" of the copyright statutes.[51] As the Supreme Court would later explain, "once the copyright owner places a copyrighted item into the stream of commerce by selling it, he has exhausted his exclusive statutory right to control its distribution."[52]

Congress codified the first sale doctrine in the Copyright Act of 1909. After reaffirming that copyright holders possessed the exclusive right to "reprint, publish, copy, and vend the copyrighted work" in Section 1,[53] Section 41 provided that "nothing in this Act shall be deemed to forbid, prevent, or restrict the transfer of any

43 *Id.* at 936–37 ("For the same reasons that *Sony* took the staple-article doctrine of patent law as a model for its copyright safe-harbor rule, the inducement rule, too, is a sensible one for copyright.").
44 *Id.* at 935.
45 *Id.* at 932, 936 n.11.
46 210 U.S. 339 (1908).
47 *Id.* at 346.
48 Act of July 8, 1870, ch. 230, § 86, 16 Stat. 198, 212.
49 *Id.* at 351.
50 *Id.*
51 *Id.* at 350.
52 Quality King Distribs., Inc. v. L'anza Research Int'l, Inc., 523 U.S. 135, 152 (1998).
53 Copyright Act of 1909, ch. 320 § 1(a), 35 Stat. 1075, 1075.

copy of a copyrighted work the possession of which has been lawfully obtained."[54] In 1947, this provision was renumbered without change.[55]

Congress recodified the first sale doctrine in 1976. Section 106 gives copyright holders six specific rights, including the right to distribute copies, explicitly subject to limitations enumerated in Sections 107–122.[56] Section 109(a) provides the following:

> Notwithstanding the provision of section 106(3) [i.e., the exclusive right to distribute], the owner of a particular copy . . . lawfully made under this title, or any person authorized by such owner, is entitled, without the authority of the copyright owner, to sell or otherwise dispose of the possession of that copy.[57]

The simultaneous enactment of another provision has created a difficult interpretive question regarding the scope of the first sale doctrine. The 1976 Act also included a provision that expanded copyright holders' ability to control importation of unauthorized copies of their works. Although the Copyright Act of 1909 directed the Customs Service to bar importation of "piratical copies" of copyrighted works,[58] it did not apply to the importation of gray-market copies authorized only for distribution only in foreign countries. Consequently, Congress enacted Section 602(a)(1), which provides that "[i]mportation into the United States, without the authority of the owner of copyright under this title, of copies . . . of a work that have been acquired outside the United States is an infringement of the exclusive right to distribute copies . . . under section 106."[59]

What was unclear was whether the first sale doctrine codified in Section 109(a) limits the right granted by Section 602(a) to block importation. Two fact patterns have emerged as important: (1) copies manufactured abroad and then imported into the United States and (2) copies manufactured in the United States, exported, and then reimported back into the United States.

With respect to the latter fact pattern, the Supreme Court's unanimous 1998 decision in *Quality King Distributors, Inc.* v. *L'anza Research International, Inc.* held that copies that were manufactured in the United States, exported, and then reimported were subject to the first sale doctrine.[60] Because the copies at issue were manufactured in the U.S., the Court had no occasion to address the former fact pattern. Indeed, Justice Ginsburg's concurrence explicitly noted that the Court did not "resolve cases in which the allegedly infringing imports were manufactured abroad" without drawing any comment or objection from the majority.[61]

[54] § 41, 35 Stat. at 1084.
[55] Act of July 30, 1947, Pub. L. No. 80–281, § 27, 61 Stat. 652, 660.
[56] 17 U.S.C. § 106(3).
[57] *Id.* § 109(a).
[58] § 30, 35 Stat. at 1082.
[59] 17 U.S.C. § 602(a)(1).
[60] 523 U.S. 135 (1998).
[61] *Id.* at 154 (Ginsburg, J., concurring).

Absent specific guidance from the Supreme Court, the lower courts were left to address the former fact pattern as best they could. The seminal case was the pre-*Quality King* district court decision in *CBS* v. *Scorpio Music Distributors, Inc.*, which held that Section 109(a) applied only to works "lawfully made under this title" and thus did not apply to foreign manufactured copies.[62] Although some courts (including the Third Circuit) questioned *Scorpio* in dicta,[63] the Ninth Circuit adopted the *Scorpio* rule.[64] Thus by 1996, one court commented, "The courts . . . appear to be in agreement that that the first sale doctrine does not apply to foreign manufactured works copyrighted in the U.S."[65] The Ninth Circuit later expressed concerns about the implications of this holding, noting that it would "render the first sale doctrine wholly inapplicable to foreign manufactured goods, even after the goods have been lawfully imported into the United States" and would give "foreign manufactured goods . . . greater copyright protection than goods manufactured in the United States."[66] The Ninth Circuit thus held the first sale inapplicable only when the copies were both manufactured and first sold abroad. Foreign manufactured copies whose first sale occurred within the United States remained subject to the first sale doctrine.[67]

After the Supreme Court decided *Quality King* in 1998, lower courts had to determine whether anything in that decision altered the existing consensus. They uniformly concluded that *Quality King* supported the conclusion that Section 109(a) does not apply to copies manufactured and first sold abroad.[68] Interestingly, the Supreme Court granted certiorari in a Ninth Circuit decision, only to split 4–4 and affirm the judgment by an equally divided Court after Justice Kagan recused herself.[69] The issue arose again in *John Wiley & Sons* v. *Kirtsaeng*, in which a divided panel of the Second Circuit again held that the first sale doctrine codified

[62] 569 F. Supp. 47, 49 (E.D. Pa. 1983).

[63] Sebastian Int'l, Inc. v. Consumer Contacts (PTY) Ltd., 847 F.2d 1093, 1098 n.1 (3d Cir. 1988); *see also* Cosmair, Inc. v. Dynamite Enters., Inc., 226 U.S.P.Q. 344 (S.D. Fla. 1985).

[64] *See* BMG Music v. Perez, 952 F.2d 318, 319–20 (9th Cir. 1991); Hearst Corp. v. Stark, 639 F. Supp. 970 (N.D. Cal. 1986). Two other cases often cited as adopting the *Scorpio* rule are not squarely on point. *See* T.B. Harms Co. v. Jem Records, Inc., 655 F. Supp. 1575 (D.N.J. 1987); Nintendo of Am., Inc. v. Elcon Indus., 564 F. Supp. 937 (E.D. Mich. 1982).

[65] Summit Tech., Inc. v. High-Line Med. Instruments Co. 922 F. Supp. 299, 312 (C.D. Cal. 1996).

[66] Parfums Givenchy, Inc. v. Drug Emporium, Inc., 38 F.3d 477, 482 n.8 (9th Cir. 1994).

[67] Denbicare U.S.A. Inc. v. Toys "R" Us, Inc., 84 F.3d 1143, 1149–50 (9th Cir. 1996).

[68] *See* Omega S.A. v. Costco Wholesale Corp., 541 F.3d 982, 987–90 (9th Cir. 2008), *aff'd by an equally divided Court*, 131 S. Ct. 565 (2011); Pearson Educ., Inc. v. Kumar, 721 F. Supp. 2d 166, 176–78 (S.D.N.Y. 2010); Pearson Educ., Inc. v. Arora, 717 F. Supp. 2d 374, 379 (S.D.N.Y. 2010); Pearson Educ., Inc. v. Liu, 656 F. Supp. 2d 407, 412–13 (S.D.N.Y. 2009); Microsoft Corp. v. Big Boy Distribution LLC, 589 F. Supp. 2d 1308, 1317 (S.D. Fla. 2008); Pearson Educ., Inc. v. Liao, No. 07-Civ-2423 (SHS), 2008 WL 2073491, at *3 (S.D.N.Y. May 13, 2008); Swatch S.A. v. New City Inc., 454 F. Supp. 2d 1245, 1254–55 (S.D. Fla. 2006); UMG Recordings, Inc. v. Norwalk Distribs., Inc., 2003 WL 22722410, at *2–*4 (CD. Cal. Mar. 13, 2003); Lingo Corp. v. Topix, Inc., No. 01 Civ. 2863(RMB), 2003 WL 223454, at *4 (S.D.N.Y. Jan. 31, 2003).

[69] 131 S. Ct. 565 (2011) (per curiam).

by Section 109(a) does not apply to copies manufactured in other countries.[70] In so holding, the Second Circuit rejected the Ninth Circuit's distinction between foreign manufactured copies where the first sale took place abroad and those where the first sale took place in the United States.[71] District Judge Murtha, sitting by designation, dissented.[72]

The Supreme Court granted certiorari in *Kirtsaeng*.[73] For the purposes of this chapter, the most interesting position was taken by the Solicitor General, who argued that the Court should resolve the case by applying the principles in embodied *Bobbs-Merrill*.[74] The government asserted in effect that *Bobbs-Merrill* continued to have vitality notwithstanding Congress's subsequent codification of the first sale doctrine, a claim that drew substantial attention during oral argument.[75] The Supreme Court eventually agreed, invoking the canon of construction that recognizes that "'[w]hen a statute covers an issue previously governed by the common law,' we must presume that 'Congress intended to retain the substance of the common law.'"[76]

II. THEORIES OF THE RELATIONSHIP BETWEEN LEGISLATIVE AND JUDICIAL LAWMAKING

All four areas of copyright law discussed earlier exhibit the courts' continuing willingness to develop the law despite the enactment of the Copyright Act of 1976 and without engaging in a close examination of the text and enactment history of the statute. The propriety of the courts' actions depends on the relevant theories of legisprudence, which span a broad spectrum. At one pole are theories that recognize broad judicial authority to revise and overturn statutes regardless of legislative intent. At the other pole are theories that suggest that codification categorically forecloses all further judicial development of the law. In between are theories that recognize limited judicial authority to continue to innovate.

A. *Broad Judicial Authority to Develop the Law in the Face of Adverse Statutory Language*

One school of thought holds that courts should feel free to overrule or revise statutes on the same terms as judicial precedents. Lord Coke offered a classic statement of this position in *Bonham's Case*, in which he stated his belief that "when an Act of Parliament is against common right and reason, or repugnant, or impossible to

70 654 F.3d 210, 218–22 (2d Cir. 2011), *rev'd*, 133 S. Ct. 1351 (2013).

71 *Id.* at 221.

72 *Id.* at 226 (Murtha, J., dissenting).

73 132 S. Ct. 1905 (2012) (mem.).

74 Brief for the United States as Amicus Curiae Supporting Respondent, *supra* note 4, at 27–29.

75 Transcript of Oral Argument at 22, 29, 38, 42, 44–49, 52, John Wiley & Sons v. Kirtsaeng, 133 S. Ct. 1351 (2012) (No. 11–697), *available at* https://www.eff.org/sites/default/files/filenode/11–697.pdf.

76 133 S. Ct. 1351, 1363 (2013) (quoting Samantar v. Yousuf, 130 S. Ct. 2278, 2289–90 n.13 (2010)).

be performed the common law will control it and adjudge such Act to be void."[77] Coke's *Institutes* lauded the common law as "the perfection of reason."[78] Under this view, law was not the product of positive enactments and declarations, but rather "a 'brooding omnipresence' of Reason, of which decisions [and presumably statutes] were merely evidence and not themselves the controlling formulations."[79] The modern consensus rejects the view that the common law is a preexisting, natural construct awaiting discovery. As Justice Holmes noted in his now famous dissent in *Southern Pacific Co.* v. *Jensen*, "The common law is not a brooding omnipresence in the sky but the articulate voice of some sovereign or quasi-sovereign that can be identified."[80]

Blackstone echoed Coke's belief in the perfection of the common law,[81] but acknowledged legislative supremacy when he conceded that "[w]here the common law and a statute differ, the common law gives place to the statute."[82] Moreover, he rejected claims "that acts of parliament contrary to reason are void," because permitting judges to reject statutes they found to be unreasonable would "set the judicial power above that of the legislature, which would be subversive of all government."[83] Blackstone concluded, however, that "the most universal and effectual way of discovering the true meaning of a law, when the words are dubious, is by considering the *reason* and the *spirit* of it.... For when this reason ceases, the law itself ought to cease with it."[84] Blackstone also allowed that "where some collateral matter arises out of the general words, and happens to be unreasonable; there the judges are in decency to conclude that this consequence was not foreseen by the parliament, and therefore they are at liberty to expound the statute by equity, and only *quoad hoc* disregard it."[85] To the extent that the statutory text is clear, "there is no court that has power to defeat the intent of the legislature."[86] Thus, in the words of the leading commentator on statutory interpretation, "[t]o the extent Blackstone saw judges as agents..., they were agents of the common law as much as agents of Parliament."[87] U.S. commentators issued similar calls for interpreting statutes in a

77 College of Physician's (Dr. Bonham's) Case, 77 Eng. Rep. 646, 652 (C.P. 1609). It should be noted that Coke offered these views before the principle of parliamentary supremacy had become established. Estreicher, *supra* note 3, at 1159 n.106; Jefferson B. Fordham & J. Russell Leach, *Interpretation of Statutes in Derogation of the Common Law*, 3 VAND. L. REV. 438, 441 (1950).

78 EDWARD COKE, FIRST PART OF THE INSTITUTES OF THE LAWES OF ENGLAND 97b (Garland 1979) (1628).

79 Guaranty Trust Co. of N.Y. v. York, 326 U.S. 99, 102 (1945); *accord* Harlan F. Stone, *The Common Law in the United States*, 50 HARV. L. REV. 4, 8 (1936).

80 244 U.S. 205, 222 (1917) (Holmes, J., dissenting).

81 1 WILLIAM BLACKSTONE, COMMENTARIES *70.

82 *Id.* at *89.

83 *Id.* at *91.

84 *Id.* at *61.

85 *Id.*

86 *Id.* at *92.

87 William N. Eskridge, Jr., *All About Words: Early Understandings of the "Judicial Power" in Statutory Interpretation, 1776–1806*, 101 COLUM. L. REV. 990, 1002 (2000).

way that preserved the capacity for expansion and adaptation associated with the common law.[88]

Arguments against judicial deference to statutes found a modern voice in Guido Calabresi, who was concerned that legislative inertia was causing the ever-growing body of statutory law to become increasingly out of step with the legal landscape and current majoritarian preferences.[89] The inability of legislatures to keep up with the pace of change leads courts to distort their reasoning either by straining to find clear statutes ambiguous or to declare statutes unconstitutional.[90] Calabresi's solution was to treat statutes the same as common law precedents,[91] even permitting judges to override statutes that have become obsolete.[92] Calabresi offered a nod toward legislative supremacy when he acknowledged that it would be "infinitely preferable" for legislatures to enact legislation authorizing courts to revise statutes. The absence of such legislative authorization did not give him much pause, however; he criticized devoting any effort to analyzing when courts could revise statutes without explicit authorization as "premature" and even "wasteful and even misguided."[93] Instead, Calabresi thought it better "to get on with the task" of considering how (rather than when) it should be done.[94]

More recently, William Eskridge has advocated a more evolutive approach that he calls "dynamic statutory interpretation," which Eskridge acknowledges is "related to, but stops far short of" Calabresi's proposal.[95] Like Calabresi, Eskridge is motivated in large part by the limits of legislative processes, using the tools of positive political theory to take this skepticism to a new level and arguing that legislative outcomes typically reflect rent seeking and special interests rather than the popular will.[96] As a result, Eskridge rejects exclusive reliance on methods of interpretation that seek to construe statutes based on the statutory text or legislative intent.[97] Instead, his approach seeks to provide a corrective to the overrepresentation and underrepresentation inherent in legislative processes that can cause enactments to deviate from majoritarian preferences.[98] He argues, "Sometimes the circumstances will be materially different from those contemplated by the statutory drafters," in which case courts can "go . . . *against* the drafters' expectations, which have been negated because important assumptions have been undone."[99] Thus, "[w]hen the

88 *See, e.g.*, John Norton Pomeroy, *The True Method of Interpreting the Civil Code*, 4 W. Coast Rptr. 109, 110–13 (1884).

89 Guido Calabresi, A Common Law for the Age of Statutes 1–7 (1982).

90 *Id.* at 38, 81.

91 *Id.* at 82.

92 *Id.* at 96–97, 121–23.

93 *Id.* at 117.

94 *Id.*

95 William N. Eskridge, Jr., *Dynamic Statutory Interpretation*, 149 U. Pa. L. Rev. 1479, 1481 n.7 (1994).

96 William N. Eskridge, Jr., Dynamic Statutory Interpretation 157–58 (1994).

97 *Id.* at 13–47.

98 *Id.* at 156–61.

99 *Id.* at 50.

assumptions of a society or culture underlying a statute are discredited," courts seeking "[t]o fulfill the original statutory functions" must "consider the new circumstances, and doing so often leads to a dramatically dynamic interpretation of the statute."[100] When faced with such changes, a statute "can change its form to deal with the policy chasm introduced by the obsolescence of some of its assumptions."[101]

Eskridge's initial statement of his theory recognized that the statutory text and the expectations of the legislature that enacted the statute represented the primary considerations when interpreting statutes, conceding that "when a clear text and supportive legislative history suggest the same answer, they typically will control."[102] Current policies and social conditions influence statutory construction only when "the statutory text is not clear and the original legislative expectations have been overtaken by subsequent changes in society and law."[103] His later work envisions a more expansive role for courts, presenting the evolutive perspective as being coequal with text and legislative history.[104] Under this approach, current norms and values can alter the interpretation of a clear text when its "plain meaning is unreasonable and apparently unanticipated by the legislature."[105]

Calls for allowing judges to negate or modify statutes based on contemporary values have met with sharp criticism. Commentators have challenged assertions that courts are better institutionally suited than legislatures to keep up with the times, noting that legislation was initially viewed as a solution to the courts' inability to keep pace with social and economic change and that judicial lawmaking has led to its share of outdated doctrines.[106] Arguments motivated by the flaws in the legislative process must also take into account that judicial processes suffer from institutional shortcomings of their own.[107] Moreover, determining when a statute is out of sync with contemporary values is likely to prove difficult, and the existing proposals fail to provide a clear basis for determining when a statute is so obsolete as to need judicial revision.[108] The absence of such criteria raises serious concerns about whether the resulting approach to interpretation will be too malleable.[109]

[100] *Id.* at 53.

[101] *Id.* at 55.

[102] Eskridge, *supra* note 95, at 1483–84.

[103] *Id.* at 1484.

[104] ESKRIDGE, *supra* note 96, at 56, 63–64.

[105] *Id.* at 56.

[106] Roscoe Pound, *Common Law and Legislation*, 21 HARV. L. REV. 383, 384, 405 (1908); Stone, *supra* note 79, at 11–12; *see also* Fordham & Leach, *supra* note 77, at 441 (citing Pound and THEODORE SEDGWICK, A TREATISE ON THE RULES WHICH GOVERN THE INTERPRETATION AND APPLICATION OF STATUTORY AND CONSTITUTIONAL LAW 270 (1st ed. 1857)).

[107] Estreicher, *supra* note 3, at 1168–69; Martin H. Redish & Theodore T. Chung, *Democratic Theory and the Legislative Process: Mourning the Death of Originalism in Statutory Interpretation*, 68 TUL. L. REV 803, 856–57 (1994).

[108] *See* Estreicher, *supra* note 3, at 1130; Redish & Chung, *supra* note 107, at 850; Robert Weisberg, *The Calabresian Judicial Artist: Statutes and the New Legal Process*, 35 STAN. L. REV. 213, 225 (1983).

[109] Abner J. Mikva, *The Shifting Sands of Legal Topography*, 96 HARV. L. REV. 534, 541–42 (1982); John Copeland Nagle, *Newt Gingrich, Dynamic Statutory Interpreter*, 143 U. PA. L. REV. 2209, 2221 (1995);

The lack of interpretive constraints risks politicizing decisions about when a statute should be overridden.[110] Most glaringly, permitting unelected and unaccountable judges to overturn the actions of the politically accountable branches raises serious problems from the standpoint of democracy.[111]

The conventional wisdom is that recent Supreme Court decisions have exhibited a tendency to favor textualism over evolutive approaches.[112] Although Eskridge denigrates legislative supremacy as a "shibboleth," he concedes that it is a "shibboleth with bite."[113] Text is given the most weight[114] and, in Eskridge's early work, is even controlling.[115] Indeed, "[t]he evolutive perspective must yield where the text and evidence of legislative expectation support another interpretation."[116] Under the Supreme Court's jurisprudence, the question has thus become how to reconcile the judiciary's role in explicating statutes with the democratic commitment to legislative supremacy.

B. *Complete Displacement of Judicial Authority to Develop the Law*

At the other extreme are schools of thought that view codification as completely displacing courts' authority to develop legal principles. In the words of the leading treatise on statutory interpretation, "general and comprehensive legislation . . . indicates a legislative intent that the statute should totally supersede and replace the common law dealing with the subject matter."[117] Areas where legislation is sometimes said to have almost entirely displaced common law include the Uniform Commercial Code, labor law, and antitrust.[118]

It would be a mistake, however, to regard all major codifications as displacing prior sources of law. As an initial matter, although some codifications aspired to be comprehensive, others were intended only to cover a portion of existing law.[119]

David E. Van Zandt, *An Alternative Theory of Practical Reason in Judicial Decision*, 65 TUL. L. REV. 775, 790–91 (1991).

110 Estreicher, *supra* note 3, at 1166; Redish & Chung, *supra* note 107, at 833, 841.

111 Estreicher, *supra* note 3, at 1129, 1137, 1158–65; Allan C. Hutchinson & Derek Morgan, *Calabresian Sunset: Statutes in the Shade*, 82 COLUM. L. REV. 1752, 1761–67 (1982); Redish & Chung, *supra* note 107, at 812; Weisberg, *supra* note 108, at 217.

112 *See, e.g.*, ESKRIDGE, *supra* note 96, at 34; Frederick Schauer, *Statutory Construction and the Coordination Function of Plain Meaning*, 1990 SUP. CT. REV. 231, 231; David L. Shapiro, *Continuity and Change in Statutory Interpretation*, 67 N.Y.U. L. REV. 921, 921–22 (1992).

113 William N. Eskridge, Jr., *Spinning Legislative Supremacy*, 78 GEO. L.J. 319, 319, 320 (1989).

114 ESKRIDGE, *supra* note 96, at 56.

115 Eskridge, *supra* note 95, at 1495, 1496.

116 *Id.* at 1495.

117 2B NORMAN J. SINGER & J. D. SHAMBIE SINGER, SUTHERLAND STATUTES AND STATUTORY CONSTRUCTION § 50:5 (7th ed. 2012).

118 Note, *The Legitimacy of Civil Law Reasoning in the Common Law: Justice Harlan's Contribution*, 82 YALE L.J. 258, 259 & n.8 (1972).

119 Mark D. Rosen, *What Has Happened to the Common Law? – Recent American Codifications, and Their Impact on Judicial Practice and the Law's Subsequent Development*, 1994 WIS. L. REV. 1119, 1131–35.

This is why, according to a leading commentary on codification, "[t]here is no *a priori* jurisprudentially correct relationship between the codes and the pre-code materials."[120] Codes can represent either "a culmination of the pre-code materials" or a self-conscious "break . . . from pre-code archaic law."[121] Even if intended to be revisionary, codifications generally leave untouched common law in areas falling outside the scope of the statute. Moreover, that courts retain some freedom to fashion equitable corrections to mitigate unfair outcomes that may arise under mechanical application of the statute.[122] In the words of a noted judge,

> A primary function of any codification of common law . . . is to displace prior *legal* rules. The same cannot be said of prior *equitable* principles. Equity was developed to do justice in individual case by carving expectations to and otherwise modifying legal rules. Thus, a codification of legal rules does not automatically displace the equitable principles which supplement them.[123]

Thus, codification does not foreclose later courts from consulting preenactment common law. Nor does it foreclose courts from continuing to make revisions to an area of law. The easiest case is when the statute itself invites continued judicial development, which poses no analytical problems.[124] The question is more difficult in the absence of such an invitation. As discussed later, the significance of such silence may depend on the background understandings that frame the codification. The omission may suggest a legislative intent not to allow courts to continue to develop the doctrine and will deter judges' willingness to do so, depending on Congress's intent.[125]

C. *Limited Authority for Judicial Development*

Between the two extremes of near-complete judicial latitude and complete judicial displacement lies a middle ground that permits a prominent role for judicial development while simultaneously paying sufficient respect to legislative supremacy. Legislatures may delegate such authority to courts. Alternatively, courts may construe statutes in light of other statutes.

1. Affirmative Delegation of Authority to the Judiciary

The strongest case for a strong judicial role in shaping the law after codification arises when the statute affirmatively confers the authority to do so on the courts. The Sherman Antitrust Act has long been regarded as a prime example of congressional

[120] *Id.* at 1176.
[121] *Id.* at 1177, 1178.
[122] *Id.* at 1164, 1179–86.
[123] Bluebonnet Warehouse Cooperative v. Bankers Trust Co., 89 F.3d 292, 299 (6th Cir. 1996) (Merritt, C.J., dissenting).
[124] *Id.* at 1187–94.
[125] *Id.* at 1196–98.

delegation of the responsibility for fashioning legal principles in a common law fashion to the judiciary.[126] Other leading examples include § 301(a) of the Taft-Hartley Act[127] and 42 U.S.C. § 1983.[128] When Congress delegates such authority to the courts, common law development poses no conflict with legislative supremacy.

Legislative delegations of lawmaking authority to courts are rarely explicit, however, which raises questions about what indicia are sufficient to signal Congress's intent to confer this power on the judiciary. Some find it sufficient that the statute employed common law concepts as the basis for liability.[129] Others look to the legislative history for indications of Congress's intention to delegate to the courts the authority to flesh out the law.[130]

Whether a statute cuts off the courts' power to continue to fashion relief is thus itself a matter of statutory interpretation. For example, the Supreme Court looked to legislative intent when determining whether Federal Rule of Civil Procedure 11 or a statute authorizing courts to sanction attorneys who unreasonably multiply proceedings abrogated a district court's inherent power to sanction bad-faith conduct by one of the parties.[131] Moreover, because the typical statute does not purport to cover all areas of law, courts' authority to continue to address areas that fall outside its scope remains unaffected.

2. Analogies to Other Statutes (Particularly Patent Law)

Another possible source for interpreting statutes that is consistent with legislative supremacy is another statute. During the early twentieth century, a number of noted scholars called for a revival of the English doctrine known as the "equity of the statute," which "treat[s] a statute much more as we treat a judicial precedent, as both a declaration and a source of law, and as a premise for legal reasoning."[132] This approach regards statutes "as sources of law which by judicial decision could be

[126] *See, e.g.*, National Soc'y of Professional Eng'rs v. United States, 435 U.S. 679, 688 (1978) (Congress "expected the courts to give shape to the statute's broad mandate by drawing on the common-law tradition." (footnote omitted)); Guardians Ass'n v. Civil Serv. Comm'n, 463 U.S. 582, 641 n.12 (1983) (Stevens, J., dissenting).

[127] *See, e.g.*, Textile Workers Union v. Lincoln Mills, 353 U.S. 448, 451 (1957).

[128] *See, e.g.*, *Guardians Ass'n*, 463 U.S. at 641 n.12 (Stevens, J., dissenting); Cass R. Sunstein, *Interpreting Statutes in the Regulatory State*, 103 HARV. L. REV. 405, 421–22 (1989); Larry Kramer & Alan O. Sykes, *Municipal Liability Under Section 1983: A Legal and Economic Analysis*, 1987 SUP. CT. REV. 249, 265.

[129] For an early classic statement, see Pound, *supra* note 106, at 382 n.2. For more recent statements, see, e.g., RICHARD A. POSNER, THE FEDERAL COURTS: CRITICISM AND REFORM 288 (1985); Thomas W. Merrill, *The Common Law Powers of Federal Courts*, 52 U. CHI. L. REV. 1, 44–45 (1985).

[130] For example, Senator Sherman indicated Congress's belief that "defin[ing] in legal language the precise line between lawful and unlawful combinations" was a task that "must be left for the courts to determine in each particular case" and that courts will apply the general meaning articulated by the legislature "so as to carry out the meaning of the law as the courts of England and the United States have done for centuries." 21 CONG. REC. 2469 (1890).

[131] Chambers v. NASCO, Inc., 501 U.S. 32, 48 n.13 (1991).

[132] Stone, *supra* note 79, at 13.

extended to apply to situations analogous to those embraced within their terms."[133] Even proponents of the principle, however, acknowledged its rejection by English and U.S. courts.[134] The doctrine still appears in judicial decisions from time to time,[135] and subsequent scholars have again called for its revival.[136] These suggestions have generally been rejected, however, as inconsistent with the legislative supremacy inherent in a constitutional democracy.[137]

Although modern law has rejected appeals to treat statutes in a manner similar to common law precedents, it has shown greater willingness to draw analogies between statutes that cover similar subject matter. A longstanding canon of construction calls for statutes that are *in pari materia* (on the same subject) to be construed in a similar manner.[138] Approaches that "consider one statute's meaning in light of other statutes . . . ha[ve] been especially influential on the Court."[139] As demonstrated in Part I, the Supreme Court analogized to patent law in *Sony* and *Grokster* when determining the scope of third-party liability.[140] The *Lasercomb* court did the same with respect to copyright misuse.[141] Other leading copyright decisions have also been based largely on patent precedents.[142]

On other occasions, the Court has warned against drawing simplistic analogies between copyright and patent. *Bobbs-Merrill*, for example, declined a call to extend patent principles to copyright in part because "there are differences between the patent and copyright statutes in the extent in protection granted by them."[143] Although the *Sony* Court based its decision on a broad analogy between patent

[133] *Id.* at 14 (citing James McCauley Landis, *Statutes and the Sources of Law*, *in* HARVARD LEGAL ESSAYS 213 (1934)); *see also* Pound, *supra* note 106, at 388–89.

[134] Eskridge, *supra* note 87, at 1007, 1106 (England); Landis, *supra* note 133, at 218 (U.S.); *see also* William S. Blatt, *The History of Statutory Interpretation: A Study in Form and Substance*, 6 CARDOZO L REV. 799, 822 (1985) (noting that "the overwhelming opinion of late classical lawyers was that the equity of a statute was dead"); John F. Manning, *Textualism and the Equity of the Statute*, 101 COLUM. L. REV. 1, 79 (2001) (observing that "federal courts sometimes applied the equity of the statute as late as the mid-nineteenth century, but that the Supreme Court had taken a decisive turn toward the faithful agent theory as early as the Marshall Court").

[135] *See, e.g., In re* Long, 519 F.3d 288, 298 (6th Cir. 2008); N.D. v. Fredericks, 940 F.2d 333, 337 (8th Cir. 1991).

[136] *See* Eskridge, *supra* note 87; William Page, *Statutes as Common Law Principles*, 1944 WIS. L. REV. 175; Roger J. Traynor, *Statutes Revolving in Common-Law Orbits*, 17 CATH. U. L. REV. 401, 403–04 (1968).

[137] *See* Manning, *supra* note 134.

[138] *See, e.g.*, United States v. Freeman, 44 U.S. (3 How.) 556, 564 (1845); SEDGWICK, *supra* note 106, at 247–51.

[139] ESKRIDGE, *supra* note 96, at 229.

[140] *See supra* Part I.C.

[141] *See supra* Part I.B.

[142] *See, e.g.*, Eldred v. Ashcroft, 537 U.S. 186, 201–02 (2003).

[143] *Id.* at 345. In support of this conclusion, the Court quoted a lower court decision noting, "'There are such wide differences between the right of multiplying and vending copies of a production protected by the copyright statute and the rights secured to an inventor under the patent statutes, that the cases which relate to one subject are not altogether controlling as to the other.'" *Id.* at 346 (quoting John D. Park & Sons v. Hartman, 153 F. 24, 28 (C.C.E.D. Ky. 1907)).

and copyright, it noted that copyright and patent were different in important ways without exploring the nature of the differences and any possible implications.[144] Moreover, in *Eldred* v. *Ashcroft*, the Court based its argument for sustaining the constitutionality of the copyright term extension primarily on patent precedents.[145] At the same time, it relied on the differences between patent and copyright when rejecting arguments that the statute failed to incorporate the quid pro quo between authors and the public.[146]

It would thus be improper for courts simply to assume that copyright and patent law are analogous in all aspects. Instead, whether two statutes should be read together is itself a matter of legislative intent.[147] Peter Menell and David Nimmer have provided a useful framework for determining when copyright laws are properly interpreted *in pari materia* with other statute. Their careful review of the legislative history of the Copyright Act of 1976 revealed that its provisions could be divided into five categories:

1. Enacted provisions that explicitly drew on patent law;
2. Proposed provisions that explicitly drew on patent law, but were not enacted;
3. Enacted provisions that self-consciously diverged from the approach taken by patent law;
4. Enacted provisions that drew on sources of law other than patent law;
5. Enacted provisions that drew on both patent and trademark law.[148]

Courts are most justified in drawing on patent law with respect to enacted provisions that were modeled on patent law in whole or in part (categories 1 and 5). Conversely, reference to patent law is inappropriate for provisions that either affirmatively rejected the approach taken by patent law (category 3) or that were based on patent law, but were not enacted by Congress (category 2). Provisions based on other laws (category 4) should be interpreted according to the nonpatent source of law actually invoked.[149]

Interestingly, related statutes can give rise to negative inferences as well as broad analogies. The Supreme Court has repeatedly recognized that the inclusion of language in one statute and the omission of parallel language in a related statute suggest that Congress did not intend the doctrine established by that language to apply to the second area of law. Consider, for example, *Meghrig* v. *KFC Western, Inc.*, in which the Court held that the government could not recover cleanup costs under the Resource Conservation and Recovery Act of 1976 (RCRA).[150] The Court

[144] Sony Corp. of Am. v. Universal City Studios, Inc., 464 U.S. 417, 439 n.19 (1984) ("The two areas of the law, naturally, are not identical twins, and we exercise the caution which we have expressed in the past in applying doctrine formulated in one area to the other.").

[145] *Eldred*, 537 U.S. at 201–02.

[146] *Id.* at 216–17.

[147] Fort Stewart Sch. v. Fed. Labor Relations Auth., 495 U.S. 641, 647–48 (1990).

[148] Menell & Nimmer, *supra* note 2, at 989–91.

[149] *Id.* at 992–93.

[150] 516 U.S. 479, 484–85 (1996).

contrasted the omission of statutory language explicitly authorizing the recovery of cleanup costs from RCRA with the inclusion of a specific provision authorizing such a recovery in the Comprehensive Environmental Response, Compensation, and Liability Act of 1980 (CERCLA), the other major federal statute addressing toxic waste.[151] In the words of the Court, "Congress thus demonstrated in CERCLA that it knew how to provide for the recovery of cleanup costs, and that the language used to define remedies under RCRA does not provide that remedy."[152]

The Court followed similar reasoning in *Gebser* v. *Lago Vista Independent School District*, in which it focused on inclusion of a particular language in one statute and the omission of that language in a related statute when addressing the applicability of *respondeat superior* under two leading civil rights statutes.[153] A previous decision holding agency principles applicable to Title VII of the Civil Rights Act of 1964 was based on statutory language imposing liability on "an employer," which was defined to include "any agent."[154] The omission of a comparable reference to agents in Title IX of the Education Amendments Act of 1972 created the negative inference that agency principles did not apply.[155] The Court has drawn similar conclusions in numerous other cases.[156]

Practical considerations suggest that courts should take care when drawing such a negative inference. Legislative silence is ambiguous in that it may signal a failure to focus on an issue rather than an affirmative rejection.[157] Moreover, the negative inference depends on what has been called the "one Congress fiction," which presumes that every instantiation of the legislature is aware of the work done by previous Congresses and works to weave all subsequent legislation into a seamless whole.[158]

The foregoing discussion underscores the dangers associated with adopting either the polar extreme of allowing judges broad authority to revise statutes or the opposite presumption that an enactment completely displaces further judicial development.

[151] *Id.* at 485.

[152] *Id.*

[153] 524 U.S. 274 (1998).

[154] *Id.* at 283.

[155] *Id.*

[156] *See, e.g.*, Central Bank of Denver, N.A. v. First Interstate Bank of Denver, 511 U.S. 164, 176–77 (1994); W. Va. Univ. Hosps., Inc. v. Casey, 499 U.S. 83, 88–91 (1991); Lukhard v. Reed, 481 U.S. 368, 376 (1987) (plurality opinion); Block v. Community Nutrition Inst., 467 U.S. 340, 345–48 (1984); Transamerica Mortgage Advisers, Inc. v. Lewis, 444 U.S. 11, 21 (1979); United States v. Culbert, 435 U.S. 371, 378 n.9 (1978); City of Greenwood v. Peacock, 384 U.S. 808, 820 n.17 (1966).

[157] ESKRIDGE, *supra* note 96, at 246–52; Daniel A. Farber, *Statutory Interpretation, Legislative Inaction, and Civil Rights*, 87 MICH. L. REV. 2, 9–14 (1988).

[158] *See* SINGER & SINGER, *supra* note 117, § 51:1; William W. Buzbee, *The One-Congress Fiction in Statutory Interpretation*, 149 U. PA. L. REV. 171, 205 (2000); William N. Eskridge, *The New Textualism*, 37 UCLA L. REV. 621, 679–81 (1990); William D. Popkin, *An "Internal" Critique of Justice Scalia's Theory of Statutory Interpretation*, 76 MINN. L. REV. 1133, 1148–52 (1992); Nicholas S. Zeppos, *Legislative History and the Interpretation of Statutes: Toward a Fact-Finding Model of Statutory Interpretation*, 76 VA. L. REV. 1295, 1320 (1990).

The former is inconsistent with the commitment to democracy. The latter is not a blanket principle, but rather a matter of legislative intent that raises questions of both how much judicial authority is displaced within the scope of the statute and of the precise location of the boundaries of the displacement. Although limiting judges to drawing on the approaches taken by related statutes is easier to reconcile with legislative supremacy, reflexively drawing broad analogies between copyright and patent would be a mistake. Instead, courts must determine whether the legislature intended the statutes to be read together and, if so, whether a positive or negative inference would be more appropriate.

III. A REEXAMINATION OF THE EXAMPLES OF CONTINUING JUDICIAL DEVELOPMENT

The various theories of legisprudence in turn inform whether continued judicial development in the areas of fair use, misuse, third-party liability is appropriate. What emerges is not a blanket approach that treats various levels of judicial involvement in a categorical manner. Instead, it yields a context-sensitive inquiry that depends on a close examination of the indicia of legislative intent with respect to the judiciary's role.

A. *Fair Use*

Of the four examples discussed earlier, fair use represents the easiest case for justifying ongoing judicial development. Both the statutory text and the context surrounding its enactment reveal a legislative intent to delegate to the courts a continuing role in developing the contours of the doctrine.

Looking first at the statutory text, both the preamble and the four-factor test enumerated by the fair use statute signal Congress's expectation that courts would continue to incorporate new considerations into the fair use analysis. For example, when enumerating examples and considerations, the text uses the terms "including," "such as," and "shall include."[159] As the Supreme Court noted in *Campbell*,[160] the inclusion of these terms indicates Congress's intent that the enumerated criteria be regarded as "illustrative and not limitative."[161] Moreover, as the Supreme Court concluded in *Harper & Row*, the legislative history similarly indicates that "[t]he factors enumerated in the section are not meant to be exclusive: '[S]ince the doctrine is an equitable rule of reason, no generally applicable definition is possible, and each case raising the question must be decided on its own

[159] 17 U.S.C. § 107.

[160] Campbell v. Acuff-Rose Music, Inc., 510 U.S. 569, 577–78 (1994); *accord* Ty, Inc. v. Publ'ns Int'l Ltd., 292 F.3d 512, 522 (7th Cir. 2002).

[161] 17 U.S.C. § 101.

facts.'"[162] The Supreme Court has noted that the legislative history indicates that "'the courts must be free to adapt the doctrine to particular situations on a case-by-case basis'"[163] and that "Congress . . . intended that courts continue the common-law tradition of fair use adjudication."[164]

Thus, the presence of clear legislative authorization renders continued judicial development of fair use unproblematic under any theory. On the contrary, the leading schools of legisprudence and constitutional theory arguably place the courts under the affirmative obligation to play an active role in determining the contours of fair use.

B. *Misuse*

At first blush, continued judicial development in the area of copyright misuse appears to be more problematic. Not only does the statute lack any provision that can be construed as an express delegation of authority to the courts; the inclusion of specific language in the Patent Act of 1952 recognizing the patent misuse defense and the omission of similar language in the Copyright Act of 1976 arguably create negative implications with respect to copyright misuse.

Again, a close analysis of the statutes and the contexts surrounding their enactment reveals subtleties that a more categorical analysis might overlook. The patent statute does not define misuse directly. Instead, it defines certain conduct that cannot constitute misuse.[165] The structure of this provision thus necessarily recognizes patent misuse as a preexisting background principle in front of which the statute was enacted. Moreover, by its own terms, the statute only exempts certain practices from patent misuse doctrine, which only makes sense if the affirmative contours of the doctrine were already established under another source of law and left undisturbed by the amendment. This provision is thus better regarded as a surgical correction to law based on a prior, nonstatutory source rather than a comprehensive displacement of existing law.

The limited nature of the statute makes it difficult to draw any strong negative inferences from the failure to include a similar provision in the copyright statute. Quite the contrary, by tacitly confirming the existence of a preexisting patent misuse doctrine, the patent statute implicitly acknowledges the possibility that misuse stems from a nonstatutory source that may well be applicable to copyright.

As the Court noted in *Morton Salt Co.* v. *G.S. Suppiger Co.*, which first presented patent misuse in its mature form, patent misuse doctrine stems from the line of precedents holding that practices designed to extend the inventor's monopoly beyond

162 Harper & Row Publishers, Inc. v. Nation Enters., 471 U.S. 539, 560 (1985) (quoting H.R. REP. NO. 94-1476, at 65 (1976).

163 Sony Corp. of Am. v. Universal City Studios, Inc., 464 U.S. 417, 448 & n.31 (1984) (quoting H.R. REP. NO. 94-1476, at 65–66).

164 *Campbell*, 510 U.S. at 577.

165 35 U.S.C. § 271(d).

the scope of the patent violate the antitrust laws.[166] The *Morton Salt* Court applied the "principle of general application that courts, and especially courts of equity, may appropriately withhold their aid where the plaintiff is using the right asserted contrary to the public."[167] The Court would later characterize patent misuse as an extension of the equitable doctrine of unclean hands, under which the courts could refuse to give aid to a party that was violating the antitrust laws.[168] The connection between patent and antirust is so strong that the Supreme Court would later note that "the patent laws . . . are in *pari materia* with the antitrust laws."[169] Moreover, the patent misuse and antitrust laws became deeply intertwined, with patent misuse cases informing antitrust law and vice versa.[170]

The Supreme Court's antitrust jurisprudence has long suggested that similar principles apply to copyright law as well. In its 1948 decision in *United States* v. *Paramount Pictures, Inc.*, the Court cited its patent misuse precedents as the primary authority for holding that bundling copyrighted movies together (a practice known as block booking) violated the antitrust laws.[171] The Court drew a similar conclusion in *United States* v. *Loew's, Inc.* with respect to the block booking of copyrighted television programs.[172] In so holding, the Court again invoked its patent misuse precedents, holding that just as patent law prohibited the use of tying arrangements to extend a legal monopoly to other products, so too were such practices impermissible under copyright.[173] Both *Paramount Pictures* and *Loew's* were antitrust cases and as such did not explicitly recognize copyright misuse, but lower courts have regarded the Court's citation of patent misuse cases in these cases as an implicit endorsement of the doctrine with respect to copyright.[174] To the extent that the interplay between antitrust and copyright is likely the same as the interplay between antitrust and patent, the same considerations supporting patent misuse arguably also support recognizing copyright misuse.[175]

[166] 314 U.S. 488, 491 (1942). For a discussion of earlier patent misuse cases, see Richard Calkins, *Patent Law: The Impact of the 1988 Patent Misuse Reform Act and Noerr-Pennington Doctrine on Misuse Defenses and Antitrust Counterclaims*, 38 DRAKE L. REV. 175, 180–82 (1988–89).

[167] 314 U.S. at 492.

[168] U.S. Gypsum Co. v. Nat'l Gypsum Co., 352 U.S. 457, 465 (1957).

[169] Simpson v. Union Oil Co., 377 U.S. 13, 24 (1964).

[170] Ill. Tool Works, Inc. v. Indep. Ink, Inc., 547 U.S. 28, 38–43 (2006); *see also* Princo Corp. v. Int'l Trade Comm'n, 563 F.3d 1301, 1307–08 (Fed. Cir. 2009) ("Tying arrangements have a long history in both the patent misuse and antitrust contexts. Much of the Supreme Court's early patent misuse doctrine was developed in cases involving a challenge to some form of tying arrangement. . . . Likewise, the early antitrust cases found that various tying arrangements violated the antitrust laws.").

[171] 334 U.S. 131, 156–59 (1948).

[172] 371 U.S. 38, 44–50 (1962).

[173] *Id.* at 44–50.

[174] Atari Games Corp. v. Nintendo of Am., Inc., 975 F.2d. 832, 846 (Fed. Cir. 1992); Lasercomb Am., Inc. v. Reynolds, 911 F.2d 970, 973–74 (4th Cir. 1990); United Tel. Co. of Mo. v. Johnson Publ'g Co., 855 F.2d 604, 611 (8th Cir. 1988).

[175] Peter M. Boyle et al., *Antitrust Law at the Federal Circuit: Red Light or Green Light at the IP-Antitrust Intersection*, 69 ANTITRUST L.J. 739, 752–53 (2002).

Holding that copyright and patent are *in pari materia* for the purpose of recognizing copyright misuse as a defense does not necessarily extend to all of the doctrine's particulars. Consider the question whether refusal to license can constitute misuse. Some courts have analogized between these two areas of law and cited the 1988 amendment explicitly providing that refusal to license cannot constitute patent misuse[176] to justify extending the same principle to copyright misuse.[177] Other courts have drawn the opposite conclusion, drawing a negative inference from Congress's failure to enact a similar amendment to the copyright statute.[178] Thus, concluding that copyright and patent are *in pari materia* with respect to recognizing the copyright misuse defense does not necessitate treating copyright and patent as *in pari materia* for all aspects of misuse.

C. *Third-Party Liability*

Compared with fair use and copyright misuse, continuing judicial development of the contours of third-party liability is more problematic. In contrast to fair use, the statute does not evince any legislative delegation of authority to courts to continue to develop the law. Moreover, unlike with misuse, Congress did enact a comprehensive statute to cover third-party liability for patent infringement.[179] The more expansive nature of the patent statute with respect to third-party liability is more likely to give rise to a negative inference regarding third-party liability with respect to copyright.

Despite the absence of a specific provision governing third-party liability, some courts have regarded the text of the 1976 amendments as supporting the imposition of third-party liability. One of the central changes effected by the Copyright Act of 1976 was its new definition of infringement providing that "the owner of copyright under this title has the exclusive rights to do *and to authorize*" the specified rights associated with copyright protection, including reproduction, the preparation of derivative works, distribution, performance, and display.[180] This language suggests that facilitation of unauthorized uses arguably constitutes direct infringement of the copyright holder's exclusive right to authorize uses of the copyrighted work. Indeed, the Ninth Circuit has concluded that the addition of the words "to authorize" "was intended to remove the confusion surrounding contributory and vicarious infringement."[181] It noted the Supreme Court's conclusion in *Sony* that this language establishes that "'an infringer is not merely one who uses a work without authorization by the

[176] 35 U.S.C. § 271(d)(4).

[177] *See* Intergraph Corp. v. Intel Corp., 195 F.3d 1346, 1362 (Fed. Cir. 1999); Advanced Computer Servs. of Mich., Inc. v. MAI Sys. Corp., 845 F. Supp. 356, 368–69 (E.D. Va. 1994).

[178] Data Gen. Corp. v. Grumman Sys. Support Corp., 36 F.3d 1147, 1187 (1st Cir. 1994); *see also* Image Tech. Servs., Inc. v. Eastman Kodak Co., 125 F.3d 1195, 1218 (9th Cir. 1997) (following *Data General* in relevant part).

[179] 35 U.S.C. § 271(c).

[180] 17 U.S.C. § 106 (emphasis added).

[181] Peter Starr Prod. Co. v. Twin Continental Films, Inc., 783 F.2d 1440, 1443 (9th Cir. 1986).

copyright owner, but also one who authorizes the use of a copyrighted work without actual authority from the copyright owner.'"[182]

This textual analysis draws further support from the enactment context. As a subsequent Ninth Circuit decision noted, the legislative history specifically provides the following:

> Use of the phrase "to authorize" is intended to avoid any questions as to the liability of contributory infringers. For example a person who lawfully acquires an authorized copy of a motion picture would be an infringer if he or she engages in the business of renting it out to others for purposes of unauthorized public performance.[183]

Another portion of the legislative history ignored by the courts but identified by Menell and Nimmer notes that the House Committee explicitly rejected an amendment to exempt dance halls from copyright liability, concluding that "no justification exists for changing existing law," which provides for vicarious liability on those who actively supervise a place where performances occur and who expect commercial gain from those performances.[184] Other courts have drawn the same conclusion.[185]

The *Sony* Court could therefore have based third-party liability squarely on the copyright statute itself and used the pre-1976 decisions to determine its contours. Instead, the Court noted the difficulty of attributing third-party liability because "[t]he Copyright Act does not expressly render anyone liable for infringement committed by another," in contrast to the patent statute, which explicitly provides for liability for inducement and contributory infringement.[186] The Court nonetheless held that "[t]he absence of such express language in the copyright statute does not preclude the imposition of liability for copyright infringements on certain parties who have not themselves engaged in the infringing activity."[187] Instead of deriving from the statute, third-party liability stemmed from broad principles that are applied in all areas of the law.[188]

Rather than follow this reasoning to its logical conclusion, the Court borrowed the "staple article of commence" and "substantial noninfringing use" tests from the patent statue.[189] Given the clear statements of desire to codify existing law and the absence of any indication of any intent to import the patent law standard, the Supreme Court would have been better served to turn to the pre-1976 copyright law

[182] *Id.* (quoting Sony Corp. of Am. v. Universal City Studios, Inc., 464 U.S. 417, 435 n.17 (1984)).

[183] H.R. REP. NO. 94-1476, at 61, *quoted in* Subafilms Ltd., v. MGM-Pathe Commc'ns Co., 24 F.3d 1088, 1093 (9th Cir. 1994).

[184] *Id.* at 159–60.

[185] Davis v. Blige, 505 F.3d 90, 106 n.13 (2d Cir. 2007); Venegas-Hernandez v. Asociacion De Compositores, Editores De Musica Latinoamericana (ACEMLA), 424 F.3d 50, 57–58 (1st Cir. 2005); Columbia Pictures Indus., Inc. v. Aveco, Inc., 800 F.2d 59, 62 (3d Cir. 1996).

[186] 464 U.S. at 434–35.

[187] *Id.* at 435.

[188] *Id.*

[189] *Id.* at 440–42.

as a guide.[190] The *Grokster* Court followed suit by relying primarily on patent law.[191] It did augment the patent analogy with a discussion of pre-1976 copyright cases.[192] The borrowing has become reciprocal. Patent cases have begun to borrow back from copyright law despite their differences (although to the extent the copyright precedents on third-party liability are in effect construing patent law, this reverse borrowing is unproblematic).[193]

Any commonality that may exist between copyright and patent with respect to third-party liability stems from the fact that they draw from the same source: tort law.[194] Some courts have recognized that third-party liability is properly based in tort law and turned to the pre-1976 copyright cases rather than patent law.[195] Analyzing how this difference in analytical approach would change copyright law is beyond the scope of this chapter. For present purposes, it suffices to note that the difference should matter to those who care about democratic legitimacy and legislative supremacy. Basing third-party liability in tort also provides greater room for judicial development than does a broad analogy to patent law. It would certainly have placed less focus on the meaning of terms such as "staple article of commerce" and "substantial noninfringing use."

D. *The First Sale Doctrine*

As the briefing and oral argument in *Kirtsaeng* demonstrated, the Supreme Court is directly confronting the extent to which codification limits the propriety of drawing on judicial sources of law when determining the scope of the first sale doctrine. Courts must determine both the extent to which they can look to precodification judicial precedents for guidance and their ability to effect additional postcodification changes in the manner associated with the common law.

As noted earlier, the role of courts in developing copyright law is itself a matter of legislative intent. In contrast to the case of fair use, there is no statutory language or legislative history indicating any intent to confer on the courts the authority to shape the first sale doctrine. Nor is the first sale doctrine a carve out enacted in front of a backdrop of preexisting extrastatutory legal principles, as was the case with the patent misuse principles that were transferred to copyright. Nor is there any basis for resolving the question by analogizing to patent law, as is the case with third-party liability. The legislative history accompanying the most recent codification of the

[190] Menell & Nimmer, *supra* note 2, at 993.

[191] Metro-Goldwyn-Mayer Studios Inc. v. Grokster, Ltd., 545 U.S. 913, 932–33 (2005).

[192] Menell & Nimmer, *supra* note 2, at 935–36.

[193] *See* Ricoh Co., Ltd. v. Quanta Computer Inc., 550 F.3d 1325, 1338 (Fed. Cir. 2008).

[194] Menell & Nimmer, *supra* note 2, at 994–1005.

[195] *See* Fonovisa, Inc. v. Cherry Auction, Inc., 76 F.3d 259, 261–62 (9th Cir. 1996); Gener-Villar v. Adcom Group, Inc., 509 F. Supp. 2d 117, 125 (D.P.R. 2007); Lifetime Homes, Inc. v. Residential Dev. Corp., 510 F. Supp. 2d 794, 807 (M.D. Fla. 2007); Peer Int'l Corp. v. Luna Records, Inc., 887 F. Supp. 560, 565–65 (S.D.N.Y. 1995); Demetriades v. Kaufmann, 690 F. Supp. 289, 291–92 (S.D.N.Y. 1988).

first sale doctrine indicated that Section 109 "restates and confirms" the principles "established by the court decisions and section 27 of the present law,"[196] including first and foremost *Bobbs-Merrill*, which explicitly disavowed drawing any analogies to patent law.

Instead, there are strong indications that Congress intended courts to look to the statute instead of the common law when determining the contours of the first sale doctrine. Section 106 enumerates six exclusive rights conferred on copyright holders, including the right to distribute that forms the basis for the first sale doctrine, subject to the restrictions enumerated in the following sections. The legislative history indicates that "[t]he approach of the bill is to set forth the copyright owner's exclusive rights in broad terms in section 106, and then to provide various limitations, qualifications, or exemptions in the 12 sections that follow. Thus, everything in section 106 is made 'subject to sections 107 through 118,' and must be read in conjunction with those provisions."[197] In addition the Report language describes Section 109 as a restatement of the first sale doctrine, which suggests that Congress intended it to be its authoritative statement.[198]

The language of the Supreme Court's decision in *Quality King* corroborates the statutory nature of the first sale doctrine under current law. It noted that although *Bobbs-Merrill* represented a judicial construction of the statutory right to "vend" the copyrighted work, the comparable right under current law is the right to "distribute," and "[t]he comparable limitation on that right is provided not by judicial interpretation, but by an express statutory provision."[199] In other words, "the basic holding in *Bobbs-Merrill* is now codified in § 109(a)."[200]

Moreover, the Court's analysis of whether the first sale doctrine restricted § 602(a) was entirely statutory in nature. Instead of prohibiting unauthorized distribution directly, Section 602(a) instead provides that unauthorized importation "is an infringement of the exclusive right to distribute copies ... under section 106." In other words, Section 602(a) simply defines one aspect of the distribution right created by section 106. According to the statutory text, all Section 106 rights are subject to the restrictions of Section 109(a). Because Section 602(a) claims are simply one type of Section 106 claim, they are necessarily subject to Section 109(a).[201] This reasoning did not invoke any form of common law decision making, but instead focused on the import of the "literal text."[202] The Court then focused on how that construction was consistent with other provisions of the copyright statute.[203] The Court closed by declaring all policy considerations to be irrelevant.[204] Similarly, the

[196] S. Rep. No. 94-473, at 71 (1975).
[197] *Id.* at 57; H.R. Rep. No. 94-1476, at 61.
[198] S. Rep. No. 94-473, at 71; H.R. Rep. No. 94-1476, at 79.
[199] 523 U.S. at 142.
[200] *Id.* at 143.
[201] *Id.* at 144–45.
[202] *Id.* at 145.
[203] *Id.* at 145–52.
[204] *Id.* at 153.

primary thrust of the Supreme Court's reasoning in *Kirtsaeng* focused on the plain meaning of the text of Section 109(a).[205]

There is an argument based on the legislative history that would treat precodification decisions as an appropriate source of law. The House and Senate Reports accompanying the 1909 Act indicated that Section 41's codification of the first sale doctrine was "not intended to change in any way existing law."[206] The House and Senate Reports accompanying the 1976 Act similarly indicated that Section 109 simply "restates and confirms" the principles "established by the court decisions and section 27 of the present law."[207] Moreover, the Supreme Court observed in *Quality King*, "There is no reason to assume that Congress intended either § 109(a) or the earlier codifications of the [first sale] doctrine to limit its broad scope."[208] This suggests that courts might be justified in basing their constructions of Section 109(a) on precodification judicial decisions. Such a conclusion would be at odds with the textualist approach adopted by the Court in *Quality King* and would not convince those who reject legislative history as a legitimate basis for statutory interpretation. Moreover, even if successful, such an argument would not give courts any authority to continue to refashion the scope of the first sale doctrine.

The Supreme Court's decision in *Kirtsaeng* recognized the continuing relevance of precedents predating the 1976 Act, albeit one based more in text than legislative history. As noted earlier, the Court invoked a canon of construction that when confronting a statute covering subject matter previously governed by common law, courts "must presume that 'Congress intended to retain the substance of the common law.'"[209] Interestingly, the Court bases most of its analysis on the law's hostility toward restraints on the alienation of chattels, which Justice Breyer traces back to Coke's *Institutes*. Only in the end does the opinion note the absence of any distinction based on geography in *Bobbs-Merrill* as well as the Solicitor General's concession that that decision "would not preclude the 'first sale' defense form applying to authorized copies made overseas."[210]

Although certainly plausible, the Court's reasoning seems incomplete. As an initial matter, no judicial decision addressed whether the first sale doctrine applied to foreign-manufactured works until the 1983 district court decision in *Scorpio*,[211] which was decided long after the 1976 Act was passed. The Court's espousal of adherence to the common law amounts to deference to postenactment lower court decisions, a practice inconsistent with the Supreme Court's usual modus operandi and unlikely to yield useful insights into congressional intent. At the same time, the Court manipulates the applicable common law baseline by shifting the focus from

[205] 133 S. Ct. at 1358–62.
[206] H.R. Rep. No. 60-222, at 19 (1909); S. Rep. No. 60-1118, at 19 (1909).
[207] S. Rep. No. 94-473, at 71; H.R. Rep. No. 94-1476, at 79.
[208] 523 U.S. at 152.
[209] 133 S. Ct. at 1363.
[210] *Id.* at 1363–64.
[211] 569 F. Supp. at 49.

restraints on the sale of copyrighted works in particular to restraints on alienation of property in the abstract.

Moreover, as Karl Llewellyn pointed out in his landmark critique of the canons of construction, the principle that statues are to be read in accordance with their common law antecedents is opposed by the canon that the common law gives way to statutes that revise an entire body of law.[212] Put a different way, the whole point of many statutes is to change the law by clarifying ambiguities, resolving inconsistencies, or framing the analysis in a more unified and analytically consistent manner. Whether any particular part of a codification simply restates existing law or effects some changes is an issue that must be analyzed, not simply presumed.

In short, the continuing relevance of precodification precedent is itself a matter of legislative intent that cannot be presumed simply by reciting a canon of construction. On the contrary, the more natural presumption is that Congress's intentions in this regard may vary from provision to provision. Instead of analyzing the issue, the *Kirtsaeng* Court simply relied on an inference from silence in *Bobbs-Merrill* and on a concession by the Solicitor General, who appeared as an amicus. A more direct analysis of legislative intent would have been more appropriate.

In its amicus brief, the U.S. government advanced a subtle argument for giving the courts a more active role that not only preserves the relevance of precodification precedent, but also leaves room for further judicial development of the first sale doctrine. Where Section 109(a) applies, it supersedes Section 106 and determines whether the conduct in question violates copyright. Where Section 109(a) does not apply, courts remain free to shape whether particular conduct violates the distribution right, just as *Bobbs-Merrill* decided whether particular conduct contravened the antecedent vending right. This would allow the courts to place some limits on copyright holders' ability to restrict the resale of foreign manufactured copies even if they are not subject to the first sale doctrine.[213] *Quality King* did not present the Court with an opportunity to address this question, because the goods were manufactured in the United States and thus were clearly governed by Section 109(a).

The success of this argument depends on whether one believes that Congress regarded the list of restrictions on the exclusive rights granted to copyright holders enumerated in Sections 107 to 122 to be comprehensive. If they were not comprehensive, then courts may well retain some role in determining the contours of copyright law. If comprehensive, such judicial involvement would be improper.

Continuing judicial innovation with respect to the first sale doctrine would require some indication that Congress only regarded Section 109(a) as a partial reification of the first sale doctrine. Although such questions are always debatable, the detailed nature of Sections 107 to 122 suggests that they represent the entirety of Congress's thinking on the subject matter that they cover. The Supreme Court's observation

[212] Karl N. Llewellyn, *Remarks on the Theory of Appellate Decision and the Rules or Canons About How Statutes Are to Be Construed*, 3 VAND. L. REV. 395, 401 (1950).

[213] Brief for the United States as Amicus Curiae Supporting Respondent, *supra* note 4, at 27–29.

that "the basic holding in *Bobbs-Merrill* is now codified in § 109(a)" would seem to contradict claims that *Bobbs-Merrill*-style innovations fall outside the scope of Section 109(a).[214]

Lastly, policy considerations offer no clear guidance to the interpretive question, because the policy implications from either construction are unattractive. Holding the first sale doctrine applicable to foreign manufactured copies would raise a host of problems. It would allow anyone to defeat the purpose of Section 602(a) simply by buying indirectly. Moreover, import restrictions facilitate price discrimination, which is widely recognized as a necessary condition to the efficient provision of copyrighted works.[215] Moreover, if companies are unable to prevent copies intended for sale outside the United States from being diverted back to the United States, they will have no choice but to charge a uniform price, which will disadvantage consumers in countries with low willingness or ability to pay.

At the same time, exempting foreign manufactured copies from the first sale doctrine would create a different set of policy anomalies. As Justice Sotomayor noted during oral argument, such a rule would prevent a U.S. resident who bought an edition of a book meant to be sold exclusively in England from bringing it home.[216] As Justice Breyer noted, it would also permit foreign companies who manufacture and sell cars with GPS systems containing copyrighted information to exercise control over the used car market.[217] It would give foreign manufactured copies greater protection than domestically manufactured copies,[218] thereby providing incentives to shift manufacturing operations offshore.[219]

The best reading of these statutes still appears to militate against recognizing broad judicial authority to refine the contours of the first sale doctrine. The legislative intent reflected in the statutory text and the legislative history and the interpretive approach reflected in Supreme Court precedent all suggest that continuing judicial innovation would be improper. Although policy considerations exist on both sides, until the Supreme Court's decision in *Kirtsaeng*,[220] courts regarded such policy considerations as illegitimate bases for statutory interpretation.[221]

More to the point, the scope of judicial authority in shaping copyright is not something that can be determined categorically. Instead, it is a contextual question that requires a careful assessment of the legislature's intent with respect to a particular

214 *Id.* at 143.

215 John M. Conley & Christopher S. Yoo, *Nonrivalry and Price Discrimination in Copyright Economics*, 157 U. Pa. L. Rev. 1801, 1814–20 (2009); *see also* Benjamin Klein & John Shepard Wiley, Jr., *Competitive Price Discrimination as an Antitrust Justification for Intellectual Property Refusals to Deal*, 70 Antitrust L.J. 599, 611–19 (2003).

216 Transcript of Oral Argument, *supra* note 75, at 27.

217 *Id.* at 28–29.

218 *See Drug Emporium*, 38 F.3d at 482 n.8.

219 *See Kirtsaeng*, 654 F.3d at 222 n.44.

220 133 S. Ct. at 1364–66.

221 *See Quality King*, 523 U.S. at 153; *Kirtsaeng*, 654 F.3d at 222 n.44.

issue. As such, the resolution may depend on the particular theory of legisprudence to which particular judges adhere. More than any other issue discussed in this chapter, the role of the courts with respect to the first sale doctrine depends on the weight placed on text, legislative history, the interpretive approach reflected in the precedents, and policy considerations.

E. *Other Doctrines Unaddressed by the Statute*

An interesting question is posed by the scope of the judiciary's authority in areas where Congress has not acted at all. A classic example is with respect to infringement, where in the absence of any legislative guidance the courts have fashioned a wide array of tests to determine whether copying has occurred.[222] Where Congress has not acted, there is no legislative intent to try to discern. Although it is conceivable that the absence of legislation may reflect an affirmative endorsement of the judicially developed law as it existed at any particular moment, at a minimum such a conclusion would require active consideration of a potential intervention and a decision not to do so on the grounds that doing so was unnecessary. And even such action would be ambiguous at best. Legislative inaction can stem from a host of reasons, with a tacit endorsement of the status quo from an affirmative desire to freeze it in place being only one (and a relatively unlikely one at that).

What inference should courts draw about their authority in areas of copyright law that Congress has left untouched? The absence of legislative intervention into an area gives rise either to an implicit delegation to the courts or at least a tolerance of continued judicial development. Moreover, as a practical matter, judges must still decide cases even in the absence of affirmative legislative guidance, so it is hard to see what alternative they would have. Such authority would not be an act of federal common law of the type invalidated by *Erie Railroad* v. *Tompkins*.[223] Instead, it would focus on interpreting broad statutory terms that have not yet received congressional attention, as typically occurred in early copyright cases. All of this would change should Congress choose to intervene. But the scope of that intervention would be subject to the type of contextual analysis undertaken earlier.

CONCLUSION

One of the signature changes of the past few decades is the Supreme Court's growing emphasis on statutory text and on formal approaches to statutory interpretation. As textualism has grown more influential, it has prompted a reaction from those who are dissatisfied with it as a methodology or with the answers that it yields. Those wishing to counter the increasing influence of textualism have begun to call for

[222] *See* Shyamkrishna Balganesh, *The Normativity of Copying in Copyright Law*, 62 Duke L.J. 203, 216–20 (2012).

[223] 304 U.S. 64 (1938).

recognizing greater judicial authority to incorporate contemporary values when construing statutes. Academic dissatisfaction with recent changes to the copyright statutes may make copyright particularly fertile ground for such entreaties.

Any evaluation of these proposals must make sure to honor the basic commitments to democracy reflected in the U.S. system of government. Any proposals that involve giving courts greater authority must also recognize that judicial decision-making processes have their shortcomings as well. A complete analysis requires a comparison of legislatures' and courts' relative institutional competencies as well as the key legitimating function played by legislative supremacy.

Furthermore, closer analysis of the relative positions in this debate reveals that the role of courts in articulating copyright law is not susceptible to simple policy inferences or sweeping generalizations. The question is not so much between judicial and legislative authority in the abstract, but rather an allocation of responsibility that leaves substantial scope for judicial lawmaking, subject to legislatively enacted limits to judicial discretion. Determining the proper balance of decision-making authority between judges and legislators in any particular case thus turns out to be a context-specific inquiry that can vary with each statutory provision and even across issues contained within the same statutory provision. A court should eschew broad categorical approaches, such as categorically analogizing to patent law, in favor of more granular analysis of the precise contours of legislative intent.

PART II

The Common Law Method in Intellectual Property

9

Legal Pragmatism and Intellectual Property Law

*Thomas F. Cotter**

INTRODUCTION

The legal pragmatism movement that came to prominence in the 1990s generated a body of scholarship that drew on a variety of intellectual sources, ranging from Aristotle's concept of practical reason and the classic American pragmatism associated with Peirce, James, and Dewey to a variety of postmodern thinkers including Hans-Georg Gadamer, Richard Bernstein, and Richard Rorty.[1] Legal scholars including Richard Posner, Margaret Radin, Thomas Grey, and Dan Farber, among many others, came to be associated with a legal pragmatism movement characterized (at a certain abstract level) by a common perspective on the relationship between law and society, coupled with what could often be quite different emphases, applications, and conclusions on the part of the individual commentator.[2] Some of my own early work focused on the relationship between legal pragmatism and the law-and-economics movement,[3] as well as on some possible applications of a pragmatist outlook to questions of intellectual property (IP) law and policy.[4] And much of what I have written since has reflected, at least implicitly, what I view as some of the leading insights associated with legal pragmatism: its understanding of human thought as contextual, "the product . . . of culture, collectively developed and

* Briggs and Morgan Professor of Law, University of Minnesota Law School. I thank Sanjiv Laud for research assistance and, for their comments and criticism, participants in the University of Pennsylvania's symposium on Intellectual Property and the Common Law held in May 2011. Any errors that remain are mine.

1 For an overview, see Thomas F. Cotter, *Legal Pragmatism and the Law and Economics Movement*, 84 GEO. L.J. 2071, 2073–98 (1996).

2 *See id.*

3 *See id.*

4 *See* Thomas F. Cotter, *Pragmatism, Economics, and the* Droit Moral, 76 N.C. L. REV. 1 (1997). For an excellent discussion of legal pragmatism and the common law of intellectual property, see Shyamkrishna Balganesh, *The Pragmatic Incrementalism of Common Law Intellectual Property*, 63 VAND. L. REV. 1543 (2010).

transmitted";[5] the (related) rejection of "foundationalism," meaning in this context the idea that any one body of law can be adequately explained by some grand theory, united by a single goal or value, or logically deduced from certain foundational principles;[6] the idea that knowledge is instrumental and that, in turn, legal rules as well should be evaluated more by their practical consequences than by their formal consistency or conformity to some abstract grand theory;[7] and the importance of practical reason – the practice of making rational decisions in light of uncertainty.[8]

In this chapter, I argue that a legal pragmatist approach to IP law has both strengths and weaknesses. Among the strengths of such an approach are its recognition of the competing values that animate IP policy and doctrine, its understanding of the limits of both instrumental and natural rights theories in explaining and shaping the contours of IP rights, and its appreciation for the common law method of incrementally adapting doctrine to changing circumstances – in the present case, to changing technological environments. At the same time, however, some versions of a legal pragmatist approach risk exacerbating certain negative trends in the evolution of IP law and policy. An approach that naively embraces totality-of-the-circumstances tests, for example, may induce IP users to overcomply with their legal obligations and thus raise social costs without a commensurate public benefit. Similarly, an approach that overemphasizes the unquantifiable and the incommensurable may inhibit the use of economic analysis as a tool (albeit an imperfect one) for precisely stating one's assumptions, predicting consequences, and testing results; more generally, it may blunt the critical edge necessary to counter the ever expanding scope of some IP rights. Policy makers, in short, should avoid the temptation to turn legal pragmatism's antifoundationalist stance into a rigidly foundational principle of IP law and policy.

5 *See* Cotter, *supra* note 1, at 2075 (quoting Thomas C. Grey, *Holmes and Legal Pragmatism*, 41 STAN. L. REV. 787, 798 (1989)). As I noted at the time, this view of knowledge as contextual need not be a mere restatement of the obvious, but rather leads some neopragmatists to challenge the conventional view of truth as correspondence with reality. *See id.* at 2075–76. For a cogent critique of some neopragmatic approaches to truth, see SUSAN HAACK, EVIDENCE AND INQUIRY: A PRAGMATIST RECONSTRUCTION OF EPISTEMOLOGY 239–61 (2d expanded ed. 2009).

6 *See* Cotter, *supra* note 4, at 29–30; Cotter, *supra* note 1, at 2083–85. Susan Haack notes that the term foundationalism has at least three distinct meanings in epistemology and that only one of them "has an analogue in legal theory: the idea that legal rules, to be (in a non-epistemic sense) justified, must be grounded in some relation to (presumably, moral) values." Susan Haack, *On Legal Pragmatism: Where Does "The Path of the Law" Lead Us?*, 50 AM. J. JURIS. 71, 104 (2005). Haack argues that legal pragmatism in the tradition of Holmes may not even be antifoundational in this third sense; although it may "repudiate[] the idea that what the law is may be deduced from some overriding set of moral principles, it also urges that judges look to the social benefits and disadvantages of their rulings." *Id.* My own view is that policy makers should be wary, though not necessarily dismissive, of attempts to ground any body of law in one overarching policy or justification. *See* Cotter, *supra* note 1, at 2083–84. In adopting a skeptical attitude toward such "grand theory," legal pragmatism has some affinity with the Burkean view of tradition as (sometimes) a repository of practical wisdom. *See, e.g.*, Thomas F. Cotter, *A Burkean Perspective on Patentable Subject Matter*, 22 BERKELEY TECH. L.J. 855 (2007) [hereinafter Cotter, *Burkean*].

7 *See* Cotter, *supra* note 4, at 29–30; Cotter, *supra* note 1, at 2078, 2083–85.

8 *See infra* note 23 and accompanying text (discussing practical reason).

Part I outlines some of the virtues of a legal pragmatist approach to law in general, whereas Part II focuses on the merits of such an approach to IP law in particular. Part III, however, cautions against a simplistic application of legal pragmatist thought in the development of IP law and policy; in some respects, IP law and policy would benefit more from adhering to firm principles than from accommodating too many, often inconsistent, values. The final part concludes.

I. LEGAL PRAGMATISM

As suggested earlier, legal pragmatists of various stripes often have stressed the virtues of a contextual, antifoundationalist approach to law. In part, their embrace of contextualism and antifoundationalism can be traced to the emphasis in (at least some versions of) pragmatist and postmodern thought on the contingent nature of human knowledge: that our knowledge of the world is shaped by our environment and experience (e.g., our time, place, culture, class); that our efforts to describe reality can be nothing more than efforts to control and shape that environment in ways that suit our (ever shifting) goals; and thus that attempts to ground our understanding of the world in some immutable set of principles or foundations are doomed to fail.[9] From this perspective, there is no "God's-eye view" from which we can judge whether our own descriptions of reality are better or worse than those of others.[10] Descriptions of reality that suffice at one time for one purpose may not be adequate – or even comprehensible – when deployed at another time or for other purposes.[11]

Epistemologists and philosophers of science have long debated the soundness of the forgoing principles and no doubt will continue to do so for years to come. To be sure, the idea that *many* of our ideas and understandings are historically and culturally contingent hardly seems radical or shocking.[12] Taken to its logical conclusion, however, contextualism might seem to imply something much deeper: that even our most cherished moral sentiments are nothing more than human conventions,[13] for example, or that human beings can never aspire to attain objective truth even in realms of science and mathematics.[14] One might therefore question how a legal theory rooted in pragmatism and its postmodern offshoots could ever be

[9] *See* Cotter, *supra* note 1, at 2075–78, 2094, 2097–98.

[10] Joan C. Williams, *Rorty, Radicalism, Romanticism: The Politics of the Gaze*, *in* Pragmatism in Law & Society at 151, 151 (Michael Brint & William Weaver eds., 1991).

[11] *See* Cotter, *supra* note 1, at 2078–79, 2096–97.

[12] *See id.* at 2075.

[13] Though as Richard Rorty observed, one may still be willing to die for beliefs that one recognizes are merely historically and culturally contingent. *See* Richard Rorty, Contingency, Irony, and Solidarity 189 (1989).

[14] To quote Mark Tushnet, "[t]he canned footnote here typically begins with T. Kuhn, The Structure of Scientific Revolutions (1970), and continues according to the author's taste and reading." Mark Tushnet, *Critical Legal Studies: A Political History*, 100 Yale L.J. 1515, 1539 n.93 (1991). For my own quondam views on the matter, see Cotter, *supra* note 1, at 2095–98. For critical responses to postmodern challenges to the philosophy of science, see, e.g., Susan Haack, Defending Science

pragmatic in the *everyday* sense of being practical or useful (in the present context, to the task of formulating and applying legal rules). Although some scholars find the radical contextualist stance intellectually persuasive, I suspect that most ordinary people – and most legal policy makers – do not. Seen in this light, pragmatism might appear to present some interesting intellectual challenges and yet seem an unpromising candidate for integration into any sort of practical legal theory.

The reality of the situation is not quite so stark, however. *Legal* pragmatism may derive its inspiration from *philosophical* pragmatism, but it need not be synonymous with any particular branch of philosophical pragmatism; its distinctive approach may be judged on the basis of pragmatic criteria (e.g., is it useful?) without necessitating (or, for that matter, precluding) any sort of buy-in to a broader pragmatic or postmodernist agenda.[15] In my view, the themes that legal pragmatists tend to stress[16] hold much promise for the enterprise of legal decision making and policy formulation. The idea that human thought (and, by extension, the legal rules that are sometimes a product of that thought) is contextual – a product of our time, place, and cultural heritage – certainly resonates with the contemporary understanding of how laws shift over time with changes in social attitudes and understandings.

Similarly, the antifoundationalist stance *as applied to law*, which calls into question the idea that any one body of law (or law generally) can (or should) rest on a single grand theoretical foundation, seems to me to be largely accurate from both a descriptive and a normative perspective. Descriptively, attempts to explain a body of law as embodying a single grand narrative (the march of economic efficiency, the dominance of the ruling class, what have you) rarely if ever succeed in explaining more than a portion of what they set out to explain. Rather, any given body of law is likely to reflect the values and interests of many disparate actors and groups; casual observation alone suggests that many bodies of law are characterized by competing values (e.g., efficiency versus equality; free speech versus protection of dignitary interests) that can generate difficult-to-resolve tensions.[17] Normatively, the existence of such tensions – coupled with the inevitable limits of human reason in predicting all of the myriad ways in which grand theory is likely to misfire in its application[18] – suggests

WITHIN REASON (2003); ALAN SOKAL & JEAN BRICMONT, FASHIONABLE NONSENSE: POSTMODERN INTELLECTUALS' ABUSE OF SCIENCE (1998).

15 Richard Posner, among others, has repeatedly stressed this theme. *See, e.g.*, RICHARD A. POSNER, LAW, PRAGMATISM, AND DEMOCRACY 24–56 (2003).

16 *See supra* notes 5–8 and accompanying text.

17 *See, e.g.*, Christopher L. Kutz, Note, *Just Disagreement: Indeterminacy and Rationality in the Rule of Law*, 103 YALE L.J. 997 (1994).

18 This has been a theme in some of my own work that, drawing on themes found in the works of authors such as Burke, Hayek, and James Scott, counsels against jettisoning certain traditional restraints on the expansion of IP property rights. *See* Cotter, *Burkean*, *supra* note 6; Thomas F. Cotter, *Memes and Copyright*, 80 TUL. L. REV. 398–401 (2005). *See also* Balganesh, *supra* note 4, at 1602–03 (perceiving legal pragmatism's tendency toward "Burkean minimalism," but arguing that pragmatism's antifoundationalism and focus on consequences can also foster significant change in the IP context, *see id.* at 1603).

that grand theoretical approaches to the law are likely to fall short from a normative perspective as well. Disparate actors and groups may actually *have* different goals, and sometimes the law operates better if it mediates among those goals than if it consistently favors one and disapproves the other. Cass Sunstein, for example, has argued that the common law approach to legal decision making (including constitutional law decision making) can be understood as embodying "incompletely theorized agreements" among judges who can agree on outcomes without necessarily sharing precisely the same underlying principles.[19] By this process, the legal system sometimes sacrifices a degree of intellectual purity for the greater good of enabling consensus on outcomes when consensus on underlying principles may be unattainable.[20] In a similar vein, Richard Posner has cautioned against overreliance on "top-down" theoretical approaches to legal decision making that overlook the particularities of reasoning from the "bottom up," that is, incrementally and on the basis of empirical fact.[21] This type of approach, in turn, ties into Posner's (and other legal pragmatists') general perspective on law as an instrument for solving concrete human problems, rather than as an exercise in formal logic or deductive reasoning.[22]

Legal pragmatism's emphasis on context and consequences also calls into question whether one can or should attempt to deduce conclusions to real-world disputes on the basis of theory alone. For this reason, many legal pragmatists tend to emphasize the use of practical reason, "a method that emphasizes the need for choice, deliberation, and communication in the face of radical uncertainty . . . a way of simultaneously affirming and mediating among our conflicting norms."[23] By emphasizing the need for deliberation, empiricism, and revision in the light of new experience, legal pragmatists foresee a legal system that is flexible, dynamic, and adaptable in its operation, while at the same time paying due regard to the virtues of

[19] *See* Cass R. Sunstein, *Incompletely Theorized Agreements*, 108 HARV. L. REV. 1733 (1995).

[20] *See id.* at 1746–50.

[21] RICHARD A. POSNER, OVERCOMING LAW 191–92 (1995); Richard A. Posner, *Guido Calabresi's The Cost of Accidents*: A Reassessment, 64 MD. L. REV. 12, 22 (2005). Posner is at least as skeptical of overreliance on "bottom-up" reasoning, however, arguing that one needs at least an intuitive theoretical framework to make analogical moves from one case to another. *See* POSNER, *supra*, at 174–75; *see also supra* note 6.

[22] *See* POSNER, OVERCOMING LAW, *supra* note 21, at 11 (describing legal pragmatism as "practical, instrumental, forward-looking, activist, empirical, skeptical, antidogmatic, experimental"). This understanding of law dovetails with philosophical pragmatism's view of human thought and concepts as being, in general, instrumental: tools for helping us satisfy certain ends. *See* Cotter, *supra* note 1, at 2078. Legal pragmatism's focus on consequences nevertheless can (and should) lead judges to take into account systemic consequences as well. *See* RICHARD A. POSNER, HOW JUDGES THINK 239 (2007) [hereinafter POSNER, HOW JUDGES THINK]; Cotter, *supra* note 4, at 29 n.153.

[23] Cotter, *supra* note 4, at 30. For various formulations of the concept of practical reason, see Cotter, *supra* note 1, at 2087–90. *See also* RICHARD A. POSNER, THE PROBLEMS OF JURISPRUDENCE 73 (1990) (defining practical reason as "a grab bag that includes anecdote, introspection, imagination, common sense, empathy, imputation of motives, speaker's authority, metaphor, analogy, precedent, custom, memory, 'experience,' intuition, and induction (the expectation of regularities, a disposition related both to intuition and to analogy)"); Balganesh, *supra* note 4, at 1597–1601 (discussing the concept of practical reason in the thought of Joseph Singer and others).

stability, predictability, and respect for (what might be) the wisdom embodied in past tradition.[24] To legal pragmatism's critics, this all sounds, at best, like a sermon[25] and, at worst, banal and indeterminate,[26] a charge that even some of pragmatism's champions sometimes have been willing to concede.[27] The charge may be irrefutable. Yet, as I have argued before, if "[j]udges and other policymakers necessarily make decisions under conditions of great uncertainty, before all of the evidence that otherwise might have some bearing on the decision can be assessed,"[28] then the exercise of practical reason (banal though it may be) would appear well nigh inevitable.[29] The question is whether one can identify better or worse applications of practical reason in specific cases (while recognizing that, from a pragmatist perspective, the terms "better" and "worse" themselves may have no meaning external to the practice).[30]

II. LEGAL PRAGMATISM AND IP

In Part I, I argued that certain themes associated with legal pragmatism have much to recommend them in relation to legal decision making generally. In this part, I argue

[24] *See* Thomas F. Cotter, *Patent Remedies and Practical Reason*, 88 TEX. L. REV. SEE ALSO 125, 128 (2010) (stating that "to live in the hope of attaining some absolute truth derived from unshakable first principles is a fool's game; the rules we devise to resolve our disputes and to structure our lives are necessarily constrained by the limitations of our knowledge, the contingency and contestability of our goals, and the need to revise and rebuild in light of new experience").

[25] *See* Steven D. Smith, *The Pursuit of Pragmatism*, 100 YALE L.J. 409, 444–47 (1990).

[26] *See* Cotter, *supra* note 1, at 2090 n.81 (citing critiques). Critiques of legal pragmatism as banal are common. *See, e.g.*, BRIAN LEITER, NATURALIZING JURISPRUDENCE 46 (2007); Ronald Dworkin, *Pragmatism, Right Answers, and True Banality, in* PRAGMATISM IN LAW & SOCIETY, *supra* note 10, at 359, 360.

[27] Richard Rorty, *The Banality of Pragmatism and the Poetry of Justice*, 63 S. CAL. L. REV. 1811, 1811 (1990).

[28] Cotter, *supra* note 1, at 2090 (stating that "[j]udges and other policymakers necessarily make decisions under conditions of great uncertainty, before all of the evidence that otherwise might have some bearing on the decision can be assessed").

[29] *See* POSNER, HOW JUDGES THINK, *supra* note 22, at 254–55 ("Even if the objections to legal pragmatism are stronger than I think they are, there is no alternative in the United States of the twenty-first century.").

[30] *See* Richard Warner, *Why Pragmatism? The Puzzling Place of Pragmatism in Critical Theory*, 1993 U. ILL. L. REV. 535, 542 (stating that "[t]he distinctively pragmatic claim about justification is that there can be no *external* standard of evaluation: our norms of justification neither have nor need a ground outside themselves"); *see also* Susan Haack, *The Pluralistic Universe of Law: Towards a Neo-Classical Legal Pragmatism*, 21 RATIO JURIS 453, 475 (2008) (stating that "neo-classical pragmatist legal theory" "offers no simple decision-procedure for legislators or judges, no legal 'theory' in the restricted, tendentious sense in which it is sometimes understood today," but rather recognizes that "it is possible to make only fallible, imperfect assessments of what arrangements will, overall, be better, and what worse"). Seen in this light, the charge that pragmatism embraces relativism (moral or otherwise) would be accurate only if conformity with some external standard were necessary for, say, a moral norm to be "true." Pragmatists are not alone, however, in denying that one can rationally conclude that some moral norms are better than others even in the absence of such an external standard of evaluation. *See, e.g.*, RONALD DWORKIN, JUSTICE FOR HEDGEHOGS ch. 4 (2011). Legal pragmatists nevertheless part company with nonpragmatists such as Dworkin on other issues, most notably with respect to his famous "one right answer" thesis. *See* POSNER, *supra* note 23, at 197.

for legal pragmatism's relevance to IP law and policy in particular. Legal pragmatism shares with IP law both a focus on consequences and (to some extent) a resistance to grand theory. Legal pragmatism's sensitivity to context and its emphasis on practical reason also resonate with IP law's penchant for context-sensitive standards that enable decision makers to mediate, over time, among conflicting values. In the following paragraphs, I elaborate on these related themes and their relevance to IP law and policy.

First, legal pragmatism's focus on consequences resonates with the traditional characterization of IP rights as being largely instrumental in nature. By way of illustration, the conventional rationale for patents is that the state confers exclusive rights in inventions *not* because inventors have a moral entitlement to reap the fruit of their labor, but rather as a means to an end – indeed, to multiple ends, including the creation and disclosure of new inventions from which the public stands to benefit but that (due to free-rider problems) might not have been invented or disclosed in the absence of the patent incentive.[31] In a similar vein, copyright is often viewed (particularly in the United States) as a means for inducing the creation and publication of original works of authorship that enrich the common stock of knowledge, art, and entertainment.[32] Other IP rights also typically find support in some sort of utilitarian rationale. Trademark law's investiture of rights in product-identifying symbols, for example, serves the mutually reinforcing instrumental purposes of reducing consumer search costs and encouraging producers to maintain consistent product quality.[33] Ideally, the content of all of these bodies of law can (and does) change over time, as circumstances (such as changes in technology) warrant.

Second, and notwithstanding the importance of consequences, legal pragmatism's resistance to grand theory also strikes a chord with much of IP law and policy as it historically has existed. Although the instrumental approach sketched earlier dominates much of the relevant scholarly and judicial discourse (particularly within the United States), natural rights theories inspired by the writings of Locke, Kant, Hegel, and others also have influenced various aspects of IP law at various times.[34] A legal pragmatist may resist buying in to such natural rights theories completely, while still recognizing that the intuitions behind them – for example, that people

[31] *See* Cotter, *supra* note 24, at 126.

[32] Cotter, *supra* note 18, at 332.

[33] *See* RESTATEMENT (THIRD) OF UNFAIR COMPETITION, § 9 cmt. c (1995).

[34] Conventionally, protection of authors' "moral rights" to attribution and to respect for their work is traced to the writings of Kant and Hegel. U.S. law has adopted moral rights protection to a limited extent, particularly in connection with the Visual Artists Rights Act of 1990. *See* Cotter, *supra* note 4, at 6–24. Although the Supreme Court rejected a Lockean justification for copyright in *Feist Publ'ns, Inc.* v. *Rural Tel. Serv. Co.*, 499 U.S. 340, 359–60 (1990), some scholars continue to find inspiration for contemporary IP law in Locke's writings. *See, e.g.*, ROBERT P. MERGES, JUSTIFYING INTELLECTUAL PROPERTY (2011); Wendy J. Gordon, *A Property Right in Self-Expression: Equality and Individualism in the Natural Law of Intellectual Property*, 102 YALE L.J. 1533 (1993). For a recent defense of the view that IP rights should be exclusively instrumental, *see* CHRISTINA BOHANNAN & HERBERT HOVENKAMP, CREATION WITHOUT RESTRAINT: PROMOTING LIBERTY AND RIVALRY IN INNOVATION 41–43 (2012).

often disapprove of others' attempts to free-ride on their labor and that they regard works of authorship as embodying something of their creator's individuality – may be widely (though perhaps not universally) shared, and that as a consequence the law should accord such concerns due consideration.[35] In a similar vein, IP law (particularly copyright and trademark) sometimes subsists in what appears to be an uneasy tension with other aspects of U.S. law relating to freedom of speech.[36] To the extent that First Amendment law reflects not only instrumental concerns but also a commitment to deontological values such as personal autonomy, intellectual property sometimes may have to accommodate these noninstrumental values even if or when they conflict with other purely instrumental norms.[37] At a more fundamental level, just as philosophical pragmatists such as John Dewey called into question the sharp distinction between means and ends,[38] my discussion thus far may have overstated the sharpness of the distinction between instrumental and deontological approaches to law. For example, it may be the case that copyright law serves the instrumental goal of promoting (or could better promote) certain distributional goals, such as a more egalitarian distribution of written works.[39] Whether such goals themselves are desirable cannot be determined solely on instrumental criteria, however, but depends rather on one's moral sentiments (which, in turn, may be rooted in a complex mix of both moral reasoning and inarticulable belief). Indeed, any instrumental or teleological approach ultimately must rest on some goal the desirability of which must be justified on other grounds; at the same time, few of us are such strict Kantians as to believe that consequences never matter to the morality of the course we choose to take. So perhaps Dewey was right in suggesting that means and ends are two sides of the same coin, and if so, a simplistic instrumental view of IP rights may be equally untenable.[40]

[35] Such notions may be merely historically and culturally contingent, as the "romantic authorship" model posits. *See, e.g.*, James Boyle, Shamans, Software, and Spleens: Law and the Construction of the Information Society (1996); *but see* Denis Dutton, The Art Instinct: Beauty, Pleasure, and Human Evolution 56 (2008) (stating that "[t]he claim that artistic individuality is a Western construct not found in non-Western and tribal cultures has been widely accepted and is certainly false").

[36] *See, e.g.*, Mark A. Lemley & Eugene Volokh, *Freedom of Speech and Injunctions in Intellectual Property Cases*, 48 Duke L.J. 147 (1998); Jennifer E. Rothman, *Liberating Copyright: Thinking Beyond Free Speech*, 95 Cornell L. Rev. 463 (2010).

[37] *See, e.g.*, Cotter, *Burkean*, *supra* note 6, at 880–82 (citing with approval the works of other scholars arguing that patent law should accommodate human liberty and autonomy interests); Jed Rubenfeld, *The Freedom of Imagination: Copyright's Constitutionality*, 112 Yale L. J. 1 (2002) (arguing in favor of stronger First Amendment protection for the creation of derivative works).

[38] *See* Cotter, *supra* note 4, at 32 & n.168 (citing sources in Dewey's writings on aesthetics); Cotter, *supra* note 1, at 2093 & n.196.

[39] *See* Molly Shaffer Van Houweling, *Distributive Values in Copyright*, 83 Tex. L. Rev. 1535 (2005).

[40] *See* Balganesh, *supra* note 4, at 1574–79 (arguing that the common law of IP exhibits value pluralism by couching concepts and terms "at a relatively high level of abstraction" that "enables courts to look at conflicting values and balance them through a form of practical reasoning"); *see also* Benjamin Zipursky, *Pragmatic Conceptualism*, 6 Leg. Theory 457 (2000) (critiquing purely instrumental accounts of tort law and proposing instead a theory that takes seriously concepts embedded in the law).

Third, even within a purely instrumentalist framework there are likely to be disagreements over *which* instrumentalist goals should take precedence when two or more conflict, or over how best to attain even those goals on which like-minded observers agree; resolving these disagreements, I believe, is where practical reason can play a useful role. As John Golden has pointed out, for example, an instrumentalist approach to patent law ideally would take into account the effect (or lack thereof) of the patent system not only in inducing invention and disclosure but also in satisfying other (possible) instrumentalist goals such as inducing commercialization, "signaling," and the coordination of follow-up invention.[41] Similarly, as I have argued in other work, the scope and content of copyright law surely have an impact not only on the quantity of works of authorship produced but also on their dissemination, diversity, and quality.[42] In both the patent and copyright arenas, then, a problem arises in determining how to proceed when one instrumental goal threatens to conflict with or undermine another. Strengthening IP rights along one metric may advance certain policies while hindering others.[43] There may be no consensus on exactly what the right mix of policies is, and even if there were there would be room for considerable disagreement on how to effectuate that mix.

Although this might seem like reason for despair, legal pragmatism, as I have sketched it out earlier, recognizes the limits of conscious instrumentalism and invites the use of practical reason as a tool for mediating among these conflicting values and beliefs. There is a great deal we do not (and perhaps cannot) know about the broader social consequences of interacting legal rules and standards; this lack of confidence invites constant reevaluation and readjustment in light of new experience (while also, at least in my view, counseling against hubris in expecting that we can accurately predict the effects of departures from tradition). Even on their own terms, none of the instrumental or deontological approaches, standing alone, may be adequate, for reasons discussed earlier.[44] Perhaps, then, Terry Fisher's call for an IP system that puts human flourishing front and center is right on the mark.[45] Such an approach may well sound vague, but some degree of vagueness may be unavoidable if the certainty promised by grand theoretical approaches is illusory.

Fourth, although much of IP law has been codified over the past decades, many aspects of the law originally were developed by judges in common law fashion and remain standard-like in application. This use of flexible, multifactor standards in turn resonates with various legal pragmatist themes, to the extent it enables courts to

In Part III, I argue that for the most part patent law *should* pursue only instrumental goals, but that even within this framework practical reason plays a role in mediating among conflicting instrumental goals and methods for achieving them.

41 *See* John M. Golden, *Principles for Patent Remedies*, 88 TEX. L. REV. 505, 509–11, 520–21 (2010).

42 *See* Cotter, *supra* note 18.

43 *See* Golden, *supra* note 42, at 527.

44 *See supra* notes 35–43 and accompanying text.

45 *See* William W. Fisher III, *The Implications for Law of User Innovation*, 94 MINN. L. REV. 1417, 1463–72 (2010); William W. Fisher III, *Reconstructing the Fair Use Doctrine*, 101 HARV. L. REV. 1659 (1988).

engage in context-sensitive analysis that draws on a variety of underlying values and interests; to mediate among these values through the exercise of practical reason; and to adapt doctrine over time, in light of new experience and with an eye toward practical consequences. In the patent arena, for example, Craig Nard has noted how courts have nurtured the evolution of patent doctrine over time – often *dehors* the statutory text – in a manner that calls to mind the parallel development of a "common law" of antitrust.[46] Nard makes a persuasive case that courts often are better poised than is Congress to adapt doctrine (relatively) quickly in response to changes in the technological environment.[47] In a similar vein, the Supreme Court in recent years has repeatedly castigated the Federal Circuit for departing from this flexible framework in various respects by imposing unwarranted bright-line rules[48] and for deemphasizing the role of "tradition"[49] and "common sense"[50] in the development of patent doctrine. Copyright's fair use doctrine presents another obvious example of a body of law codified only after a century of judicial development, and even then only to the extent of advising courts to consider four nonexclusive factors in determining whether a given unauthorized use is fair.[51] Imperfect though it has surely been in its application, the fair use doctrine nevertheless has been able to adapt over the years in response to new technological challenges[52] in a manner that has evaded some of the industry capture that is reflected in many other aspects of the statutory text.[53] Similar examples can be culled from the law of trademarks.[54] In short, IP law's frequent preference for standards over bright-line rules promises many of the benefits touted by legal pragmatists, by permitting courts to respond

46 See Craig Allen Nard, *Legal Forms and the Common Law of Patents*, 90 B.U. L. REV. 501 (2010).

47 *See id.* at 106–08.

48 Recent cases emphasizing the virtues of flexibility in the patent context include Bilski v. Kappos, 130 S. Ct. 3218, 3226–27, 3229 (2010) (patentable subject matter); KSR Int'l Co. v. Teleflex Inc., 550 U.S. 398, 415 (2007) (obviousness); MedImmune, Inc. v. Genentech, Inc., 549 U.S. 118, 127 (2007) (declaratory judgments); eBay Inc. v. MercExchange, LLC, 547 U.S. 388, 392–94 (2006) (injunctive relief); Festo Corp. v. Shoketsu Kinzoku Kogyo Kabushiki Co., 535 U.S. 722, 738 (2002) (prosecution history estoppel).

49 *See eBay*, 547 U.S. at 392–93.

50 *See KSR*, 550 U.S. at 418, 420, 421 (using the term "common sense" five times).

51 *See* 17 U.S.C. § 107.

52 *See, e.g.*, Sony Corp. of Am. v. Universal City Studios, Inc., 464 U.S. 417 (1984) (holding that home video recording for purposes of time shifting constituted fair use); Perfect 10, Inc. v. Amazon.com, Inc., 508 F.3d 1146 (9th Cir. 2007) (holding that the search engine's production of "thumbnail" reproductions of photographs likely constituted fair use); Sony Computer Entm't, Inc. v. Connectix Corp., 203 F.3d 596, 598 (9th Cir. 2000) (holding that reverse engineering of software for purposes of extracting application programming interfaces (APIs) constituted fair use).

53 *See, e.g.*, Jessica Litman, *Copyright Legislation and Technological Change*, 68 OR. L. REV. 275 (1989) (discussing capture by special interests in the context of copyright law).

54 Trademark law's "digits of confusion" are a quintessential standard, but the digits all supposedly cast light on one foundational question: the likelihood of confusion. Examples of trademark doctrines that sometimes require mediation among multiple purposes, however, might include functionality, *see* Thomas F. Cotter, *The Procompetitive Interest in Intellectual Property Law*, 48 WM. & MARY L. REV. 483, 553–56 (2006), as well as trademark's many speech-protective doctrines, *see* William McGeveran, *Rethinking Trademark Fair Use*, 94 IOWA L. REV. 49 (2008).

to circumstance and to mediate among conflicting values through the exercise of practical reason.

III. LEGAL PRAGMATISM'S LIMITS

So far, I have highlighted some of the virtues of a legal pragmatist approach as reflected in various aspects of IP law and policy. In this part, however, I argue that a naïve legal pragmatist framework can do just as much harm as good and that a more mature approach must also consider the systemic consequences of standards that are too open-ended and too accommodating in their attempt to mediate among conflicting norms. Pragmatism need not degenerate into the view that one argument is, ultimately, just as good as any other. Briefly illustrating my thesis with examples from the three major bodies of IP law, I argue that sometimes a little foundationalism, and a little less context, would do a world of good.

A. *Patents*

Legal pragmatism may counsel caution in grounding any one body of law in a single all-pervasive theory, but in past work I have expressed reservations about turning pragmatism's skeptical perspective into a foundational principle in its own right.[55] Patent law in particular is one body of law in which commitment to a single perspective – the instrumental one, of patents as nothing more than a means to an end – would be preferable to a multidimensional perspective that stresses values such as desert and fairness, on the one hand, or the sanctity of property rights and fidelity to text, on the other. Commentators sometimes express concerns about desert and fairness, invoking the image of the small inventor as a reason for retaining aspects of U.S. law, such as the first-to-invent rule and the one-year grace period, that few if any other countries follow.[56] At other times, the concern expresses itself in the idea that even relatively minor inventions "deserve" patents just as much as do lifesaving drugs,[57] as well as in the emphasis in some opinions on implicit appeals to fairness over economic considerations in awarding patent

[55] *See* Cotter, *supra* note 1, at 2083–84 & n.48.

[56] *See, e.g.*, Michael J. Meurer, *Inventors, Entrepreneurs, and Intellectual Property Law*, 45 HOUS. L. REV. 1201, 1205 (2008) (observing that "the United States maintains first-to-invent priority rules and a one-year grace period to benefit small inventors"). The recently enacted America Invents Act, however, phases out the first-to-invent rule with respect to applications filed on or after March 16, 2013.

[57] *See, e.g.*, *Media Technologies Licensing, LLC v. Upper Deck Co.*, 596 F.3d 1334, 1339–40 (Fed. Cir. 2010) (Rader, J., dissenting) (accusing the majority of "a bias against non-technical arts," and that although "the invention of the transistor or of the polio vaccine came from more scientific fields and contributed more to the welfare of humanity," the court "cannot overlook that many individuals invest vast energies, efforts, and earnings to advance these nontechnical fields of human endeavor. Those investments deserve the same protection as any other advances. The incentives for improvement and the protection of invention apply as well to the creator of a new hair-extension design as to a researcher pursuing a cure for cancer.").

damages.[58] Concerns about fairness also sometimes manifest themselves in standards that emphasize the patentee's or the infringer's state of mind, such as the inequitable conduct doctrine or the standards for awarding enhanced damages.[59] From the other end of the spectrum, concerns about the sanctity of property rights have sometimes led courts to adopt quite expansive readings of the Patent Act[60] (notwithstanding the many exceptions that often cabin in the exercise of property rights outside the patent system,[61] as well as patents' lack of many of the characteristics, such as an effective notice system, that enable other property regimes to function[62]); whereas concerns about fidelity to text have inspired courts to (for example) reject calls for a more robust experimental use doctrine[63] (notwithstanding the lack of fidelity to text that traditionally has characterized the evolution of much of patent doctrine).[64]

Space does not permit me to address each of these concerns at length. Suffice it for now to say that, in the patent context, I remain skeptical of appeals to vague and unquantifiable notions of fairness – or to strong property rights – that sometimes may serve as nothing more than a fig leaf for naked self-interest. Nor am I alone in perceiving appeals to these other values as sometimes getting in the way of developing a patent policy that recognizes both the social benefits and social costs of patent protection and that seeks to maximize (as best one can approximate) the

58 A possible example is a series of Federal Circuit cases holding that courts may award reasonable royalties that exceed the amount the infringer could have expected to earn in profits from the use of the patented invention. *See* Mars, Inc. v. Coin Acceptors, Inc., 527 F.3d 1359, 1373 (Fed. Cir. 2008); Monsanto Co. v. Ralph, 382 F.3d 1374, 1383 (Fed. Cir. 2004); Golight, Inc. v. Wal-Mart Stores, Inc., 355 F.3d 1327, 1338 (Fed. Cir. 2004).

59 *See* NAT'L RESEARCH COUNCIL, A PATENT SYSTEM FOR THE 21ST CENTURY 117–23 (Stephen A. Merrill et al. eds. 2004) (arguing in favor of limiting reliance on subjective elements in patent litigation); Thomas F. Cotter, *Four Principles for Calculating Reasonable Royalties in Patent Infringement Litigation,* 27 SANTA CLARA COMP. & HIGH TECH. L.J. 725, 740 n.70 (2011) (noting that current law on enhanced damages focuses on the infringer's state of mind and not on optimal deterrence).

60 For example, in adopting pre-*eBay* the rule that patentees were entitled to injunctive relief absent exceptional circumstances. *See eBay*, 547 U.S. at 392–93 (rejecting this rule).

61 *See* Michael A. Carrier, *Cabining Intellectual Property Through a Property Paradigm*, 54 DUKE L.J. 1, 1 (2004) (proposing that "property is not as absolute as it is often claimed to be").

62 *See generally* JAMES BESSEN & MICHAEL J. MEURER, PATENT FAILURE: HOW JUDGES, BUREAUCRATS, AND LAWYERS PUT INNOVATORS AT RISK (2008).

63 *See, e.g.*, Embrex, Inc. v. Serv. Eng. Corp., 216 F.3d 1343, 1352 (Fed. Cir. 2000) (Rader, J., concurring) (stating that "the Patent Act leaves no room for any *de minimis* or experimental use excuses for infringement" because it "confers the right to preclude 'use,' not 'substantial use'"). Scholarly opinion, by contrast, often favors an expanded experimental use doctrine of the type common in other countries. *See, e.g.*, Henrik Holzapfel & Joshua D. Sarnoff, *A Cross-Atlantic Dialog on Experimental Use and Research Tools*, 48 IDEA 123, 149–99 (2008).

64 *See* Cotter, *Burkean*, *supra* note 6, at 876–77 (noting that "[m]uch of patent law traditionally has been judge-made: consider, for example, the evolution of the nonobviousness doctrine prior to its codification in 1952; the first sale doctrine; the exclusion of laws of nature and naturally-occurring physical phenomena; [and] the doctrine of non-statutory double patenting"). In contrast, sometimes the Federal Circuit's imposition of literalism reaches absurd heights. *See* Stark v. Advanced Magnetics, Inc., 119 F.3d 1551, 1555 (Fed. Cir. 1997) (reading two otherwise similar provisions of the Patent Act differently because of the absence of a comma in the second of them).

surplus of the former over the latter.[65] To be sure, even a consciously utilitarian patent system should recognize the limits of utilitarian reasoning. Economics has its limitations too, as I have emphasized in previous work, suggesting, for example, that certain aspects of traditional patent doctrine may have played a useful role in keeping patents from invading important liberty and autonomy interests.[66] And even a predominant focus on utilitarian concerns leaves plenty of scope for the exercise of practical reason. As suggested earlier, often there may be more than one plausible instrumental goal and a variety of opinions on how best to attain them[67] – although sometimes it is surprising just how much of the discourse surrounding this body of law, one ostensibly rooted in respect for science and technology, assumes on the basis of little or no actual evidence that more patent protection is necessarily socially beneficial.[68] Nevertheless, as I have argued elsewhere, economic analysis can be an important (albeit imperfect) tool for stating one's assumptions with precision and for making and testing predictions about likely consequences.[69] With regard to patents in particular, theoretical and empirical economic analysis in recent years has made substantial contributions to the debate over patent reform.[70] A patent system that continues to evolve – in much the same way that antitrust has evolved over the

65 *See, e.g.*, Mark A. Lemley, *Property, Intellectual Property, and Free Riding*, 83 TEX. L. REV. 1031, 1046 (2005) (warning that property theory, and rhetoric, "provides intellectual heft to justify the expansion" of IP rights).

66 *See* Cotter, *Burkean*, *supra* note 6.

67 *See supra* notes 43–44 and accompanying text.

68 *See, e.g.*, F. Scott Kieff, *Coordination, Property, and Intellectual Property: An Unconventional Approach to Anticompetitive Effects and Downstream Access*, 56 EMORY L.J. 327, 414 (2006) (asserting that IP rights provide a "beacon" that assists complementary users of IP to find one other); Alan O. Sykes, *TRIPS, Pharmaceuticals, Developing Countries, and the Doha "Solution"*, 3 CHI. J. INT'L L. 47 (2002) (arguing that widespread use of compulsory licensing will reduce research incentives to develop treatments for diseases endemic to the developing world). For evidence that patents may not play such an important role in many industries, see Wesley M. Cohen et al., *Protecting Their Intellectual Assets: Appropriability Conditions and Why U.S. Manufacturing Firms Patent (or Not)*, NBER Working Paper No. 7552 (Feb. 2000), at tbl.1, available at http://www.nber.org/papers/w7552 (suggesting that firms often rank patents below other reasons for engaging in research and development, but that patents may be relatively more effective at inducing research and development in some industries, including pharmaceuticals, than in others); *see also* Thomas F. Cotter, *Market Fundamentalism and the TRIPs Agreement*, 22 CARDOZO ARTS & ENTER. L.J. 307 (2004) (responding to Professor Sykes); Julie Cohen, *Lochner in Cyberspace: The New Economic Orthodoxy of "Rights Management,"* 97 MICH. L. REV. 462, 465 (1998) (decrying, in the copyright context, "cybereconomists' arguments and proposals [that] amount to ideology, not science"). For empirical evidence on the dysfunctional nature of the patent notice system, *see generally* BESSEN & MEURER, *supra* note 62; *see also* Mark A. Lemley, *Ignoring Patents*, 2008 MICH. ST. L. REV. 19, 21 (2008) (stating that "both researchers and companies in component industries simply ignore patents. Virtually everyone does it.").

69 *See* Cotter, *supra* note 1, at 2098–2140.

70 Empirical work by scholars such as Bessen and Meurer, John Allison, Mark Lemley, Josh Lerner, and Kimberly Moore, among others, has greatly contributed to our knowledge of how the patent system actually works. Policy makers ranging from Congress to the courts to the Federal Trade Commission have begun to take the works of law-and-economics scholars into account in formulating policy recommendations. The FTC's most recent effort is its March 2011 report, *The Evolving IP Marketplace: Aligning Patent Notice and Remedies with Competition*.

past generation – toward a single focus on promoting consumer welfare (albeit by different means than the means chosen by antitrust law) would, in my view, be an improvement both over the status quo and over some more pluralistic ideal.[71]

B. *Copyright*

The claim that copyright does (or should) reflect values other than purely instrumental ones seems somewhat more intellectually defensible than does the parallel claim for patent law. As suggested earlier, for example, many people appear to share the intuition that a work of authorship embodies the unique personality of the creator and that a proper respect for human individuality and autonomy entails respect for the creator's creative output.[72] I have tentatively endorsed such a view in previous work, while recognizing that to a large extent the romantic understanding of authorship may be merely historically and culturally contingent.[73] One of the virtues of a legal pragmatist approach to copyright may be that it seeks to establish common ground between proponents and opponents of such "moral rights" theories – for example, by suggesting reforms that both instrumental and moral rights theorists might find palatable in the spirit of Sunstein's incompletely theorized agreements.[74]

Pragmatism nevertheless has its limits in developing a rational copyright policy. The totality-of-the-circumstances nature of copyright's fair use doctrine, for example, can be both a blessing and a curse. Like any standard, the doctrine can be flexible and adaptive. As I and others have argued elsewhere, however, this flexibility can

[71] Work still needs to be done, for example, to further rationalize the law of patent remedies and equitable defenses. *See* Cotter, *supra* note 61 (discussing patent remedies); Thomas Cotter, *An Economic Analysis of Patent Law's Inequitable Conduct Doctrine*, 53 ARIZ. L. REV. 735 (2011); Thomas Cotter, *Four Questionable Rationales for the Patent Misuse Doctrine*, 12 MINN. J. L. SCI. & TECH. 457 (2011).

[72] *See supra* note 35 and accompanying text.

[73] See Cotter, *supra* note 4.

[74] *See id.* One possible objection to the view expressed earlier – that copyright may embody values other than purely instrumental ones – is that it is inconsistent with the view expressed in the preceding section that instrumental concerns alone should guide the development of patent law. After all, patent and copyright law – with the exception of residual state common law copyright for, e.g., unfixed works – both arise from the same constitutional provision, which authorizes Congress to "promote the Progress of Science and useful Arts, by securing for limited Times to Authors and Inventors the exclusive Right to their respective Writings and Discoveries." U.S. CONST., art. I, § 8, cl. 8. Whether Article I forbids Congress from enacting, say, a moral rights law that lacks any instrumental purpose whatsoever presents an interesting question of constitutional law on which I offer no particular views at present – although I think it is unlikely that Congress *would* enact such a law without proposing *some* instrumental justification, to which the courts likely would defer. *See* Golan v. Holder, No. 10-545, 2012 WL 125436 (U.S. Jan. 18, 2012) (applying a highly deferential standard of review to copyright restoration legislation). As a matter of policy, however, I see no fundamental reason why different values cannot animate two bodies of law that, although they share many features at an abstract level, address different subject matter; to my mind, the noninstrumental rationales for at least some features of copyright are less implausible than proposed noninstrumental rationales for utility patents, given that the latter are directed exclusively to functional subject matter.

contribute to unpredictability and, at the margin, to the steady expansion of copyright rights through overcompliance on the part of risk-averse users of copyrighted material.[75] Efforts to solve this problem defy any easy solution, and at the end of the day an uncertain standard may be the best choice among imperfect alternatives. The potential negatives nevertheless throw some cold water on a naive embrace of standards as a means for appreciating context and for mediating among conflicting values. At least in some contexts, the development of "best practices" or other quasi-rules may be preferable to completely open-ended standards.[76]

Pragmatism also has its limits in helping us bridge the gaps among the competing values that animate copyright. A copyright system that places a high value on authors' moral rights, for example, inevitably will look quite different in some respects than a system that places a high value on the interests of users (audiences, performers, appropriation artists) to fashion new understandings of, and new works that borrow from, the existing cultural environment. At some point a copyright system must choose which values are paramount. A recent case that illustrates the (sometimes) stark nature of that choice is *Salinger* v. *Colting*.[77] J. D. Salinger, the reclusive author of *The Catcher in the Rye*, filed suit to enjoin Fredrik Colting from publishing an unauthorized sequel, titled *60 Years Later: Coming through the Rye*, that depicted Holden Caulfield as an elderly nursing home resident.[78] The district court's decision that Salinger was likely to prevail on the merits is consistent with mainstream current copyright doctrine, which generally forbids unauthorized derivative works.[79] On a policy basis, however, the decision is difficult to justify in conventional instrumental terms. On the peculiar facts of *Salinger*, the likelihood that the sequel would usurp the market for the original or for an authorized sequel seemed extremely remote; nor does it seem very likely, the district judge's protestations notwithstanding, that many future authors would be dissuaded from writing based on the remote possibility that their works someday would be the subject of unauthorized sequels.[80] From a purely instrumental vantage point, the only plausible argument in favor of an injunction is that a sequel to an iconic work may undermine the stability of cultural icons that people hold dear (e.g., the image of Holden Caulfield as a sensitive teenager) or, more generally, may affect the public's ability to appreciate the boldness and audacity

[75] *See* Thomas F. Cotter, *Fair Use and Copyright Overenforcement*, 93 IOWA L. REV. 1271 (2008); James Gibson, *Risk Aversion and Rights Accretion in Intellectual Property Law*, 116 YALE L.J. 883, 887–906 (2007).

[76] *See* Cotter, *supra* note 75, at 1313 n.125.

[77] 641 F. Supp. 2d 250 (S.D.N.Y. 2009), *vacated on other grounds*, 607 F.3d 68 (Fed. Cir. 2010).

[78] *See Salinger*, 641 F. Supp. 2d at 253, 260 n.3.

[79] *See* Thomas F. Cotter, *Transformative Use and Cognizable Harm*, 12 VAND. J. ENT. & TECH. L. 701, 750 (2010).

[80] *See id.* at 750 & n.228. To be sure, an unconditional right to make unauthorized sequels could, at least in theory, create perverse disincentives to the creation of originals or of authorized sequels; but these concerns seemed absent on the facts of *Salinger* and probably could be addressed by fashioning an appropriately limited remedy. *See id.* at 750 n.228, 752 n.232.

of the original.[81] This type of argument, however, seems impossible to reconcile with a commitment to freedom of speech, which, after all, generally permits speakers to cut cultural icons down to size even when a majority may prefer otherwise.

The principal policy reason in support of an injunction therefore would appear to be Salinger's moral-rights interest in protecting the integrity of his creation. Whether this interest *should* win out over the interest of Colting and his would-be readers to reshape Holden Caulfield to their own liking is a genuinely difficult question – one that pragmatism, unfortunately, offers little help in resolving. To be sure, the resolution of questions such as those raised in *Salinger* is a matter that may be *informed* by pragmatic commitments to context, antifoundationalism, consequences, and practical reason. At the end of the day, though, the decision maker must make a choice between two competing visions, of free speech versus authors' moral rights, based on the merits of those visions as he or she understands them in the context of the matter at hand. Pragmatism itself, however, dictates no particular end result; the values that determine outcomes in such matters must derive from other philosophical and experiential sources.[82]

C. *Trademarks*

The limits of pragmatism are also apparent in other bodies of IP law, including those that are classed together as part of unfair competition law. Space restrictions preclude a deep analysis of all the relevant issues here, but I note briefly a couple of ways in which a naive pragmatism might do more harm than good as applied to trademark law in particular.

First, antifoundationalism might suggest that the traditional view of trademarks as a means for reducing consumer search costs and encouraging consistent quality was too narrow; instead, contemporary law rightly takes other values (such as the gratification some consumers derive from trademarks as status symbols[83] or the

[81] *See id.* at 750 & n.228; *see also* MILAN KUNDERA, TESTAMENTS BETRAYED 247 (1997) (stating that "[w]ithout a doubt, this or that sentence of *À la recherche du temps perdu* could be better written. But where could you find the lunatic who would want to read an improved Proust?").

[82] *See* BRIAN Z. TAMANAHA, BEYOND THE FORMALIST-REALIST DIVIDE: THE ROLE OF POLITICS IN JUDGING 186 (2010) (noting this weakness in Posner's pragmatism). To be sure, some versions of practical reason understand the concept as embracing a theory of appropriate ends as well as means. *See, e.g.*, Elizabeth Anderson, *Practical Reason and Incommensurable Goods*, *in* INCOMMENSURABILITY, INCOMPARABILITY, AND PRACTICAL REASON 90 (Ruth Chang ed. 1997). Analogously, others have sought to transcend the sharp distinction between means and ends, as noted earlier. *See supra* notes 38–40 and accompanying text. Thus, although I am not alone in ascribing to legal pragmatism a limited role in choosing among conflicting norms, *see, e.g.*, POSNER, *supra* note 21, at 395; Rorty, *supra* note 27, at 1816, future work on the intersection of pragmatism and IP may benefit from challenging this assumption by exploring alternative conceptions of practical reason in greater depth than I am prepared to do here.

[83] *See, e.g.*, Jeffrey L. Harrison, *Trademark Law and Status Signaling: Tattoos for the Privileged*, 59 FLA. L. REV. 195 (2007) (concluding, however, that the law's subsidization of this trend is indefensible); *see also* Barton Beebe, *Intellectual Property and the Sumptuary Code*, 123 HARV. L. REV. 809 (2010) (arguing that contemporary IP law facilitates status signaling, but that this trend is unsustainable).

supposed moral entitlement of trademark owners to profit from the use of their marks as products unto themselves[84]) into the mix by, for example, extending protection against the dilution of famous marks;[85] recognizing claims based on likelihood of confusion as to sponsorship or endorsement;[86] and, more generally, not taking into account the materiality of confusion to consumer purchasing decisions.[87] As with the earlier discussion of moral rights, however, pragmatism has little if anything to say about the desirability of these other ends or values in and of themselves. Just because pragmatists are suspicious of efforts to ground bodies of law in some all-encompassing rationale does not mean that all possible competing rationales are deserving of equal weight. In the present context, according weight to consumers' desires to engage in status competition or producers' interests in profiting from sponsorship opportunities – even when consumer confusion is unlikely – must be justified on some other basis. Trenchant criticisms of these developments in trademark law convince me that a little foundationalism, in the sense of focusing on reducing consumer confusion that matters, to the exclusion of such "values" as consumer narcissism and producer rent seeking, would be preferable to an unquestioning faith in giving voice to all competing interests.[88]

Seen from another perspective, however, perhaps the antifoundationalists are onto something in that trademark law *should* pay greater heed than it currently does to some other values, such as the values of competition and freedom of speech. At some point, the marginal benefits of an additional reduction in the risk of consumer confusion begin to decrease, while the corresponding costs (in terms of restricting competition among producers and of restraining speech) increase; sometimes some degree of confusion simply must be tolerated to make way for other values. Trademark law does take these competing values into account in a variety of ways, but arguably further reforms would be desirable. Practical reason and an attention to consequences may well play a useful role in developing standards that strike the

84 *See* Robert C. Denicola, *Institutional Publicity Rights: An Analysis of the Merchandising of Famous Trade Symbols*, 62 N.C. L. Rev. 603, 640–41 (1984) (arguing that no one has a stronger moral entitlement to use of a famous logo on merchandise than does the trademark owner).

85 *See* 15 U.S.C. § 1125(c).

86 *See* Mark P. McKenna, *Testing Modern Trademark Law's Theory of Harm*, 95 Iowa L. Rev. 63, 79–81 (2009) [hereinafter McKenna, *Theory of Harm*] (discussing doctrinal evolution). In this and in other work, McKenna has also documented how the instrumental view of trademarks as reducing consumer search costs and encouraging quality investments emerged only in the twentieth century, partially displacing an earlier, natural rights-based perspective. *See id.* at 72–74; *see also* Mark P. McKenna, *The Normative Foundations of Trademark Law*, 82 Notre Dame L. Rev. 1839 (2007).

87 See Mark A. Lemley & Mark P. McKenna, *Irrelevant Confusion*, 62 Stan. L. Rev. 413 (2010) (arguing, however, that trademark doctrine *should* condemn only unauthorized uses that are material in the sense of being likely to affect consumer purchasing decisions).

88 *See, e.g.*, Beebe, *supra* note 83; Harrison, *supra* note 83; Lemley & McKenna, *supra* note 87; McKenna, *Theory of Harm*, *supra* note 86; *see also* Geoffrey Miller, Spent: Sex, Evolution and Consumer Behavior 126–27 (2009) (arguing that "branding seems iniquitous – a waste of human effort, attention, and vanity in the zero-sum game of social status").

right balance among these competing interests. In this regard, introducing into trademark law a materiality requirement, as Lemley and McKenna have recommended,[89] would be a move in the right direction. By focusing attention on reducing only confusion that matters to purchasing decisions, trademark law could free up other uses the interdiction of which at present serves no public purpose and that may, at the margin, inhibit both free competition and free speech. Similarly, efforts to delineate a trademark "fair use" doctrine that screens out nonmeritorious claims at an early stage, and thus reduces the risk of chilling protected speech, would help stem the tide of what sometimes appears, in practical terms, to be an ever-expanding regime of trademark rights.[90]

CONCLUSION

In this chapter I have argued that legal pragmatism has much to offer to the development of IP law and policy. Its focus on consequences resonates with a common understanding of the purposes of IP law, whereas its suspicion of foundationalism also pays tribute to the traditional connections between some branches of IP and noninstrumental theories. In addition, legal pragmatism's emphasis on context and on practical reason ties in with numerous IP doctrines that take the form of multifactor standards in preference to bright-line rules. In this regard in particular, legal pragmatism's emphasis on experimentation and on doctrinal evolution over time seems to sit well with a body of law that itself must constantly evolve within an ever-changing technological environment. Moreover, although this discussion has focused exclusively on the three major bodies of IP law (patents, copyrights, and trademarks), it is conceivable that legal pragmatism may have as much or more to offer to other IP regimes – such as the law of trade secrets and the right of publicity – which also may embody multiple policy rationales and which as creatures of state law may present greater opportunities for experimentation with different approaches. Further consideration of the implications of pragmatism for these bodies of law, although beyond the scope of this chapter, may bear fruit in future work.

At the same time, it is important not to oversell the virtues of legal pragmatism. Legal pragmatism provides little if any guidance in choosing among competing values – particularly when, as is sometimes the case in IP and other bodies of law, those values conflict. Pragmatism is not magic, and one cannot expect it to reconcile competing perspectives that fundamentally contradict one another. Indeed, a "pragmatic" approach that attempts to give equal weight to all potentially relevant values is likely either to lead to indecision (in which case it fails the pragmatic criterion of being useful) or by necessity to wind up privileging one view of the good (e.g., moral rights or totality of the circumstances tests) over another

89 *See* Lemley & McKenna, *supra* note 87.

90 *See* William McGeveran, *The Trademark Fair Use Reform Act*, 90 B.U. L. Rev. 2267 (2010).

(e.g., freedom of speech, predictability, or consistency). Whether such privileging results in the "right" outcome or not, however, depends on reasons and consequences, not an a priori commitment to antifoundationalism and contextualism themselves as foundational values.

Pragmatism nevertheless may serve a useful purpose insofar as it counsels distrust of grand theories, though not necessarily the discarding of them altogether; that we pay attention to consequences, including systemic consequences, using the best tools available for predicting what those consequences will be; and that we be willing to revise our theories as new evidence comes to light. Altogether not a bad fit for an IP system, even if it is – at the end of the day – a bit banal.

10

Copyright, Custom, and Lessons from the Common Law

*Jennifer E. Rothman**

INTRODUCTION

One of the foundational features of early English common law was its use of custom to set legal rules. At that time, the common law used the term "custom" to encompass the practices and norms both of the entire kingdom and of particular communities. Prior to an organized legal system, practices and norms regulated local behavior and facilitated the resolution of disputes. As legal systems in England began to develop, custom shaped, guided, and often defined the law. The incorporation of custom by courts served an important role in getting communities to support the authority of the growing judiciary. Today, custom – particularly in the form of industry practices and social norms – remains an important tool in common law adjudication.

One might think that, because of the dominance of statutory frameworks governing today's intellectual property (IP) laws, custom would have a limited or even a nonexistent role in determining the scope of intellectual property rights. Perhaps because of this initial impression scholars have often overlooked or dismissed the impact of custom on IP law. Elsewhere I have refuted this common misperception and documented the frequent consideration and incorporation of custom into IP law.[1] Custom shapes the scope of privileges afforded to IP owners, as well as the access and use rights of the public. When courts have considered custom in the context of intellectual property, they often have used industry practices to limit use and access rights. These courts, however, have not engaged with the important question of whether these particular customs are worthy of consideration and, even if they are, whether they should rise to the level of a dispositive legal rule. I contend that

* Professor of Law and the Joseph Scott Fellow at Loyola Law School, Los Angeles.

[1] Jennifer E. Rothman, *The Questionable Use of Custom in Intellectual Property*, 93 VA. L. REV. 1899 (2007).

custom should rarely be determinative of a particular legal inquiry, but it can (if appropriately cabined) provide some meaningful evidence for a number of inquiries in IP cases.[2]

In this chapter, I focus on one important facet of the subject of what role custom should play in IP law – how longstanding common law principles should inform our understanding of custom. The common law provides a number of lessons on how to appropriately limit the consideration of custom in IP law and elsewhere. In this discussion, I use copyright law and its fair use doctrine as the primary lens through which to consider custom. Copyright is a particularly important example of the incorporation of custom not only because it is representative of the treatment of custom in intellectual property more broadly but also because a number of recent efforts to expand the scope of permissible uses of others' copyrighted works have relied on custom.

I begin by considering the traditional role of custom in the common law. I then consider several of the ways that courts have incorporated custom into copyright law, particularly in the context of determining fair use. I also discuss recent efforts to use custom to ameliorate both the uncertainty of fair use and copyright's ever-expanding boundaries. I next critique the unreflective reliance on custom and consider appropriate limits on its role, taking into consideration the traditional common law limits on the use of custom. Finally, I suggest a number of useful insights (other than the provision of legal rules) that custom provides for copyright law.

I. THE TRADITIONAL ROLE OF CUSTOM AT COMMON LAW

Under common law dating at least to the late 1400s in England, "general customs" formed the basis of the law itself. William Blackstone, one of the foremost commentators on early common law, writing in the 1700s, defined the common law as "[t]hat ancient collection of unwritten maxims and customs [that] had subsisted immemorially."[3] The two main advantages of using longstanding community (either local or kingdom-wide) customs were that they were thought to be "universally known" and were viewed as originating with the communities and people rather than being imposed by the King.[4] Accordingly, communities were more willing to defer to these custom-based legal rules that largely reflected their prior understanding of appropriate conduct.

Blackstone distinguished these *general* customs from those that were *particular* to a specific locality or community. Local or particular customs could sometimes trump general custom or the common law – which governed kingdom-wide – when

[2] For a more developed critique of the use of custom in intellectual property cases, see *id.*

[3] 1 William Blackstone, Commentaries *17.

[4] *Id.* at *17, *45; *see also* J.H. Baker, An Introduction to English Legal History 1–10 (4th ed. 2002); Gerald J. Postema, Bentham and the Common Law Tradition 3–4 (2004 reprint) (1986).

applied within the relevant community. Much of the Blackstonian discussion of particular customs focused on their role in defining the scope of public use and access rights to private land. In contrast to property doctrines such as prescription, custom permitted access and use not by a particular person but by the broader public.

There are numerous examples of the public obtaining access and use rights to private property on the basis of custom; for example, English courts held – on the basis of customary use – that the public could hold annual dances, conduct horse races, play cricket, fish, gather wood, and graze animals on various private lands.[5] Carol Rose has described many of these customary uses as "recreational" in nature; they were preferred because they supported social engagement and connections in a community.[6] Many of the uses were also of a subsistence nature. During the enclosure movement in England beginning in the sixteenth and seventeenth centuries, landowners increasingly excluded citizens from land that they had previously relied on for food and fuel.[7] The English historian E. P. Thompson describes custom during this period as a response to this enclosure of land. The customary use arguments challenged efforts by property owners to move property in the direction of a virtually absolute right.[8] The concept of property providing an absolute right to exclude others now dominates property discourse, but at the time of the enclosure movement this understanding of property was still very much contested.

Having briefly considered the traditional role of custom at common law, I next consider custom in a very different context and era – copyright law and particularly more recent evaluations of the fair use defense by American courts. Although I agree with those scholars who have criticized analogies between intellectual property and real property,[9] the commonalities of the customary use discussions are significant. To the extent that they are different, the nonrivalrous nature of copyrighted works weighs in favor of more liberal rather than more restrictive customary use rights. This is so because uses of intellectual property do not deplete the resource or diminish the property itself. If unchecked, such uses may reduce the value of the intellectual property or perhaps interfere with its distribution, but greater latitude may be appropriate given the ability of multiple parties to use the same intangible work at the same time.

[5] 2 William Blackstone, Commentaries, *33–36, *263, *422; Carol Rose, *The Comedy of the Commons: Custom, Commerce, and Inherently Public Property*, 53 U. Chi. L. Rev. 711, 740–41, 758–59 (1986) (citing exemplary cases).

[6] Rose, *supra* note 5, at 723, 767–70, 779–81.

[7] E. P. Thompson, Customs in Common 106–84 (1991).

[8] *Id.* at 161–84.

[9] *See, e.g.*, Stewart E. Sterk, *Intellectualizing Property: The Tenuous Connections Between Land and Copyright*, 83 Wash U. L.Q. 417 (2005); Seana Valentine Shiffrin, *Lockean Arguments for Private Intellectual Property*, in New Essays in the Legal and Political Theory of Property 138–67 (Stephen R. Munzer ed., 2001).

II. THE INCORPORATION OF CUSTOM INTO COPYRIGHT LAW

Although custom does not have the same hallowed status as it once did, it continues to play an important role in American jurisprudence. Yet, instead of being the preferred starting point for any legal rule, the status of custom is now contested and debated. Different areas of law (and different inquiries within those areas) treat custom differently. In tort law, for example, there have been ongoing debates about whether the development of customary safety precautions by a particular industry should be an absolute defense to tort liability, no defense at all, or simply some evidence of negligence or lack thereof. The dominant contemporary principle – with a few notable exceptions – is that custom should be some evidence of reasonable care, but not its measure.[10] In property law, courts and scholars continue to debate whether the public's longstanding use of land can form the basis of a right to access and use private property. This issue has often arisen in the context of public access to beaches that are privately owned.[11] In contract law, scholars and courts have disagreed about whether industry practices should be read into contracts as implied terms and also, less controversially, whether such practices should inform the interpretation of existing contract terms.[12]

Despite longstanding discussions of custom in other areas of the law, only recently have IP scholars begun to consider in any depth the role of custom in the field. Yet, IP rules, both as a de facto and de jure matter, incorporate many practices and norms that shape the scope of IP rights. In copyright law, custom has affected determinations of authorship, ownership, copyrightability (such as whether something is original), and whether a use is infringing – especially whether something is an idea or expression, or a *scènes à faire*. Custom has most frequently been considered in evaluating whether a particular use of a copyrighted work is a fair use and therefore not infringing. I focus here on the fair use doctrine and the role of custom in defining its parameters.

If a use of a copyrighted work is fair, then a person or entity can use a copyrighted work without permission or payment. There are no bright-line rules, however, for determining when a use is fair. Instead, Congress has set forth a four-factor analysis to assist courts in evaluating fair uses. The four factors consider the purpose and character of the use (in particular, whether it is commercial or for nonprofit educational use); the nature of the underlying work; the amount and substantiality of the portion used in relation to the copyrighted work as a whole; and finally, the effect on the potential market for or value of the copyrighted work.[13] The preamble of the

[10] *See, e.g.*, The T.J. Hooper, 60 F.2d 737 (2d Cir. 1932).

[11] *See, e.g.*, Thornton v. Hay, 462 P.2d 671, 676–78 (Or. 1969); Trepanier v. County of Volusia, 965 So.2d 276, 286–293 (Fla. App. 2007); Rose, *supra* note 5, at 713–14.

[12] *See, e.g.*, Lisa Bernstein, *The Questionable Empirical Basis of Article 2's Incorporation Strategy: A Preliminary Study*, 66 CHI. L. REV. 710 (1999); Richard A. Epstein, *Confusion About Custom: Disentangling Informal Customs from Standard Contractual Provisions*, 66 U. CHI. L. REV. 821 (1999).

[13] 17 U.S.C. § 107.

statutory fair use section states that fair uses of copyrighted works "for purposes such as criticism, comment, news reporting, teaching[,] scholarship, or research, [are] not an infringement of copyright."[14] The terms of the fair use statute largely grew out of the common law development of a fair use defense.[15] The codification of fair use was intended to incorporate the common law, but still leave open room for the continued development of the doctrine by the courts.[16]

Custom most often arises in fair use analysis in two ways. First, under the codified fair use factors, courts look to custom to evaluate the market effects of a particular use of a copyrighted work. Courts often consider the failure to pay the "customary price" of a work as dispositive of the fair use determination. This focus on customary pricing in copyright decisions stems in part from the Supreme Court's 1985 decision in *Harper & Row Publishers, Inc.* v. *Nation Enters., Inc.*[17] In *Harper & Row*, the Court looked at customary practices to determine whether a use was commercial in the context of the first fair use factor: "The crux of the profit/nonprofit distinction is not whether the sole motive of the use is monetary gain but whether the user stands to profit from exploitation of the copyrighted material without paying the *customary price*."[18]

The "customary price" analysis, although ostensibly a factor-one inquiry, fits more appropriately into the logic of factor four, which evaluates harm to the actual and potential markets for a work. When there is a custom to license a copyrighted work or a genre of works, courts often hold that failure to pay that price amounts to market harm even when the uses would otherwise be good candidates for fair use. In *Ringgold* v. *Black Entertainment Television*, for example, the producers of a television sitcom used a poster of the plaintiff's artwork in the background of a set without permission. The poster was visible for less than thirty seconds, was never the focal point of any shot, was not referred to in the dialogue, and was lawfully purchased.[19] Nevertheless, the court rejected a fair use defense in the case because the producers had not followed the television and film industry practice of licensing copyrighted works used as set dressing. The defendants had therefore failed to pay the "customary price" and could not benefit from the fair use defense. Other courts, including the district court in *Ringgold*, that have not considered custom in their analyses have held to the contrary and concluded that such uses of copyrighted works in the background of television and film sets are either de minimis or fair.[20] Unsurprisingly, when courts put consideration of custom into the mix outside of

[14] Despite these specific categories, there have been rejections of fair use in each of these contexts.

[15] H.R. Rep. No. 94–1476, at 65–66 (1976); Folsom v. Marsh, 9 F. Cas. 342, 344–45 (D. Mass. 1841).

[16] H.R. Rep. No. 94–1476, *supra* note 15, at 65–66.

[17] 471 U.S. 539 (1985).

[18] *Id.* at 562 (emphasis added).

[19] Ringgold v. Black Entm't Television, 126 F.3d 70, 72–73, 81 (2d Cir. 1997).

[20] *See, e.g.*, Ringgold v. Black Entm't Television, 40 U.S.P.Q. 2d 1299, 1302 (S.D.N.Y. 1996); *see also* Sandoval v. New Line Corp., 147 F.3d 215, 216, 218 (2d Cir. 1998); Amsinck v. Columbia Pictures Indus., 862 F. Supp. 1044, 1046, 1050 (S.D.N.Y. 1994).

the context of set dressing, we also see the frequent rejection of fair use defenses if defendants fail to conform to industry licensing norms; for example, short samples of music, the incidental display of sunglasses in an advertisement, course packets for classes at universities, and copies of articles for private researchers have all been judged infringing in large part because licensing such uses is the dominant practice in each instance.[21]

A second way that courts consider custom in the fair use context is to treat custom as reflective of what is "fair" in a more colloquial, gut-check sense of the word. When defendants do not follow industry practices or community or self-developed norms, they are viewed as wrongdoers not deserving of a fair use (or First Amendment) defense to their copying. In *Roy Export Co. Establishment of Vaduz* v. *CBS, Inc.*, for example, both a district court and the Second Circuit held that failing to license film clips when it was industry custom to do so was unethical and a basis for rejecting both fair use and First Amendment defenses to copyright infringement.[22] In *Roy Export*, CBS aired a retrospective on the great film actor and director Charlie Chaplin soon after his death. CBS incorporated footage from both Chaplin's copyrighted and uncopyrighted films in its broadcast without licensing the footage. In upholding a substantial jury verdict, the district court rejected a fair use defense on the grounds that "CBS's conduct violated not only its own guidelines but also industry standards of ethical behavior." The district court pointed to the industry's licensing practices as evidence of harm to the potential market for the plaintiffs' copyrighted works and of "bad faith."[23] In affirming the district court, the Second Circuit pointed to the same lack of conformity with in-house guidelines and industry practices as evidence of "commercial immorality" and as a basis for rejecting CBS's First Amendment defense.[24]

Both courts suggested that because most similarly situated companies were paying for licenses in such circumstances, there was an existing market for such licenses – a market that would be jeopardized by CBS's nonpayment. But these markets are largely creations of the courts. They would not exist if parties were not fearful of the cost of litigation and the unpredictability of fair use. This risk aversion is exacerbated by courts' circular reasoning in these cases: the courts reject fair use largely on the basis of the existence of licensing markets – markets that but for those decisions would cease to exist.

Similarly, nonconformity with more formal industry practices, such as use guidelines, has also been viewed as unfair. Most notably, the Agreement on Guidelines

[21] *See, e.g.*, Bridgeport Music, Inc. v. Dimension Films, 410 F.3d 792, 801–02, 804 & n.19 (6th Cir. 2005); Davis v. Gap, Inc., 246 F.3d 152, 166–68 (2d Cir. 2001); *see also* Rothman, *supra* note 1, at 1932–33 & n.120.

[22] Roy Export Co. Establishment of Vaduz v. CBS, Inc., 672 F.2d 1095, 1100, 1105 (2d Cir. 1982); Roy Export Co. Establishment of Vaduz v. CBS, Inc., 503 F. Supp. 1137, 1146–47 (S.D.N.Y. 1980).

[23] *Roy Exp. Co.*, 503 F. Supp. at 1146–47.

[24] *Roy Exp. Co.*, 672 F.2d at 1105.

for Classroom Copying in Not-for-Profit Educational Institutions, usually shortened to the "Classroom Guidelines," has been very influential in determining the scope of fair use in the context of classroom use of copyrighted materials.[25] The Classroom Guidelines were developed during the drafting of the 1976 Copyright Act at the behest of Congress. They were developed and negotiated primarily by large publishers and a few author organizations with minimal to no input from educators and students. The Classroom Guidelines set forth recommended principles for determining when it is "fair" or lawful to use another's copyrighted work in an educational setting. These guidelines, which were never adopted by statute, restrict how copyrighted works are used by educators and greatly influence courts when they analyze fair use claims. The extreme specificity of the Classroom Guidelines stands in stark contrast to the open-ended nature of the statutory and common law fair use criteria, greatly restricting the possible uses of copyrighted works. Although the Classroom Guidelines purport to set forth the "minimum" allowable uses, they have come to set a ceiling on allowable educational uses of materials. Not only is there vast conformity with the standards but courts also have routinely rejected fair use and found infringement when a party has not conformed to the purported floor of the Guidelines.[26] This is true both because the nonconformity with the Guidelines is viewed as ethically unfair and also because it demonstrates that the defendant is not paying the customary price, suggesting harm to an existing licensing market.

Despite being problematic, it is not surprising that custom has been influential in the context of fair use determinations. The fair use doctrine is challenging for courts to apply. Fair use analysis has been termed "muddled," "troublesome," and "ad hoc."[27] As courts seek guidance through the fair use "thicket,"[28] they sometimes turn to custom. A similar dynamic played out in the courts over the challenging determination of what is negligent conduct. Custom is an attractive proxy, but it is ultimately not a fully satisfying basis for determining negligence or fair use. Just as custom in the context of torts may allow obsolete and dangerous practices to remain in place in the face of technological innovations, overreliance on custom in the copyright context could write fair use out of the law.

Another reason courts turn to custom in the copyright context is that at common law courts referred to fair uses as those that were both "reasonable and

[25] *See* Rothman, *supra* note 1, at 1922.

[26] *See, e.g.*, Basic Books v. Kinko's Graphics, 758 F. Supp. 1522 (S.D.N.Y. 1991). Much of the de facto compliance comes in the form of university and school policies. Individual instructors may ignore these policies, but they often do so at the express risk of losing any indemnification or legal representation from their educational institutions.

[27] Dellar v. Samuel Goldwyn, Inc., 104 F.2d 661, 662 (2d Cir. 1939); Pierre N. Leval, *Toward a Fair Use Standard*, 103 HARV. L. REV. 1105, 1105 (1990); Lloyd L. Weinreb, *Fair's Fair: A Comment on the Fair Use Doctrine*, 103 HARV. L. REV. 1137, 1138–40 (1990).

[28] Weinreb, *supra* note 27, at 1138, 1158.

customary."[29] Considering whether uses are customary has therefore long been a part of fair use analysis even though the statute no longer refers to this standard. The common law inquiry, however, was not solely about whether a use was customary but also whether the practice was *reasonable*, regardless of whether it was customary. Many courts have ignored this independent reasonableness inquiry and treat what is customary as definitional of what is reasonable.

In sum, courts routinely consider industry practices and guidelines to evaluate fair use. This reliance on custom raises several significant concerns. First, the quality and reasonableness of the customs are not considered, and therefore their incorporation risks the legal adoption of suboptimal and inappropriate practices and norms. Second, because of the dominance of a clearance culture – in which risk-averse licensing practices dominate – consideration of custom risks making fair use obsolete. Finally, the incorporation of custom in many contexts has been one-sided – with courts often pointing to nonconformity with practices to reject fair use, but dismissing conformity with norms or practices as a basis to accept a fair use defense.

III. THE PROMISE OF CUSTOM AND FAIR USE PROBLEM SOLVING

Scholars and various use communities have recently sought out custom as a basis to delineate and establish fair uses. This interest in custom is driven in part by efforts to persuade courts to accept defenses in individual cases. This custom-based approach also seeks to convince and empower individuals, organizations, and companies to assert fair use rather than to conform with the dominant, risk-averse clearance culture. Just as the enclosure movement in England sparked arguments in favor of granting customary use rights to the public in the walled-off land, concerns over the increased propertization of intangible works that can form crucial pieces of our identities and culture have generated efforts to articulate justifications for public use of these works. The same tensions exist now as did then between those who worry about the tragedy of the commons – if land or IP is not exclusively owned – and those who worry about the opposite problem, the tragedy of the anti-commons, if everything is owned. Thus, it is unsurprising to see similar arguments about customary uses percolating up at this juncture in history.

The burgeoning best practices movement is a prime example of this trend. Most notably, the best practices statements developed by Peter Jaszi, Patricia Aufderheide, and others at American University and its Center for Social Media seek to establish what should be considered fair use in particular communities based on the purported

[29] Shapiro, Bernstein & Co. v. P.F. Collier & Son Co., 26 U.S.P.Q. 40, 42 (S.D.N.Y. 1934); Richard C. De Wolf, An Outline of Copyright Law 143 (1925). The English defense of fair abridgement, which is a precursor to our fair use standard, also considered adherence to "custom and usage" as evidence of what was fair. Such customs and usages, however, were never conclusive of the inquiry. Dodsley v. Kinnersley, 27 Eng. Rep. 270, 270–71 (1761).

practices in those communities, as well as on community-generated guidelines. The Center for Social Media continues to produce more and more of these best practices statements – most recently ones for the poetry community and academic and research libraries. Harvard's Berkman Center for the Internet and Society, the American Library Association, and the Electronic Frontier Foundation also have endorsed the use of best practices statements to facilitate the assertion and support of fair use.

The most well known of the best practices statements is the *Documentary Filmmakers' Statement of Best Practices in Fair Use*. The *Filmmakers' Statement* presents four categories of uses of others' copyrighted works that are likely fair in the context of documentary films. The privileged categories are critique or commentary, illustrative quoting, incidental uses, and use in historical sequences. Each of these categories contains a number of "limitations." Such limitations include, for example, that illustrative quoting or copying should be properly attributed, derived from different sources, "no longer than necessary to achieve the intended effect," and not used to avoid "the cost or inconvenience of shooting equivalent footage."[30]

Elsewhere I have critiqued the best practices statements on a variety of grounds, including that they exhibit some wishful thinking about fair use and contain some problematic limitations that exceed those required by fair use law.[31] Here, however, I want to focus on the aspects of the statements that relate to custom. Proponents of the best practices statements and other forms of fair use guidelines have both explicitly – and sometimes implicitly – adopted a model of copyright law that incorporates custom as law. The *Filmmakers' Statement*, for example, declares that "[f]air use is shaped in part, by the *practice* of the professional communities that employ it. . . . [F]or any particular field of critical or creative activity, such as documentary filmmaking, lawyers and judges consider professional expectations and practice in assessing what is 'fair' within the field."[32] This statement oversells the impact of industry practices in determining fair use, while at the same time also underselling the incorporation of industry practices to limit the scope of permissible uses. Because the best practices statements expressly endorse the role of custom in determining the scope of fair use, they risk becoming ceilings rather than floors on fair use. Alternatively, they might simply be dismissed as outlying practices or even non-practices that are more akin to wishful thinking by piratical users. Instead, courts are likely to embrace the more dominant clearance culture practices. Rather than challenging the validity of incorporating such restrictive practices, the statements endorse a worldview that accepts the value of such practices as determinative of fair use.

30 *Documentary Filmmakers' Statement of Best Practices in Fair Use* 4–5 (2005), available at http://www.centerforsocialmedia.org/rock/backgrounddocs/bestpractices.pdf.

31 Jennifer E. Rothman, *Best Intentions: Reconsidering Best Practices Statements in the Context of Fair Use and Copyright Law*, 57 J. COPYRIGHT SOC'Y 371 (2010).

32 *Documentary Filmmakers' Statement*, *supra* note 30, at 1 (emphasis added).

The risk that the best practices statements will come, like the Classroom Guidelines, to stand for ceilings rather than floors on uses is of particular concern because some of the limitations are unwarranted and severe. For example, the *Filmmakers' Statement* limits incidental uses of music captured on film so that an editor and director cannot cut or edit a scene or sequence to the beat of the captured music or allow the music to spill over to another scene. Cutting to the rhythm of music and allowing music from one scene to spill over to the next are both important filmmaking techniques. The *Filmmakers' Statement* also concludes that documentary films cannot be designed around copyrighted works. Documentaries about war movies, the rock n' roll star Elvis Presley, or the portrayal of gays and lesbians in film and television are all legitimate projects, yet the *Filmmakers' Statement* throws them all into fair use purgatory or, worse yet, infringement hell simply because they are designed to comment on copyrighted material. Such a conclusion is out of sync with the needs of filmmakers and the public. Other best practices statements similarly constrain users – for example, the OpenCourseWare Code restricts uses of copyrighted works by educators to single examples and requires educators to remove incidentally captured copyrighted works. Moreover, the statements suggest a preference for licensing when material can be easily licensed at reasonable rates. This preference for licensing makes all unlicensed uses suspect and calls into question whether the movement's goals of encouraging fair use are furthered or in fact undermined by these statements.

Recent legal scholarship has also sought to use custom to support fair use. In Michael Madison's analysis of fair use he contends that fair use can be made more predictable if it is understood as protecting uses that fall within certain social and cultural patterns. He suggests that conformity with community practices in one of these given patterns should insulate users from liability for copyright infringement. For example, if a use is allegedly journalistic, then the norms and practices of the journalistic community should be used to assess first if the use is in fact journalistic in nature, and second, if it is, whether the use conforms with existing journalistic practice. One of the main motivations for Madison's analysis was to suggest that at least some peer-to-peer file sharing fits within an existing social and cultural pattern (of personal uses) and therefore is fair.[33]

Pamela Samuelson's recent work on fair use similarly suggests that customary uses, at least those by authors, merit fair use protection. She points to note-taking, quotations, close paraphrasing, photocopying, and sketches as examples of activities that all promote authorship and have long been considered fair when engaged in by those creating new works.[34] Samuelson declares that "whether a second author's use is reasonable and customary in the authorial community in which he or she

[33] Michael J. Madison, A *Pattern-Oriented Approach to Fair Use*, 45 Wm. & Mary L. Rev. 1525, 1530, 1672–77, 1687–90 (2004).

[34] Pamela Samuelson, *Unbundling Fair Uses*, 77 Fordham L. Rev. 2537, 2576–77 (2009).

creates" is something courts should consider when evaluating fair use.[35] Professor Samuelson views custom as an appropriate factor to consider, but she has agreed with me that custom should not be the sole measure of fair use.[36]

IV. QUESTIONABLE JUSTIFICATIONS FOR USING CUSTOM AS A PROXY FOR FAIR USE

The recent advocacy of the expansion of fair use on the basis of custom has some appeal, but there is reason to pause before advocating greater reliance on custom as a basis for expanding or protecting uses of copyrighted works. First, courts have looked to custom to cabin rather than to expand fair use. Second, the public use and access rights to land rooted in custom have largely become disfavored in the United States – our legal system instead has favored strong private property rights even when they limit longstanding public uses. It thus is quite possible that advocates of using custom may find that their efforts backfire. Even if we take a step back from this healthy dose of legal realism, there are normative and theoretical reasons to question the usefulness and appropriateness of custom as a proxy for what uses should be deemed fair.

The common law preferred custom not because it was superior, but because there was little else in its place as a starting point. As James Carter Coolidge observed, "Custom . . . is the only law we discover at the beginning of society."[37] Now that we have a developed legal system, custom should rarely be the measure of the law. Three of the primary justifications advanced today for relying on custom in various contexts suggest that consideration of custom is less justifiable in the copyright context than in many other circumstances. The first major justification for relying on custom to establish legal rules is that custom may best reflect optimal rules in a given market. In common law terms this argument might be framed as "the community knows best." In the context of copyright transactions this would mean that custom would reflect the optimal development of copyrighted works and a balance between the exclusionary owners' rights and the public's use and access rights to those works. In the context of copyright markets, there are reasons to doubt the optimality of industry practices because they are often generated by efforts to avoid litigation or preserve relationships. Licensing material or removing material from new works is common not because it is optimal, but because the outcome of fair use litigation is unpredictable and litigation itself is expensive. Moreover, guessing wrong about the likely success of a fair use defense comes with a severe downside – high statutory damages and possible criminal liability. Such a risk makes it rare that parties who can obtain permission for a reasonable (or even unreasonable) licensing fee will

[35] *Id.* at 2578.
[36] *Id.* at 2578 & n.288.
[37] James Coolidge Carter, Law: Its Origin, Growth and Function 19 (1907).

risk litigating fair use. However, this rational choice by individual actors is not an optimal or preferred choice for society.

Another reason that copyright markets are less likely to generate welfare-maximizing practices is that they are not particularly close-knit and have fewer repeat transactions between the same parties, thereby contrasting with other industries and communities in which norms and practices have been celebrated as preferential to externally imposed laws. The different economic power of players in copyright markets also suggests that customs will likely skew toward the interests of the most powerful owners of copyrighted content at the expense of others.

Despite such concerns, some, such as Richard Epstein, have argued in response to my work that negotiated licenses and other clearance culture practices actually reflect optimal private ordering based on mutual agreement as to pricing.[38] Such a conclusion has several flaws. First, negotiating licensing agreements is challenging, especially for smaller players or when a potential user has a limited amount of time to obtain permission for the use. Content owners sometimes cannot be located or do not respond at all or in a timely manner to requests for permission to license works. These challenges lead to significant transaction costs that warp the market for these licenses. Second, content owners sometimes refuse to license at any price or charge a prohibitively high or simply unreasonable fee for use. Third, because fair use works in conjunction with the exclusive rights of copyright holders to promote the overall public interest in generating more works and more knowledge, we cannot simply look at an individual transaction and evaluate the optimality between the owner and user, as compared to litigation costs – we must also consider the costs to society more broadly. Optimality in the sense of maximizing wealth is not the only consideration at issue here. We must also maximize creativity, knowledge, and liberty. Fair use is more than simply a mechanism for optimizing the production of creative works; it prevents copyright law from unreasonably interfering with the free speech and liberty rights of others. Given copyright's status as a government entitlement, such concerns are particularly appropriate counterweights.

A second justification for incorporating custom is that, even if suboptimal, the resulting legal rules are fair because they satisfy parties' expectations.[39] In the copyright context, however, expectations often do not track the relevant customs, and even when they do, it may not be appropriate to determine the scope of copyright law on the basis of such expectations given the countervailing public interests at stake. For example, the *New York Times* recently hired a talent agency to assist with

38 Richard A. Epstein, *Some Reflections on Custom in the IP Universe*, 93 VA. L. REV. IN BRIEF 223 (2008). For a more developed reply to his comments, see Jennifer E. Rothman, *Why Custom Cannot Save Copyright's Fair Use Defense*, 93 VA. L. REV. IN BRIEF 243 (2008).

39 *See* CARTER, *supra* note 37, at 18–19, 80–81, 124; Rothman, *supra* note 1, at 1946, 1961–65. Even the ardent critic of Blackstone and of custom, Jeremy Bentham, noted that custom has the most value when it furthers parties' expectations. *See* JEREMY BENTHAM, A COMMENT ON THE COMMENTARIES: A CRITICISM OF WILLIAM BLACKSTONE'S COMMENTARIES OF THE LAWS OF ENGLAND 233 (Charles Warren Everett ed., 1928).

licensing its news stories for use in television shows and movies. Neither the *New York Times*' expectation that it can extract compensation for news that is in the public domain nor the existence of an industry practice of licensing such stories should alter copyright law's exclusion of facts from its reach. Not only can expectations push the law in ways contrary to public policy but they can also lock in existing property regimes even when they are unjust and even when the parties themselves might prefer a different arrangement. Such expectations may simply reflect resignation rather than preferred rules.

The final commonly cited justification for incorporating custom is the furtherance of autonomy interests. Early justifications for the common law expressed a preference for communities being governed by their own customary laws that had evolved over a period of time. These laws not only furthered parties' expectations of how given behavior would be treated but also injected a degree of community self-governance and autonomy in what would otherwise be a suspect rulemaking process handed down from a monarchy. Today, the democratic process allows communities to contribute in a more orderly fashion to the creation of governing laws, and accordingly, the appeal of the common law has faded. But even in contemporary legal debates, the issue of whether laws should be driven by the private or public sphere continues to fuel many discussions. Given copyright's public-regarding goals, deference to private ordering is less appropriate than in other business contexts.

Moreover, there are conflicting autonomy interests at stake. As I have discussed elsewhere, non-owners have liberty and autonomy-based interests in using copyrighted works.[40] Copyright is a statutory grant of a limited property right – it is justified on a variety of bases. One of the most prominent of these is the claim that copyright will incentivize the production of works. But it is not only production that the law seeks to encourage, copyright law also provides an incentive (perhaps an even stronger one) for public disclosure and dissemination of works. There is a bargain worked by the legal protection that requires some relinquishment of autonomy interests when one makes one's copyrighted work public. Although a work is copyrighted on fixation regardless of whether it is published, infringement actions require demonstration of access to the work, which usually requires having made it public. Additionally, to the extent that a party wishes to monetize the copyrighted work it must be made public – something it is assumed that authors and copyright holders will want to do. Thus, the autonomy interests of an author must be balanced with those of his or her audience.

V. COMMON LAW LIMITS ON CUSTOM

Despite this critique of the wholesale incorporation of custom, custom continues to provide some pertinent and meaningful information, including for evaluations

[40] Jennifer E. Rothman, *Liberating Copyright: Thinking Beyond Free Speech*, 95 Cornell L. Rev. 463 (2010).

of fair use. But before considering the value of any particular custom, we need a system to distinguish the practices and norms worthy of consideration from those that should be dismissed. The common law provides some guidance on how to make such assessments.

Early common law scholars and courts had a much more moderated view of custom than contemporary scholars sometimes recognize. William Blackstone and Matthew Hale in England, and Oliver Wendell Holmes Jr. in the United States, recognized that not all customs made for appropriate legal rules. Practices and norms sometimes developed in a haphazard manner that created rules that defied logic or that became obsolete given societal or technological changes.[41] The common law therefore limited the use of custom in several important ways. Before being considered worthy of legal recognition, a custom needed to be deemed both legal and good.[42] To meet this standard, a custom had to pass a number of hurdles.

Blackstone's work provides the most famous delineation of these common law limits on custom. He provides seven express limits on custom: to be both legal and good customs must be "immemorial," "continued," "peaceable," "reasonable," "certain," "compulsory," and "consistent."[43] In this discussion I largely track Blackstone's enumeration of these limits, but I synthesize these limits into four broad conceptual categories that best reveal their continued relevance. The four conceptual categories that I use are first, limits that relate to the *certainty* of the custom; second, limits that demonstrate the *consent* of the people to the custom; third, the absence of *conflicts* between the custom and other laws and customs; and finally, the fourth limit, that the custom itself must be *reasonable*.

Certainty

There are a variety of common law limits on custom that address the *certainty* of the custom. Before deserving judicial consideration, a custom must be proven to exist, and its contours need to be clearly identifiable, definite, sufficiently detailed, and agreed on.[44]

Consent

Consent was the key justification for custom at common law, and many of the limits on custom are at their root about whether the community agreed to the alleged practice or norm. The *continuity* of the custom, its longevity, and agreement about its contours demonstrated a consensus by a community with regard to

[41] Oliver Wendell Holmes Jr., The Common Law 5 (1881).

[42] 1 William Blackstone, Commentaries *76.

[43] *Id.* at *76–78.

[44] *Id.* at *78; J.H. Balfour Browne, The Law of Usages and Customs 21–22 (1875); John D. Lawson, The Law of Usages and Customs with Illustrative Cases 32–36 (1881).

the practice that suggested likely consent.[45] The requirement that a custom must have been so longstanding or *immemorial* that no one could remember a time without that custom being in place also reflected a community's likely consent to that custom.[46] Other evidence of consent was that the custom be *peaceable*. Peaceability required demonstration that a custom was undisputed. This was an important component because disagreements over a custom's validity called into question the community's consent to that custom. The custom also needed to be *compulsory* in the sense that everyone in the relevant community needed to follow that custom rather than having obedience to the custom be at the "option of every man."[47]

Absence of Conflicts

Even if a custom were universally accepted, understood, and followed in a given community, it might still violate a superior governing rule. Common law courts would therefore analyze whether the given custom conflicted with any other custom or law.[48] This requirement was sometimes referred to as requiring *consistency*.[49] Custom could not contradict laws set forth by the King or by Parliament or other common law rules or customs in the same community.[50]

Reasonableness

The courts would also consider whether the custom was *reasonable*, regardless of its acceptance or duration.[51] The fact that something has been accepted and practiced for a long time might reflect its wisdom, but more is meant by the reasonableness inquiry than mere deference to the custom as a proxy for what is reasonable. Determination of whether a custom is reasonable has long been a challenging inquiry. Blackstone noted that courts therefore often considered a slightly different and easier inquiry – evaluating whether the custom was "unreasonable."[52] J. H. Balfour

[45] BROWNE, *supra* note 44, at 15–16.

[46] 1 WILLIAM BLACKSTONE, COMMENTARIES *67. *See also* BROWNE, *supra* note 44, at 15. The requirement of immemoriality was liberally interpreted. BENTHAM, *supra* note 39, at 221–24. By the late 1800s there was a recognition that twenty to thirty years was sufficient to meet the standard even if some recalled the start of the practice. BENTHAM, *supra* note 39, at 218, n.†. The historian E. P. Thompson suggests that the legal incorporation of customary uses in the sixteenth through eighteenth centuries was largely the incorporation of *recent* – rather than ancient – practices. THOMPSON, *supra* note 7, at 1. In the United States, the immemoriality requirement was largely dismissed for obvious reasons. As John Lawson in his treatise on usages and customs explained in 1881, custom in America could by definition not be since time immemorial. Instead, customs simply needed to have been "established." LAWSON, *supra* note 44, at 28–30.

[47] 1 WILLIAM BLACKSTONE, COMMENTARIES *78.

[48] *Id.*

[49] *Id.*; BROWNE, *supra* note 44, at 25–27.

[50] *Id.*; 1 WILLIAM BLACKSTONE, COMMENTARIES *78–79, 89–90.

[51] POSTEMA, *supra* note 4, at 5–8.

[52] 1 WILLIAM BLACKSTONE, COMMENTARIES *77; BROWNE, *supra* note 44, at 19–21.

Browne writing in 1875 suggested that, if there was no reason to the contrary, one might defer to custom, but if there was reason to question whether the custom was good, courts could reject the practice or norm. In particular, Browne focused on whether the practice benefited the people. "A custom . . . which is injurious to the public, which is prejudicial to a class, and beneficial only to a particular individual, is repugnant to the law of reason. No such custom could be capable of becoming law which is a rule for the benefit of all."[53] As Jeremy Bentham observed, "To prove the existence of a practise is one thing, to prove the expediency of establishing it by force of law is another."[54] Bentham points to Lord Bacon's advice that one should "*Let Reason be pregnant, Custom barren*" to highlight his skepticism that customary practices and norms are likely to reflect a preferred legal rule.[55] Similarly, the great justice Benjamin Cardozo suggested that "social needs" justify "sacrific[ing] custom in the pursuit of other and larger ends."[56] Cardozo noted that, although "history and custom have their place," "[e]thical considerations" and the "welfare of society" must rule the day.[57] Although Cardozo observed that social welfare was difficult to determine and ethical considerations could be contested, he pointed to fundamental underpinnings of our constitutional democracy that could not be sacrificed in the name of custom or common law.[58]

Despite these longstanding limits on custom, when courts and scholars consider the use of custom in copyright law they rarely consider these limits. Courts have simply not scrutinized the quality and value of particular practices and norms in the copyright context.

VI. RETHINKING THE ROLE OF CUSTOM THROUGH A CONTEMPORARY COPYRIGHT LENS

The ignorance of common law limits may be driven in part by a lack of awareness that courts are engaged with the analysis of custom; however, if custom is to have any influence in IP law, then a more thoughtful and nuanced view of it must be adopted. It is therefore worth considering how one should evaluate custom today. Without limits on the incorporation of custom we risk not only incorporating bad rules but also shoring up a feedback loop in which the law reinforces problematic practices and then further entrenches them into the law.[59] We have seen this problem with particular prominence in the context of licensing markets for copyrighted works.

53 BROWNE, *supra* note 44, at 20.
54 BENTHAM, *supra* note 39, at 218.
55 *Id.* at 219.
56 BENJAMIN N. CARDOZO, THE NATURE OF THE JUDICIAL PROCESS 65 (1922).
57 *Id.* at 66.
58 *Id.* at 65–77.
59 James Gibson, *Risk Aversion and Rights Accretion in Intellectual Property Law*, 116 YALE L.J. 882 (2007); Rothman, *supra* note 1, 1933–37, 1950–56.

The common law's focus on certainty, consent, lack of conflicts, and reasonableness is all relevant today. As I have elaborated elsewhere, I do not think that custom should be incorporated wholesale into determinations of fair use. Nevertheless, custom may provide some guidance into what is reasonable or appropriate in a particular context, and thereby likely fair. In the past, I have developed six vectors that should be evaluated when considering whether practices or norms are useful indicators of fairness in the context of intellectual property.[60] Here I condense these vectors into four primary areas of evaluation: (1) the certainty of the custom, (2) the motivation for the custom, (3) the representativeness of the custom, and (4) the implications of adopting the custom. I briefly elaborate on each of these considerations and their connections to the traditional common law limits on custom. As part of this analysis I consider a few relevant examples and evaluate them in the context of fair use.

Certainty of the Custom

To have any value, a custom must be identifiable, in terms of what constitutes the practice itself, and the practice must also be widely accepted and followed. This analysis tracks that of Blackstone's requirement that practices be certain before meriting judicial consideration. Several considerations help evaluate how certain a particular custom is. First, if there is unanimity as to the contours of the custom among diverse parties, it is more likely to exist and have clearly definable boundaries. Such agreement confirms the likely consent of the community. Second, customs that are longstanding are more stable and hence more certain because they have weathered the test of time.

Because the best practices statements are more wishful than descriptive and have fuzzy boundaries, they are not particularly certain. Although these statements purport to set forth the practices of the relevant communities, they instead set forth what the drafters think the community should be doing. In the context of the *Filmmakers' Statement*, for example, the report leading up to the statement and the statement itself both reveal that the dominant practice was to license or cut out copyrighted materials from documentaries. If courts take seriously the call to incorporate customary practices, then such clearance practices may narrow rather than expand fair use. Second, under the guidelines of the *Filmmakers' Statement* evaluations must be made of whether the "extent of the use is appropriate," quotes are no "longer than necessary," and attribution was "reasonably possible." These inquiries do not provide certain guidelines worthy of deference as custom. Instead, they leave the same ambiguities of the existing fair use system, but add an additional layer of complexity to the already convoluted fair use analysis.

60 *See* Rothman, *supra* note 1, at 1967–80.

In other instances, we see conflicting customs at work. For example, in the *Roy Export* case described earlier – in which a court rejected fair use and First Amendment defenses for the use of clips of Charlie Chaplin films in a news obituary of Chaplin – the court rejected fair use on the basis that the defendant did not conform to custom. The court failed to consider, however, that there was more than one custom at work. Clips were not usually licensed for obituaries even though they were often licensed in other contexts for projects with more lead time or scripted series. Such conflicting customs suggest either that the court needed to more carefully scrutinize which custom was applicable or that there was no single, dominant, and widely accepted custom worthy of consideration.

Motivation for Custom

Motivation was not a common law limit on custom; however, sitting underneath the understanding that custom was valuable was a belief that custom reflected the preferences of a particular community. In other words, if the community had been asked to sit around and agree to what the rule should be this is likely the rule they would have come up with – or at least if such a rule had been suggested to them they would have agreed to it. In the context of copyright then, the practices and norms that will be the most valuable will be those that reflect preferred allocations between copyright holders' and users' interests rather than customs driven by litigation avoidance. Litigation-avoidance norms arise when laws are uncertain or the expense of litigation discourages resort to the legal system. Such norms do not reflect a preferred or aspirational allocation between the exclusive rights of copyright owners and the ability of others to use those works. Both the licensing practices exemplified in the *Ringgold* decision and the use guidelines, such as the Classroom Guidelines, are examples of such litigation-avoidance customs. These *reactive customs* – developed to address the shortcomings of the legal regime – are not the sort of aspirational, independently developed customs that others, such as Robert Ellickson, have appreciated in other contexts.[61] When customs have developed with aspirational motivations behind them they are better indications of what is appropriate. In the context of fair use, practices and norms should primarily be relevant only to the extent that they are indicative of what is actually deemed "fair" by the relevant community rather than what that community thinks is colorable or safe under the law.

As part of considering the motivation for a particular custom, courts should particularly try to engage with whether the custom was intended to provide an appropriate balance between competing interests. As a check on this analysis, courts should independently evaluate whether reasonable people would agree to such rules if they

[61] Robert C. Ellickson, Order Without Law: How Neighbors Settle Disputes (1991).

knew neither whether they would be powerful or minor players in the market nor whether they would own or wish to use the relevant content.

Representativeness

The common law focus on the importance of custom reflecting the will and consent of the people is instructive. Customs that represent only one party's or one group's interests are suspect. By contrast, when a custom develops with input and participation of both copyright owners and users and of large and small players, it is more valuable. The best practices statements are highly unrepresentative and therefore of limited value. Like the Classroom Guidelines (which the authors of the best practices statements criticize for being one-sided), none of the best practices statements include representation by the most affected parties – the content providers whose work is most likely to be appropriated. The fact that some of the users are also authors does not remedy this one-sidedness. After all, almost everyone – if not absolutely everyone – is an author of copyrighted work. Although the proponents of the statements are likely correct that if they had invited larger content owners to the table very little would have been agreed on, the fact that the parties could not have agreed to any common principles should raise serious flags about using the articulated practices to affect entitlements outside of that community. Not only were the copyright holders that were most likely to be injured by the uses not invited to the table but the public at large was also not included even though the statements potentially limit the types of uses that we can make.

Although not an explicit consideration at common law, the application of custom was limited to the community that had developed the particular custom at issue. Customs were never supposed to be applied outside the relevant community. Doing so would fly in the face of the primary limit on custom – that it must demonstrate the consent of those governed by the practice or norm.[62] It therefore is particularly inappropriate in the context of copyright law to apply custom outside the community in which it developed.

Implications

Another way of thinking about the common law requirement that customs must be independently evaluated to determine if they are reasonable is to consider the likely implications of adopting such practices, not just in the immediate case but more broadly. Courts must independently scrutinize the implications of adopting any customary practice or norm as a legal rule. When evaluating the worth of a

[62] I note that Henry Smith's recent consideration of the role of custom in property law using an information costs analysis further supports limiting the application of custom to the community that is most familiar with the relevant customary practices. *See* Henry E. Smith, *Community and Custom in Property*, 10 THEORETICAL INQUIRIES IN LAW 5 (2009).

particular custom, a court must consider what the end result of incorporating that custom would be. If followed to its logical conclusion, will the custom result in a slippery slope, such that no uses will be allowed or, alternatively, that too many uses will be allowed? In either scenario, courts should reject customary practices. Consider, for example, two extremes. If it is customary to license everything, then no fair uses remain. On the flip side, consider the heyday of free peer-to-peer file sharing in which the custom was *not* to pay for any music downloaded from the Web. Such a custom could destroy the entire market for music online.

In the best practices statement related to user-generated content (UGC) in the context of online video, virtually any use is deemed fair because the commentary and critique category is read very broadly. For example, in the report supporting the Online Video Code, the drafters suggest that a mash-up titled Clint Eastwood's "The Office" – which mixed together clips from the television series *The Office* with the movie *Evan Almightly* to show what it would be like if Clint Eastwood directed an episode of *The Office* – falls within the favored category of negative or critical commentary. This category and its exemplars suggest that all mash-ups are fair use. This means that there can be no market for licensing such mash-ups – a conclusion that pulls the rug out from under a possible new media market and makes copyright law virtually irrelevant in the context of UGC.

In sum, if custom is certain, representative, and motivated by aspirational purposes and it would result in a reasonable allocation of use and ownership rights, then that custom will likely provide meaningful guidance for evaluating fair use in that particular context. Otherwise, such practices and norms should be met with great skepticism and little deference.

VII. RECONCEPTUALIZING THE ROLE OF CUSTOM IN COPYRIGHT

Despite the many reasons to be cautious about jumping on the custom bandwagon, custom provides several broader lessons for copyright policy. First, massive disobedience of copyright law in given categories can signal market failure or overreaching by copyright holders. The copyright system needs some public buy-in to work. Public support requires people to think that on some level copyright law is fair. When copyright law is wildly out of sync with community practices there may be value in interpreting copyright to conform to those understandings, or better yet amending the copyright act to reflect some of those norms.

Second, customary uses may demonstrate a consensus about preferred rights that may not be appropriately recognized under the law. For example, many norms in the copyright world favor giving attribution to authors when their work is used, but the law does not generally recognize such a right. Such locations of commonality suggest promising areas for advocating for legal change and the express adoption of commonly accepted principles.

Third, custom may demonstrate areas of need by users and creators that must be accommodated either through a reasonable market mechanism or through fair use. There are a number of categories of uses of copyrighted works that some scholars and courts have treated as prima facie fair because they are "customary." Although courts have mostly used custom to reject fair use defenses, on several occasions courts have pointed to "years of accepted practice" as a basis to establish fair use. In *William & Wilkins Co* v. *United States*, for example, the Court of Claims held that the practice of making copies for research purposes was a customary fair use.[63] Many of these "customary uses" are simply uses that have been established at common law and now exist because they are uncontroversial legal precedents. Over time, these precedents form categories of uses that are likely (and predictably) fair – but this is a very different understanding than that they are fair *because* they are customary. In other words, one way of thinking about customary uses is simply as precedents.

Additionally, the normative underpinnings of these decisions are much more important than their customary nature. Consider, for example, the "customary" use of copyrighted works in biographies.[64] As with personal copies for research, we have seen practices in the context of biographical works shift over time toward a permission-only culture. Instead of adopting customary uses or industry practices wholesale then, we should evaluate the specific practices that have developed and consider whether they are appropriate. Permitting some uses of copyrighted works in biographical works is necessary. The fact that such uses have been permitted over time may signal their importance, but it should not be dispositive. Similarly, if such uses cease to occur because of risk-averse publishing houses, the reasonable use of copyrighted works in biographies should nevertheless remain fair.

A fourth insight from custom and the common law comes from the common law requirement that a custom must be consented to by the relevant community. This requirement of consent suggests an important avenue for counteracting the incorporation of the clearance culture – active, vocal, and public dissent from these restrictive practices. I have previously advocated for such dissent from the dominant and restrictive practices in IP markets.[65] One of the purported values of using custom to set the law is that it reflects a "shared sense of its reasonableness and historical appropriateness."[66] When it does not, the custom is neither legal nor good.

Finally, the common law provides at least one other important insight. The acceptance of some customary uses of private lands was limited to those uses that were rooted either in subsistence or communal recreation. Similarly, public use of copyrighted works is appropriate when the uses are for subsistence rather than

[63] William & Wilkins Co v. United States, 487 F.2d 1345 (Ct. Cl. 1973), *aff'd without opinion by a equally divided court*, Williams & Wilkins, 420 U.S. 376 (1975).

[64] *See, e.g.*, New Era Publ'ns Int'l v. Carol Publ'g Group, 904 F.2d 152, 157 (2d Cir. 1990); Rosemont Enters. v. Random House, Inc. 366 F.2d 303, 307 (2d Cir. 1966).

[65] Rothman, *supra* note 1, at 1980–81.

[66] Postema, *supra* note 4, at 8.

exploitation and also sometimes when such uses facilitate community-building. What does subsistence mean in the context of copyright? From the perspective of users, certain copyrighted works cannot be substituted for and form an important part of both personal and cultural identity and expression – accordingly there must be some ability to use such works without permission or payment.[67] With this in mind, compare two different types of uses: first, the use of limited film clips for illustrative and historical purposes in a documentary (or even fiction film); second, unlicensed peer-to-peer file sharing that reflects the need to access music in digital formats quickly. The former might be an appropriate fair use even if there is a licensing market, whereas the latter might only be fair until an alternative market mechanism forms. The enumerated Section 107 categories also signal areas where subsistence rather than exploitation usually rules. For example, one must be able to quote from copyrighted works in order to provide meaningful scholarly commentary, reporting, or reviews of such works.

CODA: OVERLAPPING STATUTES AND THE COMMON LAW

There has long been disagreement among legal scholars about whether legislation – passed by a representative government – or judge-made (or judge-declared) law purportedly interpreting or incorporating community practice is more reflective of the will of the people. Today, arguments about public choice and legislative capture suggest that, even if one prefers legislative rulemaking to incorporating custom, one should be concerned about whether the public interest is being served in today's legislative bodies, especially in the context of IP law. Custom is an attractive counterpoint to such dangers, but it is also fraught with its own risks. The United States and particularly copyright law have veered toward legislation over custom, but the interpretation and application of that legislation have long been informed by practices and norms. As Justice Cardozo wrote in the 1920s with regard to the U.S. legal system, "[W]e look to custom, not so much for the creation of new rules, but for the tests and standards that are to determine how established rules shall be applied. When custom seeks to do more than this, there is a growing tendency in the law to leave development to legislation."[68] Custom can provide valuable information, but its usefulness depends on independently evaluating the worthiness of the custom and particularly scrutinizing its reasonableness and its likely reflection of a community's consent to the relevant practice or norm. The common law has told us this for hundreds of years; now all we need to do is listen.

67 Rothman, *supra* note 40, *passim*; Wendy J. Gordon, *A Property Right in Self-Expression: Equality and Individualism in the Natural Law of Intellectual Property*, 102 YALE L.J. 1533 (1993).

68 CARDOZO, *supra* note 56, at 60. Cardozo noted that Blackstone and his "[followers] likely exaggerated" the role of custom even at the time that Blackstone wrote. *Id.* at 59–60.

11

Common Law Reasoning and Cybertrespass

*Emily Sherwin**

INTRODUCTION

Recently, courts have been called on to apply common law doctrine to disputes over things that did not exist twenty years ago, such as computer systems and Internet domain names. In doing so, they turn naturally to common law precedents, invoking doctrines such as trespass and conversion. In this chapter, I do not comment on the substantive doctrinal choices courts have made in decisions involving the Internet. Instead, I address the process of decision making and the suitability of decisional strategies traditionally associated with the common law for resolution of disputes over use and misuse of the Internet. Focusing on the example of "cybertrespass," I argue that so-called analogical reasoning and the related technique of applying "legal principles" drawn from the patterns of prior decisions are not fruitful methods of resolving Internet-related disputes. At least in the early years of Internet litigation, rules laid out in prior cases are likely to be unhelpful as well. It follows that the only method of decision making suitable for the task is unconstrained natural reasoning, aimed at determining what outcome is best, all things considered.

I. CYBERTRESPASS

In a number of cases, plaintiffs annoyed by various types of electronic intrusions have claimed that the intrusions are actionable under a venerable common law tort known as trespass to chattels. Trespass to chattels provides a remedy for intentional interferences with possession of chattels that fall short of conversion.[1] As developed

* Professor of Law, Cornell Law School. Thanks to Oskar Liivak for helpful comments.

[1] *See, e.g.*, eBay, Inc. v. Bidder's Edge, Inc., 100 F. Supp. 1058, 1069–1070 (N.D. Cal. 2000).

by American courts, trespass to chattels, unlike trespass to land, does not impose liability for interference per se; there must be some adverse consequence to the owner.[2]

The initial judicial response to trespass-to-chattels claims in the Internet context was favorable. Most courts allowed the claim, treating computer systems and servers as chattels and unwanted electronic contacts as interferences with possession. These early courts acknowledged the common law requirement that the interference must cause harm, but were willing to treat fairly minor inconvenience or simply unauthorized use as harm. Accordingly, computer owners and website managers were able to enjoin mass e-mailings, use of data-gathering spiders, and similar unwanted contacts.[3]

In *Intel Corp.* v. *Hamidi*,[4] decided in 2003, the California Supreme Court changed direction. Intel sought an injunction to stop Hamidi, a former Intel employee, from transmitting hostile e-mail messages to current employees through an internal e-mail system linked to the Internet. The court denied the remedy, holding that trespass to chattels does not encompass electronic communications that do not impair the plaintiff's rights in the property itself, meaning the computer system or server. It followed that evidence of consequential loss – specifically, lost productivity due to the distractions Hamidi's messages caused and the time Intel spent on efforts to block them – was not sufficient to support Intel's claim. The effect of the decision was to cut back substantially on the types of electronic contacts that recipients can prevent by legal action against the sender.[5]

In the course of its decision, the California court took the position that an Internet address is not a form of real property; in the court's view, descriptions of the Internet as a "space" are merely metaphors, not to be given legal effect. Therefore, the rules governing trespass to land, which do not require harm as a prerequisite to relief, are

[2] The *Restatement of Torts* allows recovery

> "if, but only if,
>
> (a) the chattel is impaired as to its condition, quality or value, or
> (b) the possessor is deprived of the use of the chattel for a substantial time, or
> (c) bodily harm is thereby caused to the possessor or harm is caused to some person or thing in which the possessor has a legally protected interest."

Restatement (Second) of Torts § 218 (1977). Comments explain that the chattel owner's interest in "the mere inviolability" of the chattel is adequately protected by the availability repossession by self-help. Id., cmt. e.

[3] *See, e.g.*, eBay, Inc. v. Bidder's Edge, Inc., 100 F. Supp. 1058, 1069–1070 (N.D. Cal. 2000); Register.com, Inc. v. Verio, Inc., 126 F. Supp. 2d 238 (S.D. N.Y. 2000); Compuserve v. Cyber Promotions, Inc., 962 F. Supp. 1015 (S.D. Ohio 1997); Thrifty-Tel v. Beznick, 46 Cal App. 4th 1559 (1996).

[4] 71 P.3d 296 (Cal. 2003).

[5] The court did not expressly overrule past state and federal cases taking a more generous view of trespass to chattels in the context of Internet contacts, but its opinion casts doubt on prior judicial expressions of willingness to accept nominal harm, or harm not directly affecting the operation of the complainant's computers, as sufficient to support relief.

inapt.[6] The court's discussion of the tort of trespass indicates that, while rejecting the analogy to land, it was willing to treat websites and servers as chattels entitled to legal protection. It did not, however, define just what type of chattels they are or what possessory rights their owners can assert.[7]

In addition to assigning computer systems to the legal category of chattels, the California court touched briefly on questions of regulatory policy in Internet contexts. It declined to apply the "rigid" property rule reflected in the tort of trespass to land in the context of disputes over use of the Internet. Beyond this, the court purported to remain neutral in the controversy over whether the Internet is most valuable as a resource open to all or as a subject matter for private rights:

> Creating an absolute property right to exclude undesired communications from one's e-mail and Web servers might help force spammers to internalize the costs they impose.... But a property rule might also create substantial new benefits to e-mail and e-commerce users and to society generally, in lost openness of communication and in lost network benefits. In light of the unresolved controversy, we would be acting rashly to adopt a rule treating computer servers as real property for purposes of trespass law.[8]

The court's claim of neutrality, however, is disingenuous: by refusing to enjoin unwanted contacts in the absence of harm to the server, the court limited private control of servers and websites and lent significant support to the principle of free access.[9]

This quick review of decisions shows that courts have varied in their response to claims of Internet trespass. Some have been lenient in allowing owners of servers or websites to exclude unwanted intrusions; others have been reluctant to limit access to Internet "space." Decisions in the area have been based in part on perceived analogies – between computer servers and chattels or land, or between contacts made through the Internet and interferences with more familiar subjects of private ownership – and in part on substantive views about optimal management of Internet use.[10]

6 The court made this point in response to an amicus brief filed by Richard Epstein. For a sample of Epstein's views, see, e.g., Richard A. Epstein, *Cybertrespass*, 70 U. CHI. L. REV. 73 (2003); Richard A. Epstein, *Intellectual Property: Old Boundaries and New Frontiers*, 76 IND. L.J. 804, 818–21 (2001).

7 Shyamkrishna Balganesh makes this point more generally in his criticism of the court's treatment of Internet-related disputes. Shyamkrishna Balganesh, *Common Law Property Metaphors on the Internet: The Real Problem with the Doctrine of Cybertrespass*, 12 MICH. TELECOMM. & TECH. L. REV. 265, 323 (2006).

8 71 P.2d at 311.

9 In the context of a dispute over messages critical of Intel, the court also appeared to be concerned about the effects of liability on speech.

10 For a sample of differing views on common law regulation of Internet use, *see, e.g.*, Balganesh, supra note 7; Yochai Benkler, *From Consumers to Users: Shifting the Deeper Structure of Regulation Toward Sustainable Commons and User Access*, 52 FED. COMM. L.J. 561 (2000); Dan L. Burk, *The Trouble with Trespass*, 4 SMALL & EMERGING BUS. L.J. 27 (2000) Epstein, *Cybertrespass, supra* note 6; Epstein,

II. COMMON LAW DECISION MAKING

A. *Reasoning by Analogy and Reasoning from Legal Principles*

It is commonly believed that judges use special methods of reasoning to decide legal cases. Prominent among these is the method of reasoning by analogy: the judge consults a set of previously decided cases and determines which of these are factually similar to the case at hand.[11] The judge then conforms his or her decision to the outcomes of cases found to be analogous. Decisions in cases found to be factually dissimilar are "distinguished" and set aside. The analogical method is commonly thought to result in evenhandedness (like treatment of like cases), to preserve the continuity of law, and to constrain judicial decision making without entrenching erroneous or outdated rules.

In my view, analogical reasoning is illusory: either it simply cannot be done, or it is not a form of reasoned decision making.[12] Any two cases are both similar and dissimilar in countless ways.[13] To determine whether the two cases are importantly similar, and thus should be decided alike, something further is needed: the decision maker must refer to a general rule or principle that picks out certain facts as pivotal to outcomes. But if this is correct, the decision rests on the applicable rule or principle, not the brute similarity between cases. In fact, once the decision maker identifies an appropriate principle, the outcome of the prior decision is irrelevant to the outcome of the present case because all important work is done by the rule or principle.

From a psychological standpoint, it may be possible to reason directly from one case to another, relying on an intuitive sense of important similarity: the decision maker simply perceives that two cases are importantly alike for the purpose of

Intellectual Property, *supra* note 6; Dan Hunter, *Cyperspace as Place and the Tragedy of the Digital Anticommons*, 91 CAL. L. REV. 439 (2003); Daniel Kearney, *Network Effects and the Emerging Doctrine of Cybertrespass*, 23 YALE L. & POL'Y REV. 313 (2005); Mark Lemley, *Place and Cyberspace*, 91 CAL. L. REV. 521 (2003); R. Clifton Merrell, *Trespass to Chattels in the Age of the Internet*, 80 WASH. U. L.Q. 675 (2002); Maureen A. O'Rourke, *Property Rights and Competition on the Internet: In Search of an Appropriate Analogy*, 16 BERKELEY TECH. L.J. 561 (2001); Laura Quilter, *The Continuing Expansion of Cybertrespass to Chattels*, 17 BERKELEY TECH. L.J. 421 (2002); Richard Warner, *Virtual Border: Trespass to Chattels on the Internet*, 47 VILL. L. REV. 117 (2002).

[11] *See generally* STEPHEN BURTON, AN INTRODUCTION TO LAW AND LEGAL REASONING 25–41 (1995); EDWARD H. LEVI, AN INTRODUCTION TO LEGAL REASONING 1–6 (1948); JOSEPH RAZ, THE AUTHORITY OF LAW 813–89, 200–06 (1979); LLOYD WEINREB, LEGAL REASON: THE USE OF ANALOGY IN LEGAL ARGUMENT (2005); Scott Brewer, *Exemplary Reasoning: Semantics, Pragmatics, and the Rational Force of Legal Argument by Analogy*, 109 HARV. L. REV. 925, 925–29, 962–63 (1996); Grant Lamond, *Do Precends Create Rules?*, 11 LEGAL THEORY 1 (2005); John F. Horty, *The Result Model of Precedent*, 10 LEGAL THEORY 19 (2004).

[12] Larry Alexander and I have discussed this problem at length. *See* LARRY ALEXANDER & EMILY SHERWIN, THE RULE OF RULES: MORALITY, RULES, AND THE DILEMMAS OF LAW 125–35 (2001); LARRY ALEXANDER & EMILY SHERWIN, DEMYSTIFYING LEGAL REASONING 66–88 (2009).

[13] *See* MELVIN A. EISENBERG, THE NATURE OF THE COMMON LAW 84 (1988).

decision and decides accordingly.[14] In fact, the process just described may not be intuitive; it may represent a rapid and virtually unconscious application of rules or principles the decision maker has internalized over a lifetime of experience. Supposing, however, that decision makers can determine important similarity by a purely intuitive process, this process is not an acceptable method for judges to use in resolving legal disputes. We expect judges to reason to conclusions, not simply to arrive at them by intuition. When a decision is based on intuition alone, there are no criteria by which it can be judged right or wrong. In daily life, we may sometimes need to make decisions this way; in a legal context, doing so is no better than a coin flip.

Another supposed method of judicial decision making, closely related to reasoning by analogy, is reasoning from legal principles. This is the "chain novel" method described by Ronald Dworkin: a judge faced with a dispute builds on prior decisions in comparable cases by extracting a principle from their facts and outcomes.[15] The process by which the judge identifies a legal principle is similar to the process of analogical decision making described earlier: the judge surveys prior decisions in cases that appear factually similar and formulates a principle that is both morally attractive and capable of explaining the outcomes of most of the prior cases. The judge then applies the resulting principle to decide the current case.

This description of judicial decision making is widely accepted; moreover, reasoning from legal principles, like reasoning by analogy, appears to reconcile the goals of constraint and flexibility in law. Legal principles, however, suffer from two serious difficulties. First, they impose little, if any, real constraint on judges: because the judge is free to disregard some unspecified portion of prior decisions in constructing an ideal legal principle, the requirement of "fit" between the principle and past cases is open to manipulation. Second, to the extent that legal principles are constrained by past decisions, they are not ideal principles. Unless the judge disregards all recalcitrant precedents, some of the outcomes reflected in the principle will be wrong. It follows that the best available legal principle is not a morally correct principle, but a principle that rests on a flawed foundation.

Some degree of moral imperfection might be an acceptable price to pay for certainty and settlement of controversy, if legal principles in fact provided these goods. Legal principles, however, are not equivalent to determinate rules: they are relatively indeterminate and manipulable. Further, at least as described by Dworkin, the process of constructing legal principles begins anew in each case.

[14] *See* Weinreb, *supra* note 11, at 12–13, 77–103, 107–16. On the psychology of intuitive judgment, *see, e.g.*, Steven A. Sloman, Two Systems of Reasoning, In Heuristics and Biases: The Psychology of Intuitive Judgment 379 (Thomas Gilovich, Dale Griffen, & Daniel Kahneman, eds., 2002); Johathan Haidt, *The Emotional Dog and Its Rational Tail: A Social Intuitionist Approach to Moral Judgment*, 4 Psych. Rev. 814 (2001).

[15] *See* Ronald Dworkin, Law's Empire 228–32, 240–50, 254–58 (1986); Ronald Dworkin, Taking Rights Seriously 22–31 (1978). For further description and criticism of Dworkin's approach to adjudication, see Alexander & Sherwin, Demystifying Legal Reasoning, *supra* note 12, at 88–103; Larry Alexander, *Bad Beginnings*, 145 U. Pa. L. Rev. 57 (1996).

Legal principles, therefore, do not provide stable guides to conduct and cannot be justified as a means of minimizing controversy and coordinating conduct.

I have argued, to this point, that analogical reasoning is an illusion and that reasoning from legal principles is unreliable and flawed. It does not follow, however, that the methodology of the common law, in which judges consult the facts and outcomes of past cases, should be abandoned. At least in some circumstances, the process of consulting precedents can provide a useful corrective to judicial error. The corrective comes not from the analogies judges may find in prior cases, but from the process of reviewing prior cases in search of analogies.[16]

When a judge adjudicates a particular case, his or her attention is naturally focused on a single set of facts, presented as vividly as possible by the parties to the case. If the judge's only task were to resolve the current dispute, this might not be a significant problem. But judicial decisions inevitably affect parties who are not before the court, as well as future conduct and future judicial decisions. Accordingly, too much attention to the facts of the present case can have a negative impact on the overall quality of the decision, by distracting the judge from the broader consequences of the decisional rule he or she adopts. Immediate facts may overshadow statistically likely, but comparatively remote and disembodied, effects of the rule.[17]

Given this danger, a process in which judges habitually consult the facts and outcomes of prior cases is useful in its own right, even if prior outcomes impose no direct constraint on their decisions. Studying a wider array of concrete facts may counteract the undue influence of a single dispute and draw the judge's attention to the impact of its decisional rule in other settings. Consequently, the judge is less likely to choose a rule that produces an appealing outcome in the current case but may misfire in other, future cases.

B. *Natural Reasoning and Deductive Application of Rules*

I have suggested that there is no such thing as reasoning by analogy and that legal principles drawn from past decisions either do not or should not constrain judicial decision making. At best, these decisional strategies have a secondary procedural value, insofar as they counteract the bias of adjudication. How, then, do (or should) judges decide questions of common law?

With analogies and legal principles off the table, the two remaining possibilities are unconstrained, or "natural," reasoning and decision making according to rules.[18]

[16] *See* ALEXANDER & SHERWIN, DEMYSTIFYING LEGAL REASONING, *supra* note 12, at 118–20; Emily Sherwin, *A Defense of Analogical Reasoning in Law*, 66 U. CHI. L. REV. 1179 (1999).

[17] *See* ALEXANDER & SHERWIN, DEMYSTIFYING LEGAL REASONING, *supra* note 12, at 108–14; Frederick Schauer, *Do Cases Make Bad Law?*, 73 U. CHI. L. REV. 883 (2006).

[18] For further discussion, see ALEXANDER & SHERWIN, DEMYSTIFYING LEGAL REASONING, *supra* note 12, at 31–63.

A judge engaged in natural reasoning relies on his or her own moral and practical judgment to determine what outcome is best, all things considered. Past decisions are relevant, but only to the extent that they have generated expectations. If parties, or actors attentive to law, have relied on the conclusions courts have reached in past cases, their reliance counts for whatever it is worth in the moral balance, but no more.

Natural reasoning is best conceived of as a process of reasoning to reflective equilibrium. The judge begins with an intuitive judgment about the best outcome for the case, then formulates a more general principle that supports the initial intuition. The judge then tests the principle by considering other instances to which it might apply and adjusts both principle and intuition to reach an acceptable accommodation.[19] Notice that, although reasoning to reflective equilibrium is structurally similar to formulation of legal principles based on prior cases, the two processes are in fact quite different. The starting point for reflective equilibrium is the reasoner's best unconstrained moral judgment; in contrast, the starting point for a construction of a legal principle is a set of prior decisions, some of which the reasoner might reject as wrongly decided.

The alternative to natural reasoning is rule-based decision making. Rules have a role in natural reasoning: when prior decisions announce a relatively determinate rule to govern a class of future cases, a judge engaged in natural reasoning considers whether, based on all relevant considerations, including the value of the rule as a means of regulating and coordinating conduct, the best choice is to follow the rule. But rule-sensitive deliberation of this kind is not rule-based decision making. A judge engaged in rule-based decision making determines whether the target case meets the criteria for application fixed in the rule; if it does, the judge decides as the rule requires, without further consideration of whatever principles or policies may lie behind the rule. The judge, in other words, treats the prescriptions laid out in past opinions as authoritative and preemptive of further reasoning.[20]

Rule-based decision making is imperfect, because rules are imperfect. The rule-maker may have erred in formulating the rule, and even if the rule is well designed, it may be overinclusive. A rule is a determinate prescription applicable to a generically described category of facts, designed to carry out a less determinate principle or purpose. Because the rule is blunt and categorical, the outcome the rule requires will conflict with the rule's purpose in some of the cases to which it applies. Rule-based decision making means disregarding this conflict and adhering to the terms of the rule.

[19] This is a simplified description of the process. For more detailed philosophical discussion of reasoning to reflective equilibrium, *see, e.g.*, Norman Daniels, *Wide Reflective Equilibrium and Theory Acceptance*, 76 J. PHIL. 256 (1979); Howard Klepper, *Justification and Methodology in Practical Ethics*, 26 METAPHILOSOPHY 201, 205–06 (1995); John Rawls, *Outline of a Decision Procedure for Ethics*, 60 PHIL. REV. 177 (1951).

[20] On the preemptive effect of rules, see JOSEPH RAZ, THE MORALITY OF FREEDOM 57–62 (1986); RAZ, *supra* note 11, at 16–19, 22–23, 30–33.

Despite the defects of determinate rules, following rules is often the best available decisional strategy.[21] A well-designed rule can limit the errors of natural reasoning. A determinate rule can also provide certainty and coordination for those whose conduct it governs.[22] These are significant benefits, but they depend on consistent application of the rule. If judges treat the rule as a rule of thumb, to be applied only when the outcome it prescribes coincides with the rule's purpose or with the outcome that appears best, all things considered, the rule will neither curb error nor effectively coordinate conduct.

Thus, from a societal perspective, rule-based decision making can be superior to natural reasoning, at least in some circumstances. The question is not whether the outcome of the rule is correct in a given case, but whether, over time, the sum of errors likely to result if judges consistently follow the rule is less than the sum of errors likely to result if they rely on their own best judgment.[23] Errors resulting from unconstrained judgment include not just potential mistakes in reasoning but also loss of coordination and other benefits through dilution of the rule. When the overall balance of error favors the rule, we are better off if judges follow it without reflection. This conclusion applies not only to rules enacted by legislatures but also to rules announced in prior judicial opinions. When a common law rule is likely prevent more errors than it causes, judges should treat it as binding.

III. COMMON LAW DECISION MAKING AND CYBERTRESPASS

I have argued that there are only two sound decisional strategies open to judges: natural reasoning and strict application of rules. Decision by analogy and decision according to legal principles are not acceptable methods for resolving legal disputes. The *process* of reviewing facts and outcomes of past cases, however, may aid judges, both in natural reasoning and in formulation of rules. In this section, I consider how the general analysis I have laid out might apply to questions of Internet use and, in particular, to claims of cybertrespass. I suggest that analogical techniques are out of place in this context and that rule-based decision making is not a viable alternative. Thus, the only decisional strategy practically available to judges is unconstrained natural reasoning, all things considered.

21 For further discussion of the benefits of rules, see ALEXANDER & SHERWIN, THE RULE OF RULES, *supra* note 12, at 55–59; FREDERICK SCHAUER, PLAYING BY THE RULES: A PHILOSOPHICAL EXAMINATION OF RULE-BASED DECISION-MAKING IN LAW AND LIFE 135–66 (1991).

22 *See* RAZ, *supra* note 20; Gerald J. Postema, *Coordination and Convention at the Foundations of Law*, 11 J. LEGAL STUD. 165 (1982).

23 *See* ALEXANDER & SHERWIN, THE RULE OF RULES, *supra* note 12, at 54. For discussion of the gap between the rationality of issuing rules and the rationality of following rules, *see id.*, at 53–95; SCHAUER, *supra* note 21, at 128–34.

A. *Analogical Methods*

As discussed earlier, the benefits of analogical methods do not lie in any real guidance furnished by past outcomes, but in the process of consulting past facts and outcomes. Searching for analogies exposes judges to examples that can dilute the influence of the facts of the immediate case and better equip them to formulate rules for future cases. Yet, if potential analogies are too far afield, the process will be of little use and may even have adverse effects.

At least in the early stages of the application of trespass doctrine to Internet disputes, comparison to past cases is unlikely to be helpful. What counts as harm to a toothbrush[24] or pernicious interference with a cow[25] will not shed light on what should count as harm to an e-mail server. The items involved and, more importantly, the owner's interest in excluding others from their use are simply too different to be sensibly combined within a single rule or principle of decision. In the circumstances, consulting earlier examples is more likely to confuse judges' thinking than to aid them in formulating an acceptable rule.

In *Intel* v. *Hamidi*, the majority accused dissenting Justice Brown of overreliance on "metaphor."[26] On this point, the majority was probably correct. Justice Brown made a valiant effort to marshal analogies to support the argument that Hamidi's intrusion on Intel's e-mail server was cognizable damage, consistent with prior decisions.[27] Ultimately, however, his substantive remarks about property rights were more cogent than his arguments from precedent.

B. *Rule-Based Decision Making*

Rule-based decision making presents a different set of problems in the context of cybertrespass. In cases such as *Intel Corp.* v. *Hamidi*, courts have assumed that their task is to interpret and apply the set of common law rules defining trespass to chattels. At least in part, therefore, they have treated their decisions as rule-based. Given this assumption, the threshold question of rule application is whether the doctrine of trespass to chattels encompasses Internet-based contacts with computer systems and servers: are these things chattels, and is Internet contact an interference with the owner's possession?

At this point, it is necessary to say something about the meaning of rules. Elsewhere, Larry Alexander and I have argued that the meaning of a rule is no more or less than the meaning the rulemaker intended the rule to have.[28] Our legal system assigns rulemaking power to certain officials, including both legislatures and judges, in order to secure authoritative settlement of controversy. It follows from the

24 The *Restatement* uses this example. RESTATEMENT (SECOND) OF TORTS § 218, cmt. h (1977).
25 Farmer v. Hunt, 123 Eng. Rep. 766 (Ct. Common Pleas 1610).
26 Intel v. Hamidi, 71 P. 2d 296, 310 n.7 (Cal. 2003).
27 Id. at 318–325 (Brown, J., dissenting).
28 *See* ALEXANDER & SHERWIN, DEMYSTIFYING LEGAL REASONING, *supra* note 12, at 132–41.

settlement function we expect these authorities to perform that the content of a rule depends on their intent.

Determining the intent of rulemaking authorities is not an easy task.[29] The words the rulemaker chose to use are the primary guide to intent, but words will not provide an answer in all cases. To understand how the rulemaker used the words, the interpreter must have some sense of the rulemaker's purpose in issuing the rule. At the same time, the interpreter cannot simply refer to the principles and purposes underlying the rule, because one of the objectives of any rule is to translate indeterminate principles and purposes into a set of concrete instructions that will settle controversy about what those principle and purposes require.[30] For purposes of settlement, the rulemaker has chosen particular words.

A further challenge for intent-based interpretation is that intentions are always inchoate to some extent.[31] Necessarily, a rulemaker's intentions about how a rule should apply to future events are intentions about matters of which the rulemaker does not have full knowledge when he or she issues the rule. It follows that the scope of the intentions that define the meaning of the rule must be broader than any particular set of facts the rulemaker envisioned at the time.

The inchoate character of intentions requires interpreters to make a delicate distinction between intentions that are not fully specified in the mind of the rulemaker but nevertheless exist and can be understood, and intentions that are simply indeterminate. There are things that a rulemaker intends to include within the scope of a rule – things the rulemaker would acknowledge as members of the generic class of regulated objects named in the rule – even though the rulemaker has never seen or imagined them. In contrast, there are unimagined things about which the rulemaker would admit that he or she had no intent. In other words, the rulemaker, if confronted now with the object, would be unable to say whether the object is or is not within the scope of the rule. In such a case, the rulemaker has no intent and the rule cannot apply.

Cybertrespass probably falls into the category of cases about which the intentions of rulemakers are wholly indeterminate. A computer system or server is certainly different in kind from the chattels envisioned – specifically or generically – by the judges who formulated the rules governing trespass to chattels. The value of the system to its owner lies in its capacity to gather, sort, and transmit information, which is not equivalent to any physical features of the thing. The concept of possession is also a poor fit: what is interfered with in Internet trespass cases is not really possession but a right of control, exercised within the framework of a public communication network. Given the complexity of ownership in this context, if the judges who decided past trespass cases and fashioned the doctrine of trespass to chattels were now confronted with a world of computers linked to the Internet, they might admit

[29] I am setting aside the problem of rules issued by multimember entities. *See id.* at 171–73.

[30] *See* SCHAUER, *supra* note 21, at 53–54.

[31] *See* ALEXANDER & SHERWIN, DEMYSTIFYING LEGAL REASONING, *supra* note 12, at 141–45.

that they did not know whether to include these new objects within the scope of the trespass rules.

This observation does not imply that plaintiffs in cybertrespass cases should not have a claim to relief. It does indicate, however, that the answer is not a matter of interpretation, properly understood. The intended meaning of existing rules governing trespass to chattels does not resolve the problems of unwanted Internet contacts. Consequently, judges are on their own. Both in adjudicating disputes and in formulating rules for future cases, judges must consult their own best judgment, all things considered.

The majority in *Intel* v. *Hamidi* was reluctant to accept this conclusion: as noted, the court purported to remain neutral on questions of regulatory policy.[32] In fact, however, the court determined an outcome, adopted a decisional rule, and, in doing so, took a stance on the disputed substantive issues. The opinion might have been clearer, had the court acknowledged that it was deciding these issues by a process of natural reasoning.

CONCLUSION

The not-too-surprising implication of the arguments made earlier is that past legal decisions provide little if any help to judges who must resolve disputes about use of the Internet. Examining the facts and outcomes of prior cases in search of analogies is likely to confuse rather than clarify judicial thought. Formulating legal principles based on past decisions is unreliable and probably unwise. Common law rules developed to govern trespass to chattels are inapt because Internet disputes are outside the scope of the rulemakers' intentions. Thus, the only sensible method open to judges who must decide Internet disputes is natural reasoning, all things considered, about what results and what future rules are best.

[32] *See* note 8 and accompanying text, *supra*.

PART III

State Intellectual Property Law

12

The Intellectual Property Clause's Preemptive Effect

*Jeanne C. Fromer**

INTRODUCTION

Federal law's preemption of state power in the context of intellectual property (as well as more generally) remains unclear in several respects, even in the face of considerable scholarship and judicial decisions on the subject. As Arthur Miller observes, "Preemption in the intellectual property context . . . has received oscillating treatment over the years. . . . The result has been a body of law replete with internal tensions, distinctions, and ambiguities, making definite answers to many preemption questions impossible to divine."[1]

Much of the confusion in preemption doctrine in intellectual property comes from trying to piece together the Supreme Court's various cases in the area into a coherent analytical framework. I propose that the cases can be read consistently, with the help of the Constitution's Intellectual Property Clause (IP Clause), which grants Congress authority "[t]o promote the Progress of Science and useful Arts, by securing for limited Times to Authors and Inventors the exclusive Right to their respective Writings and Discoveries."[2] The IP Clause can help shed analytical light on when state laws are preempted.

The IP Clause is the authority pursuant to which American copyright and patent laws have been enacted. As I discuss elsewhere, it establishes the means and ends to which Congress can legislate to protect intellectual property: Congress can act with the goal of promoting progress of science and useful arts, using only the means

* Professor of Law, New York University School of Law. I thank Arnaud Ajdler, Thomas Cotter, Deven Desai, Wendy Gordon, Paul Heald, Mark Lemley, Arthur Miller, Caleb Nelson, Jennifer Rothman, Pamela Samuelson, Catherine Sharkey, Molly Van Houweling, and Benjamin Zipursky, as well as participants in the University of Pennsylvania Law School symposium on Intellectual Property and the Common Law, for balanced comments and suggestions.

[1] Arthur R. Miller, *Common Law Protection for Products of the Mind: An "Idea" Whose Time Has Come*, 119 Harv. L. Rev. 703, 745–46 (2006).

[2] U.S. Const. art. I, § 8, cl. 8.

set out therein, of securing for limited times to authors and inventors the exclusive rights to their works.[3] I argue here that, understood through the lens of the IP Clause, state laws are preempted on satisfaction of two conditions: (1) they lie within the preemptive scope of the IP Clause, and (2) they upset the IP Clause's balance, as effectuated by a federal law.

Because the IP Clause authorizes Congress to act only for the purpose of promoting progress in science and useful arts (using the means specified), when state laws (or their enforcement) are instead structurally directed to another purpose, they generally lie outside the scope of the IP Clause and therefore outside its preemptive scope. Nonetheless, transitively, state laws that piggyback off the federal laws passed pursuant to the IP Clause lie within its preemptive scope in certain ways, even if they lack structural purpose to promote progress of science and useful arts.

State laws within the IP Clause's preemptive scope ought to be preempted when they upset the IP Clause's balance, as instantiated by federal laws enacted pursuant to its authority. The IP Clause effectuates a balance between granting incentives to authors and inventors to create certain valuable works and promoting the public interest of having access to these works (by encouraging their creation and by ensuring that rights last only for limited times). Federal legislation enacted pursuant to this power instantiates this balance in particular ways (even when Congress does not expressly state as much). It is therefore problematic when state laws within the IP Clause's preemptive scope upset this balance.

Part I explains my understanding of the IP Clause and provides an overview of the patent and copyright laws enacted pursuant to its authority. Part II describes the Supreme Court's preemption doctrine, focusing on its case law with respect to intellectual property. Part III turns to the IP Clause's preemptive effect. I maintain therein that the IP Clause does not preempt state laws of its own force, yet it is helpful in making sense of Supreme Court doctrine to decipher when state laws are preempted. I argue that state laws are preempted when they both fall within the IP Clause's preemptive scope and upset the IP Clause's balance, as instantiated by federal law.

I. CONGRESSIONAL AUTHORITY

The Constitution grants Congress authority "[t]o promote the Progress of Science and useful Arts, by securing for limited Times to Authors and Inventors the exclusive Right to their respective Writings and Discoveries."[4] Pursuant to this grant of power, Congress has enacted patent and copyright laws.

Patent law grants protection to inventors of useful, novel, and nonobvious inventions.[5] Patents are granted after successfully undergoing examination by the

[3] Jeanne C. Fromer, *The Intellectual Property Clause's External Limitations*, 61 DUKE L.J. 1329 (2012).
[4] U.S. CONST. art. I, § 8, cl. 8.
[5] 35 U.S.C. §§ 101–103.

Patent and Trademark Office (PTO) to ascertain that an invention meets patentability conditions and that the description in the patent application satisfies certain disclosure requirements.[6] The patent right permits the patentee to exclude others from practicing the invention claimed in the patent for a term of typically twenty years from the date the patent application was filed.[7] Federal patent law contains no provision specifying when it preempts state laws.[8]

American copyright law looks different. It protects "original works of authorship fixed in any tangible medium of expression, now known or later developed," including literary works, sound recordings, movies, and computer software code.[9] To obtain copyright protection, authors need only create an original fixed work; there is no requirement that a work be published to be protected.[10] Protection vests in authors without any formalities, such as registration.[11] A copyright holder receives the exclusive right to reproduce the work, sell copies of it, and prepare derivative works, among other things,[12] normally until seventy years after the author's death.[13] Copyright protection extends to the expression of particular ideas rather than to the ideas themselves.[14] Yet protection actually reaches well beyond the literal work to works that are copied and substantially similar.[15]

In its 1976 revision of copyright law, Congress included a preemption provision in § 301.[16] Section 301 principally provides that state laws are preempted when two conditions are met: (1) they confer "legal or equitable rights that are equivalent to any of the exclusive rights" provided by federal copyright law, and (2) they protect "works of authorship that are fixed in a tangible medium of expression and come within the subject matter of copyright as specified by sections 102 and 103" of the

6 *Id.* § 131. The Patent Act requires disclosure of certain content within the patent by calling for a written description and enablement. *Id.* § 112. *See generally* Jeanne C. Fromer, *Patent Disclosure*, 94 IOWA L. REV. 539, 547–94 (2009) (describing these requirements and arguing that they do not suffice for useful and clear disclosures).

7 35 U.S.C. § 154(a).

8 Sharon K. Sandeen, Kewanee *Revisited: Returning to First Principles of Intellectual Property Law To Determine the Issue of Federal Preemption*, 12 MARQ. INTELL. PROP. L. REV. 299, 335 (2008).

9 17 U.S.C. §§ 101, 102(a).

10 *Id.* § 102 (requiring only that a work be fixed in "any tangible medium of expression" to be copyrightable).

11 Registration of a protected work with the Copyright Office is permissive. *Id.* § 408. To bring an infringement action, however, a copyright holder must in the ordinary case first have registered the copyright with the Copyright Office. *Id.* § 411(a).

12 *Id.* § 106 (granting the right to prepare derivative works; rent, lease, or lend works; perform works publicly; display works; and digitally transmit works).

13 *Id.* § 302(a).

14 *Id.* § 102(b); Nichols v. Universal Picture Corp., 45 F.2d 119, 121 (2d Cir. 1930).

15 Corwin v. Walt Disney Co., 475 F.3d 1239, 1253 (11th Cir. 2007); Whitehead v. Paramount Pictures Corp., 53 F. Supp. 2d 38, 46 (D.D.C. 1999).

16 For a thorough history of this provision, see Howard B. Abrams, *Copyright, Misappropriation, and Preemption: Constitutional and Statutory Limits of State Law Protection*, 1983 SUP. CT. REV. 509, 537–48.

copyright laws.[17] Although § 301 was intended to clarify copyright's preemptive reach,[18] the litigation it has generated and the often conflicting judicial decisions applying it underscore that the provision has likely muddied preemption analysis.[19] For example, when is a state right equivalent to copyright's exclusive rights, as the first factor requires? Is the state right valid when it contains an extra element not found under federal copyright protection, as most courts find;[20] if copyright holders' exercise of any of their exclusive rights does not violate the state right, as a minority of courts hold;[21] or on some other basis entirely? From the first perspective, most state rights, including laws of contract, trade secrecy, and rights of publicity, are in the clear, because they have additional elements that copyright law does not.[22] By contrast, from the second perspective, state laws can be preempted more easily.[23]

The dominant premise underlying American patent and copyright laws is that the incentive of exclusive rights is granted to creators for a limited time to encourage their productions, which are valuable to society.[24] An integral part of this understanding is that the restrictions these rights impose on the public are justified, but only for a limited time and with some limitations on right scope, so that the public can use them to create further.[25]

In fact, the power conferred on Congress by the IP Clause itself reflects a balance between granting creators rights to create (and disseminate) works that are valuable to the public to consume and build on, but restricting them so that the public is not hurt.[26] The Supreme Court, in its most recent preemption decision for intellectual property, stated as much when it underscored the balance struck by the IP Clause between encouraging innovation and competition, by permitting Congress to enact intellectual-property protection to promote the progress of science and useful arts, but only for limited durations and without removing material from the public domain.[27] This principle is longstanding. In 1896, the Supreme Court emphasized in the patent context that "on the expiration of a patent the monopoly created by it ceases to exist, and the right to make the thing formerly covered by the patent becomes public property. It is upon this condition that the patent is

17 17 U.S.C. § 301.

18 H.R. REP. NO. 94-1476, at 129–30 (1976); S. REP. NO. 94-473, at 113–14 (1975).

19 Abrams, *supra* note 16, at 512; Joseph P. Bauer, *Addressing the Incoherency of the Preemption Provision of the Copyright Act of 1976*, 10 VAND. J. ENT. & TECH. 1, 3–4 (2007).

20 Bauer, *supra* note 19, at 9, 38.

21 Jennifer E. Rothman, *Copyright Preemption and the Right of Publicity*, 36 U.C. DAVIS L. REV. 199, 229–30 (2002).

22 Bauer, *supra* note 19, at 39–42; Schuyler Moore, *Straightening Out Copyright Preemption*, 9 UCLA ENT. L. REV. 201, 203–04 (2002).

23 Rothman, *supra* note 21, at 230.

24 Jeanne C. Fromer, *Expressive Incentives in Intellectual Property*, 98 VA. L. REV. 1745 (2012).

25 Abrams, *supra* note 16, at 510.

26 *Id.* at 527; Bauer, *supra* note 19, at 108; Christina Bohannan, *Copyright Preemption of Contracts*, 67 MD. L. REV. 616, 617 (2008).

27 Bonito Boats, Inc. v. Thunder Craft Boats, Inc., 489 U.S. 141, 146 (1989).

granted."[28] On this reasoning, Congress can act to secure intellectual-property protection so long as it does not upset this calibrated balance established by the IP Clause.[29]

Therefore, when Congress enacts intellectual-property protection pursuant to the IP Clause, it is essentially effectuating a particular instantiation of this balance.[30] The Supreme Court has explained that the patent laws provide rights in a bounded set of inventions for a limited time, leave the rest in the public domain, and induce disclosure to support the public domain (and scientific and technological progress).[31] It has elaborated that

> the patent system is one in which uniform federal standards are carefully used to promote invention while at the same time preserving free competition. Obviously a State could not, consistently with the Supremacy Clause of the Constitution, extend the life of a patent beyond its expiration date or give a patent on an article which lacked the level of invention required for federal patents. To do either would run counter to the policy of Congress of granting patents only to true inventions, and then only for a limited time. Just as a State cannot encroach upon the federal patent laws directly, it cannot, under some other law, such as that forbidding unfair competition, give protection of a kind that clashes with the objectives of the federal patent laws.[32]

The Court has made the same observation about copyright law. For example, one opinion observes in light of the IP Clause that "the monopoly privileges that Congress has authorized, while intended to motivate the creative activity of authors . . . by the provision of a special reward, are limited in nature and must ultimately serve the public good."[33] This balance is particularly emphasized with respect to copyright's limited duration, doctrine of fair use limiting copyright's scope,[34] and its idea-expression dichotomy. According to the Supreme Court,

> The limited scope of the copyright holder's statutory monopoly, like the limited copyright duration required by the Constitution, reflects a balance of competing claims upon the public interest: Creative work is to be encouraged and rewarded, but private motivation must ultimately serve the cause of promoting broad public

[28] Singer Mfg. Co. v. June Mfg. Co., 163 U.S. 169, 185 (1896).

[29] *Id.*; *see also* Eldred v. Ashcroft, 537 U.S. 186, 204–08 (2003). *See generally* Fromer, *supra* note 3.

[30] *E.g.*, *Bonito Boats*, 489 U.S. at 146 ("From their inception, the federal patent laws have embodied a careful balance between the need to promote innovation and the recognition that imitation and refinement through imitation are both necessary to invention itself and the very lifeblood of a competitive economy.").

[31] *Id.* at 151; *see also* Kewanee Oil Co. v. Bicron Corp., 416 U.S. 470, 480 (1974).

[32] Sears, Roebuck & Co. v. Stiffel Co., 376 U.S. 225, 230–31 (1964).

[33] Fogerty v. Fantasy, Inc., 510 U.S. 517, 526 (1994) (internal quotation marks omitted). Scholars frequently espouse this view as well. *E.g.*, Dennis S. Karjala, *Federal Preemption of Shrinkwrap and On-Line Licenses*, 22 U. DAYTON L. REV. 511, 512–13 (1997); Mark A. Lemley, *Beyond Preemption: The Law and Policy of Intellectual Property Licensing*, 87 CALIF. L. REV. 111, 142 (1999).

[34] 17 U.S.C. § 107.

> availability of literature, music, and the other arts. The immediate effect of our copyright law is to secure a fair return for an 'author's' creative labor. But the ultimate aim is, by this incentive, to stimulate artistic creativity for the general public good.[35]

Similarly, the idea-expression dichotomy "strike[s] a definitional balance . . . by permitting free communication of facts [and opinions] while still protecting an author's expression."[36] As such, "every idea, theory, and fact in a copyrighted work becomes instantly available for public exploitation at the moment of publication."[37]

More generally, the Supreme Court strongly indicates that there is a public domain that cannot be undone. For example, in the context of discussing the relationship between federal powers under the IP Clause and state authority, the Supreme Court notes that

> the ultimate goal of the patent system is to bring new designs and technologies into the public domain through disclosure. State law protection for techniques and designs whose disclosure has already been induced by market rewards may conflict with the very purpose of the patent laws by decreasing the range of ideas available as the building blocks of further innovation. . . . To a limited extent, the federal patent laws must determine not only what is protected, but also what is free for all to use.[38]

An unfortunate outlier in this context is one of the Supreme Court's most recent decisions, *Golan* v. *Holder*.[39] In that decision, the Court maintained that the IP Clause does not impose an "impenetrable barrier to the extension of copyright protection to authors whose writings, for whatever reason, are in the public domain."[40] Justice Breyer's forceful dissent in *Golan* reveals the problems of allowing Congress to protect works that have already fallen into the public domain: doing so both "bestows monetary rewards only on owners of old works – works that have already been created and already are in the American public domain" and "inhibits the

35 Twentieth Century Music Corp. v. Aiken, 422 U.S. 151, 156 (1975); *accord* Maureen A. O'Rourke, *Drawing the Boundary Between Copyright and Contract: Copyright Preemption of Software Licenses*, 45 Duke L.J. 479, 535 (1995) ("The fair use doctrine is an essential part of [copyright's] balancing approach. It attempts to correct market inefficiencies inherent in the grant of a monopoly by sanctioning uses that otherwise might be infringing when doing so is necessary to strike the appropriate balance between the rights of authors and those of the public.").

36 Harper & Row, Publishers, Inc. v. Nation Enters., 471 U.S. 539, 556 (1985) (making this statement in the course of discussing the interaction of copyright law and the First Amendment).

37 Eldred v. Ashcroft, 537 U.S. 186, 219 (2003).

38 Bonito Boats, Inc. v. Thunder Craft Boats, Inc., 489 U.S. 141, 151 (1989); *accord* Graham v. John Deere Co., 383 U.S. 1, 6 (1966) ("Congress may not authorize the issuance of patents whose effects are to remove existent knowledge from the public domain, or to restrict free access to materials already available."). Another view of copyright and patent laws is occasionally articulated: They set out default terms that private parties (and perhaps states) can modify. Kathryn Judge, Note, *Rethinking Copyright Misuse*, 57 Stan. L. Rev. 901, 907 n.25 (2004) (articulating this position). That view is hard to square with the Supreme Court's and others' thinking on the fine-tuned balance of these laws.

39 132 S. Ct. 873 (2012).

40 *Id.* at 884.

dissemination of those works, [which otherwise] would assume their rightful places in computer-accessible databases, spreading knowledge throughout the world."[41] These concerns are reflected in the IP Clause itself, which the *Golan* majority discounted in its constitutional construction.

Related, however, to the more consistently invoked understanding of the patent and copyright laws as instantiations of the balance set out in the IP Clause is the limited reach of congressional power pursuant to the IP Clause. In other work, I rely on the text, structure, and history of the IP Clause, as well as subsequent governmental activity and Supreme Court doctrine, to show that the IP Clause operates to forbid Congress from using its other powers "[t]o promote the Progress of Science and useful Arts" through laws employing means beyond the extent of the IP Clause's power to "secur[e] for limited Times to Authors and Inventors the exclusive Right to their respective Writings and Discoveries."[42] That is, this evidence shows that if Congress seeks, via legislation, to promote the progress of science and useful arts, the only way it can do so is by enacting laws that secure to authors and inventors exclusive rights in their writings and discoveries for limited times.

Having discussed the power conferred by the IP Clause and the patent and copyright laws Congress enacted pursuant to those powers, I turn to the Supreme Court's preemption doctrine, both generally and in the context of intellectual property.

II. PREEMPTION DOCTRINE

Generally, the Supreme Court has classified three types of preemption of state law: express preemption, field preemption, and conflict preemption.[43] Express preemption occurs when Congress legislates, in a lawful exercise of authority, to state explicitly how its laws preempt state laws,[44] as Congress did with § 301 of the copyright laws.[45] The other two forms of preemption are implicit. Field preemption dictates that federal law supersedes state law when there is a "scheme of federal regulation so pervasive as to make reasonable the inference that Congress left no room to supplement it," either "because the federal interest [in the field] is so dominant or because the object sought to be obtained by the federal law and the character

[41] *Id.* at 900 (Breyer, J., dissenting).
[42] Fromer, *supra* note 3.
[43] Pac. Gas & Elec. Co. v. State Energy Res. Conservation & Dev. Comm'n, 461 U.S. 190, 203–04 (1983).
[44] *Id.* at 203; *accord* Caleb Nelson, *Preemption*, 86 VA. L. REV. 225, 226–27 (2000). Although the Supreme Court has suggested that there is a general presumption against federal preemption of state law, Viet Dinh makes the case that the Supremacy Clause's set-up of preemption confers no such presumption, but instead requires particularized evaluations in each different statutory context, if not a presumption in favor of preemption. Viet D. Dinh, *Reassessing the Law of Preemption*, 88 GEO. L.J. 2085, 2087, 2094–98 (2000). Dinh suggests as well that Congress's power to preempt state laws expressly must come, if it exists at all, not from the Supremacy Clause – which is a choice-of-law rule – but in an affirmative grant of power, such as the Commerce or IP Clause. *Id.* at 2088–91.
[45] *Supra* text accompanying notes 16–23.

of obligations imposed by it may reveal the same purpose."[46] Conflict preemption "arises when compliance with both federal and state regulations is a physical impossibility or where state law stands as an obstacle to the accomplishment and execution of the full purposes and objectives of Congress."[47] The Supremacy Clause of the Constitution provides a basis for preemption of state laws.[48] It provides that "[t]h[e] Constitution, and the Laws of the United States which shall be made in pursuance thereof; and all treaties made, or which shall be made, under the authority of the United States, shall be the supreme law of the land."[49]

In 1964, the Supreme Court ushered in its modern preemption jurisprudence in the context of intellectual property in the companion cases of *Sears, Roebuck & Co.* v. *Stiffel Co.*[50] and *Compco Corp.* v. *Day-Brite Lighting, Inc.*[51] In these cases, the Court addressed the viability of state unfair-competition laws protecting against the copying of unpatented industrial designs in the face of the federal patent laws.[52] In *Compco*, the design at issue (a lighting fixture by Day-Brite) was the subject of an invalidated design patent and a refused utility patent.[53] Likewise, in *Sears*, the design at issue was found to be entitled neither to a design nor a utility patent.[54] The *Compco* lawsuit involved a claim that Compco had unfairly competed with Day-Brite by selling similar fixtures that deceived consumers into thinking that they were Day-Brite's.[55] *Sears* involved an analogous claim.[56] The *Compco* Court saw the evidence that consumers were confused as wafer-thin at best,[57] although there was slightly more such evidence in the *Sears* case.[58] *Compco* found the state law to be preempted because "[u]nder the federal patent laws [Day-Brite's fixture] is . . . in the public domain and can be copied in every detail by whoever pleases."[59] *Sears* agreed and expanded on this reasoning:

> To allow a State by use of its law of unfair competition to prevent the copying of an article which represents too slight an advance to be patented would be to permit

46 *Pac. Gas*, 461 U.S. at 204 (internal marks omitted).

47 *Id.* (internal marks omitted). The obstacle form of conflict preemption can, in theory, be broad. Nelson, *supra* note 44, at 228–29. Caleb Nelson argues that obstacle preemption, as a general doctrine, is not a valid form of preemption. *See id.* at 231–32 ("Under the Supremacy Clause, preemption occurs if and only if state law contradicts a valid rule established by federal law, and the mere fact that federal law serves certain purposes does not automatically mean that it contradicts everything that might get in the way of those purposes.").

48 Dinh, *supra* note 44; Nelson, *supra* note 44; Rothman, *supra* note 21, at 208.

49 U.S. Const. art. IV, cl. 2.

50 376 U.S. 225 (1964).

51 376 U.S. 234 (1964).

52 *Compco*, 376 U.S. at 234; *Sears*, 376 U.S. at 225.

53 *Compco*, 376 U.S. at 234–35.

54 *Sears*, 376 U.S. at 231.

55 *Compco*, 376 U.S. at 234–35.

56 *Sears*, 376 U.S. at 231.

57 *Compco*, 376 U.S. at 236.

58 *Sears*, 376 U.S. at 226.

59 *Compco*, 376 U.S. at 237–38.

> the State to block off from the public something which federal law has said belongs to the public. The result would be that while federal law grants only [a limited number of] years' protection to genuine inventions, States could allow perpetual protection to articles too lacking in novelty to merit any patent at all under federal constitutional standards. This would be too great an encroachment on the federal patent system to be tolerated.[60]

Nonetheless fearing the undermining of legitimate state interests in promoting fair trade, the *Sears* Court stated in dicta that

> [d]oubtless a State may, in appropriate circumstances, require that goods, whether patented or unpatented, be labeled or that other precautionary steps be taken to prevent customers from being misled as to the source, just as it may protect businesses in the use of their trademarks, labels, or distinctive dress in the packaging of goods so as to prevent others, by imitating such markings, from misleading purchasers as to the source of the goods.[61]

Nearly ten years later, the Supreme Court revisited preemption in *Goldstein* v. *California*,[62] this time in the context of copyright law.[63] California had enacted a law criminalizing unauthorized copying of sound recordings with intent to sell them, and the law's constitutionality was challenged on the basis that it was preempted by federal copyright law, which at the time did not confer protection on sound recordings.[64] The Court rejected this challenge, reasoning that "[a]lthough the Copyright Clause . . . recognizes the potential benefits of a national system, it does not indicate that all writings are of national interest or that state legislation is, in all cases, unnecessary or precluded."[65] In this statement, the *Goldstein* Court seems to reject the possibility of field preemption for copyright law. The Court interpreted congressional action neither to have provided copyright protection for sound recordings nor to have required that sound recordings be freely available.[66] According to the Court,

> a conflict would develop if a State attempted to protect that which Congress intended to be free from restraint or to free that which Congress had protected. However, where Congress determines that neither federal protection nor freedom from restraint is required by the national interest, it is at liberty to stay its hand entirely. Since state protection would not then conflict with federal action, total relinquishment of the States' power to grant copyright protection cannot be inferred.[67]

60 *Sears*, 376 U.S. at 231–32.
61 *Id.* at 232.
62 412 U.S. 546 (1973).
63 At issue was copyright law predating § 301's provision of express preemption, and thus the Court did not assess express preemption.
64 *Goldstein*, 412 U.S. at 548–52.
65 *Id.* at 556–57.
66 *Id.* at 563–69.
67 *Id.* at 559.

By asking whether the state law at issue was local or national in character – a question usually asked with regard to laws enacted under the Commerce Clause instead of the IP Clause – *Goldstein* appeared to shift the focus of the Court's preemption jurisprudence,[68] an analytical move that has been widely criticized.[69]

The next year in *Kewanee Oil Co.* v. *Bicron Corp.*,[70] the Supreme Court took up preemption of state trade secrecy laws by the federal patent laws.[71] The *Kewanee* Court viewed the patent laws as effectuating the constitutionally authorized promotion of progress by providing inventors with the "high price of [many] years of exclusive use" as an incentive to invent for society's benefit in exchange for the public disclosure of their inventions, on which society could build to invent cumulatively, thereby further stimulating progress.[72] Given the strong incentive provided and the need to build on once patented inventions, the Court observed that "that which is in the public domain cannot be removed therefrom by action of the States."[73] Although the Court saw trade secrecy protection as being particularly concerned, just like patent law, with the promotion of invention (as well as commercial ethics), it held that Ohio's trade secret laws were not preempted, because they were not an obstacle to the carefully calibrated patent system.[74] The Court reasoned that Ohio's trade secrecy laws did not deter inventors from opting into the patent system with its disclosures, primarily because they protected many inventions that were not patentable and offered less secure protection to those that were, such that reasonable inventors would opt for patent law's certain, though time-limited benefits, over trade secrecy's less certain ones.[75] Moreover, the Court saw the state laws as providing a mere additional incentive to invent without removing material from the public domain; as such, it did not think that the state laws upset patent law's balance.[76]

Five years later, in *Aronson* v. *Quick Point Pencil Co.*,[77] the Supreme Court held that the federal patent laws did not preempt state contract law "to preclude enforcement of a contract to pay royalties to a patent applicant, on sales of articles embodying the putative invention, for so long as the contracting party sells them, if a patent is not granted."[78] In that case, the parties had contracted for a specific royalty rate, which would be de-escalated by half were no patent to issue within five years.[79] As with the *Kewanee* Court's view of Ohio's trade secrecy laws,

[68] Abrams, *supra* note 16, at 527.
[69] *E.g.*, Miller, *supra* note 1, at 750.
[70] 416 U.S. 470 (1974).
[71] *Id.* at 472.
[72] *Id.* at 480–81.
[73] *Id.* at 481.
[74] *Id.* at 482–83.
[75] *Id.* at 484–91.
[76] *Id.* at 482–84.
[77] 440 U.S. 257 (1979).
[78] *Id.* at 258–59.
[79] *Id.* at 261–62.

the Court thought that the contract at issue complemented, rather than interfered with, the balance effectuated by the federal patent scheme. It thought that the royalty contract provided an extra incentive to innovate, did not discourage patenting, promoted disclosure by encouraging the invention's commercialization, and did not remove any unpatented invention from the public domain (because the invention had not truly been in the public domain at the time of contracting and remained available to anyone else to use freely once the patent was not granted).[80]

In 1989, the Supreme Court considered patent law's preemptive effect in *Bonito Boats, Inc.* v. *Thunder Craft Boats, Inc.*,[81] in ruling on the constitutionality of a Florida law prohibiting the use of direct molding to duplicate for sale any manufactured vessel hull or component thereof without permission.[82] The Court held that federal patent law preempted the state law.[83] It reasoned that the IP Clause "reflects a balance between the need to encourage innovation and the avoidance of monopolies which stifle competition without any concomitant advance in the 'Progress of Science and useful Arts.'"[84] As such, the Court continued, progress of science and useful arts is promoted – and authorized – only when rights of limited duration are granted and when the public domain is guarded against removals of material therein.[85] To the Court, the patent laws effectuate this balance with their requirements of novelty and nonobviousness, which ensure that the public domain is the norm rather than the exception, and with their disclosure rules, which induce a public sharing of information for the benefit of the public domain.[86] Through this analytical lens, the Court reasoned that the Florida law was preempted, because it upset this balance. For one thing, the state law's purpose was the same as that set out in the IP Clause: to promote technological progress.[87] Additionally, it sought to accomplish that purpose by upsetting patent law's balance between promoting innovation through rights and competition, by providing producers with protection over unpatentable designs, which by the federal scheme, ought to be in the public domain.[88]

Having outlined the Supreme Court's preemption doctrine generally and with regard to intellectual property, I turn now to explicating the role of the IP Clause in preemption.

80 *Id.* at 262–64.
81 489 U.S. 141 (1989).
82 *Id.* at 144–45.
83 *Id.* at 157–66.
84 *Id.* at 146.
85 *Id.*
86 *Id.* at 151.
87 *See id.* at 157, 165–66 (observing that the state law is occupied with "the protection of producers as an incentive to product innovation").
88 *Id.* at 159–60.

III. THE IP CLAUSE'S PREEMPTIVE EFFECT

In some respects, the Constitution's role itself in preemption analysis for intellectual property has been invoked infrequently. In particular, given copyright law's express preemption provision in § 301, many courts begin and end their analysis of copyright preemption with that section.[89] However, to the extent that state laws cause an actual conflict or create a sufficient obstacle with the federal laws, the Supremacy Clause, as understood by the Supreme Court, should nullify those state laws.[90] This is true even in the presence of an express preemption provision in the relevant statute that does not nullify those state laws.[91]

That said, when discussing the Constitution's role in preempting state laws, analysis tends to focus only on the Supremacy Clause itself.[92] This Part considers the role that another constitutional provision, the IP Clause, ought to play in analyzing preemption of state laws.[93] After rejecting in Section A the possibility that the IP Clause can preempt state laws of its own force, I take up in Section B the role it serves to preempt state laws in conjunction with federal laws enacted pursuant to its authority.

A. *Preemptive of Its Own Force?*

In a 1955 dissenting opinion in *Capitol Records, Inc.* v. *Mercury Records Corp.*,[94] a case raising very similar issues to *Goldstein*, Judge Learned Hand seemed to express the view that the IP Clause could preempt laws of its own force:

> I cannot believe that the failure of Congress to include within the Act all that the Clause covers should give the states so wide a power. To do so would *pro tanto* defeat the overriding purpose of the Clause, which was to grant only for "limited Times" the untrammelled exploitation of an author's "Writings." Either he must be content with such circumscribed exploitation as does not constitute "publication,"

89 *See* Tom W. Bell, *Misunderestimating Dastar: How the Supreme Court Unwittingly Revolutionized Copyright Preemption*, 65 Md. L. Rev. 206, 228–32 (2006) (describing a possible recent shift away from this trend); Rothman, *supra* note 21, at 208.

90 P. Stephen Fardy, *Feet of Clay: How the Right of Publicity Exception Undermines Copyright Act Preemption*, 12 Tex. Intell. Prop. L.J. 443, 448–49 (2004); Rothman, *supra* note 21, at 208; *see supra* text accompanying notes 48–49.

91 *See* Geier v. Am. Honda Motor Co., 529 U.S. 861, 872 (2000) (rejecting the "argument that the presence of the express pre-emption provision entirely foreclosed the possibility of conflict pre-emption").

92 *E.g.*, 3 Paul Goldstein, Goldstein on Copyright 17:41 (3d ed. 2011); Bauer, *supra* note 19, at 9, 107–08; Bell, *supra* note 89, at 228; Fardy, *supra* note 90, at 448–49; O'Rourke, *supra* note 35, 534–35 (1995); Rothman, *supra* note 21, at 236.

93 Herein, I focus principally on its role in conflict preemption, but my analysis might also be used to help interpret express preemption provisions in laws passed pursuant to the IP Clause. A discussion of the IP Clause's role in preemption can be found in Bauer, *supra* note 19, at 108, and Malla Pollack, *Unconstitutional Incontestability?: The Intersection of the Intellectual Property and Commerce Clauses of the Constitution*, 18 Seattle U. L. Rev. 259, 326 (1995).

94 221 F.2d 657 (2d Cir. 1955).

> or he must eventually dedicate his "work" to the public. The situation is no different from that of patents, where such bilateral character of the grant is a commonplace. I would hold that the clause has that much effect *ex proprio vigore*; and that the states are not free to follow their own notions as to when an author's right shall be unlimited both in user and in duration. Such power of course they have as to "works" that are not "Writings"; but I submit that, once it is settled that a "work" is in that class, the Clause enforces upon the author the choice I have just mentioned; and, if so, it must follow that it is a federal question whether he has published the "work."[95]

Perhaps the most straightforward interpretation of Hand's view is that the IP Clause directly preempts all state laws that do not comply with the Clause's internal limitations, such as limited duration, so long as they regulate subject matter that is protectable by the Clause.[96] (There is another way to view Hand's reasoning, which I explore in the next Section and which I think – unlike this understanding – is more compatible with Supreme Court jurisprudence.)

Nonetheless, Hand's view seems difficult to accept, given that since the first federal copyright laws, the states have frequently provided common-law protection to unpublished writings.[97] As evidenced by Congress's protection of unpublished writings in its 1976 copyright statute,[98] such writings fall squarely within the scope of the power conferred by the IP Clause. Yet states' pre-1976 protection of these writings often contravened the Clause's internal limitations, by providing protection for an unlimited duration.[99] Even though Congress in 1909 made express the long implicit authorization to the states to protect unpublished writings,[100] Hand's position would deem the earliest state practices constitutionally suspect.

95 *Capitol Records*, 221 F.2d at 667 (Hand, J., dissenting); *see also* Abrams, *supra* note 16, at 519–25 (explaining Hand's view).

96 Paul Goldstein, *Federal System Ordering of the Copyright Interest*, 69 COLUM. L. REV. 49, 51 (1969); Miller, *supra* note 1, at 747. Some scholars agree with Hand that the IP Clause can be preemptive of its own force. Bell, *supra* note 89, at 232–33; *cf.* Dinh, *supra* note 44, at 2099 (recognizing "that state laws can be preempted without any congressional action," such as through the dormant Commerce Clause or federal common law); Jane C. Ginsburg, *No "Sweat"?: Copyright and Other Protection of Works of Information After* Feist v. Rural Telephone, 92 COLUM. L. REV. 338, 362 (1992) (suggesting that the Supreme Court's reasoning in its preemption decisions has been inconsistent with regard to the Clause's preemptive effect on its own).

97 John Tehranian, *Parchment, Pixels, & Personhood: User Rights and the IP (Identity Politics) of IP (Intellectual Property*, 82 U. COLO. L. REV. 1, 63–64 (2011).

98 *See* 17 U.S.C. § 102(a) ("Copyright protection subsists, in accordance with this title, in original works of authorship fixed in any tangible medium of expression, now known or later developed, from which they can be perceived, reproduced, or otherwise communicated, either directly or with the aid of a machine or device.").

99 Tehranian, *supra* note 97, at 63.

100 Copyright Act of 1909, Pub. L. No. 60-349, § 2, 35 Stat. 1075, 1076 (1909) ("[N]othing in this Act shall be construed to annul or limit the right of the author or proprietor of an unpublished work, at common law or in equity, to prevent the copying, publication, or use of such unpublished work without his consent, and to obtain damages therefor."); *see also* Paul Bender, *Product Simulation: A Right or a Wrong?*, 64 COLUM. L. REV. 1178, 1231 (1964).

Most scholars think that Judge Hand is wrong, observing that the IP Clause "neither specifically endorses nor prohibits state law [intellectual property] protection."[101] The Supreme Court has most recently in *Bonito Boats* made the same assertion: "the Patent and Copyright Clauses do not, by their own force or by negative implication, deprive the States of the power to adopt rules for the promotion of intellectual creation within their own jurisdictions."[102] As the Court observed in *Goldstein*, "[t]he [IP] clause . . . does not provide that such power shall vest exclusively in the Federal Government. Nor does the Constitution expressly provide that such power shall not be exercised by the States."[103] Although some see the Supreme Court's assertions as dicta that could be worked around in future cases,[104] it is unlikely that that Court will soon come to see the IP Clause as working on its own to preempt state laws.

B. *The Clause's Role in Statutory Preemption*

Although the IP Clause will not of its own force preempt state laws, it nonetheless has a critical role to play in preemption analysis. As this Section sets out, conflict preemption is a central aspect of the Supreme Court's decisions on preemption in intellectual property. In that light, as understood through the lens of the IP Clause, state laws are preempted when (1) they lie within the preemptive scope of the IP Clause and (2) they upset the balance set out in a federal law that effectuates the IP Clause's balance. I consider each requirement in turn. In doing so, I also show how preemption analysis ought to be considered both facially and as applied to the particular challenge.

1. The Clause's Preemptive Scope

As I discuss in this Section, only state laws that fall within the preemptive scope of the IP Clause are preemptable.

As noted earlier, the best understanding of the IP Clause is that it both grants and limits Congress's powers to enact intellectual-property protection.[105] It confers on Congress power "to promote the Progress of Science and useful Arts," but only employing the means specified in the latter part of the Clause: "by securing for limited Times to Authors and Inventors the exclusive Right to their respective Writings and Discoveries."[106] Although this interpretation has critical implications

[101] Abrams, *supra* note 16, at 517; *accord* Miller, *supra* note 1, at 746; Pollack, *supra* note 93, at 301.
[102] *Bonito Boats*, 489 U.S. at 165.
[103] *Goldstein*, 412 U.S. at 553.
[104] Miller, *supra* note 1, at 749.
[105] *Supra* text accompanying note 42.
[106] *Goldstein*, 412 U.S. at 555 ("The clause . . . describes both the objective which Congress may seek and the means to achieve it. The objective is to promote the progress of science and the arts. . . . To accomplish its purpose, Congress may grant to authors the exclusive right to the fruits of their respective works.").

for Congress's ability to use other means pursuant to its other powers,[107] it also has important consequences for the ability of states to enact laws that are not preempted.

Given that Congress's authority to act pursuant to the IP Clause limits it to the means specified for the purpose of promoting progress of science and useful arts, state laws (or enforcements) that lack the structural purpose of promoting this progress – whatever their means – ought to lie outside the preemptive scope of the IP Clause. According to the Tenth Amendment, "[t]he powers not delegated to the United States by the Constitution, nor prohibited by it to the States, are reserved to the States respectively, or to the people."[108] Therefore, when a state's law (or enforcement of such law) is not done in the service of promoting progress of science and useful arts, it is not within the preemptive scope of the IP Clause and will generally not be preemptable by Congress's patent and copyright laws.[109]

Although pinning down the precise scope of "promot[ing] the Progress of Science and useful Arts" is beyond the scope of this chapter, the purpose can generally be understood, as I have discussed elsewhere, as "encouraging the advancement of systematic knowledge, cultural knowledge, and technology."[110] It is frequently, although not always, self-evident when laws have this structural purpose. I nevertheless sketch some thoughts on how to scrutinize state laws for this purpose.

Concerns about pinpointing legislative purpose are well documented, such as the difficulty of assigning a unified purpose to a body composed of many members.[111] To circumvent these problems, I suggest ascertaining a state law's purpose from its structure. As John Manning notes, "[f]ew would deny the possibility of gleaning a statute's overall purpose from its structure or from the aims suggested by the text itself."[112] Moreover, ascertaining this purpose structurally avoids the difficulty of deciding how to measure empirically whether the state law in actuality promotes the progress of science and useful arts, by instead determining whether the law has the structural purpose of so promoting this progress.[113]

Exempting from preemption state laws with structural purposes other than promoting progress of science and useful arts is consistent with *Bonito Boats*' analysis and clarification of the reach of *Sears* and *Compco*. *Bonito Boats* suggested that states

107 Fromer, *supra* note 3.

108 U.S. CONST. amend. X.

109 This invocation of the Tenth Amendment, however, ought not to imply that the states have plenary power over all means not conferred on Congress to effectuate the goal of promoting progress of science and useful arts. Because the limitation of means in the IP Clause is done with the purpose of effectuating a balance between creators' incentives and public benefit, upsetting the particular balance implemented by Congress is a direct affront to federal law and ought to be preempted. *Infra* Part 2.

110 Fromer, *supra* note 3, at 1373.

111 William W. Buzbee, *The One-Congress Fiction in Statutory Interpretation*, 149 U. PA. L. REV. 171, 173 (2000).

112 John F. Manning, *The Absurdity Doctrine*, 116 HARV. L. REV. 2387, 2408 n.75 (2003).

113 *See generally* Fromer, *supra* note 3, at 1373–79.

can typically protect subject matter traditionally covered by federal copyright and patent laws when they have a legitimate interest in doing so apart from the ends of promoting artistic, scientific, or technological progress conferred by the IP Clause.[114] In this sense, the Florida law prohibiting the use of direct molding to duplicate for sale any manufactured vessel hull or component thereof without permission was problematically within the preemptive scope of the IP Clause because its structural purpose was to promote progress of useful arts, here, of boat hulls.[115]

Moreover, the Illinois unfair-competition law at issue in *Sears* and *Compco*, as applied to unpatentable designs, fell within the IP Clause's preemptive scope. Even though the state law is not about promoting progress of science and useful arts but about promoting fair trade, as applied in this circumstance, it sought to protect the functional aspects of a design that had passed into the public domain. The principal reason why there might have been unfair competition in these cases is that consumers might have been confused by seeing a copy of the design because of the unique functionality that had once (or might in theory have) been protected by the patent laws.[116] As such, permitting the state law to operate in this circumstance would piggyback on the federal laws passed pursuant to the IP Clause, thereby transitively (or constructively) conferring on it the purpose of promoting progress of science and useful arts. So doing places this state law, as applied, squarely within the IP Clause's preemptive scope.

By contrast, consider a hypothetical state law that prohibits the copying of computer programs containing a virus or one that forbids copying or distribution of obscene materials. The purpose of the former law is to prevent the spread of computer viruses, and the purpose of the latter is to diminish obscenity. Both laws would not facially lie within the IP Clause's preemptive scope, even though they might forbid copying beyond the federal copyright and patent laws, because neither is concerned with promoting progress of science and useful arts or is bootstrapping off of the IP Clause's purpose transitively. Similarly, the hypothetical state law mentioned in *Sears* and *Compco* requiring the labeling of designs with a source would fall outside of the IP Clause's preemptive scope.

Contrasting the analysis for the vessel hull and unfair-competition laws suggests that, to understand a state law's purpose, one ought to look both at its facial purpose

114 *See Bonito Boats*, 489 U.S. at 154 ("That the extrapolation of . . . a [very] broad preemptive principle from *Sears* is inappropriate is clear from the balance struck in *Sears* itself. The *Sears* Court made it plain that the States 'may protect businesses in the use of their trademarks, labels, or distinctive dress in the packaging of goods so as to prevent others, by imitating such markings, from misleading purchasers as to the source of the goods.'").

115 *Supra* text accompanying note 87.

116 *Cf.* Deven R. Desai & Sandra L. Rierson, *Confronting the Genericism Conundrum*, 28 Cardozo L. Rev. 1789, 1820–21 (2007) (observing that "genericide . . . was much more likely to occur where the mark was placed on a product that was or had been the subject of a utility patent," because during the patent period, "the trademark label placed on the good typically serves a dual function: to identify the sole source of the good (i.e., the trademark holder) and to identify the good itself").

and its purpose as applied in the particular enforcement scenario.[117] That is, the law struck down in *Bonito Boats* was analyzed (and preempted) facially given that (all or most of) its conceivable applications were within the IP Clause's preemptive scope, whereas the law struck down in *Sears* and *Compco* was analyzed (and preempted) merely as applied to designs denied patent protection. Thus, whether state laws seemingly unconcerned with promoting the progress of science and useful arts – such as a right of publicity or contracts – are within the IP Clause's preemptive scope likely depends on analyzing their purpose as applied in the particular enforcement scenario.

2. The Clause's Balance

If a state law is within the preemptive scope of the IP Clause, either facially or as applied, I contend that it is preempted only if it also upsets the particular balance effectuated by Congress in light of the more general balance specified in the IP Clause. In so doing, I reject an alternative understanding that state laws are never preempted by the IP Clause – as effectuated by federal laws – when they confer protection using means forbidden to Congress by the IP Clause.

One view of the IP Clause's role in preemption of state laws starts from the point that if the IP Clause does not confer particular powers on Congress, the states are not preempted from enacting laws that confer those withheld powers.[118] To take a concrete example, the Supreme Court interprets the IP Clause as not providing Congress the authority to protect the factual content in most informational works, because that content is lacking a sufficient degree of authorial creativity.[119] As such, one might conclude that states instead could protect this factual content. In *Goldstein*, in response to an argument that California had created a copyright of unlimited duration, in contravention of the IP Clause, the Supreme Court seems sympathetic to this understanding:

> [Article I,] Section 8 enumerates those powers which have been granted to Congress; Whatever limitations have been appended to such powers can only be understood as a limit on congressional, and not state, action. Moreover, it is not clear that the dangers to which this limitation was addressed apply with equal force to both the Federal Government and the States. When Congress grants an exclusive right or

[117] *Cf.* Sandeen, *supra* note 8, at 353 ("Since the basic issue of a preemption analysis is whether a state law interferes with the purposes of federal law, it would seem that a comparison of the two laws is enough. However, as common sense and the record of the Supreme Court's intellectual property preemption jurisprudence indicates, this approach does not work in IP preemption cases because the required analysis is dependent upon knowing the nature of the information sought to be protected.").

[118] Ginsburg, *supra* note 96, at 360–61 (speculating as to this possibility); *cf.* Daniel Farber, *Federal Preemption of State Law: The Current State of Play*, *available at* http://papers.ssrn.com/papers.cfm?abstract_id=1740043 (suggesting this possibility generally, rather than in the context of the IP Clause).

[119] Feist Pubs., Inc. v. Rural Tel. Serv. Co., 499 U.S. 340 (1991).

> monopoly, its effects are pervasive; no citizen or State may escape its reach. As we have noted, however, the exclusive right granted by a State is confined to its borders. Consequently, even when the right is unlimited in duration, any tendency to inhibit further progress in science or the arts is narrowly circumscribed. The challenged statute cannot be voided for lack of a durational limitation.[120]

Nonetheless, this understanding of preemption in intellectual property is too cramped. It fails to account for the Supreme Court's more capacious understanding generally of preemption to include conflict preemption.[121] Recall that conflict preemption can arise when "state law stands as an obstacle to the accomplishment and execution of the full purposes and objectives of Congress."[122] Pursuant to application of this doctrine, it is possible in the context of intellectual property for states to be preempted from doing that which even Congress cannot do. Why? A robust explanation requires an understanding of the IP Clause's balance that flows particularly from the possibility of conflict preemption.

As evaluated earlier, the patent and copyright laws created pursuant to the IP Clause's authority effectuate (distinct) constitutionally mandated balances between incentives to creators and benefit to the public in the name of promoting progress of science and useful arts.[123] It is the IP Clause itself that requires a balance within certain bounds, which the patent and copyright laws implement.[124] As such, state laws that upset this balance, say, by prolonging the duration of copyright or patent rights serve as a critical and preempted obstacle to the effectuation of Congress's powers pursuant to the IP Clause, as enacted in federal law.[125] As Maureen O'Rourke recognizes in the copyright context, an obstacle can arise when state law interferes with the federal "striking [of] a balance between providing an incentive to create through the grant of a limited statutory monopoly in the form of copyright and

[120] *Goldstein*, 412 U.S. at 560–61. This discussion can be read consistently with the view I espouse herein, that state laws within the IP Clause's preemptive scope are preempted if they upset the IP Clause's balance, as effectuated by a federal law. A reasonable way to understand this excerpt is as suggesting that states' contraventions of the means specified in the IP Clause do not necessarily upset the balance implemented in federal laws, although they might in particular cases.

[121] *Supra* text accompanying note 47.

[122] Pac. Gas & Elec. Co. v. State Energy Res. Conservation & Dev. Comm'n, 461 U.S. 190, 204 (1983) (internal marks omitted).

[123] *Supra* text accompanying notes 24–37.

[124] *Supra* text accompanying notes 26–30.

[125] *Cf.* Ginsburg, *supra* note 96, at 361 ("Under [a] view of the statute [that not protecting ideas/facts leaves them free to be copied], Congress has occupied the field of information protection: copyright covers the presentation of information (selection and arrangement), and no law may cover the information content itself. State protection of facts would therefore conflict with the congressional free-copying policy."). *But see* Livingston v. van Ingen, 9 Johns. 507 (N.Y. 1812) (Kent, J.) ("[A] patentee under the act of congress may have the time of his monopoly extended by the legislature of any state, beyond the term of fourteen or twenty-eight years allowed by that law. Congress may secure, for a limited time, an exclusive right throughout the union; but there is nothing in the constitution to take away from the states the power to enlarge the privilege within their respective jurisdictions. The states are not entirely devested of their original sovereignty over the subject matter; and whatever power has not been clearly granted to the union, remains with them.").

maintaining the free flow of the information on which such creativity is built."[126] And as Jane Ginsburg notes with regard to the protection of factual content in informational works, "the states could continue to protect information, so long as state regulation does not interfere with the general federal copyright scheme."[127]

Seen in this light, the IP Clause serves an important role in analyzing preemption. It is the provision that confers the authority under which Congress acts. As such, ascertaining copyright and patent laws' reach to preempt state laws requires reading these federal laws in light of the constitutional provision authorizing them. As the Supreme Court articulated in another context, "the mere grant of . . . power to Congress did imply a prohibition on the states to exercise the same power; . . . it is not the mere existence of such a power, but its exercise by Congress, which may be incompatible with the exercise of the same power by the states."[128] Similarly, Laurence Tribe recognizes the importance to preemption analysis of the constitutional power for Congress's legislation, coupled with the Supremacy Clause.[129] Highlighting the IP Clause's role in preemption analysis takes cognizance of the IP Clause's express set of *constitutional* balances for a particular purpose as a source of legislative power. It supplements and provides more texture to the not infrequent scholarly refrain that preemption analysis ought to account for the *statutory* balances that Congress made.[130]

Although its jurisprudence seems somewhat confused, the Supreme Court has said as much in each of its preemption decisions on federal legislation enacted pursuant to the IP Clause. In those decisions, from *Sears* and *Compco* through *Bonito Boats*, it emphasizes that state laws are invalidated only if they (fall within the IP Clause's preemptive scope and) upset the balance implemented in statutes enacted pursuant to the IP Clause.[131] In this light, a state law extending federal patent protection by one year would be preempted because it both falls within the IP Clause's preemptive scope and upsets the balance effectuated by patent law. But a state law forbidding the creation or distribution of obscenity likely would not, even if it upsets the balance of copyright law by diminishing the incentives to creators of obscene works, because it lies outside the IP Clause's preemptive scope. And a state law likely located within the Clause's preemptive scope – say, one providing a more robust right of attribution to creators – might not be preempted if it does

[126] O'Rourke, *supra* note 35, at 534–35.

[127] Ginsburg, *supra* note 96, at 360–61.

[128] Cooley v. Bd. of Wardens, 53 U.S. (12 How.) 299, 318 (1851).

[129] 1 LAURENCE H. TRIBE, AMERICAN CONSTITUTIONAL LAW 1172 (3d ed. 2000).

[130] *See, e.g.*, Bauer, *supra* note 19, at 15; Bohannan, *supra* note 26, at 620; Christopher John Brej, *A Fantastic "New National Pastime": Copyright Preemption and the Public Domain*, 48 IDEA 1, 5–6 (2007).

[131] *E.g.*, *Bonito Boats*, 489 U.S. at 146; *Kewanee*, 416 U.S. at 480–91; *Goldstein*, 412 U.S. at 569–70 (distinguishing *Sears* and *Compco* from the instant case because there state law upset the balance outlined in the IP Clause and implemented by Congress); *accord* Paul Heald, *Federal Intellectual Property and the Economics of Preemption*, 76 IOWA L. REV. 959, 961 (1991).

not sufficiently disturb copyright law's balance between creators and the public interest. In sum, state laws within the IP Clause's preemptive scope are preempted only when they disrupt the constitutionally mandated balance, as legislated in a particular federal law.

In fact, even Judge Hand's position in *Capitol Records*, which most observers understand as incompatible with this view of the IP Clause's important, but more limited, role in preemption analysis, can be read to support this take. Judge Hand's view might say more about his construction of congressional intent than his view of the IP Clause's standalone preemptive effect. That is, Judge Hand seemed to be of the view that each time Congress legislated pursuant to the IP Clause, everything it did not protect but could have protected pursuant to the full reach of the Clause was, at least constructively, a conscious omission.[132] In this light, he can readily be understood as thinking that any state laws protecting those omitted items upset the statutory balance created in light of the IP Clause's balance, rather than just the IP Clause standing alone.

Key to conflict preemption in intellectual property as just set out is an assessment of congressional intent – whether textually, structurally, or purposively – about the particular balance Congress sought to achieve between creators' and public entitlements.[133] In fact, many Supreme Court decisions that commentators see as missteps frequently are critical principally of the Court's particular assessments of congressional intent with regard to the balance. Pertinently, *Goldstein* troubles some for its conclusion that states might protect a class of articles – there, sound recordings – for an unlimited amount of time in apparent contravention of the balance set out in the IP Clause.[134] Such concerns – colorable, to say the least – seem to lie less with *Goldstein*'s analysis of the IP Clause's reach than with its restrictive reading of copyright law's balance between free and protected materials: that the lack of federal protection for sound recordings did not indicate congressional intent that sound recordings be unprotectable in some other way. Similarly, *Kewanee* troubles many for its conclusory reasoning that very few would choose trade secrecy protection over patent protection when both are available, in light of empirical evidence to the contrary.[135] One might quibble with *Aronson* in much the same way, with regard to whether requiring a promisor to pay royalties when a patent did not issue prevented free use of something in the public domain in a way

[132] *Capitol Records*, 221 F.2d at 667 (Hand, J., dissenting); *accord* Goldstein, *supra* note 1144, at 52.

[133] *See* Appellate Judges Conference, American Bar Association, The Law of Preemption 14–15 (1991) [hereinafter Law of Preemption] (emphasizing the importance of congressional intent to preemption analysis).

[134] *E.g.*, Abrams, *supra* note 16, at 530.

[135] *E.g.*, Jeanne C. Fromer, *Trade Secrecy in Willy Wonka's Chocolate Factory*, *in* The Law and Theory of Trade Secrecy: A Handbook of Contemporary Research 3 (Rochelle C. Dreyfuss & Katherine J. Strandburg eds., 2011); Sandeen, *supra* note 8, at 345–46 (discussing, also, other concerns with *Kewanee*'s analysis, including the effect of changes to patent disclosure and patentable subject matter).

that upsets the balance set out by the IP Clause, as implemented in the patent laws.[136]

As the Supreme Court underscored in *Kewanee*, a preemption analysis must include an examination of the relevant federal and state laws' underlying purposes and how they might conflict with one another.[137] The general difficulties of divining congressional intent,[138] however, prompted a group of federal appellate judges reporting on preemption to recognize that the need to assess this intent "suggests a great . . . potential for unpredictability and instability in the law."[139] Pertinently, they observe how hard it is to draw any clear conclusions as to obstacle preemption: "It is unclear when, if ever, Congress has not balanced and compromised in enacting legislation. If every state law affecting one of the many interests reconciled by a particular federal statute were preempted under a delicate balance theory, there would seem to be little if any room for state regulatory authority."[140]

This problem is less severe in the context of intellectual property because, when exercising its power under the IP Clause, Congress is legislating a balance between author and public entitlements, in light of the more general balance set out in the IP Clause. As such, the frequently articulated concern that judges are ill equipped to make broad policy decisions that tend to arise in preemption cases generally[141] is diminished to some extent by the IP Clause itself. As Justice Douglas recognized in dissent in *Kewanee*, the Clause "expresses the activist policy which Congress has enforced by statutes. It is that constitutional policy which we should enforce, not our individual notions of the public good."[142] In that vein, even when congressional intent as to the precise balance struck is less than clear, unlike other areas of law, judges ought to feel at greater ease making equitable policy – sussing out the negative space that Congress desired be left free in the context of its positive rights conferred by statute – due to the constitutional mandate of the IP Clause.[143]

[136] John Shepard Wiley, Jr., Bonito Boats: *Uninformed but Mandatory Innovation Policy*, 1989 Sup. Ct. Rev. 283, 288.

[137] *Supra* text accompanying notes 70–76; *see* Abrams, *supra* note 16, at 531–32.

[138] Buzbee, *supra* note 111, at 173.

[139] Law of Preemption, *supra* note 133, at 15. As they observe in analyzing field preemption generally, broad congressional action on its own can both demonstrate that "Congress, reflecting upon the interests of the states, intended all state laws touching the area to be superseded" and, oppositely, that "the intrusion on state prerogatives sanctioned by the comprehensive federal program represents all that Congress considered appropriate." *Id.* at 35.

[140] *Id.* at 36.

[141] *Id.* at 38.

[142] *Kewanee*, 416 U.S. at 499 (Douglas, J., dissenting).

[143] *Cf.* Henry E. Smith, *Equitable Intellectual Property: What's Wrong with Misappropriation* (in this volume) (highlighting the equitable powers that courts might exercise with regard to bad actors). In this sense, the invocation of obstacle preemption for statutes enacted pursuant to the IP Clause, with its constitutionally mandated negative space and the concomitant need to understand how Congress sought to maintain that space, seems less problematic than for those statutes enacted pursuant to other powers arguably lacking a constitutionally mandated negative space. *See generally* Catherine M. Sharkey, *Against Freewheeling, Extratextual Obstacle Preemption: Is Justice Clarence Thomas the*

An analysis of intellectual property's statutorily implemented balance between creator and public entitlements for preemption will typically require an assessment of the effect on this balance by the state law at issue both facially and as applied. For example, contract law facially has little to no effect on patent and copyright laws' balance. Yet, as applied to particular intellectual-property licenses, contract law's enforcement might upset the balance enough that it ought to be preempted in those situations, should this context also fall within the IP Clause's preemptive scope.[144] Thinking about preemption in an "as applied" manner helps diminish the problem identified by Mark Lemley in thinking about patent law's preemptive ability over contract law:

> Using preemption doctrine against contracts is something like swinging a sledgehammer at a gnat: you are likely to hit the target, but you may do some serious damage to the things around it. More likely though, and of more immediate concern for my purposes, you might decide not to swing the hammer at all, for fear of hitting the wrong thing.[145]

Lone Principled Federalist?, 5 N.Y.U. J.L. & LIBERTY 63 (2010). There is, however, an additional worry for courts ruling on preemption in the context of intellectual property that relates to the near absence of agency rulemaking in copyright and patent law. As Catherine Sharkey has suggested in the context of products liability, courts might conceivably turn to the extent of federal agency action in intellectual property to help assess preemption. Catherine M. Sharkey, *Products Liability Preemption: An Institutional Approach*, 76 GEO. WASH. L. REV. 449, 452–53 (2008). Currently, however, agency action in the field is limited given the narrow scope of congressional delegation to agencies of substantive rulemaking authority in intellectual property. *See* 35 U.S.C. § 2(b)(2) (granting authority to the Patent and Trademark Office (PTO) to regulate its internal procedures); Tafas v. Doll, 559 F.3d 1345, 1351–53 (Fed. Cir. 2009) (holding that this procedural rulemaking authority is the extent of the PTO's rulemaking power); Jessica D. Litman, *Copyright Legislation and Technological Change*, 68 OR. L. REV. 275, 356 n.446 (1989) ("The Copyright Office . . . is not viewed as administrative agency and has no adjudicatory and only very limited rulemaking authority. The Copyright Royalty Tribunal, in contrast, is an agency but its jurisdiction is limited to the setting of rates and division of fees for compulsory licenses."). As such, the relevant agencies have not engaged in usual forms of fact-finding for policy making that happens in most other substantive legal areas. Therefore, courts – in the context of intellectual-property litigation – are often the first governmental actors to make many factual determinations that affect intellectual-property policy. Courts are likely institutionally less equipped than others to make these determinations, EVAN TSEN LEE, JUDICIAL RESTRAINT IN AMERICA: HOW THE AGELESS WISDOM OF THE FEDERAL COURTS WAS INVENTED 56 (2011) (footnotes omitted), which might impair court decisionmaking regarding such factual determinations.

144 *See* Viva R. Moffat, *Super-Copyright: Contracts, Preemption, and the Structure of Copyright Policymaking*, 41 U.C. DAVIS L. REV. 45, 48–50, 65–66 (2007); Kathleen K. Olson, *Preserving the Copyright Balance: Statutory and Constitutional Preemption of Contract-Based Claims*, 11 COMM. L. & POL'Y 83, 83 (2006). *But see* O'Rourke, *supra* note 35, at 482 (arguing that there are numerous cases in which fair use rights should be alienable). One might also fruitfully think about the preemption of rights of publicity as applied. *See* Rothman, *supra* note 21, at 208 ("I set forth three situations in which the right [of publicity] must yield to copyright law: first, when a publicity holder's action is based solely on the use of his or her persona rather than on the publicity holder's name or likeness; second, when the use at issue was licensed or authorized by a copyright holder who received consent from the publicity holder for the original work; and finally, when the use at issue is explicitly authorized by the Copyright Act.").

145 Lemley, *supra* note 33, at 145.

In sum, preemption analysis in the context of intellectual property requires examination of whether a state law – either facially or as applied – upsets the balance between creator and public rights implemented by Congress in light of its powers under the IP Clause.

CONCLUSION

All in all, I argue that the IP Clause, which has long sat in the background of preemption analysis in intellectual property, deserves room in the foreground. Although the Clause does not preempt state laws of its own force, it establishes a framework for thinking about preemption by federal laws enacted pursuant to its authority. As I show, state laws are preempted when they both are within the IP Clause's preemptive scope and upset the balance between creator and public entitlements mandated by the IP Clause and effectuated in a particular way by federal law. The Supreme Court's opinions on preemption have long confused scholars. Imposing this preemption framework is consistent with these opinions and clarifies the preemption analysis. This framework sets out how to ascertain conflict preemption in the context of intellectual property.

13

Trademark Law's Faux Federalism

*Mark P. McKenna**

Federal and state trademark laws regulate concurrently. The Lanham Act[1] does not preempt state law, and in fact many states have legislatively and/or judicially developed trademark and unfair competition laws of their own.[2] This state of affairs, which is now well accepted even if it has not always been uncontroversial, distinguishes trademark from patent and copyright law, since federal patent and copyright statutes preempt state law much more broadly. The Patent Act preempts state law completely with respect to nonsecret inventions,[3] and the Copyright Act of 1976 preempts state copyright law with respect to all works fixed in a tangible medium of expression.[4]

According to the common wisdom, concurrent trademark regulation is an artifact of the historical primacy of state law, which federal law supplemented but did not supplant entirely. John Cross, for example, argues characteristically that the Lanham Act "builds upon a foundation of state-law rights, leaving states generally free to regulate the field of trademarks."[5] This chapter evaluates that claim and its

* Professor and Notre Dame Presidential Fellow, Notre Dame Law School. Thanks to Shyam Balganesh, Joe Bauer, A.J. Bellia, Eric Claeys, Graeme Dinwoodie, Pam Karlan, Caleb Nelson, Jeff Pojanowski, Jay Tidmarsh, and Rebecca Tushnet for helpful discussions of the ideas in this chapter and/or comments on an earlier draft.

1 15 U.S.C. §§ 1051 *et seq.* (2006).

2 *See* 3 J. Thomas McCarthy, McCarthy on Trademarks and Unfair Competition § 22:2 (4th ed. 2012) (citing state law cases).

3 *See* Kewanee Oil Co. v. Bicron Corp., 416 U.S. 470 (1974). In fact, it is patent law rather than trademark law that works the primary preemption of state unfair competition law. *See* Bonito Boats, Inc. v. Thunder Craft Boats, Inc., 489 U.S. 141 (1989); Sears, Roebuck & Co. v. Stiffel Co., 376 U.S. 225 (1964); Compco Corp. v. Day-Brite Lighting, Inc., 376 U.S. 234 (1964).

4 17 U.S.C. § 301 (2006). As a result, for any work created after January 1, 1978, state copyright law can apply only to unfixed works. State law is also valid to the extent that the rights it provides are not "equivalent to any of the exclusive rights" provided by the Copyright Act, or when it does not provide rights in works of authorship that "come within the subject matter of copyright." *Id.* § 301(b)(1), (3). On the difficulty of applying this preemption provision, see Joseph P. Bauer, *Addressing the Incoherency of the Preemption Provision of the Copyright Act of 1976*, 10 Vand. J. Ent. & Tech. L. 1, 3–4 (2007).

5 *See, e.g.*, John T. Cross, *Contributory Infringement and Related Theories of Secondary Liability for Trademark Infringement*, 80 Iowa L. Rev. 101, 127 (1994); *see also* Richard A. De Sevo, *Antidilution*

implied premise that state law has always played an important role in trademark law. As the chapter demonstrates, the historical role of state law is not straightforward, and the accuracy of the claim of state law primacy depends in substantial part on one's understanding of the status of general law before the Supreme Court's decision in *Erie Railroad Co. v. Tompkins*.[6]

To illustrate, this chapter describes the history of trademark and unfair competition in three periods: (1) the pre-*Erie* era, in which trademark and unfair competition claims were understood as distinct species of the same general legal right, both of which were substantively determined by the common law; (2) the period after *Erie* and straddling passage of the Lanham Act, before courts had settled on an interpretation of the new statute under which claims for infringement of unregistered trademarks could be brought under § 43(a);[7] and (3) the modern period, in which the Supreme Court and Congress have accepted and cemented that interpretation of the statute, bringing most unfair competition claims under federal statute. It argues that, although state law has played some role in each of these periods, its only significant substantive role has been to broaden the scope of rights beyond the federal statute in certain contexts in the modern period.

Nevertheless, the persistent sense that federal and state law regulate concurrently has masked a significant federalization of trademark and unfair competition law over the last forty to fifty years. That federalization deserves some scrutiny, particularly because it depended on a broad understanding of the commerce power that has been criticized heavily in some quarters. If broad federal trademark law ultimately can be justified, then we should question any continuing role for state trademark law.

I. HISTORY OF TRADEMARK AND UNFAIR COMPETITION LAW IN THREE PERIODS

Until sometime in the second half of the twentieth century, courts understood trademark and unfair competition claims as distinct legal claims that vindicated the same general right. Trademark infringement claims were available against parties who used a plaintiff's technical trademark to designate the source of their directly competing goods. Unfair competition claims, by contrast, were available against defendants who did not use the plaintiff's technical trademark, but whose actions

Laws: The Unresolved Dilemma of Preemption Under the Lanham Act, 84 TRADEMARK REP. 300, 303 (1994) ("More important, as other courts have held, and the Supreme Court has indicated, the holdings in the two early decisions [holding that the Lanham Act preempted all of state trademark law] were clearly wrong. It cannot seriously be contended that in the Lanham Act Congress intended to 'enter[] and pre-empt[] the field of trade mark law in its application to inter-state commerce' when, as Judge Kozinski has noted, in the same statute Congress 'explicitly contemplat[ed] the continued existence of state law protection.'") (citations omitted).

6 304 U.S. 64 (1938).

7 15 U.S.C. § 1125(a) (2006).

were nevertheless likely to have the same effect of deceiving consumers and diverting the plaintiff's trade. Thus, trademark infringement and unfair competition claims targeted the same ultimate harm of deceptive trade diversion; the means by which the defendant accomplished that end determined which of the claims was available in any particular case.

As this description suggests, trademark infringement and unfair competition claims were always tightly linked at the conceptual level. This is why trademark law has always been considered part of the broader law of unfair competition. But the relationship between those claims was also a function of the ultimate dependence of both on the common law. The following sections describe this historic relationship between trademark infringement and unfair competition more completely and trace their evolution over the course of the twentieth century, paying particular attention to the sources of law governing those claims.

A. *The Pre-Erie Period*

The common law of trademarks and unfair competition substantially predates adoption of any federal statutes.[8] Prior to the first federal trademark statute in 1870,[9] the only statutes governing use of a mark were highly trade-specific state statutes. Massachusetts, for example, specifically regulated the use of marks on sailcloth.[10] A handful of states later passed more general trademark statutes,[11] but overwhelmingly unfair competition law in the nineteenth century was a common law field – narrowly, in the sense that the law was decisional rather than statutory, and in a broader substantive sense.

Unfair competition law retained that common law character even after Congress began regulating in the area, because early federal trademark statutes were quite limited in scope.[12] First, registration under pre-Lanham Act statutes was available only to "technical trademarks," which were distinguished from mere "trade names" and other matter that did not indicate the source of a party's goods.[13] Second,

[8] *See* Mark P. McKenna, *The Normative Foundations of Trademark Law*, 82 Notre Dame L. Rev. 1839, 1850–63 (2007).

[9] Act of July 8, 1870, ch. 230, 16 Stat. 198.

[10] *See* Frank I. Schechter, The Historical Foundations of the Law Relating to Trade-Marks 130–32 (1925). Other states later adopted statutes dealing with trademarks in particular industries, as Kentucky did when it regulated the use of marks by distillers and union and labor associations. *See* Act of March 27, 1896 Ky. Acts 65 (codified at § 2572c, Kentucky Statutes 1915 (Carroll, ed.)); Act of March 9, 1894 Ky. Acts 68 (codified at §§ 4749–4755 Kentucky Statutes 1915 (Carroll, ed.)).

[11] *See, e.g.*, An Act to Protect Manufacturers from the Use of Counterfeit Labels and Stamps, 1895 Mass. Acts 519.

[12] The Act of 1870 was actually fairly ambitious – it even purported to allow registration of trademarks based on intent to use. *See* § 77, ch. 230, 16 Stat. 198, at 210. But it had little actual effect, because the Supreme Court promptly struck it down in the *Trade-Mark Cases*. 100 U.S. 82, 99 (1879) (invalidating the trademark legislation of 1870 and the Act of Aug. 14, 1876, ch. 274, 19 Stat. 141, which imposed criminal sanctions against one who fraudulently used, sold, or counterfeited trademarks).

[13] Arbitrary or fanciful terms as applied to particular products were considered technical trademarks, and they were protected in actions for trademark infringement. *See* Restatement (Third) of Unfair

only trademarks used in interstate commerce were registrable.[14] Together these two limitations excluded many identifying marks from federal registration, which was important because the federal causes of action that pre-Lanham Act statutes created were available only to owners of registered trademarks whose marks were used by others in interstate commerce.[15] Thus, only the owners of technical trademarks who had taken the initiative to register their marks could bring federal claims. Those claims under federal statutes were denominated trademark infringement actions because by definition they involved the use of technical trademarks.[16] Unfair competition claims, by contrast, were common law claims brought by those who did not own technical trademarks and therefore could not have received a federal registration or brought a federal claim.[17] And precisely because registration was more limited at the time, much of the conduct that we now regard as actionable under federal statute was then the province of common law unfair competition.

Even when a party owned a federal registration, its rights were substantively determined by the common law because federal statutes did not create trademark rights – those rights arose at common law through use, and the federal statutes merely created mechanisms for registering trademarks used in interstate commerce and means for enforcing those rights through a federal cause of action. Indeed, every federal trademark statute passed since *The Trade-Mark Cases* has taken for granted that the trademark rights arise at, and are defined substantively by, the common law.[18] Section 1 of the Trademark Act of 1905, for example, provided that

COMPETITION § 9 cmt. g (1995); *see also* 1 MCCARTHY, *supra* note 2, at § 4:4 (defining technical trademarks as marks that were "fanciful, arbitrary, distinctive, non-descriptive in any sense and not a personal name"). Trade names included surnames, geographic terms, and descriptive terms – what we would now refer to as non-inherently distinctive designations. 1 MCCARTHY, *supra* note 2, at § 4:5.

14 *See* Trademark Act of 1905, ch. 592, § 1, 33 Stat. 724 ("[T]he owner of a trade-mark used in commerce with foreign nations, or among the several States, or with Indian tribes . . . may obtain registration. . . . ").

15 *See* Trademark Act of 1905 § 16 (creating cause of action for infringement of registered marks); *see also id.* § 17 (granting federal courts jurisdiction in cases involving use of a registered mark in interstate commerce). The requirement that the defendant's use affect interstate commerce was, formerly, a real limitation. *See* United States Printing & Lithograph Co. v. Griggs, Cooper & Co., 279 U.S. 156, 157, 158–59 (1929) (refusing plaintiff's claim under the 1905 Act that the defendant infringed its registered "Home Brand" trademark, which the plaintiff used in "certain named States of the Northwest" by printing and selling labels containing the word "Home," on the ground that the defendant's activities took place only within the limits of the state of Ohio and did not interfere with interstate commerce).

16 Common law trademark infringement claims also existed – those involving use of the same sort of "technical" trademark, but where the mark was never federally registered. Precisely because those marks were not registered, the claims were not federal.

17 Not every mark eligible to be federally registered was in fact registered. Consequently, although all federal claims were trademark infringement claims, not all trademark infringement claims were federal claims. There were also common law trademark infringement claims, brought to vindicate exclusive rights in unregistered trademarks, though many courts conflated those claims with unfair competition claims – seeing trademark infringement claims as one category consisting of claims under the federal statute, and common law unfair competition claims as the other category consisting of any claim not based on a registered mark.

18 The Trade-Mark Cases, 100 U.S. 82, 99 (1879) (invalidating trademark statutes of 1870 and 1876 on the ground that they exceeded Congress's power under Article I § 8 cl. 8 (the IP Clause)).

"the owner of a trade-mark used in commerce . . . [could] obtain registration for such trade-mark by complying with the following requirements."[19] And according to § 29 of that statute, "[t]he term 'trade-mark' include[d] any mark which [was] entitled to registration under the terms of this Act."[20] Thus, the statute made no attempt to define a "trade-mark" that was entitled to registration when it was used in commerce; Congress merely assumed that the concept of a "trade-mark" had preexisting content and that "trade-marks" came into existence prior to registration. It could make those assumptions because trademark rights existed independently of the statute according to principles of common law, and the federal statutes merely borrowed those common law concepts.[21]

The Lanham Act similarly assumes that trademark rights arise out of use independently of the statute – the statute provides a mechanism for registration and a federal cause of action to vindicate one's rights, but it does not *create* trademark rights. Indeed, the entire statutory scheme is built on the underlying notion that trademark rights are logically prior to the statute. According to the Lanham Act, "[t]he owner of a trademark used in commerce may request registration of its trademark on the principal register."[22] For those indicators already in use, an applicant's status as the "owner" of the mark precedes registration; the applicant already "owns" the mark, and the statute makes owners eligible to register their marks.[23] Registration thus simply records and amplifies the owner's preexisting rights.[24] Indeed, the fact that

[19] § 1, 33 Stat. at 724.

[20] § 29, 33 Stat. at 731.

[21] American Steel Foundries v. Robertson, 269 U.S. 372, 381 (1926) ("[I]t reasonably may be assumed . . . that to the extent the contrary does not appear from the statute, the intention was to allow the registration of such marks as [the substantive law of trade-marks], and the general law of unfair competition of which it is a part, recognized as legitimate."); *see also* H.R. REP. NO. 3147, at 7 (1904) ("Section 5 of the proposed bill [the 1905 Act] we believe will permit the registration of all marks which could, under the common law as expounded by the courts, be the subject of a trade-mark and become the exclusive property of the party using the same as his trade-mark.").

[22] 15 U.S.C. § 1051(a)(1). It defines a trademark as includ[ing] any word, name, symbol, or device, or any combination thereof –

> (1) used by a person, or
> (2) which a person has a bona fide intention to use in commerce and applies to register on the principal register established by this Act, to identify and distinguish his or her goods, including a unique product, from those manufactured or sold by others and to indicate the source of the goods, even if that source is unknown.

15 U.S.C. § 1127.

[23] Use is ultimately dispositive even for registrations issued on intent-to-use applications, since the intent-to-use mechanism simply allows a party to apply for registration prior to making use of the mark; no registration will ever issue unless the applicant actually makes use. *See* 15 U.S.C. § 1051(b), (d) (2006). The purpose of the intent-to-use provision, then, is simply to allow the registrant to rely for priority purposes on a date certain that precedes in time the date of actual use.

[24] A certificate of registration serves as prima facie evidence of the mark's validity, shifting the burden to a defendant who wishes to contest the mark's validity. 15 U.S.C. §§ 1057(b), 1115(a) (2006). Registered marks can achieve incontestable status, making several of those presumptions irrebuttable. *Id.* §§ 1065, 1115(b). Registration also endows the owner with nationwide priority, effective

trademark rights are not created by statute is why we can speak sensibly of § 43(a) providing a cause of action for infringement of unregistered trademarks – the federal cause of action protects common law rights that have accrued through use, independent of the statute.

This understanding that federal statutes did not create trademark rights was the reason courts in the early twentieth century routinely said that the pre-Lanham Act federal statutes created only procedural, and not substantive, rights.[25] As the Eighth Circuit said,

> Mere registration under the Federal Act does not create a trade-mark and confers no new rights to the mark claimed, nor, indeed, any greater rights than already existed at common law without registration. Registration is a method of recording for the protection of dealers, the public, and owners of trade-marks. It is notice of the claims of the owner affecting his right to the mark. But the right to such a trade-mark must have accrued from actual use, because such right is not created by registration of the mark.[26]

Federal statutes were intended merely to "provide appropriate procedure and to give the described protection and remedies where property rights existed. The acquisition of such property rights in trade-marks rested upon the laws of the several States."[27] Indeed, it was not just that Congress did not mean for the federal statutes to create substantive rights; Congress *lacked the power* to legislate on the substantive law of trademarks.[28]

As a result, and particularly in light of the paucity of state trademark statutes, courts developed nearly all of trademark law's substantive rules at common law.

at the time of application, see *id.* § 1057(c), in contrast to the geographically limited, use-based rights one acquires at common law. *See* United Drug Co. v. Theodore Rectanus Co., 248 U.S. 90 (1918).

25 *See, e.g.*, American Trading Co. v. H. E. Heacock Co., 285 U.S. 247, 258 (1932) ("[T]he Federal statute did not attempt to create exclusive substantive rights in marks, or to afford a refuge for piracy through registration under the Act, but to provide appropriate procedure and to give the described protection and remedies where property rights existed. The acquisition of such property rights in trade-marks rested upon the laws of the several States."); *American Steel Foundries*, 269 U.S. at 381 ("[S]ince [Congress] has been given no power to legislate upon the substantive law of trade-marks, it reasonably may be assumed, also, that to the extent the contrary does not appear from the statute, the intention was to allow the registration of such marks as that law, and the general law of unfair competition of which it is a part, recognized as legitimate"); Estate of P. D. Beckwith, Inc. v. Comm'r of Patents, 252 U.S. 538, 543 (1920) ("The Registration Act of 1905, without changing the substantive law of trade-marks, provided, in the manner prescribed, for the registration of marks (subject to special exceptions) which, without the statute, would be entitled to legal and equitable protection.") (citations omitted); Emerson Electric Mfg. Co. v. Emerson Radio & Phonograph Corp., 105 F.2d 908, 910 (2d Cir. 1939) ("We may start by at once laying aside the plaintiff's registration of its name. That did not enlarge its substantive rights at all; all it did was to confer jurisdiction on the court and give the registrant certain procedural advantages.").

26 Walgreen Drug Stores v. Obear-Nester Glass Co., 113 F.2d 956, 960 (8th Cir. 1940) (citations omitted).

27 *American Trading*, 285 U.S. at 258 (referring to the 1905 Act).

28 *See American Steel Foundries*, 269 U.S. at 381 ("[Congress] has been given no power to legislate upon the substantive law of trade-marks.").

Federal registration gave rise to a federal claim that could, at least after 1905, always be heard in federal court, even if the parties lacked diversity of citizenship. Registration also entitled the mark owner to certain presumptions.[29] But the underlying content of trademark law, from issues of protectability to standards of infringement, was developed at common law. The common law also provided causes of action for infringement of unregistered trademarks and for unfair competition in cases where the defendant's use threatened the same harm but did not involve use of a trademark. Thus, it is no surprise that courts in this era always understood trademark infringement and unfair competition claims to be species of the same general legal right.[30] Indeed, many of the same doctrinal limitations applied in both types of cases, and courts often made explicit reference to the close conceptual relationship between trademark infringement cases and other cases of unfair competition.[31]

This description of the pre-*Erie* state of affairs uses "common law" in two different senses, both of which deserve some elaboration. The first sense describes the source of the unfair competition cause of action, under which plaintiffs who did not own rights to a federally registered mark brought claims against competitors engaged in passing off. Those unfair competition claims were common law claims in the

[29] *Emerson Electric Mfg. Co.*, 105 F.2d, at 910. Owners of technical trademarks, for example, did not have to prove intent; because use of a technical trademark was unlikely to have a legitimate explanation, intent was presumed. *See* McKenna, *supra* note 8, at 1861–62. Unfair competition plaintiffs, in contrast, were asserting rights against facially ambiguous uses – uses, for example, that might have been descriptive of the defendant's goods – so they were required to prove intent. *Id.*

[30] *See, e.g.*, James Love Hopkins, The Law of Trademarks, Tradenames and Unfair Competition, § 4, at 12 (3d ed. 1917) ("The principles involved in trademark cases and tradename cases have been substantially identical."). When trademark law began to evolve away from its traditional focus on parties in direct competition, some courts harbored uncertainty about whether the "doctrine of expansion of trade," under which a plaintiff might be able to get relief against a noncompetitor in a line of business into which the plaintiff might naturally go, applied to technical trademark cases. *See, e.g.*, *Walgreen Drugs Stores*, 113 F.2d at 963 ("It is doubtful whether the doctrine of expansion of trade is applicable in a case of alleged infringement of a technical registered trade-mark."). The uncertainty was a result of the fact that the 1905 Act made infringement turn on whether the defendant's goods were of "substantially the same descriptive properties" as the plaintiffs. Pub. L. No. 58-84, § 16, 33 Stat. 724, 728 (1905). But courts ultimately read the statute broadly and accepted the doctrine in trademark law as well. *See, e.g.*, Dwinell-Wright Co. v. National Fruit Prod. Co., 140 F.2d 618, 622 (1st Cir. 1944) ("[I]f the doctrine [of expansion] applies to trade-mark infringement cases as well as cases of unfair competition, and we see no reason why it should not in spite of the doubts which have been expressed"); *see also* Yale Electric Corp. v. Robertson, 26 F.2d 972, 974 (2d Cir. 1928) (refusing to allow registration of YALE for flashlights and batteries in light of the plaintiff's prior use of the YALE mark for locks, but admitting that the decision "[did] some violence" to the language of the statute).

[31] *See, e.g.*, Hanover Star Milling Co. v. Metcalf, 240 U.S. 403, 413 (1916) ("Th[e] essential element is the same in trade-mark cases as in cases of unfair competition unaccompanied with trade-mark infringement."); Marsh v. Billings, 61 Mass. (7 Cush.) 322, 330 (1851) ("This is an action on the case, sounding in tort. The principle involved in the merits of the case is one of much importance, not only to persons situated as the plaintiffs are, but also to the public. But this principle is by no means novel in its character, or in its application to a case like the present. It is substantially the same principle, which has been repeatedly recognized and acted on by courts, in reference to the fraudulent use of trade marks, and regarded as one of much importance in a mercantile community.").

sense that the cause of action was not created by any federal or state statute, but was instead recognized by courts in the same way courts recognized causes of action for negligence and trespass.[32] Unfair competition was a judicially created cause of action, and it was to be distinguished from trademark infringement, over which federal courts had jurisdiction because federal statutes created the cause of action.

The second sense in which unfair competition was a common law field relates to the content of the law governing trademark infringement and unfair competition cases, and not simply the source of the cause of action itself. That content was developed from the bottom up, by courts developing the law on a case-by-case basis, rather than from the top down, by interpretation of the text of a statute. And this was true, as the previous discussion suggested, not only of unfair competition claims, for which the cause of action was created entirely at common law, but even of trademark infringement claims. This is why we can say that, even if a federal statute created the cause of action for infringement of registered marks, the statute did not create substantive rights: the existence of trademark rights and the substantive rules of trademark infringement developed at common law, not through any sort of statutory interpretation or gap-filling exercise.

In the pre-*Erie* era, it was reasonably clear that this common law of trademarks and unfair competition was general law, although there is some controversy about the status of that general law. Specifically, disagreement persists over whether general law was a species of state law or was instead a separate body of law, distinct from both federal and state law. On one view, "state law came in two flavors – 'local' and 'general.'"[33] The difference between those flavors was primarily reflected in the amount of deference federal courts extended to state supreme court precedents: courts deferred on questions of local law, but they exercised independent judgment on questions of general law. But, this account holds, "despite that difference in the federal courts' practices, the 'general' law in force within any particular state on questions that lay within the state's legislative competence was properly regarded as state law."[34] On another account, however, general law "consisted of a 'body of rules and principles separate from the law of any state,' and the conflict-of-law rules applied in federal court sometimes told federal judges to draw rules of decision from this body of law rather than from state law."[35]

32 Some states did adopt trademark statutes as well, particularly near the end of the pre-*Erie* period, but those state statutes did not displace the general common law of unfair competition. *See* Articles 850–51, Title 23 – Brands and Trade-Marks, Complete Texas Statutes (1928); N.Y. Gen. Bus. Law 360–369 (Thompson 1938). Both of those states' laws were subsequently repealed and replaced by more current versions.

33 Caleb Nelson, *A Critical Guide to* Erie Railroad Co. v. Tompkins, 54 Wm. & Mary L. Rev. 921, 928 (2012).

34 *Id.*

35 *Id.* (quoting John Harrison, *The Power of Congress over the Rules of Precedent*, 50 DUKE L.J. 503, 526 (2000)). As Nelson explained, "[p]eople who took this view of the 'general' law would have

Insofar as the issue with respect to the common law of trademarks and unfair competition is whether state law was substantively important, it is not necessary to choose sides in that debate. Whatever the technical status of the general law, it is clear that neither state nor federal courts acted as if deference was due to state court decisions in this area. Federal courts sitting in diversity decided many unfair competition cases before *Erie*, but their decisions did not refer to the laws of any particular state, let alone suggest that courts were bound by the decisions of any state supreme court. Moreover, the relatively fewer state court (compared to federal court) decisions from this era were substantively indistinguishable from federal court decisions.[36] As a result, whatever its technical status, the common law of trademark and unfair competition was substantially uniform across jurisdictions (federal and state), and federal courts never faced hard questions about when they might have been obligated to defer to state court decisions.[37] Indeed, it was only after *Erie* that federal courts seem to have given any thought to the source of these common law rules.[38]

B. *The Middle Period (Post-Erie, but Premodern)*

In the years immediately following *Erie*, several courts concluded that common law unfair competition claims must be based on state law. In fact, because pre-Lanham Act statutes were widely understood to confer only procedural rather

acknowledged that with respect to matters within a particular state's legislative competence, the conflict-of-law rules applied in federal court pointed toward the 'general' law only in the absence of state statutes; if the state wanted to supersede the 'general' law, the state could pass a statute to that effect, and federal as well as state courts would then look to the statute rather than the 'general' law for rules of decision. But it was possible to acknowledge that fact without describing any portion of the 'general' law as state law." *Id.*

36 *See, e.g.*, Alff v. Radam, 14 S.W. 164 (Tex. 1890) (deciding a common law trademark infringement claim without reference to particular state law and relying extensively on Amoskeag Mfg. Co. v. Trainer, 101 U.S. 51 (1879), a Supreme Court decision on a common law trademark infringement claim, which itself made no reference to the law of any state); Amoskeag Mfg. Co.v. Spear, 2 Sand. 599 (N.Y. Super. Ct. 1849) (deciding a common law trademark infringement action without reference to the law of any state).

37 *Cf.* Nelson, *supra* note 31, at 15–16 (discussing the role of general law in promoting national uniformity); *see also* Arthur John Keeffe et al., *Weary Erie*, 34 CORNELL L.Q. 494, 504 (1949) (concluding that the Supreme Court's decisions about the content of general law "did promote uniformity to a substantial degree").

38 *See, e.g.*, Philco Corp. v. Phillips Mfg. Co., 133 F.2d 663, 665–66 (7th Cir. 1943) ("In the field of trade-mark infringement and unfair competition it has long been recognized that all rights originally existed by virtue of the common law of the Several States. Thus, in one sense, there has not been thought to be a federal general common law in the field. But in another sense there has been a federal general common law and cases have been 'governed by federal law' within the meaning of the *Erie* doctrine, for federal courts have exercised independent judgment as to what 'the common law' was in all cases in the field. The instant case requires us to draw the line between those cases still 'governed by federal law' (federal courts make an independent determination of the law) and those 'governed by State law' (federal courts are bound by the views of a particular State court).") (citation omitted).

than substantive rights, there was some question in the time between *Erie* and passage of the Lanham Act about whether state law controlled on questions of validity and infringement, even in cases involving *registered* trademarks. The Supreme Court accepted certiorari in *Pecheur Lozenge Co., Inc. v. National Candy Co., Inc.*, asking counsel to express their views as to "whether State law govern[ed] and, if so, what the applicable State law [was]."[39] It did so on the belief that the suit was "founded upon a trademark registered under the 1905 Act," which the "complaint had ma[de] it appear."[40] The Court, in other words, had accepted certiorari to determine the extent to which state law applied in cases involving registered marks. The Court never ruled on that question, however, because it vacated the decree after further examination of the record revealed that the registration referred to was a copyright registration rather than a trademark registration. And because the petitioner had not asserted a claim for copyright infringement, "[t]he only cause of action that [the] record could possibly support [was] for unfair competition and common law trademark infringement, to which local law applie[d]."[41]

Never having received a definitive answer from the Supreme Court, federal courts seem to have coalesced around the reasoning of the Seventh Circuit in its *Philco* decision, which concluded that federal law applied in cases involving registered marks.[42] They did so even though the Seventh Circuit reached that conclusion by claiming, contrary to a number of previous Supreme Court decisions, that Congress had in fact created substantive rights when it passed the Act of 1905.[43] Federal law (of unspecified variety) therefore applied in trademark infringement cases brought under the statute. This set up a hard contrast with common law trademark and unfair competition cases, in which *Pecheur Lozenge* and many other cases made clear that state law applied.[44] That distinction worried several prominent trademark practitioners, who wondered about the continuing precedential value of the many pre-*Erie* unfair competition decisions issued by federal courts. Some even claimed that a new federal statute (which would become the Lanham Act) was needed to

39 315 U.S. 666, 667 (1942).

40 *Id.*

41 *Id.* (internal quotation marks omitted).

42 *Philco*, 133 F.2d at 667 ("We believe that all such questions [relating to registrability, infringement, defenses, remedies, and validity] arising under the Act of 1905 are governed by federal law, since they involve the interpretation and application of a federal statute.").

43 *Id.* at 668 ("It is our opinion that Congress did create substantive rights in trade-marks by the passage of the Act of 1905."). The *Philco* court's conclusion regarding substantive rights under the 1905 act was transparently an attempt to avoid the consequences of the *Erie* decision in the context of registered marks. *See id.* ("If it were held that Congress created no substantive rights but only procedural rights, the *Erie* doctrine would require that State law govern substantive questions of trade-mark law, just as that doctrine would have required if it had been applied before the Act was passed.").

44 *See* Sergei S. Zlinkoff, Erie v. Tompkins: *In Relation to the Law of Trade-Marks and Unfair Competition*, 42 Colum. L. Rev. 955, 960 (1942) ("The basic policy underlying these decisions makes it clear that one class of trade-mark and unfair competition cases unmistakably comes within their scope, namely, the ordinary common law trade-mark and unfair competition action, wherein the jurisdiction of the federal court is predicated upon diversity of citizenship.").

create a federal law of unfair competition because states emboldened by *Erie* would destroy the necessary national uniformity courts had achieved.[45]

It is not clear why those advocates were so concerned about a loss of uniformity, because there was no evidence in the cases decided in the aftermath of *Erie* that uniformity was in jeopardy.[46] Some Lanham Act advocates suggested that certain states were considering statutes that would have instantiated state-specific rules, and later courts have even sometimes credited those concerns.[47] No such state statutes seem ever to have actually passed, however, and in any event the Lanham Act would have been only a partial solution to the problem of disparate state statues. Indeed, despite much discussion of the incentives the new statute would provide to encourage registration, no one suggested that registration would be required or that the Lanham Act would displace the common law or state statutory law with respect to unregistered marks.

Whatever the validity of concerns about the potential effect of *Erie*, in fact uniformity was never seriously threatened. Federal courts called on to decide unfair competition cases after *Erie* needed to look somewhere for the substantive rules of decision. Previous federal court decisions had developed a general law of unfair competition, and the few state court decisions that existed largely relied on federal precedents.[48] Thus, courts looking for a rule of decision faced a landscape devoid of state-specific law, and as a result, state and federal courts alike continued to apply the general law of unfair competition. The Fifth Circuit's decision in *El Chico, Inc. v. El Chico Café* is representative here.[49] In that case the court expressly concluded that, because the plaintiff's claim was only for unfair competition and the

45 *See* Edward S. Rogers, *Introduction* to DAPHNE ROBERT, THE NEW TRADE MARK MANUAL: A HANDBOOK ON PROTECTION OF TRADE-MARKS IN INTERSTATE COMMERCE xvi–xxi (1947) (arguing that *Erie* displaced what practitioners had assumed was federal common law).

46 In his concurring opinion in *Two Pesos, Inc. v. Taco Cabana, Inc.*, Justice Stevens credited a statement in a 1939 House Report in relation to new federal legislation that the consequence of having previously left protection of trademarks to state law was that there were "almost as many different varieties of common law as there are States so that a person's right to a trademark in one State may differ widely from the rights which [that person] enjoys in another." 505 U.S. 763, 782 (1992) (quoting H.R. REP. NO. 944 (1939)) (internal quotation marks omitted). Whether Congress actually was motivated by such a view of the common law when it later passed the Lanham Act, the statement clearly did not accurately describe the common law in practice pre-Lanham Act.

47 *See* Kohler Co. v. Moen Inc., 12 F.3d 632, 640 n.10 (7th Cir. 1993) (claiming that the "Lanham Act was drafted in *reaction* to draconian state trademark legislation that threatened to interfere with interstate commerce" and that "[t]he Lanham Act differs in many respects from the common law standards") (emphasis in original) (citing Edward S. Rogers, *The Lanham Act and the Social Function of Trade-Marks*, 14 LAW & CONTEMP. PROBS. 173, 177–84 (1949) (reporting proposed state legislation that would have required registration of marks to maintain validity)).

48 *See* Zlinkoff, *supra* note 44, at 968 (noting that the "freedom of the federal courts in relation to the decisions of state courts is particularly significant from the standpoint of the relation between the *Erie* doctrine and the law of trade-marks and unfair competition" because there was probably no other field in which the gaps in state law were as large or widespread); *see id.* at 969 (noting the extent to which state courts had relied on "federal precedents and doctrines").

49 214 F.2d 721 (5th Cir. 1954).

case did not involve a registered mark, state law applied.[50] Yet the court did not bother to say which state's law it was applying, and it cited federal and state decisions (many of them pre-*Erie*) interchangeably in rejecting the plaintiff's claim for lack of proof of likely confusion.[51]

If some greater authority were needed, we have the Supreme Court's famous decision in *Kellogg Co. v. National Biscuit Co.* In that case, the National Biscuit Company alleged that Kellogg's "manufacture and sale of the breakfast food commonly known as shredded wheat" constituted unfair competition.[52] The Court noted that "[m]ost of the issues in the case involve[d] questions of common law and hence [were] within the scope of *Erie*," but neither of the parties contended that local law differed from general law, and both relied almost entirely on federal precedents.[53] Thus, the Court proceeded to apply the general law of unfair competition, without reference to the law of any particular state.

This state of affairs largely persisted in the decades following the Lanham Act, as the *El Chico* case suggests. Just as they had before *Erie*, federal and state courts resolved unfair competition cases under the general law of unfair competition. Even when courts acknowledged that state law nominally governed, they typically made clear that the applicable state law was substantively identical to the general law.[54] States did increasingly adopt trademark statutes in this era, but those statutes tended not to have much substantive effect – with a few notable exceptions, courts generally regarded state statutes as codifications of general law principles.[55] Thus, at least in the unfair competition context, *Erie* simply led to a rearrangement of the deck chairs.

C. *The Modern Period*

Despite persistent uniformity of decisional law following *Erie*, many advocates remained interested in a federal statutory basis for unfair competition, and some claimed that the Lanham Act had in fact provided such a basis. Edward Rogers,

50 *Id.* at 724.

51 *See id.* at 725 (citing, among other cases, Hanover Star Milling Co. v. Metcalf, 240 U.S. 403 (1916) and United Drug Co. v. Theodore Rectanus Co., 248 U.S. 90 (1918) (both pre-*Erie* Supreme Court decisions), as well as Fifth Circuit, Texas, Louisiana, New York, and Pennsylvania cases). The parties in *El Chico* were from New York and Texas, but the court never suggested that cases from either of those states were more important.

52 Kellogg Co. v. Nat'l Biscuit Co., 305 U.S. 111, 113 (1938).

53 *Id.* at 113 n. 1.

54 *See* Stork Rest. v. Sahati, 166 F.2d 348, 352 (9th Cir. 1948) ("In California and elsewhere, a firmly established trade name receives the same protection from the law as a trade mark."); *id.* at 357 ("The rule [regarding confusion] has been repeatedly expounded by this and other Federal courts."); Dior v. Milton, 9 Misc. 2d 425, 434, 155 N.Y.S.2d 443, 454 (N.Y. Sup. Ct. 1956) (noting the expansion of the concept of unfair competition across a variety of courts and then stating that "[t]he doctrine of extending unfair competition beyond cases of 'palming off' has similarly been recognized and applied by the courts of this State").

55 *See, e.g., Sahati*, 166 F.2d at 352–53 (noting that "[o]wnership of a trade name is a property right. It is made so by statute in California" and that "[t]he California rule accords with general law.").

one of the Lanham Act's primary drafters, focused particularly on § 44 of the Lanham Act, which he argued could be interpreted broadly to create the federal law of unfair competition.[56] A few courts initially accepted that view,[57] but one had to read § 44 quite creatively to find in it a federal unfair competition cause of action, and most courts were not inclined to do so. That did not mean they were uninterested in finding statutory footing, however, and many courts soon turned their attention to § 43(a) – first to ground a federal unfair competition claim in cases not involving trademarks but other false statements,[58] and then eventually to allow federal claims for infringement of unregistered trademarks and trade dress.[59]

To fit these latter types of claims into the text of the statute, courts interpreted the term "origin" broadly to refer not only to geographic origin but also to origin of manufacture.[60] The Supreme Court has on occasion shown some doubts about the legitimacy of that interpretation, but it has now clearly accepted the conclusion that § 43(a) provides a cause of action for infringement of unregistered marks.[61] Over the same time period, courts began recognizing a much broader range of identifiers as trademark subject matter (and therefore potentially registrable) – including product packaging and design, colors, sounds, and even scents.[62] Many of those more exotic designators previously would not have been considered trademarks, and

[56] *See* Rogers, *supra* note 45, at xvi–xxi (arguing that § 44(h) of the statute should be understood to give courts the ability to develop a uniform body of federal unfair competition law).

[57] *See, e.g.*, Pagliero v. Wallace China Co., 198 F.2d 339 (9th Cir. 1952); Stauffer v. Exley, 184 F.2d 962 (9th Cir. 1950).

[58] *See, e.g.*, L'Aiglon Apparel, Inc. v. Lana Lobell, Inc., 214 F.2d 649 (3d Cir. 1954).

[59] *See, e.g.*, Scarves by Vera, Inc. v. United Merchants and Mfrs., Inc., 173 F. Supp. 625 (S.D.N.Y. 1959); Catalina, Inc. v. Gem Swimwear, Inc., 162 F. Supp. 911 (S.D.N.Y. 1958).

[60] Professor McCarthy suggests that this trend took root in the 1970s, and he attributes the expansion to the decision in *Federal-Mogul-Bower Bearings, Inc.* v. *Azoff*, 313 F.2d 405 (6th Cir. 1963). *See* 5 McCarthy, *supra* note 2, at § 27:7. *Federal-Mogul-Bower* might have the most explicit construction of the statute along these lines, but as the previous notes reflected, several earlier decisions allowed claims under § 43(a) for infringement of unregistered trademarks.

[61] *See* Dastar Corp. v. Twentieth Century Fox Film Corp., 539 U.S. 23, 29–30 (2003) ("Although a case can be made that a proper reading of § 43(a), as originally enacted, would treat the word 'origin' as referring only to the geographic location in which the goods originated, the Courts of Appeals considering the issue, beginning with the Sixth Circuit, unanimously concluded that it does not merely refer to geographical origin, but also to origin of source or manufacture, thereby creating a federal cause of action for traditional trademark infringement of unregistered marks."); Two Pesos, Inc. v. Taco Cabana, Inc., 505 U.S. 763, 768 (1992) ("[T]he general principles qualifying a mark for registration under § 2 of the Lanham Act are for the most part applicable in determining whether an unregistered mark is entitled to protection under § 43(a).") (citations omitted) (internal quotation marks omitted).

[62] *See, e.g.*, Wal-Mart Stores, Inc. v. Samara Bros., 529 U.S. 205 (2000) (holding that product design is protectable only with evidence of secondary meaning); Qualitex Co. v. Jacobson Prods. Co., 514 U.S. 159 (1995) (holding that colors are capable of protection when they have secondary meaning); *Two Pesos*, 505 U.S. 763 (holding that inherently distinctive, nonfunctional trade dress is protectable without evidence of secondary meaning); *In re* Clarke, 17 U.S.P.Q.2d (BNA) 1238 (T.T.A.B. 1990) (holding that a scent is capable of serving as a trademark and is therefore registrable when shown to be distinctive); *In re* Gen. Electric Broadcasting Co., 199 U.S.P.Q. 560 (T.T.A.B. 1978) (finding the

consequently, use of those designators by third parties would have been remediable only through (common law) unfair competition claims.

These interpretations, along with the broader interpretation of interstate commerce that courts embraced over the latter half of the twentieth century, substantially increased the number of marks eligible for federal registration and for enforcement under federal law. Importantly, the effect of these expansive interpretations of the Lanham Act was only partly to expand the field of trademark and unfair competition law as a whole. It was, more importantly, a shifting of subject matter (1) from common law to statutory law and (2) from state to federal law, at least as compared to the middle, post-*Erie*, period.

These shifts have not stripped trademark and unfair competition law of their common law character in every sense. Indeed, courts, rather than Congress, developed most of modern trademark law's substantive rules.[63] They expanded the scope of actionable confusion,[64] developed the functionality and nominative fair use doctrines,[65] and distinguished between product packaging and product design, allowing the latter protection only when it has developed secondary meaning.[66] Congress sometimes has ratified these rules and written them explicitly into the Lanham Act, and even in the few cases in which it has rejected court-developed rules, Congress has never questioned the appropriateness of courts developing trademark law through the common law process.[67] Thus, if "common law" is used narrowly to mean only judge-made law, then trademark law remains largely a common law field, or at least a statutory field in which courts have quite a bit of common lawmaking

sound of a series of bells capable of functioning as a service mark and registrable with evidence of secondary meaning).

63 *See, e.g.*, Robert C. Denicola, *Some Thoughts on the Dynamics of Federal Trademark Legislation and the Trademark Dilution Act of 1995*, LAW & CONTEMP. PROBS. 75, 79–80 (1996) ("Putting aside statutory innovations directly linked to the public notice provided by the Act's registration system, the Lanham Act codifies the basic common law principles governing both the subject matter and scope of protection."); Kenneth L. Port, *The Illegitimacy of Trademark Incontestability*, 26 IND. L. REV. 519, 520 (1993) ("[T]he Lanham Act's primary, express purpose was to codify the existing common law of trademarks and not to create any new trademark rights.").

64 *See* McKenna, *supra* note 8, at 1904–09 (describing this expansion).

65 *See* 1 MCCARTHY, *supra* note 2 § 7:63 ("For many decades, the functionality doctrine was followed by the courts as a matter of public policy. However, until 1998 there was no mention of it in the text of the Lanham Act."); New Kids on the Block v. News America Publishing, Inc., 971 F.2d 302 (9th Cir. 1992) (first articulating the concept of nominative fair use).

66 *Wal-Mart*, 529 U.S. 205.

67 For example, the Senate Report accompanying Congress's first substantial revision of the Lanham Act in 1988 made clear that the revisions to § 43(a) were "to codify the interpretation [the section] has been given by the courts," and that "[b]ecause Section 43(a) of the Act fills an important gap in federal unfair competition law, the committee expect[ed] the courts to continue to interpret the section." S. REP. NO. 100-515, at 40 (1988), *reprinted in* 1988 U.S.C.C.A.N. 5577, 5603. *See also* Graeme B. Dinwoodie, *The Common Law and Trade Marks in an Age of Statutes*, *in* THE COMMON LAW OF INTELLECTUAL PROPERTY: ESSAYS IN HONOUR OF PROFESSOR DAVID VAVER 331, 333 (Catherine W. Ng, Lionel Bently & Giuseppina D'Agostino eds., 2010) ("[D]espite substantial legislative intervention, both Congress and the Supreme Court appear content that the development of trademark and unfair competition law in the United States remain heavily dependent on common law law-making by the courts.").

latitude. But because so little now lies outside the reach of the Lanham Act, this "common law" is now clearly federal law. And on the assumption that those concerned about federalism mean that concern to sound at least in part in vertical choice of law terms rather than simply in separation of powers terms, they may have missed something here. Trademark law is today much more federal than it used to be.

State law claims, of course, have remained technically available even as federal law has expanded, but those state law claims are substantively irrelevant in the vast majority of cases. For infringement claims, courts overwhelmingly see state law as redundant of federal law: courts' discussions of state law claims generally consist entirely of simple statements, often in footnotes, explaining that state and federal law are identical.[68] The coincidence of state and federal law should not be particularly surprising, since courts frequently have held that state law cannot narrow the scope of federal law.[69] Where federal law reaches the same conduct – which, at this point, it essentially always does – states can implement their policy choices only in one direction: by expanding the scope of protection.[70]

This is why state law has mattered over the last several decades only when it has offered broader rights than federal law.[71] State statutory and common law dilution

68 *See* 3 McCarthy, *supra* note 2, at § 22:1 ("In most states, courts have held that the state trademark common law and statutes on trademark law are to be given the same meaning and interpretation as the mainstream principles of common law and federal trademark law."). The Model State Trademark Bill of 2007 explicitly links the substance of state law to the Lanham Act. *See* § 19(b) ("The intent of this Act is to provide a system of state trademark registration and protection substantially consistent with the federal system of trademark registration and protection under the Trademark Act of 1946, as amended. To that end, the construction given the federal Act should be examined as persuasive authority for interpreting and construing the Act."). Model State Trademark Bill of 2007, *reprinted in* 3 J. Thomas McCarthy, McCarthy on Trademarks and Unfair Competition § 22:9.25 (4th ed. 2012). A number of states have either copied this language directly into their state statutes or included such a statement in the legislative history. *See, e.g.*, N.Y. Gen. Bus. Law § 360 note (McKinney 1996 & Supp. 2012) (Historical and Statutory Notes) ("The intent of this act is to provide a system of state trademark registration and protection substantially consistent with the federal system of trademark registration and protection under the Trademark Act of 1946, as amended. To that end, the construction given the federal act should be examined as persuasive authority for interpreting and construing this act.").

69 So, for example, a state registration cannot create rights throughout a state in contravention of federal law's determination of the geographic scope of rights. *See* Teddygram Inc. v. Boyce, 53 U.S.P.Q.2d 1804, 1812 (N.D. Ga. 1999) ("[T]he mere fact that plaintiffs registered their service mark with the state of Georgia prior to the defendants' federal registration is not dispositive on the issue of which party has territorial rights within the state of Georgia.... [G]iving plaintiffs' Georgia service mark registration such effect would elevate Georgia's registration process over the federal process and would be tantamount to overruling the Lanham Act's regulations regarding continuous pre-registration usage."). This is consistent with Congress's statement of intent in the Lanham Act: "The intent of this chapter is to regulate commerce within the control of Congress by making actionable the deceptive and misleading use of marks in such commerce; to protect registered marks used in such commerce from interference by State, or territorial legislation." 15 U.S.C. § 1127 (2006). *See also* Spartan Food Sys., Inc. v. HFS Corp., 813 F.2d 1279, 1284 (4th Cir. 1987) ("[T]he Lanham Act effects a limited preemption of state law, resolving the conflict in favor of the federal registrant's rights.").

70 Ironically, given that common law claims were traditionally the default, modern state-level innovation would likely have to be accomplished statutorily, because state courts now hear trademark or unfair competition relatively infrequently, federal claims nearly always being available.

71 Broader state protection is usually only preempted if application of state law would upset a "carefully constructed regulatory compromise." Attrezzi, LLC v. Maytag Corp., 436 F.3d 32, 42 (1st Cir. 2006).

claims, for example, played important roles before Congress passed the Federal Trademark Dilution Act in 1995 because there was until that point no federal cause of action for dilution.[72] And those state claims regained significance after the Supreme Court interpreted the 1995 statute to require evidence of actual dilution, a standard most believed was impossible to meet in practice.[73] But state dilution law receded again in importance after Congress passed the Trademark Dilution Revision Act in 2006.[74] To be sure, federal law still leaves some room for state dilution law, but that is only because the new statute is (ostensibly, at least) circumscribed. Under the TDRA, dilution claims are available only for marks that are "widely recognized by the general consuming public of the United States."[75] State law may therefore make dilution claims available to some mark owners for whom federal claims are unavailable – specifically those whose marks have only local or niche-market reputations. State law also might go beyond blurring and tarnishment, the only types of dilution actionable under the TRDA.[76] So far states have not taken much advantage of this freedom to operate, however, and several states have aligned their dilution laws with federal law in recent years,[77] a development many have encouraged.[78]

Thus, courts have allowed state law to protect broader rights than the Lanham Act. *See* Golden Door, Inc. v. Odisho, 646 F.2d 347, 352 (9th Cir. 1980) (finding California law not preempted by the Lanham Act because "[b]y extending to federal registrants greater protection than is available under the Lanham Act, California law, like the Act, protects both the public from confusion about the services and products it is receiving and the public relations investment of plaintiff").

72 *See* Moseley v. V Secret Catalogue, 537 U.S. 418, 432 (2003); Nabisco, Inc. v. PF Brands, Inc., 191 F.3d 208, 227 (2d Cir. 1999); Deere & Co. v. MTD Prods., Inc., 41 F.3d 39, 42 (2d Cir. 1994).

73 *Moseley*, 537 U.S. at 433 (holding that the statute "unambiguously require[d] a showing of actual dilution, rather than a likelihood of dilution").

74 15 U.S.C. § 1125(c) (2006).

75 *Id.* at § 1125(c)(2)(A). Dilution claims at the federal level have always been limited to "famous" marks, but not until the Trademark Dilution Revision Act was "fame" defined in the federal statute. Section 1125(c)(2)(A) now states that a mark is famous when it is "widely recognized by the general consuming public of the United States as a designation of source of the goods or services of the mark's owner." *Id.*

76 Some state dilution provisions, for example, have been interpreted to provide a claim against any use that "harms the reputation" of a mark. For example, N.Y. Gen. Bus. Law § 368-d, on which the decision in *Deere & Co. v. MTD Products, Inc.*, 41 F.3d 39 (2d Cir. 1994) was based, provided that "[l]ikelihood of injury to business reputation or of dilution of the distinctive quality of a mark or trade name shall be a ground for injunctive relief in cases of infringement of a mark registered or not registered or in cases of unfair competition, notwithstanding the absence of competition between the parties or the absence of confusion as to the source of goods or services." *Id.* at 42. That section has since been repealed and replaced by the substantively identical § 360-l. N.Y. GEN. BUS. LAW § 360-l (McKinney Supp. 2012).

77 In fact, the Model State Trademark Bill's dilution language is identical to that of the current federal dilution statute. *See* Model State Trademark Bill of 2007 § 13, *reprinted in* 3 J. THOMAS MCCARTHY MCCARTHY ON TRADEMARKS AND UNFAIR COMPETITION § 22:9.25 (4th ed. 2012). California and Texas have both amended their state trademark laws since 2007 expressly for the purpose of bringing them in line with the Model State Trademark Bill. *See* 2011 TEX. GEN. LAWS 1359; CAL. BUS. & PROF. CODE § 14247 (West 2008).

78 *See, e.g.*, David S. Welkowitz, *State of the State: Is There a Future for State Dilution Laws?*, 24 SANTA CLARA COMPUTER & HIGH TECH. L.J. 681, 682 (2008) ("[S]tate law has outlived its usefulness in this area.").

One reason trademark law's federalization might have gone unnoticed is that federal statutory law expanded fairly gradually and was not easily traceable to a particular act of Congress. Federal trademark legislation was keyed to the commerce power long before the Lanham Act was passed in 1946, and even well before the New Deal. The Trademark Act of 1905 limited registration to trademarks used in interstate commerce,[79] and only the owners of registered marks could assert a cause of action under the Act.[80] Consequently, the scope of federal trademark law naturally expanded along with broader interpretation of the Commerce Clause, even without any additional legislative action.[81] Over time, a wider range of uses qualified as uses in interstate commerce, which made federal statutory claims more readily available. First, more trademarks qualified for federal registration, which made a greater number of marks eligible for enforcement under the statute. And second, a number of intrastate uses that would not have been actionable under the statute were reclassified as interstate uses and therefore subject to enforcement under federal law.[82]

Yet these expanding notions of interstate commerce were only partially responsible for the growth of federal law. Expansion of the *types* of indications eligible for registration and courts' interpretations of § 43(a) to embrace a cause of action for infringement of unregistered marks were more important contributing factors. Thus,

79 Trademark Act of 1905, ch. 592, 33 Stat. 724. The Trademark Act of 1881 was even more limited: it allowed registration only of marks used in "commerce with foreign nations, or with the Indian tribes." Trademark Act of 1881, ch. 138, 21 Stat. 502. The legislative history of the Lanham Act clearly reflects Congress's understanding that the scope of the Act would be limited by the Commerce Clause. *See* H.R REP. NO. 79-219, at 4 ("There can be no doubt under the recent decisions of the Supreme Court of the constitutionality of a national act giving substantive as distinguished from merely procedural rights in trade-marks in commerce over which Congress has plenary power."); S. REP. NO. 79-1333 at 5–6 (1946); *Hearings Before the Sub. Comm. on Patents, U.S. Senate*, 78th Cong. 43–48 (1944).

80 Trademark Act of 1905 § 16. The cause of action was similarly limited under the 1881 Act, and the restriction had even more bite under that statute because registration was so much more limited. *See* Trademark Act of 1881 § 7.

81 Richard Epstein, like many other critics of modern Commerce Clause jurisprudence, identifies the New Deal cases – particularly *Wickard* v. *Filburn*, 317 U.S. 111 (1942); *United States* v. *Wrightwood Dairy Co.*, 315 U.S. 110 (1942); *United States* v. *Darby*, 312 U.S. 100 (1941); and *NLRB* v. *Jones & Laughlin Steel Corp.*, 301 U.S. 1 (1937) – as the end of limitations on the scope of the commerce power. *See* Richard A. Epstein, *The Proper Scope of the Commerce Power*, 73 VA. L. REV. 1387, 1443 (1987) ("The New Deal cases systematically removed each of the previous limitations on the scope of the commerce clause."). Notably, Epstein argues that this expansive interpretation of the commerce power was at least partly a result of the fact that "a narrow majority of the Court was in sympathy with the dominant intellectual belief of the time that national problems required national responses" – the same belief that seems to have motivated courts to broaden the scope of the Lanham Act. *Id.*

82 *Compare* Samson Crane Co. v. Union Nat'l Sales, Inc., 87 F. Supp. 218 (D. Mass. 1949) (dismissing a Lanham Act claim against alleged misrepresentation that the defendant's store was being operated by unions or for their benefit on the ground there was no allegation of any misrepresentation in regard to the goods caused to enter interstate commerce) *with* Drop Dead Co. v. S. C. Johnson & Son, Inc., 326 F.2d 87 (9th Cir. 1963) (finding defendant's sale of aerosol furniture wax solely within California actionable because it had a substantial impact on interstate commerce).

although it may be difficult to attribute expansion of federal law to specific legislative actions, that expansion clearly is traceable to judicial interpretation of a particular federal statute and not simply to a more expansive understanding of the background concept of interstate commerce.

It is also possible that expansion of federal law seemed unremarkable because Congress has never purported to displace state law, at least not generally; as a result the extent of federalization has been obscured by the appearance of concurrent regulation. Relatedly, some who view federalism in terms of states' autonomy to legislate their policy preferences might not have seen federalization of trademark law as a problem to the extent that the irrelevance of state law is traceable to states' own decisions to cede substantive regulatory control to Congress by tying the substance of their laws to federal law. States interested in effectuating their own policy objectives could simply take the lack of federal preemption seriously and more aggressively develop their own bodies of trademark and unfair competition law.

Aside from reducing federalism to a procedural concern, however, this view grossly overstates states' ability to make substantive policy choices in the trademark area. State regulation in this area is a one-way ratchet: state law can only have a meaningful effect to the extent it grants broader rights than are available under federal law. Ironically, this means that there is a sense in which states are *less* free to act in the trademark law context than they are with respect to patent and copyright. Even though the Patent and Copyright Acts both preempt state law much more broadly than does the Lanham Act, states are more genuinely free to effectuate their policy preferences in those areas where federal patent and copyright law do *not* preempt. States are free, for example, to have whatever trade secret law they wish, and they are free to regulate unfixed performances however they would like (or to forego such protection altogether). By contrast, states are not free to deviate downward in the trademark context.

II. ENDURING UNIFORMITY AND THE CASE FOR PREEMPTION

There are two other potential explanations for the lack of controversy regarding federalization of trademark law that deserve more extended discussion. First is the possibility that federalization did not provoke concern because it did not change much as a substantive matter. Whatever its status, trademark and unfair competition law have always been essentially uniform, even if (nearly) uniformly expansionary in the Lanham Act era. As a result, the only practical effect of federalization was to assure federal jurisdiction over a wider range of cases. The second explanation is that the countervailing interest in national uniformity grew so much stronger over the last half-century that even those otherwise inclined to take a skeptical view of federal power have been persuaded that federal regulation is appropriate here. I address those explanations in turn in the next sections.

A. *Substantive Uniformity – Then and Now*

The most likely explanation for the uncontroversial nature of trademark law's federalization is that reclassification of unfair competition claims as federal claims did not result in a flattening out of previously diverse bodies of law that reflected states' varying policy judgments. Prior to *Erie*, courts understood that federal statutes created only procedural, and not substantive rights – the content of the substantive rights came from the common law, as did the law of unfair competition. And that common law was general law. Whatever the status of general law (whether it was state law or instead stood outside of the law of any state), courts in the pre-*Erie* era clearly knew that this general law was not federal law, and they did not act as though they owed any deference to the highest court of any particular state. *Erie* superficially disrupted this arrangement, and courts after *Erie* recognized that the common law of unfair competition had to be understood as state law. But that recognition had little impact on the substance of the law, which remained essentially uniform across technically distinct sources of law. Thus, even when state law ostensibly controlled, there was little substantive diversity. In this sense, expansion of federal law had few costs, at least to the extent one sees federalism in terms of enabling states to develop their own law to reflect local policy preferences or as a means of creating laboratories of policy experimentation.

This explanation does more than simply describe a possible reaction to trademark law's federalization; it poses a modest challenge to the importance of federalism principles generally, at least insofar as federalism is seen as a means to the end of states' autonomous lawmaking.[83] Federalism advocates often frame their arguments about the scope of federal law in nostalgic terms, suggesting that something was lost as a result of the Supreme Court's modern Commerce Clause jurisprudence. But in the trademark area at least, substantive variety never really existed, even in the constitutional era to which most federalism advocates would have us return. Courts in that era often did not see themselves as creating distinctive state law, so although the law they were creating was not federal law, it was as substantively uniform as common law can be.

B. *Federalization and National Uniformity*

Lack of suspicion about expanding federal law might, alternatively, reflect general acceptance of the importance of national uniformity in the trademark area, or at least agreement on the relative unimportance of state-level diversity. After all, the

83 Substantive diversity is not, of course, the only reason to be concerned about federalism values. For many, federalism is simply a check on federal power, limiting the size and scope of the federal government, irrespective of whether or how states use their autonomy. But those who view federalism in this way should have been concerned about trademark law's federalization regardless of its substantive effect, for there can be no dispute that federal power is much broader here than it once was.

legislative history of the Lanham Act suggests that Congress was motivated at least in part by its perception that uniform national trademark laws were needed. But this hypothesis is notable for at least two reasons. First, the idea that there was a felt need for national uniformity is inconsistent with the reality that trademark law has always been largely uniform, even when federal law was not compelling that uniformity. If little changed as a substantive matter when federal law expanded, then it is hard to believe that federalization was uncontroversial because it brought needed uniformity or because the need for national uniformity was perceived to be growing as the century went on – unless, of course, the perceived need for uniformity was created by the *Erie* decision itself, which drew attention to the fact that common law unfair competition law was state law. In other words, federal law may have been necessary not to make existing law more uniform, but instead because of concern that uniformity would dissipate to the extent states began to understand their prerogative.[84] Indeed, for those like Rogers who never accepted that unfair competition law was really state law in any meaningful sense, *Erie* injected unnecessary uncertainty, and broad interpretation of the Lanham Act simply guaranteed the law's historical stability.

Yet if it is true that federal law is appropriate here in the interests of national uniformity, then it is difficult to justify the present intermediate condition under which federal law controls nearly all of the time but state law is not expressly preempted. Under the current arrangement, states have latitude to effectuate their policy preferences only in the direction of broader trademark rights. Yet interests in uniformity are not only on one side of the case: would-be defendants are also often national companies, and uniform rules are important to them too. Google, for example, is equally disadvantaged by non-uniform laws whether it is a trademark plaintiff or defendant. In this sense, those who argued for preemption of state dilution laws in the years preceding recognition of a federal dilution cause of action were correct – there is no reason to think that trademark owners deserve the certainty of consistent nationwide protection, but that potential defendants should have to determine their ability to use a mark on a state-by-state basis.[85]

Nor can the lack of preemption be justified on the ground that co-regulation allows the states to serve as laboratories of experimentation through which the best

84 Hints of this concern are apparent in the House and Senate Reports accompanying the Lanham Act. *See* S. Rep. No. 79-1333, at 5 (1946) ("Many years ago the Supreme Court held and has recently repeated that there is no Federal common law. It is obvious that the States can change the common law with respect to trade-marks and many of them have, with the possible result that there may be as many different varieties of common law as there are States. A man's rights in his trade-mark in one State may differ widely from the rights which he enjoys in another. However, trade is no longer local, but is national.").

85 Milton W. Handler, *Are the State Antidilution Laws Compatible with the National Protection of Trademarks?*, 75 Trademark Rep. 269, 287 (1985) ("[W]hat greater inconsistency can there be than for one body of law to uphold the defendant's right to use the challenged mark while another body of law prohibits such use?"); *see also* De Sevo, *supra* note 5.

substantive rules might surface. First, state law is overwhelmingly redundant of federal law, so very little experimentation has ever been done. Second, states are not particularly needed for experimentation here, because the various circuit courts of appeal have long provided adequate opportunity for competition. In fact, to the extent there has been disagreement among courts, that disagreement has traditionally been more significant among circuits ostensibly applying the same law than among states applying their own laws. And now that Congress has enacted federal dilution law, there are even fewer opportunities for substantive differences to arise.

The pockets of disagreement that remain do so only because Congress has yet to resolve an issue, and they might be the areas in which state law has the least claim to legitimacy. For example, the most prominent recent example of state law relevance is in the context of the well-known marks doctrine, which is an exception to the bedrock principle that trademark rights are territorial in nature.[86] The Second Circuit, in *ITC Ltd. v. Punchgini, Inc.*,[87] held that federal law does not recognize a well-known marks exception to the territoriality principle. The holding with respect to federal law was in conflict with the Ninth Circuit's earlier decision in *Grupo Gigante SA De CV v. Dallo & Co.*,[88] which held that the well-known marks exception *did* exist under federal law, and that a foreign mark owner could therefore enforce rights against American uses under certain conditions. But federal law was not the whole story in *Punchgini*, since the Second Circuit certified to the New York Court of Appeals the question of whether New York law recognized a well-known marks exception. And in contrast to the Second Circuit's ruling regarding federal law, the Court of Appeals held that an unfair competition claim is available under New York law when a defendant "appropriates" a party's reputation in the state of New York, even if that reputation derives from use outside the country.[89]

On one level, this kind of result opens the door for states to make different policy choices, trading off the values of territoriality and protection against consumer confusion. But given the importance of the territoriality principle and the significance of the well-known marks to the United States' treaty obligations, it is hard to imagine this is the type of question on which it makes sense to allow states to develop their own law. The policy issues at stake seem precisely the ones we want resolved at a national level, and in fact the disagreement between the Second and Ninth Circuits is an example of precisely the kind of competition among venues that will either result in some consensus through the courts or will impel Congress to step in to resolve the question. The persistence of state law here promises only mischief.

[86] Thus, as the well-known marks doctrine would be applied in the United States, marks that are sufficiently "well-known" may receive protection, notwithstanding the fact that the senior foreign user of that mark has not used that mark within the United States, as is traditionally necessary to acquire legitimate rights. 3 McCarthy, *supra* note 2, at § 29:4.

[87] 482 F.3d 135 (2d Cir. 2007).

[88] 391 F.3d 1088 (9th Cir. 2004).

[89] ITC Ltd. v. Punchgini, Inc., 880 N.E.2d 852 (N.Y. 2007).

More generally, if state law matters now only in these small corners of trademark law, areas in which state law may well be least appropriate, and if otherwise states only have the option of broadening trademark rights, then it is time to recognize the extent of trademark law's federalization and question the value of carrying forward a legal structure that only superficially is concerned with state prerogatives. Unless Congress is interested in repudiating important aspects of the last fifty years of trademark jurisprudence and carving out meaningful space for state policy making, it is time to take the final step and expressly preempt state trademark and unfair competition law.

PART IV

Plural Values in Intellectual Property

14

The Normative Structure of Copyright Law

*Shyamkrishna Balganesh**

INTRODUCTION

The economic account of copyright as an inducement for creativity is today the dominant justificatory theory for the institution. According to this account, copyright law exists primarily (if not exclusively) to provide creators with a market-based incentive for creativity by assuring them of a limited exclusionary interest in their creative expression, once brought into existence and fixed in a tangible medium.[1] Courts, scholars, and legislators alike today take this account of copyright law as a given, even if they occasionally acknowledge the importance of other noneconomic values in the system.[2]

Very interestingly, the economic theory of incentives, with which copyright law is today associated, began as a positive account of the institution. Looking to copyright law's structural and functional attributes, the account posited that copyright law – in practice – works by providing creators with an inducement to create, thereby generating creativity at minimal social cost. Somewhere along the way, however, this positive account morphed into a normative one, with the incentives effect of the institution coming to be understood not just as a description of copyright law's functioning but also as its very goal/objective. Because this normative account also fit rather well with copyright's constitutional mandate of "promoting the progress of science and useful arts,"[3] which is couched in utilitarian terms, the

* Assistant Professor of Law, University of Pennsylvania Law School. Many thanks to Wendy Gordon, Jody Kraus, David Lametti, Gideon Parchomovsky, Jennifer Rothman, Ben Zipursky, and participants at the symposium on Intellectual Property and the Common Law, held at the University of Pennsylvania Law School in May 2011. All errors remain with the author.

[1] *See, e.g.*, Sara K. Stadler, *Incentive and Expectation in Copyright*, 58 Hastings L.J. 433 (2006); Shyamkrishna Balganesh, *Foreseeability and Copyright Incentives*, 122 Harv. L. Rev. 1569 (2009); Julie E. Cohen, *Copyright as Property in the Post-Industrial Economy: A Research Agenda*, 2011 Wisc. L. Rev. 141 (2011).

[2] Cohen, *supra* note 1 (describing this phenomenon).

[3] U.S. Const., Art. I, § 8, Cl. 8.

economic account came in due course to take its current place as copyright's principal justificatory and normative theory.[4] Copyright is today thought to exist *in order to* provide creators with an economic incentive to create.

The economic account of copyright law, however, is not without its own set of problems. As a descriptive account of what copyright actually does in practice, its conclusions remain largely unsubstantiated in empirical terms.[5] And as a normative theory (of optimal incentivization), it remains constitutively incomplete. When confronted with some of the peculiar structural features of the copyright system, many of which have existed since the institution's very origins, the incentives account treats them as aberrations or the result of peculiar political compromises, or it instead turns to additional values (e.g., efficiency or fairness) to account for their existence.

It is the latter of these problems that this chapter addresses. It argues that the extensive emphasis placed by both courts and scholars on the incentives-based justification for copyright law – as a normative theory – has resulted in the neglect of copyright law's fundamental *normative structure*. Under the economic account, several of copyright's core structural attributes – including its emphasis on copying (both as a probative and normative matter), the structure of its defenses, its structure as a bundle of "exclusive use privileges," and, perhaps most importantly, its extensive reliance on private enforcement to enforce its promise of exclusivity – are all viewed as contingent (rather than core) features of the system. Although they are no doubt occasionally justified in economic efficiency terms, they are hardly thought to derive directly from the incentives account of copyright law or indeed be required by it.

This chapter attempts to develop an account of copyright law's normative structure by viewing several of its aforementioned features as integral to what copyright is and indeed has always been. In so doing, the objective is hardly just to fault the dominant economic account of copyright law, especially in its descriptive/positive manifestation, which one may accept as largely true. It is instead to reveal that as a normative matter, however, copyright law merits being understood in more nuanced and perhaps less foundationalist terms than it currently is and that looking to the structure of private law is likely to aid significantly in this endeavor.[6] Copyright's

4 *See generally* Dotan Oliar, *Making Sense of the Intellectual Property Clause: Promotion of Progress as a Limitation on Congress's Intellectual Property Power*, 94 Geo. L.J. 1771 (2006); Richard A. Posner, *The Constitutionality of the Copyright Term Extension Act: Economics, Politics, Law, and Judicial Technique in* Eldred v. Ashcroft, 2003 Sup. Ct. Rev. 143.

5 *See* Ivan P. L. Png, *Copyright: A Plea for Empirical Research*, 3 Rev. Econ. Res. on Copyright Issues 3 (2006); Raymond Shih Ray Ku et al., *Does Copyright Law Promote Creativity? An Empirical Analysis of Copyright's Bounty*, 62 Vand. L. Rev. 1669, 1671 (2009).

6 I have developed a related aspect of copyright's private law structure elsewhere. *See* Shyamkrishna Balganesh, *The Obligatory Structure of Copyright Law: Unbundling the Wrong of Copying*, 125 Harv. L. Rev. 1664 (2012). There, I argued that copyright's private law structure embodied an "obligatory" element that allowed the institution to be reconceptualized around the idea of the "duty not to copy." My objective here is to mount a limited defense of analyzing copyright law through its structure. For a more general defense of this approach, see Ernest Weinrib, The Idea of Private Law (1995).

instrumental, incentives-based justification, I argue here, is neither fundamentally wrong nor palpably misguided, but rather incomplete.

In speaking of an institution's "normative structure," my reference is to the set of obligations – rights, duties, and privileges – that the institution creates between different parties and the mechanisms that it affords them to validate and enforce those obligations.[7] The structure of a legal institution is invariably, of course, normative, in the sense that it directs individuals to behave in a certain way (i.e., it guides behavior). The source of this normativity is twofold: one, the actual directives that it issues as a matter of positive law, and two, the sanctions that it imposes or the benefits that it awards for noncompliance/compliance with those directives in actual practice.[8] The institution's normative structure is thus in its widest sense the devices/mechanisms through which it seeks to guide, facilitate, and control the behavior of a relevant set of actors. Although an institution's normative structure may no doubt be usefully deployed to achieve certain instrumental goals, to the extent that it is not a contingent feature of the institution, it also independently sheds light on the goals and purposes animating the very existence of the institution in question.

As an institution that is just over three hundred years old, copyright has its own unique normative structure.[9] Much of this, rather unsurprisingly, originates in its reliance on different ideas and structures from the domain of private law specifically, and the common law more generally. Part I begins by looking to the dominant idea of economic incentives that today motivates the normative analysis of copyright law, showing how it elides over the institution's underlying structural bulwark. Part II then reorients the discussion around copyright's structural core, which originates in its use of two private law mechanisms that can be traced back to the common law – *exclusivity* and *liability* – which can in turn be understood in both nonconsequentialist and instrumental terms. In so doing, it shows how the dominant incentives account, while by no means inaccurate, is capable of addressing only a part of copyright's normative framework. Part III concludes by highlighting the consequences that are likely to flow from refocusing analytical attention on copyright's core structure.

I. THE IDEA OF INCENTIVES IN COPYRIGHT THINKING: FROM EXPLANATION TO JUSTIFICATION

What is "copyright"? Although a seemingly innocuous question, attempts to answer it often elide the distinction between an explanation and a justification. An explanatory response purports to tell us "what the nature of a thing is" or "why things are

7 *See* JULES L. COLEMAN, THE PRACTICE OF PRINCIPLE: IN DEFENCE OF A PRAGMATIST APPROACH TO LEGAL THEORY 13 (2001); Jules L. Coleman, *The Structure of Tort Law*, 97 YALE L.J. 1233, 1241–42 (1988); Jules L. Coleman & Gabe A. Mendlow, The Normative Structure of Tort Law (working paper).

8 Stephen A. Smith, *The Normativity of Private Law*, 31 OXFORD J. LEG. STUD. 1, 4–6 (2011); Lewis Kornhauser, *The Normativity of Law*, 1 AM. L. & ECON. REV. 3 (1999).

9 The first copyright statute dates back to 1710, Statute of Anne. Copyright Act 1709, 8 Anne c. 19.

as they are" and retain a facial neutrality about the desirability of the things being explained[10]: for example, an account of copyright as a simple "bundle of exclusive rights" over creative expression. A justificatory endeavor, in contrast, openly eschews claims of neutrality and purports to "defend or legitimate" the thing being accounted for.[11] It thus makes an overt claim about the desirability of the things being justified. Both explanations and justifications can in some sense be normative, since even explanations remain motivated by norms of accuracy and predictability.[12] Yet, explanations are not overtly prescriptive, in the sense of seeking to motivate reform or lawmaking. What is important to appreciate in the copyright context is how the incentives-based account of the institution underwent the transformation from being an explanation to becoming an overt justification for the institution.

The serious analysis of copyright law's incentives-based account can be traced to the early twentieth century. In a 1934 article, Arnold Plant set out to examine the economic aspects of copyright in books.[13] After surveying the motivational role of copyright, the monetary incentives that it sought to provide authors, the history of copyright law, and the market for books, he offered a set of "conclusions" that are remarkable for their marked ambivalence. Observing that copyright might serve to induce heightened risk-taking by publishers, he nonetheless noted that there is "no system of economic calculus which supports the contention that output of the type which [the copyright] monopoly induces is 'preferable' to that which emerges from the different disposition" of the same resources.[14] Indeed, he ended the article on a fairly skeptical note, observing that "[t]o the economist who studies the statements of the case for and against the copyright system as we know it, there is no document more satisfying in its logic than the minority report" of a member of the Royal Commission on Copyright, which "stated the arguments *against* the copyright monopoly" [emphasis added].[15] A far cry from being a normative defense of copyright, Plant's arguments hint at a degree of skepticism with copyright's basic incentives-based justification.

In a 1966 article published in the *American Economic Review*, the economist Robert Hurt described copyright as a "grant of the aid of state coercion to the creators of certain 'intellectual products' to prevent for a period of years the 'copying' of these products."[16] Examining different theoretical and philosophical accounts for copyright, his analysis quickly moved to the incentives account, where he concluded that "it seems fairly clear that without some device to assist authors in receiving compensation for their services, some works with high costs of creation, as well as literary creation induced by the expectation of incremental income from subsidiary

10 Coleman, *supra* note 7, at 3.
11 *Id.*
12 *Id.*
13 Arnold Plant, *The Economic Aspects of Copyright in Books*, 1 Economica 167 (1934).
14 *Id.* at 192.
15 *Id.* at 195.
16 Robert Hurt, *The Economic Rationale of Copyright*, 58 Am. Econ. Rev. 421, 421 (1966).

and reprint rights, may not be produced at all."[17] In so doing, he thus affirmed what seemed to be a descriptive, explanatory account of copyright's functioning – that in practice, it does seem to be playing a role in inducing the production of creative expression. What then of the prescriptive question? In other words, should it follow that, because copyright has this effect, one may consider the production of these effects its principal purpose? And here, Hurt surprisingly answered the question in the negative, observing that "it does not necessarily follow that the grant of a copyright monopoly is the only such device possible, nor that it is the most desirable device."[18] Hurt proceeded to conclude his paper by observing that, short of deontic, rights-based accounts for copyright law, the justification for copyright law from the need to "support the creators of literary products" is weak and that these objectives are perhaps better served by other institutional mechanisms.[19] In direct reference to the argument that copyright is justifiable because it "enhance[s] the general welfare," Hurt wrapped up his argument in rather harsh terms by noting that the claim was "subject to attack on theoretical grounds" and therefore deserving of "less self-righteous moral defense."[20]

Two decades later, Bill Landes and Richard Posner took the economic analysis of copyright forward by offering a formal economic model to explain copyright law.[21] Observing at the outset that their account was a "positive analysis" rather than a normative one (thereby purporting to explain, rather than justify), they set out to describe existing copyright doctrine as promoting the efficient allocation of resources through the creation of a socially optimal incentive structure.[22] Yet, there remained an unavoidable justificatory tone in their analysis – a form of creeping normativity. When after developing their model, they thus set out their "intuition" – that "[s]ome copyright protection is necessary to generate incentives to incur the costs of creating easily copied work . . . [t]he key issue is how the level of protection . . . is set along several dimensions," and most interestingly that "the modern law of copyright makes intelligent estimates" on these questions – they seemed to be most clearly entering the realm of justification (and prescription) rather than mere explanation.[23]

This conversion of the incentives account into a justificatory rationale reached it culmination when the Supreme Court affirmed it and used it as an interpretive tool. In *Harper & Row*, the Court observed famously that "[b]y establishing a marketable right to the use of one's expression, copyright supplies the economic incentive to create and disseminate ideas;" it went on to use that conclusion to reject the defendant's expansive reading of fair use in the case, noting that doing so would diminish the

17 *Id.* at 426.
18 *Id.*
19 *Id.* at 432.
20 *Id.*
21 William M. Landes & Richard A. Posner, *An Economic Analysis of Copyright Law*, 18 J. LEGAL STUD. 325 (1989).
22 *Id.* at 325.
23 *Id.* at 335–36.

incentive to create, which it described as "the major premise of copyright."[24] Later courts (and scholars) have followed this trend in large measure, thereby effectively converting the incentives theory into copyright's raison d'être.[25]

The economic incentives account of copyright law is not intrinsically problematic as a normative proposition. In other words, it may well be desirable to provide creators with an incentive to create in order to have them produce creative expression. But the incentives account is troubling because it adopts a very narrow view of the structure of copyright law. This narrow view in turn tracks the distinction between a sanctions-based account of the law and the intrinsic normativity of a legal institution.[26] In the economic conception of the law, the law is what it *does*. It is defined by the consequences it imposes on behavior of a certain kind. These consequences may be negative, such as liability, or they may be positive, as in the case of a reward. Copyright, in the incentives account, follows this pattern. Copyright law is, and is justifiable, simply because of what it does for creators – by rewarding them for their socially beneficial (i.e., creative) activity. As a normative matter, however, this account of copyright is problematic for at least four interrelated reasons.

First, and indeed most obviously, this incentives story treats the entire structure of copyright as largely contingent. If an economic incentive is *all* that copyright is, the precise structure of that incentive, its magnitude, or indeed how it is operationalized should matter little, unless other considerations enter the picture such as fairness, efficiency, transaction costs and the like – which the traditional incentives story does not pay sufficient attention to, except *qua* incentives. Indeed, even economists seem to concede that copyright is not necessarily the most "efficient" way of providing creators with an incentive to create.[27] Yet, instead of using this claim to question the justificatory sufficiency of the incentives account, they then proceed to take the incentives account as a normatively desirable story and try to construct a regime that does in practice provide efficient incentives.[28] A tax subsidy, a prize, or other reward structure might do just as well or indeed better than copyright law, if inducement by reward is the sole end of copyright law.[29]

Second, the incentives account focuses exclusively on the consequences of the regime on a potential plaintiff, the creator. A one-sided focus along these lines may be less objectionable in situations where the parties are likely to be highly symmetrical,

24 Harper & Row Publishers, Inc. v. Nation Enter., 471 U.S. 539, 558 (1985).

25 *See, e.g.*, Eldred v. Ashcroft, 537 U.S. 186, 219 (2003).

26 *See* Smith, *supra* note 8, at 4.

27 Hurt, *supra* note 16, at 432; Steven Shavell & Tanguy Van Ypersele, *Rewards Versus Intellectual Property Rights*, 44 J. L. & Econ. 525 (2001); Marcel Boyer, *Efficiency Considerations in Copyright Protection*, 1 Rev. Econ. Res. on Copyright Issues 11 (2004).

28 *See, e.g.*, William M. Landes & Richard A. Posner, *Indefinitely Renewable Copyright*, 70 U. Chi. L. Rev. 471 (2003); Balganesh, *supra* note 1, at 1569.

29 Hurt, *supra* note 16, at 432.

such as in certain instances of accident/negligence law.[30] This symmetry of parties is, however, far from being the case in copyright law, where creators and copiers are often pitted against each other structurally in the marketplace. Consequently, even if the system's consequences were to inform its normative purpose, the analysis ought to pay attention not just to its incentive effects on potential creators but also to its deterrent (or disincentive) effects on potential copiers. Copyright law might then, following in this exact same consequentialist line of thinking, be understood as being about the optimal deterrence of harmful copying.[31]

Third, the incentives account almost completely rules out the possibility of understanding copyright law from an internal point of view – whether on the defendant's side or the plaintiff's.[32] The "internal point of view" made famous by H. L. A. Hart in his criticism of Holmes's "bad man" approach to tort law argues that individuals often follow legal rules not from fear of the sanctions that may follow from their noncompliance, but rather because they view themselves as "obligated" to comply with the directives of the law.[33] Individuals often accept rules because of the normativity of the law and legal directives, rather than because of the mere consequences (i.e., liability or gains) that flow from compliance. An individual takes this point of view when "he accepts or endorses a convergent pattern of behavior as a standard of conduct."[34] Perhaps most importantly, it involves adopting a particular "normative attitude" to a legal directive, deriving from its legitimacy and structure.[35]

Approaching copyright law from an internal point of view would entail paying closer attention than before to the nature of the legal directives that it communicates, both to potential creators and copiers. More than anything else, what the internal point of view tells us is that an individual's reasons for action need not be consequence-driven or, translated into economic terms, incentive-driven.[36] Note that this does not mean that the law itself is without effect – just that the consequences of compliance/noncompliance may assume secondary relevance to an individual's acceptance of certain behavior being obligatory because of the law's normative structure. To a user of someone else's expression, copyright law might thus communicate a normative practice of avoiding the unauthorized, harmful copying of creative

[30] *See* Louis Kaplow & Steven Shavell, Fairness Versus Welfare 100–23 (2002) (arguing that in situations of "reciprocal" harm, a focus on individual welfare ought to dominate the normative analysis of tort law).

[31] For a more general account of deterrence in copyright law, *see* Pamela Samuelson & Tara Wheatland, *Statutory Damages in Copyright Law: A Remedy in Need of Reform*, 51 Wm. & Mary L. Rev. 439 (2009). For a general account of the idea of "optimal deterrence" *see* Cass Sunstein et al., *Do People Want Optimal Deterrence?*, 29 J. Legal Stud. 237 (2000).

[32] For just such an account, see Balganesh, *The Obligatory Structure of Copyright Law*, *supra* note 6, at 1664.

[33] *See* H. L. A. Hart, The Concept of Law 82–91 (2d ed. 1994); Benjamin Zipursky, *Legal Obligations and the Internal Aspect of Rules*, 75 Fordham L. Rev. 1229 (2006).

[34] Scott J. Shapiro, *What Is the Internal Point of View?*, 75 Fordham L. Rev. 1157, 1159 (2006).

[35] Hart, *supra* note 33, at 89; Shapiro, *supra* note 34, at 1159.

[36] Smith, *supra* note 8, at 2.

expression. To the creator of original expression, it might thus symmetrically communicate a realization that others are unlikely to harmfully appropriate his or her expression without authorization. In both constructions, however, the effects of the law have to be understood independent of the possibility of liability/recovery (i.e., the deterrent/incentive).

Fourth and connectedly, describing, and justifying, copyright law in terms of a simple economic incentive to create ignores the question of who copyright law's target audience really is – namely, creators – and the mechanism through which they *internalize* the incentive – the promise of exclusivity.[37] Copyright's law grant of exclusivity is seemingly directed at creators and copiers, yet its mechanism for rendering that exclusivity operational – that is, the provision for exclusionary enforcement – is directed at courts. Does this tell us something about its attempt to segregate the two? In similar vein, the fair use doctrine sets out factors "to be considered" in determining whether something is a fair use, but is unclear on who is to consider these factors.[38] Courts routinely take the fair use doctrine to be directed at them. Paying closer attention to the structure of copyright's legal directives might reveal the extent to which it attempts to engage in what Meir Dan-Cohen famously called "acoustic separation": the practice of separating conduct rules – directed at actors – from decision rules directed at courts engaged in adjudicating claims.[39]

In summary then, the economic incentives account of copyright – as a normative justification for the institution – glosses over several important elements of copyright's structure as a *legal* institution. Additionally, unlike in some areas of the common law, where distinctively legal terms have come to acquire a consequentialist or economic meaning because of their semantic evolution in that direction, the incentives theory has thus far found little meaningful instantiation at the conceptual level in copyright law.[40] It thus remains most meaningful, and indeed less incomplete, only when it operates as a broad-based, explanatory account of copyright law, rather than a normative ideal that is individually instantiated into the system's functioning.

II. THE PRIVATE LAW CORE OF COPYRIGHT

Having examined some of the inadequacies of the extant use of economic incentives as copyright's motivating normative idea, this part moves to suggesting an alternative means of conceptualizing copyright by taking its normative structure seriously. Two important caveats are in order before proceeding. First, the suggestion that we take copyright's normative structure seriously should not be taken to imply a purely

37 Shapiro, *supra* note 34, at 1159.

38 17 U.S.C. §107 (2005).

39 Meir Dan-Cohen, *Decision Rules and Conduct Rules: On Acoustic Separation in Criminal Law*, 97 Harv. L. Rev. 625 (1984). For an analogous idea extended to private law see Dale A. Nance, *Guidance Rules and Enforcement Rules: A Better View of the Cathedral*, 83 Va. L. Rev. 837 (1997).

40 *See* Jody S. Kraus, *Transparency and Determinacy in Common Law Adjudication: A Philosophical Defense of Explanatory Economic Analysis*, 93 Va. L. Rev. 287, 326 (2007).

"formalist" approach to copyright law – or the idea that "copyright law is what copyright law is," no more no less.[41] To the contrary, the argument is that copyright's formal structure contributes to the realization of its normative goals and that an understanding of these normative goals needs to pay attention to constraints both external to the copyright's legal apparatus (e.g., whether we need incentives) and those internal to it. Copyright's logic as a mechanism of liability (in private law) ought to play a more important role in the analysis – and this insight forms the core of the argument here. Or, as Hanoch Dagan observes in a related context, copyright law should be viewed as "neither wholly autonomous, nor purely instrumental," but rather as a combination of both.[42]

Second, the push in the direction of paying more attention to copyright's normative structure need not detract from the overall desirability of having copyright function as an incentive for creativity. In other words, focusing on copyright's mechanisms of normativity will often remain perfectly compatible with an incentives-based account for copyright law, and the argument here should not be viewed as attempting to set them up as being in some kind of indelible tension with each other.[43] It will, however, reveal that our understanding of copyright's incentives story needs to be far more nuanced and tentative than it currently is, while also emphasizing that the incentives account will remain constitutively incomplete within copyright's overall framework.

A. *Exclusivity and Liability*

The institution of copyright has always operated by providing creators with a set of "exclusive" privileges in relation to their creations and with a mechanism by which to enforce these privileges against any interference by third parties.[44] Although on the face of things, the grant of a set of exclusive privileges (i.e., to copy, distribute, perform, publish, etc.) may seem to be the equivalent of property's "bundle of rights," in reality it does something very different.[45] Property's bundle of rights consists of a set of use privileges in relation to a resource. These privileges provide the bundle-holder (i.e., the owner) with an affirmative basis on which to interact with the resource in an

[41] For a general overview of formalism in the law see Frederick Schauer, *Formalism*, 97 YALE L.J. 509 (1988); Leo Katz, *Form and Substance in Law and Morality*, 66 U. CHI. L. REV. 566 (1999). For a critique of formalism as applied to tort law *see* Robert L. Rabin, *Law for Law's Sake*, 105 YALE L.J. 2261 (1996).

[42] Hanoch Dagan, *The Limited Autonomy of Private Law*, 56 AM. J. COMP. L. 809, 811 (2008).

[43] *See* Smith, *supra* note 8, at 26–27 (alluding to the fact that these positions need not be in direct conflict).

[44] *See* 17 U.S.C. §106 (2005) (observing how the copyright holder "has the exclusive rights to do" a set of activities in relation to the work); Statute of Anne, 8 Anne c. 19, §II (1710) (conferring on authors the "sole right and liberty of printing" the work in question for a specific duration).

[45] The use of the bundle idea to describe copyright's grant is quite common today. *See, e.g.*, Zechariah Chafee, Jr., *Reflections on the Law of Copyright: I*, 45 COLUM. L. REV. 503, 505 (1945).

infinite varieties of ways – the gravamen of ownership.[46] By vesting these privileges in an owner, property law declares that others (i.e., the world at large) have "no right" to stop the owner from interacting with the resource in the ways so privileged, by themselves using the resource.[47] The authorization to interact with the resource thus derives from property law's vesting of a bundle of rights with the owner. With copyright, however, the set of exclusive privileges are not necessary to enable the owner to affirmatively interact with the resource in question, the expression. This is a direct consequence of the resource being nonrivalrous and nonexcludable in nature, as a result of which others (non-owners) hardly need to be denied any right to use the resource *in order to* facilitate the owner's use.[48] Consequently, an affirmative grant of "use privileges" is hardly what copyright's bundle does. Instead, its emphasis lies in its rendering of such privileges *exclusive*.[49]

Copyright's declaration of exclusivity now fills in for the intrinsically nonexcludable nature of expression, and it endows its use privileges with a similar effect as property's use privileges – by requiring non-owners to refrain from using the expression in a certain way. Unlike property however, it is not doing so to facilitate the owner's own use, but for independent reasons, which are fully explored later. This exclusivity is then best understood in its negative connotation – that is, in terms of what it implies cannot be done. By declaring that the copyright holder has a set of exclusive entitlements in relation to the resource, copyright law is simultaneously speaking to both the copyright holder (the author) and to others who may be considering interacting with the expression in question.[50] It declares that the copyright holder is the only one who may exercise the privileges explicitly identified, in the process forbidding others from doing so. Copyright's normative directive thus lies in this declaration of exclusivity.[51]

The most important feature of this directive, however, is that it operates *relationally*. In other words, it operates by directing someone to avoid doing something in relation to another – "do not copy creative expression created by X" – rather than in absolute terms: "do not copy." Relational directives are directives that require people not to treat others in a certain way, rather than just imposing a prohibition.[52]

46 J. E. Penner, *The "Bundle of Rights" Picture of Property*, 43 UCLA L. Rev. 711 (1996).

47 *See* Wesley Newcomb Hohfeld, *Some Fundamental Legal Conceptions as Applied in Judicial Reasoning*, 23 Yale L.J. 16, 32–44 (1913).

48 *See* Yochai Benkler, *An Unhurried View of Private Ordering in Information Transactions*, 53 Vand. L. Rev. 2063, 2064–65 (2000).

49 For an early identification of this point, see T. Cyprian Williams, *Property, Things in Action, and Copyright*, L. Quart. Rev. 223, 232 (1895) (making a similar point about the centrality of forbearance to copyright law).

50 I have made this argument elsewhere before. *See* Shyamkrishna Balganesh, *Demystifying the Right to Exclude: Of Property, Inviolability, and Automatic Injunctions*, 31 Harv. J.L. & Pub. Pol'y 593, 627 (2008).

51 *Id.* at 628.

52 *See* John C. P. Goldberg & Benjamin Zipursky, *Torts as Wrongs*, 88 Tex. L. Rev. 917, 945 (2010); Benjamin Zipursky, *Rights, Wrongs, and Recourse*, 51 Vand. L. Rev. 1, 59 (1998).

In effect then, copyright's directive mimics the structure of a relational legal wrong – the content of tort law – rather than a wrong against the state or the public in the abstract.[53] What explains copyright's structure as a grant of exclusive use rights to a creator rather than a simple prohibition against copying (á la criminal law) is indeed the relational dimension of what it communicates to individuals – not just that copying is a wrong but also that it is wrongful only when in relation to another's original creation.[54]

This relational structure of copyright's directive is also of deep functional significance. On the one hand, it effectively imposes a duty of non-interference on individuals in relation to an original work of expression. Yet, it also does more. Most importantly, it provides a copyright holder with the right to commence an action – a mechanism of recourse – against a defendant who interferes with this grant of exclusivity.[55] Its grant of exclusivity is thus not just a nominal declaration but also the very core of the *liability* mechanism that it creates. Exclusivity thus generates the liability regime that copyright law fundamentally is. Now we begin to see why copyright law's analytical framework begins with its declaration of exclusivity – which is hardly mandated by the nature of the subject matter it is protecting.[56] It is perhaps precisely to the analytical structure of this directive that Justice Holmes was alluding when he observed that exclusion in copyright law operates "*in vacuo*" and unlike tangible property is not directed at an object, but is instead "a prohibition on conduct" that restrains the "spontaneity of men" artificially.[57] It operates *in vacuo* (i.e., in isolation) precisely because it remains a declaration in the abstract that is only ever realized through the framework of liability. In other words, it can afford to remain *in vacuo* because its content is only ever determined relationally in the context of liability.

To speak of copyright's "grant of exclusivity" is thus little more than an allusion to the liability apparatus that it creates, centered around the abstract duty of non-interference. Copyright in effect grants its holder the bare ability to commence a legal action to enforce the exclusivity. Although this simplification may seem somewhat radical, in reality this was precisely the idea of copyright that existed through much of the nineteenth century.[58] Indeed, this basic observation at one point led to copyright's grant being characterized by common law lawyers as a

53 Avihay Dorfman & Assaf Jacob, *Copyright as Tort*, 12 Theoretical Inquiries in the Law 59, 62 (2010) (identifying the normative structure of copyright law with tort law).

54 *See* Zipursky, *Rights, Wrongs, and Recourse*, *supra* note 52, at 60.

55 Indeed, Robert Hurt (a nonlawyer) too understood copyright precisely in these terms. *See* Hurt, *supra* note 16, at 421.

56 Balganesh, *supra* note 50, at 628 (noting how the idea of exclusion is a legal fiction in copyright law).

57 White-Smith Music Pub. Co. v. Apollo Co., 209 U.S. 1, 19 (1908).

58 W. S. Holdsworth, *The History of the Treatment of Choses in Action by the Common Law*, 33 Yale L.J. 997, 998 (1920); Williams, *supra* note 49, at 223; Spencer Brodhurst, *Is Copyright a Chose in Action?*, 11 Law Quart. Rev. 64 (1895).

mere "chose in action."[59] The grant to its holder could hardly be described as "possessory," because the privileges it afforded them need little de jure validation owing to the nonrivalrous nature of expression.[60] Exclusivity was thus perceived to be the gravamen of its grant, and rightly so. This exclusivity in turn was understood to be little more than a commitment from the legal system that it would afford its holder (i.e., the copyright holder) the ability to use the state's coercive apparatus as a mechanism of redress for invasions of this exclusivity.[61] Exclusivity was thus intricately connected to liability.

What this analysis might reveal then is that copyright's basic normative structure originates in a framework of "corrective justice" – a theory often traced to Aristotle and originating in the idea that morality identifies a "normative equilibrium," which the defendant's wrongful action disturbs, and in response to which the law provides a plaintiff with a mechanism to restore this equilibrium.[62] A reason for some caution, however, in relying on corrective justice, is that it identifies the source of this equilibrium in morality. A defendant's wrongdoing is thought to generate a moral obligation to repair the harm it creates, which the law in turn mirrors.[63] In relation to copyright however, it is hard (and indeed somewhat implausible) to assert that the obligation to compensate a creator for the unauthorized copying of his or her original work is a "moral obligation" – pre-legal and in some ways independent of the law. Indeed, courts' early rejection of the idea of common law copyright, at least facially, put this idea to rest.[64] Copyright's normativity is thus entirely legal. Far from implying that its liability structure is rendered contingent because of this, it reveals that the normative basis of this liability apparatus must be understood independent of any moral obligation that preexists copyright law.

A possible answer lies instead in viewing copyright law through the lens of what some tort theorists call the idea of "civil recourse," an idea rooted entirely in the legal normativity of private law mechanisms.[65] Although closely aligned with corrective justice, the principle of civil recourse argues that private law mechanisms such as tort law exist primarily to provide individuals who have been "wronged" with a mechanism of redress through the legal system. It suggests that providing individuals with a "right of action" on a wrongful act forms private law's principal unifying characteristic.[66] Very importantly, the "wrong" here originates entirely in the law's determination that certain interests of an individual are worthy of protection against

59 *See* T. Cyprian Williams, *Is a Right of Action in Tort a Chose in Action?*, 10 LAW QUART. REV. 143 (1894); Williams, *supra* note 49, at 223; Holdsworth, *supra* note 58, at 998.

60 *Id.* at 223.

61 Hurt, *supra* note 16, at 421.

62 WEINRIB, *supra* note 6, at 80; ARISTOTLE, NICOMACHEAN ETHICS, Bk V.4 (Ostwald trans. 1962).

63 Benjamin Zipursky, *Civil Recourse, Not Corrective Justice*, 91 GEO. L.J. 695, 718 (2003).

64 Donaldson v. Beckett, 98 Eng. Rep. 257 (1813).

65 The idea of civil redress was developed by Benjamin Zipursky and John Goldberg in their work. For an exhaustive account see Zipursky, *Civil Recourse*, *supra* note 63.

66 Zipursky, *supra* note 63, at 733.

interference, regardless of whether such interference gives rise to an equivalent moral obligation of reparation.[67] It is thus a creation of positive law. The individual's right is thus in reality a privilege that the state affords him or her to invoke a coercive legal mechanism to redress the interference so identified.[68]

Copyright's normative structure begins to make much more sense when viewed through this framework. The declaration of "exclusivity" remains the law's abstract interest that it vests in an author. It then treats a copier's interference with that exclusivity as a legal wrong, whereupon it vests the author with a mechanism of redress, or a right of action, against the defendant. However, the promise of exclusivity – copyright's "right" – is little more than a promise of making available to the author an avenue of redress against potential defendants. In this analytical framework then, we begin with the law's directive of exclusivity, which creates an abstract duty of non-interference on all but the author (or those authorized by the author). It is in turn the breach of this duty, the legal wrong, that creates copyright's "right," the real Hohfeldian correlative of which is a duty imposed on the state to enforce its initial promise of exclusivity against the defendant.[69] Until the wrongdoing (i.e., the copying) occurs, a plaintiff's "right" is a mere place-holder for a potential entitlement to commence a legal action. This analytical structure is as true in copyright as it is in property, where to speak of a "right to exclude" obfuscates the reality that the real normative work of the institution originates in what it directs potential defendants to do.[70] And the idea of civil redress provides a plausible account of precisely this framework. In this liability-focused account of copyright then, copyright's true "right" remains its provision of a mechanism of redress to authors against copiers. A defendant's legal wrong, the act of copying, activates the right and renders it fully operational.

What distinguishes copyright from other private law claims, however, is that, unlike elsewhere, the law allows (and actively encourages) a market for the claims themselves, regardless of their stage: unmatured, nascent, or matured.[71] "Choses in action," the term that the common law came to use to denote legal claims, were historically, barring a few limited exceptions, treated as unassignable.[72] The law's principal rationale for this treatment appears to be the fear that such assignments would result in a multiplication of lawsuits.[73] Over time however, this fear was

[67] *See* Goldberg & Zipursky, *supra* note 52, at 931, 937–41.

[68] Zipursky, *Civil Recourse*, *supra* note 63, at 736–37.

[69] *See id.* at 739.

[70] *See* Balganesh, *Right to Exclude*, *supra* note 50 (making this argument in relation to property law more generally).

[71] 17 U.S.C. §201(d) (2005); Statute of Anne, 8 Anne c. 19, § II (1710).

[72] James Barr Ames, *The Inalienability of Choses in Action*, *in* LECTURES ON LEGAL HISTORY 210 (1913); Walter Wheeler Cook, *The Alienability of Choses in Action*, 29 HARV. L. REV. 816 (1916).

[73] This arose in conjunction with the common law's rules against maintenance and champerty, which sought to prevent officious intermeddling in legal disputes. *See* Percy H. Winfield, *Assignment of Choses in Action in Relation to Maintenance and Champerty*, 35 LAW QUART. REV. 143 (1919); Ari Dobner, *Litigation for Sale*, 144 U. PA. L. REV. 1529, 1543 (1996). *See also* Ames, *supra* note

shown to be somewhat misplaced, and the law began to allow some transfers of legal claims. Yet, it did so primarily in relation to matured claims: claims against a specific defendant who had committed some act that triggered an entitlement to sue in the plaintiff. Transfers to insurance companies were paradigmatic of this category.[74] Unmatured claims, in contrast – such as a pedestrian's probabilistic entitlement to bring a tort claim against a negligent driver – remained (and continue to remain) completely inalienable.[75] Nascent claims lie somewhere in between matured and unmatured claims, with the defendant having been identified, but the possibility of the claim coming to fruition still remaining uncertain (e.g., the entitlement to recover a debt). Some jurisdictions, though not all, allow these claims to be transferred. Copyright law breaks with the common law here and allows the right to be alienated at *any* stage – perhaps as a result of the peculiar political compromise that the first copyright statute reflected (between authors and publishers).[76] As long as some part of what constitutes *the copyright* in a work is transferred (i.e., some part of its exclusive rights apparatus), the alienation is treated as perfectly valid.[77] A transfer of copyright before infringement is thus an assignment of an unmatured legal claim, whereas a post-infringement transfer operates as an assignment of a matured claim. None of this, very importantly, alters copyright's basic analytical structure as a mechanism of civil redress, where the right is in reality only ever triggered by a defendant's copying (i.e., wrongdoing).

In summary then, copyright's normative structure originates in its declaration of exclusivity, which in turn operates as a relational directive, on the infraction of which the author can invoke the coercive mechanism of the state. Exclusivity and liability form two sides of the same normative structure and go hand in hand, even though they are often mistakenly analyzed in isolation.

B. *Exclusivity, Responsibility, and Ascription*

The discussion thus far has focused on copyright's directive of exclusivity, which forms the analytical basis for its provision of a mechanism of civil redress to plaintiffs on an unauthorized interference with such exclusivity. Yet, it has not addressed an obvious question: *why exclusivity?* Why, in other words, does copyright law find the need to structure its liability regime around the idea of exclusivity? Answering this

72, at 211 (noting the dominant rationale for the inalienability of choses in action, but concluding that the real reason may have to do with the personal nature of the legal action).

74 *See* Deborah L. Rhode & David Luban, Legal Ethics 698 (3rd ed. 2001).

75 Robert Cooter, *Towards a Market in Unmatured Legal Claims*, 75 Va. L. Rev. 383, 383 (1989).

76 *See* Mark Rose, Authors and Owners: The Invention of Copyright 46 (1995).

77 The exception is obviously an attempt to transfer the bare right to sue, without any of copyright's exclusive rights either in whole of part. The law forbids such transfers. *See* Silvers v. Sony Pictures Entertainment, Inc. 402 F.3d 881 (9th Cir. 2005). For a critique of the *Silvers* case, *see* Shyamkrishna Balganesh, Copyright Infringement Markets, 113 Colum. L. Rev. (forthcoming 2013).

question, in turn necessitates understanding what exactly copyright's directive of exclusivity entails.

A point that is often ignored in discussions of copyright law is that copyright's grant of exclusivity is in essence the exclusive entitlement *to copy*.[78] It is not a grant of open-ended market exclusivity in the nature of a use monopoly, commonly associated with patent law. The standard economic analysis of copyright law takes its focus on copying (within its entitlement structure) to be a largely administrative one.[79] In this analysis, copyright's focus on copying does no more than economize on the administrative costs to the public of having to avoid generating the same expression as that contained in the protected work, especially in situations where the expression in question is so commonplace as to be intuitive, and therefore independently created by multiple individuals.[80] In the process it also avoids wasteful litigation.[81] Copying, in other words, is thought to have no independent normative significance within the structure of copyright law.

Descriptively sound as it may be, this account has two major problems. First, it cannot account for the fact that copyright's examination of "copying" entails a large normative dimension, where a court/jury is often called on to determine if the defendant's copying was "wrongful," measured entirely in terms of the similarity between the works.[82] Second, as a structural matter, it also cannot explain why, if copying is entirely a matter of proof, liability in copyright law should depend on a plaintiff's showing of copying, instead of the entitlement being rendered defeasible by a defendant's showing of no copying or of independent creation.[83]

The failure to appreciate the normative significance of "copying" to copyright law has also had an additional and potentially pernicious effect on copyright thinking, and this is the propertarian turn in copyright jurisprudence.[84] Exclusivity, deriving from the idea of exclusion, is thought to represent copyright law's normative commitment to the institution of property – or the idea that it converts one's expression into a form of "literary property."[85] Consequently, the answer to the question of why copyright law is structured in terms of a directive of exclusivity is thought to derive from the straightforward fact that copyright creates a form of property. In essence, this argument relies on what is best described as a form of "property essentialism" – or the belief that describing the entitlement as a property interest is both non-ideological

78 *See* Shyamkrishna Balganesh, *The Normativity of Copying in Copyright Law*, 62 DUKE L.J. 203 (2012).
79 Landes & Posner, *supra* note 21, at 344–47.
80 *Id.*
81 *Id.* at 346 n.30.
82 *See, e.g.*, Arnstein v. Porter, 154 F.2d 464, 468 (2d Cir. 1946).
83 4 MELVILLE B. NIMMER & DAVID NIMMER, NIMMER ON COPYRIGHT §13.01[B] (2010).
84 *See* Shyamkrishna Balganesh, *Debunking Blackstonian Copyright*, 118 YALE L.J. 1126 (2009).
85 For discussions of the idea of "literary property" and its evolution in copyright history, *see* Jane C. Ginsburg, *A Tale of Two Copyrights: Literary Property in Revolutionary France and America*, 64 TUL. L. REV. 991 (1990); Justin Hughes, *Copyright and Incomplete Historiographies: Of Piracy, Propertization, and Thomas Jefferson*, 79 S. CAL. L. REV. 993, 1021 (2006).

and does not necessitate an independent justification.[86] Yet, if one begins from the understanding that the idea of property in copyright law is at best a metaphor, and at worst a misleading trope, the normative basis for the "exclusive entitlement to copy" as the central idea behind copyright's directive must be found elsewhere.

The answer might instead lie in the idea of authorship and its connection to outcome responsibility. The idea of outcome responsibility, made famous by Tony Honoré, posits that we live in a system of community norms where actions and outcomes are assigned to individuals on a causal basis to effectuate the recognition that they are indeed independent moral agents.[87] "[A]ctions and outcomes," according to Honoré, are assigned to individuals based on their bodily movements and mental accompaniments, to give them "continuing history or character," without which they would cease to have any identity as people.[88] To Honoré, life consists of a series of bets – some with positive outcomes and some with negative ones – forcing the individual to face the consequences of his or her choices.[89] "Responsibility" is thus the identification of an individual as causally responsible for a particular outcome. It is important to note that the idea of responsibility, as used by Honoré, is not a legal one.[90] In other words, the notion of outcome responsibility and the assignment of outcomes that he posits is entirely a feature of social morality rather than the law – and his argument then turns to how tort law (strict liability specifically) builds on that premise of social morality. Consequently, the underlying premise of his theory need not be restricted to his defense of strict liability or indeed tort law at all, but could instead be extended to other domains – or, more specifically, to the idea of assigning individuals positive outcomes rather than negative ones.[91]

The roots of Honoré's idea can be traced back to H. L. A. Hart's idea of "ascription" as a way of understanding the mechanisms by which actions and outcomes are in ordinary usage (and in the law) attributed to individuals.[92] Very interestingly, property formed the paradigm example for Hart, and the idea that "object *o* belongs to A" was to him a mechanism of *ascribing* the object to the person, even though at times it was used as a descriptive statement of fact.[93] Hart sought to differentiate ascription from the process of description, in that the former was an inherently normative exercise, performative in nature and directed at bringing about certain consequences, whereas the latter was outcome-neutral.[94]

86 Balganesh, *Blackstonian Copyright*, *supra* note 84, at 1133; Hanoch Dagan, *The Distributive Foundation of Corrective Justice*, 98 MICH. L. REV. 138, 150 (1999).
87 TONY HONORÉ, RESPONSIBILITY AND LUCK 26 (1999).
88 *Id.* at 29.
89 *Id.* at 24–26.
90 *Id.* at 27.
91 Indeed, Honoré himself extends the idea to fault-based liability as well. *See id.* at 29.
92 H. L. A. Hart, *The Ascription of Responsibility and Rights*, *in* 49 PROCS. ARISTOTELIAN SOC.: NEW SERIES 171 (1949).
93 *Id.* at 171.
94 *Id.* at 185–87.

The idea of outcome responsibility provides us with a plausible account of copyright's structure as an exclusive entitlement to copy original expression. "Expression" is by its very nature both an action and an intangible (notional) object – both originating in the idea of speech. Allowing expression to be assigned and attributed to individuals who originate it is thus an ascriptive exercise and one that is at least partially integral to recognizing such individuals as independent moral agents. Copyright is, in this understanding then, a simple mechanism of causation. The conceptual inseparability of the act of *expressing* oneself and the notional product of that act, the *expression*, lends itself to a situation where ascribing the latter to an individual (as author) is crucial to affirming the agency of that individual in acting to bring it into existence. Conversely, a failure to adequately ascribe expression (via the idea of authorship) to an individual might be viewed as a denial of an individual's moral agency as represented in the act of expressing oneself. It is perhaps in recognition of this failure that the law associates a directive of exclusivity with expression that is causally attributable to an individual. The act of copying in this construction thus amounts to a denial of the author's expressive activity and thereby his or her moral agency, which the law in turn seeks to avoid through its directive of exclusivity.[95]

This ascriptive account of exclusivity in copyright law may, on the face of things, come across as an oversimplification and appear to disregard a host of nuanced distinctions that copyright law and policy traditionally make. Yet, it can be shown to account for several of these nuances as well. One of these is the distinction between copying and plagiarism, which copyright law is agnostic to – the latter involves the use of another's expression without attributing its origins to him or her, whereas the former need not involve such misattribution. If we view the act of copying (unauthorized publication, but without misattribution) as being in itself an act of communicating another's expression to the public – that is, as an act of speech – then the same ascriptive logic seems to hold true to blur this distinction. Indeed, a variant of this argument is to be seen in a little known essay by Kant, where he views the act of publication (publishing) as involving the communication of another's speech to the public through an agent (the publisher).[96] An unauthorized publication (i.e., copying) seems to be problematic to Kant, because among other things, it interferes with the author's ability to dictate both what to say to the public and through whom it is to be said.[97]

The ascriptive story can also account for the possibility of overlapping expression.[98] Indeed, one may argue that it is precisely because ascription is about expression

[95] For a related, yet distinct, attempt to understand copyright law in terms of speech-acts *see* Abraham Drassinower, *A Rights-Based View of the Idea/Expression Dichotomy in Copyright Law*, 16 CAN. J.L. & JURIS. 3 (2003).

[96] Immanuel Kant, *On the Wrongfulness of Unauthorized Publication of Books* (1785), *in* PRACTICAL PHILOSOPHY 23, 34 (Mary J. Gregor trans. & ed. 1999).

[97] *Id.* at 34–35.

[98] *See also* Drassinower, *supra* note 95, at 10.

originating in an individual author that copyright law has always recognized and permitted a defense of independent creation. In viewing independent creation as a defense, however, what is often missed is the fact that independent creation also allows a putative defendant (i.e., the independent creator) to assert the same exclusive entitlement to copy that the plaintiff does. In other words, the defendant's work is eligible to obtain copyright protection through the framework of exclusivity, just as the former's is.

In sum then, the ascriptive account grounds copyright's grant of exclusivity in a theory about causation and in being responsible for speech as individual moral agents in society. Exclusivity in copying is crucial to realizing this measure of outcome responsibility, and infractions of it operate as interferences with the ascription of agency to actors, rendering it wrongful and worthy of redress by the legal system. This provides a plausible account for why copyright law structures its private-law–based liability regime around the idea of the "exclusive right to copy" by treating infractions with this exclusivity as a legal wrong and allowing the invocation of the state's coercive machinery to redress it. It also goes some distance in explaining why copyright law is in the end a private law mechanism: for it is only by investing in the original speaker (i.e., the author) the unilateral power to eliminate an impediment to moral agency (manifested in exclusivity) through a mechanism of redress that the law exhibits its commitment to agency at both the substantive and structural levels. Thus, to have a public-law-based enforcement mechanism for such infractions would amount to the state indirectly (through such enforcement) ascribing to some authors expression potentially even in situations where the authors (speakers) have no desire to be so assigned the responsibility for the expression. Leaving the discretion to commence an action with the author helps realize the idea of individual agency and responsibility at two independent levels.

The ascriptive account also reveals how it is easy to confuse the idea of exclusivity with property/ownership. Indeed, Hart's original example to illustrate the idea of ascription was the institution of property and the oft-noted conflation of its descriptive and ascriptive strands.[99] The statement that "this is O's" can either be a descriptive statement of ownership, which in the absence of a reason for the ownership relies on essentialist logic; or it can be an ascriptive statement of responsibility, which, although nonetheless normative, derives its support from the ideas of moral agency and responsibility rather than ownership. Yet, because they both entail "control" in some measure, they tend to be routinely conflated in copyright thinking.

C. *Incentives Redux*

The ascriptive/outcome-responsibility–based account of copyright's emphasis on exclusivity in expression operates principally in nonconsequentialist terms. At the

99 Hart, *supra* note 92, at 183–87.

same time, however, it can be reinforced by a purely consequentialist account. At the end of his elaborate discussion of outcome responsibility as the moral basis of strict liability in tort law, Honoré pauses to note that "responsibility" as such does not imply that the law needs to step in with a liability (or in our context – an entitlement) regime; he also observes that some "extra element" is necessary to "ground the legal sanction" – such as "fault" or the "special risk of harm" – and that such grounding that may come about for purely consequentialist (i.e., social policy) reasons.[100] In such situations the consequentialist and nonconsquentialist accounts serve to "reinforce" each other – with the former building on the structure entailed by the latter.[101]

Honoré's additional elements for strict liability, however, seem to remain exogenous considerations that operate largely in deterrent terms. Society's belief that an "uncooperative disposition" needs to be deterred, or that taking a "special risk of harm" needs to be accompanied by a more careful consideration of its consequences, are measures of social policy that the law adds onto the idea of outcome responsibility to create a regime of strict liability.[102] Outcome responsibility thus forms the fundamental, yet incomplete normative basis of liability, with secondary (or "additional") elements derived from social policy adding to it at a functional level.

The question for us is whether a similar framework can be constructed for copyright's commitment to outcome responsibility or ascription that also finds a role for the incentives account. If we begin with the understanding that copyright law's inner normative core originates in the need for exclusivity in copying in order to ensure that the ascription of speech (and its consequences) to a speaker remains unhindered, the next question is why such exclusivity and interferences with it need to be rendered actionable through the mechanics of a liability regime. One obvious explanation, internal to the outcome responsibility account, is that private law, which delegates to the speaker (i.e., author) the decision of when the ascriptive process is being impeded, is the best way of operationalizing the ideal of outcome responsibility. Yet an equally valid consequentialist explanation may be advanced for this structure as well. And here we return to the incentives account.

Speech and expression, as Neil Netanel has persuasively pointed out, serve important structural purposes in a democratic society, such that it is legitimate to presume that, as a matter of democratic social policy, a state is committed to encouraging expressive behavior and conduct of various kinds.[103] This expression extends beyond obviously political speech. If we view this policy goal – of encouraging speech – together with the ascriptive ideal that derives from a commitment to outcome responsibility, we begin to see the semblance of a normative account for copyright

[100] Honoré, *supra* note 87, at 27–28.
[101] *Id.* at 28.
[102] *Id.* at 27.
[103] Neil Weinstock Netanel, Copyright's Paradox 84–88 (2008).

law that is at once both consequentialist and nonconsequentialist. The mechanics of liability in copyright law allow for the ascription of expression and its consequences to individual actors through a directive of exclusivity, which also serves as an added incentive for the very production of such expression/speech. Now the key point to bear in mind, however, is that the consequentialist account (i.e., encouraging speech) enters the structure of the institution only after the lexically prior ideal – of ascription.[104] This explains why, even when the incentives argument is conceded to remain normatively desirable, economists (and copyright scholars more generally) are hard placed to explain why the institution's core apparatus does not seem to be directed entirely (if at all!) at realizing this normative goal.[105] The answer is simply the lexical and structural priority of ascription and outcome responsibility over inducement.

A close analogy is to be seen in what some call the "mixed" approach to tort law, which seeks to affirm both rights-based (normally corrective justice driven) and utilitarian/deterrence ideals as legitimate normative goals.[106] A persuasive argument for such an accommodation is to be found in a mechanism of normative reasoning known as "conceptual sequencing."[107] In this method, the individual components of an institution are analyzed to reveal a core commitment to a certain normative ideal at the granular level, while the system as a whole in practice serves the additional purpose of realizing another, seemingly incommensurable goal.[108] Conceptual sequencing, as a method of reasoning, can indeed even be found in the work of Kant, where he seeks to accommodate concerns for a defendant's rights with criminal law's overall commitment to deterrence.[109] The logic of conceptual sequencing can thus accommodate two independent (and incommensurable) normative goals for an institution – one at the structural level and the other at the functional level.

The obvious problem with this set-up occurs in situations where the two normative ideals point in different directions. In such situations, the overwhelming tendency among courts has been to treat the incentives account as copyright's "true normative" ideal and its rights structure as either contingent or, at best, lexically inferior. The Court's previously quoted observation in *Harper & Row* is telling, where it notes that

104 I rely on Jody Kraus's "vertical integration strategy" here as a mechanism to explain copyright's reconciliation of consequentialist and nonconsequentialist values. *See* Jody S. Kraus, *Reconciling Autonomy and Efficiency in Contract Law: The Vertical Integration Strategy*, 11 PHIL. ISS. 420, 422–26 (2001).

105 *See, e.g.*, Stewart E. Sterk, *Rhetoric and Reality in Copyright Law*, 94 MICH. L. REV. 1197 (1996).

106 Gary T. Schwartz, *Mixed Theories of Tort Law: Affirming Both Deterrence and Corrective Justice*, 75 TEX. L. REV. 1801 (1997); Ernest J. Weinrib, *Deterrence and Corrective Justice*, 50 UCLA L. REV. 621 (2002).

107 Weinrib, *Deterrence, supra* note 106, at 629; Bruce Chapman, *Pluralism in Tort and Accident Law: Toward a Reasonable Accommodation, in* PHILOSOPHY AND THE LAW OF TORTS 276 (Gerald J. Postema ed., 2001).

108 *Id.*

109 Immanuel Kant, *The Metaphysics of Morals* (1797), *in* PRACTICAL PHILOSOPHY 353, 391 (Mary J. Gregor trans. & ed., 1996).

"[b]y establishing a marketable right to the use of one's expression, copyright supplies the economic incentive to create and disseminate ideas."[110] As we noted, after making this observation, the Court immediately proceeded to decide the case on a questionable theory of economic incentives, without saying anything at all about the "right" that it acknowledged to be analytically central to its account.[111] In the account sketched here, the content of that right and indeed the nonconsequentialist reasons for it assume major (even if not singular) significance in the analysis.

III. CONCLUSION: IMPLICATIONS FOR COPYRIGHT ANALYSES

"The purpose of copyright is to create incentives for creative effort."[112] The analytical structure of this observation is of course hardly inaccurate, yet it remains grossly incomplete. It is the equivalent of saying that "the purpose of tort law is to deter wrongs." Both statements gloss over *how* the law attempts to realize this deterrence/incentive effect, *why* it chooses to do so, and additionally *why* it chooses to do so in a very particular way that derives from the kind of activity (i.e., "creative effort" or "wrong") that it is seeking to regulate. In this chapter, I have sought to provide an outline of what an account of copyright law that is at once both sensitive to its underlying private-law–based structural apparatus and its instrumental goals might look like.

In the account offered here, copyright's normative structure can be seen as affirming both the purposes of inducing the creation of original expression and the ideal of expressive ascription/moral agency – or outcome responsibility. Admittedly, it does not tell us how individual cases have to be decided, but at the very least it points to four important lessons that future analyses of copyright law ought to take seriously: (i) that the institution's substructure of an "exclusive right to copy" can be understood in normative, nonconsequentialist terms; (ii) that the incompleteness of the incentives account of copyright law is not an *inadequacy* of the particular incentives theory, but is instead a reality of copyright's unique normative structure and the plurality of normative goals that inform it; (iii) that copyright decision making should remain sensitive to this plurality and the possibility that a nonconsequentalist purpose may be lexically prior to its consequentialist goals as a normative ideal; and perhaps most importantly (iv) that adopting a nonconsequentialist structural explanation for the institution need not render the incentives argument redundant or ineffective – merely constitutively incomplete.

[110] *Harper & Row*, 471 U.S. at 558.
[111] *Id.* at 559.
[112] Sony Corp. of Amer. v. Universal City Studios, Inc., 464 U.S. 417, 450 (1984).

15

Trade Secret and Human Freedom

*Madhavi Sunder**

"[N]ot so very long ago there used to be thousands of people working in Mr. Willy Wonka's factory. Then one day, all of a sudden, Mr. Wonka had to ask every single one of them to leave, to go home, never to come back."

"But why"? asked Charlie.

"Because of spies."

– *Roald Dahl*, Charlie and the Chocolate Factory[1]

Employers can go to extremes to protect their trade secrets. Roald Dahl's fictional chocolate maker Willy Wonka was so distrustful of human employees that he fired them all, opting instead to power his factory with subhuman slaves called "Oompa Loompas." The Oompa Loompas were not free laborers but glorified prisoners. In Wonka's chocolate factory, "[t]he gates are locked" and "[n]obody ever comes out!"[2] Stories of overprotective, indeed inhumane, employers going to great lengths to protect their trade secrets are legion. Legend has it that the Moghul emperor Shah Jahan who commissioned the construction of the Taj Mahal ordered the architect's hands chopped off after the monument was completed. Though likely a myth, the story's powerful hold on the imagination stems from the real worry that employers, left to their own devices, will protect economically valuable trade secrets in ways that may violate employees' freedom. As the old English court in the classic eighteenth-century case of *Mitchell* v. *Reynolds* stated, covenants

* Professor of Law, University of California, Davis. Thanks to all of the participants in the Intellectual Property and the Common Law symposium held at the University of Pennsylvania Law School on May 6–7, 2011, and especially to convener and editor extraordinaire, Shyam Balganesh, for insightful comments.

1 Roald Dahl, Charlie and the Chocolate Factory 15 (1964). For an engaging peek into real-life industrial espionage and trade secrecy in the global chocolate industry see Jeanne C. Fromer, *Trade Secrecy in Willy Wonka's Chocolate Factory*, *in* The Law and Theory of Trade Secrecy 3, 9–11 (Rochelle C. Dreyfuss & Katherine J. Strandburg, eds. 2011).

2 Dahl, *supra* note 1, at 17.

not to compete in the employment context are subject to "great abuses . . . from masters."[3]

This chapter considers the role of trade secret law in protecting employee freedom. The dominant legal literature on trade secret rationalizes this law as promoting innovation and the efficient disclosure of information. But this dominant vision of trade secret law's normative contours is incomplete. Although trade secret is a tool for incentivizing the production of valuable information and efficient disclosure, it is also more than that. Trade secret law regulates *social relations between employers and employees*. This is the law of nondisclosure agreements and implied duties on employees not to reveal working knowledge learned and developed on the job. In short, trade secret law implicates fundamental human freedoms, namely the freedom to move, to work, to compete, and to think. In this chapter, I question the narrow law-and-economic analysis of trade secret and call for complementing that understanding with a pluralist view that sees trade secret law as implicating multiple values, including efficiency but also freedom. As my review of intra- and interdisciplinary scholarship on trade secret law reveals, trade secret implicates fundamental values, from freedom to democracy to dignity.

The pluralist account of trade secret developed here resists the move to recast a freedom-based analysis in efficiency terms. This is not to say that freedom and efficiency are not related. Modern-day Silicon Valley illustrates the important connection between these two values. Recent studies suggest that the success of Silicon Valley as compared to high-tech areas in other states is related to California's refusal to recognize employee agreements not to compete.[4] Alan Hyde credits California's law and culture for Silicon Valley's rise as a premier center for innovation and economic growth; both frown on prohibitions on employee mobility and have led to a "high velocity labor market."[5]

However, in this chapter I go further, arguing that employee freedom is valuable in its own right. Part I considers the vision of trade secret law offered by contemporary law and economic scholars. Scholars such as Richard Posner and, more recently,

[3] Mitchell v. Reynolds, 1 P. Wms. 181, 190, 24 Eng. Rep. 347, 350 (Q.B. 1711).

[4] *See* Edwards v. Arthur Andersen, LLP, 8 Cal.Rptr. 3d 282, 290 (Cal. 2008) (holding that noncompetition agreements are invalid in California under Section 16600, even if narrowly drawn, unless they fall within applicable statutory exceptions). *See generally* Mark A. Lemley & James H.A. Pooley, *California Restrictive Employment Covenants After* Edwards, 23 CAL. LAB. & EMP. L. REV. 3 (2009).

[5] Alan Hyde, *The Wealth of Shared Information: Silicon Valley's High-Velocity Labor Market, Endogenous Economic Growth, and the Law of Trade Secrets* (1998), *available at* http://andromeda.rutgers.edu/~hyde/WEALTH.htm. *See also* ANNALEE SAXENIAN, REGIONAL ADVANTAGE: CULTURE AND COMPETITION IN SILICON VALLEY AND ROUTE 128 (1994) (comparing Silicon Valley and the Route 128 high-tech region in Massachusetts); Ronald J. Gilson, *The Legal Infrastructure of High Technology Industrial Districts: Silicon Valley, Route 128, and Covenants Not to Compete*, 74 N.Y.U. L. REV. 575 (1999). *See generally* Matt Marx et al., *Noncompetes and Inventor Mobility: Specialists, Stars, and the Michigan Experiment* (2007), *available at* http://www.hbs.edu/research/pdf/07-042.pdf (finding notable decrease in innovation of Michigan technology companies after state courts began enforcing noncompete agreements in 1985).

Mark Lemley understand trade secret law as promoting two values: innovation and efficient disclosure of information. For the purposes of this chapter, I am particularly interested in Lemley's recent theorization of trade secret law published in 2008 in the *Stanford Law Review*.[6] There, Lemley characterizes these two goals – promoting innovation and efficient disclosure of information – as the foundations that constitute modern intellectual property (IP) rights. Lemley supports modern trade secret law to the extent that the law promotes these two goals. But he is skeptical of and uncomfortable with a trade secret law that does more, and he specifically associates a broader trade secret law with the common law, which is typically concerned with plural values, from fairness to commercial morality. Lemley's arguments have important implications for our consideration of IP and the common law.

First, I consider how a dichotomous view of IP and the common law as distinct legal frameworks may lead to a dangerous IP exceptionalism, obscuring the plural values at stake in all intellectual property conflicts. For all of its uniqueness, IP law is also in large part *common* law, teeming with plural values.

My second concern is that in the quest to reimagine trade secret law as in line with other forms of intellectual property, such as patents and copyrights, we may lose sight of what makes trade secret special. In Part II, I turn to recent work of contemporary labor law scholars, Catherine Fisk and Katherine Stone, and also to the political theorist Kim Lane Scheppele, who provide valuable insights into the broader social, cultural, economic, and political effects of trade secret law on American innovation, free labor, and democratic society more broadly. The chapter concludes that modern trade secret law ought to take into account the plural values at stake in the legal regulation of workplace knowledge, which range from the central role of free labor in a democratic society, to new understandings of employment as the development of human capital, to basic human rights, such as the freedom of movement. To repeat, my central argument is not that the dominant law-and-economics account of trade secret law is false, but that it is incomplete and can be usefully supplemented by sociolegal accounts of workplace knowledge regulation.

I. TRADE SECRET AS INCENTIVES TO INNOVATE AND DISCLOSE INFORMATION

Contemporary American trade secret law, exemplified by the Uniform Trade Secrets Act (UTSA), which has been adopted by all but a handful of states, defines a trade secret broadly as any information that derives economic value from being a secret and that is the subject of reasonable efforts to maintain its secrecy.[7] Many kinds of information can qualify under this definition, from customer lists to pricing information to formulas, recipes, design plans, and even the management structure

[6] Mark Lemley, *The Surprising Virtues of Treating Trade Secrets as IP Rights*, 61 STAN. L. REV. 311 (2008).

[7] Unif. Trade Secrets Act, § 1(4), 14 U.L.A. 437, 438 (1985).

of an enterprise. Absolute secrecy is not required for trade secret protection; modern corporations routinely share information with their employees and business partners, without losing legal rights over their trade secrets. The crucial requirements are that, to be protected, the information must not be generally known in the industry and the employer must take reasonable precautions to prevent disclosure of the secret. Typically this requirement is satisfied by showing that the employer required employees to sign nondisclosure agreements, regulated employee access to the secret information, and/or kept the information under lock and key. This requirement prevents any legal remedy for negligent employers who leave their secrets lying around for all to see. Furthermore, the requirement serves as further evidence that the employer really did believe the information was secret and that the defendant likely obtained the information wrongfully.

Having a protectable secret is only half the game under the UTSA. A trade secret is only infringed if the defendant wrongly acquired the information, either by breaching a confidential relationship with the plaintiff (such as the employer/employee relationship), or by acquiring the information through "improper means" or deviousness. Trade secret law does not impose liability for secret information if that information is obtained by *proper* means. It allows competitors to obtain a rival's secret trade information by independent discovery or by reverse engineering. Trade secret law also does not protect information that can be readily ascertained by sight or taste. It only provides a legal remedy against persons who obtain another's trade secrets by a breach of confidence (typically departing employee cases) or some other "improper means." Although the latter category often covers actions prohibited by independent laws, such as trespass or theft, this is not a requirement. In the famous textbook case, *E.I. duPont de Nemours & Co.* v. *Christopher*,[8] for example, the Christopher brothers had been paid by an unknown competitor to fly over a DuPont chemical plant while it was under construction to take aerial photos of its interior. Although the Christophers violated neither trespass nor criminal laws, the court nonetheless found them liable under trade secret law, holding that the law protects against the loss of valuable secrets by trickery.[9]

Trade secret cases typically involve one of three scenarios: (i) allegations of theft between competitors (such as the *DuPont* case), (ii) breach of confidential relations during business transactions, and (iii) departing employees who seek to take with them secret information generated or obtained during the course of their employment. Each of these cases implicates different values and common law doctrines. Notwithstanding the fact that modern trade secret law is based on a uniform statute, the UTSA, the law's roots are undisputedly in the common law. Common law principles continue to drive courts' trade secret analyses. Cases involving competitors, such as the *DuPont* case, resound in tort and unfair competition, establishing rights

[8] E.I. duPont de Nemours & Co. v. Christopher, 431 F.2d 1012 (5th Cir. 1970).

[9] *Id.* at 1015.

and duties among strangers, as well as norms of commercial morality. The breach of confidential relations cases involve parties in some sort of relationship – either a business relationship or an employment relationship – and thus sound in contract law, including both express agreements and implied duties between parties. Trade secret law is thus in various parts contract, property, tort, and even criminal law.

The law's mongrel origins themselves suggest that trade secret law is about many things – from freedom of contract, to implied duties, rights to exclude, incentives, morality, and fault. Shyam Balganesh, calling trade secret law "perhaps the most robust common law intellectual property form today,"[10] observes that "[i]n the process, it endorses multiple values: incentives, allocative efficiency, autonomy, commercial morality, corrective justice, and other distributive goals."[11]

Until recently, trade secret's common law roots were not considered a problem. One of trade secret law's prominent critics, Robert Bone, has not argued against the plural purposes of the law. Bone argues instead that the common law doctrines underlying the law already do so much that an additional claim called "trade secret" is redundant.[12] In a seminal 1991 paper titled "Some Economics of Trade Secret Law," David Friedman, William Landes, and Richard Posner acknowledge the diverse common law roots of American trade secret law, but survey the case law and doctrine to conclude that the common law of trade secrets bends toward a single value: efficiency.[13] Posner et al. argue that trade secret protection facilitates two goals: legal protection incentivizes innovation and facilitates efficient disclosure of information. Because patents involve high fixed costs (including lengthy and expensive examination processes and litigation costs), trade secret protection is more efficient for companies with valuable and novel information that nevertheless may not yield results sufficient enough to justify the high costs of patent protection. In these cases, the authors argue trade secret law offers a cheaper incentive to invent and invest in valuable and novel information.[14]

Posner et al. also argue that trade *secret* law is, counterintuitively, a tool for incentivizing companies to *disclose* information to others. Consider, for example, the *DuPont* case mentioned earlier. Without legal protection against the "school boy's trick" of aerial photography, DuPont would have had to spend exorbitant amounts

[10] Shyamkrishna Balganesh, *The Pragmatic Incrementalism of Common Law Intellectual Property*, 63 VAND. L. REV. 1543, 1553 (2010).

[11] *Id.* at 1576. *See also* Robert Denicola, *The Restatements, the Uniform Act and the Status of American Trade Secret Law, in* THE LAW AND THEORY OF TRADE SECRECY 18, 44 (Rochelle C. Dreyfuss & Katherine J. Strandburg, eds. 2011) ("Trade secret law is now largely statutory law, but despite the widespread adoption of the Uniform Trade Secrets Act, the subject retains the basic character of its common law roots.").

[12] *See* Robert G. Bone, *A New Look at Trade Secret Law: Doctrine in Search of Justification*, 86 CALIF. L. REV. 241, 243–45 (1998).

[13] David D. Friedman, William M. Landes, & Richard Posner, *Some Economics of Trade Secret Law*, J. ECON. PERSPECTIVES 62 (Winter 1991) ("[A]s in a number of other areas of common law, the common law approach to trade secrets appears to make good . . . economic sense.").

[14] *Id.* at 63.

of money to cover its roof during its renovation. In such cases trade secret law steps in, the authors argue, to avoid "the most costly means of unmasking commercial secrets."[15] Trade secret law discourages companies from overinvesting in secrecy and in "defensive maneuvers" that may be inefficient. Without legal protection of trade secrets, Posner et al. worry that companies may "reorganize their businesses in inefficient forms – perhaps by splitting up tasks among more employees so that each knows less, or by bringing in family members (even though they may be less competent) as employees, counting on them to be loyal out of altruism or because the family setting often enables effective, informal retaliation against the disloyal."[16] They conclude that, where normally secrecy imposes social costs, particularly on competition, the benefits of allowing for more efficient organization within the corporation outweigh those social costs and justify the current law.

More recently, Mark Lemley has extended the argument, arguing that a "surprising virtue" of trade secret law is that, in protecting secrecy, the law facilitates the disclosure of information. Lemley, too, makes the point that legal protection of trade secrets discourages employers from overinvesting in secrecy. Rather than expending great sums to conceal information, not licensing information to parties who could more efficiently use it, or employing only loyal family members rather than those most qualified for the job, legal protection of trade secrets that corporations make reasonable efforts to protect gives those corporations the confidence they need to share information more widely.[17] Additionally, Lemley agrees that trade secret law incentivizes the development of valuable technology and information, especially in cases where patent protection is too expensive. In short, both Posner and Lemley envision trade secret law as fundamentally focused on efficiency. Furthermore, in their view, trade secrets are more like than unlike traditional forms of intellectual property. Like patents and copyrights, trade secrets promote investment in valuable information and efficient disclosure of that information to others.[18]

I do not disagree with these descriptions of some of the virtues of trade secret law. Surely, legal protection of trade secrets encourages employers to share their information with employees and potential business partners, and to hire the best qualified employees. The question I explore here is whether this view is too limited and ultimately obscures many other values at stake in this law.

Furthermore, I consider the relationship between the common law and plural values. Notably, where Posner et al. did not reject the common law – they sought to rationalize it as promoting a single value, efficiency – Lemley is much more skeptical of the common law in the context of trade secret law and, presumably,

15 *Id.* at 67.

16 *Id.*

17 *See* Lemley, *supra* note 6, at 313.

18 *See id.* at 326 ("We grant rights over secret information for the same reason we grant rights in patent and copyright law – to encourage investment in the research and development that produces the information.").

with respect to modern IP law generally. Indeed, Lemley's project seems to be to *distinguish* the common law of trade secret from what he conceives as the specialized law of *intellectual property*. He characterizes two, in his view competing, rationales for modern trade secret law. The first view, what he calls an "intellectual property" approach, understands trade secret law as a tool for innovation and disclosure, and no more. According to Lemley, "the basic purpose of IP laws"[19] is to "promote inventive activity and [to] promote disclosure of those inventions."[20] He spends much of his article elaborating how trade secret accomplishes both of these goals and is deserving of a space in the intellectual property canon.

Lemley identifies a second view, the tort approach, which focuses not on incentivizing or protecting information, but rather on prohibiting "bad actors" from misappropriating or wrongly acquiring or using information. While acknowledging the strong influence of the tort approach and related common law doctrines of "commercial morality," "unjust enrichment," and "unfair competition" on the law of trade secret, Lemley repudiates these approaches as "ultimately empty"[21] and suggests that they should be abandoned in favor of his intellectual property approach. Lemley calls the torts approach vague and unpredictable; courts provide little guidance for what they find to be moral or immoral behavior.[22] The flexibility of the common law to respond to new forms of corporate espionage and trickery also proves to be its Achilles heel.

Here, Lemley's argument is more normative than descriptive. He suggests that, although common law courts are equally concerned about efficiency and morality, incentives and fairness, courts analyzing *intellectual property* law should not be. Under that approach, IP rights are defined as Not Common Law. IP law is modern; common law is the *ancien régime*. Intellectual property is a creature of rational legislative rulemaking tailored to promoting certain policy ends; the common law is irrational, unruly, and focused on mushy concepts such as morality and ethics. Where Bone says we should scrap trade secret but keep the common law, Lemley argues we should scrap the common law but keep trade secret.

To be fair, Lemley's goal of rearticulating trade secret law in this narrow way is to cabin the law, limiting its application in ways that could ultimately prove beneficial for departing employees. Lemley is particularly wary of common law "unfair competition" claims, which are open-ended and could potentially discourage employees from starting out on their own. An IP theory of trade secrets would "preempt 'unjust enrichment' theories and other common law ways courts are tempted to give private parties legal control over information in the public domain,"

[19] *Id.* at 329.

[20] *Id.*

[21] *Id.* at 321; *id.* at 327 (arguing that the tort-based theory of trade secret is rife with "defects").

[22] *Id.* (expressing the concern that the tort-based approach "is context and time dependent; normal behavior in one industry may end up being illegal in another. Those norms may change over time in ways that make protection unpredictable.").

Lemley writes. In this way, trade secret law would focus on preempting overreaching by employers and corporations that own secrets. "As a result, the unified trade secret approach does not expand, but rather cabins, the overbroad reach of the common law."[23] Lemley is also critical of courts' preoccupation with bad actions while failing to inquire into whether there is even a protectable secret in the first place.[24]

These concerns are understandable. Nevertheless, there are some problems with the argument. First, a dichotomous view that presents the common law as the opposite of intellectual property is simply not true as a descriptive matter. For better or for worse, trade secret law was not only born of common law doctrines but is infused through and through with the plural concerns of the common law. As Justice Holmes wrote in *The Common Law*, "The law of torts abounds in moral phraseology. It has much to say of wrongs, of malice, fraud, intent, and negligence."[25] So, too, does trade secret law focus not only on promoting efficient firms but also on legally structuring social relations built on values of sharing and trust. As the political theorist Kim Scheppele demonstrated in her 1988 book, *Legal Secrets*,[26] the economic analysis of trade secret law overemphasizes efficiency at the expense of the other values also at stake in the case law. After studying hundreds of trade secret cases, Scheppele concludes that they are driven far less by efficiency concerns than they are by concerns about preserving the sanctity of confidential *relationships*. Scheppele concludes that "the presence of a confidential relationship can be said to be at the heart of the protection of trade secrets."[27] The law does not protect trade secrets per se: recall that accidental release of the information, independent discovery, and reverse engineering do not raise any liability under trade secret law. Justice Holmes has gone so far as to say in *DuPont de Nemours Powder Co.* v. *Masland*, "The property may be denied but the confidence cannot be. Therefore, the starting point for the present matter is not property or due process of law, but that the defendant stood in confidential relations with the plaintiffs, or one of them."[28] State courts have articulated the same concerns. "California does not treat trade secrets as if they were property," the federal Court of Appeals for the Ninth Circuit opined in *Monolith Portland Midwest Co.* v. *Kaiser Aluminum and Chemical Corp.* "It is the relationship between the parties at the time the secret is disclosed that is protected."[29] As Scheppele concludes, "The common law does not use trade secrecy to protect investment; it does prevent abuse of relationships of trust or particularly

[23] *Id.* at 314.

[24] *Id.* at 342 ("[A] number of cases and commentators that have applied the tort theory of trade secrecy have minimized or even ignored [the secrecy] requirement.").

[25] Oliver Wendell Holmes, Jr., The Common Law 79 (1881).

[26] Kim Lane Scheppele, Legal Secrets: Equality and Efficiency in the Common Law (1988).

[27] *Id.* at 240.

[28] DuPont de Nemours Powder Co. v. Masland, 244 U.S. 100, 102 (1917). *See* Scheppele, *supra* note 26, at 240–41.

[29] Monolith Portland Midwest Co. v. Kaiser Aluminum and Chemical Corp., 407 F. 2d 288, 293 (9th Cir. 1969).

inappropriate prying. . . . What the law seems to protect is relationships of trust in and of themselves."[30]

In the quest to modernize trade secret and recast it as just like copyright and patent, we may be giving away too much of what is special about trade secret law. Trade secret law regulates relations between employers and employees. This is the law of nondisclosure agreements, nonsolicitation agreements, and implied duties on employers not to unreasonably limit employee mobility and freedom. Focusing just on incentives for employers to invest in valuable knowledge and its disclosure obscures the broader effects of the law not only on employment relationships but also on individual freedom, the economy, and democratic society writ large. In the next section, I turn to recent work by labor law scholars to elaborate these connections and to urge IP lawyers and scholars to consider them in explaining and evaluating trade secret law.

One obvious implication of Lemley's argument is that modern IP law, limited to promoting innovation and disclosure, should be devoid of concerns about morality and ethics, fairness and fair play. Lemley notes favorably that "one study found no evidence that courts actually took ethics into account in rendering their trade secret decisions."[31] Like Lemley, I am concerned about vague definitions of "morality" as a means of avoiding "deviousness." But I am also wary of an IP law that would ignore morality or values such as fairness altogether. The concern is particularly acute in the context of employer/employee relations, which as courts have noted, is rife with unequal bargaining power between parties and has social, economic, and political implications far beyond the individual parties themselves. The argument for IP exceptionalism and minimalism is one that many, even those who do not adopt a broad, pluralist view of intellectual property, will reject. In Chapter 2, Henry Smith, for example, embraces the common law's role in IP law, albeit a minimalist one. Smith suggests that equity "has an ongoing role as a backstop to more central laws of intellectual property such as patent, copyright, and trademark," specifically by preventing opportunist actions by those who seek to find loopholes or dance around bright-line rules. Smith conceives equity as a "safety valve to protect against these tricksters."[32]

In the pages that follow, I adopt a broader view of trade secret and IP law as laws (not unlike other laws) that regulate social relations and promote multiple values, from innovation to democracy, from equality to liberty. Trade secret law promotes not only efficiency but also *freedom* – the freedom of employees to develop their human capital and to use their workplace knowledge in fair ways. Trade secret law affects equality, the dispersal of ownership, and the mobility required for a free and democratic society. As Scheppele argued in her early critique of the law-and-economics analysis of trade secret, the dominant law-and-economics account

30 Scheppele, *supra* note 26, at 254–55.

31 Lemley, *supra* note 6, at 328.

32 Henry Smith, *Equitable Intellectual Property: What's Wrong with Misappropriation?* (in this volume).

obscures the centrality of *relationships* and *trust* in trade secret law and conceals – or simply sacrifices – *individual rights* in the name of the social welfare. But, Scheppele argues, plural values have not escaped the courts. Her study found that courts followed the general rule that employers "cannot use the claim of trade secrets to shackle a former employee."[33] Scheppele concludes, "When the claim of trade secrets starts to interfere with former employees' abilities to remain in the same line of work, courts decide in favor of the liberty of the employees rather than in favor of the sanctity of trade secrets. In other words, one cannot use the claim of a confidential relationship to put significant limits on someone else's freedom. Confidential relationships have limits."[34] In a case involving employer A sharing trade secrets with employee B, and employee B later pursuing her own dreams, where an efficiency analysis focuses on A's incentives to over- or underinvest in secrecy, a freedom-based analysis focuses on B. Scheppele concludes, "When B's sharing of A's secret becomes a barrier to B's liberty in critical ways, the law seems to emphasize liberty over loyalty."[35] In short, trade secret law balances efficiency, fairness, and freedom.

Lemley's efficiency analysis sees employee mobility and freedom as an important consequence of the law. He recognizes that in the absence of trade secret law, employers are likely to go to extremes in protecting their workplace knowledge. "There is empirical evidence that overinvestment in secrecy is a real problem in the absence of trade secret protection," writes Lemley. "Examples can be found as far back as the guild system that pervaded Western economies in the Middle Ages. Guilds were places that could and did develop technical knowledge, but in the absence of legal means to protect that knowledge they went to great lengths to prevent others from learning of it, imposing draconian limits on the mobility of employees and the development of competing firms."[36] He acknowledges that today, in countries such as Mexico and Brazil, where little if any legal protection for trade secrets exists, knowledge is held close, resulting in inefficiencies. The "legal protection trade secret law provides serves as a substitute for investments in physical secrecy that companies might otherwise make."[37] He concludes that "a world without trade secret protection is likely to have more, not less, secrecy."[38]

But the law's motives matter. The theory of decision making affects outcome. Under the law-and-economics approach, draconian measures to protect trade secrets ought to be avoided because they are inefficient. "Trade secret law reduces investments in secrecy and encourages the dissemination of the secret to more people who can make productive use of it."[39] Whereas Lemley would keep modern trade secret

33 Scheppele, *supra* note 26, at 244.
34 *Id.*
35 *Id.* at 245.
36 Lemley, *supra* note 6, at 334.
37 *Id.* at 333–34.
38 *Id.* at 336.
39 *Id.* at 353.

law to a narrow regimen – promoting innovation and disclosure alone – I submit that trade secret must also take into account employees' *freedom* to move, to think, to innovate, and to compete and also the question of what kind of *social relations* we want and demand in a free and democratic society. I elaborate this position in the next section, building on the insights of labor law scholars.

II. TRADE SECRET AS PROMOTING FREE LABOR, DEVELOPMENT, AND DEMOCRACY

In an illuminating new book on the legal regulation of workplace knowledge in America from 1800 to 1930, labor law scholar Catherine Fisk describes profound changes in the way American courts and lawmakers have understood rights over employee innovations and know-how.[40] For much of the nineteenth century, American law forbade competitors from enticing away the employees of others who were under an obligation of service, but otherwise left employees free to change jobs and take their workplace knowledge with them. Fisk sums up the law this way: "If the employee 'was permitted to acquire, and did acquire, a full knowledge' of the trade secret to enable him to perform his duties, the employer could not afterward 'restrain him from using any knowledge so acquired or any secret so disclosed.'"[41] Enticement laws protected the right to the continued service of the employee, but not the employee's *knowledge*.[42] Know-how was considered the "personal attribute"[43] of the employee, free for him or her to take along to a future employment. Common law courts simply would not enforce contractual agreements between employers and employees to keep such knowledge confidential.

The explosives manufacturer E. I. du Pont de Nemours & Co. was one such employer that found itself struggling to control its workplace knowledge during this period without much help from the law. In 1800, Éleuthère Irénée du Pont de Nemours came with his family from France to the United States with knowledge of gunpowder technology that was superior to anyone else's in the United States. Du Pont had studied under the famous French chemist Lavoisier. The family bought property along the Brandywine River near Wilmington, Delaware, and by 1808 DuPont had already become a leading explosives manufacturer. Competitors yearned to learn Du Pont's manufacturing secrets and offered enticing wages to Du Pont's senior employees to get them to leave their employer and spill Du Pont's secrets. Although the law banned outright enticement, Du Pont had little else to ensure that employees would not reveal confidential information about machinery

40 See Catherine Fisk, Working Knowledge: Employee Innovation and the Rise of Corporate Intellectual Property, 1800–1930 (2009).

41 *Id.* at 56 (citing *Morison* v. *Moat*, 68 Eng. Rep. 492, 501 (1851)).

42 *Cf.* A. Arthur Schiller, *Trade Secrets and the Roman Law: The Actio Servi Corrupti*, 30 Colum. L. Rev. 837 (1930) (describing Roman law protecting a master against the corruption of his slave by a third party for the purpose of learning the master's trade secrets).

43 *Id.* at 23.

and factory designs; as Fisk reports, few if any common law courts were disposed to enforce nondisclosure agreements between employers and employees at that time. This left Du Pont and his competitors to engage in a war of words by appealing to public opinion. Du Pont complained that competitors were unfairly driving up wages and trying to poach information they had not worked to develop.

Competitors accused Du Pont of being un-American, trying to stifle the capabilities of his skilled laborers, prohibiting their advancement and the nation's advancement, to boot.[44] As one competitor wrote to Du Pont's employee, "you possess information – and I want it immediately. There is no impropriety in yr. parting with this. It is your right – all men sell it – and the man must be a fool who will complain of your doing it."[45] Although the author's honesty may be disconcerting, as Fisk writes, "At the time, this was a correct statement of what the law permitted."[46] Du Pont wrote a scathing reply to his competitor, whose actions he labeled "villainy." He wrote, to "fair competition . . . we will never object, but to be stealing in the dark the improvements of others is a mean unworthy action which inevitably annihilates all kind of useful exertion."[47] Yet Du Pont had no more than harsh words in his arsenal. When a former partner left to start a rival company, Du Pont could not object, because it was both the legal right and accepted business practice "for a man of his status to do so."[48]

A. *Free Labor in the Antebellum Period: Prohibitions on "Slavery of the Mind"*

Why did common law courts for nearly all of the nineteenth century refuse to protect employee knowledge – the very information that by 1930 would firmly be protected as corporate intellectual property? "An employee's agreement to relinquish the products of his mind struck courts as the sort of contract that should be subject to retraction for it restricted future freedom and constrained creativity," concludes Fisk.[49] Fisk shows that judges and political leaders during the antebellum period were particularly influenced by the idea that middle-class mobility and freedom were fundamental to a successful democracy; thus they looked skeptically on corporate claims of owning the knowledge of professional and well-educated workers. Critics of slavery also linked employee mobility to economic development and growth. As Abraham Lincoln elaborated in a pair of speeches in 1858 and 1859, slavery had taught the American republic that democracy and economic development both depended on individuals being able to move freely and put to use their knowledge for

44 *See* Fisk, *supra* note 40, at 51–52.
45 *Id.* at 51.
46 *Id.*
47 *Id.* In 1812, Du Pont published a pamphlet called "Villainy Detected," exposing the actions of his competitors. *Id.* at 53.
48 *Id.* at 54.
49 *Id.* at 7.

invention and improvement of the self and society.[50] A fluid labor force was necessary for economic development, or else markets would stagnate. (Slaves lacked control over their physical *and* intellectual labor. As Keith Aoki has written, Eli Whitney may have stolen the operative idea for the cotton gin from his slave, identified only by the name Sam, who invented the machine to ease the labors of his family. Ironically, Whitney not only stole the invention but the cotton gin also prolonged the institution of slavery itself.[51]). America, Lincoln argued, had "broken the 'shackles' of the 'slavery of mind' and had established a 'habit of freedom of thought' that was necessary to the 'discovery and production of new and useful things.'"[52] Lincoln elaborated the deep links between "free labor, freedom of thought, protection for inventions and discoveries, and political freedom."[53]

Following a similar logic, covenants not to compete and agreements not to disclose acquired knowledge of the trade struck courts as unreasonable restraints on human freedom. U.S. Supreme Court Justice Joseph Philo Bradley expressed this concern in 1887, when sitting by designation as a circuit judge he declared that "a mortgage on a man's brain, to bind all its future products – does not address itself favorably to our consideration."[54] As Fisk writes, "restrictions on the use of knowledge and on intellectual property ownership were characterized in quasi-slavery terms, as if they deprived the employee of his freedom and independence."[55] One court deciding the case of *Continental Car-Na-Var Corp.* v. *Moseley* affirmed "the right inherent in all people . . . to follow any of the common occupations of life. . . . Every individual possesses as a form of property, the right to pursue any calling, business or profession he may choose."[56]

Prohibiting creative individuals from owning their own innovations and knowledge further deprived them of capital and threatened the dispersal of property ownership in a democratic society. "The reluctance of courts throughout the nineteenth century significantly to limit employee use of workplace knowledge and intellectual property was attributable to the perception of the employee litigants' middle class status," writes Fisk. "[E]mployee independence was an essential bulwark against the tyranny that characterized both chattel slavery and the degraded wage labor of the factory system."[57]

Finally, the creative thinking that employee ownership of knowledge was thought to spur was valued not only in its own right but also as a core component of democratic citizenship. Entrepreneurship spurred both economic development *and* critically

50 *Id.* at 75–78.

51 *See* Keith Aoki, *Distributive and Syncretic Motives in Intellectual Property Law (with Special Reference to Coercion, Agency, and Development)*, 40 U.C. Davis L. Rev. 717, 745–47 (2007).

52 Fisk, *supra* note 40, at 77.

53 *Id.* at 76.

54 *Id.* at 6.

55 *Id.*

56 Scheppele, *supra* note 26, at 244 (citations omitted).

57 Fisk, *supra* note 40, at 7.

engaged democratic citizens who, in Lincoln's view, were not afraid to think new thoughts and throw off the shackles of "Old Fogy" institutions and ways of life.[58]

B. *Freedom as Freedom of Contract*

As Fisk describes, however, within the scope of just fifty years, this conception of employee freedom gave way to a new vision of freedom itself, now understood as the liberty of the employee to contract away the right to his or her knowledge in exchange for a comfortable salary and job security. Fisk captures well the paradoxical position of turn-of-the-century courts, which reluctantly began to approve agreements by employees not to compete and use trade secrets. Consider how one court put it: "if these mill owners desire to cripple a man's enterprise and his energy and intelligence, to hamper him in his future employment by requiring that he shall not give to that future employer the benefit of his skill or the things that he has developed for the former master, they must contract to that effect."[59]

By the 1930s, as craft guilds and entrepreneurship gave way to industrialization and modern corporations, courts grew even more sympathetic to the claims of corporate employers such as Du Pont and Eastman Kodak that made significant investments in technical improvements.[60] By 1930, a revolution in labor law was complete. Workplace knowledge came to be governed almost exclusively by contract law. Courts routinely approved nondisclosure agreements and willingly implied obligations of confidentiality on employees where no express agreements had been made.[61]

In short, trade secret law, which only formally emerged during the latter period of Fisk's study, 1890–1930, reflected very different notions of freedom from those articulated by common law courts confronted with similar questions in the antebellum era. This is a good place to remind ourselves that the flexibility of the common law means it may adopt the prevailing mores of the time, for better or for worse. Here, the common law evolved to reflect the changing American workplace. The rise of corporate intellectual property at the start of the twentieth century reflected not only the needs of corporations but also the new desires of laborers, who were willing to trade entrepreneurship and mobility for stability and the creature comforts of a middle-class lifestyle.

Fisk's brilliant account of these changes reveals the deeper social, economic, and political links between trade secret law, freedom, economic development, and democracy. As she points out, tight corporate control over workplace knowledge was not always the best innovation policy, let alone effective for developing democratic citizens. By 1911, DuPont had virtually all of its employees under contract

58 *Id.* at 77.
59 *Id.* at 106.
60 *Id.* at 188.
61 *See id.* at 99.

to assign their inventions and to keep confidential all technical knowledge. But as Fisk explains, this tight-fisted approach to securing the company's corporate property sapped the motivation of the firm's most talented salaried employees.[62] What's more, the "Company Man" lacked the entrepreneurial spirit that had stood as the foundation of democratic society.

C. *Silicon Valley and the Return of American Entrepreneurship*

Today we are again at a turn-of-the-century crossroads with respect to the American workplace and the laws that govern employer/employee relations. The Company Man is giving way to the high-tech entrepreneur. Where in the last century employees contracted away their mobility and ownership of their workplace knowledge in exchange for security and salaries, today's high-tech workers prefer mobility and flexibility and consider the knowledge they develop on the job their own human capital to develop and use.[63] Nevertheless, trade secret law at the start of the twenty-first century continues to assume the same workplace as existed a century ago, leading to a disconnect between law and social practice. Current trade secret law, with its broad definition of what constitutes trade secrets (*any* information that derives economic value from being a secret) and some problematic new doctrines, is out of step with changing workplace social relations and with current understandings of human dignity, property, equality, innovation, and democracy. Labor law scholar Katherine Stone describes current employee expectations, writing that "[n]etworking, training, and lateral mobility are a fundamental aspect of today's employment system."[64] Employees today expect to be treated with dignity; their work is understood as an investment in their own human capital and capability. The irony, however, is that acquiring knowledge is the very thing that can get employees in trouble legally. And with the subject matter of trade secret law so broad, "it becomes increasingly difficult for an employee to avoid learning them," Stone observes.[65]

More recently, courts in many states have begun recognizing the problematic "inevitable disclosure" doctrine, which further jeopardizes employee freedom. The doctrine, which first emerged in American courts as early as 1919,[66] "permits a trade secret owner to prevent a former employee from working for a competitor ... by

62 *Id* at 198–99.

63 *See id.* at 254.

64 Katherine V. W. Stone, From Widgets to Digits: Employment Regulation for the Changing Workplace 154–55 (2004).

65 *Id.* at 150.

66 Brandy L. Treadway, *An Overview of Individual States' Application of Inevitable Disclosure: Concrete Doctrine or Equitable Tool?*, 55 SMU L. Rev. 621, 623 (2002) (referring to *Eastman Kodak Co.* v. *Powers Film Products*, 179 N.Y.S. 325, 330 (N.Y. App. Div. 1919) ("The mere rendition of the service along the lines of his training would almost necessarily impart such knowledge to some degree. Warren cannot be loyal both to his promise to his former employer and to his new obligations to the defendant company.")).

demonstrating the employee's new job duties will inevitably cause the employee to rely upon knowledge of the former employer's trade secrets."[67] What is particularly troubling about the doctrine is that some employees who are deemed to know too much may be prohibited altogether for working for a competitor, even in the absence of any evidence that they would disclose the information to their future employer. In *International Business Machines (IBM)* v. *Papermaster*,[68] for example, Mark Papermaster was an executive at IBM who left the company to work for Apple, Inc. IBM requested a preliminary injunction against Papermaster based on the inevitable disclosure doctrine. In granting the injunction, U.S. district court Judge Kenneth Karas of the Southern District of New York concluded that "[b]ecause Mr. Papermaster has been inculcated with some of IBM's most sensitive and closely-guarded technical and strategic secrets, it is no great leap for the Court to find that Plaintiff has met its burden of showing a likelihood of irreparable harm."[69] In *Pepsico, Inc.* v. *Redmond*,[70] the U.S. Court of Appeals for the Seventh Circuit enjoined former Pepsico employee Redmond from assuming a position with competitor Quaker based on the inevitable disclosure of trade secret doctrine. More recently, a high-level employee, one of just seven people worldwide who knew the secret recipe for Thomas' English Muffins, was enjoined by a federal district court in Pennsylvania from working for competitor Hostess under the same theory.[71] In this case, however, the employee's actions appeared more dishonorable: Botticella, a vice president and holder of the secret information, copied non–muffin-related trade secret documents to an external hard drive before he left his employer to work for a rival. Even though both Botticella and Hostess testified that no secrets would be misappropriated, the district court granted plaintiff's injunction based on inevitable disclosure, reasoning that Botticella's actions had undermined his trustworthiness.[72]

To date, the inevitable disclosure of trade secret doctrine has been considered by twenty-two states. Six states, including California, have outright rejected the doctrine (the California Supreme Court considered the doctrine tantamount to agreements not to compete, which are illegal in the state).[73] Thirteen states, however, have

67 Whyte v. Schlage Lock Co., 125 Cal.Rptr. 2d 277, 277 (Cal. Ct. App. 2002).

68 International Business Machines (IBM) v. Papermaster, No. 08-CV-9078, 2008 WL 4974508, at *1 (S.D.N.Y., Nov. 1 2008).

69 *Id.* at 8.

70 54 F.3d 1262, 1264 (7th Cir. 1995).

71 Bimbo Bakeries USA, Inc. v. Botticella, 613 F.3d 102, 107 (3d Cir. 2010).

72 *Id.* at 105–08, 114–17.

73 *See* Whyte v. Schlage Lock Co., 125 Cal.Rptr. 2d 277, 293 (Cal. Ct. App. 2002). Kentucky, Louisiana, Maryland, Massachusetts, and Virginia have also rejected the doctrine. Tracy Farrell, *Applicability of Inevitable Disclosure Doctrine Barring Employment of Competitor's Former Employee*, 36 A.L.R.6th 537 (2008). As a state that prohibits any kind of postemployment restriction, California is a center for industry efforts at restricting current employee mobility. One such method is the nonsolicitation agreement among rival companies. In September 2010 the Justice Department filed an antitrust complaint in court against six Silicon Valley companies: Apple, Adobe, Google, Intel, Intuit, and Pixar. For five years, these six companies had abided by an unwritten agreement to not

applied the doctrine on at least one occasion.[74] Contemporary trade secret law thus presents a paradox: "Under current trends, the most successful employee in the new workplace is the one who is most at risk from the inevitable disclosure doctrine. The more successful an employee is on the employer's own terms, the more likely she is to be penalized for obtaining information when she departs."[75] The disconnect leads Stone to conclude, "In this area, the law is clearly out of step with business practice."[76]

III. THE WAY FORWARD

Incentives to invent and disclose are important, but they do not encompass the full range of values at stake in the law of trade secrets. There are deep connections between law, innovation, freedom, and democracy. Too strong trade secret law hampers the ability of employees to move, to work, to learn, to think, and to develop their own human capital. These freedoms, in turn, promote innovation, economic development, dispersal of property ownership, and a culture of critical thinking that is essential to a robust democracy.

As the histories provided by Scheppele, Fisk, and Stone illustrate, common law courts have long regulated employee agreements regarding workplace knowledge to promote employee freedom, not efficiency alone. Stone describes how the earliest common law courts stepped in to prevent masters from overreaching and unduly prohibiting competition by apprentices, leading to the Statute of Apprentices of 1563. Before passage of the statute, masters were seeking to extend the period of apprenticeship beyond the customary period of seven years.[77] Although the progressiveness of the Statute of Apprentices can be debated – it is surely problematic to characterize an act that reinforced the guild system and *required* apprenticeships to last for seven years as a law promoting employee mobility![78] – we must recognize the context in

cold-call each other's employees. The companies had intentionally limited the mobility of current employees by having potential competitors withhold potential offers of employment. *See* P. May, M. Swift, & J. Boudreau, *Apple, Google, Intel, Other Tech Firms Admit Secret Agreements to not Poach Employees*, CONSUMER WATCHDOG (Sept. 27, 2010), http://www.consumerwatchdog.org/story/apple-google-intel-other-tech-firms-admit-secret-agreements-not-poach-employees.

74 These states are Arkansas, Connecticut, Delaware, Illinois, Indiana, Iowa, Michigan, Minnesota, New Jersey, North Carolina, New York, Ohio, Pennsylvania, Texas, Utah, and Washington. *See* Farrell, *supra* note 73.

75 Stone, *supra* note 64, at 152.

76 *Id.*

77 *Id*, at 153.

78 *See* Harlan M. Blake, *Employee Agreements Not to Compete*, 73 HARV. L. REV. 625, 632 (1960) ("If the early cases represent, in fact, the courts' attempt to assist the guilds and legislative bodies in shoring up the crumbling values of the medieval economic system, they cannot fairly be described as indicative of an attitude of economic liberalism. Thus, the usual statement of the early common law of restraints appears to require revision.... [R]estraints of future employment were originally held invalid without regard to the scope of the restriction, and this was so because they involved circumventions of the customary rules of apprenticeship."); *id.* at 634 (arguing that intervening common law courts and

which the law was passed. In light of the context of a seven-year apprenticeship norm, courts sought to curb employer excesses.[79] To this day, covenants not to compete are closely examined by state common law courts for reasonableness, if not rejected entirely by some states, such as California. Courts' underlying acceptance or rejection of these covenants turns on their assessment of the effect of these covenants on competition, innovation, freedom, and democracy, and not on efficiency alone.

Covenants not to compete are distinct from trade secret law. California, for example, has long rejected covenants not to compete as inhibiting freedom of movement and trade, yet nevertheless recognizes trade secret protection like any other state.[80] Although California's rejection of restrictive covenants has led the state courts to reject the problematic inevitable disclosure doctrine,[81] nondisclosure agreements in California are enforceable. California's state trade secret statute[82] adopts the broad definition of trade secret recommended under the UTSA.[83]

The broader social and political accounts I have presented here elaborating the links between labor, innovation, economic development, and democracy provide an important backdrop against which we should reconsider trade secret law today. Whereas contemporary law-and-economics accounts focus on promoting efficiency, Fisk and Stone's broader accounts of the law regulating workplace knowledge elaborate multiple effects and interests at stake in the enterprise. Their work suggests some reforms, such as narrowing the legal definition of trade secrets. Today's broad definition of trade secrets leaves knowledgeable employees at risk of legal liability simply for doing their jobs.

One alternative to the problematic inevitable disclosure of trade secrets doctrine may be a wider implementation of "garden leave" policies. In an employment contract with a garden leave clause, the employee promises to give a certain amount of notice to the employer in advance of his or her resignation from employment.[84] In exchange, the employee stays at home with little to no company work so he or she can focus on "tending the garden."[85] During this set time at home, the employee is still employed and paid a regular salary by the employer.[86] The garden leave clause has

legislatures were driven more by moral outrage that "unethical" masters were subverting the customary order); *id.* at 637 ("If, as seems likely, these cases represent reactions by the judges against erosions in the customs of the guilds by aggressive craftsmen, they have a significance almost the reverse of that usually attributed to them.").

79 Stone, *supra* note 64, at 153 ("Thus in the seventeenth century, courts became suspicious of covenants not to compete because they viewed them as attempts by employers to breach customer understandings of the terms of the employment relationship.").

80 Cal. Civ. Code § 3426.

81 *Whyte*, 125 Cal.Rptr.2d at 293 (Cal. Ct. App. 2002).

82 Cal. Civ. Code § 3426.

83 *See* Lemley & Pooley, *supra* note 4, at 9.

84 Jeffrey Klein & Nichols Pappas, *'Garden Leave' Clauses in Lieu of Non-Competes*, 241 N.Y. L.J. 1 (2009).

85 *Id.*

86 *Id.*

some of the same benefits of a noncompete clause: if the employee begins working for another employer during the time of the leave, the employer may request an injunction that would enforce the provision or make a separate claim of breach of employee loyalty.[87] Moreover, because garden leave is paid leave, employers are not faced with the prospect of asking a court to enjoin an employee from pursuing his or her chosen field of endeavor or to prevent an employee from earning a living.[88]

To be sure, leaving trade secret adjudication to common law courts is less than predictable, and whether and how courts advance freedom and efficiency is a matter for debate. A virtue of the common law is its flexibility and context dependency,[89] which allows courts to alter law to reflect the changing workplace and evolving ideologies. But this flexibility can also lead to radically different legal policies over time as conceptions of freedom evolve. At the same time, allowing for common law adjudication, which takes into account multiple theories and values, from fairness to freedom, can give more consideration to the complex and interrelated interests of multiple parties, from individual rights to corporate concerns to the interests of a free and democratic society.

87 Tyler Paetkau, *Paetkau on the Case for "Garden Leave" in California*, Lexis-Nexis Emerging Issues Analysis 4513 (2009).

88 *Id. See, e.g.*, Estee Lauder Companies Inc. v. Batra, 430 F. Supp. 2d 158, 182 (S.D.N.Y. 2006) (upholding a restrictive covenant containing a garden leave clause because the loss of livelihood was mitigated by the continual payments of the annual salary during the running of the noncompete agreement).

89 *See, e.g.*, Balganesh, *supra* note 10, at 1572.

16

Laying Bare an Ethical Thread

From IP to Property to Private Law?

*David Lametti**

INTRODUCTION

To what extent is law supposed to be moral? Holmes famously said that law was for the bad man, or, I suppose, had to at least be comprehensible as being in those terms. H. L. A. Hart did not go that far but certainly posited, like either positivists "soft" or "hard,"[1] at least some degree of separation between law and morality. Fuller, in contrast, challenged that notion, claiming that law had a "morality of aspiration."[2] Some natural law theorists have gone further, claiming that law is a moral exercise, whether or not they make the claim that *lex injusta non est lex*.[3]

I wish to make a more limited claim: that how we, as a society, deal with property resources – objects of social wealth, to use the term employed by the late Jim Harris[4] –

* Director, Centre for Intellectual Property Policy, Associate Professor of Law, and former Associate Dean (Academic), Faculty of Law, McGill University. I wish to thank D. Gordon Cruess, Sarah Huggins, Michael Bookman, Keiran Gibbs, Ellen Bourque, Ian Dahlman, and Abby Shepard for research and editorial assistance, as well as the Dobson Fund and Wainwright Trust of the Faculty of Law, McGill University and the Social Sciences Humanities Research Council of Canada for research support. I would also like to thank participants in the Canadian Private Law Workshop, and especially Lisa Austin, Dennis Klimchuk, Giorgio Resta, Helge Dedek, Lionel Smith, and Catherine Valcke, as well as participants at the University of Pennsylvania symposium, Intellectual Property and the Common Law, in particular Hanoch Dagan, Gideon Parchemovsky, Gregory Alexander, and Madhavi Sunder. Email: david.lametti@mcgill.ca.

1 There is a wealth of writing on positivism and its various subclassifications, and their differences, real and perceived. To begin, see MATTHEW H. KRAMER, IN DEFENSE OF LEGAL POSITIVISM: LAW WITHOUT TRIMMINGS (2003).

2 LON L. FULLER, THE MORALITY OF LAW 3–32 (1964).

3 *See, e.g.*, Michael S. Moore, *Law as a Functional Kind, in* NATURAL LAW THEORY: CONTEMPORARY ESSAYS (Robert P. George ed., 1992); and A *Natural Law Theory of Interpretation* 58 S. CAL. L. REV. 277 (1985). On *lex injusta non est lex, see* JOHN M. FINNIS, NATURAL NAW AND NATURAL RIGHTS 351–66 (1980).

4 The term is from J. W. HARRIS, PROPERTY AND JUSTICE 1 (1996). I have used the term "property-as-object" to describe the use of the word "property" in reference to such objects. Similarly, I use the term "property-as-relationship" to refer to instances where the word "property" is used to describe a relation

is part of a moral context that reflects our values as a society or community.[5] Indeed, I would go further to add that such a moral context imports what have been called the "social obligations"[6] of property. Property rights are not unlimited. In examining how and why private property institutions ranging from ownership of land to ownership of a copyright are limited and indeed *channeled* or *directed*, and in analyzing what justifications are offered for this in practice and theory, we inevitably expose larger ethical and moral principles: the common good, the development of individual goods, and the like.

Social obligations are most obvious in the various areas of intellectual property, even though we have grown accustomed to using individual, right-based vocabularies to frame IP discourse. As I argue, the areas of IP, especially copyright and patent, are all in some way subservient to a very ethical teleology. This teleology is present in the very foundational documents of intellectual property. The same kind of teleology is equally pervasive for private property, as a number of scholars are beginning to point out.[7] This point, however, requires more excavation to unearth, and the bulk of this chapter is focused on that task. This is the "ethical thread" that I wish to expose. Once this thread is laid bare and understood, we have reached a point where we can begin to rethink private law in these terms: beginning with elements fundamental to the law of property, then moving to nuisance (on the cusp of property and civil responsibility), and expanding that scope into contract and tort, we can begin to see more fully what Fuller might have called the "aspirational morality" of private law.

This stance taken is from the perspective of "virtue ethics."[8] Drawing support from the work of Aristotle and, to a lesser extent, Aquinas and recast by a new generation of scholars,[9] virtue ethics purports to provide guidelines or the right questions to ask in a situation of ethical decision making. These situations challenge us as actors to adopt an ethical stance and act accordingly, and in doing so they force us in effect to define

between or among individuals through a given object of social wealth: *see* D. Lametti, *The Concept of Property: Relations Through Objects of Social Wealth* 53 U. TORONTO L.J. 325 (2003), *available at* http://ssrn.com/abstract=1758871.

5 D. Lametti, *The Objects of Virtue*, *in* PROPERTY AND COMMUNITY 1 (Gregory S. Alexander & Eduardo Peñalver, eds., 2010).

6 To be discussed *infra*. *See, e.g.*, Gregory S. Alexander, et al. *A Statement of Progressive Property*, 94 CORNELL L. REV. 743 (2009); G. S. Alexander, *The Social-Obligation Norm in American Property Law*, 94 CORNELL L. REV. 745 (2009); and Eduardo M. Peñalver, *Land Virtues*, 94 CORNELL L. REV. 821 (2009). *See also* PROPERTY AND COMMUNITY (G. S. Alexander & E. M. Peñalver, eds., 2010); and Lametti, *supra* note 4.

7 See the various works cited *id*, and especially, Lametti, *supra* note 5; Peñalver, *supra* note 6 (property cannot be understood without a relatively thick theory about the sorts of values that people are likely to pursue).

8 For an introduction to virtue ethics see STAN VAN HOOFT, UNDERSTANDING VIRTUE ETHICS (2006); ROSALIND HURSTHOUSE, ON VIRTUE ETHICS (1999); VIRTUE ETHICS: A CRITICAL READER (Daniel Statman ed., 1997); and Virtue Ethics (Roger Crisp & Michael Slote eds., 1997). *See also* Onora O'Neill, Towards Justice and Virtue (1996) and Charles Taylor, The Sources of the Self (1989). *See also* D. Lametti, *The (Virtue) Ethics of Private Property: A Framework & Implications*, *in* New Perspectives on Property Law, Obligations and Restitution 39 (Alastair Hudson ed., 2003), *available at* http://ssrn.com/abstract=1758893.

9 As identified, *id*.

and better ourselves. Such decisions, following Aristotle's concept of practical reasonableness and attention to context, makes the context or "positionality" of the ethical decision maker central to deciding how to act in any given circumstance.[10] That is to say, first, all norms are culture-relative and supported by intuitions that are grounded in these community traditions, and second, these norms are understood and inculcated in the members of a community over time. The hermeneutic tradition that supports this understanding of normativity and the transmission of norms will not necessarily tell agents – us – what the right answer is in all cases, but rather will help us find the right answer for ourselves. Although set rules form part of the basis for what it means to act virtuously,[11] rules are often less than clear, incomplete, contradictory, and opaque; hence rule following is incomplete as an ethical stance, outlook, or way of life.[12] Put simply, we need to do more than follow rules in order to do what is right.[13] Finally, this approach allows for the ethics of a set of legal norms to evolve over time, as societal contexts and underlying moralities (usually slowly) evolve.

The strength of virtue ethics and its contextual positionality is that it helps individuals order their daily decision making. It demands enlightened, self-reflective, and self-critical individual judgment, all in service of the balanced decision making that Aristotelians and neo-Aristotelians have favored in their ethics. Of course, the drawback of contextual analysis is that it might be used to justify less than virtuous behavior. But within an interpretive community, these types of decisions will go against the grain of the ever-evolving moral base and the formal and informal norms that it supports and will be identified as outliers or as just plain wrong. So notwithstanding this sort of "situational ethics critique," the ethical stance based on virtue is sufficiently thick, known, and understood to be an effective guide. Therefore, as I argue, it helps inform current practice in both intellectual and common law property (the descriptive claim) and also points to the direction in which these areas ought to evolve (the normative claim).

I. THE ETHICS OF INTELLECTUAL PROPERTY

The virtue ethics of intellectual property are in plain view.[14] First, IP rights are clearly limited. Although most citizens, legislators, and scholars are now comfortable with the idea of labeling IP rights as *property* rights in the sense that they have economic

10 The best discussion of "positionality," in my view, remains Katherine Bartlett, *Feminist Legal Methods*, 103 HARV. L. REV., no. 4, 829–88 (1990).

11 Bartlett notes that rules act as a check on arbitrariness and represent past wisdom: *id.* at 850.

12 According to Bartlett, all truth is situated and partial: *id.* at 851.

13 Of course, following Aristotle and seeing "law" as a combination of "law" and "equity" (*epikeia*), then a virtue ethics is necessary for all law (or indeed law ought to be an instantiation of virtue ethics), and especially for judging. *See* Lawrence Solum, *A Virtue-Centered Account of Equity and the Rule of Law*, *in* VIRTUE JURISPRUDENCE 142–66 (Colin P. Farrelly & L.B. Solum eds., 2008).

14 This discussions tracks in part what I have written in D. Lametti, *The Virtuous P(eer): Reflections on the Ethics of File Sharing*, *in* NEW FRONTIERS IN THE PHILOSOPHY OF INTELLECTUAL PROPERTY 284 (Annabelle Lever ed., 2012).

value,[15] have an in rem and partly exclusive nature, and are treated as such in statutes[16] as well as in practice,[17] this labeling is by no means accompanied by the underlying idea that such rights must be absolute.[18] Numerous courts and scholars have noted, in the common law tradition, the statutory origins of the rights in question and the fact that such rights are not rights in gross. In theory and in practice, there are serious limits on all forms of intellectual property. Moreover, various substantive doctrines, notably fair use or fair dealing in copyright or patent misuse in patent law, have further emphasized this seemingly banal point by limiting even more specifically the exercise of rights by a right-holder. Even those IP rights that have their origins not in statute but in the common law, such as passing off, are by no means unlimited.[19]

More than merely accepting the presence of limits on IP rights, one needs to acknowledge and underscore the very explicit, very ethical teleology of the various kinds of intellectual property, especially that of patent and copyright. The self-stated purpose of these IP rights is to favor artistic creativity and the promotion of useful inventions, as evidenced in a variety of foundational documents. The Statute of Anne, the first copyright statute in the United Kingdom and the common law tradition, in its preamble states that the Act's purpose is for "the Encouragement of Learning."[20] The Constitution of the United States, in protecting patent and copyright under federal jurisdiction, does so "to promote the Progress of Science and useful Arts, by securing for limited Times to Authors and Inventors the exclusive Right to their respective Writings and Discoveries."[21] The first U.S. federal Copyright Act of 1790, picking up the language of the Statute of Anne, was "an Act for the

[15] Or, in civil law terms, are "patrimonial."

[16] The Canadian Copyright Act, R.S.C. 1985, c. C-42, Trade-mark Act, R.S.C. 1985, c. T-13 and Patent Act, R.S.C. 1985, c. P-4 all use the term "ownership."

[17] Think only of the use of IP rights as collateral for secured lending.

[18] D. Lametti, *The Concept and Conceptions of Intellectual Property as Seen Through the Lens of Property*, *in* Scienza e Diritto nel Prisma del Diritto Comparato 269 (G. Comandé & G. Ponzanelli eds., 2004), *available at* http://ssrn.com/abstract=1758894.

[19] Passing off, of course, is limited by the use of the mark and the context in which it was used. But it should always be or have been understood as not going beyond these limited parameters. See e.g. Jessica Litman, *Breakfast with Batman: The Public Interest in the Advertising Age*, 108 Yale L.J. 1717 (1999); Mark A. Lemley, *The Modern Lanham Act and the Death of Common Sense*, 108 Yale L.J. 1687 (1999); and Stacey L. Dogan & M. A. Lemley, *The Merchandising Right: Fragile Theory or Fait Accompli?* 54 Emory L.J. 461 (2005). Shyamkrishna Balganesh has argued that we might return, fruitfully, to the methodology and substance of the common law of intellectual property, still present in interstitial state law. This too is not an argument for absolute IP rights across the various domains, but rather posits a system in which rights are discerned through a process of "pragmatic incrementalism": *see* Shyamkrishna Balganesh, *The Pragmatic Incrementalism of Common Law Intellectual Property*, 63 Vand. L. Rev. 1543 (2010).

[20] An Act for the Encouragement of Learning, by Vesting the Copies of Printed Books in the Authors or Purchasers of such Copies, During the Times therein mentioned, 1710, 8 Anne, c.19.

[21] U.S. Const. Art. I, § 8, cl.8. Note that this provision also underscores the limited nature of these exclusive rights by positing a limited time on exclusivity and focusing on the utility of the invention (even if the U.S. Supreme Court has in effect held that even lengthy terms of copyright protection are still "limited": *see* Eldred et al. v. Ashcroft, 537 U.S. 186 (2003), 239 F.3d 372).

encouragement of learning, by securing the copy of maps, charts, and books, to the authors and proprietors of such copies, during the times therein mentioned." Thus in both copyright and patent there is an idea that, in its barest terms, IP protection is overtly consequentialist: the according of certain and limited exclusive (and thus property-like) rights is done to foster specific desirable and indeed ethical goals.

Certainly, one might take an impoverished view of these goals and reduce the idea of progress and incentives simply to economic terms. This reduction, however, would not accurately describe the full amplitude of the notion of progress or creativity that underlies intellectual property. A fuller idea would include intellectual, innovative, technical, and artistic progress and their ties to the promotion of knowledge, learning, and the advancement of scientific and artistic ideas,[22] human flourishing,[23] social benefits,[24] or to the role that a robust public domain of ideas necessarily has in providing the backdrop for progress.[25] These institutions are not uniquely about according economic rights to the creator, but rather are about the process or "bringing about" of the creation itself: the promotion of the useful arts and science and the encouragement of learning. This is not something that can be measured in simple *utils*. Rather, there is an ethical direction to the whole of these institutions. This direction is exemplified in the balance of according rights limited scope in exchange for promoting the public's access to the arts and providing incentives for authors, all in service of the public good.

Perhaps the best illustration of this point is the discussion regarding a central limitation of copyright: fair use or fair dealing. That voluminous discussion of what is either a central limit to copyright's property-like rights or an instance of "users' rights"[26] is an explicitly moral discussion. A glance at § 107 of the U.S. Copyright Act and its criteria for fair use brings out this ethical picture quite nicely. The purposes that justify fair use – "criticism, comment, news reporting, teaching (including multiple copies for classroom use), scholarship, or research" – are purposes that go

[22] *See, e.g.*, Michael J. Madison, *Beyond Creativity: Copyright as Knowledge Law*, 12 Vand. J. Ent. & Tech L. 817 (2010) (knowledge and learning as the central goals of copyright norms); *Beyond Invention: Patent as Knowledge Law*, 15 Lewis & Clark L. Rev. 71 (2011) (knowledge and learning as the central goals of patent); and *Knowledge Curation*, 86 Notre Dame L. Rev. 1957 (2011).

[23] *See, e.g.*, William W. Fisher III, *The Implications of Law of User Innovation*, 94 Minn. L. Rev. no. 5 1417, 1463 (2010) (human flourishing as a part of the law of copyright); Abraham Drassinower, *Copyright Infringement as Compelled Speech*, *in* New Frontiers in the Philosophy of Intellectual Property (Annabelle Lever ed., 2011).

[24] *See* Brett M. Frischmann, *Spillovers Theory and Its Conceptual Boundaries*, 51 Wm. & Mary L. Rev. 801 (2009) (how social benefits of IP depend on spillovers for which standard economic utilitarian theories cannot account).

[25] *See* Jessica Litman, *The Public Domain* 39 Emory L.J. 965 (1990); J. Boyle, The Public Domain: Enclosing the Commons of the Mind 179 (2008) (on the intellectual commons as a source for creative work); Lawrence Lessig, The Future of Ideas: The Fate of the Commons in a Connected World (2001); and Brett Frischmann, Infrastructure: The Social Value of Shared Resources 333 (2012).

[26] CCH Canadian Ltd. v. Law Society of Upper Canada, 1 S.C.R. 339 (2004) (effectively importing into Canadian "fair dealing" jurisprudence a U.S.-like "fair use" test and pitching fair dealing not as a mere limitation but as a user right).

to the heart of what we feel our society is about: knowledge and knowledge transfer, public debate and discourse, teaching, scholarship, and learning. The enumerated factors that follow in that provision are meant to provide a basis for making such determinations: in its channeling of factors, the fair use test is necessarily embedded in positionality or context.

Another interesting example is the emerging doctrine of copyright misuse. Based on the notion of patent misuse, copyright misuse has increasingly been cited as a check or a brake on the unfettered rights of copyright holders, *even within the normal scope of rights held.* The parameters of the doctrine are being worked out, but what is of significant interest is the focus on the actions of the right-holder and the purposes for which the actions were taken.[27] Thus in Canada, the actions of a chocolate maker were scrutinized under this doctrine when copyright was used to vindicate a putative right where neither trademark nor competition law afforded a remedy and where the competitor broke no laws.[28] In the views of some scholars, in this David and Goliath scenario, the large chocolate maker was merely being unethical as regards the competition from the smaller (legal) importer.[29] An obvious parallel is the concept of abuse of rights, or *abus de droit,* in the civil law tradition (a doctrine that, as is argued later, may very well be seeping into the common law or has indeed already crept in from time to time).[30]

This teleology in intellectual property norms is discernible at the formal level – copyright statutes, cases, treaties and such. However, increasingly in IP circles, a great deal of behavior that is being channeled by virtue ethics is being done via informal norms,[31] or "copynorms."[32] This helps foster the ethic of sharing and exchange in the

[27] *See generally* Kathryn Judge, *Rethinking Copyright Misuse*, 57 STAN. L. REV. 901 (2004): in her view any attempt by a copyright holder to effectively expand the purview of copyright protection to gain control over an idea or deter fair use constitutes misuse. For an application to digital copyright, see Dan L. Burk, *Anti-Circumvention Misuse,* 50 UCLA L. REV. 1095 (2003). For a specific application to the idea of asserting nonexistent (copy-) rights, *see* Jason Mazzone, *Copyfraud* 81 N.Y.U. L. REV. 1026 (2006).

[28] Euro-Excellence Inc. v. Kraft Canada Inc., 3 S.C.R. 20 (2007), 2007 SCC 37 (Can.) (concurring reasons of Bastarache J. and the warning expressed regarding copyright over reach in the concurring reasons of Fish J.) The majority dismissed the copyright "abuse" claim on technical grounds.

[29] Pierre-Emmanuel Moyse, *Kraft Canada c. Euro-Excellence: l'insoutenable légèreté du droit,* 53 MCGILL L.J. 74 (2008), *available at* http://ssrn.com/abstract=1761002; and A. Drassinower, *The Art of Selling Chocolate: Remarks on Copyright's Domain, in* FROM "RADICAL EXTREMISM" TO "BALANCED COPYRIGHT": CANADIAN COPYRIGHT AND THE DIGITAL AGENDA 121 (Michael Geist ed., 2010).

[30] *Contra* Larissa Katz, *A Jurisdictional Principle of Abuse of Right* (8 February 2010), *available at* http://ssrn.com/abstract=1417955.

[31] *See generally* Richard H. McAdams, *The Origin, Development, and Regulation of Norms,* 96 MICH. L. REV. 338 (1997); Mark Schultz, *Copynorms: Copyright Law and Social Norms, in* INTELLECTUAL PROPERTY AND INFORMATION WEALTH: COPYRIGHT AND RELATED RIGHTS 201, 309 (Peter Yu ed., 2007); Lior J. Strahilevitz, *Charismatic Code, Social Norms, and the Emergence of Cooperation on the File-Swapping Networks,* 89 VA. L. REV. 505 (2003); and Dan M. Kahan, *The Logic of Reciprocity: Trust, Collective Action, and Law, in* John M. Olin Center for Studies in Law, Economics, and Public Policy Working Papers, paper 281 (2002).

[32] The term is employed by M. Schultz, *id.* and L. Solum, *The Future of Copyright* (Review of Lawrence Lessig, FREE CULTURE), 84 TEX. L. REV. 1137 (2005).

context of creative commons, open access publishing, and open source computing.[33] In many of these cases, the informal norm not only contradicts the formal norm but also takes precedence within the practicing community of programmers, creators, gamers, and the like.

What is critical to all of these discussions – the scope of rights, the nature of limitations, doctrines such as fair use and misuse – is context. In all of these instances, there is a requirement to look at the context of right-holders and non–right-holders and come up with a balanced answer based on context or positionality. There is often no clear, bright-line answer that is easily discernable in advance; hence the resort to a contextualized, ethical assessment. And part of the contextual assessment – a guidepost, if you will – is precisely identifying the ultimate goal or goals to be fostered by the IP norms in question and applying them to the specific circumstances.

Context and positionality *are* the stuff of virtue ethics. In other words, it is a small step from these relatively uncontroversial descriptive points about the nature of patent and copyright to an understanding of their teleology and context or to the classification of the ethics of these institutions as an ethics of virtue. My central point here is that this discussion of the teleology of IP is explicitly *moral*, and although it is very much teleological, any discussion that purports to reduce this teleology to merely acontextual, economic terms will miss much, if not most, of its richness and import, as well as its evolution.[34]

Thus the "virtues" of IP have been rather explicit; they are found in foundational texts and elaborated in cases and scholarly writing. The question then becomes, if IP is a species or subset of larger property rights, whether we can find traces of these kinds of ethical considerations in the common law of property. And if so, what impact would the presence of this underlying ethics of the common law – this moral teleology, if you will – have on both the current understanding and the law of property or on its future development?[35]

II. THE ETHICS OF PRIVATE PROPERTY

In the preceding discussion of IP norms – formal and informal – we found that these norms helped promote, serve, foster, care for, or nourish virtues such as creativity, knowledge, education, and sharing, as well as individual development and expression. The category of IP did so by recognizing formally in its very foundational texts a direction or teleology meant to enhance such virtues. It does so explicitly by

33 See generally the sources cited *supra* note 25, as well as in Lametti, *supra* note 14.

34 Indeed, this might very well be the *ethical* problem with the DMCA and other copyright-plus or para-copyright initiatives: they depart markedly from the traditional teleology of copyright.

35 For example, I have applied this analysis in helping resolve the problems raised by "digital copyright" reforms in Canada that have been inspired by the U.S. Digital Millennium Copyright Act, 17 U.S.C. § 1201 (1998): *see* D. Lametti, *How Virtue Ethics Might Help Erase C-32's Conceptual Incoherence, in* From "Radical Extremism" to "Balanced Copyright": Canadian Copyright and the Digital Agenda 309 (M. Geist ed., 2010).

recognizing that IP rights are not unlimited, but rather are specific packages of rights tempered with duties and obligations. Particular formal norms such as fair use are explicitly contextual. Where formal normativity may occasionally tend to emphasize an absolute rights-based approach, other sorts of formal and informal normativity operate to counterbalance.

Can an ethical thread (or ethical threads) be located or be drawn through traditional property discourse? I would argue that such a thread most definitely can be identified and teased out of current and past property norms and understandings, pushing us to the very core of our understanding of the institution of private property. The same method of looking at foundational concepts and justificatory discourses would be employed.

The starting point in all such discussions is the notion of absolute ownership, but further investigation readily reveals that this notion is limited at its very core. In particular, ownership is an institution that serves important societal and individual goals and indeed can only be justified when it does so. So as part of the justificatory discourse we find limits and duties associated with resource holding in traditional private property discourse. However, this chapter argues more than the obvious assertion that private property rights have limits, and even more than the related but now equally obvious conclusion that private property is necessarily a limited concept.[36] Rather, it argues that an examination of the *reasons* for such limits that are offered explicitly or implicitly will explain aspects of the underlying ethics of the institution that are not explicable in simply rights-based terms. These limits on property rights generally, and the specific duties imposed on certain property rights, will be seen to serve larger ethical and moral principles: the common good, the development of individual goods, and the like. Hence, one must resort to an understanding of the kind of goals – here I would insert *virtues* among them – that are served by the institution of private property. These principles govern how human beings should interact with scarce resources.

I have already dealt with many of these issues in theoretical, conceptual terms.[37] The ensuing discussion in this chapter focuses on selective aspects of the practice of private property in the common law. These examples build a strong prima facie case for the claim that there is an ethical thread running through traditional private property that is similar to the one already seen running through intellectual property, although of course the nature of the virtues served may differ. This chapter is a survey of a few private property institutions and thus is not meant to be an exhaustive description of the common law of property; indeed, I am "cherry-picking" easy examples – or, even better in property terms, picking low-lying

[36] Funnily, this was one of my strongest points of disagreement with Jim Harris, who argued that, despite all forms of private property being limited in practice by property-limitation rules, it was not a limited concept: *see* D. Lametti, *Property and (Perhaps) Justice*, 23 McGill L.J. 665 (1998).

[37] Lametti, *supra* note 4; Lametti, *supra* note 5.

fruit – to identify aspects of what I have earlier called the "*virtue (ethics) of private property*."[38]

The starting point is ownership. The basic underlying assumption or starting point of the common law is that ownership entails rights that are relatively absolute[39] – Blackstone's "sole and despotic dominion"[40] – and that "property law" is about the identification, description, and enforcement of these rights. This assumption is deemed to be true notwithstanding the fact that the dominant bundle metaphor for property is not necessarily so rights oriented or indeed so inflexible. Thus, adjectives such as "full liberal" (Becker) or "full-blooded" (Harris) are the norm in describing the paradigmatic concept of ownership. Even framing the concept of property in terms of exclusivity can lead to this result.[41] Such is the case, even though most writers, practical and theoretical, recognize that private property is not unlimited.[42] A cursory glance at virtually any common law text will find this predisposition toward rights to some degree.[43] This focus should come as no surprise, given our intuitive and deeply held understanding of the property relationship in the Western world. Further, it is evidence of an undeniable fact that modern property law systems reflect quite explicitly the continuing primacy of rights-based explanations for private property, a point that has been elaborated elsewhere.[44]

Such a view is clearly deficient, both in theory and practice: it does not explain all that needs to be explained or understood about the nature of private property, missing important descriptive elements of an institution. I draw support from a growing number of property scholars who recognize this deficiency in rights-based property discourse. A group of property writers have begun to focus on the social

[38] This discussion contains selected and revised excerpts from a more extensive discussion contained in the first part of chapter 3 of my unpublished doctoral thesis: D. Lametti, The Deon-Telos of Private Property: Ethical Aspects of the Theory and Practice of Private Property (1999) (unpublished D.Phil. thesis, Oxford University). I called this idea the *deon-telos* of property in my doctoral thesis. The term was meant to be a place-holder for the idea of "non–rights-based." In the intervening period, the term "virtue ethics" became current for the same kinds of considerations and with the same theoretical sources, and it was close enough in application to what I had wanted to convey. Since 2003, I have used the rubric of virtue ethics more widely: Lametti, *supra* note 8.

[39] Specifically, *dominium*: see an extended discussion in Lametti, *supra* note 4.

[40] 2 William Blackstone, Commentaries *2, though this right was qualified elsewhere "by the laws of the land": 1 William Blackstone, Commentaries *138.

[41] James E. Penner, The Idea of Property (1997); Lametti, *supra* note 36. *See also* Thomas W. Merrill & Henry E. Smith, *The Morality of Property*, 48 Wm. & Mary L. Rev. 1849 (2007); and Thomas Merrill, *Property and the Right to Exclude*, 77 Neb. L. Rev. 730 (1998).

[42] *See, e.g.*, Charles R. Noyes, The Institution of Property 299 (1936); and Harris, *supra* note 4, at 33. Becker, in his later work, appears to go even further: *see* Lawrence Becker, *The Moral Basis of Property Rights*, *in* Nomos XXII: Property 231 (J. Rolland Pennock & John W. Chapman eds., 1980).

[43] *See for example* F. H. Lawson & Bernard Rudden, The Law of Property 8 (3d ed. 2002) for how property confers rights, whereas other parts of private law impose duties. Notable exceptions are Bruce Ziff, Principles of Property Law (5th ed. 2010) and Kevin Gray, Elements of Land Law (2d ed. 1993), as well as the articles by Gray and Lucy & Mitchell discussed *infra* note 49. *See also* Kevin Gray & Susan Francis Gray, Elements of Land Law (5th ed. 2009).

[44] Lametti, *supra* note 38, at chs. 4–5.

obligations of property, analyzing property relations in a contextual fashion and paying attention to an underlying theoretical discourse that is not rights based.[45] This "progressive" property school is now well established intellectually[46] and, in a sense, physically.[47] These writers have injected a variety of different ethical concerns into theoretical and practical property discourse.[48]

This chapter reinforces this position by demonstrating that accepted limitations on private property rights are less than random, all the while trying to tease out the underlying ethical threads. Property limitations and duties reflect a profound and fundamental fettering of property rights by the larger idea of an underlying morality manifested in property law. This underlying morality in property law is, in my view, partly explained by this emerging concept of *virtue ethics*, along with other moral discourses, as well as traditional utilitarian and rights-based narratives. An "ethics of virtue" helps channel property rights, as well as property duties, in the service of functional and principled goals.

These ethical or virtuous aspects of formal property rules are manifested generally in two ways. First, notwithstanding the existence of a grand principle expressed in a common law maxim, the rights to or the rights granted by title of ownership (let alone lesser entitlements) are never absolute. Indeed, in practice it is quite the opposite, with ownership subjected to various restrictions either in codified law, in rules and principles of the common law or equity, in public policy, or in statutory and regulatory restrictions. The point is not merely that private property is limited, but rather *why* and *how* it is limited. Most fundamentally, these restrictions reflect non-individuated "goods" that at times can "trump" rights that individuals might otherwise claim in private property in some circumstances. In some cases, these restrictions might even positively channel the property rights one has by fostering or requiring a certain use, or by imposing duties of stewardship in the exercise of these rights. Contrary to the argument advanced by William Lucy and Catherine Mitchell,[49] private property rights do not conflict with stewardship; rather, both

45 For an introduction, see G. S. Alexander & E.M. Peñalver, *Properties of Community*, 10 THEORETICAL INQUIRIES IN LAW 127 (2009), as well as PROPERTY AND COMMUNITY, *supra* note 6. See also the special edition of 94 CORNELL L. REV. (2009).

46 Alexander et al., *supra* note 6.

47 At the Cornell Law School, where three of the four signatories to the Statement – Gregory Alexander, Laura Underkuffler, and Eduardo Peñalver – teach. The fourth is Joseph William Singer of the Harvard Law School.

48 See the work of Singer, for example: ENTITLEMENT: THE PARADOXES OF PROPERTY (2000). *See also* Eric Freyfogle, *Ownership and Ecology*, 43 CASE W. RES. L. REV. 1269 (1993); *The Construction of Ownership*, U. Ill. L. REV. 173 (1996); William N. R Lucy & Catherine Mitchell, *Replacing Private Property: The Case for Stewardship*, 55 CAMB. L.J. 3, 566 (1996); K. Gray, *Equitable Property*, 49 CURR. LEGAL PROB. 157, 161 (1996); and Edward J. McCaffery, *Must We Have the Right to Waste?*, *in* NEW ESSAYS IN THE LEGAL AND POLITICAL THEORY OF PROPERTY 76 (Stephen R. Munzer ed., 2001). *See also* Lametti, *supra* note 5; Alexander, *supra* note 6; Peñalver, *supra* note 6.

49 Lucy & Mitchell, *supra* note 48.

are a fundamental part of property properly understood and are subservient to the teleology of private property.

Second, there are explicit provisions in the common law that are best grasped only in terms of proper or good behavior – and hence some form of virtue (via a duty or an obligation to other holders of real rights or as subservient to some global or local teleology). Although these legal norms do not necessarily form part of a coherent taxonomy in the common law – indeed they often appear to be quite idiosyncratic – their presence is enough to illustrate that the law of private property is not only about or explainable in terms of individual rights or protecting the reciprocity of individual rights. As such, these elements and fragments are better understood, along with rights, as an integral element of an explanation or series of justifications for private property containing both rights and duties, and undertaken in pursuit of certain non-individualistic goals. Thus the threads are not so disparate or exceptional; woven together they exemplify property's virtue ethics.[50]

At this point it is important to underscore the argument that is central to this chapter. It is of no great surprise that the rights and powers of private property, as manifested most completely in ownership, are limited, as a number of writers have pointed out. Indeed, it is a fact admitted in all property texts, where it is now trite to say that private property rights are always restricted by specific laws, regulations, and the like. The more interesting question, and one that is rarely discussed in depth, is *why* this is the case. That is, in examining how and why private property – specifically the most absolute form of property, namely, ownership – is limited, and in analyzing what justifications are offered in practice and theory for limiting property rights (rights that are of capital metaphoric importance to Western society), one goes beyond the merely trite. Indeed, it is in this examination that the teleology of private property becomes clearer. So the limits on property rights generally, and the specific duties imposed on certain property rights, will be seen to serve larger ethical and moral principles: the common good, the development of individual goods, and the like. These principles govern how human beings should interact with scarce resources. In other words, I am arguing more than the obvious assertion that private property usually has limits; rather, the argument is that private property is necessarily a limited concept. An examination of the reasons for such limits that are offered explicitly or that are implicit will explain underlying aspects of the institution that are not explicable in rights-based terms: this is property's social dimension, of which virtue ethics is one part. The argument is not that rights have no role or that duties, goals, and virtues are presently excluded from property discourse; rather, the

[50] Ultimately, these rules are reflective of the larger ideas exposed in other parts of my work, which purport that, to the extent that there are any natural rights to private property, there are also natural duties that flow from some idea of "destination" of the resource; and to the extent that some private property is a creation of the state, its substantive rights, powers, and duties can be given out, modified and taken away by the state. At bottom, private property rights and duties, far from being absolute, are part of a larger functional and virtue-oriented morality.

claim is that the role of virtue ethics is presently not properly understood and is thus underincluded. As such, we need to rebalance the virtue ethics with the rights-based and utilitarian perspectives, in the same way that copyright and patent have to balance interests: this is property's social dimension, of which an ethic of virtue is a component part. A parallel discussion exists at the level of ethics and justice and underlies this analysis.[51]

Despite the potentially wide-ranging nature of the types of resources we call property (property-as-object, as seen elsewhere[52]), the focus of this part is on ownership generally and on land ownership in particular. The discussion is so limited for several reasons. First, the fragmented forms of ownership or "lesser estates" are de facto limited. In effect, they represent the easy case where duties and obligations to other holders of real rights (in this case, in the same property-as-object) are not only explicit but are also subservient to an ethical teleology.[53] In restating the idea that the more expansive notion of ownership is limited and, more importantly, in going on to give the reasons behind these limits, this argument will have met the burden of proof. Second, land ownership has until very recently been the most valuable form of ownership. As a result, much of the legal literature on property law centers around land. Partly as a result of this historical value and critical focus, most of the teleological and deontological elements and fragments I seek to identify deal specifically with land law.[54] Finally, the principles behind these elements and fragments might then be applicable to the other forms of social wealth traditionally governed by "private property"[55] (and, as seen earlier, are also present in IP governance regimes).

Before looking at some of the specific rules and principles regarding ownership, the aspects of the institution on which the discussion focuses should be clarified more precisely. These aspects divide roughly into what I call ethical "elements" and "fragments" of the institution of private property. Aspects of an ethics of virtue are present in all of these component parts of private property and are critical to their understanding.

51 The virtue ethics sources have already been cited; *supra* note 8. The "justice" writers include AMARTYA SEN, THE IDEA OF JUSTICE (2009); MARTHA C. NUSSBAUM, CREATING CAPABILITIES: THE HUMAN DEVELOPMENT APPROACH (2011); and MICHAEL SANDEL, JUSTICE: WHAT'S THE RIGHT THING TO DO? (2009).

52 Lametti, *supra* note 4.

53 This is usually manifested by the use and preservation of the resource; for example, usufruct and emphyteusis in the civil law.

54 See JEREMY WALDRON, RIGHT TO PRIVATE PROPERTY 34 (1990), who also focuses on corporeals.

55 Hanoch Dagan has identified other regimes, such as marital property, in a larger "property-as-institutions" approach to property. *See* HANOCH DAGAN, PROPERTY: VALUES AND INSTITUTIONS 37–75 (2012). I would argue that these kinds of community property schemes are easier cases through which to illustrate property's virtues. Hence, my focus is on the traditional ownership paradigm. As regards a conceptual definition for private property, I believe that the institutions approach, while relying on family resemblances (*id.* at xi), is still too loose a concept to withstand the criticisms of the property-as-exclusion theorists. An open-ended, pluralist definition – but still conceptual enough to demarcate property from other areas of law – is possible: *see* Lametti, *supra* note 5.

By elements, I mean the more general, first-order duties and obligations that form part of the concept of ownership at its core or in its essence. These elements can only be explained and justified coherently by acknowledging certain overarching deontological or teleological principles, or indeed virtues. These principles are often common to a number of private property systems and across different jurisdictions within the same paradigm. The full explanation of these core elements provides evidence that private property is a concept that serves various functional ends and ethical purposes, a number of which might be called virtuous. These values and virtues are not monist, but rather form part of a plurality of virtues (and other rights) served by the institution of private property.[56]

By fragments, I mean specific duties attached to more particular incidents of ownership or with regard to particular objects of property. They appear to be less coherent than the core elements in their demonstration of virtues, being more particular to different jurisdictions or even to different physical settings. They appear, if you will, idiosyncratic. Nevertheless, any one of these fragments, as well as their sum, might exemplify a more general basic duty or goal, even if that goal is more localized; for instance, if tied to a specific resource. And, as seen in the context of intellectual property, such fragments exhibit the "positionality" that is necessary to understanding facts "on the ground." The difference may be explained by borrowing from James Penner's original articulation of property norms: an element is one that may be a criterion of family resemblance for the identification of property in most cases, whereas a fragment is a criterion only in some cases.[57] Grafting this ethics of virtue onto this Wittgensteinian stance, one might say the rationale underlying an element is a more direct, coherent, and systematic example of property's functional goals and duties, illuminating aspects of private property of a more general nature, whereas a fragment is an example of particular principles applied to a specific resource.

As with any dichotomy, the lines of demarcation between elements and fragments are not all that precise; a specific duty may go to limiting ownership at its root. The criterial, family resemblances approach clearly evokes this type of overlap.[58] The main purpose of this taxonomy is to serve as a pointer that helps identify and organize the argument. The distinction also illustrates that some duties, goals, or functions may be more fundamental than others in identifying and understanding private property's virtue ethics. This classification is also to some extent temporary. If this project is successful, many of the disparate fragments might be bolstered or

56 Here I am clearly following Dagan's characterization of property as pluralist: see DAGAN, *supra* note 55, at 57.

57 James E. Penner, *The "Bundle of Rights" Picture of Property*, 43 UCLA L. REV. 711 (1996). The possibility for Wittgensteinian family resemblances as a means to understanding property had been first identified by Tony Honoré, in his famous article, *Ownership*, *in* OXFORD ESSAYS IN JURISPRUDENCE 107 (A. G. Guest ed., 1961). It is now followed by, inter alia, myself and Dagan, *supra* note 55. Penner's more famous work seems to focus more on exclusion than family resemblance.

58 Penner, *supra* note 57.

supplemented or given a theoretical foundation such that they will in fact illustrate larger, more coherent underlying principles of virtue.

A. *Ethical Threads in the History of Land Ownership*

To understand the basic structure of common law property one must trace, at least superficially, the beginnings of the common law system of landholding.[59] Any discussion of the historical origins of private property in the common law pointedly illustrates that the modern tendency to equate private property only with rights was not always the case, at least with respect to land and fixtures.

The evolution of the law of real property in the common law is a story well known to every common law lawyer.[60] The structure and details of the law in this area have their origins in the nature of feudal landholding, particularly as manifested in England after the Norman conquest of 1066. The two central organizing concepts of that property system were the web of legal relations known as "tenure" and the means of defining the intensity and duration of interests in land known as the "doctrine of estates." This system of symbiotic relationships and defined interests in land resources lay at the heart of the feudal system and formed the basis for the common law of property, and indeed the whole of the common law. The key was that the feudal network was a system of effective government; property relations were a component of social ordering and were subservient to its larger functional goals.

The notion of seisin is worth some emphasis. The concept entailed more than legal possession; its substance focused on proprietary rights based on actual physical possession or being in a position to so enjoy. As Gray states, "Seisin thus expressed the organic element in the relationship between man and land and as such provided presumptive evidence of ownership within the medieval framework of rights in land."[61] Rights and duties are thus based on a very close, objectively intrinsic relationship with the resource – a relationship that is predicated on being able to derive direct benefits from the object. In addition to the doctrine's application throughout the law of real property is the built-in tendency it demonstrates toward the facts and the factual relationship of being seized. It draws attention to the substance of physical possession – what it entails and what it does not – by virtue of which rights it protects and obligations it requires, and those that it does not.

Perhaps most importantly, the doctrine of estates allowed for multiple interests to be held in the same land at the same time. These interests were not arbitrary;

[59] *See* Charles Donahue, Jr., *The Future of the Concept of Property Predicted from Its Past*, *in* NOMOS XXII: PROPERTY 37 (J. Rolland Pennock & John W. Chapman eds., 1980).

[60] The ensuing discussion loosely follows and summarizes the general outlines of the more detailed historical analysis in the following works: A. W. B. SIMPSON, A HISTORY OF THE LAND LAW c. I, II, & IV (2d ed. 1986); J. H. BAKER, AN INTRODUCTION TO ENGLISH LEGAL HISTORY Part II, c. 13–15 (3d ed. 1990); S. F. C. MILSOM, HISTORICAL FOUNDATIONS OF THE COMMON LAW c. 5–8 (2d ed. 1981).

[61] Gray, *supra* note 43, at 61.

estates in land were limited to those recognized by the common law.[62] The fact that multiple interests in the same resource could exist makes the practice of common law property less than absolute at the outset, at least with respect to relations between interested title holders. What is crucial is that a multiplicity of estates in the same land recognizes, of necessity, correlative duties and rights as between and among the various estate holders. What is obvious in the doctrine of estates is indicative of the larger system of feudal tenure: every instance of tenure has duties attached to it and serves functional goals.

There is a larger point to be taken from this familiar discussion of origins. First, both the doctrines of tenure and of estates, at a conceptual level, explicitly acknowledged the general limitations of private property by recognizing the function of property within the organic structure or chain of society and within a context of reciprocal rights and duties. Within this structure, certain virtues were fostered – loyalty being the most obvious, but also generosity on the part of a superior lord – and certain types of behavior were expected, forming the basis for duties and obligations through the property relationship. These general limitations were particularized in the specific duties that were a precondition to landholding. Moreover, through a doctrine of estates, which recognizes multiple interests in the same resource, one's interest might be further limited. That is not to say that a form of powerful property "ownership" *right* did not exist in the common law; a number of writers have pointed out that indeed it has and does.[63] Rather, the context for property ownership, as well as its structure, evinces *virtues* as well as rights: there were manners of conduct, duties, and obligations that were expected and had normative force. Second, and more importantly, the system and its base values and virtues themselves served larger goals: the effective organization of society, the productive use of land, the raising of revenues, and the ensuring of the polity's overall security and political stability. These goals were recognized explicitly in the personal relations and pledges of loyalty, as well as in the nature of the services provided to each ascendant and descendant within the structure. They were recognized implicitly in the productive use to which the land was put and the system of order protected. Thus, at the outset, property holding in the common law had an explicit teleology and was reinforced by a system of duties and rights. Third, in a point related to the second, despite the admission that only the shell of the system of tenure exists today in common law systems, its theoretical existence still points to the larger, unstated goals that continue to be fostered by the landholding system of the common law.

[62] Keppell v. Bailey, 2 My. & K. 517, 39 ER 1042 (Ch. 1834) (Eng.). *See* Bernard Rudden, *Economic Theory Versus Property Law: The* Numerus Clausus *Problem, in* OXFORD ESSAYS IN JURISPRUDENCE 239 (J. Eeekelaar & J. Bell eds., 3d Series, 1987). *See also* Thomas H. Merrill & Henry E. Smith, *Optimal Standardization in the Law of Property: The Numerus Clausus Principle*, 110 YALE L.J. 1 (2000).

[63] *See* HARRIS, *supra* note 4; and GEORGE W. PATON, A TEXT-BOOK OF JURISPRUDENCE 516–17 (G. W. Paton & D. P. Derham eds., 4th ed., 1972). This is also implied, in my view, by the discussion in LAWSON & RUDDEN, *supra* note 43, at 6–11, even if never formally stated as such.

If ownership of land explicitly served societal goals and fostered virtues in the past, then it likely still does so, although perhaps more implicitly. The same is also true of the private property institution more generally: it still serves similar kinds of goals, although in an understated manner. And to the extent that there has been a change in societal structure, there may also have been a change in the underlying teleology of private property. The past has left its imprint on our collective memory and shapes our legal imagination. It is from this last point that we move from past to present.

B. *Ethical Threads in the Practice of Land Ownership*

What ethical or virtue-oriented elements exist in the modern system of property law in the common law as it relates to land? In terms of the elemental or core structure of property, it is restating the obvious to underscore that there are restrictions on most modes of exercising the rights of private property, whether in the most powerful estate, the fee simple, or other lesser estates. As regards what I have called fragments of such ethical threads, one would look at a number of context-specific, land-based duties that do not appear to fall into any sort of coherent conceptual regime of reciprocal rights. Rather, these duties appear to be tied to owning a specific physical resource, and the vocation of destination of that resource. Far from being idiosyncratic, these examples – often on the conceptual boundaries of property law, especially nuisance examples on the border with tort – have much to offer to our understanding of the nature of property rights.

At this point, I focus only on the most powerful estate, that of fee simple ownership of land. In the common law, the fee simple estate is the greatest and most durable interest one can have in land. It has the largest number of metaphorical sticks in its bundle.[64] It is infinite in duration and can be alienated in whole or in part, vertically or horizontally; in addition, some of its rights can be parceled off and alienated through the granting of easements.[65] But even where no other concurrent lesser estate exists in a certain real property (the Crown's interest or eminent domain still exists in theory as a greater estate), the remaining rights and powers of fee simple are still not absolute.[66]

Although it is quite evident in practice that "low-level" restrictions impinge on ownership – zoning rules, regulations, and the like – the larger conceptual point is that the nature of fee simple is limited at the very outset by common law doctrine. A pertinent example, applying to all common law jurisdictions, is the common law's restriction of the very physical scope of ownership as stated in the *cuius est solum eius est usque ad coelum et ad inferos* rule, a maxim whose origins trace back to the

64 *See* GRAY, *supra* note 43, at 58 n.16.

65 *Id.* at c. 5.

66 It should be noted that "absolute" in the term *fee simple absolute* refers to duration only: the estate is not limited in time. I am discussing "absolute" in the sense of unlimited more generally.

medieval glossator Accursius.[67] The import of the *cuius ad coelum* rule is that the owner of the soil in theory owns a column proceeding downward to the center of the earth and upward to the heavens. However, contrary to the wide scope implied by this rule, the common law has restricted the full impact of this defining element of ownership to something far less extensive. Thus, in terms of air or aerial space above one's land, a person can only claim exclusive ownership of what he or she can reasonably use and enjoy.

Oft-cited cases present a familiar story; what is of current theoretical interest is why and how the limits are understood and justified. In the case of *Bernstein of Leigh (Baron)* v. *Skyviews & General Ltd.*,[68] a wealthy landowner attempted to sue in trespass a company that routinely took aerial photographs of properties and then tried to sell them to the respective owners for having taken an aerial photograph of his estate. Griffiths J. held that no property right was being trespassed on by the overhead flight of aircraft at high levels. In doing so he explicitly stated that the scope of the maxim was not unlimited, but rather was a question of balance:

> The problem is to balance the rights of an owner to enjoy the use of his land against the *rights of the general public* to take advantage of all that science now offers in the use of air space. *The balance is in my judgment best struck in our present society by restricting the rights of an owner in the air space above his land to such height as is necessary for the ordinary use and enjoyment of his land and the structures upon it,* and declaring that he has no greater rights in the air space than any other member of the public.[69]

Several observations emanate from these reasons. The first is that a traditional right or power of ownership is not unlimited; the extent of ownership will in large measure *depend on the resource*. This passage is best understood as a way of drawing lines around the objects of property or resources in question, as opposed to mere qualification of rights. It is the nature of the resource that will determine the scope of the rights and duties. Second, and more importantly, is the speculation on how and why the right is limited. Here, the balancing of interests undertaken by Griffiths J. is of capital import. He states that the limit is one of "ordinary use," which implies some idea of a standard destination for this particular resource – whether it is a "natural" or ordinary use, or whether there is an agreed-on, conventional use; in turn, this destination delimits the way in which the resource should be used. Implicitly, one might even infer the notion of "destination" for the civil law: some objects of property are classified or change classification according to their function (or a change in function), or some resources should be used in specific ways.[70] In this case, the "historical use" or "vocation" of the land appears to be tied to some idea of utility.

[67] *See* K. Gray, *Property in Thin Air*, 50 CAMB. L.J. 252, 253, n.1 (1991).

[68] 1 QB 479 (High Ct. 1978) (Eng.).

[69] *Id.* at 487–88 [emphasis added].

[70] D. Lametti, The *Destino* of Destination in Civil Law Property (unpublished manuscript) (on file with the author). *See also* Peñalver, *supra* note 6.

The employment of the concept of utility might be evidence that there still exists, in part, a consequentialist teleology to private property. That is, if it is seen as one of the explanations for private property that all of society will benefit economically from putting land to productive use, then utility does have at least one non-individual, non–rights-based aspect.[71] Yet, utility on its own is insufficient to capture the robust ethical nature of the balance struck in this decision. The idea of how a resource ought to be used is based on more than simply productive or allocative efficiency. The idea of "rights of the general public" implies not only a benefit to individuals but also to the community as a whole. It necessarily entails neither merely correlative rights and duties nor reciprocal rights. Rather, there is an asymmetry in the relationship between owners and non-owners mediated through the resource. If use or utility is often used to justify restrictions on core ownership rights, it might be evidence that tenurial ownership, even in the absence of personal duties, fits into a larger, goal-oriented structure. Yet utility on its own is insufficient to capture the robustness of the balance struck in the decision; the idea of how a resource should be used is the more profound understanding of the process.

The same types of balances between the individual landholder and the community or neighborly interests are drawn when applying the same maxim downward, toward the center of the earth. Another well-known case is equally enlightening. One set of reasons in *Edwards* v. *Sims*[72] does appear to apply the *cuius est solum* rule in an absolute way. In that case, a plaintiff landowner was attempting to bar a neighbor from having an underground survey undertaken of a scenic cave that existed under the plaintiff's own land. The survey was supposed to ascertain if the cave, whose mouth opened onto the plaintiff's land and was economically exploited by the plaintiff, was also situated beneath the land of his neighbor.[73] The plaintiff cave-mouth owner ultimately failed in preventing the survey from being undertaken, even though the defendant neighbor could not have exploited the cave on his own in any event. So the neighbor's right *ad inferos* was seemingly upheld, at the expense of the trespassory rights of the plaintiff. Nevertheless, even with respect to the neighbor's rights, the *cuius est solum* rule was not given its largest potential reading. Although the majority decision of the Court used the maxim as the starting point for discussion, it did note that the scope of the rule was not unlimited, subject as it was to "certain limitations on the right of enjoyment of possession of all property, such as its use to the detriment or interference with a neighbour and burdens which it must bear in common with property of a like kind."[74] In the end, the majority of the Court fixed

[71] Of course, I do not deny a whole host of factors promoting individual utility or individual self-development.

[72] 24 S.W.2d 619 (Ky. Sup. Ct. 1929); 232 Ky. 791.

[73] The plaintiff was actually seeking a writ of prohibition, barring a judge from ordering the completion of the survey: *id.* at 620.

[74] *Id.*

on what it felt was an analogous provision in the law pertaining to the surveying of mines and then applied the provision to caves.

More illuminating is the dissent of Logan J. to the effect that the maxim and indeed ownership were not unlimited. In particular, he focuses on potential "use" as a limitation circumscribing the ownership rights protected by the maxim:

> It is well enough to hang to our theories and ideas, but when there is an effort to apply old principles to present-day conditions, and they will not fit, then it becomes necessary for a readjustment, and principles and facts as they exist in this age must be made comfortable. For these reasons the old sophistry that the owner of the surface of land is the owner of everything from surface to nadir must be reformed, and the reason why a reformation is necessary is because the theory was never true in the past, but no occasion arose that required the testing of it. . . . *It should not be held that he owns that which he cannot use and which is of no benefit to him,* and which may be of benefit to others.[75]

There are a number of relevant points to draw from this statement of principle. First, as in *Bernstein*, the scope of the *cuius est solum* rule is not unlimited. The maxim was never true, according to Logan J., but in effect was tolerated because it could not be challenged. Second, the scope of private property is contextual. New resources and new means of exploitation open up different possibilities and hence different kinds of property rights. These rights, and their limitations, will evolve as the conditions of societies change. As the nature of private property (as both resource and relation) changes, so might its underlying principles. This is a step toward some recognition of a larger functional purpose: to some extent, the institution of private property reflects the needs of society. Third, one limiting principle in the view of Logan J., and to a lesser extent the minority, is once again utility. Use, or potential use, is the factor that determines the scope of ownership rights. There is recognition that potential benefits falling within "the centre to the heavens" might be owned by others if indeed they can derive the benefit but the owner cannot, or might be beyond the ambit of anyone's *dominium,* if no one can derive a benefit from it. In short, Logan J. presents a very functional, use-oriented approach to the scope of property rights.

This statement of limitation according to uses is potentially very wide and reflects a larger theory that land ownership is for the benefit of human beings; if an individual cannot benefit from the use of a land resource, others should not be so prevented. Indeed, Logan J. in a lavish piece of rhetorical flourish goes on to describe the exploration, development, and opening of the cave in near-epic terms: allowing the defendant neighbour to succeed would kill all incentives to develop.[76] This last point, that of individual interest, coupled with the second point, recognizing changing conditions, leaves open to speculation whether one could go further than Logan J.

[75] *Id.* at 622 (emphasis added).

[76] *Id.*

went by explicitly stating that putting land to productive use and development is also a communal good and as such susceptible to regulation by the community, even if it is individual landowners who benefit. Moreover, one might see this as a condition of ownership for an extremely scarce and precious resource. Although the passage cited earlier does not go that far explicitly, certainly the rhetorical tone in other parts of the judgment indicate that Logan J. was favorably disposed to such a view.[77] The point is that limitations on ownership rights are very much tied to questions of the characteristics of the resource and the manner in which it is used and to whether that is a productive use.

The obvious point of the narrative so far is that even the rights associated with the most absolute estate in common-law land law are in fact not so absolute. Hence, even land ownership in fee simple was never treated as absolute; this is true not only in the sense of a correlative limit – in that in overextending one's rights another's rights were undermined – but also, more importantly, in the noncorrelative sense that there are larger, non-individualized interests at stake in the resource. In these cases, the community's interests in the proper use and development or protection of a resource might be undermined by a characterization of the property relation that is too strictly rights based.

The more profound general point that begins to emerge, even using the example of fee simple, is that these limitations are tied both to the resource itself and to some immanent teleology (or teleologies), whether explicitly or implicitly, that serves to justify or explain the limits. From these two examples, utility is an obvious candidate that helps illuminate a consequentialist teleology. To some extent, a notion of utility helps explain why we impose limits on fee simple ownership (as well as on lesser rights). But a purely economic calculus fails to capture the teleology of private property in its fullest sense.

Another example of a limit on the basic concept of property ownership that exemplifies a larger sense of direction or vocation to private property is that of the possibility of adverse possession leading to a change in ownership. A fee simple owner might lose the whole of the bundle of rights because of non-use: the doctrine of adverse possession. Under this doctrine, a non-owner who has an intention to possess a piece of land as an owner, as well as a sufficient degree of possession for a specified period of time, may eventually extinguish the rights of the true owner. Historically, the required conditions enabling a claim of title through adverse possession to be successful have been onerous; in general they require the continued public use of the property without the consent of the owner, often in a way inconsistent with the owner's

77 Morton Horwitz has argued that judges in the United States in the nineteenth century used law in an effort to favor all sorts of economic development. *See* M. Horwitz, The Transformation of American Law: 1780–1860, 31 (1977). I am not sympathetic to any theory of conspiracy of elites, while recognizing that utility has always played a large role in analyzing property rules. There are other systemic goals – the stewardship over and protection of the natural world (for religious or secular reasons), for example – that have existed in addition to individualistic utility.

intended use.[78] As a result, these requirements in fact provide a great deal of protection for ownership. Nevertheless, the possibility remains for one to lose one's land completely.

The possibility of adverse possession has several practical functions: it provides protection for settled interests and allows for the quieting of titles. It might also reflect, at least in part, the idea that land should be put to productive use, and if it is not so used and someone else puts it to an alternative use, then title will flow to the new user. It rewards the "purposeful" at the expense of the "sluggard."[79] This last function in particular illustrates a teleological aspect to the rule: land is an important resource of objective value, and given its finite quantity and relative scarcity, certain types of uses will be favored over others. Conversely, certain types of non-use will put one's ownership rights at a risk of loss. This particular rationale is not watertight, as has been pointed out.[80] One might frame the same argument more gently in terms of stewardship.[81] If stewardship entails a duty to preserve and use, one might interpret the law of adverse possession as either punishing the owner's lack of stewardship or rewarding the squatter's.[82] We reward the virtuous party. Whatever the case, acquisition through adverse possession certainly cannot be explained in terms of absolute rights of ownership, because an owner's rights in theory cannot be compared to those of a mere possessor. Thus, there must be some other functional justification – historical contingency, utility, stewardship, or even a self-developmental argument,[83] possibly virtue-based[84] – that allows us to compare the benefit that the use of the resource confers to the owner and the possessor as well as to society, thus serving to explain adverse possession.

What may be equally telling from the example of adverse possession is that the teleologies informing a particular legal property norm can evolve over time. Environmental concerns actively challenge the notion that land must be used productively in the traditional sense; protective non-use may be more beneficial to society than the depletion of a particular resource.[85] Thus the process of determining the value of the nature of the resource is similar, but the underlying teleological and deontological

[78] *See generally* ZIFF, *supra* note 43, at 118–26. *See also* M. Lubetsky, *Adding Epicycles: The Inconsistent Use Test in Adverse Possession Law*, 47 OSGOODE HALL L.J. 497 (2009) (challenging the validity of the notion of inconsistent use).

[79] Gray, *supra* note 43, at 285.

[80] *See* Ziff, *supra* note 43 at 120, n.20–24. To reiterate, my claim is that adverse possession is "in part" so explained.

[81] There is a more detailed discussion of stewardship later in this part.

[82] I am indebted to Jim Harris for this reading. For a lengthier theoretical discussion on the moral status of the possessor vis-à-vis the owner in Quebec civil law, see generally, D. Lametti, "Prescription *à la recherche du temps*: In Search of Past Time (or Recognizing Things Past)" *in* M. DÉVINAT ed., *Les livres du Code Civil du Québec* (Yvon Blais, 2013) (forthcoming). The argument applies *mutatis mutandis* to the common law.

[83] *See* A. RYAN, PROPERTY AND POLITICAL THEORY *passim* (1984).

[84] Lametti, *supra* note 89.

[85] John G. Sprankling, *An Environmental Critique of Adverse Possession*, 79 CORNELL L. REV. 816 (1994).

considerations have moved. In one case, forests are seen as a valuable source of wood and pulp; in another they are seen as objectively valuable for their beauty as part of a wilderness area or according to their role in an ecosystem (perhaps even with a standing independent of human beings).[86] Coupled with the perceived harshness of the rule, some jurisdictions are further restricting the scope of adverse possession.[87] Thus, as the larger goals of societies change as underlying moralities evolve, the scope of ownership changes.

It is from these sorts of examples that the social dimension of private property, expressed in moral terms as the social obligations of property or the virtues of property, becomes visible. In terms, or property's virtues, I have elsewhere noted that Aristotle had seen the promotion of friendship through liberality as one of the virtues fostered by the institution of private property.[88] Eduardo Peñalver adds industry, justice, and humility.[89] Gregory Alexander and Madhavi Sunder, following Martha Nussbaum, posit the virtues in terms of human flourishing.[90] Or these dimensions can be framed within specific kinds of property institutions.[91]

C. *Ethical Elements in the Ownership of Lesser Estates*

If such virtuous aspects of private property – gleaned through a fuller understanding of *why* ownership is limited – exist in the common law's most absolute estate, then one would expect the same to be true for lesser estates. Using only one example, I think that the expectation is a fair one. A life estate is another long-term freehold interest, but it too is modified rather obviously at its core by the idea that there is someone who has an estate in the same land, which will go in remainder over to that person at the end of the present freeholder's life estate. So with respect to alienation, because one cannot alienate more than one's own interest in land, alienation at common law is restricted.[92] This, however, is trite. The important aspect of the life estate is the life tenant's relation to the resource. Life tenants at common law are governed by a set of rules preventing them from permanently altering the physical

86 See the influential article by Christopher D. Stone, *Should Trees Have Standing? – Toward Legal Rights for Natural Objects*, 45 S. Cal. L. Rev. 450 (1972).

87 For example, Ontario, which has abolished adverse possession for land under land titles registration: Land Titles Act, R.S.O. 1990, c. L-5, s. 51(1).

88 Lametti, *supra* note 4.

89 Peñalver, *supra* note 6, at 876–86.

90 *See* Gregory S. Alexander & Eduardo M. Peñalver, An Introduction to Property Theory 80–104 (2012); Madhavi Sunder, From Goods to a Good Life: Intellectual Property and Global Justice (2012).

91 *See generally*, Dagan, *supra* note 55 and Singer, *supra* note 48.

92 This fettering of sale and mortgage had a negative impact on the maintenance of land, often preventing the life tenant from making major repairs. Alienation is now allowed under certain conditions designed to protect the ultimate interest of successive owners; this is now governed by different rules in different common law jurisdictions.

condition of the land: the doctrine of waste. The doctrine involves a number of diverse strands, but in general the life tenant is prohibited from making alterations that diminish the value of the freehold (voluntary waste) or that are severe and malicious acts of destruction (equitable waste). Damage resulting from the failure to preserve or repair (permissive waste) and waste that actually improves the value of the land (ameliorating waste) can (but does not always) result in compensating the person holding the remaining interest. In short, a balance is struck between the person with the life estate and the person holding the remainder interest.[93] The life tenant is, in effect, a steward of the land in question, preserving its value for the ultimate owner. These common law provisions, which identify the estate holders and attempt to settle their respective rights and obligations, explicitly illustrate a limited concept, at least with respect to the life estate.

As it stands, the importance of the particular example of the life estate to my overall argument is limited. As a formally limited type of freehold interest with relatively well-defined limits and duties, its intrinsic characteristics are not immediately applicable to property theory more generally. The notion of stewardship, however, both in the life estate and latent in the doctrine of adverse possession, has a larger import that is only beginning to be acknowledged more widely. Given the contours or characteristics of landholding in the common law, the explicit notion of stewardship present in the life estate might well be applicable to the larger concept of ownership as well. That is, the virtuous aspects evinced or required by the relationship of the life tenant to the ultimate owner might be applicable to ownership of land generally. The fundamental premise of the life estate is that one turns over the resource at the end of the tenure to someone with a stronger claim. The resource is valuable over the long term and requires protection and preservation to maintain this value.

One might say the same is true with respect to ownership. If one determines that land is a scarce and valuable resource, necessary for the survival and flourishing of the human race, then one might be compelled to conclude either that its distribution into private hands is predicated on the obligation to preserve the resource for future generations; or on the requirement to put the resource to certain productive uses, the benefit of which accrue to the individual and society, directly or indirectly; or equally on the requirement to avoid uses that will destroy the resources or harm other individuals. Thus all landowners might be classed as stewards of a valuable resource, holding with regard to a higher claim held by society and the human race, present and future.

The formal structure of the life estate also applies to the formal structure of ownership. A remnant of feudal landholding is that the ultimate reversionary interest in land is in the Crown or the state. Although "holding of" the Crown is only symbolically true today in a doctrine such as eminent domain, it does represent the ultimate

[93] Ziff, *supra* note 43, at 155–64.

interest that the state has in determining how land is used: land can be expropriated or rezoned, for example. The Crown or the state embodies the collective interests of those who might in fact be analogous to holders of the remaining interest, namely everyone. Thus, the life estate has greater metaphorical application generally to the whole of property law than is strictly considered to be the case, and the paradigm of stewardship exemplified in the life estate acquires even greater persuasive force. In my view, we can apply this metaphor to land ownership generally. If Kevin Gray is correct about the emerging importance of "equitable property,"[94] in particular equitable property in the natural environment, perhaps the usufructuary relationship of the life estate is a more appropriate metaphor for land entitlement than is ownership: indeed, one pair of writers has advocated stewardship as a *replacement* of ownership in land.[95]

My understanding of stewardship lies in what one might call its "theological" conception.[96] That is to say, human beings might benefit personally from the goods committed to them, unlike a trustee, for instance. Thus, they can use the resource. In addition, however, they also have a duty to preserve the resource, and if Gray is correct, perhaps even to share it in some way; for instance, by allowing access. Stewardship does not replace ownership in this form, because – as the practice is revealing – ownership is in part stewardship. Seen in this light, ownership in practice comprises a rights element (uses to which the owner may suit him- or herself) and elements of *virtue ethics* (goals that must in some way orient the owner's use, or duties to preserve), both of which comprise stewardship in the fullest sense. Over time the specific duties and goals can evolve – feudal incidents to productive use to environmental concerns – depending on the resource in question and the stage of development.

This argument – *virtue ethics* both as a third *ethical methodology*, between the poles of utilitarianism and rights-based views, and as explaining part of the *ethical substance* of property relations – ties into the role played by another overarching set of principles in the evolution of the common law: equity. In addition to the explicit mention thus far of productive use and utility, the limitation of ownership is also consistent with some of the larger, ethical principles found generally in the past and present of the common law legal world through the ever-evolving principles of equity. The term "equity" is here used in the Aristotelian sense of the general principles of justice behind specific and unarticulated laws,[97] as well as their specific manifestations in the law of equity, which traces its origins to the moderation of the harshest elements of the common law by the Lord Chancellor and Chancery Courts.

94 K. Gray, *Equitable Property*, 47 CURR. LEG. PROBS. 157 at 204–05 (1994).

95 Lucy & Mitchell, *supra* note 49. It is also an argument made from outside the Western paradigm, by native peoples for example, but I submit that a similar argument can be made on Western terms.

96 The late Jim Harris had helped me frame this point.

97 ARISTOTLE, NICOMACHEAN ETHICS bk. V, at 133 (David Ross trans., 1980) (c. 384 BCE).

Equity thus has a general, all-pervasive supporting function – which can have the effect of limiting ownership rights.

Most basically, equity has provided for the splitting of ownership interests between legal owners and beneficial owners or interest-holders. This fragmentation was effected by the development of the trust. Its standard structure is well known: in this institution there is an estate created for a specific purpose vested in a trustee who is the legal owner. It is, however, an estate where the legal owner is charged with fiduciary duties to certain other persons, called beneficiaries. They are the objects of the specific terms of the trust. These persons to whom the duties of the trustee are owed, the owners of the beneficial estate, may owe nothing in return to the trustees and indeed may have certain common law and statutory rights against the trustees. Thus, we see two types of ownership: the first, the legal ownership recognized at common law in the trustee, and the second, recognized in equity as the beneficial ownership in the beneficiary.

There are two features of the trust that are crucial to illustrating the underlying concept of virtue ethics. First, trust ownership recognizes a limited idea of ownership, coupled with a specifically stated teleology – the purpose or goal of the trust – and a set of general duties and obligations. It is a most complete institution in terms of balancing rights, duties, and goals, all the while maintaining a flexibility that is envied – and adopted – in civil law jurisdictions.[98] The institution embodies a view of ownership that is explicitly consistent with stewardship in its most stringent manifestation, setting very onerous standards for the maintenance of the trust property. Thus trustees are stewards as well as owners; moreover, unless also a beneficiary, they will have no personal interest at all in the corpus. Second, the fiduciary relationship that finds its source in the trust and principles of equity has found wider application in all areas of private law dealing with property[99]: family, corporate law, and restitution. It thus serves as a metaphor for a more moral institution of private property, representing the conscience of the property institution.

Equitable remedies specifically have influenced the law of property and the concept of ownership in several areas. In particular, equitable remedies have protected certain rights a person might have in another's land, as well as protecting the duties that might be owed by an owner to these lesser right-holders. These remedies posit a formal role for the concept of virtue – here expressed as loyalty or fidelity,[100]

[98] Such as Quebec: see CIVIL CODE OF QUEBEC arts. 1261 ff.

[99] *See*: Lionel Smith, *The Motive, Not the Deed*, *in* RATIONALIZING PROPERTY, EQUITY AND TRUSTS: ESSAYS IN HONOUR OF EDWARD BURN 53 (Joshua Getzler ed. 2003); Lionel Smith, *Philosophical Foundations of Proprietary Remedies*, *in* PHILOSOPHICAL FOUNDATIONS OF THE LAW OF UNJUST ENRICHMENT 281 (Robert Chalmers, Charles Mitchell, & James Penner eds., 2009).

[100] *See* Smith, *supra* note 106; and Lionel Smith & Remus D. Valsan, *The Loyalty of Lawyers: A Comment on 3464920 Canada Inc. v. Strother*, 87 CAN. BAR REV. 247 (2008).

stewardship, responsibility, or duty. If other property theorists are correct, the concept of the trust may have deeper import for all of property relations.[101]

D. *Ethical Fragments Relating to Land Ownership*

I now turn briefly to the discussion of what I have called ethical fragments: those property rules that might be traced to or understood in fragmented terms of an underlying concept of virtue. They are those norms that, while restricting and channeling property, do so not widely and generally, but rather more directly and specifically – often by imposing specific duties on landowners in specific circumstances. As such, they even appear idiosyncratic and haphazard. Although these piecemeal duties do not appear to be a coherent part of the common law of property – indeed the substantive rules often change in different jurisdictions – they do illustrate the idea that such duties can be imposed to serve some non–rights-based purpose. They are examples where specific rights and duties might attach to specific resources: resources with a traditional destination or teleology. For instance, if one has a certain specific duty toward one's neighbor that is unique given the situation of one's land, such a duty is in no way reciprocal – other landowners do not have such a duty – and therefore difficult to justify under some sort of reciprocal or "golden" rule for property owners. Put another way, such rules cannot be universalized in some a priori, Kantian fashion; these duties do not exist because all owners are bound by similar formal rules or could be bound if similarly situated. Context and virtue, or some ethical goals, must supply the answer to the question "why" in a way not permitted by some categorical imperative.

Here I do not go into detail on these examples, leaving that task for another occasion. It suffices for now to claim that the rules to which I wish to attach some significance deal with the duties a landholder might owe to his or her neighbors. There are, in the common law, certain neighborly duties that are specific to landholders: duties of support or riparian duties, for example. Thus, a landholder can expect that land in its natural state will attract duties of both lateral and vertical support from his or her adjoining neighbors. Or, a landowner will owe certain duties to other downstream landowners as regards the water flowing in a river or stream through their lands. Typically framed as a right of landowners against other adjacent landowners, these are best thought of as duties, which may not even be correlative to a right, depending on the nature and destination of the land.

Care must be taken from the outset to distinguish these types of property norms from those pointing to extracontractual responsibility (i.e., the law of tort). This is not always a clear distinction to draw, because it is also true that one cannot act completely independently on one's own land without regard for one's neighbors. The doctrine of nuisance is a limiting idea in this regard with respect to property

[101] *See* R.A. Macdonald, *Relational Ownership*, *in* Cross-Examining Private Law 167 (2008).

law, as it would be in other areas of private law.[102] So there is some question as to when the duty or obligation restricting ownership comes from a private property rule or principle itself and when it is imposed because of a standard in tort. Waldron, as I have pointed out in "The Concept of Property,"[103] argues that justifications for private property rules do not generally encompass uses, but only allocation.[104] Presumably, this might lead him to apply tort rules in all of these cases. I disagree; at least in this type of case, there is some direct link or characteristic in the rule that gives the norm a specificity that is uniquely tied to a resource and hence invokes property rules.[105] The distinction can be stated as a use whose consequential damage to neighbors is reasonably foreseeable (tort) versus a common law rule that gives one a right to reasonably use, often regardless of damages, or a duty to reasonably use in the limiting sense (property). These latter property rules are tied to some notion of destination, natural or artificial.

There are three points to note for these kinds of adjacent duties cases. First, each case would be determined according to its unique facts and circumstances. Second, the specification or instantiation of this overarching teleology – for example, a balanced use of water resources between individuals and the ultimate benefit to the community through the protection of the resource – can change from place to place, time to time, and technology to technology. Given that these rights are so closely tied to the character of the land on which they arise, rules change to affect the larger purpose. Third, especially as regards water, there is a clear teleology here with respect to how riparian water must be used. But the same is also true for the use of land. Most of the time, the *telos* emanates from some natural destination, anchored in timeless basic needs. Sometimes, however, the meeting of basic needs is manifested in different ways in unique settings. Thus, even particular rules such as prior appropriation are indicative of some larger systemic goals at play, all of which are "grounded" on the lie[106] of the land.

[102] *See, e.g.*, Bradford v. Pickles, A.C. 587 (H.L. 1895) (Eng.); Hollywood Silver Fox Farm v. Emmett, 2 K.B. 468 (1936) (U.K.); T. H. Critelli v. Lincoln Trust 86 D.L.R.3d 724 (Ont. High Ct. 1978) (Can.); and Rylands v. Fletcher L.R. 3 H.L. 330 (H.L. 1868) (Eng.). *But see* Katz, *supra* note 30. On things such as spite walls, a virtue ethics approach would (and should) allow us to go further than Katz allows, indeed allowing the common law to be (Razian) "perfectionist" in its pluralism. Of course, the civil law tradition is well acquainted with the idea of "abuse of right." In the French-language tradition the *locus classicus* is LOUIS JOSSERAND, DE L'ESPRIT DES DROITS ET DE LEUR RELATIVITÉ: THÉORIE DITE DE L'ABUS DES DOITS (2d ed. 1939). *See also* R. A. Macdonald, *id.*; and P.-E. Moyse, *L'abus de droit: l'anténorme – Réflexions sur l'application de l'abus de droit aux droits intellectuels*, 57 MCGILL L.J. 859 (2012).

[103] Lametti, *supra* note 4.

[104] Waldron, *supra* note 54, at 32.

[105] In any event, we should hesitate to impose tort standards willy-nilly and try to find the demarcating lines between these areas of private law. See the brief discussion, *supra* note 55, on what conceptual definition of property is still required.

[106] Even this very term is contextual, depending on where one learns to speak English: it is also "lay" of the land!

III. CONCLUSION: SPECULATING ON THE ETHICS OF PRIVATE LAW

It seems fair to conclude with the descriptive claim that those teleological and virtuous elements of ethics (and, hence, of *virtue ethics*) that are explicitly present in the IP regimes of copyright and patent are also implicitly present in the common law regimes covering land law and personal property, and especially in the former. Whether as part of the recognition that the notion of ownership of land is limited, with some attention paid to the care or stewardship of the resource through a contextually limited package of rights and social obligations; whether as part of the recognition that the very fragmentation of property rights at common law was a product of an ethical teleology; or whether we see the numerous fragmentary limits on ownership in service of neighbors, the neighborhood, and the lie of the land as part of a larger moral picture about how we use resources, there can be little doubt that the fullest understanding of property rules has pushed us into an analysis of how we understand and value, and then how we distribute, redistribute, and care for these resources. There are few governance challenges that are more fundamentally grounded in ethics than this; how we regulate resources will say a great deal about us as a society. And here we slide into the normative claim: the better, the more virtuously, or the more ethically we regulate resources, the better will be our property system and our ability to build a more ethical society and citizenry. It should even be the case that attention to virtues will provide us not only with better norms, but in understanding, formulating, and justifying property rules we will achieve more stable norms as they are calibrated to context. Property and IP law force a society to deal with important ethical questions and thus are an important place to begin.[107]

What if any of these threads might be woven through other parts of private law? Regarding the descriptive claim, it is certainly true that, at the very least, the Aristotelian-Thomistic notion of *epikeia* or *aequitas* that underlies both the common law doctrine of equity and its civil law analog, *équité*, is explicit evidence that this ethical direction – explicit in IP and increasingly being understood in property law – is also present in the larger private law tradition. As regards the common law, the central point is an obvious one: the common law system as we know it is comprised of both the common law doctrines *and* doctrines of equity. Together, there is a strong ethical element that has always been present in the structure of the common law system. Of course, as regards the civil law, such doctrines are quite clear, with good faith and *abus de droit* being the most obvious. In other words, the very fact of

[107] According to James Penner, to understand these ethical questions, "we must transcend the outlook of the individual owner of property vis-à-vis others if we are to understand with any sophistication the ethical community in which humans live, or rather must live to be fully human." *See* James E. Penner, *Property, Community and the Problem of Distributive Justice*, 10 THEORETICAL INQUIRIES IN LAW 193, 208 (2008). I would add that the inverse is true; we can better understand the ethical community by understanding the norms it has erected to interact with and through resources of value, whether scarce or not.

a doctrine of equity points to a set of guiding and determinative considerations that in turn are tied to the morality of society.

At the very least, asking ethical questions and trying to foster virtuous actions force us to build a system that *aspires* to the good and to the virtuous. So we are back to Fuller's aspirational morality of law, at least in formal terms of how to understand and to structure property norms, but perhaps also in the substantive terms that appeared to have eluded Fuller.

PART V

Parallels between the Substantive Common Law and Intellectual Property

17

Technology and Tracing Costs

Lessons from Real Property

*Molly Shaffer Van Houweling**

INTRODUCTION

Intellectual property (IP) scholars often contrast tangible and intangible property schemes on the basis of how much information is readily available about the identity of property owners and the nature of their rights. Typically, the comparison holds up tangible property – real property in particular – as the model of successful information provision. Physical signs can provide clues that a piece of land is owned by someone (often the person in possession). Public records indicate exactly who that someone is and reveal details about the physical dimensions of the parcel, how its ownership has changed over time, and whether express encumbrances (liens, servitudes, etc.) complicate ownership. These sources of information help prevent inadvertent trespass by those who wish to avoid invading private land; they facilitate consensual transactions for those who seek permission to use or buy it.

IP rights, by contrast, do not so neatly correspond either to physical things in the world or to public records signifying ownership and identifying owners. Of course, physical objects can embody intellectual works – a book can embody a copyrighted story, for example. But ownership of the physical object does not necessarily (or even usually) correspond to ownership of the IP right or vice versa.

Indeed, readily observable indicia of ownership of physical objects (possession of books, for example) are more likely to mislead than to inform about ownership of the embedded intangible rights. Although some such objects are marked with signs of copyright or patent ownership, a practice that is encouraged by the relevant federal statutes in the United States, marking is not a prerequisite for protection. In many cases neither the physical object nor any record to which it is expressly tied provides

* Professor of Law, University of California, Berkeley. Thanks to Shyam Balganesh and other participants in the University of Pennsylvania symposium on Intellectual Property and the Common Law for their feedback on my initial presentation of these ideas, and to the University of Colorado School of Law faculty for feedback on a subsequent draft. Thanks to Nicholas Fram for excellent research assistance.

much indication about whether the intellectual work is owned or by whom. A story embodied in a book may be copyrighted or it may be in the public domain; the copyright may be held by the author or by an employer, heir, devisee, or transferee; some elements of the story may be free and others owned; and the like. In the patent realm there is at least a centralized record of issued patents, but the scope of their coverage can be maddeningly unclear.

Anxiety about the inadequacy of information about IP rights has increased in recent years due to statutory changes that have worsened the situation (e.g., the elimination of registration and notice as prerequisites for copyright protection) and to technological changes that have raised the stakes and thickened thickets of (often hidden) rights. In copyright, this anxiety is manifest, for example, in policy debates about the status of "orphan works" whose owners cannot be identified and located and the (related) fate of the Google Book Search project.[1] In patent, critics are alarmed when innovators' investments are jeopardized by allegations that they have infringed unclear and thus difficult-to-avoid patent claims – especially in the new-fangled realms of software and Internet business methods.[2] In both the copyright and patent contexts, informational inadequacies can contribute to inadvertent infringement and then to surprising and costly disputes; fear of potential infringement – combined with the inability to identify, locate, and negotiate with relevant rights-holders – can chill productive endeavors.[3]

Critics of this current state of affairs lament what they see as unnecessarily faulty information provision and suggest that intellectual property should aspire to replicate the superior informativeness of real property. For example, copyright reformers have called for statutory changes modeled on the centralized ownership information provided by land recording systems and the title-clearing function performed by

1 Pamela Samuelson has written extensively on the relationship between the orphan works problem and the Google Book Search controversy. *See, e.g.*, Pamela Samuelson, *The Google Book Settlement as Copyright Reform*, 2011 WIS. L. REV. 479; Pamela Samuelson, *Legislative Alternatives to the Google Book Settlement*, 34 COLUM. J.L. & ARTS 697 (2011); Pamela Samuelson, *Google Book Search and the Future of Books in Cyberspace*, 94 MINN. L. REV. 1308 (2010).

2 *See, e.g.*, Bilski v. Kappos, 130 S.Ct. 3218, 3256 (2010) (Stevens, J., concurring in the judgment); eBay Inc. v. MercExchange, L.L.C., 547 U.S. 392, 397 (2006) (Kennedy, J., concurring); JAMES BESSEN & MICHAEL J. MEURER, PATENT FAILURE: HOW JUDGES, BUREAUCRATS, AND LAWYERS PUT INNOVATORS AT RISK (2008); Clarisa Long, *Information Costs in Patent and Copyright*, 90 VA. L. REV. 465, 487–88, 543–44 (2004); Peter S. Menell & Michael Meurer, *Notice Failure and Notice Externalities*, 5 J. LEGAL ANALYSIS 1, 2–4 (2013).

3 *See generally* FEDERAL TRADE COMMISSION, THE EVOLVING IP MARKETPLACE: ALIGNING PATENT NOTICE AND REMEDIES WITH COMPETITION 3 (2011) (observing that where patent notice is poor, "collaborators or licensees may not find relevant patents, or they may hesitate to invest in technology when the scope of patent protection is unclear"); U.S. COPYRIGHT OFFICE, REPORT ON ORPHAN WORKS 15 (2006) ("In the situation where the owner cannot be identified and located . . . the user faces uncertainty – she cannot determine whether or under what conditions the owner would permit use . . . Concerns have been raised that in such situation, a productive and beneficial use of the work is forestalled – not because the copyright owner has asserted his exclusive rights in the work, or because the user and owner cannot agree on the terms of a license – but merely because the user cannot locate the owner.").

marketable title acts.[4] As for patents, although the public availability of issued patents (and of most applications eighteen months after they are filed) already provides a relatively comprehensive centralized source of information, critics complain that vague patent claims do too little to clarify inventions' "metes and bounds."[5]

Ironically, while IP scholars and activists have been coveting the information-providing mechanisms of real property, developments in the land context have triggered skepticism about the functioning of those mechanisms. The mortgage foreclosure crisis has revealed to the public weaknesses in land recording that have long been lamented by real property scholars[6] – who have issued renewed calls to bring antiquated local recording systems into the digital age.[7] At the same time, private entities (most notably the Mortgage Electronic Recording System) have arisen that interact with the public recording system in controversial ways.[8]

The formal, centralized, and sometimes error-prone information mechanisms associated with land titles are not the only models offered by the law of tangible property, however. As other recent scholarship has observed, these structures coexist with common law adjudication that is sometimes explicitly attentive to and often seems implicitly shaped by information-cost concerns.[9] This common law tradition features a wide variety of doctrinal tools. Even – or perhaps especially – if the formal, centralized informational structures of the land law are never fully replicated for intangible property, this rich common law tradition may prove a valuable source of ideas for addressing contemporary IP challenges.[10]

4 *See, e.g.*, Lawrence Lessig, *For the Love of Culture: Google, Copyright, and Our Future*, NEW REPUBLIC, Feb. 4, 2010, at 24.

5 *See, e.g.*, BESSEN & MEURER, *supra* note 2, at 46–72; Long, *supra* note 2, at 505–06.

6 *See, e.g.*, Dale A. Whitman, *Digital Recording of Real Estate Conveyances*, 32 J. MARSHALL L. REV. 227, 227 (1999).

7 *See, e.g.*, Gerald Korngold, *Legal and Policy Choices in the Aftermath of the Subprime and Mortgage Financing Crisis*, 60 S.C. L. REV. 727, 739–46 (2009); Tanya Marsh, *Foreclosures and the Failure of the American Land Title Recording System*, 111 COLUM. L. REV. SIDEBAR 19 (2011); Christopher L. Peterson, *Foreclosure, Subprime Mortgage Lending, and the Mortgage Electronic Registration System*, 78 U. CIN. L. REV. 1359, 1366 (2010).

8 *See generally* Peterson, *supra* note 7.

9 Stewart Sterk has documented this phenomenon, with particular attention to judicial adjustment of remedies in both the real property and IP contexts. Stewart E. Sterk, *Property Rules, Liability Rules, and Uncertainty About Property Rights*, 106 MICH. L. REV. 1285 (2008). In a similar spirit, Henry Smith explains equitable analysis of patent remedies as a response to notice problems in patent law. Henry E. Smith, *Institutions and Indirectness in Intellectual Property*, 157 U. PA. L. REV. 2083, 2125–32 (2009); *see also* Mark P. Gergen, John M. Golden, & Henry E. Smith, *The Supreme Court's Accidental Revolution? The Test for Permanent Injunctions*, 112 COLUM. L. REV. 203, 239–40 (2012) (describing the special role that notice plays in property and in equity).

10 *Cf.* Smith, *Institutions*, *supra* note 9, at 2121 (observing that "[a]lthough systematic and centralized property records often do provide effective notice (most notably in the case of land), it is an empirical question as to how they stack up against other methods in any given situation. Other methods include standardization, equitable doctrines of notice . . . and doctrines absolving from liability those who encounter rights.").

In this chapter I offer some doctrinal examples that illustrate the common law practice of crafting and adjusting rules about tangible property ownership to account for information-cost problems. I draw primarily from the law of servitudes, which I find a particularly enlightening source of insights for thinking about intellectual property.[11] Like intellectual property rights, servitudes are nonpossessory property rights that often allow their owners to constrain what other people can do with resources that they rightfully possess. Servitudes are thus not characterized by the coincidence of possession and property rights that provides an easy source of important information in many other tangible property contexts. Their nonpossessory character creates special information-cost challenges quite similar to those we encounter in the IP context.

Here, I focus on a particular kind of information-cost problem addressed in the law of servitudes: the potential difficulty of tracing servitude ownership, by which I mean identifying and locating the beneficial owner(s) of a nonpossessory interest in land (for the purpose, typically, of renegotiating the servitude's terms).[12] Traditional limits on the eligible subject matter and beneficiaries of servitudes reflect anxiety about this problem (among others).[13] So understood, these limits are amenable to common law adjustments that account for changes in the rest of the property information infrastructure that make tracing easier or more difficult. Where recording systems have made servitude owners easier to identify and locate, for example, some information-cost-motivated limitations on subject matter and beneficiaries become harder to defend.

[11] *See* Molly S. Van Houweling, *Touching and Concerning Copyright*, 51 SANTA CLARA L. REV. 1063 (2011); Molly S. Van Houweling, *The New Servitudes*, 96 GEO. L. J. 885 (2008); Molly S. Van Houweling, *Cultural Environmentalism and the Constructed Commons*, 70 LAW & CONTEMP. PROBS. 23 (2007); Molly S. Van Houweling, *Cultivating Open Information Platforms: A Land Trust Model*, 1 J. TELECOMM. & HIGH TECH. L. 309 (2002).

[12] At the risk of courting confusion with other, somewhat different uses of the term, I borrow this notion of "tracing costs" from William M. Landes & Richard A. Posner, *Indefinitely Rewnewable Copyright*, 70 U. CHI. L. REV. 471, 477 (2003) ("[I]mmense tracing costs would be required to determine the ownership of a parcel of land if titles to land were not recorded in a public registry.").

[13] In prior work I have identified three constellations of concerns that have triggered anxiety about servitudes: those related to notice and information costs, those related to dead-hand control and other aspects of the "problem of the future" (borrowing a term from Julia Mahoney), and those related to harmful externalities. Van Houweling, *The New Servitudes*, *supra* note 11. Some problems transcend these categories, and tracing is one of them. It is a type of information cost, but one that is troubling because of problems that are exacerbated by the passage of time. As servitudes age, tracing ownership for purposes of renegotiation is likely to become both more desirable (because changing circumstances have made the original arrangements obsolete, etc.) and difficult (because relevant parties have died, relocated, forgotten, etc.). In thinking about tracing I have found it useful to augment my own way of organizing ideas about servitudes with Carol Rose's framework, which groups servitude concerns into three slightly different categories: those related to information or notice, those related to renegotiability, and those related to value (i.e., costs versus benefits). Carol M. Rose, *Servitudes*, *in* RESEARCH HANDBOOK ON THE ECONOMICS OF PROPERTY LAW 296 (Kenneth Ayotte & Henry E. Smith eds., 2011).

My examination of the evolving doctrinal approaches to tracing and related information costs in the servitude context is enlightening to IP scholars for several reasons. First, it illustrates specific information-cost-management mechanisms that could also be deployed in the IP realm through "interstitial" common law rulemaking.[14] Second, it provides a general model of doctrinal adjustment in reaction to a changing information-cost landscape that could be especially useful in this era of legal and technological change. Third, the law of servitudes is part of the doctrinal heritage of – and can therefore help explain and shape – the law of IP "exhaustion," a frustratingly undertheorized doctrine that continues to confound courts and commentators.

I. NOTICE, TRACING, AND THE COMMON LAW OF SERVITUDES

When IP scholars emphasize the relative difficulty of noticing and tracing intangible versus tangible property rights,[15] they often seem to have in mind possessory tangible property rights – where the person in possession of the resource has the right to object to physical invasions of it and where the possessor's superior rights can be signaled by his or her own occupation and by fences and other physical signs.[16] The contrast between intangible and tangible property rights is not so stark, however, when the tangible property right is a *nonpossessory* interest in land or some other physical thing. In this context, as in the IP context, a person in rightful possession of a resource must sometimes use it (or refrain from using it) in accordance with the rights of someone else who is often *somewhere* else – sometimes next door, but other times far away and without any personal connection with the person whose behavior is constrained.

In land law, nonpossessory property rights are exemplified by servitudes. Among the various permutations, the easiest servitude to grasp is the affirmative appurtenant

[14] *See generally* Shyamkrishna Balganesh, *The Pragmatic Incrementalism of Common Law Intellectual Property*, 63 VAND. L. REV. 1543, 1595 (2010).

[15] *See, e.g.*, BESSEN & MEURER, *supra* note 2, at 46–72; WILLIAM M. LANDES & RICHARD A. POSNER, THE ECONOMIC STRUCTURE OF INTELLECTUAL PROPERTY LAW 16 (2003); David Fagundes, *Crystals in the Public Domain*, 50 B.C. L. REV. 139, 158 (2009); Jeanne C. Fromer, *Claiming Intellectual Property*, 76 U. CHI. L. REV. 719, 725–26 (2009); Long, *supra* note 2, at 482–89; Henry E. Smith, *Intellectual Property as Property: Delineating Entitlements in Information*, 116 YALE L.J. 1742, 1799–1819 (2007); Christopher Sprigman, *Reform(aliz)ing Copyright Law*, 57 STAN. L. REV. 485, 500–01 (2004); Sterk, *Property Rules*, *supra* note 9, at 1296–99; Menell & Meurer, *supra* note 2, at 2.

[16] *See, e.g.*, BESSEN & MEURER, *supra* note 2, at 64 (observing that "[i]n general, in order to own, one must possess" and that simple possession rules "make it easier for third parties to recognize the existence an scope of a property right"); Fagundes, *supra* note 15, at 158 ("If I want to know where someone's land begins and ends, I need not venture a trespass to discover this fact. Rather, I can eyeball the tract and identify where the landowner has fixed a boundary fence."); Long, *supra* note 2, at 482–83 ("Although each parcel of land is unique, real property law can reduce information costs for observers by codifying existing customs and social relations. Social norms also underlie boundary markers such as fences."); Menell & Meurer, *supra* note 2, at 2 (observing that "[l]andowners can usually determine who their neighbors are, the boundaries of their land, and restrictions on land dev relatively easily"). *But cf.* Sterk, *supra* note 9, at 1296 (noting how unclear property rights can be even in the real property context, which is "often treated as a refuge for clear legal rights").

easement, which gives the possessor of one piece of land the right to use a (typically adjoining) piece of land – as a right of way, for example. The right to cross and the obligation to yield to the crossing run with the benefited and burdened parcels. The recognition and enforcement of this type of running, nonpossessory property right facilitate land-use control and planning through decentralized private ordering – without the recurring transactions that would be required if landowners had to renegotiate mutually beneficial contracts with neighbors every time land changed hands.[17]

In addition to easements, two other types of servitudes have emerged over the last two centuries or so: real covenants and equitable servitudes.[18] The existence of these three categories reflects in part the establishment and then the erosion of subject-matter limitations: running restrictions that courts refused to recognize as easements were enforced (subject to different limitations) as real covenants, limitations on real covenants were overcome when the Court of Chancery recognized equitable servitudes, etc.[19] But some limitations on the types of servitudes that courts will enforce have persisted within and sometimes across these categories.[20]

To get a sense of these limitations, it is helpful to recall a few labels and distinctions. For an interest to be classified as a servitude at all, the burden and/or the benefit must run with land – that is, "the right or obligation passes automatically to successive

[17] *See generally* RESTATEMENT (THIRD) OF PROP.: SERVITUDES ch. 1, intro. note (2000) ("Servitudes may be used whenever an arrangement that does not require renegotiation on transfer of the land is desired."); Rose, *supra* note 13, at 297 ("The greatest overall advantage of servitudes is that they give stability to property arrangements over both time and space."); *see also* Robert C. Ellickson, *Alternatives to Zoning: Covenants, Nuisance Rules, and Fines as Land Use Controls*, 40 U. CHI. L. REV. 681, 713–14 (1973).

[18] Easements existed in Roman law and running covenants were recognized as early as *Spencer's Case* in 1583. But widespread attempts to impose servitudes and the resulting doctrinal tangles arose with the land-planning needs of the Industrial Revolution. *See* Susan F. French, *Design Proposal for the New Restatement of Property – Servitudes*, 21 U.C. DAVIS L. REV. 1213, 1214 (1998); *see also* Uriel Reichman, *Toward a Unified Concept of Servitudes*, 55. S. CAL. L. REV. 1177, 1183 (1982).

[19] *See generally* DUKEMINER ET AL., PROPERTY 764 (7th ed. 2010) ("The functional overlap among the different doctrinal categories is the result of history, not policy.... The law of servitudes is a study of how the tides of urbanization and the demands of the market for efficient control of externalities swept around the artificial barriers limiting one form of servitude and forced courts to recognize and develop other forms."); Susan F. French, *Servitude Reform and the New Restatement of Property: Creation Doctrines and Structural Simplification*, 73 CORNELL L. REV. 928, 929 (1988) ("[J]udicial controls have evolved in true common law fashion over many centuries. To escape controls that had become too restrictive, lawyers cast transactions in different forms and drew arguments from different areas of the law. Judges accommodated the demands for development by accepting these new forms and arguments, and by designing or using new types of controls made available by developments in other areas of the law. However, the old forms and controls did not disappear, and as the old continued alongside the new, the gradually accreting layers of doctrine became ever more complex.").

[20] On the complex evolution of servitude law, see generally Rose, *supra* note 13, at 296–97 (describing evolution of servitude law toward simplification, but noting that "this happy sequence is not quite the whole story," as "streamlined servitude doctrines assisted in great expansions of servitude use during the twentieth and now twenty-first centuries" and that "newly-expanded servitude uses triggered a resurgence of traditional concerns, albeit in new guises").

owners or occupiers of the land or the interest in land with which the right or obligation runs."[21] A benefit that runs with land is classified as "appurtenant,"[22] and the interest with which it runs is called the "dominant estate."[23] A burden that runs with land is likewise characterized as appurtenant, and the relevant interest in land is called the "servient estate."[24] Often both the burden and benefit are appurtenant and run with land. The paradigmatic easement of way, introduced earlier, burdens the possessor of one piece of land (and his successors to that servient estate) for the benefit of the possessor of the neighboring piece of land (and her successors to that dominant estate). This easement is further classified as "affirmative" (because it gives the owner of the dominant estate the right to use the land as opposed to a "negative" right to object to some use of it).[25]

Easements were the first type of recognized servitudes, and early controversies tested the enforceability of easements that did not fit the classic paradigm. One question was whether an easement could be enforced that would not give the owner of the dominant estate an affirmative right to do something on the land of the servient estate (e.g., pass over a right of way), but instead a right to object to some use of that land (e.g., to object to industrial as opposed to agricultural uses).[26]

Courts have traditionally recognized only a handful of such "negative easements."[27] Some new types of restrictions that do not fall within the closed list of negative easements have since been enforced as "restrictive covenants" or "equitable servitudes." But within those categories, too, courts have imposed subject-matter restrictions. These include the notorious "touch and concern" doctrine,[28] which

[21] Restatement (Third) of Prop.: Servitudes § 1.1(1) (2000) ("A servitude is a legal device that creates a right or an obligation that runs with land or an interest in land. . . . Running with land means that the right or obligation passes automatically to successive owners or occupiers of the land or the interest in land with which the right or obligation runs.").

[22] *Id.* § 1.5 ("(1) 'Appurtenant' means that the rights or obligations of a servitude are tied to ownership or occupancy of a particular unit or parcel of land. . . . (2) 'In gross' means that the benefit or burden of a servitude is not tied to ownership or occupancy of a particular unit or parcel of land.").

Although benefits and burdens that run with land are "appurtenant" under the Restatement definition, it is possible for a benefit or burden to be appurtenant and yet to not run with the land. "Only appurtenant benefits and burdens run with land, but the terms are not synonymous. Running with land means that the benefit or burden passes automatically to successors; appurtenant means that the benefit can be used only in conjunction with ownership or occupancy of a particular parcel of land, or that only the owner or occupier of a particular parcel is liable for failure to perform a servitude obligation. Appurtenant benefits and burdens ordinarily run with land, but they may be made personal to particular owners or occupiers of the land." *Id.* at cmt (a).

[23] *Id.* § 1.1(1).

[24] *Id.*

[25] The *Restatement* uses a somewhat streamlined classification scheme in which easements are affirmative by definition. What have sometimes been referred to as "negative easements" are now classified by the *Restatement* as "restrictive covenants." *Id.* § 1.2.

[26] *See* Reichman, *supra* note 18, at 1187 & nn.42–43.

[27] *Id.*

[28] As *Restatement* Reporter Susan French helpfully summarizes, "[t]raditional servitudes doctrine requires that covenant burdens and benefits touch and concern the land if they are to pass automatically to successors of the original covenanting parties. The doctrine . . . applies regardless of the

insists that what the burdened party is required to do (or to refrain from doing) must be connected to his or her land and also to the land of the party enforcing the servitude.[29]

As other commentators have noted, and as I have discussed in previous work,[30] one justification for the touch and concern doctrine is that it promotes notice to the public and (more importantly) to people who acquire land subject to restrictions or obligations.[31] The logic is that restrictions and duties tied to land use are relatively easy to discover on physical inspection.[32]

Note that "touch and concern" was first articulated by English courts operating in what seems in retrospect like an especially challenging information environment. There was at the time no official system for recording interests in land. Furthermore, some types of servitudes were recognized as arising from prescription – that is, not from an express agreement between landowners but merely from longstanding use of a right of way, for example. In a context in which servitudes could be so easily created and in which there was no centralized system for keeping track of them,

parties' intent, limiting the kinds of covenants that can be made into servitudes." Susan F. French, *The Touch and Concern Doctrine and the Restatement (Third) of Servitudes: A Tribute to Lawrence E. Berger*, 77 NEB. L. REV. 653, 653 (1998) (citing Spencer's Case, (1583) 77 Eng. Rep. 72 (K.B.)); *see generally* GERALD KORNGOLD, PRIVATE LAND USE ARRANGEMENTS: EASEMENTS, REAL COVENANTS AND EQUITABLE SERVITUDES 349 (2d ed. 2004) ("The authorities mostly agree that touch and concern means that in order for a covenant to run, there must be some fundamental link between the promise and the burdened and benefited land. The question of touch and concern must be analyzed on both sides of the covenant.").

29 One widely cited articulation of the test is whether the servitude "operate[s] to make more valuable some of the rights, privileges, or powers possessed by the covenantee or to relieve him in whole or in part of some of his duties." Harry A. Bigelow, *The Content of Covenants in Leases*, 12 MICH. L. REV. 639 (1914). A variation provides that "[i]f the promisor's legal relations in respect to the land in question are lessened – his legal interest as an owner rendered less valuable by the promise – the burden of the covenant touches or concerns that land; if the promisee's legal relations in respect to that land are increased – his legal interest as owner rendered more valuable by the promise – the benefit of the covenant touches and concerns the land." CHARLES E. CLARK, REAL COVENANTS AND OTHER INTERESTS WHICH "RUN WITH LAND" 97 (2d ed. 1947).

30 Van Houweling, *The New Servitudes*, *supra* note 11, at 395; Van Houweling, *Touching and Concerning Copyright*, *supra* note 11, at 1072.

31 Touch and concern has also been interpreted as a rough test for whether covenants and equitable servitudes are sufficiently value-enhancing to justify their enforcement. Even so understood, the doctrine is related to both notice and renegotiability. Servitudes that are both surprising and inefficient are especially problematic, as are servitudes that are inefficient and difficult to renegotiate. *See* Rose, *supra* note 13, at 304–05.

32 *See* Henry Hansmann & Reinier Kraakman, *Property, Contract, and Verification: The Numerus Clausus Problem and the Divisibility of Rights*, 31 J. LEGAL STUD. 373, 402 (2002) (noting that servitudes touching and concerning the land "are much easier to verify upon physical inspection of property"). *See generally* Antony Dnes & Dean Lueck, *Asymmetric Information and the Law of Servitudes Governing Land*, 38 J. LEGAL STUD. 89, 93 (2009) ("Our general argument is that because complex divisions of property, such as those defined by servitudes, can often be hard to measure, verify, and enforce contractually, limits on their use can actually clarify rights to land and thus support market transactions."); Susan F. French, *Toward a Modern Law of Servitudes: Reweaving the Ancient Strands*, 55 S. CAL. L. REV. 1261, 1289–92 (1982).

strict judicially imposed limitations on the substantive subject matter was one way to limit the instances of unfairly and inefficiently surprising servitudes.[33]

Thomas Merrill and Henry Smith have drawn our attention to the touch and concern doctrine as an example of a broader phenomenon of subject-matter limitations that serve to standardize property rights and thus to limit the information costs that might otherwise be imposed by the proliferation of idiosyncratic property forms.[34] They cite a classic articulation of this view in *Keppell* v. *Bailey*, in which the English Court of Chancery refused to enforce a covenant that purported to bind the operators of an ironworks (not original parties to the covenant) to purchase all of the limestone they used in their furnaces from a particular quarry and to use a particular railroad to carry it. In refusing to enforce the covenant beyond the original parties, Lord Brougham opined,

> [G]reat detriment would arise and much confusion of rights if parties were allowed to invent new modes of holding and enjoying real property, and to impress upon their lands and tenements a peculiar character, which should follow them into all hands, however remote. Every close, every messuage, might thus be held in a several fashion, and it would hardly be possible to know what rights the acquisition of any parcel conferred, or what obligations it imposed.[35]

Merrill and Smith emphasize the *Keppell* court's concern with the "confusion of rights" that comes with "new modes of holding and enjoying real property." Buyers of assets subject to novel restrictions may not understand what they are buying, and third parties may also suffer from the increased confusion that arises in a world in which idiosyncratic property rights are enforced.[36] This type of information-cost concern – which Merrill and Smith document across various areas of property law – could be heightened in the nonpossessory servitude context if courts did not impose doctrinal substitutes for the notice that possession and other physical signs often

[33] *See generally* Dnes & Lueck, *supra* note 32, at 108 ("In England the resistance to extending the list of four negative easements saves the costs of judicial supervision in a country in which land title can be ancient and easements can be created not only by grant but also by implication and, in particular, by prescription."); Rose, *supra* note 13, at 301 ("With respect to the content of rights and obligations running with the land, then, what now seem formalistic anachronisms are instructive in showing the relevance of information. Particularly in England, where recording was not generally used, it was important that information-poor obligations be characterized as covenants, because one of the major features of the covenant designation was to push such claims into a more information-rich structure."); French, *supra* note 32, at 1282–83.

[34] Thomas W. Merrill & Henry E. Smith, *Optimal Standardization in the Law of Property: The Numerus Clausus Principle*, 110 YALE L.J. 1, 17 (2000).

[35] Keppell v. Bailey, 2 Myl. & K. 517, 546–47, 39 Eng.Rep. 1042, 1053 (1834).

[36] *See generally* Merrill & Smith, *supra* note 34, at 8 ("When property rights are created, third parties must expend time and resources to determine the attributes of these rights, both to avoid violating them and to acquire them from present holders. The existence of unusual property rights increases the cost of processing information about all property rights."); *id.* at 26 ("In modern terminology, the Lord Chancellor thought that permitting interests like the covenants in *Keppell* to be established as property rights would create unacceptable information costs to third parties.").

provide. Touch and concern and other subject-matter limitations on servitudes can thus partly be explained as attempts to limit the number of servitude types and to ensure that those that are recognized are relatively easy to notice and understand on physical inspection of the burdened land.[37]

Servitudes raise an additional type of information-cost concern to which the key passage from *Keppell* also alludes: the nonpossessory nature of the property right increases the likelihood that the property owner will be far removed from the restricted resource as it passes into a succession of different "hands, however remote." This remoteness matters in part because of the problems with confusion and lack of notice just discussed: where the owners are far away it may be difficult to ask them to offer their interpretation of terms of the restrictions or obligations that servitudes impose. But another reason for concern relates not to how well the servitude can be noticed and understood, but rather to how easily it can be renegotiated.[38] This too could be especially challenging where the parties are remote, because the beneficiary of the servitude might be difficult to *trace* – that is, to identify, locate, and contact in order to engage in renegotiations.[39]

This concern with tracing costs is manifest in another persistent question within servitude doctrine: to what extent the benefit of a servitude can be in gross as opposed to appurtenant – that is, whether it can benefit someone without regard to his or her ownership or possession of a particular piece of land. Imagine, for example, an easement allowing a railroad company to run its tracks and trains across an owner's land. The burden of this easement would be appurtenant, imposed on the servient estate, but the railroad company would like the benefit to be in gross – enjoyable by the company regardless of what it owns (and perhaps even transferable to others

37 Consistent with this view, the least controversial servitude type – the affirmative easement – is easy to notice and to understand. *See, e.g.*, *Keppell*, 2 Myl. & K. at 536 ("The right of way or of common is of a public as well as of a simple nature, and no one who sees the premises can be ignorant of what all the vicinage knows.").

38 *See generally* Rose, *supra* note 13, at 298 ("Some transaction costs derive from information issues, matters that were especially prominent in the doctrines that constrain servitudes. A second source of transaction costs revolves around what I will call 'renegotiability' – that is, protecting the capacity to renegotiate these instruments from a potentially disparate and fragmented set of interest-holders."); *id.* at 301 ("Information dissipation was clearly one of the chief concerns that drove traditional servitude law toward information-producing constraints. But a concern that the parties be able to modify or escape servitude obligations was another important consideration.").

39 Additional complications – and doctrinal corrections – arise when the beneficiaries are numerous. *See generally* Michael Heller, *The Tragedy of the Anticommons: Property in the Transition from Marx to Markets*, 111 HARV. L. REV. 621, 664 (1998) ("In the American law of property, numerous restraints limit an individual's capacity to break up property bundles too much."); *see also* Rose, *supra* note 13, at 302 ("The concern for renegotiability links servitude law to a much-discussed issue in modern property scholarship: the worry that excessive fragmentation of interests will quash value-enhancing transactions and leave property unusable.... The anticommons standoff is especially problematic where a property would have higher value in some *new* use, since the fragmentation of interests impedes what would otherwise be a normal transaction from less to more valuable uses."); David A. Dana, *The Foreclosure Crisis and the Antifragmentation Principle in State Property Law*, 77 U. CHI. L. REV. 97, 110–13 (2010) (describing doctrines that "enhance alienability... by limiting fragmentation of interests in land").

regardless of what they own). English courts refused to recognize this variation on the classic easement.[40] Courts in the United States eventually allowed easements with benefits in gross, but remnants of the traditional hostility to all servitudes with benefits in gross remain – especially within the other servitude categories of real covenants and equitable servitudes.[41]

The case law limiting benefits in gross tends to be conclusory and to reveal little about judicial rationales for the hostility.[42] But Gerald Korngold draws our attention to an opinion by Justice Holmes for the Massachusetts Supreme Judicial Court that offers helpful insights.[43]

In *Inhabitants of Middlefield* v. *Church Mills Knitting Co.*, the court enforced a servitude that required the owner of a bridge to maintain it for the benefit of the town.[44] The benefit was in gross, held by the town regardless of its ownership of any particular piece of land. Justice Holmes's opinion acknowledges the traditional hostility to this type of servitude, but suggests that the rationale for skepticism about benefits in gross falls away where the beneficial owner is easy to track down:

> [A]lthough ordinarily the corresponding right could not exist in gross, yet, in the case of a way which a town is bound to keep in repair for the benefit of the public, the town is the natural and convenient protector of the obligation, and being immortal, and locally fixed, may enforce a covenant originally made to it, without being shown to be strictly the owner of the highway.[45]

In the course of enforcing the servitude in this case, Justice Holmes thus implicitly recognizes the tracing and renegotiation problems associated with benefits held by entities that are neither associated with a particular piece of land nor otherwise "locally fixed" or "immortal."

Commentary on the issue of benefits held in gross articulates this concern more fully. Susan French, Reporter for the *Restatement (Third) of Property: Servitudes*, explains as follows:

> If the benefit holder is the owner of an identified parcel of land, then she can be identified (and probably located) through the land records. If the property is taxable, the demise or disappearance of the owner will eventually provoke a tax

[40] RESTATEMENT (THIRD) OF PROP.: SERVITUDES § 2.6 cmt. A (2000) ("Early law prohibited the creation of servitude benefits in gross and the creation of servitude benefits in persons who were not immediate parties to the transaction. . . . English law adopted the prohibition on benefits in gross from Roman law, but applied it only to easements and equitable servitudes. American law recognizes easements in gross, but has retained remnants of the prohibition against interests in gross with respect to covenants.").

[41] *See generally* French, *supra* note 19, at 941–47.

[42] Gerald Korngold, *Privately Held Conservation Servitudes: A Policy Analysis in the Context of in Gross Real Covenants and Easements*, 63 TEX. L. REV. 433, 470–71 (1984) (lamenting that most opinions refusing to allow running covenants with benefits in gross "are troubling for their lack of a clear rationale and their failure to consider the relevant policies. Most rely on stare decisis or precedents from other jurisdictions.").

[43] *Id.* at 476–77.

[44] 35 N.E. 780 (Mass. 1894).

[45] *Inhabitants of Middlefield*, 35 N.E. at 782.

> sale which will again produce an identifiable and locatable benefit holder. The importance of having identifiable and locatable benefit holders lies in enabling the party owning the burdened land to negotiate a release or modification of the servitude. The concern here is that the holder of a benefit in gross will be difficult to locate and may even disappear.[46]

Other commentators have similarly observed how restrictions on benefits held in gross help ease tracing and thereby promote servitude flexibility through consensual modification.[47]

These are just some of many examples of judicially imposed limitations on servitude subject matter and beneficiaries, justified in part by concerns with information costs – including both the difficulty of noticing and understanding the burdens that servitudes impose and the difficulty of tracing servitudes' beneficiaries for purposes of renegotiating their terms. As we see later, the common law techniques of limiting subject matter and beneficiaries could be, and sometimes have been, deployed to address the analogous problems that plague IP law. Before turning to the dynamic field of intellectual property, however, let us understand the dynamism of servitude law and how these common law mechanisms for addressing information costs have been adjusted over time to account for changes in the property information infrastructure with which they interact.

II. THE DYNAMISM OF THE COMMON LAW OF SERVITUDES

If traditional judicial skepticism about servitudes has been motivated in part by concern with information costs related to notice and tracing, then one might expect the doctrine to become more accommodating as those costs fall.[48] Indeed, a

46 French, *supra* note 19, at 945–46.

47 Rose, *supra* note 13, at 317 ("[T]he linkage of a servitude to benefitted land conveys information about the character of the servitude obligations. . . . [T]his linkage also reveals the identify of claimants and reduces their numbers, thus preserving renegotiability."); Korngold, *supra* note 42, at 468 (noting that renegotiation is relatively easy among neighboring landowners "because neighbors, especially in adjoining residential lots, usually try to accommodate one another to maintain good relations" and that "[i]n contrast, the owner of an in gross servitude often is not near the land; the chances of flexibility through compromise are accordingly reduced"); James L. Winokur, *The Mixed Blessings of Promissory Servitudes: Toward Optimizing Economic Utility, Individual Liberty, and Personal Identity*, 1989 Wis. L. Rev. 1, 37 ("Consensual removal or modification of servitudes may also be hindered if the enforcement power is held 'in gross' – separate from ownership of any benefited land interest. . . . Neighbors are more easily located and more likely to be reasonable than others in seeking mutually agreeable resolutions of land use conflicts."); Stewart E. Sterk, *Freedom from Freedom of Contract*, 70 Iowa L. Rev. 615, 651 (1985) ("At least with a servitude whose benefit is appurtenant to ownership of a particular parcel of land, a party seeking to negotiate for removal has a greater chance of locating the holder of the benefit by locating the benefited land. Thus, the difficulty of locating holders of benefits in gross produces transaction costs that inhibit removal of unwanted servitudes.").

48 *See, e.g.*, Rose, *supra* note 13, at 307 ("[I]t has been something of a puzzle why courts in the United States retained some of the British formal categories at all, given the wide use of recording."). *See generally* Merrill & Smith, *supra* note 34, at 41 ("As the costs of standardization to the parties and the government shift, we expect the optimal degree of standardization to rise or fall. Consider the rise of registers of interests in real property, that is, recording acts. This device lowers the costs of notice; it

principal and recurring argument in favor of liberalizing servitude law is that all U.S. states have recording systems and marketable title acts that help both to ensure notice and to facilitate the identification and location of servitude beneficiaries for purposes of renegotiation. These developments, reformers have argued, justify jettisoning restrictive doctrine that was originally developed in large part by English courts operating in a much less orderly information environment.[49] Courts have been less responsive to these arguments than some reformers would like. Yet certainly the general trend in the United States has been toward liberalization (if not necessarily rationalization) of servitude law and – in particular – the falling away of limitations on subject matter and beneficiaries discussed earlier.[50]

The *Restatement (Third)* and its reporter Susan French urge abandonment of the touch and concern doctrine, limitations on benefits held in gross, and various other restrictions as inferior to alternative methods of addressing information-cost concerns. French argued in advance of the *Restatement* revision that "[s]ervitudes law may be simplified substantially because particular rules designed to give notice are no longer needed. The modern technology of record systems and title search procedures, together with the protection recording acts afford, have made these rules superfluous."[51]

As for limitations on benefits held in gross and the problem of renegotiability in particular, French concludes that "[e]qually effective solutions would be providing parties who want to terminate servitudes with procedural methods to foreclose the interests of those who cannot be located or requiring periodic filing of a notice of claim to keep in gross servitudes alive."[52] Consistent with this view, the revised *Restatement* describes a procedure for judicial modification or termination of these orphan servitudes.[53]

is an alternative method of lowering information costs."). *But cf.* Henry E. Smith, *Standardization in Property Law*, *in* Research Handbook on the Economics of Property Law 148, 166 (Kenneth Ayotte & Henry E. Smith eds., 2011) ("The position that notice cures all overlooks some of the functions of the *numerus clausus* as well as empirical evidence that suggests that standardization and title records are not always substitutes.").

49 *See, e.g.*, French, *supra* note 32, at 1284 ("[R]ecording systems in the United States serve the notice function adequately and it therefore need not be separately addressed by the law of servitudes. In every state, a purchaser for value who properly records an instrument of title is protected against interests created by unrecorded instruments of which the purchaser has no notice. A purchaser can thus be certain of the encumbrances to which specific property is subject by inspection of the property and the public records."); Richard Epstein, *Notice and Freedom of Contract in the Law of Servitudes*, 55 S. Cal. L. Rev. 1353, 1364 (1982) ("Record notice obviates the need for the touch and concern requirement.").

50 On this evolution and its consequences, see generally Rose, *supra* note 13.

51 French, *supra* note 18, at 1225.

52 French, *supra* note 19, at 947; *see also* Sterk, *supra* note 46, at 652 ("[R]ules better tailored to the problem of removing outdated servitudes might serve to reduce transaction costs at less sacrifice than the various restrictions on servitudes in gross.").

53 Restatement (Third) of Prop.: Servitudes § 7.13 (2000) ("If it has become impossible or impracticable to locate the beneficiaries of a servitude held in gross, a court may modify or terminate the servitude with the consent of those beneficiaries who can be located, subject to suitable provisions for protection of the interests of those who have not been located.").

III. TRACING, TECHNOLOGY, AND THE DEVOLUTION OF INTELLECTUAL PROPERTY

Although yet to be fully embraced by courts, the *Restatement*'s proposals for the evolution of servitude law offer an illuminating model for common law evolution in a changing information-cost environment. The traditional rules – the touch and concern requirement, limitations on benefits held in gross – can be understood as prophylactic mechanisms that limit the creation and recognition of property rights that will become difficult to notice, trace, and renegotiate. The *Restatement*'s position is that these rules can safely be abandoned when alternative notice and tracing techniques – including the "modern technology of record systems and title search procedures" – improve.

In the late 1990s, IP scholars expected that the modern technology of electronic commerce might similarly improve our ability to trace and transact in intellectual property rights.[54] And it has done so, to some extent. But what was not fully evident when the Internet was first emerging as a mass medium was how it would simultaneously complicate the IP landscape. The copyright environment is becoming more complex as technology empowers users to create and distribute new copyright-protected works, to acquire digital copies of works subject to novel and often opaque terms of use, and to undertake mass digitization projects for which the information costs associated with tracing ownership impose unprecedented challenges.[55] Meanwhile, rapidly proliferating patents on software and Internet business methods are subject to especially troublesome problems of definition, comprehension, and overlap.[56]

If improvements in rights-tracing technology justify loosening common law rules about the subject matter and beneficiaries of servitudes, might technological changes that have increased information costs in the IP environment justify *tightening* analogous rules – that is, to become less accommodating of unruly IP rights?[57] I think so.

54 *See, e.g.*, Tom W. Bell, *Fair Use v. Use: The Impact of Automated Rights Management on Copyright's Fair Use Doctrine*, 76 N.C. L. Rev. 557, 583 (1998); *see also* Jane C. Ginsburg, *Authors and Users in Copyright*, 45 J. Copyright Soc'y U.S.A. 1, 15 (1997); Edmund W. Kitch, *Can the Internet Shrink Fair Use?*, 78 Neb. L. Rev. 880, 881 (1999). *Cf.* Robert P. Merges, *The End of Friction? Property Rights and Contract in the "Newtonian" World of On-Line Commerce*, 12 Berkeley Tech. L.J. 115, 116 (1997) (drawing careful distinctions between different types of transaction costs and recognizing that "[c]yberspace does not eliminate all of these sources of transaction costs," specifically, "cyberspace does not appear to lower negotiation costs in most cases").

55 *See generally* Molly S. Van Houweling, *Author Autonomy and Atomism in Copyright Law*, 96 Va. L. Rev. 549 (2010).

56 *See, e.g.*, Bilski v. Kappos, 130 S.Ct. 3218, 3256 (2010) (Stevens, J., concurring in the judgment); eBay Inc. v. MercExchange, L.L.C., 547 U.S. 392, 397 (2006) (Kennedy, J., concurring); Bessen & Meurer, *supra* note 2; Long, *supra* note 2, at 487–88, 543–44.

57 As I hope this chapter's exploration of the dynamism and pluralism of common law approaches to information costs makes clear, there are various mechanisms by which the law could accomplish this task. *See generally* Menell & Meurer, *supra* note 2 (articulating a variety of solutions to "notice failure"). Among other commentators, some suggest withholding property rights from certain especially

For example, the doctrine of "exhaustion" is one tool that courts have used to define IP rights in a way that avoids some tricky information-cost dilemmas (although the doctrine serves other purposes as well).[58] Broadly construed, this doctrine forbids copyright and patent owners from interfering with ordinary uses of objects that embody IP rights.[59] So, for example, it allows the owner of a book to share it with or sell it to another reader without having to track down the copyright owner and seek his or her permission.[60] Consider how valuable this is for libraries and other owners of large collections of books.

Exhaustion can be understood as a limitation on the substance of the property right (analogous to the touch and concern doctrine) or as a limitation on the enforceability of that right by an IP owner who no longer owns a particular physical embodiment (analogous to limitations on servitude benefits in gross). The limitations on tangible property servitudes provide more than just an analogy. Exhaustion is in fact an outgrowth of the common law of servitudes – specifically, of cases grappling with the question of whether running restrictions could be imposed on items of personal property as well as land.[61]

amorphous subject matter. *See, e.g., id.* at 46 ("[A]s the costs of identifying and avoiding property rights rise, then policy should move away from propertization. We have long questioned the wisdom of patent protection for computer software and business methods on notice and other grounds."). Some focus on remedial adjustments. For example, several observers have justified (if not necessarily embraced) the Supreme Court's rejection of automatic injunctive relief for patent infringement in *eBay, Inc.* v. *MercExachange*, L.L.C., 547 U.S. 388 (2006), by reference to information-cost problems that plague the contemporary patent system. *See, e.g.*, Sterk, *supra* note 9, at 1333–34; Smith, *supra* note 9, at 2125–32; Menell & Meurer, *supra* note 2, at 45–46. *Cf.* Gergen, Golden, & Smith, *supra* note 9 (criticizing *eBay* but emphasizing the value of equitable adjustment of remedies to account for notice problems and the opportunities for opportunism they create).

For an example of a court adjusting the land law to account for new problems with the property information infrastructure, see *Bynum* v. *Barker*, 39 So.3d 1013 (Ala. 2009), in which the Supreme Court of Alabama held that a purchaser was protected against a prior mortgage that was recorded but improperly indexed (because of a minor mistake in how the mortgager was listed on the mortgage deed). In concluding that the purchaser was not on constructive notice of the mortgage, the court seemed to suggest that the county's digitization of land records had, ironically, made it more difficult than it had been in the era of bound paper record books to locate a mislabeled deed. As the court explained, "a computerized database relies on the alphabetical storage of names entered, and when someone incorrectly describes a mortgagor, neither the computer nor the probate clerk has any way, or duty, to ascertain the mistakes. . . . " Bynum, 39 So.3d at 1022. This strikes me as a strangely pessimistic view of the capabilities of computerized databases. But the court's willingness to account doctrinally for what it perceives to be a newly challenging information environment is laudable.

58 *See generally* Aaron Perzanowski & Jason Schultz, *Digital Exhaustion*, 58 U.C.L.A. L. Rev. 889 (2011).

59 Aaron Perzanowski and Jason Schultz develop such a broad construction, documenting and explaining the common law evolution of the doctrine. *Id.*

60 This aspect of the exhaustion concept is codified in the Copyright Act's so-called first sale doctrine. 17 U.S.C. § 109.

61 *See* Van Houweling, *The New Servitudes*, *supra* note 11, at 907–14; Van Houweling, *Touching and Concerning Copyright*, *supra* note 11, at 1068; Glen O. Robinson, *Personal Property Servitudes*, 71 U. Chi. L. Rev. 1449, 1449 (2004); *see also* Kirtsaeng v. John Wiley & Sons, Inc., 568 U.S. ___ (2013) 133 S.Ct. 1351, 1354 (2013) ("The 'first sale' doctrine is a common law doctrine with an impeccable historic

This chapter does not provide a thorough treatment of ongoing controversies about the scope of the exhaustion principle – which is the subject of litigation, policy debate, and important recent scholarship.[62] Instead, what I emphasize here is that this doctrine – like the tangible property doctrines that are its intellectual forebears – is justified in part by concerns about the difficulty of tracing and negotiating IP rights.[63] The exhaustion principle's evolution – like the evolution of servitude law – should therefore remain attentive to that difficulty and should respond dynamically to changes in the information-cost calculus.

Other observers have linked these intellectual histories in order to argue in favor of jettisoning exhaustion – following land servitude law's example by removing limitations on the subject matter and beneficiaries of IP-based restrictions on resource use.[64] But this logic does not hold. Although systems for recording interests in land have improved (at least since the English origins of servitude law) in ways that arguably justify liberalizing the law of land servitudes, systems for recording IP interests have deteriorated. Ironically, then, we may now be justified in deploying the old-fashioned common law limitations associated with land servitudes only in the new-fangled statutory realm of intellectual property.

There is something fundamentally sound, however, about the observation that limitations on property rights that are justified by information-cost concerns should be reconsidered if technological or other developments alleviate those concerns. Ongoing efforts to lower the costs of tracing and negotiating with IP owners may therefore eventually trigger adjustments to limiting doctrines.[65] These efforts include both legal reform initiatives – proposed legislation to address the problems posed

pedigree. In the early 17th century Lord Coke explained the common law's refusal to permit restraints on the alienation of chattels.").

62 *E.g.*, Bowman v. Monsanto Co., 133 S.Ct. 1761 (2013); *Kirtsaeng*, 133 S.Ct. 1351; Costco Wholesale Corp. v. Omega, S.A., 131 S.Ct. 565 (2010); Quanta Computer, Inc. v. LG Electronics, Inc., 553 U.S. 617 (2008); Apple Inc. v. Psystar Corp., 658 F.3d 1150 (9th Cir. 2011); UMG Recordings, Inc. v. Augusto, 628 F.3d 1175 (9th Cir. 2011); Vernor v. Autodesk, Inc., 621 F.3d 1102 (9th Cir. 2010); MDY Industries, LLC v. Blizzard Entertainment, Inc., 629 F.3dc 928 (9th Cir. 2010); Perzanowski & Schultz, *supra* note 57; Herbert Hovenkamp, *Post-Sale Restraints and Competitive Harm: The First Sale Doctrine in Perspective*, 66 N.Y.U. Ann. Surv. Am. L. 487 (2011); Van Houweling, *Touching and Concerning Copyright*, *supra* note 11; Aaron Perzanowski & Jason Schultz, *Copyright Exhaustion and the Personal Use Dilemma*, 96 Minn. L. Rev. 2067 (2012).

63 *See* Van Houweling, *The New Servitudes*, *supra* note 11, at 917 (explaining early exhaustion cases as "part of an effort to maintain the informational simplicity of commerce in things that 'pass from hand to hand,' even when those things are burdened with intellectual property rights"); Perzanowski & Schultz, *supra* note 57, at 896–96, 906.

64 *See, e.g.*, Robinson, *supra* note 60.

65 *Cf.* Landes & Posner, *supra* note 12, at 477 ("Enormous tracing costs would be incurred by any would-be publisher of a new translation of the *Iliad* if the heirs of Homer could enforce copyright in the work, but that is only because no one knows who those heirs are.... [T]here need be no great difficulty in identifying copyright owners a century or for that matter a millennium hence if, for example, the law required copyright owners to reregister their copyrights every ten or even twenty-five years in some central registry under the name of the copyright holder and to notify the registry in the event the copyright was transferred.").

by orphan works, for example – and private efforts to keep better track of owners and their preferences, using both centralized registries and decentralized techniques such as embedding copyright management information in digital works.[66]

Two notes of caution are in order. First, recent experience in land law suggests that private provision of property-related information may not alone justify abandoning doctrines that protect the public from untraceable rights. The mortgage crisis has revealed imperfections in the public land recording system.[67] It has also brought public attention to private attempts to transact over interests in land without fully relying on that system, but instead resorting to the more nimble private-sector information processing offered by title plants[68] and, more recently, the Mortgage Electronic Recording System (MERS).[69] As some courts and commentators have noted in assessing MERS, private institutions for tracing property rights may lack the transparency necessary to ensure that everyone potentially affected by those rights has the opportunity to investigate and transact in them.[70] Similar concerns have

[66] *See, e.g.*, Pamela Samuelson, et al., *The Copyright Principles Project: Directions for Reform*, 25 BERKELEY TECH. L.J. 1175, 1198–1202 (2010); Sprigman, *supra* note 15, at 546–68; Molly S. Van Houweling, *Atomism and Automation*, 27 BERKELEY TECH. L.J. 1471 (2013); Menell & Meurer, *supra* note 2.

Robert Merges has written extensively on the topic of private efforts and institutions designed to overcome transaction costs in the IP context. *See, e.g.*, Robert P. Merges, *Contracting into Liability Rules: Intellectual Property Rights and Collective Rights Organizations*, 84 CAL. L. REV. 1293 (1996); Robert P. Merges, *Intellectual Property Rights and the New Institutional Economics*, 53 VAND. L. REV. 1857, 1864–67 (2000); Robert P. Merges, *A New Dynamism in the Public Domain*, 71 U. CHI. L. REV. 183, 184 (2004).

[67] *See* sources cited *supra* at notes 6 & 7. *See generally* Benito Arruñada, *Property Titling and Conveyancing*, in RESEARCH HANDBOOK ON THE ECONOMICS OF PROPERTY LAW 237, 242 (Kenneth Ayotte & Henry E. Smith eds., 2011) (noting, from a comparative perspective, the poor organization of land records in many U.S. counties); Gary D. Libecap & Dean Lueck, *Land Demarcation Systems*, in *id.* at 257, 257 (describing a variety of systems for defining land boundaries including meets and bounds systems, which are "necessarily vague and imprecise . . . , temporary . . . , idiosyncratic, . . . and . . . subject to dispute and conflict").

[68] *See generally* Arruñada, *supra* note 67, at 242 ("When the records are poorly organized (as in many US counties), it seems natural to develop private 'title plants,' that is, well-organized replicas of the public records.").

[69] *See generally* Phyllis K. Slesinger & Daniel Mclaughlin, *Mortgage Electronic Registration System*, 31 IDAHO L. REV. 805, 808 (1995) (promoting MERS for its promise to "greatly simplify a terribly cumbersome, paper-intensive, error-prone, and therefore costly process for transferring and tracking mortgage rights" that is "derived from seventeenth century real property law and is not at all suited to late twentieth century mortgage finance transactions"); Korngold, *supra* note 7, at 742 (praising MERS for "facilitat[ing] an efficient secondary market in mortgages by allowing the easy transfer of beneficial rights" and characterizing as "unfortunate[]" that "some judicial decisions during the recent spike in subprime and conventional foreclosures have questioned MERS" (citing, *e.g.*, Landmark National Bank v. Kesler, 192 P. 3d 177 (Kan. Ct. App. 2008)).

[70] *See, e.g.*, Peterson, *supra* note 7, at 1407 (critiquing MERS because "[t]he shift away from recording loans in the name of actual mortgagees and assignees represents an important policy change that erodes not only the tax base of local governments, but also the usefulness of the public land title information infrastructure"); Korngold, *supra* note 7, at 743–44 (defending MERS but acknowledging "the importance of transparency in the recording system" and raising "a legitimate concern if unrecorded mortgage assignments in secondary market transactions are not placed on the public record"); *see also* David R. Greenberg, Comment: *Neglected Formalities in the Mortgage Assignment Process and the*

been raised in the copyright context with regard to the private information and rights-clearance functions performed by ASCAP and by the Books Rights Registry proposed as part of the failed settlement to the Google Book Search controversy.

Second, as courts consider adjusting (tangible or intangible) property's limiting doctrines to take account of changes (innovations and deteriorations) in the relevant information-cost environments, they should also bear in mind the continued relevance of other justifications for those doctrines.[71] In both contexts, property rights that are perfectly clear and traceable can nonetheless contribute to holdouts and other transactional failures;[72] they can also be enforced in ways that unduly sacrifice distributional fairness (including intergenerational fairness) and harm third parties.[73] The progress-promotion justification for IP protection should trigger especially keen attention to intergenerational fairness in the copyright and patent contexts.[74]

CONCLUSION

IP observers and reformers have drawn our attention to ways in which formal information infrastructures – for copyrights, in particular – suffer in comparison to systems for recording and otherwise signaling and tracing interests in land. One approach to alleviating the information-cost challenges that plague intellectual property would be to try to replicate those formal systems of centralized information provision. It is also valuable, however, to consider how such systems interact with the common law

Resulting Effects on Residential Foreclosures, 83 TEMP. L. REV. 253 (2010); Robert E. Rodan, *Mortgage Electronic Registration System (MERS), Its Recent Legal Battles, and the Chance for Peaceful Existence*, 12 LOY. J. PUB. INT. L. 177 (2010). For a statutory response, see Minn. Stat. § 507.413 (2008).

71 *See generally* Rose, *supra* note 13, at 319 (observing that, as servitude law has liberalized, "a streamlined set of servitude doctrines helped these devices to expand to proportions that made them threatening to outsiders or dictatorial to participants").

72 Thanks to Victor Fleisher for prompting me to highlight this distinction. *See generally* Menell & Meurer, *supra* note 2, at 12 (observing with an example of a complicated copyright license renegotiation that "after the owners have been located, the hold-out problem remains"). Some of Robert Merges's work on this topic suggests, counterintuitively, that transaction-cost problems attributed to overpropertization might in fact be alleviated by making property rights *stronger*, not weaker. *See, e.g.* Merges's articles cited *supra* at note 66; Robert P. Merges, *A Transactional View of Property Rights*, 20 BERKELEY TECH. L.J. 1477 (2005); Robert P. Merges, *Of Property Rules, Coase, and Intellectual Property*, 94 COLUM. L. REV. 2655 (1994).

73 Note that the *Restatement* acknowledges this. Although it abandons most limitations on servitude subject matter on the grounds that they are no longer justified by information-cost concerns, it articulates narrow subject-matter limitations for servitudes that violate public policy (including by unreasonably burdening fundamental constitutional rights). RESTATEMENT (THIRD) OF PROP.: SERVITUDES § 3.1 (2000).

74 *Cf.* Van Houweling, *Touching and Concerning Copyright*, *supra* note 11, at 1085 (arguing that "beyond concern with notice – and thus even in cases with actual notice by the party who would bear the burden – intellectual property law's animating principles provide courts with a touchstone for deciding what restrictions deserve to be enforceable via copyright (or patent) law"). *See generally* Brett Frischmann & Mark P. McKenna, *Intergenerational Progress*, 2011 WIS. L. REV. 123 (2011).

of tangible property, and in particular to focus on the dynamic way in which land law has responded to changing information-cost calculations. Servitude law provides an example in which common law dynamism has taken the form of doctrinal liberalization in response to the establishment and improvement of recording systems. The logic of this progression might suggest, ironically, quite a different evolution in the law of intellectual property, where digital age developments appear thus far to have exacerbated rather than alleviated information-cost problems. Doctrines such as intellectual property exhaustion, whose analogs and progenitors in the land law are being discarded, may remain important as tools for managing IP rights in an increasingly complex information environment.

18

Intellectual Usufructs

Trade Secrets, Hot News, and the Usufructuary Paradigm at Common Law

*Eric R. Claeys**

INTRODUCTION

Contemporary American intellectual property (IP) scholarship assumes that a right is a property right if it confers a "right to exclude." In IP conventional wisdom, a "right to exclude" refers to a right to monopolize any use, copying, or commercial gain from the thing clothed with property protection. According to that definition, patents and copyrights are property rights, but trade secrets and rights over gathered news are not.

There are three problems with this conventional wisdom. Most fundamentally, it misunderstands the conceptual character of property in American common law. "Property" is conceived of most accurately not as a right to exclude but as a right securing normative interests in exclusively using or determining the use of an external asset.[1] That general conceptual error then leads to two more specific ones. One has been identified elsewhere[2]: conventional IP wisdom classifies patent and copyright correctly, but for the wrong conceptual reasons. What IP scholars assume are rights to exclude are actually one kind of property right, to which this chapter refers as a right of exclusive control and disposition or (for short) a trespassory right. Such rights entitle owners to exclude most non-owners from their assets without needing to show that the former's intended uses deserve priority over the latter's. In real property, the law confers such rights on land and chattels. With adjustments,

* Professor of Law, George Mason University. I thank the George Mason University Law and Economics Center for a grant supporting my research and writing of this chapter. I also thank Shyam Balganesh, Joe Dellapenna, Wendy Gordon, Paul Heald, Mark McKenna, Adam Mossoff, Chris Newman, and Henry Smith for helpful comments and criticisms.

1 *See* Eric R. Claeys, *Exclusion and Exclusivity in* Gridlock, 53 ARIZ. L. REV. 9 (2011) (book review). *Cf.* Larissa Katz, *Exclusion and Exclusivity in Property Law*, 58 U. TORONTO L.J. 275 (2008) (property consists of a domain of exclusive agenda-setting); Adam Mossoff, *What Is Property? Putting the Pieces Back Together*, 45 ARIZ. L. REV. 371 (2003) (property consists of a right of exclusive use).

2 *See* Adam Mossoff, *Exclusion and Exclusive Use in Patent Law*, 22 HARV. J. L. & TECH. 321 (2009).

IP law confers similar rights on inventions (in patent) and works of authorship (in copyright).

This chapter focuses on one last conceptual error: conventional IP wisdom uses the wrong concepts to put trade secrets and interests over gathered or (henceforth in this chapter) "hot" news in the wrong classifications. Trade secrets and hot-news interests are property rights. They do not confer rights of exclusive control and disposition, but they confer another kind of property right – a usufruct. A usufruct refers to a proprietor's right to use an asset, to continue using it, and to be free from attempts to divert his or her efforts to extract benefits from it. In contrast with trespassory rights, the owner of a usufruct may not exclude from an asset other claimants who extract similar benefits from it by their own independent efforts.

Trade secrets and hot-news interests apply the usufructuary paradigm to IP. IP law and scholarship, however, seem unfamiliar with that paradigm.[3] To correct that shortcoming, this chapter advances two claims. The first is conceptual: if property is defined conceptually as a right of exclusive use determination, trade secrets and hot-news interests are property rights. (Although the possibility needs to be explored elsewhere, the right of first publication may also be such a usufructuary property right.)

This chapter's second claim is historical. In several key authorities that laid the groundwork for American IP law, leading judges or treatise writers described and grounded rights in trade secrecy and hot-news interests as usufructs. (Some of these authorities described and grounded the right of first publication as a usufruct as well.)

I. THE RIGHT TO EXCLUDE IN INTELLECTUAL PROPERTY

Most leading contemporary authorities in IP assume that a right is not a property right unless it confers a monopolistic right to exclude. The U.S. Supreme Court relied on this assumption in the 1974 decision *Kewanee Oil Co.* v. *Bicron Corp.*: "In return for the right of exclusion – this 'reward for inventions,' the patent laws impose upon the inventor a requirement of disclosure."[4] In *The Economic Structure of Intellectual Property Law*, William Landes and Richard Posner introduce intellectual property with a primer on the general economic theory of property rights. In their primer, a "property right is a legally enforceable power to exclude others from using a resource – all others . . . , and so with no need to make contracts with would-be users of the resource forbidding their use."[5]

This assumption is informed by several sources. In lay perceptions, the quintessential class of "property" is land, and property certainly does confer on land broad rights

[3] For two significant exceptions, see Mossoff, *supra* note 2, at 333–35; Mark P. McKenna, *The Normative Foundations of Trademark Law*, 82 Notre Dame L. Rev. 1839 (2007). This chapter's insight in relation to trade secrets has been anticipated by McKenna, *see id.* at 1883 n.198, and also by Mossoff, *supra* note 1, at 415–18.

[4] 416 U.S. 470, 480 (1974) (quoting Universal Oil Co. v. Globe Co., 322 U.S. 471, 484 (1944)).

[5] William M. Landes & Richard A. Posner, The Economic Structure of Intellectual Property Law 12 (2003).

to exclude. Separately, because leading IP scholarship tends to prefer functionalist and utilitarian foundations, the scholarship often assumes conceptual foundations propounded by leading Legal Realist theorists. Prominent Realists and fellow travelers reconceived of property from a right of exclusive use determination into a right to exclude.[6]

The right-to-exclude conception conditions how scholars approach IP rights. At one extreme, scholars unanimously agree that patent rights are property rights. Any unauthorized manufacture, use, or sale of an invention under patent infringes the patent,[7] no matter whether the person engaging in the infringement discovered the idea embodied in the invention by his own independent research or development. Although federal copyright law does not bar subsequent authors from re-creating independently works similar to those of earlier authors, it does generally confer on authors rights to control the copying or distribution of their works of authorship.[8]

By contrast, in mainline IP scholarship, trade secrets are assumed *not* to confer property rights. A trade secret confers on its owner a right to prevent rivals from acquiring a secret by spying or by bribing her employees or licensees. Yet a trade secret does not entitle the owner to exclude rivals from using the substance of the secret if they discover that substance by independent research.[9] Leading lawyers and scholars conclude that trade secrets confer neither rights to exclude nor property rights. For example, in the 1917 case *E.I. du Pont de Nemours Powder Co.* v. *Masland*, Justice Oliver Wendell Holmes suggested that "[t]he property may be denied" in a trade secret, and he favored a theory grounded in the confidential relation between a trade secret's claimant and his employee or other confidante.[10] Holmes's view of trade secrecy accorded with his more general (and proto-Realist) assumptions about property. In his scholarly writings, Holmes maintained that a property owner is one who is "allowed to exclude all, and is accountable to no one."[11] Although practitioners and scholarly dissenters maintain that trade secrets constitute property rights,[12] in scholarship, the mainline view follows Holmes.[13]

6 *See* Adam Mossoff, *The Use and Abuse of IP at the Birth of the Administrative State*, 157 U. PA. L. REV. 2001 (2009); Eric R. Claeys, *Property 101: Is Property a Thing or a Bundle?*, 32 SEATTLE U. L. REV. 617, 634–38 (2009) (book review).

7 *See* 35 U.S.C.A. § 271(a) (2013).

8 17 U.S.C.A. § 102, 106 (2013); Feist Publications, Inc. v. Rural Tel. Serv. Co., 499 U.S. 340, 345–46 (1991).

9 *See, e.g.*, RESTATEMENT (FIRST) OF TORTS § 757 & cmt. a (1939).

10 244 U.S. 100, 102 (1917).

11 OLIVER WENDELL HOLMES, JR., THE COMMON LAW 246 (1881).

12 *See, e.g.*, 1 ROGER M. MILGRIM & ERIC E. BENSEN, MILGRIM on TRADE SECRETS §§ 2.01 to -.06 (2010); Eric R. Claeys, *Private Law Theory and Corrective Justice in Trade Secrecy*, 4 J. TORT L. 1, 30–39 (no. 2, art. 2, 2011), http://www.bepress.com/jtl/vol4/iss2/art2/; Mark A. Lemley, *The Surprising Virtues of Treating Trade Secrets as IP Rights*, 61 STAN. L. REV. 311 (2009).

13 *See* Pamela Samuelson, *Privacy As Intellectual Property?*, 52 STAN. L. REV. 1125, 1153 n.1248 (2000); Robert G. Bone, *A New Look at Trade Secret Law: A Doctrine in Search of Justification*, 86 CAL. L. REV. 241, 241–43 (1998).

A parallel debate recurs in law and scholarship about hot news. Hot-news law makes it actionable for a copier to appropriate without authorization information published by the gatherer, republish that information in her own writing or format, and then sell the republished information, during its commercial life, in a market in which the gatherer is publishing it for commercial gain.[14] When the Supreme Court endorsed this doctrine (in the 1918 case *International News Service* v. *Associated Press*, or, hereinafter, "*INS* v. *AP*"), it was ambivalent about whether the right it was declaring counted as a property right. In dissent, Justice Holmes (joined by Justice McKenna) argued that "[p]roperty depends on exclusion by law from interference, and a person is not excluded from using any combination of words merely because someone has used it before." Also in dissent, Justice Brandeis (another proto-Realist) insisted that "[a]n essential element of individual property is the legal right to exclude others from enjoying it." Somewhat sheepishly, Justice Pitney (the author of the Court opinion) assumed that rival news-gathering agencies could not have "any remaining property interest as against the public in uncopyrighted news matter after the moment of its first publication." Nevertheless, he still insisted that "as between [the rivals], it must be regarded as quasi-property."[15] Yet the term "quasi-property" seems oxymoronic. No wonder that most commentators conclude that Holmes and Brandeis had the better of the argument.[16]

II. PRACTICAL PROBLEMS WITH THE RIGHT TO EXCLUDE

Yet this received wisdom cannot explain many aspects of contemporary IP law and policy. Because the main claim of this chapter is conceptual, space and focus prevent me from recounting all the possible discrepancies.[17] Let me focus here on one clear and representative example – the interfaces at the edges of property, contract, and antitrust.[18]

[14] *See, e.g.*, Nat'l Basketball Ass'n v. Motorola, Inc., 105 F.3d 841, 850–53 (2d Cir. 1997).

[15] 248 U.S. 215, 236 (1918); *id.* at 246 (Holmes, J., dissenting); *id.* at 250 (Brandeis, J., dissenting).

[16] Douglas G. Baird, *Common Law Intellectual Property and the Legacy of* International News Service v. Associated Press, 50 U. Chi. L. Rev. 411, 414 (1983). For accounts more sympathetic to the property in gathered information, see *NBA*, 105 F.3d at 853; Richard A. Epstein, International News Service v. Associated Press: *Custom and Law as Sources of Property Rights in News*, 78 Va. L. Rev. 85 (1992).

Shyamkrishna Balganesh is also sympathetic to the case for encouraging the gathering of hot news, but he thinks that the law provides this encouragement not through property protection but rather through unjust enrichment. *"Hot News": The Enduring Myth of Property in News*, 111 Colum. L. Rev. 419 (2011). This chapter's conceptual criticisms of anti-property views toward hot news apply to Balganesh, but its policy criticisms of those views do not. Balganesh's views on unjust enrichment will need to be treated in separate scholarship. My reservations relating to unjust enrichment are similar to criticisms I have made of restitutionary interpretations of trade secrecy in Claeys, *supra* note 6, at 26–28, 59–62.

[17] For a more discursive analysis of the problems in trade secrecy, see Claeys, *supra* note 12, at 6–13, 41–62.

[18] *See id.* at 12–13, 55–56.

Ordinarily, contract law presumes that parties are competent to contract on most subjects of their choosing. Yet contract law declares some contractual provisions – especially noncompete clauses and territorial restrictions – to be void against public policy. Ordinarily, courts review particular clauses using a case-specific interest balancing test.[19] Yet if a challenged restraining clause merely bars the unauthorized disclosure of trade secrets, it is automatically "valid and enforceable."[20] The same holds true for restraints imposed in an agreement selling or licensing the use of hot news.[21] In these cases, property concepts set a baseline shaping how courts evaluate parties' conduct. If the party bargained for the restraint to profit from IP she owns, she is merely "using" her "property" commercially; if she has no IP in play, then the restraint may illegitimately "restrain" others' legitimate "liberties" to contract or compete.

For example, in *Vickery* v. *Welch*, the earliest reported American trade secrecy case of which I am aware, the Supreme Judicial Court of Massachusetts rejected a restraint-of-trade challenge to a secret formula for chocolate. Vickery had bought a chocolate factory and the secret formula from Welch. In the contract of sale, Welch conveyed "the exclusive use" of the secret and pledged a bond in case of nonperformance. After Welch sold the secret a second time to another party, Vickery sued to recover the bond, and Welch argued that the exclusivity provision was an invalid restraint of trade. The court dismissed Welch's argument summarily, because Vickery became the "proprietor" of the chocolate formula when he bought it. For the court, that insight settled the restraint-of-trade challenge: "The public are not prejudiced by the transfer of it to the plaintiff. . . . [I]t is of no consequence to the public whether the secret art be used by the plaintiff or by the defendant."[22] "Property" in the secret meant the "exclusive use" of the secret. That domain of exclusive use included the right to make commercial use of the secret, and particularly the right to profit from selling the rights to use or license the use of the secret. The discoverer and first user of a secret could not threaten the public's legitimate interests in trade by assigning the right to profit from the secret to a higher-valuing buyer. The property rights that justified such a transfer gave the buyer ample incentive to use the secret commercially (i.e., share the secret's benefits with members of the public in commercial transactions).

Robert Bone argues that trade secrecy ought to be grounded not in property but in contract.[23] The black-letter principles recounted in the last paragraph prompt an

19 *See, e.g.*, Fla. Stat. Ann. § 542.335 (2012); RESTATEMENT (SECOND) OF CONTRACTS §§ 186–88, at 239–44 (2007).

20 *Winston Research Corp.*, 321 P.2d at 459; *see, e.g.*, GTI Corp. v. Calhoon, 309 F. Supp. 762, 767–73 (S.D. Ohio 1969).

21 *See* Morris Comm. Corp. v. PGA, 364 F.3d 1288, 1296–98 (11th Cir. 2004) (summarily rejecting and dismissing antitrust claims, and distinguishing *INS*, because the defendant was legitimately using contracts to prevent the plaintiff from free-riding on its information-gathering efforts).

22 Vickery v. Welch, 36 Mass. (19 Pick.) 523, 527 (1837).

23 *See* Bone, *supra* 13, at 297.

objection to Bone's proposed reconstruction: if the law gives competitors a reasonable chance of getting a trade secrecy restriction invalidated ex post in an ad hoc restraint-of-trade analysis, will that legal regime deter businesses from researching and developing new secrets ex ante? This cycle occurred in women's fashion in the early twentieth century. A federal court refused to extend the *INS* hot- news principle to the designs of silk clothing and accessories.[24] When the designers tried to circumvent that ruling with an agreement to boycott department stores that bought from style pirates, federal regulators prosecuted the parties to the agreement and had it declared a violation of federal antitrust law.[25] After that prosecution, high-end designers produced fewer new designs.[26]

A thorough policy analysis of common law IP doctrines would need to consider systematically whether what happened to high-end designs might happen to trade secrets or hot news if courts internalized the conceptual teachings of anti-property skeptics. Bone does not consider this possibility, even though he is aware of *Vickery* and its holding.[27] How could Bone have missed the problem? And why do courts avoid the problem by classifying trade secrets and hot-news interests – routinely – as property?

III. PROPERTY AT COMMON LAW

A. *Blackstone*

To start answering that latter question, it is helpful to consider how the *Vickery* court spoke of the property rights in question. The Massachusetts Supreme Judicial Court referred not to a "right to exclude" but to the owner's "exclusive use," "an exclusive art" for making chocolate, an "exclusive right" over the chocolate formula, and the owner's power "to have, use and enjoy the right or secret art exclusively."[28] The court assumed property was exclusive, but property's exclusivity was keyed to various attributes of the power to *use* the object of property.

One can see the same contrasts in Blackstone's *Commentaries*. Blackstone described the "right of property" as "that sole and despotic dominion which one man claims and exercises over the external things of the world, in total exclusion of the right of any other individual in the universe." That quotation seems to confirm the "right to exclude" portrait. Nevertheless, elsewhere, Blackstone defined property

24 *See* Cheney Bros. v. Doris Silk Corp., 35 F.2d 279 (2d Cir. 1929).

25 *See* Fashion Originators' Guild of Am. v. FTC, 312 U.S. 457 (1941).

26 Randal C. Picker, *Of Pirates and Puffy Shirts*, VA. L. REV. IN BRIEF (2007), http://www.virginialawreview.org/inbrief.php?s=inbrief&p=2007/01/22/picker.

27 *Compare* Bone, *supra* note 13, at 252 & n.56 (citing *Vickery* and discussing the restraint-of-trade principle associated with the case) *with id.* at 260–83 (analyzing economic arguments for trade secrecy without considering whether restraint-of-trade defenses might undermine a contract-based account of the field).

28 *Vickery*, 36 Mass. at 525–26.

in relation to various incidents of use – "the free use, enjoyment, and disposal of all [one's acquisitions], without any control or diminution, save only by the laws of the land." And at the end of the "despotic dominion" chapter, Blackstone conceded that "after all, there are some few things, which . . . must still unavoidably remain in common; being such whereas nothing but a usufructuary property is capable of being had; and therefore they still belong to the first occupant, during the time he holds possession of them, and no longer." Among these he listed air, light, wild animals – and water.[29] So to appreciate property's conceptual range, we need a definition that reconciles the exclusion evident in land law with Blackstone's references to "use" and "enjoyment" and with the "usufructuary" features of water rights.

B. *Property as a Right of Exclusive Use Determination*

As an alternative, consider this entry for "property," from an 1892 encyclopedia of English and American law: "property" refers to "that dominion or indefinite right of user and disposition which one may lawfully exercise over particular things or subjects, and generally to the exclusion of all others."[30] Obviously, this definition builds interpersonal normative relations around a "thing" or "subject," which is to say an *external asset* – not around, say, one's personal ability to make promises, one's reputational interest, or one's interest in someone else's affections and support.

These normative social relations are ordered through the concept of a "right." In doctrine and background concepts, the term "right" does not mean "any entitlement conferred by the state." Rather, rights presume a community in which different individuals have parallel concurrent normative interests. Rights settle conflicts among the interests of non-owners and owners of different resources. A property "right" confers on an owner a moral power to use or otherwise engage with the propertized asset within certain outer parameters delineated by the scope of the right. The right also entitles the owner to exclude or repel others who interfere with his moral power within those parameters. The parameters, however, are drawn to encourage different owners and non-owners to pursue their own interests concurrently, in using their own assets or personal talents to enlarge their own individual and concurrent well-beings.[31]

Last, a property right secures an owner's interest in *using* the propertized asset. In the narrowest possible case, "use" refers only to a right to consume an asset – to eat fruit one has picked. Usually, however, the right to "use" confers on an owner a meta-right: to decide *how* to use. This meta-right may incorporate not only the privilege to consume but also some combination of the privileges to deploy as a

[29] 2 William Blackstone, Commentaries of the Laws of England 2 (A.W. Brian Simpson 1979) (1766); 1 *id.* at 135; 2 *id.* at 14.

[30] 19 The American and English Encyclopedia of Law 284 (John Houston Merrill ed., 1892).

[31] See Claeys, *supra* note 12, at 17–19. For my usage of "right," see Joel Feinberg, *The Nature and Value of Rights*, 4 J. Value Inquiry 243, 255–56 (1979). For my usage of "interest," see Joel Feinberg, Harm to Others: Moral Limits of the Criminal Law 33–34 (1984).

tool instrumental to another goal, to save for later consumption, to merge with another asset to create an even more useful asset, to give away, or to exchange.[32] The 1892 definition suggests as much by speaking not of "use" but of "disposition" and "user" (an archaic term for deciding how to use) – and of a sphere of "dominion" or an "indefinite" right to dispose or enjoy user. In my definition, that sphere consists of a right of "use *determination*."

Although this domain of use determination is exclusive, here "exclusivity" is derivative, not fundamental. An owner may exclude others only within the legitimate bounds of the powers and rights entitling him to use the asset or set the agenda for its future use. For each species of property, the relevant powers and rights are limited in general ways to accord with the interests of different owners of the same species of property, owners of different species of property whose uses overlap considerably with uses of the species in question, and the liberty interests of others who may want to use the propertized asset without owning it.[33]

C. *Land*

When property consists of a right securing a normative interest in using or determining exclusively the use of a thing, the right and the interest may be configured differently for different propertizable assets. For example, in relation to land, all societies with moderately developed economies accentuate the "exclusivity" and "determination" in property. Trespass law does so by conferring on an owner a right to exclude any unconsented entry, with virtually no questions asked. Land may be deployed for residential homes, farms, apartments, factories, businesses, and many other uses, and a boundary rule lets any one owner decide among all these uses.[34]

Yet the right to direct the use of land is not and cannot be absolute. Nuisance law qualifies background boundary rules. By forcing owners to tolerate low-level pollution, these qualifications limit all owners' autonomy over their lots, to free them all to use their lots in ways that will probably benefit them all.[35] A right of exclusive use determination explains land law's exclusion as well as a right to exclude, and it explains nuisance and other similar qualifications better.

D. *Water Flow*

Although IP scholars know the general features of the property law regulating land, they tend *not* to know the general features of water law. If they did, they would appreciate better that real property and intellectual property present many similar

[32] For a complete list of incidents and responsibilities of ownership, see Anthony M. Honoré, *Ownership*, *in* OXFORD ESSAYS IN JURISPRUDENCE 107 (A.G. Guest ed., 1961).

[33] *See* Claeys, *supra* note 12, at 23–25.

[34] *See id.* at 30–34.

[35] *See* Eric R. Claeys, *Jefferson Meets Coase: Land-Use Torts, Law and Economics, and Natural Property Rights*, 85 NOTRE DAME L. REV. 1379 (2010); Richard A. Epstein, *Nuisance Law: Corrective Justice and Its Utilitarian Constraints*, 8 J. LEG. STUD. 49 (1979).

tradeoffs. To be sure, the tradeoffs tend to generate different stable solutions in real and intellectual property. But that is not the same thing as saying that IP is so special that it has nothing to learn from "RP" about "P's" pros and cons.[36]

To appreciate the character of water law, one must appreciate the distinguishing features of usufructs. In my conceptual definition of property, usufructs downplay the "exclusivity" and the "determination"; they emphasize the "interest" and the "use." As an ideal type, a usufruct consists of a right not to possess or deplete an asset but to use it or consume it without depleting it. The usufruct emerged in Roman law as "the right to use and take the fruits and profits of another's property . . . without fundamentally altering its character."[37] "Usufruct" derives from the Latin phrase *usus fructus*, or "use and enjoyment." In Roman law, these were two of the three powers associated with absolute ownership of property; the third, *abusus*, consisted of the powers to consume the asset, even to the point of destruction, and also to alienate it. Thus, as an ideal type, a usufruct included the powers to use and to enjoy the fruits of an asset but not the powers to waste, destroy, or sell it.[38]

Anglo-American law expanded the usufruct's range. The usufruct came to encompass not only a use right in someone else's property – *A*'s profit to pick fruit from *B*'s tree – but also a legal interest in undivided absolute ownership. For assets clothed with such an interest, a claimant enjoys a usufruct only as long as she is actually using or extracting benefits from the propertized asset. (In Blackstone's terms, access to the asset "belong[s] to the first occupant, during the time he holds possession of" it.) In addition, a usufruct does not entitle a claimant to exclude others from acquiring similar rights on the same asset. Instead, it gives the claimant some assurance (though not an iron-clad one) that she may continue using a resource at the intensity at which he has been consuming it regularly. A usufruct also gives such a claimant a (stronger) assurance that no one else will divert her efforts to extract benefits from a resource without engaging in similar extraction efforts of his own.

Different jurisdictions institute different rules for river water depending on whether they have "humid" or "arid" climates.[39] Humid jurisdictions institute riparian rights. Such rights hold that the owner of riparian land acquires title to riparian rights by operation of the principle of accession. Presumptively, then, humid jurisdictions typically withhold from a riparian the right to alienate water rights separate from the land.[40] The same principles of accession, however, entitle a riparian to exclude nonriparians from diverting any water from his river, without needing to

[36] *See* Richard A. Epstein, *Intellectual Property: Old Boundaries and New Frontiers*, 76 Ind. L.J. 803 (2001).

[37] Barry Nicholas, An Introduction to Roman Law 144 (1962).

[38] Joseph W. Dellapenna, *The Right to Consume Water Under Pure Riparian Rights*, *in* 1–7 Waters and Water Rights § 7.04 (Robert E. Beck and Amy L. Kelley eds., 3rd ed. LexisNexis/Matthew Bender 2010); 1 The Digest of Justinian VII.1.1, at 216–17 (Theodor Mommsen ed. & Alan Watson trans. 1985).

[39] *See* A. Dan Tarlock, Law of Water Rights and Resources ch. 1, at 1–1 (1990).

[40] In many modern jurisdictions the presumption described in text is overridden. *See* Dellapenna, *supra* note 38, at § 7.04.

show that the diversion frustrates any ongoing use or causes him any other special harm. Similarly, one riparian may exclude another from diverting water for non-riparian uses from their common river. Otherwise, in relation to other riparians, a riparian has only an equal right of reasonable use. To lodge a claim against another riparian, a riparian must demonstrate as a threshold matter that he is suffering harm in the form of an interference with an ongoing river use.[41] When a claimant makes that threshold showing, the law then instead rates his and the defendant's uses depending on how "reasonable" they are. In nineteenth-century law, uses were judged on how "essential" they were in relation to drinking, bathing, animal feeding, irrigation, power generation, or other "wants of man";[42] in contemporary law, uses are prioritized by comparing their social utilities.[43] In short, the riparian lacks a right to alienate the riparian rights separate from the land, he has a right of exclusive control in relation to non-riparians – but he has only usufructuary rights in relation to other riparians.

By contrast, in arid climates, jurisdictions institute prior-appropriation rights. An appropriator acquires property only in "the amount of water that he puts to beneficial use," and "[b]eneficial use . . . represents a continuing obligation which must be satisfied in order for the appropriation to remain available."[44] The appropriator is not required to own riparian land, but appropriates water rights simply "on the application of water to a beneficial use."[45] Prior-appropriation rights confer on a claimant a right to continue appropriating and using water beneficially in the future at volumes marked off by previous use. That right gives earlier appropriators priority to exclude water extraction by later appropriators. In addition, prior-appropriation rights (with qualifications and jurisdictional variations) are transferrable separately from the riparian land to which the extracted water is appurtenant.[46] In short, prior-appropriation rights are usufructuary in that they have a "use it or lose it" character, they are trespassory in that earlier claims operate to the exclusion of later claims, and they are generally transferrable.

E. *Riparian Usufructs and the in Rem/in Personam Distinction*

To be fair, lawyers and courts have vacillated somewhat about water usufructs. Prior-appropriation rights are clearly held to count as property rights.[47] In riparian systems,

41 Dumont v. Kellogg, 29 Mich. 420, 423 (1874); Tyler v. Wilkinson, 24 F. Cas. 472, 474 (C.C. D.R.I. 1827).

42 *See* Evans v. Merriweather, 4 Ill. 492, 494–96 (1842).

43 *See* Restatement (Second) of Torts §§ 850–54 (1979). *See generally* Dellapenna, *supra* note 38, at § 7.03.

44 Tarlock, *supra* note 39, at § 5.05[2], at 5–21 (quoting Basin Electric Power Cooperative v. State Board of Control, 578 P.2d 557 (Wyo. 1978)).

45 *Id.* § 5.07[1], at 5–33.

46 *See id.* § 5.17[2], at 5–71; Robert E. Beck, *Reallocations, Transfers, and Changes*, *in* 2–14 Waters and Water Rights, *supra* note 38, at § 14.04.

47 Coffin v. Left Hand Ditch Co., 6 Colo. 443, 446 (1882).

however, some courts have insisted that riparian rights are "right[s] of property,"[48] whereas others have denied "a property in the water itself" and called riparian rights "a simple use of it" or a mere "incident" of ownership "annexed . . . to the land" adjacent to the river.[49] Blackstone confirms the same equivocation when he contrasts property's "sole and despotic dominion" with a mere "usufructuary property." Nevertheless, a usufruct can still count as *a* form of property even if it does not seem the quintessential form of property.

The confusion here is understandable, for lawyers and scholars have a hard time deciding whether usufructs generate in rem or in personam legal obligations. Doctrinally, however, usufructs have long been understood as being in rem.[50] And conceptually, usufructs may be understood as in rem consistent with the two most influential definitions of in rem and in personam.

According to one pair of definitions, rights are in rem if their mandates are indefinite and "good against the world" and not (as in personam rights are) binding in relation only to one or a few people.[51] This standard can be difficult to apply in borderline cases, when legal mandates obligate a numerous but still finite class of identifiable individuals. Riparian rights fall near such a borderline. Nevertheless, when A owns riparian land in a regime of riparian rights, A's rights institute three conditional duties: "(1) If you are a stranger to A's watershed, do not divert any of A's water. If you are a fellow riparian, (2) do not divert water from your and A's common river for non-riparian uses, and (3) do not divert water for riparian uses at volumes or for uses less reasonable than A's." These duties attach to everyone else in the world. They bind other citizens even if those citizens must determine which particular duty or duties apply to them. It makes no difference that riparian rights have built-in reasonability limits in relation to other riparians. In land law, nuisance duties are qualified by reasonability limits, but that qualification does not stop them from remaining in rem.[52]

In another usage, a right is defined as in rem if rights- and duty-holders come into normative relations with one another only through the medium of a res – some thing. By contrast, a right is in personam if individuals acquire rights and duties in relation to one another through their actions, past promises, their past history with one another, or other similar aspects of their personalities.[53] Under this definition,

[48] *See* Southern California Inv. Co. v. Wilshire, 88 P. 978, 981 (1907).

[49] Tyler v. Wilkinson, 24 F. Cas. 472, 474 (C.C. D.R.I. 1827).

[50] *See* Ulpianus, *Ad Edictum*, book XVII, *reprinted and translated in* 3 The Civil Law Including the Twelve Tables, the Institutes of Gaius, The Rules of Ulpian, The Opinions of Paulus, The Enactments of Justinian, and The Constitutions of Leo 266 (The Lawbook Exchange, Ltd., 2006) (S.P. Scott ed. & trans. 1932).

[51] Wesley Newcomb Hohfeld, Fundamental Legal Conceptions as Applied in Legal Reasoning and Other Essays 72 (Walter Wheeler Cook ed., 1923).

[52] *See* Claeys, *supra* note 35, at 1405–11.

[53] *See* J. E. Penner, The Idea of Property in Law 22–31 (1997). *See also* Nicholas, *supra* note 37, at 99–105.

riparian rights are in rem beyond any reasonable doubt. Nonclaimants owe duties to A not by virtue of any promise they make or action they take, but by virtue of normative relations emanating from A's entitlement to her water flow.

IV. THE CONCEPTUAL CASE FOR INTELLECTUAL USUFRUCTS

The concepts explained in the last part leave room in IP for intellectual usufructs. Consider trade secrecy. A valuable and secret business discovery counts as an external asset. If a business wants to decide how to deploy a secret to enhance the competitive advantage of products or services it sells separately from that secret, it claims a normative interest in determining the secret's use. That interest generates in the business a right to exclude competitors from diverting its use of the secret by stealing it and using it for their own purposes. Under the definition of "property" set forth in Section III.B, that right is a property right. Hot news grounds a similar interest and right. As J. E. Penner explains, a news gatherer has a conceptual property right protecting "his publication of the news he has gathered by the imposition of a legal duty on all others (not just between him and other news agencies) not to publish for consideration (*i.e.*, a *market* monopoly, not a total monopoly) said news, unless that other has gathered the same news himself."[54]

IP scholars resist these conceptual classifications on two grounds relevant here. I respond here only to the objections as they apply to trade secrecy, but the responses apply (with appropriate adjustments) to hot-news doctrine.[55] First, as Pamela Samuelson argues, "A does not have the right to exclude *B* from the trade secret, he merely has the ability to prevent *B* from taking certain actions to obtain it."[56] Yet trade secrecy institutes a right to exclude. A may exclude *B* when *B* uses or discloses A's secret "wrongfully." *B* acts wrongfully if he uses or discloses A's secret in breach of a duty of confidentiality to A, uses or discloses the secret on inquiry notice that it was disclosed accidentally or by some third party's prior misappropriation, or acquires it by circumventing A's reasonable precautions to keep the discovery secret and proprietary. These rules excuse *B* in borderline cases, when *B* has no reason to know that A's secret was disclosed accidentally or by previous misappropriation. They definitely excuse *B* when *B* discovers the substance of A's secret by independent research. Yet these rules still allow A to exclude *B* in situations in which common sense suggests *B* is free-riding on A's research and use of the discovery.[57] When Samuelson argues otherwise, she assumes a standard according to which a right is a "property right" only if it confers on its owner a "right to exclude" with no qualifications. Yet property institutes many rights to exclude that are more contextual than this absolute right.

[54] J. E. Penner, *The "Bundle of Rights" Picture of Property*, 43 UCLA L. Rev. 711, 816 (1996).
[55] *See* Balganesh, *supra* note 16, at 435–36.
[56] Samuelson, *supra* note 13, at 1154 n.148 (italics added).
[57] *See* Claeys, *supra* note 12, at 30–37.

Separately, critics insist that trade secrecy's misappropriation norms are not good "against the world."[58] This criticism is harder to pin down. Perhaps the argument is that a right does not generate a property right unless the duties it generates apply in a uniform manner to all non-owners. Yet riparian rights defy such characterizations, and so do use rights grounded in nuisance, easements, and other fields not covered here. Perhaps the argument trades on the fact that many trade secrecy norms arise out of "relational" agreements, especially licensing agreements or employer/employee confidentiality clauses.[59] For example, in trade secrecy misappropriation cases litigated in federal court between 1950 and 2008 and generating a reported opinion, 90 percent or more of the cases involved an employee, former employee, or a business partner.[60]

This argument, however, puts the cart before the horse. An in rem account explains the facts just cited at least as well conceptually as in personam accounts of trade secrecy. In trade secrecy, the in rem right (the claimant's right to the exclusive use of its discovery) creates a correlative duty: all non-owners must refrain from acquiring the business's iteration of the secret or research except by consent, independent discovery, or pure accident. Not only does the in rem duty apply to strangers but it also sets a baseline for contracting with employees or licensees. Owner A may waive his in rem right to exclude prospective employee or licensee B from A's iteration of a secret discovery if B agrees to in personam promises to use the secret for A's ends and under A's direction. Here, however, the in personam promises accord with, specify, and reinforce logically prior in rem duties.

Conversely, in personam interpretations of trade secrecy cannot explain many important features of trade secrecy that can be explained by the in rem interpretation. The property/contract/antitrust interface is one such feature. Another is the in rem feel to trade secrecy contracts. For example, if an in personam license or employment contract were primary in establishing a trade secret, it would be extremely difficult to explain why trade secrecy nondisclosure clauses are extremely easy to enforce in equity.[61] More fundamentally, in personam accounts of trade secrecy cannot explain why three of the four theories of trade secrecy misappropriation establish in rem duties. If A's employees throw out an intact customer list mistakenly and contrary to A's standard document-shredding policy, garbage-hauler *B* breaches a duty to A if he uses the list with any reason to know that it was disclosed accidentally.[62] If A tries to build a building to conceal machinery that will embody a secret process for making a chemical, *B* uses "improper means" and breaches a duty to A if she pays a

[58] Bone, *supra* note 13, at 243; Samuelson, *supra* note 13, at 1153 n.148.

[59] *See* Bone, *supra* note 13, at 244.

[60] *See* David S. Almeling et al., *A Statistical Analysis of Trade Secret Litigation in Federal Courts*, 45 Gonz. L. Rev. 291, 302 & Table 2 (2010).

[61] *See* Claeys, *supra* note 12, at 57–58.

[62] B.C. Ziegler & Co. v. Ehren, 414 N.W.2d 48 (Wis. App. 1987); Restatement (Third) of Unfair Competition § 40(b)(4), at 453 (1995).

commercial pilot to fly over the half-built building and photograph its interior. (This result was announced in the leading 1970 decision *E.I. du Pont Co.* v. *Christopher*.[63]) If *B* acquires A's trade secret from *C* after *C* misappropriated it from A, *B* owes a duty not to use or disclose it if he has any reason to know he is benefiting from C's prior misappropriation.[64] The two relevant *Restatements* and the Uniform Trade Secrets Act all restate four theories of misappropriation,[65] and these theories comprise three of the four. One could say *B* triggers an in personam obligation in each of these cases by the "personal" action of engaging with a secret discovery he does not own. In each of these cases, however, *B*'s personality cannot trigger an in personam obligation except by flouting a prior in rem duty, owed by everyone besides A, not to engage with A's secret if he has any reason to know it may be proprietary.

V. THE NORMATIVE CASE FOR INTELLECTUAL USUFRUCTS

A. *Form, Function, and Legal Concepts*

Some readers may associate the conceptual analysis conducted in the previous part with austere legal formalism, in which "[t]he purpose of private law is simply to be private law."[66] Such formalism has little purchase in IP scholarship, which favors instrumentalist utilitarian foundations.[67] Yet there is a middle ground, for "pragmatic conceptualism." Legal concepts that seem formal can in reality promote sound policy goals by indirect consequentialist means.[68]

Consider what it would take for IP law to promote policy directly, by considering Justice Brandeis's dissent in *INS* v. *AP*. Among other arguments, Brandeis suggested that the Court's holding made it more difficult for legislatures to subject news gatherers to common-carrier rate regulation.[69] With respect, this suggestion is ludicrous. INS had misappropriated news reports gathered by AP papers about

63 *See* E.I. du Pont de Nemours Co. v. Christopher, 431 F.2d 1013, 1016 (5th Cir. 1971), *cert. denied*, 400 U.S. 1024 (5th Cir. 1971); RESTATEMENT (THIRD) OF UNFAIR COMPETITION § 43 cmt. b, illus. 2, at 494, cmt. c, illus. 3, at 494–95.

64 *See* RESTATEMENT (FIRST) OF TORTS § 757(c).

65 *See* RESTATEMENT (THIRD) OF UNFAIR COMPETITION § 40; UNIF. TRADE SECRETS ACT § 1(2); RESTATEMENT (FIRST) OF TORTS § 757.

66 ERNEST J. WEINRIB, THE IDEA OF PRIVATE LAW 21 (1995).

67 *See, e.g.*, Lemley, *supra* note 12, at 326.

68 Benjamin C. Zipursky, *Pragmatic Conceptualism*, 6 LEGAL THEORY 457 (2000); *see* Eric R. Claeys, *Exclusion and Private Law Theory: A Comment on* Property As the Law of Things, 125 HARV. L. REV. F. 133, 137–38 (2012). In text, I refrain from highlighting another major limitation of instrumentalist utilitarian interpretations of IP: such interpretations do not account satisfactorily for how law's internal content relates to human morality and sociability. *See id.* at 135–38; Claeys, *supra* note 12, at 17–27. The criticisms that flow from this limitation do not need to be developed here.

69 *See* International News Serv. v. Associated Press, 248 U.S. 215, 265–67 (1918); *id.* at 267 (citing New York & Chi. Grain & Stock Exch. v. Board of Trade, 19 N.E. 855 (Ill. 1889)).

events during World War I in the Atlantic, Europe, and the Middle East.[70] Ex ante, it would have been extremely difficult for AP to have forecast what marginal additional profit its member papers should have expected from their marginal investments in news reporters covering World War I or *it* should have expected from its marginal investments in transcontinental telegraph cables. And ex post, it would have been extremely difficult to determine how much INS's misappropriation of World War I news diminished the marginal demand for papers of AP members. How would a trier of fact determine how much of the profit of any daily edition was attributable to war news – and not domestic news, sports, or the funnies?[71] The right declared in *INS* circumvents these and many other informational problems. In instrumentalist utilitarian terms, assume that a news gatherer invests substantial time and effort in gathering news, the news is commercially valuable for a limited time, and the gatherer is selling the news. Society will benefit more from incentivizing the gathering and reporting of new news with an intellectual usufruct, the *INS* rule presumes, than it will from leaving the news subject to copying and limiting the gatherer only to the business advantages it accrues by reporting the news earlier than any other news company.[72]

B. *The Proper Functions of Trespassory and Usufructuary Forms*

All property rights make such presumptions. In rights-based terms, property rights presume that people deserve autonomy over property to effectuate all the plans their autonomy entitles them to make in the course of living their own lives. In utilitarian terms, a society cannot increase net social utility without delegating to individuals broad zones of discretion in relation to external assets about which they have especially strong local knowledge. Equally important, property rights also prioritize and accommodate the use interests of *non*-owners. That is why, for example, in *INS*, the Court entitled AP only to property in the exclusive use of its reports for commercial purposes – *not* the exclusive use of the news in those reports for any purpose. The *INS* called the information embodied in news "*publici juris*,"

[70] *See* Associated Press v. International News Serv., 240 F. 983, 986 (S.D.N.Y. 1917), *modified by* 245 F. 244 (2d Cir.), *aff'd*, 248 U.S. 215 (1918).

[71] Geoffrey A. Manne & Joshua D. Wright, *Innovation and The Limits of Antitrust*, 6 J. COMPETITION L. & ECON. 153 (2010). Some contemporary scholars criticize broad distinctions between "IP" and "antitrust" on a ground similar to Brandeis's: that "IP rights work better in some circumstances and competition works better in others." Mark A. Lemley, *Industry-Specific Antitrust Policy for Innovation*, 2011 COLUM. BUS. L. REV. 637, 640. Like Brandeis, such scholars do not adequately consider whether judicial and regulatory proceedings could identify the IP-appropriate and the competition-appropriate circumstances well enough on a case-by-case basis to organize IP and antitrust law that way.

[72] *See International News Serv.*, 248 U.S. at 237–39. The Second Circuit interpreted *INS* to require the trier of fact to find that the competitor's free-riding undermines the gatherer's news-gathering. National Basketball Ass'n v. Motorola, Inc., 105 F.3d 841, 852–53 (2d Cir. 1997). Yet the *INS* Court basically presumed that the free-riding would undermine news gathering, and I believe on this point *INS* remains good law and policy.

translated literally as "belonging to the public's right" or, more loosely, as "affected with a public interest."[73] This term is commonly used to refer as well to the public's interest in using and having unimpeded access to public ways – highways, navigation servitudes, and fishing servitudes. The owner may deserve the residuary value of a parcel of land, but in the right circumstances he or she may legitimately be required to recognize others' easements of passage, sailing, fishing, and so forth. By using this term in *INS*, the Court showed concern for the interests of nonproprietors in engaging with and using news for their own benefit.

So to justify usufructs and rights of exclusive control and possession, one must understand how they secure and enlarge the normative interests of owners and non-owners both. In extremely telescoped form, trespassory rights make the most sense when the asset in question can be deployed to many wide and high-value uses, when those uses require considerable investment to realize, and when such uses are rivalrous.[74] Land, farming, apartment buildings, retail malls, and other high-value uses require considerable investment and security from outside interference. To secure the investment, trespass law and other doctrines guarantee to owners not only the right to continue existing uses but also broad control over entry to their lots.[75] Similar principles apply to patents. Patent law does not need trespassory rights to prevent outside interference, because inventions are not rivalrous. Yet when an invention makes a sufficiently large advance over the prior art, it is reasonable to presume that it would not have been discovered or reduced to practice unless the discoverer were guaranteed to recoup not only the marginal cost of producing the invention but also a share of the fixed costs of discovering it.[76] Here, patent law secures and encourages the "use" of the invention simply by encouraging the invention to be created in the first place. And to give inventors the appropriate incentive, patent law gives them broad property rights, with broad power to "determine" the uses of their inventions while they remain under patent.

By contrast (and also in telescoped form), usufructuary rights make sense when an asset lends itself at least to some public-good uses. Riparian rights make sense when a river may support not only private uses but also navigation, fishing, and other public uses. Usufructs also make sense when private uses are nonrivalrous, when uses tend to be homogeneous, and when such uses can be supported without considerable investment. Riparian rights thus make sense when water is abundant enough that riparians can divert water for drinking, livestock, and basic irrigation without consuming most of the available water. These facts explain why, in "humid" jurisdictions, property's "determination" then recedes, and the underlying "use" interests

73 *See International News Serv.*, 248 U.S. at 234; *id.* at 267 (Brandeis, J., dissenting) (referring to news as "affected with a public interest").

74 *See* Richard A. Epstein, *On the Optimal Mix of Private and Common Property*, 11 Soc. Phil. & Pol'y 17 (1994).

75 *See* Claeys, *supra* note 35, at 1405–09.

76 For this generalization to apply, one would need to show that the novelty and obviousness requirements in patent law require the degree of advancement described in text. *See* 35 U.S.C.A. §§ 102–03 (2013).

loom large. The "use" claims of fellow riparians, fishermen, and navigators all get status comparable to the rights of any given riparian. Of course, when "humid" conditions cease to apply, public officials may and should apply a different conceptual paradigm. In "arid" climates, rivers have too little water to support navigational or other public uses, and they generate too little water to support basic uses sustaining life or benefiting land. To generate supplies of water in useful quantities, rivers must be diverted by canals into larger dams or rivers. Such canals require considerable investment, and the water is scarce enough to be rival. These factors explain why prior-appropriation regimes have more trespassory features than riparian rights.[77]

C. *The Proper Functions of IP Usufructs*

It makes considerable sense to apply the usufructuary paradigm to interests in the use of hot news and in trade secrets. (Here, too, I state the general case in relation to trade secrets and then qualify it as necessary to adjust for hot news.[78]) To begin with, discoveries, such as inventions under patent, are not rivalrous. That fact creates a weak starting presumption against any sort of property, on the ground that discoveries may be used concurrently by many different individuals without diminishing the enjoyment of any user. As patent law confirms, however, this presumption can be overridden if it can be shown that a certain class of information will not be created without legal protection.[79] At that point, however, policy makers must determine whether usufructuary rights or trespassory rights give intellectual discoverers the correct incentives. For extremely beneficial discoveries, the law may need patent's monopolistic protections to provide researchers with adequate incentives to research. For many less innovative discoveries, however, those protections are not necessary. By common law definition, discoveries are eligible for trade secrecy if a competitor would need to expend some effort, time, or capital to discover them. To satisfy this requirement, the discoverer of a secret does not need to expend the costs associated with producing "genius," only the costs of mere "industry."[80] Many companies can incur those costs simultaneously in competition with each other, each recouping the costs from its own sales to its own customers.

Obviously, IP law sorts very crudely when it distinguishes between trade-secrecy–level "industry" and patent-level "genius." Yet the distinction does make sense as a simple proxy for the forecasted future social value of the intellectual work. Given such forecasts, it makes sense that the proprietors of trade secrets are limited only to usufructuary rights. Because many competitors can readily produce different iterations of the same discovery, it would be a mistake to endow any one with a

[77] *See* Carol M. Rose, *Energy and Efficiency in the Realignment of Common-Law Water Rights*, 19 J. Leg. Stud. 261 (1990).

[78] The following discussion relies on Claeys, *supra* note 12, at 30–37; Eric R. Claeys, *The Use Requirement at Common Law and Under the Uniform Trade Secrets Act*, 33 Hamline L. Rev. 583, 594–97 (2010).

[79] *See* Robert Merges, Justifying Intellectual Property 37–38 (2011).

[80] *See* A.O. Smith Corp. v. Petroleum Iron Works Co., 73 F.2d 531, 538–39 (6th Cir. 1934).

monopoly over the discovery. It is preferable to endow each with a limited (though still in rem) right to use the discovery, exclusive from efforts by others to steal the research by which it made the discovery.

At the same time, the usufruct concept explains how the law distinguishes between trade secrecy licenses and restraints of trade. If a discovery is already common knowledge, it is illegitimate for the proprietor to restrict the "use" by members of the public of information they have a right to use. By contrast, if the discovery is still private property, that property includes the normative power to "use" the secret as necessary to recoup and profit from the investments the proprietor originally made. It makes huge practical sense for such "use" to include commercial uses on terms set by the discoverer: unrestricted sales and assignments of the discovery; licenses to use the secret for royalties; licenses to produce goods with the secret for compensation; contracts with independent contractors; or employment agreements with employees in a firm.[81] On that basis, it is no more significant that 90 percent or more of reported trade secrecy cases involve confidentiality agreements than that there are contracts in 100 percent of real-covenant lawsuits and in 100 percent of landlord-tenant disputes.[82]

As should be clear by now, although the usufruct concept determines and settles many doctrinal rules, it does not settle all relevant legal questions. Although riparian rights were (again, traditionally) treated as nonseverable accessories to riparian land, trade secrets are discrete objects of property and may be alienated.[83] These rules raise doctrinal questions about accession and policy questions about how most effectively to scale the "resources" or "entities" to which property rights apply.[84] It is perfectly reasonable that these questions might be answered differently for riparian rights (accessories to riparian land), trade secrets (no accession), and trademarks (accessories to the business that uses them).[85] Because the usufructuary concept has little to say about the policies relevant to these choices, the concept does not and should not significantly influence how these choices are resolved in law or policy.

D. *The Function of Secrecy in IP Usufructs*

One other significant issue deserves attention. Why does trade secrecy require a proprietor to prove that a discovery is secret and protected with reasonable precautions,

[81] *Cf.* Armen A. Alchian & Harold Demsetz, *Production, Information Costs, and Economic Organization*, 62 AMER. ECON. REV. 777 (1972).

[82] *Cf.* Claeys, *supra* note 12, at 57; Epstein, *supra* note 36, at 812–13 (both making the same observation about leases).

[83] *See* 1 MILGRIM ON TRADE SECRETS, *supra* note 12, § 2.02, at 2–38 to -44.

[84] *See* Thomas W. Merrill, *Accession and Original Ownership*, 1 J. LEG. ANAL. 459 (2010); Eric R. Claeys, "Productive Use in Accession, Acquisition, and Labor Theory," in PHILOSOPHICAL FOUNDATIONS OF PROPERTY LAW (James E. Penner & Henry E. Smith eds., forthcoming), http://ssrn.com/abstract=2066166.

[85] *See* 15 U.S.C. § 1060 (2012).

especially when the hot-news doctrine has no comparable requirement? In the absence of a conventional marker such as a patent number or the © sign, secrecy is the best marker practicable to keep information that is proprietary separate from information that is *publici juris*.

To this point, I have focused on property doctrine's connection to investment and commercial use. Property relates to other important normative priorities as well. In particular, property is structured to provide clear notice of ownership, to avoid conflicts, and to create a clear baseline for contracts and cooperative relations between owners and non-owners. In the early English copyright case *Millar* v. *Taylor*, Lord Justice Yates made this point by analogy to "[t]he air, light, the sun, [which] are of value inestimable: but who can claim a property in them?" He made similar analogies to wild animals: "nothing can be an object of property, that is not capable of distinguishing proprietary marks." (Note how Yates repeated the same examples that Blackstone cited when explaining usufructs.) Applying the general principle to intellectual works, Yates concluded that the touchstone of property was secrecy: ideas "are yours, while they continue in your possession; but no longer. So, from the time of publication, the ideas become incapable of being any longer a subject of property: all mankind are equally intitled to read them; and every reader becomes as fully possessed of all the ideas, as the author ever himself was." Although Yates made this argument in dissent, the argument prevailed later and became a bedrock principle of IP common law in England and the United States.[86]

To be sure, the Supreme Court dispensed with the secrecy requirement in *INS* for functional reasons. Elsewhere, however, the common law sometimes institutes doctrines of "constructive possession" for functional reasons. For example, for fast-moving whales, courts have sanctioned rules of constructive possession, which assign ownership to the first whaling ship that lands a marked harpoon lance in a whale. This rule relaxes the ordinary standard for "capture" – manual capture – to encourage gainful investment and effort to catch whales.[87] In *INS*, the Supreme Court circumvented the secrecy requirement by allowing the Associated Press to sue in unfair competition; the unfair competition theory circumvented the secrecy requirement worked out by Yates and many later authorities. Yet the Court did so to accomplish the same policies at issue in "constructive possession" disputes. It was inequitable to enforce the secrecy requirement, the Court reasoned, when INS's use of the stories interfered

> with the normal operation of [AP's] legitimate business precisely at the point where the profit is to be reaped, in order to divert a material portion of the profit from those who have earned it to those who have not; with special advantage to [INS]

[86] Millar v. Taylor, 98 Eng. Rep. 201, 230, 233, 234, 235 (K.B. 1769) (opinion of Yates, J.); *see* Donaldson v. Becket, 98 Eng. Rep. 257 (1773); Wheaton v. Peters, 33 U.S. 491 (1834); Bone, *supra* note 13, at 255 & sources cited nn.70–75.

[87] *See, e.g.*, Ghen v. Rich, 8 F. 159 (D. Mass. 1881); Robert C. Ellickson, *A Hypothesis of Wealth-Maximizing Norms: Evidence From the Whaling Industry*, 5 J.L. ECON. & ORG. 83 (1989).

> in the competition because of the fact that it is not burdened with any part of the expense of gathering the news.[88]

Of course, by dispensing with the secrecy requirement, hot-news doctrine creates inconsistencies with and threatens to undermine the requirement as it applies to trade secrets and other common law intellectual property. Yet maybe it is still preferable to encourage the investments needed to gather and process information in commercially useful form. And perhaps the entitlement-delineation costs are not that great. After all, the hot-news interest creates in rem duties only in competitors, those competitors may be deemed to know their obligations constructively, and in any case such duties are time limited. Here, two points suffice. First, even if these presumptions about secrecy and publication are crude, they are easy to apply and they are plausible enough to support presumptive property concepts. Second, we are interested here in how background concepts channel normative arguments into doctrine. The usufructuary paradigm frees courts from reconsidering from scratch all the pros and cons related to the business of news gathering; it frees them to focus on the pros and cons on the margins involving secrecy and publication.

VI. THE HISTORICAL CASE FOR INTELLECTUAL USUFRUCTS

A. *Intellectual Property in Kent's* Commentaries

Let us turn to this chapter's historical claim: seminal American common law authorities have classified trade secrets and hot-news interests using the usufructuary concept described in the two preceding parts. New York Chancellor James Kent's *Commentaries on American Law* was the first home-grown American treatise covering American public and private law as comprehensively as Blackstone's *Commentaries* covered the parallel English sources. Although most of Kent's section on IP concentrates on patent and copyright, it begins as follows:

> Another instance of property acquired by one's own act and power, is that of literary property, consisting of maps, charts, writings, and books; and of mechanical inventions, consisting of useful machines or discoveries, produced by the joint result of intellectual and manual labour. As long as these are kept within the possession of the author, he has the same right to the exclusive enjoyment of them, as of any other species of personal property; for they have proprietary marks, and are a distinguishable subject of property. But when they are circulated abroad, and published with the author's consent, they become common property, and subject to the free use of the community. It has been found necessary, however, for the promotion of the useful arts, and the encouragement of learning, that ingenious men should be stimulated to the most active exertion of the powers of genius, in the production of works useful to the country, and instructive to mankind, by the hope

[88] International News Serv. v. Associated Press, 248 U.S. 215, 240 (1918).

> of profit, as well as by the love of fame, or a sense of duty. . . . We have, accordingly, in imitation of the English jurisprudence, secured by law to authors and inventors, for a limited time, the right to the exclusive use and profit of their productions and discoveries.[89]

In this passage, Kent covers patents, copyrights, trade secrets, and the right of first publication over a work of authorship. A few features of his survey should seem familiar to modern IP lawyers and scholars. Kent takes for granted that most ideas belong in the public domain (the realm of "common property, . . . subject to the free use of the community"). Although he justifies patent and copyright in terms of "intellectual labour," he also does so in terms of a reward theory ("stimulat[ing] the most active exertion of the powers of genius") consonant with the terms of the Constitution's Intellectual Property Clause ("the promotion of useful arts, and the encouragement of learning").[90]

Kent's portrait of trade secrets and the right of first publication may seem less familiar to contemporary readers. In the context of the concepts recounted here, however, Kent's portrait makes sense. Kent declares and confirms that trade secrets and rights of first publication are usufructs. Although I examine only the passages on patent and trade secrets, consistently with this chapter's focus, the same basic contrasts probably apply between copyright and the right of first publication.

Readers may doubt whether Kent recognizes any intellectual property in trade secrets. When he speaks of "property" in "mechanical inventions," he may be referring only to the common law principle that a person keeps absolute ownership of any chattel he or she creates. Yet Kent specifies that such machines may consist of "machines" *or* "discoveries" and that both are "produced by the joint result of intellectual and manual labour." So the "property acquired by one's own act and power" generates two species of property. The creator acquires not only absolute ownership over the machine created by "manual labour" but also some sort of property over the "intellectual labour" for the machine's design.

Kent treats secrecy in the same terms in which Lord Justice Yates did in *Millar*. In Kent's terms, it is secrecy that establishes "proprietary marks" over a business design or unpublished writings, and it is secrecy that makes the design "a distinguishable subject of property."

Kent tracks the basic policy distinctions recounted in the last part. As a first approximation, Kent presumes that ideas should remain "common property, and subject to the free use of the community." A person is entitled to keep an idea *out* of the commons only if it reflects some "intellectual labour," understood as a positive and productive contribution over and above common social knowledge. He then distinguishes between two possible legal entitlements for intellectual labor. One is the "right of exclusive use and profit," which is associated with patents. That

89 2 James Kent, Commentaries on American Law 298–99 (Da Capo Press reprint, 1971) (1827).

90 U.S. Const. Art. I, § 8, cl. 8.

entitlement clearly refers to what I have called here a right of exclusive control and disposition – a legal monopoly over any commercial profits flowing from an invention. And consistent with the last part's account, Kent reserves such rights for major contributions to public knowledge – "the promotion of the useful arts, and the encouragement of learning, that ingenious men should be stimulated to the most active exertion of the powers of genius."

Most important here, Kent assumes that the other legal option, for trade secrets, is a usufruct. When Kent describes the property in trade secrets, he refers to "exclusive enjoyment." This property is narrower than the right to exclusive use and profit; it is only the right to extract benefits from the invention without interference or diversion.[91] Kent confirms as much by referring to the right in relation to "enjoyment" – the most common translation of *fructus*. The structure of his argument reinforces the same point. If any business acquired hard-edged rights to exclude by virtue of "exclusive enjoyment," multiple competitors' rights would be mutually inconsistent, as blocking patents can be. By contrast, if these rights are usufructs, they can coexist easily.

B. *Intellectual Usufructs at Common Law*

Prominent nineteenth-century and early twentieth-century American IP precedents used the same conceptual distinctions as Kent had.[92] *Peabody* v. *Norfolk*, an 1868 trade secrecy case decided by the Massachusetts Supreme Judicial Court, is probably the best known nineteenth-century American trade secrecy decision. Cook, the main defendant, hired away Norfolk from Peabody's cloth-making factory and allegedly paid him to disclose Peabody's secret cloth-making process. When Peabody's devisees sued Cook in equity for misappropriation, he raised a laundry list of objections, all grounded in the argument that a trade secret cannot be property. In response, Chief Justice Gray began his opinion for the court with a general overview of IP:

> It is the policy of the law, for the advantage of the public, to encourage and protect invention and commercial enterprise.... If [an inventor] makes a new and useful invention of any machine or composition of matter, he may, upon filing in a public office a description which will enable an expert to understand and manufacture it, and thus affording to all persons the means of ultimately availing themselves of

[91] Elsewhere, Kent assumed that riparian rights and other incorporeal hereditaments count as property rights. *See* 3 KENT, *supra* note 89, at 344, 353–67.

[92] A decade after Kent's *Commentaries*, an early American treatise of patent law suggested that trade secrets were not property. *See* WILLARD PHILLIPS, THE LAW OF PATENTS FOR INVENTIONS; INCLUDING THE REMEDIES AND LEGAL PROCEEDINGS IN RELATION TO PATENT RIGHTS 333 (1837). However, the author cited English law for this proposition, *see* RICHARD GODSON, PRACTICAL TREATISE ON THE LAW OF PATENTS FOR INVENTIONS AND OF COPYRIGHT WITH AN INTRODUCTORY BOOK ON MONOPOLIES 170–71 (1823), *cited in* PHILLIPS, *supra*, at 333. As this part shows, American trade secrecy case law followed Kent.

it, obtain letters patent from the government securing to him its exclusive use and profit for a term of years. If he invents or discovers, and keeps secret, a process of manufacture, whether a proper subject for a patent or not, he has not indeed an exclusive right to it as against the public, or against those who in good faith acquire knowledge of it; but he has a property in it, which a court of chancery will protect against one who in violation of contract and breach of confidence undertakes to apply it to his own use, or to disclose it to third persons.[93]

In this passage, Gray describes the property in a patent using the same terms as Kent – the right to "exclusive use and profit." In his discussion of trade secrecy, Gray also confirms this chapter's conceptual starting point: property consists not of a right to exclude but a right to determine use exclusively. In his portrait, trade secrecy's "exclusivity" is derivative. A secret discovery is not "exclusive" in relation to those who discover it independently or otherwise "in good faith acquire knowledge of it." Because those individuals could publish the secret, that substance is not "exclusive" as against the world, as a patent is. Nevertheless, Gray also insists that the owner still has a "property" in the discovery. Peabody had an "exclusive" in rem right in relation to Norfolk and other employees. Because Peabody had a right in the exclusive use of the cloth-making process, he could exclude his employee Norfolk from "undertak[ing] to apply it to his own use, or to disclose it to third persons." Because that right was in rem, it also bound Cook and explained why he had breached a duty not to acquire the process in bad faith, by bribing Norfolk instead of discovering the process independently. That qualified in rem right makes perfect sense as an intellectual usufruct. As Adam Mossoff explains, in trade secrecy, "[t]he fundamental right is the possessor's 'own use' of the information, which thus dictates the extent of the 'exclusive enjoyment' of that information."[94]

Courts reasoned in the same spirit in seminal hot-news disputes. The New York Supreme Court considered one early hot-news case in 1876, in *Kiernan* v. *Manhattan Quotation Telegraph Co.*[95] Kiernan enjoyed a license with the Associated Press and an intermediary giving him the exclusive use of all "foreign financial news" received by AP wires for fifteen minutes after the intermediary's receipt of such news from AP. Manhattan Quotation employed Abbot to collect the same news, and he did so by procuring ticker tapes from Kiernan's customers and reprocessing the information on the tapes. Kiernan petitioned for a judgment restraining Manhattan Quotation from republishing the substance of the foreign financial news that Abbot was procuring

93 98 Mass. 452, 457–58 (1868). In the passages omitted by ellipsis, Gray also described trademarks and rights to business goodwill as IP usufructs. Those passages confirm McKenna's portrait of those fields, *supra* note 3, at 1884–86.

94 Mossoff, *supra* note 1, at 418 (quoting Vickery v. Welch, 19 Pick. 523, 527 (Mass. 1837), *cited in Peabody*, 98 Mass. at 460).

95 50 How. Pr. 194 (N.Y. Supr. 1876). On the development of American hot-news doctrine, see Robert Brauneis, *The Transformation of Originality in the Progressive-Era Debate Over Copyright in News*, 27 Cardozo Arts & Entertainment L.J. 321 (2009).

from Kiernan's ticker tapes; Abbot argued that an injunction was inappropriate because Kiernan lacked property in the news.[96]

Supreme Court Judge van Brunt conceded "that no person could be restrained from the publication of this news in Europe," because the news was already in common circulation. Here, he followed the same lines Kent had drawn between secret information and information published and released into the public domain. Van Brunt also conceded that "in respect to news, its publication cannot be interfered with where the party procures the intelligence by the diligence of his own agents." Here, he applied the principle that a usufruct does not entitle one user to exclude others from using the same resource with their own independent effort. Nevertheless, after canvassing two English hot-news unfair competition disputes, he concluded "that a man may impress upon materials, which are open to all the world, a right of property when he has, as the result of his own efforts and expenditure, collected and reduced to a form serviceable to the public such material." He also found it "an atrocious doctrine to hold that dispatches, the result of the diligence and expenditure of one man, could with impunity be pilfered and published by another."[97] In other words, a news gatherer is entitled to exclude others from diverting the fruits of her gathering without doing their own gathering independently. That entitlement is one of the signature features of a usufruct.

For van Brunt, the harder question was whether Kiernan waived his claims of property by publishing the information he got from AP and AP's intermediary. Here, van Brunt appealed to the same distinction as had Yates and Kent: between secret (proprietary) versus published (common) information. Van Brunt qualified that distinction to institute a rule of "constructive secrecy" corresponding to whale law's doctrine of "constructive capture." Van Brunt relied on precedents from New York's common law of copyright, which suggested that an author did not necessarily waive copyright by mailing a letter to a recipient.[98] To encourage the beneficial investment in the gathering of ticker-tape information, Van Brunt concluded it was appropriate to let Kiernan "restrain the publication by" recipients of his ticker tapes "of such intelligence" as those tapes contained.[99]

This account also helps explain why Justice Pitney's Court opinion in *INS* seems so sheepish about whether hot-news interests belong in the conceptual class of "property." When Pitney used the term "quasi-property," perhaps he conceded, in the face of Holmes and Brandeis's criticisms, that property really is just a conceptual right to exclude. If so, his opinion simply provides another confirmation of how arguments made by Legal Realist academic scribblers discredited and replaced important concepts well established in legal practice.

[96] *See Kiernan*, 50 How. Pr. at 195–96.
[97] *Id.* at 196, 198.
[98] *Id.* at 201.
[99] *Id.* at 201.

Yet another interpretation is possible. In *INS*, the AP had claimed not only a right to be free from misappropriation under unfair competition precedents in *Kiernan*'s spirit but also a copyright under federal copyright law. When Pitney conceded that hot news was not "property" but "quasi-property," perhaps he was saying simply that hot-news interests were not as quintessentially "property" as copyrights were. Here, he may have been repeating Blackstone's contrast between mere "usufructuary property" and paradigm "property" in land. Nevertheless, by describing hot-news rights as "quasi-property," Pitney still recognized that such rights belong in the class "property" even they do not belong in the genus "rights of exclusive control and possession."

VII. CONCLUSION AND IMPLICATIONS

Let me restate this chapter's theses by clarifying the most significant problems in how most IP scholars understand the "right to exclude." According to conventional wisdom, the category "property" applies narrowly and deeply. When a legal relation is conceptual "property," it automatically institutes one general legal template, the template for trespassory rights. Property law supposedly institutes this template to encourage the widest and greatest commercial use of a resource that needs to be supported by considerable investment.

In existing law, however, the category "property" applies more widely. "Property" encompasses many different social relations that encourage individuals to appropriate and use external assets beneficially. Yet the category "property" also has consequences shallower than most IP scholars appreciate. When an asset is clothed with the status of property, the law presumes that the owner has some legal rights – especially the right to contract with others to use of the thing, without running afoul of antitrust or restraint-of-trade norms. "Property" also entitles owners to *some* protection for their investments into and beneficial uses of their assets. Yet the category "property" does not automatically require that covered assets be protected by trespassory rights. Instead, it requires public officials to make a new round of more finely grained normative classifications. As Part V explained, officials must consider the likely public and private uses of the asset, as well as the degree of investment generally needed to exploit the likely private uses of the asset. As Parts III and IV explained, officials may then mix and match different features of the trespassory and usufructuary paradigms to encourage the most beneficial uses of the asset practicable by all the likely parties with stakes in it.

In that light, this chapter's theses are fairly straightforward. Conceptually, the account presented here explains why, *and in what precise respects*, trade secrets and hot-news rights are "property." They are property as intellectual usufructs. Historically, materials seminal in the development of Anglo-American IP law also assumed that trade secrets, hot-news interests, and common law rights of first publication are usufructs.

To be sure, the conceptual account presented here, especially in Parts III and IV, is normatively conditional on the policy justification sketched in Part V. Yet Part V's policy justification is plausible, to say the least. There are strong reasons to create two ideal types delineating how assets may be controlled and used, one for resources with high-investment private uses and another for resources with a mix of public and low-investment private uses. Again, existing trade secrecy and hot-news doctrines declare themselves to applying "property" doctrines that correlate with the policies explained in Part V. If skeptics want to continue to challenge trade secrecy and hot-news interests' status as property, the burden lies on them to explain why that status implements irrational policy. That is the first major implication of this chapter.

Separately, this chapter refutes previous conceptual arguments about trade secrecy and hot news. For example, Robert Bone has claimed that "the historical roots of trade secret law provide no reason to endorse the doctrine today" and that the field does not make sense as a field of property law because of "the relational focus of trade secret's liability rules." Bone also reads seminal decisions such as *Peabody* anachronistically and skeptically. When he confronts the *Christopher* case, a significant counterexample to his argument, he proposes that the case be repudiated and kicked out of trade secrecy.[100] Bone's conceptual and historical arguments are unpersuasive if the IP usufruct is a viable conceptual category. He assumes that an IP interest counts as conceptual "property" only if it confers on an owner "an exclusive right to it as against the public;" this assertion is unpersuasive in light of the conceptual and historical context recounted here. Of course, Bone and like-minded scholars remain free to criticize trade secrecy or hot-news law normatively. Yet such normative criticisms must earn their own keep strictly as normative arguments.

Finally, IP scholars had better watch out for the possibility that conceptual blinders have distorted previous normative anti-property scholarship on trade secrecy and hot-news interests. In trade secrecy, Bone overlooks the way in which property regulates the interface between IP licensing and restraint-of-trade principles from contract and antitrust.[101] Similarly, in hot-news doctrine, Douglas Baird has argued that "granting individuals exclusive rights to the information they gather conflicts with other rights in a way that granting exclusive rights to tangible property does not."[102] These and other authors focus on false-positive error costs, the social costs of classifying trade secrecy and other usufructs as property rights. Such authors overstate the false-positive costs because they assume mistakenly that the "property" category automatically creates legal monopolies. In reality, because intellectual usufructs give all news gatherers or business-secret discoverers parallel usufructs in

[100] Bone, *supra* note 13, at 244, 296, 254; *see id.* at 296–304, 253–59, 261; *accord* Samuelson, *supra* note 13, at 1153–54 n.148. *Contra* Claeys, *supra* note 12, at 49–50, 52–55.

[101] *See supra* notes 19–22 and accompanying text.

[102] Baird, *supra* note 16, at 414; *see* Bone, *supra* note 13, at 263–65.

the information they assemble, no single gatherer or discoverer acquires a legal monopoly. In addition, the same scholarly works do not adequately consider the false-negative social costs. If trade secrets and hot-news interests were not property rights, restraint-of-trade challenges might deter businesses from discovering secrets or gathering news. Sometimes formal legal rules do promote good policies. And sometimes scholars miss the good policies because they do not understand the precise scope of the forms.

19

The Fault Liability Standard in Copyright

*Steven Hetcher**

INTRODUCTION

This chapter sets out one particularly interesting connection between the common law and intellectual property: namely, that as a result of the emergence of fair use doctrine, the liability standard for infringement in copyright is now a fault standard. On first blush, this may seem a dubious proposition, given that the orthodox view is that the liability standard in copyright is not even a fault standard in the first place, but rather is strict liability.[1] Closer scrutiny will show this orthodoxy to be an anachronism, however, once true but no longer so. My argument is not a normative one – that copyright infringement *should* employ a fault standard – but an analytic or interpretive one: that due to the fair use doctrine, *copyright infringement*, properly understood, *already employs a fault standard*.[2]

In this important respect, U.S. copyright law is distinct both from that of civil law countries and other common law countries that have not adopted a fair use doctrine in copyright law. Fair use is sometimes compared to similar sounding doctrines of other countries' copyright regimes.[3] There is a crucial distinction, however, which is

* Visiting scholar at the University of Tennessee, Knoxville School of Law.

[1] Gener-Villar v. Adcom Group, 509 F. Supp. 2d 117, 124–25 (D. P.R. 2007); A. Samuel Oddi, *Contributory Copyright Infringement: The Tort and Technological Tensions*, 64 NOTRE DAME L. REV. 47, 52 (1989) ("Liability for direct infringement is imposed on a strict liability basis.").

[2] Elsewhere I have argued normatively against the application of strict liability in the context of non-commercial creative content, arguing instead for a fault standard. *See* Steven Hetcher, *The Kids Are Alright: Applying a Fault Liability Standard to Amateur Digital Remix*, 62 Fla. L. Rev. 1275 (2010).

[3] *See, e.g.*, JAP International Copyright Law and Practice JAP § 7 ("First, the Copyright Act provides various types of fair use which are exempt from copyright liability and legal licenses conditioned upon payment of compensation in Articles 30 to 49, but makes clear that these provisions do not affect the moral rights of authors."). Teruo Doi, *Availability of the "Fair Use" Defense Under the Copyright Act Of Japan: Legislative and Case Law Developments for Better Adapting it to the Digital/Network Environment*, 57 J. COPYRIGHT SOC'Y OF THE U.S.A. 631, 634–36 (2010) ("In at least two copyright infringement actions filed with the Tokyo District Court and Nagoya District Court in 1994 and in 2004 respectively, the court denied the alleged infringer's defense of non-infringement based on the

that notions such as fair deling are well-delineated, statutory carve-outs. By contrast, the fair use test is a creature of the common law, formulated broadly as a multifactor equitable test, such that a potentially unlimited diversity of activities might qualify. And as is discussed later, a growing number of them do.

In this chapter I argue that there is an important policy implication of this doctrinal interpretation – that the burden of proof with regard to this fault standard should be shifted from defendant to plaintiff. In other words, I am proposing that alleging an absence of fair use – that is, an unfair use – should be added to plaintiff's prima facie cause of action for infringement. Courts are well placed to shift this burden so that legislative change is not necessary.

Finally, I argue that, if this policy proposal is implemented, two important legal consequences are likely to follow. First, shifting the burden of proof with regard to fair use will result in fewer instances of default judgments against defendants in copyright infringement suits. Second and correlatively, fewer infringement suits will be brought in the first place. Before directly engaging in these main arguments, it is helpful to first explore some general connections between tort and copyright.

I. THE TORT OF COPYRIGHT INFRINGEMENT

Copyright infringement is a tort.[4] That is orthodoxy,[5] although what precisely it means or entails is less often discussed. Indeed, the opposite position might appear

"fair use" doctrine other than those instances of limitations and exceptions provided in the Copyright Act."; In KK Gakushu Kenkyusha v. KK Daisan Shokan, (Hanrei Jiho (No. 1567) 126 (Tokyo District Court, Dec. 18, 1995)) the court held "the Copyright Act sets forth, in Article 30 to Article 49, various instances of limiting copyrights and conditions for such limitations in detail, for the purpose of balancing the private rights of authors, etc. and the public interest of allowing other persons to exploit works of authorship in fair and equitable terms, and, therefore, the Act does not contain a general provision equivalent to the 'fair use' doctrine with the legislative intention to provide limitations in instances provided in these provisions" and in JASRAC v. K.K. Tsuge et al. the court held that "[t]he Nagoya District Court held that, in view of the objective of the Copyright Act provided in Article 1, and a set of provisions, beginning from Article 30, to provide limitations on copyright in accordance with the objective of the Act, under the legal system of Japan limitations must be expressly provided in the statute, and there should be no instances of fair use of works aside from such express statutory provisions.").

4 Ted Browne Music Co. v. Fowler, 290 F. 751, 754 (2d Cir. 1923) ("Courts have long recognized that infringement of a copyright is a tort."); Southwestern Bell Tel. Co. v. Nationwide Indep. Directory Serv., Inc., 371 F. Supp. 900, 907 (W.D. Ark. 1974) ("Copyright infringement is a tort."); Screen Gems-Columbia Music, Inc. v. Mark-Fi Records, Inc., 256 F. Supp. 399, 403 (S.D.N.Y. 1966) ("Since infringement constitutes a tort, common law concepts of tort liability are relevant in fixing the scope of the statutory copyright remedy, and the basic common law doctrine that one who knowingly participates in or furthers a tortious act is jointly and severally liable with the prime tortfeasor is applicable in suits arising under the Copyright Act."); Lawrence v. Dana, 15 F. Cas. 26, 61 (C.C.D. Mass. 1869); Hetcher, *supra* note 2, at 1275, 1283 (2010) ("Courts have long recognized that infringement of a copyright is a tort, and all persons concerned therein are jointly and severally liable as such joint tort-feasors.").

5 Given this fact, it is an oddity that torts casebooks – the main means by which new lawyers are taught tort – typically make no mention of IP torts such as copyright, trademark, or patent infringement.

more intuitive, namely that copyright infringement is one aspect of a general carve-out from the state common law of tort for those wrongs specified in the Copyright Act. On this view, the dividing line between common law torts and copyright infringement would be the preemption clause of the Copyright Act, according to which there can be no common law torts that are duplicative of those wrongs specified in the Act.[6] Given the division, one might not think it unreasonable to inquire as to whether we can even denominate the sort of wrongs specified in the Copyright Statute as torts. After all, is not judge-made law often contrasted with statutory law as distinctive species of a genus?[7] Although this latter statement is true, on closer inspection, it would appear not to gainsay the former legal proposition, namely, that not all torts are common law torts. There are common law torts and there are statutory torts.[8] To state the issue succinctly, why else call copyright infringement a tort unless it shares the features of a tort?[9] This raises the question as to what are the common features of torts, whether they be common law or statutory in origin.

For example, Goldberg, Sebok and Zipursky give the following examples of torts in the introduction to their casebook: "These include assault, battery, conversion, defamation, defective product sales (products liability), false imprisonment, fraud, intentional infliction of emotional distress, intentional interference with contract or economic advantage, invasion of privacy, negligence, nuisance and trespass to land or chattel." Tort Law: Responsibility and Redress, 3 (2d. ed. 2008).

6 17 U.S.C. § 301(a) (2010) ("On and after January 1, 1978, all legal or equitable rights that are equivalent to any of the exclusive rights within the general scope of copyright as specified by section 106 in works of authorship that are fixed in a tangible medium of expression and come within the subject matter of copyright as specified by sections 102 and 103, whether created before or after that date and whether published or unpublished, are governed exclusively by this title. Thereafter, no person is entitled to any such right or equivalent right in any such work under the common law or statutes of any State.").

7 Goldberg, Sebok, & Zipursky, supra note 6, at 12 ("In most U.S. jurisdictions, torts such as negligence are common law causes of action. This means that the plaintiff's ability to sue in the first place, and the terms on which she can obtain redress, are established by *judicial decisions*, rather than by a statute passed by a legislature and authorized by a chief executive." (emphasis added).

8 *Id.* at 14 ("Tort law need not be judicial in origin."). Integrated Solutions, Inc., v. Serv. Support Specialties, Inc., 193 B.R. 722, 727 (D. N.J. 1996) ("Although copyright infringement is fundamentally a tort, it arises under federal law."). Abbott Laboratories v. NutraMax Products, Inc., 844 F. Supp. 443, 446 (N.D. Ill. 1994) ("Infringement of intellectual property rights sounds in tort."). Taylor v. Meirick, 712 F.2d 1112, 1117 (7th Cir. 1983) ("This principle applies to a statutory tort such as copyright infringement.") Copylaw § 14:47 ("In most cases, copyright law poses no special problems with regard to liability for copyright infringement. The infringer, as any tort-feasor, is liable for the infringement. In general, issues of liability will follow the more general rules of tort liability."). Porter v. U.S., 473 F.2d 1329, 1337 (5th Cir. 1973) (citing Twentieth Century-Fox Film Corp. v. Dieckhaus, 153 F.2d 893 (8th Cir. 1943); Turton v. U.S., 212 F.2d 354 (6th Cir. 1954)) ("Rather, it has always been held that infringement of copyright, whether common law, or statutory, constitutes a tort."). Glidden Co. v. Zdanok, 370 U.S. 530, 574 (1962) ("to determine the liability of the United States for patent or copyright infringement and for other specifically designated torts").

9 *See* Caroline E. Johnson, *A Cry for Help: An Argument for Abrogation of the Parent-Child Tort Immunity Doctrine in Child Abuse and Incest Cases*, 21 Fla. St. U. L. Rev. 617, 657 (1993) (citing Streenz v. Streenz, 471 P.2d 282, 286 (Ariz. 1970) (McFarland, J., dissenting)) ("Nevertheless, Justice McFarland of the Arizona Supreme Court said it best in proclaiming, 'a tort is a tort is a tort.'"); Jeffrey A. Van Detta, *Le Roi est Mort; Vivi Le Roi!": An Essay On the Quiet Demise of McDonnell Douglas and the Transformation of Every Title VII Case After Desert Palace, Ind. v. Costa into a "Mixed-Motives" Case*, 52 Drake L. Rev. 71, 81–82 (2003) ("[A] tort is a tort – no matter how well the legislative and judicial branches may have sought to disguise its nature.").

In other words, what features does copyright infringement share with its sibling torts from the tangible world?

As noted in the introduction, it is orthodoxy to describe the liability standard in copyright law as strict liability. Established copyright doctrine provides no significant allowance for the notion of a fault-based liability standard. To the extent that fault enters the picture on the orthodox view, it is in the distinction between "intentional infringement" and "innocent infringement."[10] The distinction has an impact on the mitigation of damages but not on liability itself.[11]

By contrast, tort law is uniformly conceived of as having three liability standards, as is witnessed by the fact that torts casebooks are typically organized around the tripartite distinction of intentional torts, negligence or fault-based torts, and strict liability torts.[12] Note that, although tort orthodoxy views the tripartite liability standards as pivotal to the organization of tort law, this distinction is not essential to tort itself. Goldberg, Sebok, and Zipursky characterize a tort as follows:

> In sum, to commit a tort is to act in a manner that is wrongful toward and injurious to another. Torts in turn refers to the collection of recognized legal claims that enable a person (or entity) to obtain redress from another on the ground that he (or it) has suffered injury by virtue of having been wronged by that other.... Tort law consists of the rules and principles that determine right conduct, as well as the circumstances under which a victim can obtain redress, and the form that such redress may take.... [T]ort law articulates legal responsibilities or duties that persons owe to one another and provides victims of conduct breaching those duties with redress against those who have wronged them.[13]

Note that this definition does not mention liability standards at all, much less whether there should be some specific number of them. If some particular doctrine with regard to the correct number and type of liability standards is not part of an exemplary definition of a tort, then the fact that copyright infringement has a

[10] *Compare* Bright Tunes Music Corp. v. Harrisongs Music, Ltd., 420 F. Supp. 177, 180–81 (S.D.N.Y. 1976) (finding former Beatle George Harrison to be an innocent infringer when he unintentionally and unconsciously copied the tune of another song), and N. Music Corp. v. Pacemaker Music Co., No. 64 Civ. 1956, 1965 U.S. Dist. LEXIS 6864, at *3 (S.D.N.Y. Nov. 5, 1965) ("[I]f copying did in fact occur; it cannot be defended on the ground that it was done unconsciously and without intent to appropriate plaintiff's work."), *with* Metro-Goldwyn-Mayer Studios Inc. v. Grokster, Ltd. 545 U.S. 913, 941 (2005) (reversing summary judgment and remanding for further proceedings on whether defendants were liable for intentionally inducing infringement).

[11] New Line Cinema Corp. v. Russ Berrie & Co., 161 F. Supp. 2d 293, 300 (S.D.N.Y. 2001); *see also* David Hricik, *Remedies of the Infringer: The Use by the Infringer of Implied and Common Law Federal Rights, State Law Claims, and Contract to Shift Liability for Infringement of Patents, Copyright, and Trademarks*, 28 TEX. TECH. L. REV. 1027, 1087 (1997) ("No scienter need be shown to prove infringement. Intent is relevant only to the decision whether or not to increase damages. A finding of willful infringement permits the court to increase statutory damages. Negligence or recklessness has no relevancy to determining whether copyright infringement has occurred.").

[12] *See, e.g.*, MARC A. FRANKLIN & ROBERT L. RABIN, TORT LAW AND ALTERNATIVES: CASES AND MATERIALS Chs. II, VII, XII (6th ed. 1996).

[13] GOLDBERG, SEBOK, & ZIPURSKY, *supra* note 6, at 3.

different number than torts generally would appear not to disqualify infringement as a tort.

My dispute with the orthodoxy is not with whether it is indeed accurate to understand copyright as containing a unified liability standard. My contention, however, is that this unitary standard is a fault standard, not a strict liability standard. A strict liability tort requires mere causation – that the defendant caused a justiciable injury to the plaintiff. If causation is shown, intention or fault need not be shown. This is the case for saying that infringement is a strict liability tort, because the plaintiff need merely allege causation; namely, that the defendant caused a substantially similar copy of a protected work owned by the plaintiff to be made.

Despite these doctrinal features of copyright, infringement is best understood as a fault standard because it is in fact not enough to establish causation in order to establish infringement, *tout court*. Rather, a plaintiff must establish causation in circumstances in which the copy is not legally recognized as a fair use.[14] But because fair use may potentially be interposed in any infringement dispute, it is always a contingent matter whether a showing of prima facie infringement is legally equivalent to actual infringement. This means that there are really only two kinds of potential infringement actions: those in which the use was fair and those in which it was not. In either situation, it is fairness or fault that is dispositive – one consults the standard and either determines that by its lights the particular use is or is not fair and, thus, whether or not the use is infringing.

To fully appreciate the significance of this point, consider the fault standard in tort, generally speaking. It works by interposing a moral test – fault – between the bare test of one party causally acting in some way that injures another and a finding of liability. Fair use functions in precisely this manner to interpose a moral test – fair use – between an act by the defendant and its causal impact on the plaintiff, as being sufficient for liability. Just as one is not liable in negligence or intentional tort if one is not at fault, in copyright, one is not an infringer if one's act is fair.[15]

[14] It might be retorted that, although this is true in theory, in practice the outcome will turn as well on unrelated and problematic factors such as the fact that large commercial entities are able to threaten and legally browbeat users into unfavorable default judgment outcomes, such that they are never allowed to vindicate the fair use status of their behavior. This is true and important, but is a distinct issue and one that receives attention later. Indeed, this state of affairs serves in part as a predicate for the policy argument developed later that favors shifting the burden of proof to plaintiffs.

[15] 17 U.S.C. § 107 (2010) ("Notwithstanding the provisions of sections 106 and 106A, the fair use of a copyrighted work, including such use by reproduction in copies or phonorecords or by any other means specified by that section, for purposes such as criticism, comment, news reporting, teaching (including multiple copies for classroom use), scholarship, or research, is not an infringement of copyright."); Gaylord v. United States, 595 F.3d 1364, 1385 (2010) ("Clear error has not been shown in the Court of Federal Claims' factual findings supporting the statutory factors of fair use. A transformative work is generally deemed a fair use of a copyrighted work. This finding of fair use of itself establishes the right of the United States to use a picture of the Memorial on a United States postage stamp, without liability for copyright infringement." (internal citations omitted)); A.V. ex rel. Vanderhye v. iParadigms, LLC, 562 F.3d 630, 637 (2009) ("Thus, the copyright owner's 'monopoly . . . is limited and subject to a list of statutory exceptions, including the exception for fair use provided in 17 U.S.C. § 107.' A person

A fair use is not an excused infringement, as plaintiffs sometimes claim, but rather a justified use; that is, not an infringement at all.[16]

A fairness test is by definition a normative test. Fairness is not only an inherently normative concept but also one that is crucial to the law.[17] This is prominently seen in John Rawls's famous phrase: "justice as fairness."[18] It is in this simple way that the common law emergence of the fair use test adds an additional moral element to what was previously a strict liability test for causation regardless of fault. The fair use test is best viewed as a species of the genus fault standard, because tort law offers other fault standards as well, such as whether an injurious act passes the Hand Test, the Reasonable Person Standard, or the test for due care in the case of negligence torts,[19] or, in the case of dignitary torts, whether the act was intentional and lacked consent.[20]

who makes fair use of a copyrighted work is not an infringer even if such use is otherwise inconsistent with the exclusive rights of the copyright owner." (internal citations omitted)); Eldred v. Ashcroft, 537 U.S. 186, 219 (2003); *see also* Sony Corp. of Am. v. Universal City Studios, 464 U.S. 417, 433 (1984) ("Conversely, anyone who is authorized by the copyright owner to use the copyrighted work in a way specified in the statute or who makes a fair use of the work is not an infringer of the copyright with respect to such use.").

16 On the notion of being authorized by the law, *see* Lenz v. Universal Music Corp., 572 F. Supp. 2d 1150, 1154 (N.D. Cal. 2008) ("Here, the Court concludes that the plain meaning of 'authorized by law' is unambiguous. An activity or behavior 'authorized by law' is one permitted by law or not contrary to law. Though Congress did not expressly mention the fair use doctrine in the DMCA, the Copyright Act provides explicitly that 'the fair use of a copyrighted work . . . is not an infringement of copyright.'" (internal citations omitted)).

17 Indeed, some justifications of the fault standard have been stated in terms of "fairness." Oliver Wendell Holmes, The Common Law 76, 110–13 (1909).

18 John Rawls, A Theory of Justice 11 (15th ed. 1999).

19 United States v. Carroll Towing Co., 159 F. 2d 169, 173 (1947) ("[I]f the probability be called P; the injury, L; and the burden, B; liability depends upon whether B is less than L multiplied by P: i.e., whether B is less than PL."); Dan B. Dobbs, The Law of Torts 280 (Vol 1. 2001) ("The reasonable person whose standards the defendant must meet is said to have these attributes: (1) Normal intelligence; (2) normal perception, memory, and at least a minimum of standard knowledge; (3) all the additional intelligence, skill, or knowledge actually possessed by the individual actor; and (4) the physical attributes of the actor himself.").

20 *See, e.g., Dobbs,* supra *note* 20, at 54 ("The central core of the battery rules is simple. Subject only to the most limited exception, the defendant must respect the plaintiff's apparent wishes to avoid intentional bodily contact."); Restatement (Second) of Torts: Battery: Harmful Contact § 13 (1965) ("An actor is subject to liability to another for battery if (a) he acts intending to cause a harmful or offensive contact with the person of the other or a third person, or an imminent apprehension of such a contact, and (b) a harmful contact with the person of the other directly or indirectly results."); Restatement (Second) of Torts: Battery: Harmful Contact § 13 cmt. d (1965) ("In particular, the plaintiff's consent to the contact with his person will prevent the liability. The absence of such consent is inherent in the very idea of those invasions of interests of personality which, at common law, were the subject of an action of trespass for battery, assault, or false imprisonment."); Nelson v. Carroll, 735 A.2d 1096, 1100 (Md. 1999) (citing Prosser & Keeton, The Law of Torts § 8, at 36 (5th ed. 1984) ("The intent with which tort liability is concerned is not necessarily a hostile intent, or a desire to do any harm. Rather it is an intent to bring about a result which will invade the interests of another in a way that the law forbids."). Jurisdictions differ on whether consent is properly a burden for plaintiffs or for defendants, although most appear to place the burden on the plaintiff and not the defendant. *See* 6A Ca. Jur. Assault & Other Wilful Torts 3d § 45 (2011) ("Since lack of consent is an

The moral intuition behind the fault standard generally is that it is unjust to hold someone liable for an injury that occurred through no fault of his or her own. So stated, this moral premise is broadly deontological in form. In this vein, Jules Coleman writes, "In the received view, the substitution of fault for causation marked an abandonment of the immoral standard of strict liability under Trespass (which, after all, imposed liability without regard to fault) in favor of a moral foundation for tort liability based on the fault principle."[21] A consequentialist approach may arrive at the same result, however. Richard Posner writes, "Perhaps then, the dominant function of the fault system is to generate rules of liability that if followed will bring about, at least approximately, the efficient – the cost-justified – level of accidents and safety."[22]

Moreover, within the category of deontological approaches, there are variations. Most famously, in *Palsgraf*, Judge Cardozo espouses a reasonable foreseeability of injury standard as a moral prerequisite to liability, whereas Judge Andrews espouses a multifactor approach in which reasonable foreseeability may be a salient or even determinative factor in particular cases but is not necessary for liability.[23] Contemporary tort theorists differ regarding the necessity of the foreseeability requirement in tort generally.[24] Recent case law has been divided as well.[25] Within copyright doctrine, foreseeability has not been an element either of prima facie infringement or of the four-factor fair use test.[26]

It is instructive to consider the emergence of a fault standard in copyright in historical perspective. Consider first the manner in which the fault standard arose in tort. This tripartite schema of liability set out earlier replaced the ancient tort schema of the writs of trespass and trespass on the case.[27] Trespass torts required injurious actions that were direct and forcible.[28] Trespass on the case, which developed later, allowed trespass actions for injuries whose cause was less forcible or direct.[29] For

essential element of assault and battery, the burden of proving lack of consent is on the plaintiff"); Ill. Jur. Personal Injury & Torts § 7:38 (2007) ("A plaintiff in an assault or battery action has the burden of proving every element of the cause of action, including the absence of consent."); 6 Am. Jur. 2d *Assault & Battery* § 166 (2011) ("While the plaintiff need not negate any affirmative defense, the plaintiff's burden is to prove lack of consent when it is an essential element of the claim."). *But see* State of Washington v. Buzzell, 200 P.3d 287, 291–92 (Feb. 9, 2009) ("Consent negates forcible compulsion; the burden to establish consent is on the defendant.").

21 Jules L. Coleman, *Moral Theories of Torts: Their Scope and Limits* (pt. 1), 1 L. & PHIL. 371, 374 (1982).

22 *See* Richard A. Posner, *A Theory of Negligence*, 1 J. LEGAL STUD. 29, 32–33.

23 *See generally* the Andrews dissent, Palsgraf v. Long Island R. Co., 162 N.E. 2d 99 (N.Y. Ct. App. 1928).

24 *See*, John C. P. Goldberg & Benjamin C. Zipursky, *The Moral of MacPherson*, 146 U. PA. L. REV. 1733, 1812–24 (1998); W. John Cardi, *Purging Foreseeability*, 58 VAND. L. REV. 739 (2009).

25 *See* Cardi, *supra* note 25.

26 Recently, the foreseeability doctrine has been extended to copyright. *See* Shyamkrishna Balganesh, *Foreseeability and Copyright Incentives*, 122 HARV. L. REV. 1569 (2009).

27 GOLDBERG, SEBOK, & ZIPURSKY, *supra* note 6, at 47.

28 *Id.* In the famous formulaic phrase from the old cases, acts of trespass were committed "vi et armis," with force of arms. *See, e.g.*, Rhodes v. Collins, 150 S.E. 492, 494 (N.C. 1929).

29 DOBBS, *supra* note 20, at 25–26 (Vol. 1, 2001) ("The defendant throws a log in the plaintiff's path and he trips over it after it has come to rest. A claim on those facts does not justify the use of the writ of

our purposes, the key to the ancient torts is that fault was not an element in the cause of action.[30] The directness and force of an injurious act, per se, say nothing regarding whether the act was the result of faulty behavior. Accordingly, the ancient torts were strict liability in the sense of liability without fault – all that was required was causation of an injury by the tortfeasor to the victim, so long as the injury was sufficiently forcible and direct.[31]

trespass. Nevertheless, the claim might appeal to one's sense of justice and in the late 14th century the Chancellor began to issue writs to cover such indirect injuries. The new kind of writ was called *trespass on the case*.").

30 This is not to say that fault-based injuries could not be trespasses, however, but just that it was not the fault but instead the force and directness that formally mattered.

31 In modern tort generally, strict liability is the exception to the rule – it is applied to "unreasonably dangerous activities," such as using explosives or keeping wild animals. RESTATEMENT (SECOND) OF TORTS: ABNORMALLY DANGEROUS ACTIVITIES § 520 (1977) ("In determining whether an activity is abnormally dangerous, the following factors are to be considered: (a) existence of a high degree of risk of some harm to the person, land or chattels of others; (b) likelihood that the harm that results from it will be great; (c) inability to eliminate the risk by the exercise of reasonable care; (d) extent to which the activity is not a matter of common usage; (e) inappropriateness of the activity to the place where it is carried on; and (f) extent to which its value to the community is outweighed by its dangerous attributes."); RESTATEMENT (THIRD) OF TORTS: LIABILITY FOR PHYSICAL HARM § 20 cmt. e (2001) ("Courts frequently state that blasting is a paradigm of an abnormally dangerous activity."); *E.g.*, Hargrove v. Billings & Garrett, Inc., 529 S.E.2d 693, 694–95 (N.C. Ct. App. 2000) ("Blasting is recognized as an ultra-hazardous activity in North Carolina and parties whose blasting causes injury are held strictly liable for damages, regardless of negligence."); RESTATEMENT (SECOND) OF TORTS: LIABILITY OF POSSESSOR OF WILD ANIMAL § 507 (1977) ("(1) A possessor of a wild animal is subject to liability to another for harm done by the animal to the other, his person, land or chattels, although the possessor has exercised the utmost care to confine the animal, or otherwise prevent it from doing harm. (2) This liability is limited to harm that results from a dangerous propensity that is characteristic of wild animals of the particular class, or of which the possessor knows or has reason to know."). *E.g.*, Scorza v. Martinez, 683 So. 2d 1115, 1117 (Fla. Dist. Ct. App. 1996) ("The owner, keeper, or possessor of a wild animal is strictly liable if the animal injures another."). It is also applied in product liability cases. RESTATEMENT (SECOND) OF TORTS: SPECIAL LIABILITY OF SELLER OF PRODUCT FOR PHYSICAL HARM TO USER OR CONSUMER § 402A (1965) ("(1) One who sells any product in a defective condition unreasonably dangerous to the user or consumer or to his property is subject to liability for physical harm thereby caused to the ultimate user or consumer, or to his property, if (a) the seller is engaged in the business of selling such a product, and (b) it is expected to and does reach the user or consumer without substantial change in the condition in which it is sold. (2) The rule stated in Subsection (1) applies although (a) the seller has exercised all possible care in the preparation and sale of his product, and (b) the user or consumer has not bought the product from or entered into any contractual relation with the seller."). RESTATEMENT (SECOND) OF TORTS: SPECIAL LIABILITY OF SELLER OF PRODUCT FOR PHYSICAL HARM TO USER OR CONSUMER § 402A cmt. a (1965) ("The rule is one of strict liability, making the seller subject to liability to the user or consumer even though he has exercised all possible care in the preparation and sale of the product."). Once one considers this list, it seems obvious that copyright infringement is nothing like these activities as it would seem far-fetched to call copyright infringement unreasonably dangerous. Perhaps there are some infringement activities that are unreasonably dangerous, but clearly most are not. Just as other types of property may be injured in different ways – namely, a person can be hurt by dynamite, a punch in the nose, or a banana peel left on the floor, such that the first might be an unreasonably dangerous activity calling for the application of a strict liability standard, the second may be a purposeful injury calling for an intentional tort standard, and the third might be best seen as a negligent harm calling for a fault standard, so too, it makes sense to conceptualize copyrightable content as capable of being

The fault standard emerged in the case law, perhaps most famously in *Brown* v. *Kendall*. There, the court wrote as follows:

> What constitutes ordinary care will vary with the circumstances of cases. In general, it means that the kind and degree of care, which prudent and cautious men would use, such as is required by the exigency of the case, and such as is necessary to guard against probable danger.[32]

My suggestion is that a parallel historical shift in liability standards away from strict liability has occurred in copyright, as well as in tort generally, the difference being that there is not a general awareness of this shift in the domain of copyright infringement: the orthodox understanding has not caught up with the new reality marshaled in by the blossoming of fair use.[33]

One feature of infringement adjudication that may make fair use not seem to be a fault standard is the procedural posture in which it arises, namely, as an affirmative defense. But this fact does not mean that fair use is not a fault standard, but instead that it is one for which the burden of proof lies with defendants, who carry the burden to establish lack of fault due to the fairness of the copying. Doing so does not have the implication that these are no longer fault liability cases, however, as is apparent from the fact that courts that shift evidentiary burdens in other sorts of tort

injured in different ways. Ironically, despite the fact that the orthodox infringement standard is seen to be a strict liability standard, it is hardest to imagine how the requirement standard of "unreasonably dangerous" behavior can be met; it is not as if one can use dynamite to blow up copyright-protected works, because they are intangible, nor can such works be torn apart by domestically kept wild animals for the same reason. Nor can defective products easily harm copyrights; a defectively designed ski hill might lead to Sonny Bono's demise, but his songs will live forever. If one is creative, one can come up with an example, such as a defective photocopy machine that as a result creates unauthorized copies. This hypothetical of infringement through a defective product is best viewed as the exception that proves the rule, however, because as a rule, infringements do not result from unreasonably dangerous behavior.

32 Brown v. Kendall, 60 Mass. (6 Cush.) 292, 296 (1850); *see also* Brown v. Collins, 53 N.H. 442, 451 (1873) (rejecting strict liability in favor of the negligence rule); Losee v. Buchanan 51 N.Y. 476, 488 (1873) ("No one in such case is made liable without some fault or negligence on his part, however serious the injury may be which he may accidentally cause; and there can be no reason for holding one liable for accidental injuries to property when he is exempt from liability for such injuries to the person."); *See also* Ind. Harbor Belt R.R. Co. v. Am. Cyanamid Co., 916 F.2d 1174, 1177 (7th Cir. 1990) (holding that strict liability is only imposed when the high degree of risk associated with an activity cannot be eliminated through due care). Lawrence M. Friedman, A History of American Law 350 (3d ed. 2005) ("The old common law had very little to say about personal injuries caused by careless behavior. A good many basic doctrines of tort law first appeared before 1850; but it was in the late nineteenth century that this area of law (and life) experienced its biggest spurt of growth.").

33 Indeed, from its humble beginnings in case law from the nineteenth century, fault has passed from being the upstart, to being the ascendant liability principle, to arguably being the leading one currently. This leap to predominance can be seen, for example, in the organization of a more recent and more theoretically oriented casebook such as the one authored by Goldberg, Sebok, and Zipursky, which begins with fault liability, in contrast to established tradition whereby torts casebooks started with the intentional torts. The fact that fault has come to assume this pivotal role in tort generally, but barely appears to merit mention in copyright doctrine, cannot but cause any copyright theorist to at a minimum seek to better understand how this odd state of affairs came to pass.

cases do not in consequence shift liability standards. As is discussed in greater detail in the next part, in tort, courts sometimes shift some burdens onto the defendant, including the burden regarding fault.[34]

One of the distinctive features of fair use is that, although Congress codified the doctrine in the 1976 Act, it went out of its way to note that, in doing so, it did not mean to freeze fair use doctrine from further evolution as a result of judicial interpretation.[35] This can be seen as an invitation to courts to expand or curtail fair use doctrine when they deem it appropriate to do so. Indeed, courts often quote the statutory history for the proposition that it provides the court with greater latitude with regard to fair use.[36] This explicit invitation to courts to continue adapting the fair use doctrine is an unusual provision in a statute. It is worth highlighting in the present context because the policy prescription that I endorse comes within the doctrinal penumbra of fair use – which party has the burden of proof with regard to its establishment – and thus, I claim, is a beneficiary of Congress's invitation to innovate.[37] Consider next the argument in favor of the burden-shifting proposal.

34 *See* Summers v. Tice, 33 Cal. 2d 80 (1948) (shifting the burden of proof to the defendants who needed to show which of them caused the harm); *see also* Byrne v. Boadle, 159 Eng. Rep. 299 (1863) (where *res ipsa loquitur* shifts the burden to the defendant to prove that the injury would have otherwise occurred in some manner other than through his or her negligence).

35 Copyright Act of 1976, § 107, Pub. L. No. 94–553, 90 Stat. 2541, 2546 (codified as amended at 17 U.S.C. § 107 (2006)); *see* Campbell v. Acuff-Rose Music, Inc., 510 U.S. 569, 576–78 (1994). In his hornbook, UNDERSTANDING COPYRIGHT LAW (4th ed.) (2005). Marshall Leaffer states, "The doctrine of fair use is codified in Sec. 107 of the 1976 Act. The statute, however, does not provide a tight definition of the doctrine. Instead, it sets forth in its preamble the kinds of uses that usually prompt the defense, followed by four criteria that must all be applied to determine whether the defense succeeds. The legislative history of § 107 indicates no intent to freeze the doctrine, but rather to allow its continuing development through the case law and its adaptation to changing times and technology." H.R. Rep. No. 94–1476, 94th Cong., 2d Sess. 66 (1976).

36 *See, e.g.*, Atari Games Corp. v. Nintendo of Am., Inc., 975 F.2d 832, 843 (Fed. Cir. 1992) ("The legislative history of section 107 suggests that courts should adapt the fair use exception to accommodate new technological innovations.").

37 There is precedent with regard to secondary liability. *See* Craig A. Grossman, *The Evolutionary Drift of Vicarious Liability and Contributory Infringement: From Interstitial Gap Filler to Arbiter of the Content Wars*, 58 SMU L. REV. 357 (2005). Peter S. Mennell & David Nimmer, *Unwinding Sony*, 95 CALIF. L. REV. 941, 993 (2007) ("The question of secondary liability fits into its own niche in the law, which the legislative history specifically declined to alter from established case law."). Peter S. Menell & David Nimmer, *Legal Realism in Action: Indirect Copyright Liability's Continuing Tort Framework and Sony's De Facto Demise*, 55 UCLA L. REV. 143, 167, 203 (2007) ("Prior to the Supreme Court's Sony case, copyright law had already developed an elaborate jurisprudence for determining secondary liability. To prove vicarious liability, the plaintiff had to demonstrate that the defendant possesses (1) an obvious and direct financial interest in the exploitation of the copyrighted materials; and (2) the right and ability to supervise the infringing conduct. To prove contributory infringement, the plaintiff had to demonstrate that the defendant, with knowledge of the infringing activity, induced, caused, or materially contributed to the infringing conduct of another. The innovation of Sony, of course, was to depart from the framework by adopting patent law's staple article of commerce doctrine. . . . Although Sony nominally crowned patent law's staple article of commerce doctrine as the decisor for copyright cases, as a practical matter, the ancien régime reigns sovereign. The inherent logic of the tort framework still dominates actual analysis, as opposed to the nominal fealty to *Sony* that courts

II. SHIFTING THE BURDEN OF PROOF

My initial argument for shifting the burden with regard to fault onto plaintiffs is simple: if one buys the argument that fair use introduces a fault standard into copyright, then, other things equal (and to the extent that there is a unity to tort), one should expect that the same burden of proof should prevail in copytort, as in tort generally. In other words, if in tort, plaintiffs must allege fault, why not in copytort as well?[38]

As noted earlier, currently, copyright infringement plaintiffs are able to establish a prima facie cause of action simply by establishing copying and substantial similarity of protected expression.[39] Note that such a showing goes only to establishing causation; namely, that the defendant caused a copy of the plaintiff's protected expression to be made. This is strict liability. If the gravamen of an action for infringement is a rights violation and a fair use is not a rights violation because it is not an infringement,[40] then it certainly would seem sensible to make it an element of an infringement action that the allegedly infringing act was not a fair use; that is, a rights violation.

Another way to look at the suggested proposal is to imagine how strange and unwelcome it would seem to put the burden on defendants in tort suits generally to establish the absence of fault, instead of placing the burden on plaintiffs, as is currently done in all U.S. jurisdictions. Arguably, it once may have made sense for the burden to rest with defendants in copyright. Fair use grew up in the case law, and one of the hallmarks of common law processes is the value placed on incremental change.[41] Early on, there was no fair use doctrine in copyright law, and when it

outwardly profess. As shown above, various jurists have gravitated away from the *Sony* test and toward a tort-based analysis over the years since the case was decided.")

38 Grenier v. Med. Eng'g Corp. 243 F.3d 200, 204 (5th Cir. 2001) ("Under Louisiana law, 'A cause of action accrues when a plaintiff may bring a lawsuit. In a negligence action, for instance, the claimant must be able to allege fault, causation, and damages.'" (internal citations omitted); Clark-Aiken Co. v. Cromwell Right Co., 323 N.E.2d 876, 877 (Mass. 1975).

39 Feist Publications, Inc. v. Rural Tel. Serv. Co., Inc., 499 U.S. 340, 361 (1991) ("To establish infringement, two elements must be proven: (1) ownership of a valid copyright, and (2) copying of constituent elements of the work that are original."); Bouchat v. Baltimore Ravens, Inc., 241 F.3d 350, 353 (4th Cir. 2001) ("To prove copyright infringement, a plaintiff must show first that he owned the copyright to the work that was allegedly copied, and second, that the defendant copied protected elements of the work.").

40 *See* Sony Corp. of Am. v. Universal City Studios, Inc., 464 U.S. 417, 433 (1984) ("[A]nyone who . . . makes a fair use of the work is not an infringer of the copyright with respect to such use.").

41 *See* Dennis Sweene, *The Common Law Process: A New Look at an Ancient Value Delivery System*, 79 Wash. L. Rev. 251, 268 (2004) ("Rather, it is the common law process of making law by arriving at principled decisions in real cases, based not upon a single rule or statute, but upon a whole tradition of looking at and thinking about law and legal problems that both yields a decision and incrementally adds to the body of common law. The common law approach remains the single most effective mechanism for adapting the law incrementally to society's changing values."); Shyankrishna Balganesh, *The Pragmatic Incrementalism of Common Law Intellectual Property*, 63 Vand. L. Rev. 1543, 1545 (2010) ("Additionally, the common law method that [courts] employ develops the law incrementally, recognizing the need for caution in a rapidly changing social and technological

appeared, the doctrine started life as a small limited exception to infringement.[42] The conventional starting point is *Folsom* v. *Marsh*, although the opinion does not explicitly mention "fair use."[43] The explicit test for "fair use" first appears in *Lawrence* v. *Dana*.[44] From there, the doctrine evolved in the case law for more than a century before being codified in the 1976 Act. It is plausibly seen as more incremental for this doctrine to have begun life as a defense, as it did in these cases, inasmuch as doing so does not entail a change in the elements of the prima facie cause of action. This sort of small, incremental step may seem particularly appropriate given that, early on, fair use was a difficult test to satisfy and thus can be aptly characterized as a small exception to a general rule of strict liability. Indeed, some commentators have viewed *Folsom* as a de facto strengthening of owners' rights.[45]

Although copyright scholars are fond of noting that the modern four factors of the fair use test each bears its correlate in Justice Story's landmark elucidation of the test in *Folsom v. Marsh*,[46] this superficial similarity hides a fundamentally more important dissimilarity; namely, that the scope of fair use has grown dramatically over time.[47] Several choice examples easily demonstrate this point.

environment, and allowing future courts to extend, limit, or at times altogether deny protection when circumstance and context change. I call this method of adjudication and rule development 'pragmatic incrementalism,' in that it exhibits the characteristics of both legal pragmatism and common law incrementalism.").

42 Patterson, Copyright in Historical Perspective, 227 (1968) ("And only the nebulous and uncertain doctrine of fair use, the idea that one may reproduce a small part of a copyrighted work for a limited purpose, protects the individual who wishes to extend his use of the work beyond the reading of it.").

43 Folsom v. Marsh, 9 F.Cas. 342 (Mass. 1841).

44 Lawrence v. Dana, 15 F. Cas. 26, 58, 61 (C.C.D. Mass. 1869) (No. 8136) (A date-based search on WestlawNext for the term "fair use" returned *Lawrence* as the earliest case using the term of art in relation to copyright; this fact is also noted in Barton Beebe, *An Empirical Study of U.S. Copyright Fair Use Opinions, 1978–2005*, 156 U. Pa. L. Rev. 549, 624 n.42 (2008) ("The term of art apparently first appeared in reported federal case law in *Lawrence v. Dana*.")).

45 Lydia Pallas Loren, *Redefining the Market Failure Approach to Fair Use in an Era of Copyright Permission Systems*, 5 J. Intell. Prop. L. 1, 16 (1997) ("Because the first Copyright Act in the United States gave a copyright owner *only* the right of 'printing, reprinting, publishing and vending' the copyrighted work, the judicially created fair use doctrine actually created an expansion of the rights given to the copyright owner. If the new work was found not to be a fair use, the copyright owner could prohibit its publication, despite the fact that it was not a verbatim printing of the copyrighted work. In other words, by showing that a particular publication was not a 'fair use,' the copyright owner could prohibit uses that were not otherwise within the grant of exclusive rights."); Patterson, *supra* note 43, at 227. ("Given that a bona fide abridgment of a copyrighted work was not considered an infringement, [Justice] Story could not summarily hold that the defendant's use was piratical. Instead, he did the next best thing by narrowing the principles applicable to abridgment and making those principles applicable to a use of the copyrighted work generally. He repeated in Folsom what he had said in Gray and, without acknowledging it, reinforced his earlier narrowing of the fair abridgment doctrine. The result of Story's opinion in Folsom was to enlarge protection for the copyright owner.").

46 *See* Leaffer, *supra* note 36, at 475 n. 26.

47 *See* Beebe, *supra* note 45, at 549, 560, 622 ("The language of section 107's factors was largely drawn from Justice Joseph Story's 1841 circuit court opinion in Folsom v. Marsh, an opinion whose influence on American fair use case law up to the 1976 Act we have probably overestimated, or so the data

In a few important recent cases, courts have upheld the functioning of search engines such as Arriba Soft's image search engine and Google's search engine as fair uses.[48] They have done so despite the fact that, in their normal functioning, these search engines cause thousands or even millions of unauthorized copies to be made.[49] Google Books is a project that raises the level of unauthorized copying to world-historic proportions. First, Google engaged in the digitization of 15 million books, an indeterminate but clearly large number of which were still protected by copyright.[50] Once these books are copied onto Google's proprietary servers, portions of these texts are displayed millions of times per day, pursuant to user search requests. A group of leading copyright scholars convened to discuss the issue and concluded that Google Books was fair use.[51] Let me assume for purposes of argument that

suggest, but whose influence since is quite clear.... Where the nonleading cases declined to follow the leading cases, they repeatedly – and systematically – did so in ways that expanded the scope of the fair use defense."). *But see* Gideon Parchomovsky & Philip J. Weiser, *Beyond Fair Use*, 96 CORNELL L. REV. 91, 93–94 (2010) ("The second problem plaguing the fair use doctrine is that, sadly, the best of times are long gone. The golden era of fair use – if one ever existed – ended about a decade ago with the enactment of the Digital Millennium Copyright Act (DMCA). This legislation prohibited users from circumventing technological protection measures (TPMs) employed by rights holders to control access to their works. Furthermore, the legislation famously banned the production and provision of circumvention technologies. Taken together, these two prohibitions changed the traditional balance between rightsholders and users. As is clear from the legislative history, Congress made a conscious decision not to recognize fair use as a defense in circumvention cases. In so doing, Congress significantly limited the scope of fair use for copyrighted works in digital media; notably, Congress did not grant users fair use privileges for TPM-protected content.").

48 Kelly v. Arriba Soft Corp., 336 F.3d 811, 819–20 (9th Cir. 2003); Field v. Google Inc., 412 F. Supp. 2d. 1106, 1118 (D. Nev. 2006) ("Based on the balancing of the relevant fair use factors, the Court finds that to the extent that Google itself copied or distributed Field's copyrighted works by allowing access to them through "Cached" links, Google engaged in a "fair use" of those copyrighted works.").

49 Perfect 10 v. Amazon, 487 F.3d 701, 713 (9th Cir. 2007) ("Some website publishers republish Perfect 10's images on the Internet without authorization. Once this occurs, Google's search engine may automatically index the webpages containing these images and provide thumbnail versions of images in response to user inquiries. When a user clicks on the thumbnail image returned by Google's search engine, the user's browser accesses the third-party webpage and in-line links to the full-sized infringing image stored on the website publisher's computer. This image appears, in its original context, on the lower portion of the window on the user's computer screen framed by information from Google's webpage."); Perfect 10 v. Google, 416 F.Supp.2d 828, 831 (C.D. Cal. 2006).

50 Miguel Helft, *Judge Rejects Google's Deal to Digitize Books*, N.Y. TIMES, Mar. 22, 2011, at B1 ("Google's ambition to create the world's largest digital library and bookstore has run into the reality of a 300-year-old legal concept: copyright.").

51 *See* Pamela Samuelson, *Google Book Search and the Future of Books in Cyberspace*, 94 MINN. L. REV. 1308, 1347–48, 1374 n.33 (2010) ("In February 2006, I hosted a workshop of about fifteen copyright professors to discuss Google's fair use defense in the *Authors Guild* case. The general consensus at that meeting was that this fair use defense was likely to succeed. Scholarly commentary has generally been supportive of Google's fair use defense."). *See also* Hannibal Travis, *Google Book Search and Fair Use: iTunes for Authors, or Napster for Books?*, 61 U. MIAMI L. REV. 87, 91 (2006) ("This Article maintains that the courts will best serve intellectual property and antitrust policy by concluding that Google is making fair and permissible uses of copyrighted works when it enhances the efficiency with which they are marketed and sold. The key fact for purposes of a fair use analysis, I will argue, is that there is no evidence, and it is unlikely that there will ever be any evidence, that Google Book Search is causing a decline in sales of either printed books or e-books.... Indeed, if there were any

this distinguished group is correct. The implication of making this assumption is that an extraordinary number of uses unauthorized by owners are fair. A third large category of fair uses are user-generated content (UGC). I have argued elsewhere that a great deal of user-generated content that incorporates elements of commercial works in an evenly mildly transformative manner will be fair uses as long as the use is not commercial, there is no or marginal real harm, and not overly much is taken quantity-wise. Although these conditions may sound exacting, I argue that in fact a great deal of user-generated content fits the bill.[52]

These instances together bear evidence for the fact that fair uses now number in the millions per day. Moreover, there is good reason to think that uses of these general sorts will continue to grow dramatically, as new business models that are functionally analogous to search engines, Google Books, and UGC-aggregation sites are likely to continue to emerge, given the apparent green light given by courts.

As fair use becomes increasingly common, it is increasingly unfair to place the burden of proof on defendants, because that rule unduly favors plaintiffs, who are smaller in number and are often large corporate entities, willing and able to pursue scorched-earth legal strategies that put everyday users with little or no realistic ability to defend themselves at an unfair disadvantage.[53] As fair use becomes more common, the likelihood that a plaintiff's being able to satisfy the elements of a prima facie case of infringement will predict or correlate with an actual instance of infringement goes down. Especially under such general uncertainty and with large numbers of fair users, the burden should rest with the party seeking to assert the wrong of another.

The placement of the burden goes philosophically deep. If one considers the preservation and promotion of liberty as a core virtue of a regulatory regime, this arguably implies that defendants would have their liberty unduly constrained if they are required to take the first step regarding whether their use is fair, because that

justifiable criticism of Google Book Search, it would be that copyright law has unduly hampered its development and utility."). My own view all along has been that this activity constituted infringement on a never before seen scale. Steven Hetcher, *The Half-Fairness of Google's Plan to Make the World's Collection of Books Searchable*, 13 MICH. TELECOMM. TECH. L. REV. 1, 10 (2006).

52 Steven Hetcher, *Using Social Norms to Regulate Fan Fiction and Remix Culture*, 157 U. PA. L. REV. 1869, 1900–28 (2009).

53 Ned Snow, *Proving Fair Use: Burden of Proof as Burden of Speech*, 31 CARDOZO L. REV. 1781 (2010) ("A copyright holder who pursues an individual fair user will nearly always be successful at achieving the desired silence. The burden of proof imposes a high financial cost on the fair user to gather evidence and persuade a fact-finder of its correct interpretation. This cost becomes prohibitive as individual fair users often lack economic means to defend their speech. In the absence of any promised reward or financial backing for fair-use speech, the costliness of the burden quickly drowns out protected speech. In short, individuals who blog for fun will not even contemplate a fair-use fight given the expensive cost of prevailing."); Jessica Litman, *Lawful Personal Use*, 85 TEX. L. REV. 1871, 1873 (2007) ("Fifty years ago, copyright law rarely concerned itself with uses that were not both commercial and public."); Rebecca Tushnet, *Copy This Essay: How Fair Use Doctrine Harms Free Speech and How Copying Serves It*, 114 YALE L.J. 535, 584 (2004) (observing that copyright holders did not target past practices of innocuous copying, whereas now those copiers are becoming subject to suit owing to online technology).

rule impinges on their liberty to copy, despite the fact that this act may very well be a fair use and thus not an infringement. Switching the burden would count against plaintiffs' interests; yet between the two parties, it is more legally appropriate to place this burden on plaintiffs. This situation is the private law equivalent of innocent until proven guilty, not civilly wrongful until proven so. After all, having the burden of proof is a form of cost to the user.

In addition to this basic fairness argument, there is a distinct economic argument for shifting the burden as fair uses become more prevalent. The greater the percentage of fair uses, the more socially costly it is for defendants on average to have to get sued and then have to defend themselves, rather than making it harder to sue in the first place. After all, as mentioned earlier, having the burden of proof is a form of cost to the user.[54] Thus, on efficiency grounds, there is greater reason to shift the burden of proof as the percentage of uses that are fair grows, as doing so will reduce overall social costs.

Despite these arguments, in this early stage of inquiry, we should be open to the idea that there are other arguments as to why the burden should be with defendants. I want to consider one possibility: the argument that defendants are better situated with regard to evidence.[55] After all, this is the sort of justification that has been offered by courts in other types of tort cases. For instance, in the well-known case, *Summers* v. *Tice*, the court shifted the burden of proof regarding causation to the defendant.[56] In the doctrine of *res ipsa loquitur*, courts shift the burden with respect to fault for evidentiary reasons.[57] These cases involve fact patterns in which it is hard to imagine how the injury could have occurred absent negligence on the part of the injurer. An analogous claim does not appear to hold true for copyright infringement generally, and yet the burden is generally shifted to defendants nevertheless. Courts

[54] Campbell v. Acuff-Rose Music, 510 U.S. 569, 590 (1994) ("Since fair use is an affirmative defense, its proponent would have difficulty carrying the burden of demonstrating fair use without favorable evidence about relevant markets.").

[55] M.B.W. Sinclair, *Fair Use Old and New: The Betamax Case and Its Forebears*, 33 BUFF. L. REV. 269, 325–26 (1984) ("Thus, fair use arises in litigation as an affirmative defense. Common sense and procedure permit no other stance. It would appear to follow that '[i]f fair use is viewed as a defense, or a form of excused infringement, the burden of proof lies with the defendant.' But one should not reach hasty conclusions on mere appearances. As Congress noted, 'any special statutory provision placing the burden of proving fair use on one side or other would be unfair and undesirable.'").

[56] *See* Summers v. Tice, 33 Cal.2d 80 (Cal. 1948) (shifting the burden of proof to the defendants who needed to show which of them caused the harm); *see also* Byrne v. Boadle, 159 Eng.Rep. 299 (1863).

[57] GOLDBERG, SEBOK, & ZIPURSKY, *supra* note 6, at 204 ("*Res ipsa loquitur* is an evidentiary doctrine applicable to certain tort causes of action, including negligence. When applicable in negligence actions, it permits a jury to infer that the plaintiff's injury was caused by defendant's carelessness even when the plaintiff presents no evidence of particular acts or omissions on the part of the defendant that might constitute carelessness."). ("Notice the effect of *res ipsa*, once successfully invoked. It relieves the plaintiff of the burden of producing evidence as to what exactly the defendant did wrong. As Byrne notes it is still open to the defendant to introduce evidence to rebut the inference of carelessness that *res ipsa* permits. In this way, *res ipsa* can be understood in part as an information-gathering rule. It asks the party in the better position to identify what happened to come for with evidence as to what really did happen.").

do not simply find for plaintiffs in such cases, however, but instead shift the burden of proof to a defendant to show that he or she was not negligent. In other words, courts shift the burden due to an informational asymmetry between plaintiffs and defendants.

In *Ybarra* v. *Spangard*, famously, the plaintiff was injured during a medical procedure in which he was unconscious.[58] Because he was unconscious, the plaintiff was not in a position to possess knowledge regarding the cause of the injury, whereas the defendants were especially well positioned in this regard, having been in the operating room when the injury occurred. Under these circumstances, the court shifted the burden of proof to the defendants.

For present purposes, it is important to note that when courts invoke *res ipsa loqitor*, they continue to treat the case as involving a fault standard. For example, in *Ybarra*, the court did not shift away from a fault liability standard when it shifted the burden of proof. In other words, the question of whether a fault standard is operative is logically distinct from the issue of who carries the burden of proof with respect to fault; that is, whether the burden is on the plaintiff to show fault or on the defendant to show the lack of fault.

The question of who is best suited to carry the burden regarding fault in a copyright infringement context came before a court in a recent case, *Lenz* v. *Universal*.[59] Although the specific issue arose with regard to a court's interpretation of certain language in the Digital Millennium Copyright Act (DMCA) § 512 safe harbor provisions, nevertheless, the manner in which the court treated the issue can plausibly be seen to give the decision broader import. The issue involved the interpretation of the statutory language that called for the plaintiff to have a good faith belief that there was an infringement when instigating a Notice of Takedown against an online service provider.[60] The defendant argued that the plaintiff could not have had such a belief because the defendant's use was clearly fair.[61] The plaintiff argued that the defendant was better suited to carry the burden because it was better placed with regard to the key facts relevant to fair use.[62] The court said little directly in response

[58] 25 Cal.2d 486, 488 (Cal. 1944).

[59] Lenz v. Universal Studios Music Corp., 572 F. Supp. 2d 1150, 1154 (N.D. Cal. 2008).

[60] *Id.* ("Thus the question in this case is whether 17 U.S.C. § 512(c)(3)(A)(v) requires a copyright owner to consider the fair use doctrine in formulating a good faith belief that 'use of the material in the manner complained of is not authorized by the copyright owner, its agent, or the law.'"); 17 U.S.C.A. § 512(c)(3)(A)(v) (West, Westlaw through P.L. 112–17) ("A statement that the complaining party has a good faith belief that use of the material in the manner complained of is not authorized by the copyright owner, its agent, or the law.").

[61] *Id.* at 1152 ("Lenz asserted that her video clearly constituted fair use of "Let's Go Crazy" and thus did not infringe Universal's copyrights.).

[62] *Id.* at 1154 ("Universal contends that copyright owners cannot be required to evaluate the question of fair use prior to sending a takedown notice because fair use is merely an excused infringement of a copyright rather than a use authorized by the copyright owner or by law. Universal emphasizes that Section 512(c)(3)(A) does not even mention fair use, let alone require a good faith belief that a given use of copyrighted material is not fair use. Universal also contends that even if a copyright owner were

to the plaintiff's claim, but rejected the argument by placing the burden with the plaintiff to allege the lack of fair use.[63] Doing so implicitly states that there is no principled reason why plaintiffs cannot be made to carry this burden. Moreover, the court admonished that, in the future, it would be inclined to view a failure to do so as "misrepresentation."[64]

A rejoinder might be to observe that the court's analysis is restricted to the particular context of the DMCA's provisions concerning the meaning of "authorized" by law.[65] There is an effective response to this rejoinder, however, which is that, as noted earlier, the Copyright Act does not require that the defendant carry the burden with respect to fair use.[66] In other words, the status quo placement of the burden of proof is not grounded in the Copyright Act and so is open to common lawmaking. It is a canon of the relationship between the common law and statutory law that judges will feel freer to move the law when doing so does not require overtly contravening statutory text.[67] In addition, as noted earlier, the statutory history to § 107 makes it clear that fair use should continue to evolve through its traditional common law roots. Shifting the burden of proof would indeed be a step in the development of the fair use doctrine, and there is no reason courts cannot mandate this shift by requiring plaintiffs to allege the lack of fair use in their prima facie case.[68]

required by the DMCA to evaluate fair use with respect to allegedly infringing material, any such duty would arise only after a copyright owner receives a counter-notice and considers filing suit.").

63 *See* Lenz v. Universal Studios Music Corp., at 1156 ("A good faith consideration of whether a particular use is fair use is consistent with the purpose of the statute.").

64 *See id.* at 1154–55 ("An allegation that a copyright owner acted in bad faith by issuing a takedown notice without proper consideration of the fair use doctrine thus is sufficient to state a misrepresentation claim pursuant to Section 512(f) of the DMCA."). On the need for fair use safe harbors generally, *see* Gideon Parchomovsky & Kevin A. Goldman, *Fair Use Safe Harbors*, 93 VA. L. REV. 1483, 1502–03 (2007) (suggesting that because of overdeterrence and uncertainty, fair use should be reformed to recognize certain types of copying as per se fair).

65 *See id.* at 1154 ("Whether fair use qualifies as a use 'authorized by law' in connection with a takedown notice pursuant to the DMCA appears to be an issue of first impression.").

66 The language of Sec. 501 gives leeway for a court. It simply states, "Anyone who violates one of the exclusive rights of the copyright owner . . . is an infringer." Similarly, Section 107 is silent as to which party carries the burden. *See also* Sony Corp. of America v. Universal City Studios, Inc., 464 U.S. 417, 434, 451–52, 483–84 (1984); Karen Bevill, *Copyright Infringement and Access: Has the Access Requirement Lost Its Probative Value?*, 52 RUTGERS *L. REV.* 311, 336 (1999) (quoting Overman v. Loesser, 205 F.2d 521 (9th Cir. 1953)) (discussing the independent creation burden borne by the defendant and the Copyright Act: "The general rule is that '(t)he burden of proof . . . remains on the plaintiff throughout the presentation of the case, unless it is declared to be elsewhere by statute or practice.' Since the statute does not announce a burden-shifting effect, if there is one, it must be established through practice. The practices in the circuits differ.").

67 Lisa A. Kloppenberg, *Avoiding Serious Constitutional Doubts: The Supreme Court's Construction of Statutes Raising Free Speech Concerns*, 30 U.C. Davis L. Rev. 1, 9–10 ("The 'avoidance canon' is one of a large group of techniques used to avoid 'unnecessary' constitutional questions, as explicitly set out in Justice Brandeis's famous concurrence in *Ashwander v. Tennessee Valley Authority*. These techniques, constituting the 'general avoidance doctrine,' are closely related to other doctrines of justiciability and jurisdictional limitations.").

68 Note that in contrast to the situation with the burden of proof, regarding damages, the Copyright Act contains specific doctrine, distinguishing willful infringement and innocent infringement. This

The fair use test is sometimes derided for being uncertain in its application and in its results.[69] An opponent of my position might potentially argue that this vagueness ill suits fairness in serving as an element in the infringement cause of action. But when one sees that the same claims are made regarding the vagueness of the Hand Test and the Reasonable Person Standard in tort generally, one may reasonably conclude that vagueness of this sort comes with the territory for variants of the fault standard and is not dispositive concerning the determination of which party should carry the burden of proof for establishing fault or lack thereof.[70]

Moreover, fair use is plausibly seen as more uniformly applied across jurisdictions than is the case for fault in tort generally. All federal circuits apply the four-factor test for infringement, with two of these factors each containing two subfactors.[71] By contrast, in tort generally, some courts apply a Reasonable Person Standard, others employ a Hand Test, and still others appear to use a seemingly inchoate amalgam of the two. Plausibly, the greater degree of specificity and uniformity of the fair use test is due to the fact that it was codified in the 1976 Act. Although codification is plausibly part of the explanation for the uniformity of fair use doctrine across jurisdictions, clearly it cannot be the whole story because fair use doctrine has continued to evolve in the case law since its codification. This is vividly seen by

distinction serves as a different basis for damages than is the case in tort generally, where damage awards turn on the distinctions between simple negligence versus some higher form of negligence such as reckless disregard, versus torts that are intentional. The Copyright Act thus is in tension with the general damages doctrine in copyright, as "innocent" infringers are liable, as the tripartite punctuated continuum of culpability found in tort generally has no "innocent" slot. It is evident that copyright has not taken tort seriously when the very notion of innocent infringement is found in copyright doctrine. Infringement is a tort and a tort is a wrong. A wrong cannot be innocent; that would be a contradiction in terms. Thus, from the perspective of tort generally, it is incoherent to talk about innocent infringement. Nevertheless, a court cannot simply disregard the distinctions related to damages drawn in the Act, even if they are in tension with the goal of following through on the normative implications of the recognition of a fault standard. Hence, common law courts will not have the same freedom to change the damages rules so as to preclude damages for innocent copiers, preclude statutory damages for negligent infringers, or for that matter, to preclude disproportionately large statutory damages for willful and unfair infringers.

69 *See, e.g.*, Jessica Litman, *Reforming Information Law in Copyright's Image*, 22 U. DAYTON L. REV. 587, 612–13 (1997) (stating that the uncertainty of the application of the fair use doctrine as a defense may result in a substantial chilling effect).

70 Steven Hetcher, *Non-Utilitarian Negligence Norms and the Reasonable Person Standard*, 54 VAND. L. REV. 863, 864 (2001) ("The reasonable person standard is an empty vessel that jurors fill with community norms."); *see also* John Cirace, *A Theory of Negligence and Products Liability*, 66 ST. JOHN'S L. REV. 1, 39 ("But in the real world of uncertain knowledge, it is difficult to quantify the Hand test.").

71 Pamela Samuelson, *Unbundling Fair Uses*, 77 FORDHAM L. REV. 2537, 2541–42 (2009) ("[F]air use law is both more coherent and more predictable than many commentators have perceived once one recognizes that fair use cases tend to fall into common patterns, or what this Article will call policy-relevant clusters. The policies underlying modern fair use law include promoting freedom of speech and of expression, the ongoing progress of authorship, learning, access to information, truth telling or truth seeking, competition, technological innovation, and privacy and autonomy interests of users. If one analyzes putative fair uses in light of cases previously decided in the same policy cluster, it is generally possible to predict whether a use is likely to be fair or unfair.").

contrasting how the Supreme Court applied the fair use test in *Sony* v. *Universal* to how it applied the test years later in *Campbell* v. *Acuff-Rose*. Significant changes in substantive doctrine as seen in *Campbell* are the result of common law processes.[72] One of the features of common law, often given as a virtue, is its ability to adapt to changing circumstances in a morally nuanced manner as Congress recognized in its commentary on § 107. Allowing wider scope for this sort of moral nuance is particularly appropriate in the context of an equitable doctrine such as fair use.[73]

Relatedly, Judge Posner argues that the legislative process is more subject to industry capture than is common law rulemaking. Along with his co-author, he makes explicit the implication for copyright law, which is that we should not expect the IP statutes to be efficient to the same degree as rules produced by courts.[74] This is yet another reason to think courts should be emboldened to take a proactive role in ensuring that fair use doctrine continues to evolve by shifting the burden of proof regarding fair use to plaintiffs.

Finally, it is significant that shifting the burden is practically feasible. In cases in which infringement is clear cut, the plaintiff will be able to simply allege the absence of the factors necessary for fair use: that the use was not sufficiently transformative if transformative at all, that what was taken was creative or not published, that too much was taken, or that market harm has occurred or is occurring.[75] By contrast,

72 For instance, in *Sony*, the Court noted that a commercial use was presumptively unfair and that the fourth factor was the most important factor. By contrast, in *Campbell*, the Court stated that the first factor was the most important factor and in addition did away with the presumptions from earlier cases. *See* Sony Corp. of America v. Universal City Studios, 464 U.S. 417, 451 (1984) ("[E]very commercial use of copyrighted material is presumptively an unfair exploitation of the monopoly privilege that belongs to the owner of the copyright."). *But see* Campbell v. Acuff-Rose Music, 510 U.S. 569, 578–85 (1994) ("In giving virtually dispositive weight to the commercial nature of the parody, the Court of Appeals erred.").

73 *See* Lyman Ray Patterson, Copyright in Historical Perspective 220 (1968) ("The problem of the author's creative interest is a delicate subject which, by its nature, can best be developed by judges in the case-by-case method of the common law, for its development will require perceptive analysis and careful distinction."); Craig Nard, *Legal Forms and the Common Law of Patents*, 20 B.U. L. Rev. 51, 56–58 (2010) ("The common law compares favorably to punctuated and, potentially more distortive, congressional action. The judge, in the Hayekian sense, is closer to the "inside baseball" dynamic that is unique to each of the divergent industries that participate in the patent system. Each industry has its own norms and customs, each relies on the patent system to varying degrees, and the common law is more likely to develop doctrine that reflects an industry's legitimate expectations. As Lon Fuller wrote, the common law 'projects its roots more deeply and intimately into human interaction than does statutory law.' Relatedly, the common law demands that the judge look backward in the interest of individual fairness (namely, the parties before the court), but also requires a prospective mindset that is more inclusive in its deliberations. Moreover, judicial primacy acts as a bulwark against the more politicized legislative process or capture-prone administrative rulemaking.") (internal citations omitted)).

74 *See* William Landes & Richard Posner, The Political Economy of Intellectual Property Law 25–26 (2004).

75 17 U.S.C.A. § 107 (West, Westlaw through P.L. 112–17) ("In determining whether the use made of a work in any particular case is a fair use the factors to be considered shall include – (1) the purpose and character of the use, including whether such use is of a commercial nature or is for nonprofit educational purposes; (2) the nature of the copyrighted work; (3) the amount and substantiality of the

with respect to those fact patterns in which fair use is not so straightforward, is it not a good thing that plaintiffs are put to their proof?

Shifting the burden of proof has an important practical implication: an owner can no longer win an infringement lawsuit by default judgment, where the defendant cannot afford to dispute, on a simple prima facie showing of strict liability, as is now the case. Copyright scholars have often commented on the unfairness of the situation of losing or potentially losing by default.[76] Thus, the reduction in the number of situations in which defendants might lose simply by default judgment after a showing of prima facie infringement presumably will be welcome to many.

CONCLUSION

The copyright case law has numerous instances in which appeals courts explicitly draw from common law principles as a source of law. My normative claim is that courts *should* do this with respect to copyright law, and for fault principles in particular. First, courts should recognize that fair use doctrine means that the operative liability standard in copyright law is not strict liability, but instead a type of fault standard. Then, courts should recognize that this legal finding has policy implications. As this discussion indicated, arguing from general tort principles, there appears to be sufficient reason to shift the burden of proof of fault to plaintiffs in copyright infringement cases. Because in tort generally the burden with regard to fault lies with plaintiffs, the presumption should be that copyright should have the same burden unless sufficient reason is provided otherwise. Such a reason appears to be lacking or, at any rate, is in need of establishment. In light of these considerations, courts handling copyright cases *should* seek to change the burden of proof with respect to fair use. They should do this both because it is the equitable thing to do in substantive legal terms and because they are empowered to do so, as it is part of the common law of tort that courts can and do shift burdens of proof.

As the earlier discussion indicated, it is relevant as well that shifting the burden regarding fair use is an aspect of fair use doctrine and so is squarely within the ambit of Congress's intended scope of meaning for its stated desire not to freeze fair use doctrine but instead to let it evolve. Typically, when the statutory text regarding the desire to not freeze fair use is evoked, it is in the context of a discussion of some doctrinal element within the four-factor test.[77] But there is no reason that the

portion used in relation to the copyrighted work as a whole; and (4) the effect of the use upon the potential market for or value of the copyrighted work.").

[76] *See, supra*, note 54.

[77] Perfect 10, Inc. v. Amazon.com, Inc., 508 F.3d 1146, 1166 (9th Cir. 2007) (specifically analyzing the "transformative" element of the first factor and noting "the importance of analyzing fair use flexibly") Fisher v. Dees, 794 F.2d 432, 435 (9th Cir. 1986) (discussing the desire not to "freeze" the doctrine immediately before discussing the four factors) Triangle Publ'n, Inc. v. Knight-Ridder Newspapers, Inc., 626 F.2d 1171, 1174 (5th Cir. 1980) (same as *Fisher*) SunTrust Bank v. Houghton Mifflin Co., 136 F. Supp. 2d 1357, 1371 n.6 (N.D. Ga.) (noting the four-factor list is not exhaustive and that courts

congressional invitation to innovate should be limited to this context. If innovation with regard to the fair use burden of proof would serve the goals of copyright, then it is reasonable to assume that Congress's invitation to common law innovation with regard to fair use would countenance this aspect of fair use as well.

This discussion in the body of the text concluded by noting that this legal change provides an important practical benefit: plaintiffs will not be able to win by default without having had to allege a lack of fair use and hence an infringement. Unless the shift is made, plaintiffs will continue to be able to win on default without even having had to allege facts sufficient to rule out non-infringement due to fair use and hence authorized use.

have applied different tests to reach different conclusions), *rev'd* by 268 F.3d 1257 (11th Cir. 2001) KB; Lewis Galoob Toys, Inc. v. Nintendo of America, Inc., 780 F. Supp. 1283, 1292 (N.D. Cal. 1991) (stating the four factors "are intended to guide but not to limit analysis") DC Comics, Inc. v. Unltd. Monkey Bus., 598 F. Supp. 110, 119 n.2 (N.D. Ga. 1984).

20

The Concept of "Harm" in Copyright

*Wendy J. Gordon**

The possibility of harm plays a significant role in copyright law, as does fault. Their roles are concealed or understated in part because of the rhetorical power of the often described parallels between the torts of copyright infringement on the one hand, and trespass to land on the other.

On the surface, copyright infringement indeed shares some structure with trespass to land. They appear to have parallel acts of breach: entry for trespass and copying for copyright infringement. Both torts are commonly termed strict liability, in that once volitional entry or volitional copying occurs, the defendant cannot use reasonable mistake as a defense. Further, both torts appear to allow plaintiffs to prevail without proving harm.

However, the differences between the two causes of action may be more important than the similarities.[1] This chapter emphasizes the *dis*analogies between copyright and trespass as a device to interrogate the roles that harm and fault play in copyright.

* Copyright 2013 Wendy J. Gordon, William Fairfield Warren Distinguished Professor, Boston University, and Professor of Law, Boston University School of Law. For illuminating discussions and suggestions, I thank Oren Bracha, Gary Lawson, David Lyons, Mike Meurer, Jessica Silbey, Ken Simons, Ben Zipursky, our editor Shyam Balganesh, and the (other) participants at the venues where earlier versions of this chapter were presented: the Harvard Law Review's "Symposium on the New Private Law," the Institute for Law and Philosophy's "Philosophical Foundations of Intellectual Property Conference" at the University of San Diego School of Law, and the *Texas IP Law Journal*'s "12th Annual Intellectual Property Law Symposium." Able research assistance was provided by Josh Beldner, David Bachman, Matthew Shayefar, and especially Adam Winokur. Responsibility for errors rests of course with me.

1 I admit to having overstated the similarities in the past. *See, e.g.*, Wendy J. Gordon, *Trespass-Copyright Parallels and the Harm-Benefit Distinction*, 122 Harv. L. Rev. Forum 62 (2009), *available at* http://www.harvardlawreview.org/media/pdf/gordon.pdf (last visited May 13, 2013) (arguing that copyright should differ from trespass to land, but conceding existing similarity); *see also* Wendy J. Gordon, *An Inquiry Into the Merits of Copyright, The Challenges of Consistency, Consent and Encouragement Theory*, 41 Stan. L. Rev. 1343–94 (1989) (arguing that copyright and conventional property share consistent forms).

What would copyright infringement look like if it were structured like trespass? In trespass, the landowner's prima facie case is complete upon proof that the defendant entered the land. This is almost always a purely binary (yes/no) question of fact.[2] Reasonable mistake is not a defense. Should the defendant be able to prove that he or she entered the land out of necessity, that *does* count as a defense, but the trespass defendant – while not technically a trespasser if he or she entered out of necessity – is still responsible for paying for damage done.[3]

What would copyright look like if it followed this model? One could debate the precise contours such a parallel tort would take,[4] but I think the following the most plausible translation of the trespass model onto copyright.

The copyright plaintiff's prima facie case would be complete upon proof that the defendant copied. This would be a purely yes/no question of fact. Reasonable mistake would be (as now) no defense. Should the defendant be able to prove that his or her copying serves the public interest (because, for example, he or she copied only 'ideas' and diffused them effectively, or because his or her copying fell within the domain that current doctrine calls 'fair use'), the copyright defendant would nevertheless have to pay for any negative monetary impact.

What the tort of copyright infringement actually looks like is far different. The copyright plaintiff's prima facie case only *begins* with proof of factual copying; she must also prove that protected expression was copied and that 'substantial similarity in expression' resulted. The latter are nonbinary questions (standards rather than rules), largely normative in nature. Further, should the plaintiff prove no more than the copying of 'ideas', he or she collects nothing. Similarly, should the defendant prove that his or her use of the plaintiff's expression was a "fair use", the copyright plaintiff collects nothing.[5]

To summarize the differences, which are further detailed in Parts I and II below: trespass requires only proof of entry, while copyright requires more than proof of

[2] Occasionally, borderline questions of policy arise, such as whether the deposit of small particles of pollutant should constitute trespass, or whether entry into airspace far above the owned land should constitute trespass.

[3] The classic case is Vincent v. Lake Erie Transp. Co., 109 Minn. 456, 124 N.W. 221 (1910) (defendant's employees reinforced his boat's ties to a dock, without the dock owner's permission, in the face of a major storm). The defendant's behavior was seen as reasonable, but the court nevertheless made the defendant pay for damage that resulted when storm waters slammed the defendant's boat against the plaintiff's dock.

[4] Defining an IP parallel to the notion of bare "entry upon land" could go in two different directions. One would premise liability on copying without regard to recognizability or similarity. This I think matches what a copyright-as-trespass model would look like. The other would premise liability on a defendant's producing something recognizably similar to the plaintiff's work, without regard to whether the defendant had copied. The latter resembles the patent standard. But one of these elements – copying or similarity – would seem to be necessary. In its real form (not twisted into a trespass analog), copyright has both.

[5] Moreover, in cases where the plaintiff fails to prevail, the defendant may able to collect costs and attorney fees. 17 USC § 505 (2006). If the plaintiff prevails, his or her ability to collect costs and attorney fees depends on having registered the copyright in a timely fashion. 17 USC § 412.

copying. The cause of action in trespass requires a binary inquiry into whether a rule ('do not enter') has been broken. The cause of action in copyright requires an application of normative judgment into whether complex standards ('substantial similarity', 'use of expression versus ideas') have been satisfied. Also, trespass imposes liability for harm done in pursuit of socially desirable ends while copyright does not.

It should be clear from this summary that owner interests are less important in copyright law than in trespass. (1) It is harder for a copyright plaintiff to make a prima facie showing than is for a trespass plaintiff and (2) liability is more easily defeated by social interests in copyright than in trespass.

Were copyright law to impose an explicit requirement that plaintiffs prove harm, or (relatedly) that plaintiffs prove foreseeability, such requirements would further limit the reach of owner interests. Such changes are attractive to many commentators, in part because of copyright's absurdly overlong duration. One rhetorical obstacle to making such changes is the trespass analogy, which this chapter hopes to undermine by showing *inter alia* that copyright is already halfway to requiring proof of harm, and already requires far more than proof of entry. But this chapter also cautions against rushing to impose a harm requirement before the conceptual and policy issues inherent in "harm" are fully fleshed out.

The chapter describes some roles already played by harm and fault in copyright law. It argues that a role for harm is implicit in the copyright plaintiff's cause of action, and notes that a role for harm is explicit but much-disputed in the defense of "fair use". The chapter also essays some tentative prescriptions about how copyright law should treat harm in the future. The chapter borrows some of the tools that philosophers have offered to explicate the notion of harm in order to clarify some of the policy choices that Congress and courts would face – or at least *should* face – if "harm" is to be deployed in copyright law more explicitly and systematically than it is now. Among other things, the chapter identifies some of the issues that need resolution before we can answer a perennial question of fair use doctrine, namely, whether a defendant's failure to pay license fees should count as a harm under the fourth fair use factor.[6]

I. STRICT LIABILITY

Let us examine the first purported parallel between trespass to land and copyright infringement, namely, the supposed strict liability nature of each tort. It is true that, for both trespass and copyright, reasonable mistake is no excuse. A builder who

[6] Fair use is a defense that allows the unconsented use of copyrighted works. The determination of what is "fair" is a multifactorial inquiry. Among the matters of importance are the question of whether the social benefit served by the defendant's use could or should come through market purchase and the question of whether the defendant's use is transformative. For the doctrine's statutory embodiment, see 17 U.S.C. § 107 (2006). The fourth fair use factor is "the effect of the use upon the potential market for or value of the copyrighted work." 17 U.S.C. § 107(4) (2006). Varying notions of harm play a strong role in courts' assessments of this fourth factor.

erroneously but reasonably thinks his title extends further than it does is a trespasser when he innocently crosses another owner's boundary; a publisher who erroneously but reasonably believes she has purchased a license from a manuscript's copyright owner is an infringer when she innocently prints the plagiarized text. Neither the builder nor the publisher has a defense based on his or her reasonable mistake.

Yet "strict liability" connotes more than the absence of one particular defense. "Strict liability" means "liability without fault." In copyright law, fault of a particular kind is very relevant to liability. It appears most obviously in two substantive contexts[7]: fair use and substantial similarity.

Steven Hetcher in the previous chapter uses fair use to argue that copyright is not a strict liability tort. He correctly emphasizes the "fault" inquiry inherent in the doctrine of fair use and goes so far as to suggest that proving lack of fair use be made part of the plaintiff's case in chief.[8] What should be added to Hetcher's analysis is the acknowledgment that fault (or its close cousin) is already part of the case in chief.

It is sometimes said that copyright plaintiffs need prove only ownership and copying of protected elements.[9] However, mere copying is in fact insufficient for liability. In all but rare cases, the plaintiff cannot succeed unless he or she also proves that the defendant's product is "substantially similar" to the plaintiff's own work of authorship.[10] The test has many forms, all involving the ability of an observer (sometimes the ordinary person, sometimes the audience) to recognize the similarity.[11]

Although recognizing a similarity is necessary for liability, it cannot be sufficient, because similarities resulting from the copying of ideas violate no copyright.[12] Something more is needed. Most judicial uses of "substantial similarity" exhibit a normative, fault-like nature;[13] substantial similarity is even known as the test for "improper appropriation."[14] The Second Circuit's approach in *Arnstein* v. *Porter* is iconic:

> Assuming that adequate proof is made of copying, that is not enough; for there can be "permissible copying," copying which is not *illicit*. . . . The question . . . is whether defendant took from plaintiff's works *so much* of what is pleasing to the ears of lay listeners, who comprise the audience for whom such popular music is

7 Fault is also relevant to remedies and of course to criminal copyright liability.

8 Stephen Hetcher, *The Fault Liability Standard in Copyright* (in this volume).

9 Robert C. Osterberg and Eric C. Osterberg, Substantial Similarity in Copyright Law § 1:1 (PLI 2011).

10 *Id. See also* 2 Paul Goldstein, Goldstein on Copyright § 9.3.1, at 9:34 (3d ed. 2012).

11 "[T]he appropriate test for determining whether substantial similarity is present is whether an average lay observer would recognize the alleged copy as having been appropriated from the copyrighted work." Ideal Toy Corp. v. Fab-Lu Ltd. (Inc.), 360 F.2d 1021, 1022 (2d Cir. 1966).

12 17 U.S.C. § 102(b) (no copyright in ideas).

13 Shyamkrishna Balganesh, *The Normativity of Copying in Copyright Law*, 63 Duke L. J. 203, 206 (2012).

14 Sometimes the elements of a copyright cause of action are described as proof of valid copyright, copying in fact, and "improper appropriation," with substantial similarity being a sub-element of the latter. Goldstein, *supra* note 10, at § 9.3.1, at 9:34. As the cause of action is presented by Paul

composed, that defendant *wrongfully* appropriated something which belongs to the plaintiff.[15]

Although the inquiry into "so much" sounds merely factual (a matter of quantity), the fault-like nature of words like "improper", "illicit" and "wrongfully" is obvious.

Admittedly, improper appropriation is not equivalent to moral fault; it is an objective rather than subjective fault concept. But the law counts such concepts – including the objective conception of 'unreasonable' behavior in negligence law – as a kind of fault and far from strict liability.

Thus, the inquiry into substantial similarity is a matter for the fact-finder's normative judgment.[16] Substantial similarity "is a term to be used in a courtroom to strike a delicate balance between the protection to which authors are entitled under an act of Congress and the freedom that exists for all others to create their works outside the area protected by infringement."[17] It is very unlike the physical question of whether a defendant has crossed a land boundary.

Moreover, the substantial similarity requirement makes clear that copyright law requires something more than copying – "copying plus."[18] Trespass to land imposes no such additional element.

Admittedly, one case did abandon the requirement of "substantial similarity." For a subset of copyright disputes, those involving digital sampling, the Sixth Circuit

Goldstein, a plaintiff must prove "improper appropriation," and this in turn has two components: first, that the defendant has copied protected matter (e.g., expression rather than ideas) and second, that audiences will find the expression in the two works substantially similar.

Harm avoidance is not the only explanation for the substantial similarity requirement. Another might be the notion that a defendant infringes only when he or she "expresses" what plaintiff should have control over expressing. But here too is a notion of wrongfulness – and here too, recognizability is essential. Without similarity to what plaintiff said or sang there is no expression of what plaintiff said or sang. In addition, of course, one can conceptualize the loss of control over one's expression as "subjective distress," which might count as a harm. For discussion of copyright not as an economic device but as control over expressing one's self publicly, see Abraham Drassinower, *Authorship as Public Address: On the Specificity of Copyright vis-à-vis Patent and Trade-Mark*, 2008 Mich. St. L. Rev. 199, 224 (2008) ("[T]he test for copyright infringement must be understood not as an inquiry into whether the defendant has reproduced the plaintiff's work, but rather as an inquiry into whether, under the circumstances, such reproduction supports the inference that the defendant has abrogated the plaintiff's authorship to himself – that is, whether the reproduction is in the service of public presentation."). *Cf.* Matthew Sag, *Copyright and Copy-Reliant Technology*, 103 Nw. U. L. Rev. 1607, 1627 (2009) ("[T]he guiding principle of copyright is that one should generally not be entitled to offer the author's copyrighted expression to the public as a substitute for the work of the author.").

15 Arnstein v. Porter, 154 F.2d 464, 472–73 (2d Cir. 1946) (emphases added; footnotes omitted). What constitutes "so much" is of course much debated. But the controversies over the different versions of the substantial similarity test should not obscure what they all have in common: the ability of an observer to recognize plaintiff's work within the defendant's product.

16 Balganesh, *supra* note 13, at 256. To the extent that "substantial similarity" has objective components, that characteristic does not make it less fault-like than negligence law. Negligence law uses an objective standard of what counts as "reasonable" behavior, yet is known as a "fault"-based cause of action.

17 Steinberg v. Columbia Pictures Industries, Inc., 663 F. Supp. 706 at 711 (S.D.N.Y. 1987) (citation omitted).

18 Whereas trespass imposes liability for the mere fact of volitional entry, copyright law imposes liability for copying-in-fact plus this extra element of "substantial similarity."

Court of Appeals held that even an unrecognizable use of copyrighted expression would give rise to liability. The opinion, *Bridgeport Music, Inc.* v. *Dimension Films*,[19] has been much criticized.[20] Tellingly, the *Bridgeport* court in jettisoning "substantial similarity" was influenced by an erroneous belief it was dealing with a *physical* borrowing.[21] Unlike *Bridgeport*, the ordinary case of copyright infringement requires a normative decision, based on recognizable similarity, which is lacking in trespass to land.

II. WHETHER THE PLAINTIFF MUST PROVE HARM

On the surface, neither copyright law nor trespass to land requires proof of harm. However, in copyright, the "substantial similarity" analysis seems premised on at least the *possibility* of harm. That is, when a plaintiff proves "substantial similarity,"

[19] Bridgeport Music, Inc. v Dimension Films, 410 F.3d 792 (6th Cir. 2005).

[20] Saregama India Ltd. v. Mosley, 687 F. Supp. 2d 1325, 1339 (S.D. Fla. 2009), *aff'd*, 635 F.3d 1284 (11th Cir. 2011); EMI Records Ltd. v. Premise Media Corp. L.P., 2008 WL 5027245 (N.Y. August 8, 2008); 3 PATRY ON COPYRIGHT § 9:61 (calling Bridgeport "disturbing"); David M. Morrison, *Bridgeport Redux: Digital Sampling and Audience Recoding*, 19 FORDHAM INTELL. PROP. MEDIA & ENT. L.J. 75, 141 (2008) ("Courts reviewing digital musical sampling cases ought to reject Bridgeport in favor of traditional substantial similarity and de minimis use principles.").

[21] The *Bridgeport* lawsuit charged infringement because a movie soundtrack employed music that had sampled a couple of seconds from a George Clinton song recording. "Sampling" is a musical practice that involves the direct, mechanical, or electrical copying of sound. A "sound recording" is a copyrightable work of authorship whose artistry resides in the manner in which notes are sung or words are spoken.

In *Bridgeport*, a few seconds of sampled sound were looped and distorted in such a way that the court found "that no reasonable juror, even one familiar with the works of George Clinton, would recognize the source of the sample without having been told of its source." Nevertheless, the Sixth Circuit rocked the copyright world by holding that infringement could nevertheless result. That is, a lack of recognizable similarity was not a barrier to recovery, and for "digital samples" there was no such thing as de minimis copying. 410 F.3d 792, 798, 801–802.

The Sixth Circuit's attempted justifications were many, including an egregiously expansive reading of a statutory provision that Congress had meant to narrow, not broaden, sound recording rights. One important key to the decision can be found in the court's errors about the supposedly physical nature of sound recordings and sampling.

The court opined that the copying was "a physical taking rather than an intellectual one." *Bridgeport* at 410 F 3d 802. But nothing physical was taken; a pattern of laser-read bumps or electrical signals was duplicated and recorded, the same way the pattern of curved and straight lines that comprise the alphabet can be photocopied. The *Bridgeport* court's error probably began when the court treated a "sound recording" as if it were a physical medium, equivalent to a book. Recognizing that for books "it is not the book, i.e., the paper and binding, that is copyrightable, but its contents," 410 F.3d 800, the court went on to imply that for sound recordings by contrast it is the physical that somehow partakes of copyright. Wrote the court, "[T]he decision was made by Congress to treat a sound recording differently from a book even though both are the medium in which an original work is fixed rather than the creation itself."

It is incorrect to say that a sound recording is "the medium in which an original work is fixed rather than the creation itself." Under the Act, a "sound recording" is indeed a creation in itself, 17 U.S.C. § 102(a)(7), an intangible pattern capable of being embodied. The physical media in which sound recordings are embodied are called phonorecords. 17 U.S.C. § 101 (definition of phonorecords).

he or she has proved something that is essential to virtually any plausible conception of harm.[22]

To see this, note that "substantial similarity" is measured by whether the plaintiff can persuade the finder of fact (judge or jury) that an ordinary observer, or an ordinary audience member, would perceive enough similarity between the plaintiff's and defendant's work that the borrowing is wrongful.[23] An obvious preliminary piece of this similarity analysis is whether the fact-finder concludes that the ordinary observer or audience member could *recognize* the plaintiff's work within the defendant's work.[24] I argue later that, as a descriptive matter, the ability of the audience to perceive similarity – the requirement I call "recognizability" – is necessary (though not sufficient) for harm to arise.

The substantial similarity requirement is a judge-made rule that has remained consistent over time as a number of copyright statutes were amended and replaced.[25] It shows many ties to notions of harm in its history.[26] Moreover, I speculate that the importance of at least the potential for harm is part of what sustains the requirement's viability. That is because harm *matters* to most people on a moral level,

22 The reader might object that entry, too, is essential to virtually any conception of harm. That is true. But copyright requires more than proof of an entry-equivalent, that is, it requires more than mere factual copying. Copyright requires something (recognizable expression) from which the possibility of harm flows more strongly than it would from mere proof of (unrecognizable or non-expression) copying.

23 The courts tend to avoid the word "wrongful" – "illicit" and "improper" are more likely. Although I might agree that "wrongful copying" is at the core, *see* Balganesh, *supra* note 13, at 228, I bracket the question of whether wrongfulness is part of what plaintiff must prove. Whatever the definition of "substantial similarity," it clearly requires some normative judgment coupled with recognizability. Beyond that lies ground not necessary for the contentions made in this chapter.

24 I place outside the scope of this chapter cases where a defendant engages in "intermediate copying" of expression – such as a computer programmer who makes exact copies of a copyrighted computer program in order to reverse engineer it, and whose final product contains no copied expression. Such cases have their own intricacies.

25 Congressional enactments that leave judge-made rules unaffected are often viewed as endorsing those rules. *See, e.g.*, United States v. Rutherford, 442 U.S. 544, 554 n.10 (1979) (Once "an agency's statutory construction has been 'fully brought to the attention of the public and the Congress,' and the latter has not sought to alter that interpretation although it has amended the statute in other respects, then presumably the legislative intent has been correctly discerned."); Apex Hosiery Co. v. Leader, 310 U.S. 469, 488 (1940) ("The long time failure of Congress to alter the Act after it had been judicially construed, and the enactment by Congress of legislation which implicitly recognizes the judicial construction as effective, is persuasive of legislative recognition that the judicial construction is the correct one.").

26 In explaining substantial similarity, which the Goldstein treatise calls the "audience test," Goldstein uses as a touchstone this classic reference to the harmful potential for copying: "The audience test... resonates in Justice Story's earlier observation in Folsom v. Marsh that improper appropriation will be established if 'so much is taken, that the value of the original is sensibly diminished, or the labors of the original author are substantially to an injurious extent appropriated by another.'" GOLDSTEIN, *supra* note 10, at § 9.3.1, at 9:34 (3d ed. 2012) (footnotes omitted). *See also* Sag, *supra* note 14, at 1607, arguing that "the tests of substantial similarity provide further evidence that copyright primarily protects the author against expressive substitution." *Id.* at 1633. Sag's focus is not on harm, but harm is inherent in the notion of substitution.

and prohibitions against doing harm are deeply embedded in our legal and cultural fabric.

Harm has a special importance for the common law and for many ethical theories. Both libertarians[27] and liberals[28] place an emphasis on avoiding harm. The normative preference for harm avoidance is probably based on a combination of considerations, such as a respect for the separateness and autonomy of persons, a desire to prevent bad states of welfare, a preference for equality, and the suspicion that a person who causes harm is subordinating another person to his or her own ends.[29] It has strong historical and cultural roots: the Ten Commandments are primarily addressed to avoiding harm; Locke's theory of property was based in a biblically based injunction against causing harm;[30] and the common law has long been more willing to impose liability for harms done than it is to impose liability for benefits not paid for.[31]

In addition, this preference for avoiding harm expresses itself in an asymmetry: commonsense morality places more importance on avoiding harm than it does on providing an equivalent amount of benefits. Under many deontological approaches, it is also thought wrong to impose harm to obtain a *greater* amount of benefit.[32]

Of course, many acts of harm are not actionable or wrongful in any way; the harm done by honest competition is the classic example. But as Shelly Kagan writes, "the significance of harm doing is so great – according to commonsense moral intuition – that all other things being equal, if an act involves doing harm, it is

27 Robert Nozick, Anarchy, State and Utopia (1974) at 28–35 & passim (on "side constraints").

28 John Stuart Mill, On Liberty (1869), at ch. 1, Para. 9 ("[T]he only purpose for which power can be rightfully exercised over any member of a civilized community, against his will, is to prevent harm to others."), *available at* http://www.bartleby.com/130/1.html (last visited March 20, 2012).

29 Different philosophers emphasize different aspects. For Nozick, the key is the separateness of persons. Nozick, *supra* note 27, at 28–35. In addition, the prohibition tends to be stronger against doing harm than against allowing harm to happen. *See, e.g.*, Shelly Kagan, Normative Ethics (1998) at 94–100.

30 John Locke, Two Treatises of Government, Second Treatise (1690) at, e.g., §6 ("[N]o one ought to harm another in his Life, Health, Liberty, or Possessions"); *see also* § 332 ("He that in obedience to this command of God, subdued, tilled and sowed any part of it, thereby annexed to it something that was his property, which another had no title to, nor could without injury take from him.") *available at* http://www.gutenberg.org/ebooks/7370 (last visited March 20, 2012).

For a more detailed argument, *see* Wendy J. Gordon, *A Property Right in Self-Expression: Equality and Individualism in the Natural Law of Intellectual Property*, 102 Yale L.J. 1533, 1544–49 (the harm-based structure of Locke's argument for property).

31 Saul Levmore, *Explaining Restitution*, 71 Va. L. Rev. 65, 71 (1985) ("[T]he legal remedies available to victims of harms are far superior to those enjoyed by the analogous providers of nonbargained benefits."). I have argued that the common law asymmetry can be explained by factors other than the asymmetry between harm and benefit themselves, Wendy J. Gordon, *Of Harms and Benefits: Torts, Restitution, and Intellectual Property*, 21 J. Legal Stud. 449 (1992), but I think in that article I understated the functional significance of the harm/benefit distinction.

For other explorations of the asymmetry with which the common law treats positive as compared with negative externalities, *see, e.g.*, Scott Hershovitz, *Two Models of Tort (and Takings)*, 92 Va. L. Rev. 1147 (2006).

32 See Kagan, supra note 29, at 72–79. This may be one reason why a finding of substantial injury is often sufficient to defeat fair use claims of even publicly beneficial acts of copying.

simply forbidden."[33] Were copyright fully untethered from harm, I suspect it would be even less palatable to popular taste than it is.

Some might argue that because copyright is primarily instrumental and economic in its purposes, the distinction between harm and benefit has no relevance. In the consequentialist calculus of economics, "cost" is the usually the relevant variable, not "harm." Neoclassical economic theories aim at value maximization and do not privilege harm avoidance.[34] Out-of-pocket costs (what a deontologist or ordinary language might call "harm") are seen as largely symmetrical[35] in their effects with the "opportunity costs" of foregoing possible income. (A deontologist might call opportunity cost a "foregone benefit.") An economic actor will weigh against a desired purchase both out of pocket cost and opportunity cost, giving no special weight to the prospect of paying X from his pocket if it means he will reap X + 1. Moreover, unlike most deontogical approaches, in economics a given amount of cost can be outweighed by a slightly larger amount of benefit.[36]

As part of this attack on the notion that harm should be important to copyright, it might be pointed out that the birth of "law and economics" was due in part to the Coase Theorem, and the Coase Theorem argued that out-of-pocket costs (harms) and the opportunity costs of losing an available revenue (benefits foregone) have equivalent power to motivate.[37]

In his classic article, Ronald Coase argued that, from an economic perspective, causation (and what one might call harm) is virtually always reciprocal.[38] The polluter harms the downstream neighbor, and if the neighbor wins an injunction, the neighbor harms the polluter. (By contrast, for Aristotle and for most commonsense views today, there is a clear difference between harm done by the thief and the harm done by his punisher; when the authorities force the thief to disgorge, the result is a "correction" rather than a new harm.[39]) Neo-classical economics has, however,

33 *Id.* at 72.

34 At least, economics has different reasons for giving greater weight to harm than it does to foregone gains, namely, the growing experimental literature suggesting that people value what they have more than equivalent things they do not yet possess. Although economics might weigh costs more heavily than opportunity costs (a position that has changed since Coase wrote), economists still do not give to costs anything like the strong force that typical deontologists give to "harm."

35 Research over the last several decades suggests that the symmetry is less than perfect. See the discussion *infra* at notes 37–41.

36 Thus David Lyons writes of J. S. Mill, "The Principle of Liberty permits some 'trade-offs,' but it never sanctions the impositions of burdens on some for the sake of others' positive benefits." David B. Lyons, *Liberty and Harm to Others*, 5 (suppl.) CAN. J. PHIL. 1, 16 (1979), *appearing as* NEW ESSAYS ON JOHN STUART MILL AND UTILITARIANISM (Wesley E. Cooper, Kai Nielsen and Steven C. Patten eds., 1979).

37 Recent literature suggests that opportunity costs have less power than out-of-pocket costs. *See, e.g.*, Russell Korobkin, *The Endowment Effect and Legal Analysis*, 97 NW. U. L. REV. 1227 (2003).

38 *See* R.H. Coase, *The Problem of Social Cost*, 3 J. L. & ECON. 1 (1960).

39 Writes Aristotle,

> [I]n the case . . . in which one has received and the other has inflicted a wound, or one has slain and the other been slain, the suffering and the action have been unequally distributed; but the judge tries to equalize by means of the penalty, taking away from the gain of the assailant. For the term 'gain' is applied generally to such cases, even if it be not a term appropriate to certain

opened up to new findings that bring its assumptions closer to ordinary expectations about how the world works. In what is now called 'behavioral law and economics,' it is seen that harms and losses can play a special role in incentives, one that is stronger than or different from the role played by benefits and gains. Not only are people usually risk averse, as evidenced by the strength of the insurance industries, but, in addition, experimental evidence suggests that people put a higher price on losing what they own than they would spend to acquire something similar.[40]

This is not merely a matter of attitude or emotion. Loss tends to be more disruptive – more generative of what Guido Calabresi called "secondary costs"[41] – than either opportunity cost[42] or the loss of benefits tends to be.

Not only has economics opened to the possibility that loss might be asymmetric with foregone gain; in addition economics is not all of copyright law.[43] A prohibition

> cases, e.g. to the person who inflicts a wound and 'loss' to the sufferer; at all events *when the suffering has been estimated, the one is called loss and the other gain.* Therefore the equal is intermediate between the greater and the less, but the gain and the loss are respectively greater and less in contrary ways; more of the good and less of the evil are gain, and the contrary is loss; intermediate between them is, as we saw, equal, which we say is just; therefore *corrective justice will be the intermediate between loss and gain.* This is why, when people dispute, they take refuge in the judge . . . *the judge restores equality*; it is as though there were a line divided into unequal parts, and he took away that by which the greater segment exceeds the half, and added it to the smaller segment. And when the whole has been equally divided, *then they say they have 'their own'*-i.e. when they have got what is equal.

Aristotle, Nichomachaen Ethics (W.D. Ross, trans.) Vol. 5at 4b, available at http://classics.mit.edu/Aristotle/nicomachaen.5.v.html (emphasis added and typographical error corrected ["woundand" to "wound and"]).

40 A classic article is Daniel Kahneman et al., *Anomalies: The Endowment Effect, Loss Aversion, and Status Quo Basis*, 5 J. ECON. PERSPECTIVES 193, 194–97 (1991) (discussing experiments). For criticisms of this literature, *see, e.g.*, Gregory Klass & Kathryn Zeiler, *Against Endowment Theory: Experimental Economics and Legal Scholarship*, working paper, *available at* http://scholarship.law.georgetown.edu/facpub/1181 and http://ssrn.com/abstract=2224105.

41 GUIDO CALABRESI, THE COSTS OF ACCIDENTS: A LEGAL AND ECONOMIC ANALYSIS 27–28 (1970).

42 An opportunity cost is the "cost" of not receiving a benefit that is otherwise available. For example, a student not only pays the out-of-pocket cost of tuition but also bears the opportunity cost of the wages she could have earned had she not been involved in her schoolwork.

43 There are echoes of moral entitlement even in the Federalist Papers, written to encourage adoption of the U.S. Constitution. In Number 43, James Madison defended the Constitution's grant of copyright and patent powers to the federal government on the ground that "[t]he public good fully coincides in both cases [copyright and patent] with the claims of individuals." In modern terms, it sounds as if Madison is praising the government's IP powers on the ground that they simultaneously serve consequentialist (e.g., economic) and nonconsequentialist (e.g., deontological) ends.

Of course, it is possible that Madison was referring to legal claims rather than moral claims, because in the paragraph preceding the language just quoted, he (erroneously) wrote that "[t]he copyright of authors has been solemnly adjudged, in Great Britain, to be a right of common law." But the respectful choice of words ("solemnly") suggests that he was appealing to his audience on grounds that went beyond mere consistency with positive law. Similarly, when Madison continued that "[t]he right to useful inventions seems with equal reason to belong to the inventors," the implication is that the reasons for giving such protection were good ones – again, a normative judgment. THE FEDERALIST No. 43 (James Madison), *available at* http://thomas.loc.gov/home/fedpapers/fed_43.html (last visited March 19, 2012).

against harm (whether absolute, conditional, or limited in various ways) is embedded in many deontological approaches, and deontological concerns (whether of "just deserts" or otherwise) are often either voiced[44] or silently honored[45] by both judges and legislators in copyright. This is another reason why it is not surprising that an element in the copyright cause of action has a connection with the possibility of harm.

So let us return to my descriptive claim that the recognizability of "substantial similarity" is a necessary prerequisite for harm to arise. To assess that claim, let us consider the primary possible sources of harm in copyright.

First, there is substitutionary harm resulting from rivalry with preexisting markets. Here the evidence is likely to consist in proof of the plaintiff losing current or potential customers to the defendant. This harm of diverting customers is probably the central kind of harm with which copyright is concerned. Let us call this "substitutionary rivalry." The potential harm here is the loss of third-party revenues, rather than the loss of revenues from the defendant him- or herself.

A second candidate for copyright harm is the loss of revenues from the defendant: the empty cash drawer resulting from the failure of a defendant to obtain permission and pay negotiated fees for his or her use. Let us call this "foregone defendant license fees," or "foregone fees" for short. For this category to be fully distinct from substitutionary rivalry, let us limit the term "foregone fees" to occasions when the defendant's use is outside plaintiff's expected stream of customer uses or licenses.

A third candidate for copyright harm is less easily measured monetarily and is likely to be the most controversial: the subjective experience of distress, frustration, discouragement, anger, or suffering that a copyright owner might feel from witnessing his or her work of authorship being copied by another. The Supreme Court has at least once said that a "*personal* interest in creative control" should matter.[46] Let us

44 The high-water mark was probably the declaration in *Harper & Row* that "[t]he rights conferred by copyright are designed to assure contributors to the store of knowledge a fair return for their labors." Harper & Row, Publishers v. Nation Enters., 471 U.S. 539, 546 (1985). In a later case, Feist Publications, Inc., v. Rural Telephone Service Co., 499 U.S. 340 (1991), the Court made clear that labor alone – uncreative labor – did not entitle one to copyright. Some might interpret *Feist* as a rejection of *Harper & Row*'s emphasis on "fair return." But the Court in *Feist* did not repudiate the notion that creative labor might lead to a claim to deserve reward. So the possibility of our courts recognizing deontological morality as one of the grounds underlying copyright might remain open. *See generally* Robert P. Merges, Justifying Intellectual Property (2011) (exploring noneconomic bases for intellectual property); Gordon, *supra* note 1, at 1343, 1446–50. The Court usually takes care to accompany any allusion to notions of "just deserts" with an implicit acknowledgment of the primacy of incentives. Thus, the Court wrote in *Mazer v Stein*: "The economic philosophy behind the clause empowering Congress to grant patents and copyrights is the conviction that encouragement of individual effort by personal gain is the best way to advance public welfare through the talents of authors and inventors in 'Science and useful Arts.' Sacrificial days devoted to such creative activities deserve rewards commensurate with the services rendered." Mazer v. Stein, 347 U.S. 201, 219 (1954) *See also* Whelan Assocs. v. Jaslow Dental Laboratory, Inc., 797 F.2d 1222, 1235 n.27 (3d Cir. 1986) ("just merits" and public benefit both a concern) (citation omitted).

45 *See* Balganesh, *supra* note 13, at 210 (ordering the different norms).

46 Harper & Row Publishers, Inc. v. Nation Enterprises, 471 U.S. 539, 555 (1985) (emphasis added).

call this candidate "subjective distress."[47] Again, whether it should count as "harm" is addressed later – Mill implicitly taught that distress resulting from one's beliefs is a dangerous thing to call harm[48] – but for now please simply note that this subjective experience is a *candidate* for "harm."

A fourth potential candidate might be "loss of exclusivity." When another version of a copyrighted work appears, the authorized version might lose value. People in the media industries put a great value on exclusivity, and the possibility exists that the mere presence of a new and nonrivalrous version of the plaintiff's work might cause an economic injury of some kind (perhaps lowering the price at which plaintiff's copyright can be sold) that is not easily captured in the other categories. But it is hard to pin down what this loss consists of that would not be covered by the rivalrous substitution effect, the copyist's failure to pay license fees (since those fees could capture loss of exclusivity), and the category of "subjective distress." The following analysis therefore does not treat the loss of exclusivity as a separate category.

Having canvassed the likely candidates for harm, we have found three: substitutionary rivalry, foregone fees, and subjective distress. The question now arises: what role do "substantial similarity" and its component, recognizability, play in all these forms of potential harm?

As to the first kind of two kinds of effect, substitutionary rivalry and foregone fees, recognizability plays a key role. Unless the plaintiff's work and the defendant's work are recognizably similar, the latter is highly unlikely to substitute for the former, and the defendant making a nonrival use is unlikely to see any purpose in copying that's unrecognizable.[49] There may be some cases where substitution could occur without a recognizable similarity between the defendant's product and the plaintiff's protected expression, but those will either be cases where the defendant has taken the plaintiff's idea or functional advance (which are not protected by copyright) or cases where the substitution is coincidental and not meaningfully related to any invisible copying of expression that might be embedded in it.[50] So recognizability

47 This form of harm fits ill with the largely corporate nature of the copyright industries, because how does one assess the state of mind of an abstract entity such as a corporation?

48 *See* the discussion of belief-mediated distress in JUDITH JARVIS THOMSON, THE REALM OF RIGHTS (1990) at 251–60; Seana Shiffrin, in her recent publication, makes the proposition that some belief-mediated distresses may be harms, but recognizes issues inherent in making such categorizations. Shiffrin, *Harm and Its Moral Significance*, 37, 39 (2012) *available at* http://journals.cambridge.org/repo_A862Ssc5. This article has been published with different pagination in 18 J. LEG. THEORY 357. The pagination used in citations throughout this chapter refers to the version posted at the referenced web address.

49 Please recall that cases of intermediate copying are outside the scope of this chapter; *see supra* note 24.

50 To illustrate what I mean by coincidence, consider this far-fetched example provided by Nimmer: "[I]magine a defendant who buys plaintiff's poetry anthology to use as an inspiration, ultimately producing her own work by focusing on a poem written by plaintiff, crossing out every word except "The End," and producing a poem original in every other regard. It can hardly be doubted that defendant in this scenario has not infringed." 4 MELVILLE B. NIMMER & DAVID NIMMER, NIMMER ON COPYRIGHT § 13.03[B][1][b], at 13–70 (Matthew Bender, Rev. Ed.) (footnotes omitted).

seems to be a necessary component of the kind of harm (vel non) that results from substitutionary rivalry and foregone fees.

Recognizability also would seem to be a necessary component of the third harm candidate, what I have termed "subjective distress." It is hard to imagine authors caring deeply if their work is used unrecognizably. Much greater impact is likely to result from a stranger's using an author's ideas, and, as mentioned, the free use of other people's ideas is something copyright law explicitly privileges[51] and copyright policy encourages.[52] There might be some attenuated sense of injustice if they learn of the unrecognizable use, but without anyone, including the author, being able to perceive a similarity between the author's work and the defendant's, it is hard to see serious emotional impact.

So for these three categories of potential harm, "substantial similarity" and its recognizability component are likely essential to the possibility of harm arising. However, I must concede that under the Supreme Court's current view of the constitution, this need not be the case.

As the law stands now, a defendant owes no license fees for an unrecognizable use (except for digital sampling under the exceptional *Bridgeport* case mentioned earlier).[53] But the law can change. Given the extreme deference the Supreme Court showed to Congress in *Eldred*,[54] it would take something truly outrageous – perhaps giving copyright owners a right to royalties every time the weather turned cold – before a congressional grant of exclusive right would be found constitutionally invalid. So, under the Court's current approach, Congress probably *could*, if it wished, impose liability even for copying of protected expression that was unrecognizable in the defendant's product.

Were Congress to choose such a course, lack of recognizability would be *un*necessary as a prerequisite to recovery. In such a case, I would see little connection between copyright and harm. To have any normative bite for legal policy, harm

At the point where the two works are so different, the possibility of substitution seems unrelated to the fact of copying even should the defendant's poem happen to compete with the plaintiff's.

A more realistic example is provided by music sampling, where chunks of borrowed sound are routinely looped, stretched, and distorted in unrecognizable ways.

51 17 U.S.C. § 102(b) (no copyright in ideas).

52 Admittedly, copyright law's tolerance and encouragement for use of others' ideas do not "prove" a lack of emotional impact from either the nonrecognizable use of expression or the use of ideas. It may be that authors do suffer significant emotional harm from the use of their ideas by others, with the law making that harm non-actionable simply because the cost of doing otherwise (the cost of allowing suit for the use of ideas) is too high. Nevertheless, that copyright law regularly requires authors to tolerate whatever distress results from seeing their ideas used by others has three implications: first, that emotional harm from copying is not legally actionable without some further showing; second, that avoiding authors' emotional harm ranks below other goals of copyright; and third, that regular exposure to the practice of having their ideas copied may enable authors to develop habits of mind – coping mechanisms – that reduce whatever emotional harm might otherwise have resulted from learning they have been copied.

53 *See* notes 10–20 and accompanying text.

54 Eldred v. Ashcroft, 537 U.S. 186, 204–05 (2003).

must mean more than 'a shortfall from a legal entitlement.' Thus, I disagree with the assumption of many writers[55] that any violation of a statute itself causes "harm."[56]

To sum up: I contend that recognizability as a necessary component of "substantial similarity" functions in part to bring considerations of potential harm into the copyright calculus.[57] If that is correct, then this aspect of substantial similarity is another ground for distinguishing copyright infringement from trespass to land.

A. *What is Harm?*

Harm is usually considered a shortfall from some baseline. This raises at least two questions: what baseline should be used and how should a shortfall be measured? Although there are potentially an infinite number of possible baselines, depending on one's normative commitments,[58] we consider three here: a baseline of minimum incentives, a set of baselines that relate to the plaintiff's actual status quo position prior to the defendant's copying, and a baseline of welfare set without regard to the plaintiff's actual pre-copying holdings. The first (incentives) already plays some role in copyright, particularly in fair use cases; the second (reference to change in status quo) is the typical common law baseline for harm; and the third (general welfare level) is an unusual but philosophically respectable possibility. After examining those baseline options, we turn to the question of how to measure the shortfall.

Note that the question of how to measure the shortfall can be restated as a baseline question. Thus, people who measure the shortfall by asking how the plaintiff would

55 Copyright can be seen as a conceptual outgrowth of restitution, the branch of common law that sometimes requires payment for benefit received. *See generally*, Wendy J. Gordon, *On Owning Information: Intellectual Property and the Restitionary Impulse*, 78 VA. L. REV. 149 (1992). Restitution law is often said to order payment only when the defendant "has been unjustly enriched at the expense of another." RESTATEMENT OF RESTITUTION, QUASI CONTRACTS AND CONSTRUCTIVE TRUSTS § 63 cmt. a (1937) (First Restatement), § 1; *see* 1 ARTHUR L. CORBIN, CORBIN ON CONTRACTS, § 19A, at 64 (Supp. 1991) ("detriment to plaintiff" said to be crucial to quasi-contract).

Some judges see the requirement of expense or detriment – what I call *harm* – as capable of being satisfied by showing a nonharmful violation of a "legally protected interest." 1 GEORGE E. PALMER, THE LAW OF RESTITUTION § 2.10, at 133 (1978). I think it is an important conceptual error to equate a violation of right (an abstraction) with temporal harm (a real-world effect). It is better to see violation of a preexisting legal right as an independently sufficient basis for restitution.

56 Defining harm in terms of legal entitlements leads to disabling "harm" as an independent criterion to use in deciding what legal entitlements to award. To define any shortfall from a statutory entitlement as a "harm" just leads to an unhelpful circularity. (Thanks to Oren Bracha for making me think more deeply about circularity issues.)

57 Potential harm is admittedly not actual harm. It is nevertheless meaningful that the courts require plaintiffs to prove that defendants have done something that is a necessary if not sufficient element of harm. Among other things, the requirement that defendant made or distributed or performed something that was "substantially similar" to plaintiff's work preserves the relation of correlativity between plaintiff and defendant that is necessary under the corrective justice model of common law adjudication. *Cf.*, the "likelihood of confusion" that is a prerequisite for relief under the federal trademark law, the Lanham Act. 5 U.S.C. § 1125(a) (2006) (setting out the likelihood of confusion standard for trademark infringement).

58 An egoist might argue that his baseline is to be king of the world, and anything that kept him from that exalted position "harmed" him.

have fared but for the interaction with the defendant are implicitly setting their baseline at the level the plaintiff would have achieved had there been no copying by the defendant. People who measure harm by historical worsening[59] are using a baseline consisting of the plaintiff's actual status quo position prior to the interaction with the defendant. People who measure harm noncomparatively (looking at levels of distress regardless of comparison) are employing a baseline of a given level of welfare[60] that is independent of any level of welfare that the affected person had attained or could have attained but for the defendant.

B. *Baselines: Incentives versus the Plaintiff's Actual Position*

In 1983, the then Register of Copyrights, David Ladd, presciently attacked the use of "harm" to limit the reach of copyright.[61] Since then, a growing number of commentators have indeed suggested limiting copyright by reference to harm and related notions.[62] Interestingly, Register Ladd described the relevant concept of harm this way:

> The Constitution authorizes copyright "To promote the Progress of Science."[63] From that phrase, the exponents of harm declare that where the imperatives of

[59] Stephen Perry favors the historical-worsening test for an abstract definition of harm, but a different test for legal liability. Stephen Perry, *Harm, History, and Counterfactuals*, 40 San Diego L. Rev. 1283 (2003). By contrast, the instant essay is looking for definitions of harm that suit the context of copyright law.

[60] I use "welfare" here in the broadest possible sense. Even philosophers who concur on a noncomparative approach can differ strongly on what should count as harm.

[61] David Ladd, *The Harm of the Concept of Harm in Copyright: The 13th Donald C Brace Memorial Lecture*, 30 J. Copyright Soc'y USA 421 (1983).

[62] In 1982 I had argued that one basis for fair use could be the impossibility of a plaintiff collecting license fees: that is, that position might be restated as an argument that nonliability should flow from showing an absence of harm to plaintiff. Wendy J. Gordon, *Fair Use as Market Failure: A Structural and Economic Analysis of the Betamax Case and its Predecessors*, 82 Colum. L. Rev. 1600 (1982). More recently I have explored the possibility that harm be made an explicit part of the plaintiff's case. Wendy J. Gordon, *Harmless Use: Gleaning from Fields of Copyrighted Works*, 77 Fordham L. Rev. 2411 209 (with introduction by Sonia Katyal). Stephen Hetcher, in his argument that fair use be made part of plaintiff's case, similarly would make proof of no-harm part of plaintiff's obligation. Shyam Balganesh in his article on foreseeability looks at something closely related to harm, namely, whether the plaintiff foresaw and was aiming at the market the defendant served, as a method of limiting copyright's overreach. *See* Shyamkrishna Balganesh, *Foreseeability and Copyright Incentives*, 122 Harv. L. Rev. 1569 (2009). These are only some examples.

[63] The "progress" language comes from the constitutional clause that empowers Congress "[t]o promote the Progress of Science and useful Arts, by securing for limited Times to Authors and Inventors the exclusive Right to their *respective* Writings and Discoveries." U.S. Const. Art. I, § 8, cl. 8 (emphasis added). By speaking only of the "Progress of Science" and not of the "Progress of Science and the useful Arts," Register Ladd follows the usual interpretation of the constitutional language: Adopting a parallel construction for each of the three dual phrases in the Constitution, he is assuming that "Science" goes with "authors" and "writings," whereas "useful Arts" goes with "inventors" and "discoveries." Thus, when Ladd writes of copyright furthering only the "Progress of Science," he is following a standard interpretation. But that standard interpretation may be incorrect.

maximum distribution clash with property rights, the latter must yield; and that copyright should extend no further than to what is financially indispensable to motivate creation and publication.[64]

Thus, Ladd accused copyright skeptics of misusing the Constitution's "Progress clause" to argue "that copyright should extend no further than to what is financially indispensable to motivate creation and publication."[65] In doing so, Ladd implicitly defines "harm" as any shortfall beneath what is financially indispensable to induce authorship and distribution.[66] An amount of money equal to minimal incentives is the baseline he attacks. And normative support for such a baseline is indeed quite visible in the literature.[67] Thus, Christopher Sprigman asserts that "we understand copyright's concept of harm"; "copyright 'harm' arises from any use that threatens to suppress author incentives significantly below the optimal level."[68]

The incentive approach remains distinct from trespass; among other things, an incentive approach should emphasize the importance of inquiring into "recognizable" rather than "mere" copying. Unrecognizable copying, like unforeseeable copying, is not something an author would have taken into account in deciding how much to invest in creation.

Foreseeability is a necessary but not sufficient basis for incentive effects; Shyamkrishna Balganesh has suggested that foreseeability *in general* be made a part of the plaintiff's case.[69] Courts have not so far followed suit. Recognizability and similarity,

The rhetorical device of "chiasmus" (a rhetorical pattern of ABBA instead of ABAB) is a standard alternative to parallelism, well known to educated men (gender deliberate) of the eighteenth century. The use of the word "respective" before "Writings and Discoveries" therefore makes a difference. In this one subclause that uses the word "respective," the authors of the Constitution are making clear they do intend a construction of parallelism and not chiasmus: "authors" go with "writings," and "inventors" with "discoveries." But no signal such as "respective" applies to the "Science and useful Arts" language, throwing in doubt the usual interpretation that the drafters intended a parallel construction throughout.

Because no "respective" is applied to "Science" and the "Useful Arts," the progress preamble is capable of applying as a whole to the remainder of the clause. That is, instead of "the progress of Science" applying to copyright and the "progress of useful Arts" applying to patent, the progress of *both* Science and the useful Arts could have been intended to apply to copyright *and* patent.

64 Ladd, *supra* note 61, at 422.

65 *Id.*

66 The notion of what is "financially indispensable" not only could serve as a baseline from which to measure harm but it could also serve to define fault. Fault could be the failure to pay such fees (or to do such copying) as causes a shortfall from the baseline.

67 Thus, Shyam Balganesh contends that "creators . . . need to be given just enough incentive to create in order to balance the system's benefits against its costs." Balganesh, *Foreseeability*, *supra* note 62, at 1571 (abstract). Note, however, that Balganesh does not recommend denying copyright protection to any author whose outlay has been compensated; his recommendation is that foreseeability be made part of plaintiff's obligation of proof.

68 Christopher Sprigman, *Copyright and the Rule of Reason*, 7 J. TELECOMM. & HIGH TECH. L. 317, 320 (2009).

69 Balganesh, *Foreseeability*, *supra* note 62.

too, are necessary but not sufficient bases for incentive effects. These the courts *do* require, as part of the inquiry into actionable copying.

Let us return to the notion of harm that Ladd describes. If "what is financially indispensable" for creativity[70] could be determined, and the appropriate multipliers for uncertainty and the like could be defined,[71] then some of us who are indeed worried about copyright's overreach might well want to implement the suggestion that Ladd so disdained. The courts or Congress could change the current rule that the plaintiff need not prove harm and might adopt "what is financially indispensable" as the baseline from which harm would be measured.[72]

There is something to be said for including into the copyright plaintiff's prima facie case some notion of incentive and the plaintiff being entitled to recoup his or her investment. Consider the prisoner's dilemma, one form of which I have described as the source of the economic impetus for copyright: in a world without copyright law it is the fear of harm – the fear that unauthorized copying will cause bankruptcy or the loss of years of investment – that discourages creativity.[73] Enacting copyright law changes the payoff structure, making unauthorized copying less likely, so that investments of effort in popular works can lead to survival rather than ruination. Awarding copyright only when necessary to effectuate that change in payoff structure might indeed be a good measure of minimal copyright.

But even advocates of this incentive notion of harm acknowledge that "this theory [of harm] is exceedingly difficult to apply in many cases."[74] Empirical investigation of copyright's effects is notoriously difficult and is further complicated by the important

70 I question the relevance of publishers' incentives to the analysis; despite the importance that publication incentives may have played in Eldred v. Ashcroft, 537 U.S. 186 (2003), the Copyright Clause of the Constitution speaks of "writers" not "publishers."

71 *Cf.* Richard Craswell, *Deterrence and Damages: The Multiplier Principle and Its Alternatives*, 97 Mich. L. Rev. 2185, 2186–87 (1999) (a broad discussion of multipliers in deterrence).

72 Ladd's notion is actually closer to what we know as the "fault" or "reasonableness" determination in negligence than it is to a finding of "harm," because the approach he describes defines what duties are cost-justified. However, what is at issue in his targeted definition of copyright harm is a duty to pay rather than a duty to act, so the parallel to "reasonableness" in negligence law is only partial.

73 *See* Wendy J. Gordon, *Intellectual Property*, in The Oxford Handbook of Legal Studies 617 (Peter Cane & Mark Tushnet eds., 2003); Wendy J. Gordon, *Asymmetric Market Failure and Prisoner's Dilemma in Intellectual Property*, 17 U. Dayton L. Rev. 853 (1992). Whether in fact the fear of negative financial payoffs will discourage creativity is much debated. See the literature addressing the importance of nonfinancial considerations in the decision to create works of authorship, including, for example, Jeanne Fromer, *Expressive Incentives in Intellectual Property*, 98 Va L. Rev. 1745 (2012); Diane Leenheer Zimmerman, *Copyrights as Incentives: Did We Just Imagine That?*, 12 Theoretical Inq. L. 29, 35 (2011); Julie E. Cohen, *Copyright as Property in the Post-Industrial Economy: A Research Agenda*, 2011 Wis. L. Rev. 141 (2011); Roberta Rosenthal Kwall, *Inspiration and Innovation: The Intrinsic Dimension of the Artistic Soul*, 81 Notre Dame L. Rev. 1945, 1970 (2006); Roberta Rosenthal Kwall, The Soul of Creativity: Forging a Moral Rights Law for the United States (2010); Jessica Silbey, *Harvesting Intellectual Property: Inspired Beginnings and "Work-Make-Work," Two Stages in the Creative Processes of Artists and Innovators*, 86 Notre Dame L. Rev. 2091, 2112 (2011); Rebecca Tushnet, *Economies of Desire: Fair Use and Marketplace Assumptions*, 51 Wm. & Mary L. Rev. 513, 522 (2009); Wendy J. Gordon, *Render Copyright Unto Caesar: On Taking Incentives Seriously*, 71 U. Chi. L. Rev. 75 (2004).

74 Sprigman, *supra* note 68.

fact that much creativity needs motivation of a nonfinancial kind.[75] Moreover, deciding "how much incentive is necessary" calls for normative as well as empirical judgments, because someone needs to decide what works, and what quality of works, need to be incentivized. In addition, using a number representing minimal incentives as a baseline for determining harm causes fairness problems as between litigants otherwise similarly situated.

The fairness problem arises in part because, unlike the negligence inquiry, where the cost-benefit balancing of incentives[76] is typically limited to a particular act by the defendant,[77] in copyright the particular defendant's action is only one of many acts of copying that can contribute to whether the plaintiff receives enough income to meet the economic baseline. That would lead to giving perhaps unwarranted significance to the question of *timing*, for nonpayment by a defendant who copies early in the copyright's life is likely to do damage to the "financially indispensable" amount, whereas a defendant who copies later is likely to escape liability on the ground that the "financially indispensable" amount has already been collected.[78]

Although proposals to allow timing to affect copyright liability have been thoughtfully made,[79] and consideration of the plaintiff's incentives appears in many cases,[80] common law notions of horizontal fairness ("treating like defendants alike") make

[75] *See* Zimmerman, *supra* note 73, and the other sources cited in the immediately preceding footnote.

[76] United States v. Carroll Towing Co., 159 F.2d 169, 173 (2d Cir. 1947).

[77] Also note that the cost-benefit balancing of negligence law pertains to the costs and benefits of the defendant's action, over which the defendant has a good deal of control. By contrast, the Ladd picture of "harm" focuses on the costs and benefits related to plaintiff's productivity, about which the defendant has comparatively little control. It better fits common law notions of fairness to hinge defendants' liability on factors they can control, rather than on factors they cannot.

[78] A more flexible use of incentives, not tied to a specific monetary amount, can be more useful. I try to use such a flexible account of injury to incentives in Wendy J. Gordon, *Fair Use as Market Failure*, 82 COLUM. L. REV. 1600 (1982).

[79] Justin Hughes, *Fair Use Across Time*, 50 UCLA L. REV. 775, 781 (2003) ("Viewing the market across time has one important effect: When a work is new, unauthorized uses are less likely to be fair uses; when a work approaches the end of its copyright term, unauthorized uses are increasingly likely to be fair."); Joseph P. Liu, *Copyright and Time: A Proposal*, 101 MICH. L. REV. 409, 425 (2002) ("The proposal is simple: in deciding whether a given use of a copyrighted work is fair use, courts should take into account how much time has passed since the work was created. The more recent the work, all other things being equal, the narrower the scope of fair use; the older the work, the greater the scope of fair use.") For other proposals to adjust copyright to reflect a plaintiff's situation, see e.g., Shyamkrishna Balganesh, *supra* note 13, *at* 203 (2012); Lydia Pallas Loren, *The Pope's Copyright? Aligning Incentives with Reality by Using Creative Motivation to Shape Copyright Protection*, 69 LA. L. REV. 1 (2008).

[80] The fourth fair use factor, "the effect of the use upon the potential market for or value of the copyrighted work" 17 U.S.C. § 107(4) (2006), has been interpreted both as referring to plaintiff's private harm, and as referring to impact on incentives. Many fair use cases seem to be groping for a sense of how badly defendant's behavior would hurt incentives of people such as the plaintiff.

For explicit consideration of incentives *see, e.g.*, Williams & Wilkins Co. v. U. S., 487 F.2d 1345, 1357–58 (Ct. Cl. 1973), aff'd by an equally divided Court, 420 U.S. 376 (1975) (discussion of the health of the publishing industries); Nat'l Basketball Ass'n v. Motorola, Inc., 105 F.3d 841, 845 (2d Cir. 1997) (whether defendant's behavior would so impair incentives as to render a service unavailable to the public, ruled relevant to preemption).

rigorous employment of the incentive-oriented baseline as described by Ladd problematic. That does not mean that the incentive-baseline test is fatally flawed: eventually our legal system might decide that the timing of the defendant's copying is just one more species of acceptable "moral luck" that the law rewards or penalizes.[81] And employing an incentive baseline might have a salutary effect; if defendants imagine that the later they are sued, the better are their chances for prevailing, then they are likely to postpone their copying until after the period when the plaintiff's work has its highest popularity. Nevertheless, the issue of horizontal fairness (and the difficulty of determining what *number* to use as "financially indispensable") must give us pause.

Nor can we know what was "financially indispensable" with any certainty. Even a measure of the plaintiff's customer base does not yield determinate answers standing alone. That is because the stream of customers may bring revenues in excess of what was needed to induce the work to come into existence, even if one takes into account discounts for probabilities.[82] Parents have long been concerned that the extremely high salaries paid to sports stars could distract their children from pursuing non-sports careers; over-reward can exist in the copyright sphere as well.

Mention of the copyright owner's customer stream brings us to our second candidate for baseline. In countless common law cases, a distinction is made between plaintiffs that are harmed and those that are not – with harm being measured not by a global inquiry into ideal incentives, but rather by a much more *local* inquiry into how the defendant has affected the plaintiff's de facto welfare. This local inquiry into the defendant's effect on the plaintiff is not thought to violate horizontal fairness.

When viewed from this local perspective on "harm" as used by the common law, harm is not as vague as Register Ladd believes. Admittedly, for this local inquiry, the law still needs to make policy decisions. (For example, is the plaintiff's current customer and licensee base the only baseline that should count, so that only decreases in that current base should count as harm? If the baseline is broader than that, should a copyist's failure to pay fees for new and unexpected uses count as local harm? How

[81] Common law notions of horizontal equity are not violated by making the amount a defendant pays depend on other luck-related aspects of the plaintiff's condition. The negligent driver who luckily hits no one has no liability in tort. The unlucky negligent driver who hits someone must pay. Moreover, the driver who negligently runs down a high-earning pedestrian must pay more compensation than the somewhat luckier driver who negligently runs down a low earner. These differences in outcomes are not attributable to differences in the defendant's behavior, and as to him or her are matters of luck. The importance of such "moral luck" to the law may be a failure of consistency, but it is one that our traditions accept.

[82] What an author sees as her monetary remuneration is (very roughly) the range of possible revenue streams, each discounted by various possibilities of nonsuccess. The higher the chance of nonsuccess, the higher the actual amounts earned by successful authors of her type need to be. Here is a simple example: If an author's cost of production (including opportunity cost) is $1,000, and similar authors have a 50–50 likelihood of making $2,002, then a new author will (very roughly) be willing to produce the creative work because she sees her likely income, $1,001 ($2,002 discounted by the 50% likelihood of failure), as greater than the costs she would have to bear. A market reward of $1,000 would fall drastically below what is needed to incentivize her; a reward of $20,000 would fall drastically above. Revenues in excess of what is needed to bring forth a resource are usually called "rent."

should shortfalls from whatever baseline is chosen be measured – e.g., by historical worsening or counterfactually?) But they are decisions upon which it is easier to get a handle than are the complex factual inquiries necessary identify ideal incentives.

In the following, I do not employ the incentive baseline, but instead examine three alternative interpretations of local "harm." From these interpretations we will find much of use in understanding copyright. Among other things, parsing the various meanings of harm gives us information about how to handle the problem of foregone license fees in the doctrine of fair use. The next part addresses how localized concepts of individual harm could be applied to the various potential sources of loss in the copyright context.

III. THREE PRIMARY DEFINITIONS OF HARM

There are three primary ways a plaintiff's welfare can diverge from a designated baseline, and accordingly there are three major competitors for the definition of "harm." One set of definitions involves counterfactual comparisons, one involves comparison by historical positioning, and one involves the existence of a noncomparatively defined state of being. The three approaches can also be used to define the converse term, "benefit."

Most of American tort law uses a counterfactual approach, asking *what would have happened* but for the interaction with the defendant. This approach compares how the plaintiff fared in the real world after the interaction with the defendant, with how the plaintiff *would have fared* had the interaction not occurred. If the affected party would have been better off absent the interaction with the defendant, then the defendant has "harmed" him or her. If the affected party would have been worse off absent the interaction with the defendant, the defendant has "benefited" him or her. So when a negligent actor breaks a plaintiff's leg, the broken leg is something that would not exist "but for" the interaction and is a harm.

This counterfactual or but-for test has variants. It is sometimes linked with violation of right[83] and is sometimes defined independently of whether there has been a rights violation. Additionally, although usually one inquires counterfactually into what "*would* have happened without the interaction with the defendant," occasionally some find it appropriate to inquire into "what *should* have happened if the defendant had acted properly."[84] In yet another variant, foreseeability is incorporated: "we could say that A harms B only if his wrongful act leaves B worse off than he would

[83] Joel Feinberg, *Wrongful Life and the Counterfactual Element in Harming*, 4 Soc. Philos. & Pol. 145, 148 (1986); Hershovitz, *supra* note 31, at 1147. In my view, it makes little sense to say a harm can only arise where there has been a violation of right. Many harms are done that our law does not forbid. To the extent we wish to use concepts of "harm" as a tentative guide to deontological moral reasoning, we need an independent definition of "harm." Defining "harm" in terms of "wrongs" makes the inquiry into harms fairly useless for determining what might constitute a wrong.

[84] Feinberg, *supra* note 83 at 153, tentatively explores the alternative inquiry of what "should" have happened; I argue later against that interpretation, at least for use in law.

be otherwise *in the normal course of events insofar as they were reasonably foreseeable in the circumstances.*"[85] Feinberg calls the latter "doubly counterfactual."[86]

A second popular set of approaches to defining harm adopts a "historical- worsening" approach. It asks whether the plaintiff's interests are in worse shape after the interaction than they were before. Like the counterfactual approach, the historical-worsening approach is comparative. It has two primary variants. In one, the plaintiff's condition before the interaction is assessed simply by what he or she has. In the other, the plaintiff's condition before the interaction is assessed also by looking at what options – what possibilities – were open to him or her at that time. (That is, this approach would consider the plaintiff's options as part of the baseline from which harm is to be measured.) The latter approach would count some loss of options as a historical worsening.[87]

The third major set of definitions is noncomparative. Here "harm" has to do with states of suffering, impairment of central interests, or interference with autonomy.[88] These definitions can differ one from another, but they have in common that the designated state of being can count as harm, *without comparison to* what came before. Under this view, for example, starvation is a harm even for a child who has never known any other condition. David Lyons[89] implicitly attributes a noncomparative approach to John Stuart Mill.

Lyons argues that Mill's Liberty Principle, which prohibits the state from acting except to avoid harm, would allow the government to alleviate "harms" "such as malnutrition and starvation, emotional disturbances, illness and disease, vulnerability to attack, homelessness" by requiring cooperation. He argues that Mill would approve

85 Feinberg, *supra* note 83, at 153.

86 *Id.*

87 Perry adopts the "options" approach. *See* Perry, *supra* note 59.

88 It might feel natural to call noncomparative views of harms "state-based" views, because under the noncomparative approaches a finding of harm depends not on a change in position but on a person occupying a negative state, regardless of whether or not that negative state is worse than something experienced earlier. However, Matthew Hanser points out that comparative accounts are also state-based, in that they treat "suffering harm [as] a matter of coming to be in a comparatively bad state." Hanser, *The Metaphysics of Harm*, 77 PHIL. & PHENOMENOLOGICAL RES. 421, 422 (2008). Hanser himself urges an event-based view of harm. *Id.* at 440–49.

89 Lyons, *supra* note 36. Although Lyons does not explicitly disclaim comparative accounts, their abandonment is implicit in his position. Mill's principle is sometimes interpreted as allowing the state to use coercion only to prevent the "doing of harm," but Lyons makes a persuasive case that Mill would also approve state action to alleviate harmful states themselves. Further, consider his examples.

Writes Lyons, "Harms . . . are not to be understood in terms of mere existing preferences but rather as conditions that must be satisfied if one is to live well as a human being; they include physical necessities, personal security, social freedom (from oppressive custom as well as others' interference), and a variety of experiences and opportunities for self-development. To the extent that one is denied or deprived of such conditions, one suffers what Mill counts as "harm." *Id.* at 14.

Among "significant harms," Lyons includes examples "such as malnutrition and starvation, emotional disturbances, illness and disease, vulnerability to attack, homelessness, and so on." *Id.* at 8. He distinguishes the prevention of such harms from provision of "benefits in general," *Id.* at 7, such as "providing greater comforts and conveniences for relatively comfortable members of society." *Id.* at 8.

governmental coercion to reduce harm, and not simply against the *doing* of harm.[90] By implication, it does not matter under this interpretation how a harm arises; therefore, whether or not the state of being is different from a prior state would be immaterial. This noncomparative stance also is capable of distinguishing "harms" from "benefits." Lyons argues that for Mill the compulsions permissible to alleviate harms would not be permissible if their goal were to provide "benefits in general;"[91] Lyons provides as illustration, "providing greater comforts and conveniences for relatively comfortable members of society."[92]

If one's inquiry into "harm" is motivated by Mill's question – namely, what criteria must be met for government coercion to be justifiable – then the noncomparative view of "harm" makes perfect sense. The government is indeed justified in taxing us to help relieve the poverty of others (at least in my view). But the noncomparative view of "harm" has the disadvantage of not meeting the normal expectation of English speakers, for whom "harm" is a basically comparative notion.

A much-discussed noncomparative view is that of Seana Shiffrin, who emphasizes harm as the impairment of autonomy.[93] For her, the moral significance of harm comes not from its changing someone's position but rather from a situation's grave impact on someone's ability to form his or her own life.[94] What distinguishes a "harm" from a "pure benefit" seems to be that the benefit has a comparative lack of impact on autonomy: a "pure benefit" is "a benefit that is not also a prevention of, removal from, or alleviation of harm."[95] Shiffrin lists the following as examples of a pure benefit: "a new stereo, a coveted bicycle, or a large amount of desired, but unneeded cash,"[96] or remarkably enhanced physical attributes.[97] Although "pure benefits" should not be trivialized – pursuit of pure benefits can be an important part of "building a distinctive life"[98] – they differ from harm avoidance.

90 *Id.* at 8.

91 *Id.* at 7.

92 *Id.* If one imagines the inquiry into "harm" to be motivated by Mill's question – namely, what criteria must be met for government coercion to be justifiable – then the noncomparative view of "harm" makes perfect sense. The government is indeed justified in taxing us to help relieve the poverty of others (at least in my view). But the noncomparative view of "harm" has the disadvantage of not meeting the normal expectation of English speakers, for whom "harm" is a basically comparative notion.

93 Seana Valentine Shiffrin, *Harm and Its Moral Significance*, *supra* note 48, at 9; Seana Valentine Shiffrin, *Wrongful Life, Procreative Responsibility, and the Significance of Harm*, 5 LEGAL THEORY 117, 123 (1999). In the latter, she writes, "[o]n my view, harm involves conditions that generate a significant chasm or conflict between one's will and one's experience, one's life more broadly understood, or one's circumstances. Although harms differ from one another in various ways, all have in common that they render agents or a significant or close aspect of their lived experience like that of an endurer as opposed to that of an active agent." *Id.* at 123.

94 *See generally* Shiffrin, *Harm and Its Moral Significance*, *supra* note 48.

95 *Id.* at 8.

96 *Id.* at 20.

97 *Id.* at 8.

98 *Id.* at 34.

Thus in seeking to define "harm" and "benefit" we have counterfactual approaches, historical-worsening approaches, and noncomparative approaches. There are also combinations of them. For example, some authors suggest disjunctively combining the counterfactual and historical-worsening approaches. Or when seeking to figure out who caused harm for purposes of liability, one can combine a comparative account (did the defendant cause worsening in some counterfactual and/or historical sense) with a requirement, perhaps drawn from the noncomparative accounts, that the harm be serious and grave. Many philosophers indeed add a "gravity" component to their accounts, although, as one would expect, each defines the gravity differently. Interestingly, the *Bridgeport* case rejected a gravity inquiry altogether; it not only refused to adhere to the substantial similarity test but also turned its back on the rule that de minimis copying was not actionable.[99]

Results from the three main groupings of ways to define "harm" – counterfactual, historical worsening, and noncomparative – need not diverge. In a typical tort case, all three of these definitions are simultaneously satisfied.

Consider a careless driver who runs down a pedestrian. But for the driver's action the pedestrian would be healthy. So the counterfactual test is met. The plaintiff is in worse shape after the accident than he was before. So the historical-worsening test is met. And as a matter of objective welfare, he is seriously suffering, from a broken leg. So a noncomparative account is also probably satisfied.

But sometimes the results of the different definitions can diverge. What if, in the absence of this careless driver, another equally careless driver would have come from another direction a minute later and broken the plaintiff's leg? In that case, there would be no harm (except a minute's worth) under the counterfactual test, because "but for" the first driver, the pedestrian would have a broken leg anyway. (This is sometimes called the problem of "overdetermination." The common law has various approaches to dealing with the situation.) Although there is an absence of harm on the counterfactual test, there is significant harm under the historical-worsening test.

One reason for spelling out the alternative tests is that a finding of "harm" might weigh in the copyright plaintiff's favor. If what the defendant had done has harmed the plaintiff, a judge is more likely to find against the defendant (particularly if fair use is the issue).[100] If, in contrast, what the defendant has done is more properly defined as depriving the plaintiff of a benefit, the weight against the defendant is lighter. Harm is a standard part of the inquiry into whether the defendant's use is "fair" and thus non-infringing under copyright doctrine, and perhaps the philosophers' explorations

[99] Bridgeport Music Inc. v. Dimension Films, 410 F.3d 792, 798, 801–802.

[100] Harm to the plaintiff's potential markets is factor four in the statutory fair use inquiry and is often said to be the most important of all the factors. Barton Beebe's empirical work suggests that factor four's importance lies less in its own salience than in the way it serves as a place for the court to summarize its reactions on all factors. Barton Beebe, *An Empirical Study of U.S. Copyright Fair Use Opinions, 1978–2005*, 156 U. Pa. L. Rev. 549, 620–21 (2008) (footnotes omitted).

can help us decide what should count as harm for this purpose. Choosing how we define "harm" with open eyes is thus crucial.

To make a preliminary taxonomy, the following applies the three types of harm definitions (counterfactual, historical worsening, and noncomparative) to the three copyright scenarios: rivalrous diversion of customers, foregone defendant-license fees, and subjective distress. Unless otherwise specified, the baselines utilized will adopt the dominant common law approach of referring to the plaintiff's actual or likely position, rather than to a notion of ideal or minimal incentives.

A. *Rivalrous Diversion of Customers*

The inquiry into rivalrous harm might help us examine nonconsequentialist reasons for copyright law. Admittedly, the formulation of the Intellectual Property Clause – with its preamble specifying the purpose of "promot[ing] Progress" – suggests it was primarily the need for economic incentives that persuaded the Founders to give Congress the power to enact copyright. The economic rationale puts comparatively little importance on the harm/benefit distinction. But if in addition copyright law prevented harm to authors, there might be an additional, deontological weight on the scale in favor of granting copyright protections.[101]

If one uses a counterfactual notion of causation – often known as the "but-for" test – and applies it to the world as it is usually envisaged without copyright,[102] we see a likely scenario of overdetermination: that the unconsented and unremunerated copying of the author's manuscript by particular publisher A does not seem to cause the author harm. If A had not reprinted the manuscript, then probably publishers *B*, *C*, or *D* would have done so. Without copyright, there may nothing to discourage any number of reprintings.[103] If A's copying caused no shortfall from what would otherwise have come to the author, the copying causes no harm. Therefore, what the author wants in a world without copyright would be best described not as freedom from harm, but as a right to capture some of the benefits the publisher is capturing; the author wants to be better off than his or her baseline. We call a change that brings welfare *above* the baseline a "benefit." The law gives copyright to authors to

[101] Not all harms should give rise to legal action, of course, and deontological concerns other than harm avoidance could be operating.

[102] Copyright is premised on the supposition that, without a legal prohibition on copying, an author's baseline level of welfare is low.

[103] This is of course empirically subject to challenge; other constraints – from "gentlemen's agreements" to audience loyalty to lead time advantage – can make unconsented copying unlikely or unprofitable. For the classic warning that copyright might not be as necessary as the standard story suggests, see generally Stephen Breyer, *The Uneasy Case for Copyright: A Study of Copyright in Books, Photocopies, and Computer Programs*, 84 HARV. L. REV. 281 (1970). For an argument that unconsented copying can actually benefit the affected industry, see the discussion of how fashion thrives in the face of extensive (and lawful) copying of clothing design in KAI RAUSTIALA & CHRISTOPHER SPRIGMAN, THE KNOCKOFF ECONOMY 1–55 (2012).

remedy the possibility that "but for" the law of copyright, insufficient payment would be forthcoming. Those extra payments are, by definition under the counterfactual approach, "benefits" to authors; they will not come to the authors except if the law is enacted. If the right to be paid for benefits generated is weaker than the obligation to pay for harms inflicted – and our intuitions suggest it is weaker – then using the counterfactual test makes the justification for copyright not as strong as it might be. Under the historical-worsening approach, however, the first publisher who diverts the plaintiff's customers is doing a harm, regardless of how many other publishers stand ready to make unconsented copies. And under the noncomparative approach, it may well be (depending on circumstances) that it erodes an individual's basic interests or autonomy to devote a chunk of his or her life to creating a work of authorship that another plagiarizes and sells.

In this context, the historical-worsening test has some advantages. The counterfactual test is useful in contexts where a court is seeking to identify a particular person or persons to be liable; choosing a legal regime is less a matter of pinning responsibility on individuals than it is of raising the boat for all persons. Therefore, if a copyist interferes with an author's own plans for his or her work by diverting the author's customers, and the interference is grave enough to meet the demands of the historical-worsening or noncomparative approaches, it seems legitimate to say that the copyist harms the author.

At least two caveats apply, however. First, to the extent that avoiding the harmfulness of copying justifies copyright, the law must also be crafted so that assertions of copyright do no harm to the audience.[104] Second, if the author has not actually lost customers in whose pursuit he or she has invested heavily, the conception of harm is fairly weak as a moral matter.

Once copyright law is adopted, the diversion of customers is likely to satisfy both the counterfactual and historical-worsening approaches. Overdetermination becomes much less likely because the presence of liability and penalties discourages additional copyists from entering the field. And because we are speaking of *diverting* customers, the author has already invested in serving their interests, and so some progress has already been made to satisfy any gravity requirement.

Admittedly, a test that finds harm only where an existing customer base exists can have bad economic effects. Such a rule could entice companies to enter markets prematurely to set up the basis for claiming "harm" if the need came to sue. Landes and Posner sensibly advise against adopting laws that push owners to rush into

[104] This is the point of Locke's proviso that appropriation from the common becomes private property only if "enough and as good" is left for others. The laborer's claim to property rests on his right not to be injured (biblically based), and the public has just as good a right not to be injured. So the basis for the individual property right also limits it. *See generally* Gordon, *supra* note 30 (arguing that to the extent that Lockean theory might justify some IP rights in speech, it also demands an extensive freedom for the public to use speech authored by others.).

deploying their property before they are ready.[105] But it is likely that interference in an ongoing enterprise, with established customers, is likely to be more disruptive than would be interference with a business possibility that has not yet eventuated. One compromise that has been proposed is to require plaintiffs to prove that their entry into the claimed market was at least "foreseeable."[106]

B. *Foregone Defendant-License Fees*

As you recall, the category of "foregone fees" includes those cases where the copyist is not impairing already existing or impending markets of the plaintiff. If the defendant serves no customers whom the author would have served, the historical-worsening test is not satisfied. Except for the abstract issue of losing exclusivity, the author would be no worse off after the copying than she was before the copying began. So nonrivalrous copying does not "harm" the author/plaintiff under the historical-worsening approach, and the failure of the copyist to pay license fees does not count as a "harm" under that test.

The plaintiff also has no harm under the counterfactual test, because in the absence of the defendant's actions, the plaintiff would be no better off than he or she is. The customers the defendant is serving are by definition not customers the plaintiff would have served. So when the plaintiff copyright owner seeks license fees from a nonrivalrous defendant, the copyright owner is merely seeking payment for "benefits" the defendant has reaped,[107] and any payment the copyright owner receives is also a "benefit" to the copyright owner. No harm is involved under the counterfactual test, just as no harm was involved under the historical-worsening approach.[108] So far it seems as if the harm inquiry will weigh in the defendant's favor when the court evaluates the fairness of a nonrivalrous use.

As for how the foregone license fee situation would fare under the noncomparative approaches to defining harm, each case would depend on its own facts. In some

105 William M. Landes & Richard A. Posner, The Economic Structure of Intellectual Property Law 93 (2003).

106 *See generally* Balganesh, *Foreseeability*, *supra* note 62.

107 If the baseline is what the copyright owner could do on her own, without the defendant's causal contribution, then collecting fees from a nonrivalrous copyist would raise the copyright owner's welfare above her baseline.

108 I suppose one might argue that the revenues from the unlawful copying constitute a new baseline for the copyists, so that *they* are harmed in a comparative sense if a court makes them pay. It is to guard against such results that some philosophers, such as Feinberg, want to link "harm" to the violation of a right. (In Feinberg's view, it would be inappropriate to say a judge "harms" a thief if the judge orders the thief to return a stolen television set, because the judge is not violating any rights of the thief.) I think Perry and Hanser have the better view, when they separate harm from violation of right.

In my view, even if the copyists are "harmed" by being made to pay, violation of law constitutes a justification for inflicting the harm. One might also work with the relevance of time frame and gravity: being given a benefit, and then being made to pay for it or return it before one has begun to rely on it, is merely the divesting of a benefit.

instances the author might be left destitute if he or she lacks the ability to collect license fees from the defendant; in such a case the plaintiff might be able to claim noncomparative (grave) "harm." In other instances the author might be prospering and providing an encouraging incentive model for other aspiring authors. In such a case it is hard to see a prospering plaintiff as suffering noncomparative harm, even though he or she might be an attractive candidate for legal protection under non–harm-based theories of liability.

Under the noncomparative approach, then, a prosperous author is merely seeking a "benefit" (payment) from the defendant. By contrast, under that same approach, a suffering author is seeking to be relieved from "harm."[109]

This pair of characterizations intersects well with economic concerns. Any successful copyright lawsuit is likely to raise prices, and restrict distribution, of the work to the public. Where the plaintiff is suffering economically badly enough to be existing in a state of noncomparative harm, allowing him or her to succeed in a lawsuit against the defendant is likely to generate enough incentives to outweigh the costs of enforcement.[110] Counting the plaintiff as "harmed" is thus likely to be consistent with economic goals. By comparison, where a plaintiff is prosperous, it is less likely that allowing him or her victory in a lawsuit would serve the public's economic good.[111] Although such an inquiry may raise concerns regarding corrective justice,[112] it might nevertheless make sense to look at the plaintiff's situation and motivations.[113] Under current copyright doctrine, these observations are most likely to be helpful in cases where the question is whether a new use by a defendant is "fair."[114] The fairness of the use depends in part on "the effect of the use upon the potential market for or value of the copyrighted work."[115] The issue here is harm;[116] using the noncomparative approach to defining harm helps us distinguish the copyright

[109] I put to one side the question of whether there is a causal relation, sufficient to satisfy the correlativity concerns of corrective justice, between the defendant's failure to pay and the plaintiff's suffering.

[110] Or, speaking more strictly, the prospect of such a rule is likely to help generate incentives in the future. It may also permit the plaintiff to continue work as an author rather than seeking a day job.

[111] *See* Wendy J. Gordon, *Fair Use Markets: On Weighing Potential License Fees*, 79 Geo. Wash. L. Rev. 1814 (2011).

[112] American lawyers have long assumed that judges must treat rich and poor alike (with distributional issues being left to the legislature), and that one party must have had some causal impact on the other for them to have a correlative relation necessary for a lawsuit. The correlative relation is here (because the defendant may be depriving the plaintiff of a benefit to which he or she is entitled), but the differential treatment of rich and poor raises specters of inequality and arbitrariness.

[113] *See generally*. Balganesh, *Foreseeability*, *supra* note 62; Loren, *supra* note 87.

[114] Arguably the doctrine of fair use should have a distributional component. *See generally* Molly Van Houweling, *Distributive Values in Copyright*, 83 Texas L. Rev. 1535 (2005).

[115] 17 U.S.C. § 107(4) (2006).

[116] Harm is not the only issue relevant to the fairness of a nonrivalrous defendant's fair use status. See 17 U.S.C. § 107 (only one of whose factors directly concerns harm); *see also* Wendy J. Gordon, *Excuse and Justification in the Law of Fair Use: Transaction Costs Have Always Been Only Part of the Story*, 50 J. Copyright Soc'y U.S.A. 149, 154–55 (2003) (describing several considerations regarding market failures/limitations whose resolutions should affect the fair use determination, only one of which is harm).

owner who is seeking to collect benefits from the copyright owner who is seeking to be relieved of harm. The copyright owner who seeks a fee from someone who caused no substitutionary harm is merely seeking a benefit.

One final note on foregone fees. It is sometimes said that the "harmful" status of foregone fees is a circular inquiry.[117] The argument goes like this: if the defendant is infringing, then the failure to pay is a harm. If the defendant is not infringing, then the failure to pay is not a harm. Because everything depends on the law, and the question to be decided is whether the law makes the defendant's use "fair" or infringing, inquiry into harm is merely circular and cannot be of assistance.

However, this accusation of circularity is valid only under one sub-definition of harm, one that is not much used: namely, that "harm" arises whenever the plaintiff is less well off than he or she would have been had the defendant acted properly. This is indeed circular, because the definition of proper action will depend on what the law requires.

But this variant of the counterfactual approach is rarely used. Feinberg mentions the possibility of such a variant to solve a particular problem, but other resolutions of the problem are available. The troublesome hypothetical is this: a doctor helps his patient somewhat, but not as much as the doctor should have done.[118] To say that such a doctor "harmed" the patient is difficult under the usual counterfactual test, because without the interaction the patient would be worse off. The doctor actually improved the patient's health, albeit not as much as he should have done.[119]

Feinberg takes the usual question, of whether an affected party's condition was "in a worse condition . . . than it would be had A not acted as he did," and says what happened to the patient can be called a harm "provided we interpret 'as he did' to refer in part to the defective aspects of A's actions."[120] Consistent with that potential approach, Feinberg goes on to speculate in a footnote that "the counterfactual condition should perhaps be revised to read: *B's* personal interest is in a worse state than it would be had A acted as he *should have* instead of as he *did*."[121] Under such a revised test, the patient would be said to be "harmed" if he received care that was helpful but below a reasonable standard.

There are real difficulties with Feinberg's tentatively revised definition. (I say "tentative" because in the article Feinberg does not commit to it; he uses the locutions of "provided" and "perhaps"). As noted, a definition of harm that refers to what the other party *should* have done invites circularity; this is true in morals as well as in law. Whether an action causes "harm" sometimes usefully contributes to a decision regarding whether the action is wrongful, but a definition based on

[117] *See, e.g.*, Lydia Pallas Loren, *Redefining the Market Failure Approach to Fair Use in an Era of Copyright Permission Systems*, 5 J. INTELL. PROP. L. 1 (1997).

[118] Feinberg, *supra* note 83, at 149–50.

[119] *Id.*

[120] *Id.* at 149.

[121] *Id.* at 150 n.5.

what the other party "should have done" undercuts that possibility by disabling "harm" from serving as an independent criterion. Further, as a legal matter, little is advanced by calling what happened to the patient a harm, because wrongs can exist *without* harms. (Trespass to land is an example.) In this case, the patient probably had no need to prove harm as philosophers define it; he was probably entitled under contract or the law of medical malpractice to the "benefit" of a standard of reasonable treatment.

A defender of Feinberg's tentative revision might say that if the law gives someone an entitlement to a benefit, then that entitlement becomes the person's new baseline, and any shortfall from a baseline is a harm. That is conceivable, but not helpful. Calling the doctor's partial assistance a "harm" seems like a misuse of everyday speech. Calling foregone license fees a "harm" in the absence of rivalry for customers similarly seems like a misuse of ordinary speech.[122]

C. *Subjective Distress*

Subjective distress easily meets the historical-worsening test. After the unconsented copying, plaintiffs feel worse than they felt before it; they feel anger or some other form of emotional reaction that to them feels like it requires recompense.[123] Similarly, subjective distress easily meets the counterfactual test. Without the interaction with the defendant copyist, there would be no distress. Should there be additional copyists in the wings, there are standard moves to cure the overdetermination (such as adding a disjunctive historical-worsening test or counting as a harm-causer any act that was "sufficient" to bring about the loss).

There are many problems with counting subjective distress as a "harm." For one thing, subjective distress does not have a sensible analogue when addressing copyright owners that are corporations. Another difficulty with subjective distress is that it may lack the gravity that gives harm its usual moral significance.[124] Distress at being copied might be so widespread that, if it is given legal weight, it could squelch autonomous development in other persons. Much of what John Stuart Mill attacks in writing *On Liberty* is paternalistic and moralistic social control; the judgment of the state about what was good for people deprived the affected individuals of

[122] Defenders of the tentative revision might also point out that tort law, including medical malpractice, usually involves proof of plaintiff's harm. I would reply that "harm" in that context merely means "a physical result that was less than the result to which the patient was entitled" and that harm in moral discourse usually means something other than that. *See* Perry, *supra* note 59, who uses quite different standards for legal and moral definitions of harm. The instant essay contends that moral conceptions of "harm" can be useful in certain legal disputes, but does not contend that legal and moral conceptions of harm are always and necessarily the same.

[123] Thompson points out that some forms of emotional reaction to misfortune are not unpleasant; self-righteous anger can be one such. JUDITH JARVIS THOMPSON, THE REALM OF RIGHTS (1990) at 251–60. But because anger can conceivably discourage productivity, it is worth including it on a list of relevant subjective distress.

[124] This seems to be an important part of Shiffrin's point, though she would put the analysis in terms of autonomy rather than welfare.

the opportunities for self-development that choice affords. Moralistic laws seem to be motivated by the anger, sense of outrage, and psychological distress that some classes of people seem to feel at the "deviant" behavior of other groups of people. For reasons such as these, philosophers have a hearty doubt about whether "distress" should count as harm. Judith Jarvis Thompson goes so far as to say that any distress that rests on a belief should not count as harm.[125]

Distress experienced by copyright owners when their work is copied without their permission is indeed mediated by beliefs. Respecting their distress is unlikely to result in the kind of sexual moralizing legislation against which Mill's Harm Principle was probably intended to operate; nevertheless, if copyright law gave too much weight to their distress, that would pose strong dangers to free speech.

This is not to claim that subjective distress at being copied is inevitably minor. Jessica Silbey, in her interviews with creative persons, reports that emotional or dignitary harm arising out of reputational injury is more likely than minor loss of profits to trigger a desire to sue.[126] Feeling that one is taken advantage of unjustly is part of the emotional distress. Ernst Fehr and others have proven that many people are willing to pay to satisfy their sense of justice,[127] suggesting that the taste for justice is not trivial. But whether justice seekers are paying to redress harm to themselves or merely to satisfy a taste (for a "benefit") is a harder question. Jessica Silbey's interviews with the creative community suggest these noneconomic perceptions of harm really matter to the artists, filmmakers, and the like she has queried.[128] If incentives matter, then these frustrations and sources of anger might matter.

One question on this chapter's agenda is what kinds of harm should make a difference to a copyright infringement case, particularly when fair use is the issue. Given the dependence of many subjective reactions on an author's expectations and beliefs, allowing subjective distress to count as a harm would seem to run afoul of the destructive feedback loops that James Gibson[129] and others have identified. Further, in Seana Shiffrin's terms, we want to avoid counting any frustration of desire as a harm.[130] Such an equation between frustration and harm would wipe out the distinction between harm and benefit and would be inconsistent with the moral significance usually give harm. So deciding how to treat these noneconomic harms is very difficult.

125 THOMPSON, *supra* note 123; Shiffrin, *Harm and Its Moral Significance*, *supra* note 48.

126 Silbey, supra note 73, at 2121. Ironically, Professor Silbey's respondents tended to phrase their sense of injury in such instances by using images and rhetoric from tangible property, *id.* at 2121–22.

127 *See, e.g.*, Ernst Fehr & Simon Gachter, *Cooperation and Punishment in Public Good Experiments*, 90 AM. ECON. REV. 980 (2000).

128 Conversation with Jessica Silbey (March 5, 2012); *see also* Silbey, *supra* note 73.

129 James Gibson, *Risk Aversion and Rights Accretion in Intellectual Property Law*, 116 YALE L.J. 882, 884–885 (2007).

130 Shiffrin, *Harm and Its Moral Significance*, *supra* note 48, at 42 n43.

One issue here is gravity: whether it is appropriate to use the term "harm" to describe emotional reactions of distress and indignation in circumstances where the emotions (being related to one's work being copied) do not usually cause physical harm. Are such emotions grave and serious enough to warrant restraints to compel third parties to avoid causing the distress? Another issue is copyright tradition. I know of no case where compensation for emotional impact proved part of a copyright owner's remedy. (But traditions are changing; § 106A of the Copyright Act does give some protection to reputation, injuries to which are in part psychological.) Also important is the potential for expansion if subjective distress is recognized as harm. Belief-based emotional reactions are something over which people ordinarily have some control[131] – and beliefs are subject to manipulation. As for copyright's incentive purposes, we have information that distress at being copied exists, but whether such distress discourages future creativity is a more open question. Finally, being restrained from speaking in another's voice may be as subjectively distressing to the putative defendant (or even more distressing) as being copied is to the plaintiff; consider for example how, to be effective, someone badly affected by a literary work might need to employ that work's characters or tropes to undo the damage done him or her.[132]

For all these reasons, my own instinct is that subjective distress should not be counted as harm. Belief-mediated harms are particularly dangerous for us to honor. If there are emotional reactions that are not belief-mediated – if, perhaps, there is a basic human instinct to feel hurt if one's creative work is copied – I would come to the same conclusion. Subjective distress may be "harm" in some contexts, such as in the tort of intentional infliction of emotional distress, but should not count as such in copyright. The purposes for which we use "harm" as a moral category – a concern inter alia with gravity, with the separateness of persons, with autonomy, and with parsing the proper role of state coercion – do not seem to justify weighing a plaintiff's emotional distress against fair use.

CONCLUSION

Introducing additional requirements into the plaintiff's cause of action raises enticing possibilities for trimming copyright overgrowth. Unfortunately, one tempting candidate – requiring plaintiffs to prove "harm" – is currently insufficiently specified to accomplish the task. This chapter unpacks the current structure of the infringement tort, and lays out conceptual and policy questions that should be addressed before

[131] See the sources cited in notes 108–10.

[132] For examples see Gordon, *supra* note 30, at 1583–1605. As a child, writer Alice Randall was badly affected by the depiction of African Americans in the novel *Gone with the Wind*; to respond effectively, she needed to use some of the novel's characters in her own book. Suntrust Bank v. Houghton Mifflin Co., 268 F.3d 1257 (11th Cir.), *reh'g en banc denied*, 275 F.3d 58 (Table) (11th Cir. 2001).

"harm" is given a more prominent place in the world of copyright. The chapter also suggests some answers for the challenges so outlined.

The chapter begins by using the tort of "trespass to land" to highlight the roles that "fault" (in the sense of disserving social welfare) and "harm" already play in copyright infringement. A trespass plaintiff only need prove entry. Fault is so irrelevant to trespass that a landowner can collect money even from a defendant acting rightfully. (E.g., someone who enters another's land out of necessity, and non-negligently causes some harm, must pay.) By contrast, copyright plaintiffs must stand ready to disprove a defendant's showing of faultlessness (social merit) under the doctrinal category of "fair use." Moreover, copyright law requires plaintiffs to prove more than an entry-equivalent; inherent in the current doctrinal requirement that "substantial similarity" be shown lays a requirement to prove at least a possibility of harm. So, I argue, harm and fault already play some role in copyright.

The chapter then investigates what shape the copyright tort should take were it to be ideally reformulated. In particular, I investigate what kinds of "harm" might properly be cognizable. The chapter examines four candidates: losses imposed by rivalry, revenue foregone because of a nonrivalrous defendant's failure to pay license fees, loss of exclusivity, and subjective distress. Of these, the chapter argues that copyright should recognize only the effects of rivalry as constituting "harm." The chapter also canvasses three philosophic approaches to harm, namely, historical-worsening, counterfactual, and noncomparative.

It is popular to urge the use of "minimum incentives" as the baseline from which to calculate authorial harm. Advocates of a minimum-incentives baseline are implicitly urging a partly noncomparative approach to defining harm. If a plaintiff had to prove injury to minimum incentives in order to prevail, courts might give defendants who did the same kind of copying different treatment depending not on how each differentially affected a plaintiff's welfare, but rather on how a plaintiff's temporal welfare compared with some standard of need. The result would be a lack of horizontal equity. This might not be fatal – after all, other forms of tort law tolerate "luck" factors such as a plaintiff's pre-existing health affecting the extent of liability. Nevertheless, the chapter cautions against generally employing a minimum-incentives baseline.

The chapter itself adopts, in one context, a noncomparative concern with gravity. The chapter suggests that the failure of a nonrivalrous defendant to pay license fees is a "benefit foregone" rather than "harm." Nevertheless, I argue, when a plaintiff can show grave need, that should serve (in our future amended tort of copyright infringement) to make foregone fees weighable against that defendant in the fair use calculus.

21

The Role of Unfair Competition in the Common Law

Shyamkrishna Balganesh and Gideon Parchomovsky***

INTRODUCTION

Does the idea of "unfair competition" present the law with a viable alternative to thinking about the regulation of information and informational resources, independent of the traditional categories of the common law (e.g., property/tort) and the assumptions that these categories entail? In this chapter, we argue that, although the answer to that question is no, unfair competition nevertheless plays an important role in complementing the categories of property and torts as they apply to competitive settings. Specifically, unfair competition allows courts to both broaden and narrow the traditional notions of property and torts – especially as they apply to the regulation of information and intangibles – by infusing the values of fairness and ethics into business interactions characterized by rivalry and a desire to maximize one's profits. Unfair competition law grants common law judges the discretion and flexibility needed to ensure constructive competition, on the one hand, and to thwart destructive competitive tactics, on the other. Essentially then, unfair competition functions as a safety valve or residual category that enables equity and common law courts to expand the relatively rigid rules of property and torts in appropriate cases.

It is precisely for this reason that unfair competition has historically never lent itself to easy classification. At the same time, the complementary and composite nature of unfair competition also guarantees, we believe, its long-term sustainability. Although the role of unfair competition has diminished relative to what it was in the past due to the expansion of related areas such as trademark, antitrust law, and federal preemption, rumors about the demise of unfair competition are somewhat

* Assistant Professor of Law, University of Pennsylvania Law School.

** Professor of Law, University of Pennsylvania Law School and Bar-Ilan University School of Law. We would like to thank the participants at the symposium on Intellectual Property and the Common Law, held at the University of Pennsylvania Law School on May 6–7, 2011, for helpful comments and suggestions. Eric Hague, Penn Law class of 2013, and Jane Marie Russell, Penn Law class of 2014, provided very helpful research assistance. All errors are our own.

premature. Indeed, we believe that unfair competition will continue to serve in its traditional complementary role and to provide a useful benchmark for courts in delineating the scope of property, tort, and trademark doctrine in this area.

In Part I, we discuss the evolution of unfair competition law from its origins in equity until its codification in the *Restatement*. In Part II, we set out to place unfair competition in the broader scheme of the common law. Specifically, we explore the role of unfair competition both as a common law structural category and as an independent normative goal within the common law. In Part III, we reflect on the future on unfair competition.

I. THE EVOLUTION OF UNFAIR COMPETITION LAW AS AN IDEA IN THE COMMON LAW

The law of unfair competition has a long, albeit confusing, history. The body of law that has become known as unfair competition developed from two categories of cases, those involving "Rights Analogous to those of Trade-Marks" and those involving "The Action for 'Passing off.'"[1] The difference between the two categories of cases that gave birth to unfair competition is so subtle that it is probably lost on most, if not all, contemporary scholars. And for a good reason: scholars intent on getting to the bottom of the issue will find themselves caught in a legal vicious cycle.

As Rudolph Callmann explains, "the concept of Unfair Competition in the United States is the equivalent of 'passing off' in England."[2] He then proceeds to note that "in England the judicial approach to an action to restrain a defendant from 'passing off' his goods as the plaintiff's goods is identical with that pursued in an action to restrain the infringement of a technical trade-mark."[3] In the United States too there existed an inexorable relation between unfair competition and the law of trademarks, as "an action for trademark infringement is the legal remedy for the protection of technical trademarks, and unfair competition is the analogous remedy for the protection of trade names."[4]

Substantively, however, as befits a doctrine that has been developed by the courts of equity, unfair competition served a broader purpose than technical trademark or trade-name protection. Originally, unfair competition complemented trademark law by affording protection to trade names that failed to comply with the mandates of statutory trademark law.[5] It stood as a general bar against passing off, embodying the principle "that no one should be allowed to sell his goods as those of another."[6] Over time, however, the law of unfair competition was expanded to cases in which

[1] Oliver R. Mitchell, *Unfair Competition*, 10 HARV. L.REV. 275 (1896).
[2] Rudolph Callmann, *Unfair Competition Without Competition?*, 95 U. PA. L. REV. 443, 444 (1947).
[3] *Id.* at 444.
[4] *Id.* at 444.
[5] *Id.* at 444.
[6] White Tower Sys. v. White Castle Sys. of Eating Houses Corp., 90 F.2d 67, 69 (6th Cir. 1937).

there was no actual passing off, and it developed into a general set of principles that regulated competition in the business realm. In this part, we discuss the historical development of unfair competition, place it within the broader scheme of private law, and unearth its normative foundations.

The classic case of *Keeble* v. *Hickeringill*[7] of 1707 is considered by some theorists as the first unfair competition case.[8] This is not technically correct. As any first-year law student would recall, in *Keeble*, the owner of a decoy duck pond brought an action of trespass on the case against a neighbor who intentionally fired off his gun to scare the ducks away. The court found that the neighbor's actions constituted malicious interference with the trade or livelihood of another. The court further stated that Hickeringill could have set up his own decoy pond and competed over wild fowl with Keeble; had he done so, there would be no cause of action against him.

As Judge Holt elucidated,

> This is like the case of 11 Hen. IV p. 47. One schoolmaster sets up a new school to the damage of an ancient school, and thereby the scholars are allured from the old school to come to his new. (The action there was held not to lie.) But suppose Mr. Hickeringill should lie in the way with his guns and frighten the boys from going to school and their parents would not let them go thither sure that schoolmaster might have an action for the loss of his scholars. 29 Edw III p. 18.

It is perhaps for this reason that commentators viewed this decision as the progenitor or, at least, the harbinger of unfair competition law. But the parties were not in fact competitors. Hence, it is problematic to attribute to it the onset of unfair competition law. The fact that *Keeble* involved no trademark claim should give one an additional reason to doubt that pedigree of *Keeble* as an unfair competition case because there is virtually a scholarly consensus among commentators that unfair competition and trademark law developed in tandem.[9]

Another interesting tidbit about the case is that it is pegged under the rubric of property rather than torts; it should be noted that the court did not award Keeble compensation for the value of lost fowl, but rather for the interference with his use of his property. In modern terminology, the case would have been brought as a nuisance case and could therefore be fitted either under the category of property or torts.

As we show, the challenge of classifying unfair competition cases is still very much with us today. Unfair competition never lent itself to easy classifications. We return to this point later in this chapter.

7 Keeble v. Hickeringill, (1707) 11 East 574, 103 Eng. Rep. 1127 (Q.B.).

8 *E.g.*, Zechariah Chaffee, Jr., *Unfair Competition*, 53 HARV. L. REV. 1289, 1290–91 (1940) (opening his discussion of unfair competition law with *Keeble*).

9 Charles Grove Haines, *Efforts to Define Unfair Competition*, 29 YALE L.J. 1, 2 (1919) (noting that "[u]nfair competition appears to have been used at first in connection with the efforts of the courts to protect trade-marks."). But he also notes that some of the first cases involved inducement of breach of a competitor's contract, interference in a contractual relationship, and disclosure or use of trade secrets. *Id.* at 6.

But if not *Keeble*, what was the first unfair competition case? A less famous but more likely candidate for the title is the 1836 case of *Knott* v. *Morgan*.[10] There, the plaintiffs, operators of a bus service, sued and secured an injunction against a competing service that copied the distinctive color pattern of the plaintiffs' buses, as well as the uniforms of its employees. In ruling for the plaintiffs, Lord Langdale reasoned that the defendants "could not deprive the plaintiffs of the fair profits of their business by attracting custom upon the false representation that carriages, really the defendants', belonged to, and were under the management of, the plaintiffs."[11]

The decision was innovative in two important respects: first, it awarded the plaintiffs protection, even though they did not have a formal exclusive right in the paint patterns of the buses or the uniforms of the employees and therefore could not sue for a trademark infringement. Second, the protection in this case did not attach to a good that was sold on the market, a sine qua non for bringing a trademark infringement suit.[12]

Although *Morgan* broadened the legal protection granted to business beyond the traditional scope of trademark law, it was predicated on the same legal philosophy that underlined trademark infringement cases, namely the desire to prevent businesses from passing off other's goods and services as their own. This principle stood at the foundation of all early unfair competition decisions.

In his classic article on the subject, Oliver Mitchell noted that the rationale behind unfair competition decisions was to protect the good will of business. As he wrote, "That good will is a thing of value, and a subject of property, was very early recognized, and it is now well settled."[13] In elaborating on this point, Mitchell explained the contours of unfair competition as it was developed by the equity courts:

> The notion of property in good will, and the constituent parts of good will, is of the highest importance, as upon it from the first the jurisdiction of equity has been solely based, and from this idea has flowed the fundamental rule that to recover the plaintiff must show a right at the very least as against the defendant. The courts have proceeded upon the theory of protecting property where the legal remedy was inadequate or illusory, or irreparable damage possible. Protection of the public from deception has been more than once put forward as a ground for interference, but it is well settled that equity has no jurisdiction upon this ground. Deception of the public is material only as the test of infringement, and as bearing upon the question of damages.[14]

Furthermore, Mitchell then divided the first generation of cases into five prototypes: dressing up cases, substitution cases, business names cases, trade name cases, and trade secrets cases. Dressing up cases rested on accumulated resemblances between

10 2 Keen, 213 (1836).
11 *Id.* at 219.
12 Mitchell, *supra* note 1, at 277.
13 *Id.* at 280.
14 *Id.* at 281.

the defendant's business and the plaintiff's cases. *Knott* v. *Morgan* provides an example of a dressing up case. Indeed, the court there noted that the "accumulation of resemblances" in this case entitled the plaintiff to a remedy.[15]

Weinstock v. *Marks*[16] is another case falling into this category. There, the defendant set up his business to look exactly the same as the plaintiff's building. As a result, customers wandered into the defendant's business believing that they were actually frequenting the plaintiff's. The court ordered the defendant to alter the appearance of its business in a way that would make it distinguishable from the plaintiff's.

Over time, courts abandoned the requirement for accumulation of resemblances and awarded remedy in cases in which the resemblance was limited to a *single* particular business aspect. For example, in *Von Mumm* v. *Frash*,[17] the court enjoined the defendant from using a rose-colored capsule. Likewise, in *Cook* v. *Ross*,[18] the court recognized an exclusive right in the plaintiff to use an unusually shaped bottle.

The second category, substitution cases, was essentially the mirror image of dressing up cases. It consisted of cases in which a business used the package of another, but substituted the original product for an inferior one. The cases of *Hennessy* v. *Horgan*[19] and *Hennessy* v. *White*,[20] which share the same basic facts, provide a useful illustration. In both cases, the plaintiff, a liquor manufacturer who sold two types of brandy – premium brandy in bottles and inferior quality brandy in bulk – brought suits against two competitors that bought the bulk brandy, poured it into bottles, and offered it for sale as the premium brandy. The court granted the plaintiff an injunction.

The third category involved protection for business names. It should be noted at the outset that business names received more qualified protection than other trade names because others with the same name were allowed to use it. However, where the use of a name by two different businesses was likely to result in confusion, courts intervened. Consider the case of *Johann Hoff* v. *Tarrant & Co.*,[21] where the plaintiff who sold "Hoff's Malt Extract" in the United States brought suit against the defendant after he started to import and sell malt extract made by Leopold Hoff. The court ordered the defendant to label his products "Leopold Hoff's Malt Extract," and not "Hoff's Malt Extract."

The fourth category consisted of cases in which one competitor attempted to benefit from the trade name of another. For instance, in *Merriam* v. *Texas Sifting Publishing Co.*,[22] the plaintiff, publisher of the Webster Dictionary, sued another business that advertised a reprint of the 1847 edition after its copyright expired as

[15] Knott v. Morgan, 2 Keen, 213.
[16] 109 Cal. 529, 42 P. 142 (1895).
[17] 56 Fed. Rep. 830 (C.C.D.N.Y. 1893).
[18] 73 F. 203 (C.C.S.D.N.Y. 1896).
[19] (1869) 6 W.W. & A'B. 225 (Austl.).
[20] (1869) 6 W.W. & A'B. 216 (Austl.).
[21] 71 F. 163 (C.C.S.D.N.Y. 1896).
[22] 49 F. 944 (C.C.S.D.N.Y. 1892).

"the latest edition" for one-eighth of the original price – $1 instead of $8. The court enjoined the defendant from continuing to publish such advertisements in the future.

Likewise, in *Orr, Ewing & Co.* v. *Johnson*,[23] the plaintiffs had an unregistered trademark for yarn featuring an illustration of two elephants. The trademark was denied registration because elephants were deemed generic to the trade. The defendant began to export yarn and attached to it a ticket similar in shape and color to that of the plaintiff, featuring two elephants with a different appearance. Despite the differences in the appearance, the court found that consumers in India may be deceived and issued an injunction.

The fifth category included cases of misappropriation of trade secrets. The courts of equity strove to prevent disclosure of trade secrets by employees or their appropriation by fraudulent or illegal means by competitors. The classic case of *Peabody* v. *Norfolk*[24] is illustrative. The plaintiff brought suit against a former employee, alleging that he left him to join a competitor and undertook to build his new employer a factory with machines that were copies of the plaintiff's and that used his secret processes. The court found for the plaintiff.

It is important to clarify that, although unfair competition law was originally closely related to trademark law, it soon expanded far beyond trademark law. Mitchell correctly summarized the relationship between the two bodies of law when he observed: "[l]ogically speaking, the fact is that Unfair Competition is a generic title, of which trademark is a specific division."[25] This view was echoed by Justice Pitney in *Hanover Star Milling Co.* v. *Metcalf*,[26] when he wrote that "the common law of trade-marks is but a part of the law of unfair competition."

Indeed, the law of unfair competition evolved so fast that it reached far beyond the five categories enumerated by Mitchell.[27] Unfair competition has been considered a very broad legal category in which courts were given very broad discretion. As one commentator pointed out, the law of unfair competition expanded over time to cover all remedies at law and equity relating to "the entire field of infringement in patent law, trade-marks, and copy-rights; the protection of goodwill, trade-names, and trade secrets; and all undue interferences with the normal current of a business enterprise."[28] This description was endorsed by Charles Haines, who characterized the evolution of unfair competition as follows: "unfair competition was used in a general sense to include trade-mark infringement, passing off, and other business

[23] 40 L. T. 307.

[24] 98 Mass. 452 (1868).

[25] Mitchell, *supra* note 1, at 275.

[26] 240 U.S. 403, 413, (1915).

[27] To be fair to Mitchell, it should be noted that his enumeration was not meant to be exhaustive. In fact, his article contains references to other cases in which unfair competition law has been employed by courts.

[28] 13 Ill. L. Rev. 708, 717 (1919).

practices regarded illegal. And this general, all-inclusive meaning seems to be gaining ground."[29]

It is therefore, not surprising, that unfair competition law was extended to business practices that had originally lain outside its purview. In other areas, the role of unfair competition was gradually increased to regulate economic activities. Two such developments are of particular interest for our discussion.

The first one was the extension of unfair competition to afford a remedy to famous businesses whose trademarks were imitated by *non*competitors. The assertion of unfair competition claims against noncompetitors puzzled commentators and struck them as a contradiction in terms. It prompted Callmann to write an article titled "Unfair Competition without Competition?"[30] that opened with this statement: "[i]t should be elementary even to a 'Dr. Watson' that, absent competition, there can be no unfair competition, and that the phrase unfair competition without competition contains a basic contradiction in terms."[31]

Yet, the courts had little difficulty in assuaging the strictures of formal logic and permitted businesses to bring unfair competition claims against noncompetitors. For example, in *Wall* v. *Rolls-Royce of America*,[32] the famous automobile manufacturer brought suit against a radio tube maker that operated under an identical name. Even though the plaintiff and defendant were not in the same trade, the court found the suit meritorious and found for Rolls-Royce. In *Vogue Co.* v. *Thompson-Hudson Co.*,[33] the famous fashion magazine sued a department store that offered hats for sale under the vaunted name of the magazine. The court enjoined the practice, reasoning that the public may be deceived to think that the magazine is somehow associated with the hats, whereas in fact it was not. Similarly, in *Tiffany & Co.* v. *Tiffany Productions*,[34] the renowned jeweler sought remedy against a motion picture theater that operated under the same name. The court awarded the requested remedy, explaining that the use of the name by the defendant may lead to whittling away or dispersion of the name, which was also the plaintiff's mark.

As any contemporary reader will surely recognize, these and other similar cases presaged the doctrine of dilution in trademark law. And although the extension of unfair competition law to noncompetitors seems to be problematic from the standpoint of formal logic, substantively this development was a natural step forward in keeping with the underlying rationale of all unfair competition cases. At the basis of the extension of unfair competition law to cases involving noncompetitors stood the desire to protect good will and prevent other business entities from appropriating

[29] Haines, *supra* note 9, at 9.
[30] Callmann, *supra* note 2, at 443.
[31] *Id.*
[32] 4 F.2d 333 (3rd Cir. 1925).
[33] 300 F. 509 (6th Cir. 1924), reh'g denied, 12 F.2d 991 (6th Cir. 1926), cert. denied, 273 U.S. 706 (1926).
[34] 147 Misc. 679, 264 N.Y.S. 459 (Sup. Ct. 1932), 260 N.Y.S. 821 (App. Div. 1932), aff'd, 262 N.Y. 482, 188 N.E. 30 (1933).

or capturing the value inherent in good will. A reading of the opinions reveals that the judges were worried about the twin risks of passing off and consumer deception.

The second development that deserves mention here is the expansive use made of unfair competition to combat agreements in restraint of trade. Unfair competition was once the legal instrument of choice in the battle against various practices intended to dampen competition in the marketplace. Virtually all the activities currently addressed by antitrust law came under the aegis of unfair competition law. The enactment of the Sherman Act supplanted to a large extent this function of unfair competition law. Indeed, it can be counted as one of the primary reasons for the decline in the import of unfair competition. However, antitrust law did not render unfair competition redundant even in this context; it did not fully preempt unfair competition. Businesses can still rely on unfair competition doctrine to bring claims that are not covered by the Sherman Act.[35]

But what happened with the Sherman Act is emblematic of the general trend. It is not the process of codification as such that eroded the status of unfair competition. True, many states codified the law of unfair competition, but this is not what led to the decline in its import. The expansion of other legal doctrines, such as antitrust, trade secrets, and, of course, trademark law, pushed unfair competition to the backstage. Unfair competition claims can still be found in most cases of trademark infringements and trade secrets misappropriation, but it plays a secondary role.

Yet the effect of the expansion of adjacent fields on unfair competition should not be overstated. Unfair competition has not been condemned to exist in a legal Purgatorium, nor has it been relegated to a secondary role in all legal contexts. Even after the expansion in the scope of antitrust, trademark, and trade secret laws, those laws fall short of addressing all unethical and illegal business practices. Some such practices, such as fraudulent misrepresentations, are covered by the law of torts and perhaps even by securities regulation law. More subtle deviations from business norms and practices, especially if espoused in bad faith, remain in the exclusive domain of unfair competition.

As an illustration consider the case of *Tuttle* v. *Buck*,[36] where a banker who harbored a profound dislike for the local barber resolved to open a rival business for the sole purpose of ruining the barber's business and depriving him of his livelihood. The court ruled for the barber and awarded him substantial damages. *Tuttle* brings us full circle; it is considered the modern-day version of the antiquated case of the

[35] *See e.g.*, Natural Design, Inc. v. Rouse Co., 302 Md. 47, 485 A.2d 663 (1984) (discussing illegal restraints on trade as a form of unfair competition); Ron Tonkin Gran Turismo, Inc. v. Wakehouse Motors, Inc., 46 Or. App. 199, 611 P.2d 658 (Ct. App. 1980) (same); C.E. Services, Inc. v. Control Data Corp., 759 F.2d 1241 (5th Cir. 1985), *cert. denied* 474 U.S. 1037, 106 S.Ct. 604, 88 L.Ed.2d 583 (1985) (discussing allegations of predatory pricing as unfair competition); SuperTurf, Inc. v. Monsanto Co., 660 F.2d 1275 (8th Cir. 1981) (discussing allegation of collusion between architect and bidder as unfair competition).

[36] 107 Minn. 145, 119 N.W. 946 (1909).

schoolmaster who threatened students of a rival school, which we discussed at the beginning of this part. This is not accidental. As we explain later, unfair competition law embodies a rich set of values that lie at the foundation of our legal tradition, and therefore it cannot be easily replaced by other legal doctrines.

II. FORM AND SUBSTANCE IN UNFAIR COMPETITION LAW

The idea of using "unfair competition" as a common-law–based organizing principle for the regulation of informational resources is hardly new.[37] Yet, there remain two independent analytical ways in which the idea of unfair competition is deployed in these contexts. This part attempts to disaggregate these two methods and set out the consequences that flow from adopting one or the other.

Determining how and why categories evolve in the common law remains a puzzle that continues to confound courts and scholars.[38] On the one hand, the common law's historical insistence on parties' use of very specific "forms of action" to commence a lawsuit had the effect of allowing courts to classify the rules and principles that they developed into categories that tracked these forms (e.g., "trespass," "case," "assumpsit," etc.).[39] The classification was thus largely structural and, without question, rigidly formalistic. In due course, however, the common law came to relax its strict insistence on these different forms. When it also came to be merged with the law of equity, the forms of action ceased to provide courts with an a priori basis on which to classify newly developed rules. Here, a mixture of path dependence, instrumentalism, and structural argumentation resulted in courts (and scholars) developing their own set of principles and norms by which to classify and understand the common law.[40] This part argues that one can in fact discern a nascent analytical framework that courts and scholars came to deploy in classifying a distinct set of common law rules under the head of "unfair competition."

The two basic analytic mechanisms of categorization identified here are (i) categorization based on *structural principles* and (ii) categorization around a *normative ideal* (or set of ideals). Structure-based classification was for long thought to be the

37 Indeed this development is usually traced back to trademark law and the law of misappropriation originating in the Supreme Court's decision in *International News*. *See* Edward S. Rogers, *Unfair Competition*, 17 Mich. L. Rev. 490 (1919); *infra* Part II (for a fuller history of the idea and its development).

38 *See, e.g.*, The Classification of Obligations (Peter Birks ed., 1997); Saul Levmore, *A Theory of Deception and then of Common Law Categories*, 85 Tex. L. Rev. 1359 (2007).

39 Frederick William Maitland, The Forms of Action at Common Law 1 (A. H. Chaytor & W. J. Whittaker eds., 1936).

40 *See, e.g.*, Oliver Wendell Holmes, Jr., *The Path of the Law*, 10 Harv. L. Rev. 457 (1897); Paul H. Rubin, *Why Is the Common Law Efficient?*, 6 J. Legal Stud. 51 (1977); Oona A. Hathaway, *Path Dependence in the Law: The Course and Pattern of Legal Change in a Common Law System*, 86 Iowa L. Rev. 601 (2000).

hallmark of the common law – given its origins in very specific forms of action.[41] The law of contract was for instance taken to be principally about consensual obligations, where the existence of consent (in some form) formed the structural basis around which the law recognized a set of enforceable obligations.[42]A consensual/voluntary undertaking is in this conception taken to be the structural basis of contract law. Classification based on the function/purpose of the law is, by contrast, rarely ever seen in actual common law opinions, even though it assumes prominence in scholarly writing.[43] Judge Hand's approach to the law of negligence – as the law of optimal precautions – is perhaps a good example of a strictly functional approach to the common law seen in judicial opinions.[44] One might also argue that the law of restitution for unjust enrichment represents a similar functional commitment to the principles of distributive justice, broadly understood.[45]

It should be emphasized that the two categories are not mutually exclusive. In fact, all common law structures advanced some normative purpose. The two categories are thus hardly watertight and are offered here largely for analytical precision. The focus of our investigation is to determine whether courts view unfair competition as an independent structural category of the common law or, rather, as a branch of law representing a unique set of normative goals.[46]

A. *Unfair Competition as a Structural Mechanism*

Even when unfair competition was at the peak of its import, commentators struggled to place it within the general framework of the common law. The following statement made by Callmann more than sixty years ago captured the challenge of classifying unfair competition:

> The law of unfair competition is still in a disordered and incompletely developed state. It is not yet on a par with the exclusive fraternity of such respectable legal families as contracts, torts, trusts, agencies, etc.[47]

In particular, it was unclear whether unfair competition belonged under the rubric of property or the rubric of tort. Initially, unfair competition seemed to be grounded

[41] *But see* Guido Calabresi, *Toward a Unified Theory of Tort Law*, 1 J. TORT L. 1, 4–7 (2007) (arguing that the common law's structural categories did have a functional significance).

[42] ANDREW ROBERTSON, THE LAW OF OBLIGATIONS: CONNECTIONS AND BOUNDARIES 112 (2004) (discussing the categorization of contract law around the idea of consent).

[43] *See* Levmore, *supra* note 38, at 1371, 1375 (making this point in relation to judicial opinions and observing common law judges as minimalists). For a prominent scholarly example of a functional classification see Richard A. Posner, *A Theory of Negligence*, 1 J. LEGAL STUD. 29 (1972).

[44] *See* U.S. v. Carroll Towing Co., 159 F.2d 169, 173 (2d Cir. 1947); Allan M. Feldman, & Jeonghyun Kim, *The Hand Rule and* United States v. Carroll Towing Co. *Reconsidered*, 7 AMER. L. & ECON. REV. 523, 524 (2005) (noting how Judge Hand threw rational cost-benefit analysis into the law).

[45] *See* HANOCH DAGAN, THE LAW AND ETHICS OF RESTITUTION xi (2004).

[46] For an obvious criticism of this approach, *see* Duncan Kennedy, *Form and Substance in Private Law Adjudication*, 89 Harv. L. Rev. 1685, 1724 (1976).

[47] Callmann, *supra* note 2, at 444.

in the notion of property. Property rhetoric featured prominently in the early unfair competition cases. For example, in his attempt to capture the essence of unfair competition, Haines listed an invasion of a property right as a prerequisite for bringing legal action.[48]

The association between unfair competition and property grew out of the tendency of the English courts to view trademarks as property. Lord Cottenham introduced this view in the 1838 case of *Millington* v. *Fox*.[49] It was subsequently affirmed by Lord Westbury in *Edelsten* v. *Edelsten*, where he wrote, "[a]t law the proper remedy is by an action on the case for deceit: and proof of fraud on the part of the defendant is of the essence of the action: but this Court will act on the principle of protecting property alone, and it is not necessary for the injunction to prove fraud in the defendant, or that the credit of the plaintiff is injured by the sale of an inferior article."[50] It was also adopted by Lord Blackburn, who opined in *Hall* v. *Barrows* that "both trade-marks and trade names are in a certain sense property."[51]

A similar approach was initially taken by the U.S. courts. In the Trade-Mark cases, the Supreme Court pronounced that the right to appropriate and use a trademark

> is a property right for the violation of which damages may be recovered in an action at law, and the continued violation of it will be enjoined by a court of equity, with compensation for past infringement. This exclusive right was not created by the act of Congress, and does not now depend upon it for its enforcement. The whole system of trade-mark property and the civil remedies for its protection existed long anterior to that act, and have remained in full force since its passage.[52]

However, in a series of decisions Justice Holmes cast doubt on the classification of trademarks as property. Holmes himself went back and forth on this issue. In *Chadwick* v. *Covell* he wrote that "[w]hen the common law developed the doctrine of trade-marks and trade names it was not creating a property right in advertizing more absolute than [a copyright]; but the meaning was to prevent one man from palming off his good as another's."[53] In *Du Pont Powder Co.* v. *Masland*,[54] he famously expressed the view that "the word property as applied to trade-marks and trade secrets is an unanalyzed expression of certain secondary consequences of the primary fact that the law makes some rudimentary requirements of good faith." But in *Bourjois & Co.* v. *Katzel*, he seemed to have oscillated to the other side and

48 Haines, *supra* note 9, at 8 and n.24.

49 (1836) 3 Myl. & C. 338.

50 (1863) 1 De G. J. & S. 185, 199, 10 L. T. 780; *see also*, Leather Cloth Co. v. Am. Leather Cloth Co., (1863) 4 De G. J. & S. 137, 142 where Lord Westbury stated "[t]he true principle therefore would seem to be, that the jurisdic-tion of the Court in the protection given to trade-marks rests upon property, and that the Court interferes by injunction, because that is the only mode by which property of this description can be effectually protected."

51 (1863) 4 De G. J. & S. 150.

52 100 U.S. 82, 92 (1879).

53 151 Mass. 190, 193, 23 N.E. 1068, 1069 (1889).

54 244 U.S. 100, 102 (1917), *rev'd* 224 Fed. 689.

stated that there is no sufficient reason for holding that the monopoly granted by a trademark is less complete than that conferred by a patent.[55] Finally, in *Beech-Nut Packing Co.* v. *P. Lorillard Co.*, he went back to the more skeptical or qualified view that he endorsed in his early decisions, explaining that a "trademark and business may start together, and in a qualified sense the mark is property, protected and alienable, although as with other property its outline is shown only by the law of torts, of which the right is a prophetic summary."[56]

Commentators too have found the task of defining unfair competition by reference to common law categories quite tricky. After conducting a thorough review of the case law, Callmann concluded that, although courts often used property language in reference to trademarks, they did so in a very loose and abstracted way;[57] in fact the courts adopted "the so-called Holmes-Hand doctrine of the 'qualified nature' of property in a trade-mark, i.e., that a trade-mark is only a symbol of the good will of the business of the trade-mark owner"; that "a trade-mark is not property in the ordinary sense but only a word or symbol indicating the origin of a commercial product."[58]

The difficulty of pegging unfair competition in any of the traditional common law categories is not surprising. After all, the law of unfair competition law as it pertained to trademark and trade names grew out of the tort of passing off. Of course, there was an underlying asset that courts sought to protect, namely, goodwill. But, at least initially, protection was afforded only if there was a risk that consumers would be deceived. Hence, unfair competition evolved subject to two gravitational forces – that of property and that of torts.

The expansion of unfair competition to cases in which the defendant was not in direct competition with the plaintiff seemed to mark a victory for the property view of trademark protection. Claims of dilution are clearly predicated on concepts of property. This development presented a challenge to legal commentators. Seeking to rationalize this development, Callmann proceeded to introduce a distinction between the relationship governing rules and exclusive rights.[59] Specifically, he suggested that, although the mutual rights, privileges, and liabilities of a business vis-à-vis its competitors are governed by a set of rules designed to govern competitive relationships, its dealings with *non*-competitors with whom the business has no relationship are controlled by exclusive rights similar to the rights of a property against strangers.[60] This analytical distinction is evocative of the work of Henry Smith, who divided property law into exclusion rules and governance rules.[61]

55 260 U.S. 689, 43 S. Ct. 244 (1923).
56 273 U.S. 629, 47 S. Ct. 481 (1927).
57 Callmann, *supra* note 2, at 457–58.
58 *Id.* at 458.
59 *Id.*
60 *Id.* at 451 ("Where there is no relationship but an exclusive right, the rights and duties are determined by the exclusive right itself, according to the scope of protection afforded it by the law.").
61 Henry E. Smith, *Property and Property Rules*, 79 N.Y.U. L. Rev. 1719 (2004).

It bears emphasis that the discussion has so far focused on the subset of trademark and trade names cases of unfair competition law. But unfair competition also included other categories that made it even harder to classify. Indeed, the well-known case of *International News Service* v. *Associated Press* can be understood as setting up "unfair competition" as an alternative to property along precisely these terms. Responding to the concern that an in rem entitlement in the news would stifle speech and impede the free exchange of information, the court there chose to create an entitlement that would only ever operate between "competitors" and never against the public and strangers who are not competitors in the structural sense – that is, of operating in the same market and satisfying the same demand. Facially at least, understanding unfair competition as an independent structural principle seemed to make sense.

Yet, the reality has turned out to be something quite different from what was envisaged in theory. Over time and to accommodate the growing variety of commercial actors that operated in the marketplace, the idea of "competition" itself began to expand – to effectively cover any interaction that was in some sense commercial. When this occurred, competition ceased to remain a limiting feature of the doctrine, because anyone could be a competitor as long as he or she was gaining some commercial value from the activity in question. The law of misappropriation is again a good example here, with the "competition" requirement set up by the court in *International News* today having very little cabining effect on the reach and scope of the doctrine.

It is noteworthy that unfair competition has typically tended to rely on a traditional common law category for its structure. The parts of unfair competition intended to ensure healthy competition in the marketplace were modeled to a large extent on notions taken from the law of torts and to a lesser extent on concepts taken from the law of contract, such as good faith. The aspects that dealt with the protection of trade secrets were likewise influenced by tort and contract law. Another legal category that exerted influence over the development of unfair competition was unjust enrichment. The principle of preventing passing off that informed such a large part of unfair competition law epitomizes the central dictate of unjust enrichment that ill-gotten gains should be disgorged.

B. *Unfair Competition as a Normative Ideal*

Classifying an area of law around a normative ideal or functional variable entails associating a set of doctrines and causes of action with the realization of particular normative values. In this conception then, unfair competition represents no more than a set of common law actions that strive to realize a set of goals or values in a particular domain (i.e., the competitive marketplace).

In viewing unfair competition as a normative ideal, we must therefore begin with the fundamental question – what is unfair competition law trying to achieve? It is clear that the simple idea of efficiency is doing far less work in this area than in others, because numerous actions that are regarded as the staple forms of unfair competition are capable of resulting in palpably efficient results and outcomes. It thus often is the particular means employed by a defendant that the law of unfair competition today focuses on. Indeed, one of the earliest definitions of unfair competition sought to understand it as the body of law aimed at preventing businesses from performing what Edward Rogers called "dirty tricks" on each other.[62]

What thus seems to be at play in this understanding of unfair competition law is some kind of a commitment to the idea of "market fairness" – or the belief that competition in the marketplace is socially acceptable (and welfare maximizing) when it is "free" and "fair." The functional idea we then see comes to be described in negative, rather than positive terms. Zechariah Chafee's early article on the subject is a vivid example of this approach.[63] In it, he describes unfair competition law as the body of rules that disallow competitive behavior that is without some independent justification. The absence of "justification" for the competitor's actions is thus doing the normative work in this understanding.[64] Where then does this justification derive from? And here, unsatisfactorily, he falls back on broad palliatives – noting that all competition is prima facie actionable and needs some independent justification in terms of social policy for it to be exempted. The circularity is but obvious.

As we demonstrate later, unfair competition law did not intend to preserve the commercial status quo. Its goal was not to protect poorly run businesses that faced competition from superior rivals. In fact, courts always understood that competition was desirable and that economic harm resulting from competition is not generally actionable. This did not mean, however, that the business environment was one of all-out war, where the end always justified the means.

In fact, Callmann advances and rejects the war analogy in his attempt to distill the essence of unfair competition.[65] He begins his examination with the statement that "[t]he law of unfair competition might well be called the book of rules of the business game."[66] Adopting the game analogy, Callmann proceeds to compare the rules of competition to the rules of sports games or races. He then introduces the distinction

62 Chaffee, *supra* note 8, at 1289.

63 *Id.*

64 *Id.* at 1304.

65 Callmann characterizes competition as a "struggle." He then proceeds to ask what kind of "struggle" it is. In answering this question, he writes, "Shall that struggle be considered as the biological *bellum onmium contra omnes*, as the predatory war of beasts of prey? That view is, beyond question, incompatible with the essence of a civilized world. Hobbes' maxim, *homo homini lupus*, has never been adopted. Or should the struggle be considered as the war between nations, the *ultina ratio* employing force and fraud? This last idea would be strange, but it is not impossible. The rule of thumb seems to be the simple economic conception of the institution of free competition." Rudolph Callmann, *What is Unfair Competition?*, 28 Geo. L. Rev. 585, 594 (1940).

66 *Id.* at 596 (quoting Harry Dwight Nims, The Law of Unfair Competition and Trade Marks viii (3d ed. 1929)).

between constructive efforts and destructive efforts as the key to understanding unfair competition:

> Everyone who tries to enlarge the productivity of his business enterprise through transactions not in accordance with the conduct of reasonable businessmen introduces circumstances into his business sphere capable of falsifying the basis of comparison. As in the game, the winner will not be the competitor who wangled an advantage by means which had nothing to do with his ability to run the race.[67]

This line of reasoning leads us to the classification, which should be the pole-star in the law of "unfair competition": the distinction between competition embracing constructive effort and competition embracing nonconstructive effort. The former will always be allowed; there can be no *constructive competition* that might be unlawful. The latter should fundamentally be forbidden.[68] Unfair competition was therefore actionable because it was a wrong. Yet, what is also worth mentioning – and of direct relevance to the thesis here – is that, in order to turn to the vague ideas of fairness and honesty, courts came to deploy the mechanisms of tort law. Beginning with the understanding that tort law represented the law of actionable wrongs – nothing more, nothing less – courts and scholars began to approach the classification of all torts based on three primary variables: (i) harm, (ii) responsibility, and (iii) justification (or the absence of it). Applying this metric to instances of unfair competition then, fairness and honesty began to matter only because they created some kind of "market harm" that the law held the defendant responsible for, and was often without independent justification. Yet, there remained an analytical circularity in this analysis, because the determination of whether something was a harm was often entirely a consequence of the presence/absence of some justification for the action, which in turn related back to the vague ideas of fairness and honesty.

The reliance on "harm" also raises an additional problem. Is the harm purely notional, such that unfair competition is conduct-oriented; or is it actual, such that unfair competition is result-oriented? Support for the former view may be found in the fact that unfair competition law was often invoked to protect consumers. For example, in the trademark and trade-names cases, courts often expressed concern that certain deceptive practices, if allowed, would adversely affect consumers – even when actual harm was not shown in the individual case. Likewise, by banning a myriad of anti-competitive practices, unfair competition law clearly enhanced consumer welfare.

Other aspects of unfair competition determined the norms of acceptable conduct in competitive environments. The bans on misappropriation of trade secrets and on ruthless or ruinous business practices are cases in point. Of course, it is possible to argue that these aspects of unfair competition are also result-based because they are intended to protect businesses from other businesses. This interpretation cannot be

67 *Id.* at 600.
68 *Id.*

readily dismissed. But it appears this interpretation is not the correct one, because courts rarely ever focused on the effects of the action beyond speculating about them.

According to Callmann, one of the earliest theorists of unfair competition law, it is clear that unfair competition is not concerned with avoiding a certain undesirable result, but rather with regulating competitive conduct.[69] As he explains, "competition is not 'unfair' because the result of the commercial effort is neutral or even disadvantageous for the whole community from an objective, economical point of view unless the latter knowledge has led to a legal prohibition. 'Unfair competition' on the other hand, is not legal merely because its result is considered to be beneficial to the public."[70] Harm is thus irrelevant in the factual sense.

Tuttle v. *Buck* is a perfect example of Callmann's argument that unfair competition was purely conduct-oriented. As noted earlier, the defendant there, a village banker, decided to drive the local village barber out of business and sets up a shop in its vicinity, offering customers deep discounts. The Supreme Court of Minnesota found the defendant's actions to constitute an act of unfair competition and awarded the plaintiff damages on the reasoning that, even if the act were otherwise lawful, it was accompanied by an evil motive – which necessitated policing by the courts. The court's excursus on the role of the common law and its reliance on courts to police unfair competition are paradigmatic of a functional, normative ideal-oriented approach to unfair competition law:

> It must be remembered that the common law is the result of growth, and that its development has been determined by the social needs of the community which it governs.... To be an efficient instrument, and not a mere abstraction, it must gradually adapt itself to changed conditions. Necessarily, its form and substance have been greatly affected by prevalent economic theories. For generations there has been a practical agreement upon the proposition that competition in trade and business is desirable, and this idea has found expression in the decisions of the Courts as well as in statutes. But it has led to grievous and manifold wrongs to individuals, and many Courts have manifested an earnest desire to protect the individual from the evils which result from unrestrained business competition. The problem has been to so adjust matters as to preserve the principle of competition and yet guard against its abuse to the unnecessary injury to the individual.... *The purpose for which a man is using his own property may thus sometimes determine his rights.*[71]

Essentially then, unfair competition constituted a legal safety net that enabled courts to impose norms of fair dealing and ethical behavior on market participants. At

[69] Callmann defines constructive effort as "the effort of a man who strives to obtain commercial advantages only by the honestly exercised means of his own strength, his own ingenuity, skill, and capital." *Id.* at 601.

[70] *Id.*

[71] Tuttle v. Buck, 119 N.W. 946, 947 (Minn. 1909) (emphasis supplied).

the core of unfair competition lies a set of norms of behavior that govern interactions in the commercial realm. Or, more succinctly, it can be said that unfair competition is about transactional justice. Neither judges nor commentators in the years since have managed to reduce unfair competition to a single principle. Haines, in tackling the challenge of defining unfair competition, settled for the following summary:

> The grounds for giving relief in cases of unfair competition are held to be: to promote honesty and fair dealing; 'to protect the purchasing public;' to protect the rights and property of individuals.[72]

III. THE LAW AND LORE OF UNFAIR COMPETITION

In this part we assess the future of unfair competition in the modern legal environment. We submit that unfair competition will continue to perform three important functions: an anchoring function, an expanding function, and a limiting function. In its anchoring capacity, unfair competition law is invoked alongside other causes of actions. Although, in such cases the unfair competition claims may seem superfluous in light of the other causes of action raised by plaintiffs, they actually help bolster the plaintiffs' cases and add a moral dimension to them. In its expanding function, unfair competition broadens the menu of causes of action available to plaintiffs by providing them with independent causes of action that cannot be raised based on other legal areas. It allows courts to provide redress for harms arising from conducts that are not actionable under property, intellectual property, tort, or even antitrust law. *International News Service* v. *Associated Press* (*INS* v. *AP*) provides a prominent example of such a use of unfair competition. Finally, unfair competition law may be invoked as a limiting principle for the purposes of delineating the scope of torts or property liability. For example, courts can use the canon of unfair competition law to put constraints on the expansion of trademark law by deciding that the scope of protection granted to trademark owners will be limited to cases in which defendants engaged in unethical or deceitful practices, but not otherwise. We elaborate on these possibilities in the following sections.

A. *The Framing Effect of Unfair Competition*

In practice, claims of unfair competition are as ubiquitous as ever. In many cases, plaintiffs include a cause of action under state unfair competition law together with claims for patent, copyright, or trademark infringement. These unfair competition claims are no doubt subsidiary to the main federal claims, but we believe that they have an unappreciated influence on courts' approach to the main claims. This impact derives from their "anchoring" of the substance of the main claim in terms of the ideals and values of unfair competition. Courts then begin to view a defendant's

[72] Haines, *supra* note 9, at 9.

actions in a patent or copyright infringement claim through the lens of unfair competition law. As a result there is a greater focus on the propriety and motives behind the defendant's actions – potentially moving liability away from notions of strict liability. It also thereby allows judges to focus on remedies independent of those delineated in the statute.

Additionally, this framing effect may come about even when a plaintiff does not explicitly raise an independent unfair competition claim, but the relationship between the parties forces courts to focus their attention on the unfair competitive effects of the copying. This effect is seen rather commonly in cases involving compilations and databases under copyright law where the fact that the parties are operating in the same market – and as direct competitors – seems to have an appreciable impact on courts' willingness to find the defendant liable, despite formal arguments to the contrary.

B. *The Broadening Effect of Unfair Competition*

Unfair competition law also performs a broadening function, serving as the source of independent claims that are not available in other legal fields. As we discussed earlier, unfair competition was used in this fashion by the courts of equity to broaden trademark doctrine. It is still serviceable in this capacity today. A concrete example can be found in contemporary idea submission cases. Ideas qua ideas are not subject to copyright protection, and in many instances they do not qualify for trade secrecy protection or contractual protection. Nevertheless, idea conceivers have frequently been able to obtain relief by showing that the defendants' actions constituted an act of unfair competition.[73]

The classic case of *INS* v. *AP* provides an even more famous example of the same phenomenon. Hot news, very much like ideas, is not subject to copyright protection (only their expression is). Nor was AP able to come up with a property doctrine to support its claims against INS. Unfair competition came to its rescue. It was the driving force that motivated the Supreme Court to craft the concept of "quasi-property" and grant AP the sought-after relief. Many commentators have inveighed against this innovation of the Court, arguing that it was an improper creation of a new property right in factual information. However, from a legal standpoint, these criticisms are largely misguided because the reasoning was a direct application of unfair competition law. For our purposes, the case provides an example of how unfair competition values were effectively used to create a new form of action that had the effect of broadening the traditional common law.

Unfair competition had the same effect in other cases involving other forms of information. Information is notoriously subject to manipulation. Parties to business transactions may manipulate information in subtle ways that do not necessarily

[73] *See, e.g.*, Nadel v. Play-By-Play Toys & Novelties, Inc., 208 F.3d 368, 373 n.2 (2d Cir. 2000).

amount to fraud, deceit, or misrepresentation. Yet, by presenting information in a certain way, embellishing it, or omitting various informational aspects, businesses can lead their competitors astray and cause them harm. Traditional torts doctrine may not be readily adjusted to cope with such practices because, as we explained, the business environment is different from other settings. Unfair competition, by contrast, offers a viable legal mechanism for handling such practices and enabling courts to engage in nuanced line drawing capable of preserving competition while deterring abusive uses of information.

C. *The Cabining Effect of Unfair Competition*

In direct contrast to courts using the idea of unfair competition to broaden the traditional categories of the common law and offer plaintiffs relief in new situations, unfair competition may also provide courts (and policy makers) with an important limiting mechanism to scale back existing intellectual property and exclusionary protection in areas where the law seems to be expanding at the cost of social welfare. In these situations, it is likely to provide the law with an important "normative hook" with which to scale back a doctrinal area.

This cabining effect derives from the basic idea that unfair competition requires "competition" between the parties for the action to be sustained. It thus performs a role very similar to the "antitrust injury" rule in antitrust law, where courts allow the action to proceed only when assured that the harm actually/likely to be sustained by the plaintiff is the same as the harm that the particular doctrine in question was intended to prevent. In similar fashion unfair competition would enable courts to force plaintiffs to make a showing of actual or potential harm that was anti-competitive in the ways understood by the common law of unfair competition.

An obvious example is the possibility of scaling back trademark protection to situations where the defendant's use competes with that of the plaintiff. Indeed, as we noted, trademark law required this scaling back in many instances. Although the current propertarian turn in trademark law has undoubtedly resulted in courts all but abandoning this idea, there is perhaps good reason to believe that it will provide courts with a suitable basis by which to limit trademark infringement actions should they choose to in the future. The creeping expansion of trademark dilution in particular would stand to benefit from such a limitation.

Publicity rights represent another area. As originally understood, the law required a plaintiff to show that his or her likeness was appropriated by the defendant and used for a commercial purpose. This commercial purpose seemed to matter because it was presumed to impede the plaintiff's ability to commercialize his or her likeness – to be a form of competitive harm. In this area, the idea of unfair competition (via a commercial use requirement) might have a much needed cabining effect.

CONCLUSION

Unfair competition has played a key role in shaping commercial morality and ethics. We believe it will continue to do so in the future. It provides courts with extensive flexibility and discretion to match the law to the complexity of the business world. The breadth of unfair competition and its independence of rigid formal requirements are its principal virtues, but at the same time they are also potential vices. They raise the danger that judges may start imposing their own individual perceptions of business ethics in an inconsistent manner that may cause competition to grind to a halt. This is especially true when unfair competition is invoked in its broadening role. To counter this risk, judges should employ a considerable degree of restraint in using unfair competition. They should not rush to condemn or prohibit every business practice resulting in harm to competitors. Quite the contrary, for the most part economic harms should not be actionable, and businesses should be given a wide margin to compete against each other. Intervention via unfair competition should come only in extreme cases representing drastic deviations from accepted business practices. The business judgment rule in corporate law can serve as a useful benchmark for judges.

Unfair competition should be thought of as the "shotgun behind the door." Like the proverbial shotgun, unfair competition should not be overused; its presence in the legal arsenal should suffice to discourage unsavory business practices. Of course, for there to be a credible threat of intervention on unfair competition grounds, it should be put to use in those cases in which competition causes businesses to go too far.

22

The Fractioning of Patent Law

*Mark A. Lemley**

Patent owners might seem to have everything stacked in their favor in modern law. They are entitled to a strong presumption that their patents are valid, a presumption that can be overcome only by clear and convincing evidence.[1] That presumption exists despite the fact that patent applicants never bear the burden in the Patent and Trademark Office (PTO) of showing they are entitled to a patent; the burden is on the PTO to show that they should not get a patent.[2] This presumption is so strong that it applies even to prior art and arguments that we know for certain the PTO never considered at all.[3] Patent owners can draft an unlimited number of claims in each patent, each of which must be evaluated separately and continues to be valid even if the others are invalidated. They can return to the PTO to modify their claims, either using reissue or reexamination, or by filing an unlimited number of continuation applications in an effort to tailor their patent claims to cover whatever a particular defendant is doing.[4] They get wide latitude to choose where they want to sue, and they actively engage in forum shopping, picking the most favorable districts.[5] There

* William H. Neukom Professor, Stanford Law School; partner, Durie Tangri LLP. Thanks to Dennis Crouch, Rose Hagan, Jonathan Masur, Joe Miller, Ray Niro, Josh Sarnoff, Dave Schwartz, and participants in the Intellectual Property and the Common Law symposium at the University of Pennsylvania Law School for comments on an earlier draft of this chapter.

1 Microsoft Corp. v. i4i Ltd., 131 S.Ct. 2238 (2011).

2 *See, e.g., In re* Morris, 127 F.3d 1048 (Fed. Cir. 1997).

3 *Microsoft*, 131 S.Ct. at 2238. For criticism of that rule, see, e.g., Doug Lichtman & Mark A. Lemley, *Rethinking Patent Law's Presumption of Validity*, 60 Stan. L. Rev. 45 (2007).

4 For a discussion of these continuations, see, e.g., Mark A. Lemley & Kimberly A. Moore, *Ending Abuse of Patent Continuations*, 84 B.U. L. Rev. 63 (2004).

5 *See, e.g.*, Kimberly A. Moore, *Forum Shopping in Patent Cases: Does Geographic Choice Affect Innovation?*, 79 N.C. L. Rev. 889 (2001); Mark A. Lemley, *Where to File Your Patent Case*, 38 AIPLA Q.J. 401 (2010). Some recent decisions have limited the ability of patentees to choose whatever jurisdiction they want. *See., e.g., In re* Genentech Corp., 566 F.3d 1338 (Fed. Cir. 2009); *In re* Link-A-Media Devices Corp., 662 F.3d 1221 (Fed. Cir. 2011).

is even suspicion that some districts are actively seeking to attract patent plaintiffs.[6] They have a right to take their case to a jury, and all evidence indicates that juries tend to favor patent owners. Jurors tend not to second-guess the patent office, and they are often swayed by the personal stories of inventors.[7] And if patentees win their cases, they have been entitled to wide latitude in calculating damages, leading to arguably excessive awards of damages.[8]

Notwithstanding these seemingly dramatic advantages, patent owners overwhelmingly lose their cases. Nearly half of all patents litigated to judgment are held invalid.[9] Overall, patentees win barely more than a quarter of their cases.[10] This figure is remarkable, given that civil plaintiffs overall win 58 percent of their cases in the federal courts, and even more of their copyright cases.[11] And the very patents that economic evidence predicts as the most valuable – the ones that are litigated in multiple cases – overwhelmingly lose in court; less than 10 percent of those patentees in fact win when a case goes to judgment.[12] Forum shopping helps, but not much; even the most plaintiff-friendly district rules for the plaintiff only

[6] *See* Julie Creswell, *So Small a Town, So Many Patent Suits*, N.Y. Times (Sept. 24, 2006), http://www.nytimes.com/2006/09/24/business/24ward.html?scp=1&sq=marshall%20texas%20patent&st=cse (last visited Feb. 27, 2012).

[7] Juries are substantially more likely to rule for patent owners than are judges. *See, e.g.*, Kimberly A. Moore, *Judges, Juries, and Patent Cases: An Empirical Peek Inside the Black Box*, 99 Mich. L. Rev. 365 (2000); John R. Allison & Mark A. Lemley, *Empirical Evidence on the Validity of Litigated Patents*, 26 AIPLA Q.J. 185 (1998) (finding that patentees win 67% of jury trials on validity, compared with 56% of bench trials and 28% of summary judgment rulings).

[8] For evidence and criticism of these awards, see, e.g., Mark A. Lemley & Carl Shapiro, *Patent Holdup and Royalty Stacking*, 85 Tex. L. Rev. 1991 (2007) (documenting royalty awards in court decisions averaging 13.1% and arguing that this was out of proportion to the value of the invention); *cf.* Daralyn J. Durie & Mark A. Lemley, *A Structured Approach to Calculating Reasonable Royalties*, 14 Lewis & Clark L. Rev. 627 (2010). A number of critics have attacked the Shapiro-Lemley article, generally by arguing not that those high royalties didn't exist but that disproportionately high royalties were good for innovation. *See, e.g.*, John M. Golden, *"Patent Trolls" and Patent Remedies*, 85 Tex. L. Rev. 2111 (2007); Einer Elhauge, *Do Patent Holdup and Royalty Stacking Lead to Systematically Excessive Royalties?*, 4 J. Competition L. & Econ. 535 (2008). For defenses of the original claims, see Mark A. Lemley & Carl Shapiro, *Patent Holdup and Royalty Stacking: Reply*, 85 Tex. L. Rev. 2161 (2007); Thomas F. Cotter, *Patent Holdup, Patent Remedies, and Antitrust Responses*, 34 J. Corp. L. 1151 (2009).

The Federal Circuit has recently tightened up considerably on the evidence that can be considered in damages cases. *See, e.g.*, Uniloc USA, Inc. v. Microsoft Corp., 632 F.3d 1292 (Fed. Cir. 2011); Lucent Techs., Inc. v. Gateway, Inc., 530 F.3d 1801 (Fed. Cir. 2009).

[9] Allison & Lemley, *supra* note 9, at 185 (finding that 46% of litigated patents are held invalid).

[10] Paul M. Janicke & LiLan Ren, *Who Wins Patent Infringement Cases?*, 34 AIPLA Q.J. 1 (2006).

[11] Kevin M. Clermont & Theodore Eisenberg, *Do Case Outcomes Really Reveal Anything About the Legal System? Win Rates and Removal Jurisdiction*, 83 Cornell L. Rev. 581, 594 (1998). The win rate is 52–57% in trade secret cases in federal court, David S. Almeling et al., *A Statistical Analysis of Trade Secret Litigation in Federal Courts*, 45 Gonz. L. Rev. 291, 313 tbl.10 (2010), and perhaps as high as 73% in copyright cases, William M. Landes, *An Empirical Analysis of Intellectual Property Litigation: Some Preliminary Results*, 41 Hous. L. Rev. 749, 773 tbl.5 (2004), suggesting that it is not IP cases more generally that have low win rates.

[12] John R. Allison et al., *Patent Quality and Settlement Among Repeat Patent Litigants*, 99 Geo. L.J. 677 (2011).

about half the time.[13] Systematically, patent owners lose more often than they win.

This result is a puzzle. Why is it that patent owners, despite seemingly having every advantage, cannot seem to win their cases?[14] While the law has changed in the last five years to be less favorable to patent owners, that can't be the explanation, because patentees were losing the vast majority of their cases even in the late 1990s and early 2000s, when patent-friendly jurisprudence was at its height and the PTO was most lax in issuing patents. Nor does it appear to be that plaintiffs are all small or poorly funded and lose to bigger defendants; while Allison et al. do find that nonpracticing entities (which tend to be small) fare particularly poorly in litigation,[15] Colleen Chien has shown that patent litigation is just as likely to involve big plaintiffs and small defendants as the reverse.[16]

The answer, I think, can be found in part in the structure of the modern patent law. We have moved over the past 150 years from a holistic approach to patent cases, in which we compared the plaintiff's product to the defendant's, to a fractional patent system. In our fractional patent system, we break the patent infringement lawsuit into an enormous number of different inquiries, and in most circumstances, the patentee has to win *each* of those arguments to win its case. Patentees lose most of their cases because they might need to win ten different issues to prevail, while defendants generally need only win one. Put in electrical engineering terms, the legal issues in a patent case must be decided in series, not in parallel. One break in the chain – one patentee loss – and the game is up.[17]

The origins of this systematic imbalance can be found in the nineteenth century in the move from central to peripheral claiming. In the first several decades of the republic, and in England at common law, we treated patents as signposts, rather than the boundary-defining fence posts of a peripheral claiming system.[18] The patent focused on the actual device the patentee had built or described. Indeed, it was not

[13] *See* Lemley, *supra* note 7 (finding that the most plaintiff-friendly district, the Northern District of Texas, ruled for patentees 55% of the time).

[14] George Priest and Ben Klein hypothesized decades ago that plaintiff win rates in litigation should approach 50% because of selection effects. George L. Priest & Benjamin Klein, *The Selection of Disputes for Litigation*, 13 J. LEGAL STUD. 1, 24 (1984). Whether or not this is true in other areas of the law, see Steven Shavell, *Any Frequency of Plaintiff Victory at Trial is Possible*, 25 J. LEGAL STUD. 493 (1996), every empirical study of patent law refutes it; each shows systematic variation from a 50% win rate. Whether that is a problem with the theory or represents something specific about patent law is beyond the scope of this chapter. But the argument in this chapter provides one possible explanation.

[15] Allison et al., *supra* note 14.

[16] Colleen V. Chien, *Of Trolls, Davids, Goliaths, and Kings: Narratives and Evidence in the Litigation of High-Tech Patents*, 87 N.C. L. REV. 1571 (2009).

[17] Dennis Crouch suggested this analogy, and I really wish I had thought of it first.

[18] *See* Dan L. Burk & Mark A. Lemley, *Fence Posts or Sign Posts? Rethinking Patent Claim Construction*, 157 U. PA. L. REV. 1743 (2009). For other discussions of this history, see, e.g., Jeanne C. Fromer, *Claiming Intellectual Property*, 76 U. CHI. L. REV. 719 (2009); William Redin Woodward, *Definiteness and Particularity in Patent Claims*, 46 MICH. L. REV. 755, 757 (1948); Karl B. Lutz, *Evolution of the Claims of U.S. Patents*, 20 J. PAT. OFF. SOC'Y 457 (1938).

until the middle of the nineteenth century that patentees even began writing patent "claims" to specify what it is they thought they had contributed to the world.[19]

In a central claiming system, invalidity was less of a problem, and infringement and invalidity were more closely intertwined. A patent that covered what the inventor had actually designed was unlikely to present enablement problems as long as the patentee had actually described his or her invention. Novelty and nonobviousness were less significant, because both doctrines focused on what the patentee actually built rather than on the full scope of a genus claim, and there was room to preserve the validity of the patent even while affording it a narrow scope.[20] And determining infringement was a matter of comparing what the patentee described to what the accused infringer built, and deciding whether the two were close enough. The result was that patent infringement looked very much like a common law tort.[21] Courts considered infringement and validity as a whole and usually together.[22] So while the patentee had to win two issues – validity and infringement – the risk of invalidity was not all that great. Something of the sort is still true today in other areas of IP law, including copyright, trade secrets, and design patents, and we see a higher plaintiff win rate in those areas.

The growth of peripheral claiming in the latter half of the nineteenth century began the process of fractioning this integrated common law approach to patent infringement. Peripheral claiming replaced what the patentee built with what the lawyer claimed as the basis for analyzing infringement and anticipation. As we increasingly focused our attention on patent claims, we had to develop a theory of enablement and disclosure that controlled undue breadth in patent claims. Now there were three basic hurdles a patentee had to clear: Were the claims infringed? Were the claims anticipated or obvious? And were the claims broader than the scope of what the patentee disclosed?

The problem for patentees is worse than that, however. The courts have also divided the disclosure doctrines in section 112. It is not enough to teach a person of skill in the art to make and use the invention; the Federal Circuit has read that section to require a separate "written description" requirement, defined by proof of possession of the invention. While there are circumstances in which we might genuinely worry about proof of possession, notably where the patentee changes its claims over time, *Ariad Pharmaceuticals* v. *Eli Lilly & Co.* made it clear that the

[19] Burk & Lemley, *supra* note 20.

[20] *See, e.g.*, Mark A. Lemley, *Why Do Juries Decide Whether Patents Are Valid?* VA. L. REV. (forthcoming 2014); B. Zorina Khan, *Property Rights and Patent Litigation in Early Nineteenth-Century America* (working paper 2010) (noting that many fewer patent validity litigations in the early 1800s involved novelty disputes than today).

[21] For a discussion of the role of common law in intellectual property, see Shyamkrishna Balganesh, *The Pragmatic Incrementalism of Common Law Intellectual Property*, 63 VAND. L. REV. 1543 (2010).

[22] Burk & Lemley, *supra* note 20. For further discussion of the history, see Joshua D. Sarnoff, *The Historic and Modern Doctrine of Equivalents and Claiming the Future*, 87 J. PAT. & TRADEMARK OFF. SOC'Y 371, 441 (2005).

written description doctrine is not limited to those cases.[23] Nor is it limited to particular technologies, such as DNA, that present heightened risks of "gun-jumping" in patent claiming. The result is that patentees must survive two overlapping inquiries, and courts may end up finding a violation of the written description requirement in circumstances where the patentee has in fact taught people of skill in the art to make and use the invention. So now there are at least four different doctrines the patentee must win. And there are many others, from unenforceability to inventorship.

But it is the focus on patent claims that has had the most significant fractioning effect. Claims are composed of words, and they are easier to break down into component parts than are inventions themselves. As a result, patent litigation has increasingly become not about the overall degree of overlap between the patentee's invention and the defendant's product, but instead about matching the words of the patent claim to the defendant's product. And for the patentee to win an infringement case, *all* the words need to match to the defendant's product.[24] Suddenly the patentee needs to win not just one infringement issue, but ten different sub-issues. Lose one, and there would be no infringement. True, the same effect works in the opposite way when it comes to validity; there, the patentee benefits from fractioning, because the absence of even one claim element in the prior art prevents a finding of anticipation. But because the patentee needs to win both invalidity and infringement, the net effect of the move to element-by-element claim analysis is to make it harder for patentees to win.[25]

The express separation of claim construction into a distinct legal inquiry in 1995 made this problem much worse.[26] Once claims started to be construed in separate legal proceedings, the courts were determining the meaning of individual disputed terms, often without knowing the impact their definitions would have.[27]

[23] 598 F.3d 1336 (Fed. Cir. 2010) (en banc).

[24] The statement in text is complicated by the inability of courts to agree on the size of an "element" in a patent claim. Some courts treat each word in a claim as a separate element, while others are willing to aggregate large chunks of the claim together in a single "element." Neither side articulates any standards for deciding what an element is. For a discussion of the problem, see Dan L. Burk & Mark A. Lemley, *Quantum Patent Mechanics*, 9 LEWIS & CLARK L. REV. 25 (2005).

[25] To see this, imagine a patent that has five claims, each of which has five elements, and that the patentee's chance of prevailing on any given argument was 50%. The patentee's likelihood of having at least one claim survive a validity challenge would be quite good (96.88%), assuming the odds were strictly independent. But its odds of winning infringement of any one of those patent claims would be correspondingly small – only 3.13% for any given claim. So for each claim, the odds of winning the suit would be only 1.56% – the odds of winning infringement on that claim times the odds that that claim turned out to be a valid one. In practice, of course, the odds of prevailing in each suit are not independent, so the numbers cannot be calculated with precision.

[26] Markman v. Westview Instruments, Inc., 52 F.3d 967 (Fed. Cir. 1995) (en banc), *aff'd*, 517 U.S. 370 (1996).

[27] Early post-*Markman* cases took a firm line that claim terms were to be construed without resort to the accused device. NeoMagic Corp. v. Trident Microsystems, Inc., 287 F.3d 1062, 1074 (Fed. Cir.2002); SRI Int'l v. Matsushita Elec. Corp. of Am., 775 F.2d 1107, 1118 (Fed. Cir.1985) (en banc) ("Claims may not be construed with reference to the accused device."). But the Federal Circuit backed away from this theoretically pure but impractical rule in Wilson Sporting Goods v. Hillerich &

If the defendant has a good lawyer, each dispute over claim terms should be tied to a way that the patent claim either was invalid or was not infringed. So unless the patentee wins *every* claim construction dispute, it is probably going to lose the case on one ground or another. This is not a universal rule – sometimes a defendant needs to win several different claim construction arguments together to establish a non-infringement position. But that is the rare case. Thus the division of patent law into formal categories and, in particular, the focus on individual words in claim construction have stacked the deck against patentees.

But what of the various doctrines and rules that seem designed to give patentees multiple bites at the apple? Patentees can file multiple patents, and each patent has multiple claims. And if they cannot show literal infringement, they can fall back on the doctrine of equivalents. Surely these rules should balance out the patentee-must-win-everything characteristic of validity doctrines and claim construction.

In fact, however, the practical realities of litigation make these safety valves much less effective than one might expect. Although patentees can (and often do)[28] sue on many different patents and assert many different claims in each patent, courts are generally unwilling to adjudicate many different claims. District courts regularly limit the number of claims that patentees can assert at trial, requiring patentees to pick "representative claims."[29] Usually the patentee is only able to assert a few claims, even if they plausibly cover different inventions. The Federal Circuit has upheld the constitutionality of refusing to consider additional claims.[30] And while in theory multiple claims might allow patentees the freedom to wait and see how claim construction goes, in fact courts also impose limitations on the number of claim terms they will construe.[31] The result is that the multiplicity of patent claims seems to give patentees the option at the outset to pick the claim that looks best, but they will still have to win many different arguments to prevail on that claim.

Bradsby Co., 442 F.3d 1322 (Fed. Cir. 2006) ("[I]n reviewing claim construction in the context of infringement, the legal function of giving meaning to claim terms always takes place in the context of a specific accused infringing device or process.").

28 *See* Allison et al., *supra* note 14 (documenting instances of litigation on multiple patents).

29 This practice is fairly standard. See Panduit Corp. v. Dennison Mfg. Co., Inc., 836 F.2d 1329, 1331 (Fed. Cir. 1987) ("The term 'representative claims' is well understood in patent litigation."). For a discussion of the practice, see Patricia E. Campbell, *Representative Patent Claims: Their Use in Appeals to the Board and in Infringement Litigation*, 23 SANTA CLARA COMP. & HIGH TECH. L.J. 55,68 (2006) ("In patent infringement litigation, it has become a relatively common practice for the outcome of a case to be determined on the basis of a few representative claims selected by the patent owner."). The practice is so common that parties often agree in advance to identify those claims, knowing that they will be forced to do so. But courts have no hesitation in ordering unwilling parties to pick their favorite claims. *See, e.g.*, Kearns v. Gen. Motors Corp., Civ. No. 85–70461 (E.D. Mich. April 21, 1993) (issuing an order restricting patentee to one representative claim per patent-in-suit and five representative accused products).

30 *In re* Katz Interactive Call Processing Patent Litigation, 639 F.3d 1303 (Fed. Cir. 2011).

31 For a collection of local rules to this effect, see http://www.iplawalert.com/2010/01/articles/patent-1/limits-on-number-of-claim-terms-to-be-construed/ (last visited Feb. 27, 2012). That fact can actually benefit patent owners, because it reduces the fractioning of patent decisions. But it means that it is effectively impossible to vet more than a couple of claims in the average claim construction process.

And after *Katz*, courts are likely to resist efforts by patentees who have lost on one claim to come back and assert a different claim.

The doctrine of offensive non-mutual collateral estoppel compounds the patentee's problem. A patentee who faces infringement by multiple defendants, and sues them all in individual proceedings, confronts an asymmetry: if the patentee wins suit #1, it still needs to win the same arguments in suits #2, #3, and #4. In contrast, if one of the defendants wins a suit, the effects of that win will bar the patentee from relitigating the same issue against the other defendants. If the patent is ruled invalid even once, the patentee loses across the board.[32] Patentees might reasonably respond by consolidating claims against multiple defendants into a single suit.[33] In fact, there is evidence that patentees before 2011 were increasingly suing multiple defendants in the same case.[34] But some courts have resisted the idea that multiple defendants can be joined in a single suit merely because they are accused of infringing the same patent.[35] And Congress changed the patent statute in 2011 to preclude patentees from joining multiple defendants together merely because they are accused on infringing the same patent, or from consolidating separately filed cases for trial.[36] As a result, many patentees end up enforcing the same patent in multiple suits,[37] and that is likely to be even more true in the future.

What of the doctrine of equivalents? This is a doctrine whose very purpose is to avoid having excessive literalism unfairly disadvantage patent owners.[38] For each claim, it would seem to give the patentee a second bite at the apple. In fact, however, the courts have narrowed the doctrine of equivalents to the vanishing point, largely in tandem with the rise of a fractioned claim construction system. The scope of the doctrine was restricted beginning in the late 1980s when courts held that it must be applied element by element rather than to the patent claim as a whole.[39]

32 *See* Blonder-Tongue Labs. v. Univ. of Illinois Found., 402 U.S. 313 (1971). A non-infringement ruling will not prevent enforcement of the patent altogether, but collateral estoppel will prevent the patentee from making the same infringement or claim construction arguments, and the practical effect of that may be to make it trivial to avoid infringing the patent.

33 *See* Allison et al., *supra* note 14 (discussing this approach).

34 James Pistorino finds that, while the number of lawsuits filed in the Eastern District of Texas has declined from 2009 to 2011, the number of defendants sued there has increased dramatically. http://www.patentlyo.com/patent/2011/04/concentration-of-patent-cases-in-the-eastern-district-of-texas.html (last visited Feb. 27, 2012).

35 *See, e.g.*, Finisar Corp. v. Source Photonics, Inc., CV 10–00032 WHA (N.D. Cal. 2010); WiAV Networks, LLC v. 3Com Corp., No. C 10–03448 WHA (N.D. Cal. 2010). Separately filed cases can be related for pretrial purposes, however, and in extreme situations they can be brought together pretrial using the multidistrict litigation (MDL) procedure. *See* John R. Allison et al., *Patent Quality and Settlement Among Repeat Patent Litigants*, 99 Geo. L.J. 677 (2011) (reporting significant use of MDLs among the most litigated patents).

36 Leahy-Smith America Invents Act, 35 U.S.C. § 299(a) (2011).

37 *Id.*

38 *See* Graver Tank & Mfg. Co. v. Linde Air Prods., Inc., 339 U.S. 605 (1950) ("Outright and forthright duplication is a dull and very rare type of infringement. To prohibit no other would place the inventor at the mercy of verbalism and would be subordinating substance to form.").

39 Pennwalt Corp. v. Durand-Wayland, Inc., 833 F.2d 931 (Fed. Cir. 1987) (en banc).

An element-by-element doctrine of equivalents is narrower than a general doctrine of equivalents, and it does not avoid the fractioning problem. If the patentee must show the presence in the accused device of ten different elements to show literal infringement, the element-by-element equivalents test still requires the patentee to win on each of those ten elements, although it may make it easier to do so.

In the years immediately after *Pennwalt*, judicial application of the element-by-element rule was uneven at best.[40] As a result, the doctrine of equivalents still retained some force during those years.[41] But in 1997 the Supreme Court cemented the element-by-element nature of the doctrine.[42] Further, the move to pretrial claim construction after *Markman* gave district courts a very strong incentive to minimize the doctrine of equivalents, because it required a jury trial and threatened to undo the work the district judge had done in claim construction. Empirical work that John Allison and I did in 2007 shows that district judges responded by ruling against the doctrine of equivalents in the overwhelming majority of cases, to the point where the doctrine is all but dead today.[43] *Markman*, which is perhaps most responsible for the fractioning of patent law, also sounded the death knell for the doctrine best positioned to avoid the effects of that fractioning.

There is one final point to consider. Fact-finders, especially juries, tend to vote in all-or-nothing patterns. Patentees who sue on multiple patents usually win on all the patents or lose on all of them; only one in eight decided cases involving multiple patents results in a split verdict.[44] That tendency might be expected to come to the rescue of patentees by reducing the effect of the fractioning I have just described. But it has not. The reason is not entirely clear, but the most likely explanation is that juries, not judges, primarily vote in this all-or-nothing pattern, and the courts have been actively taking decision-making authority in patent cases out of the hands of juries and putting it in the hands of judges. *Markman* is again the most significant example; that decision vested in judges not only power over claim construction but (because there is rarely a dispute over how the defendant's product works) effectively over infringement as well. But there are other examples. The scope of patentable subject matter is a pure question of law that presumably should be resolved on summary judgment in all cases.[45] Courts treat both obviousness and enablement as

40 Hughes Aircraft Co. v. United States, 140 F.3d 1470 (Fed. Cir. 1998) (finding that "element" included more than fifty words in three subsections of patent claim); Corning Glass Works v. Sumitomo Elec. USA, Inc., 868 F.2d 1251 (Fed. Cir. 1989) (finding that element was entire claim).

41 John R. Allison & Mark A. Lemley, *The (Unnoticed) Demise of the Doctrine of Equivalents*, 59 STAN. L. REV. 955 (2007).

42 Warner-Jenkinson Co. v. Hilton Davis Chem. Co., 520 U.S. 17 (1997).

43 Allison & Lemley, *supra* note 44, at 955.

44 John R. Allison & Mark A. Lemley, *Empirical Evidence on the Validity of Litigated Patents*, 26 AIPLA Q.J. 185, 245 & tbl.18 (1998). The results are even more striking where different claims of the same patent are at issue: only 2.3% of cases involved different results for different claims in the same patent. *Id.* at 238.

45 *See, e.g., In re* Comiskey, 554 F.3d 967 (Fed. Cir. 2009).

questions of law despite their quintessentially factual nature,[46] with the result that they are often resolved on summary judgment,[47] and some courts no longer even pose the ultimate question to the jury.[48] Courts, not juries, decide inequitable conduct, and they can do so even when they must resolve disputed factual questions that bear on invalidity as well.[49] A number of commentators have accused the Federal Circuit of insufficient deference to fact-finders;[50] one consequence of that tendency has been to put more questions in the hands of judges, which in turn makes fractioning more likely.[51] Certainly that has been the experience with the Federal Circuit and claim construction, where the number of construction issues appealed has led to a particularly high reversal rate post-*Markman*.[52]

In short, the move from a common law (or more accurately, an equity) system focused on what the patentee and the accused infringer actually did to a hyper-technical system focused on strict compliance with various rules and claim language has had the unintended consequence of making life harder for patentees.

My goal in this chapter is descriptive, not normative. One might naturally conclude from the history I have described that we would be better off with a more flexible (and more patent-friendly) common law system. That may well be true. But as I have suggested elsewhere, there are other respects in which the patent system is set up to favor patentees; the question of which of these tendencies is stronger is not one I can resolve here. We would want to know whether the problem is that good patents are losing in court today or instead that bad patents were winning in the past. I have my own views on this question, but there is not sufficient evidence to answer it definitively. Further, there are some advantages to literalism in some

46 Graham v. John Deere Co., 383 U.S. 1 (1966); KSR Int'l Co. v. Teleflex Inc., 550 U.S. 398 (2007).

47 A study by Lex Machina found that district courts were nearly three times as likely to grant summary judgment of obviousness in the eighteen months after *KSR* than they were before *KSR*.

48 United States District Court for the Northern District of California, Model Patent Jury Instructions, www.cand.uscourts.gov/filelibrary/5/Model-Patent-Jury-Instructions.pdf. *Cf.* Microsoft Corp. v. i4i Ltd., 131 S.Ct. 2238, 2253 (2011) (Breyer, J., concurring) (noting that the presumption of validity applies only to factual questions, and many of the most important validity disputes are legal, not factual, issues).

49 *See, e.g.*, Agfa Corp. v. Creo Prods., Inc., 451 F.3d 1366 (Fed. Cir. 2006).

50 William C. Rooklidge & Matthew F. Weil, *Judicial Hyperactivity: The Federal Circuit's Discomfort with Its Appellate Role*, 15 BERKELEY TECH. L.J. 725 (2000). On the history of the Federal Circuit and how it affects that court's decision making, see Jeffrey A. Lefstin, *The Constitution of Patent Law: The Court of Customs and Patent Appeals and the Shape of the Federal Circuit's Jurisprudence*, 43 LOY. L.A. L. REV. 843 (2010).

51 To be sure, judges are not immune from the sorts of biases that lead them to vote for one party on an all-or-nothing basis. But they are less likely to be affected than juries because of how they understand their institutional role and because of the issue-by-issue nature of legal training. This is an empirical claim, and while I believe it to be true from my own experience, I have not tested it. Caveat emptor.

52 *See, e.g.*, David L. Schwartz, *Pre-Markman Reversal Rates*, 43 LOY. L.A. L. REV. 1073 (2010); David L. Schwartz, *Practice Makes Perfect? An Empirical Study of Claim Construction Reversal Rates in Patent Cases*, 107 MICH. L. REV. 223 (2008); Kimberly A. Moore, *Markman Eight Years Later: Is Claim Construction More Predictable?*, 9 LEWIS & CLARK L. REV. 231 (2005).

contexts. It may provide greater public notice, at least in the minority of industries in which patent claims are understandable to those in the industry.[53]

Whatever the right policy, it is worth understanding that patentees today lose most of their cases and that the most likely reason is our effort to take a broad equitable system and turn it into a rule- and text-based one.

[53] James Bessen & Michael Meurer, Patent Failure: How Judges, Lawyers, and Bureaucrats Put Innovation at Risk (2008).

23

Permanent Injunctions as Punitive Damages in Patent Infringement Cases

*Paul J. Heald**

Although much ink[1] has been spilled over the decision by the Supreme Court in eBay v. MercExchange[2] to modify the test for equitable relief in patent cases and to nullify the longstanding presumption that victims of infringement are always entitled to permanent injunctions, an obvious point is never pursued: injunctions in patent cases can function like punitive damages[3] at common law. A straightforward example suffices:

Greensweep, Inc., a manufacturer of lawn mowing equipment, invents a cleverly shaped mower deck that increases the suction and bagging function of its mowers. It anticipates net profits of $10 million due to its innovation. After Greensweep has built an expensive new manufacturing plant and produced thousands of new and improved mowers, it is sued successfully by Airwings, Inc., a helicopter manufacturer who had patented the same decking shape used by Greensweep. Airwings suffered no lost profits due to the infringement, but is awarded a reasonable royalty of $8 million for Greensweep's past infringement and permanent injunctive relief against Greensweep. The cost to convert its manufacturing facility to produce a non-infringing product would be $4 million. No cheaper non-infringing alternative technologies are available to Greensweep. Armed with a good estimate of Greensweep's switching costs, Airwings is able to negotiate a $3 million payment from Greensweep for a post-litigation license to use the patent.

* Professor of Law, University of Illinois; Visiting Professor, Centre for Intellectual Property Policy and Management, Bournemouth University.

[1] A search for "title (eBay & Mercexchange)" in the Westlaw JLR (law journals) database returns forty-three articles with the case name in the title. A search for "eBay/s Mercexchange" returns 1,290 documents with the case name in the text. *See* WESTLAW, www.westlaw.com (last visited Jan. 30, 2012).

[2] *See* 547 U.S. 388 (2006).

[3] The term "punitive" damages is used interchangeably with extra-compensatory and exemplary damages, regardless of the rationale for their application.

Note that Airwings, a party that has suffered no actual damages (i.e., lost profits in its own line of business), receives an ultimate reward of $11 million, whereas Greensweep, an unintentional infringer, suffers a net loss of $1 million. A permanent injunction[4] in a patent infringement case sometimes allows a successful patent owner to negotiate an amount up to the infringer's cost of complying with the injunction (hereinafter "switching costs") as an extra-compensatory bounty.

Indeed, the provision of the bounty in the Greensweep hypothetical seems to be the primary effect of injunctive relief. After all, if an infringer can switch to a cheaper, equivalent non-infringing technology, then an injunction has no value to the patent owner.[5] Even in cases where there is no alternative, the availability in the United States of treble damages for intentional infringement is enough to deter infringement postjudgment. A permanent injunction, therefore, only benefits the patent owner when the infringer is vulnerable due to significant switching costs. For this reason, Mark Lemley advocates that in many situations a court should award an ongoing future royalty to the patent owner instead of an injunction.[6]

This phenomenon of "patent hold up" is well known in the patent literature,[7] generally referring to the plight of infringers such as Greensweep in the hypothetical described earlier.[8] Even after *eBay*, permanent injunctive relief is common.[9] A "hold up," however, need not occur in every case. If Greensweep's switching costs were only $500,000, compared to $4 million, then the negotiated post-injunction royalty would presumably be less than $500,000. Airwings' post-injunction licensing fee would then allow Greensweep an overall profit of $1.5 million, probably closer

4 This chapter does not discuss the rationale for, nor the effect of, preliminary injunctive relief.

5 *See* Grain Processing Corp. v. American Maize-Prods. Co., 185 F.3d 1341, 1351 (Fed. Cir. 1999) ("Without the infringing product, a rational would-be infringer is likely to offer an acceptable non-infringing alternative, if available, to compete with the patent owner rather than leave the market altogether. The competitor in the 'but for' marketplace is hardly likely to surrender its complete market share when faced with a patent, if it can compete in some other lawful manner. Moreover, only by comparing the patented invention to its next-best available alternative(s) – regardless of whether the alternative(s) were actually produced and sold during the infringement – can the court discern the market value of the patent owner's exclusive right, and therefore his expected profit or reward, had the infringer's activities not prevented him from taking full economic advantage of this right.").

6 *See* Mark A. Lemley, *The Ongoing Confusion Over Ongoing Royalties* (Stanford Pub. Law Working Paper No. 793361), *available at* http://ssrn.com/abstract=1793361 (posted Apr. 4, 2011).

7 Mark A. Lemley & Carl Shapiro, *Patent Hold Up and Royalty Stacking*, 85 TEXAS L. REV. 1991 (2007); Einer Elhauge, *Do Patent Hold Up and Royalty Stacking Lead to Systemically Excessive Royalties?* 4 J. COMP. L. & ECON. 534 (2008); Gregory Sidak, *Hold Up, Royalty Stacking and the Presumption of Injunctive Relief: A Reply to Professors Lemley and Shapiro*, 92 MINN. L. REV. 714 (2008).

8 A different problem, known as "royalty stacking," can also be caused by injunctive relief. An injunction may give the patentee of a relatively minor component disproportionate bargaining power if switching costs are high enough. *See supra* note 7. In fact, if more than one patent is infringed, then "stacked" royalties may result in a net loss to an innocent infringer, as in the Greensweep hypothetical.

9 *See Post EBay Injunctive Relief*, PATENTLY-O BLOG (Nov. 17, 2009), http://www.patentlyo.com/patent/2009/11/post-ebay-injunctive-relief.html (reporting permanent injunctions granted in 72% of cases); *Success Rates for Permanent Injunction after eBay v. MercExchange*, PRIOR SMART.COM, http://news.priorsmart.com/success-rates-permanent-injunction-after-ebay-v-mercexchange-bVN/ (last visited Feb. 2, 2012) (reporting 72% of cases granted at least a partial permanent injunction).

to the likely result of an ex ante bargain. In such a case, an injunction does not look punitive, but rather merely prompts an arms-length, post-infringement royalty negotiation. Consistent with the academic papers commenting on patent hold up, this chapter focuses on the situation where an injunction allows the patent owner to obtain compensation beyond what it would expect from an ex ante arms-length negotiation.

The debate so far has focused on how granting or failing to grant injunctions affects incentives to invent or how they affect economic efficiency in a broad sense.[10] Some commentators have also examined the question from the standpoint of the history of equitable relief.[11] No one has yet exploited the obvious analogy that extra-compensatory injunctions in hold-up cases can bear to punitive damages nor has asked this question: When would extra-compensatory relief typically be authorized under common law? The confusion over how courts should deal with the patent hold-up phenomenon can be substantially clarified by examining the justifications provided at common law for extra-compensatory relief. Part I of this chapter proceeds by examining the common law rationales for the award of punitive damages, including the speculation of economists seeking to make sense of the common law cases. Part II explains how the test applied by the Supreme Court in *eBay* should be interpreted to accommodate the most applicable wisdom of the common law.

I. DESCRIPTIVE ANALYSIS OF INJUNCTIONS AS PUNITIVE DAMAGES

At first cut, one might approach the patent hold-up phenomenon by mechanically applying the black-letter rules stating when punitive damages are an appropriate remedy. The focus in treatises and the *Restatement (Second) of Torts* is squarely on the reprehensibility of the defendant's conduct. "According to the usual formulation, punitive damages can be awarded when the defendant's behavior is malicious, oppressive, gross, willful and wanton, or fraudulent."[12] For example, the *Restatement* requires "conduct involving some element of outrage similar to that usually found in crime."[13] In this sense, punitive damages function as a "tool to punish [a wrongdoer] for his outrageous conduct and to deter him and others like him from similar conduct in the future."[14] If this language told the whole story of punitive damages, then the analogy to the law of patent injunctions would be straightforward: a court would need only assess the defendant's mental state in deciding whether to award an injunction when significant switching costs created a hold-up situation. A least one

[10] *See id.*

[11] H. Tomas Gomez-Arostequi, *Prospective Compensation in Lieu of a Final Injunction in Patent and Copyright Cases*, 78 FORDHAM L. REV. 1661 (2010).

[12] Robert Cooter, *Punitive Damages, Social Norms and Economic Analysis*, 60 LAW & CONTEMP. PROBLEMS 73, 75 (1997).

[13] *See* RESTATEMENT (SECOND) OF TORTS § 908, cmt. b (1979).

[14] *Id.* at § 908(1).

commentator has already suggested that the defendant's intent to infringe should be a factor in the post-*eBay* patent injunction analysis.[15]

Of course, if injunctions were available only in situations where the infringer's conduct was malicious or outrageous, few injunctions would issue. Cotropia and Lemley found that only 31.1 percent of the patent cases they studied involved an allegation that the defendant knew of the patent before the lawsuit was filed, and only 10.9 percent alleged that the infringer knowingly copied.[16] More tellingly, only 1.76 percent of the cases in their sample resulted in a finding of intentional copying by the infringer.[17] Most infringement is committed unknowingly, as in the earlier Greensweep hypothetical, or is committed with knowledge of the patent but with legitimate doubts as to its enforceability. After all, the patent invalidity rate hovers around 30 percent.[18] In addition, the black-letter rule suggests something more than mere knowledge of a right being invaded; it envisions intent to harm the victim. Mere knowledge of committing infringement might not be enough,[19] although one can certainly imagine an infringer, especially of a process patent, seeking to commit the infringement in secret, compete with the patent owner, and intentionally cause a devastating loss of profits. Injunctions would rarely issue in hold-up cases if willful conduct were required. Of course, that might be the proper result.

Interestingly, trademark law already has added a willfulness requirement onto a class of cases where the victim of the infringement requests extra-compensatory equitable relief. In trademark law, unlike in patent law, the victim of the infringement can request a recovery of the infringer's profits (the equitable award of an "accounting"), even when it cannot prove its own losses.[20] In such cases, the award of an accounting can act like the award of punitive damages, in that the recovery may exceed any harm done to the plaintiff.[21] Therefore, in line with the common law's insistence on willful conduct as a predicate to punitive damages, many jurisdictions require a showing of willful and intentional infringement before awarding

[15] William Everding, *"Heads-I-Win, Tails-You-Lose": The Predicament Legitimate Small Entities Face Post Ebay and the Essential Role of Willful Infringement in the Four-Factor Permanent Injunction Analysis*, 41 J. MARSHALL L. REV. 189 (2007) (willfulness should be a factor after *eBay*).

[16] *See* Christopher A. Cotropia & Mark A. Lemley, *Copying in Patent Law*, 87 N.C. L. REV. 1421, 1424 (2009).

[17] *Id.*

[18] *See* Mathew D. Henry & John L. Turner, *The Court of Appeals for the Federal Circuit's Impact on Patent Litigation*, 35 J. LEG. STUD. 85, 117 (2006) (noting that from 1982–2002 the rate at which courts found patents invalid was 28%).

[19] *See In re* Seagate Tech., 497 F.3d 1360, 1371 (Fed. Cir. 2007) (en banc) ("[T]o establish willful infringement, a patentee must show by clear and convincing evidence that the infringer acted despite an objectively high likelihood that its actions constituted infringement of a valid patent.... If this threshold objective standard is satisfied, the patentee must also demonstrate that this objectively-defined risk (determined by the record developed in the infringement proceeding) was either known or so obvious that it should have been known to the accused infringer.").

[20] *See* Lindy Pen Co., Inc. v. Bic Pen Corp., 982 F.2d 1400 (9th Cir. 1993).

[21] *See* Paul J. Heald, *Money Damages for Corrective Advertising*, 55 U. CHI. L. REV. 629, 640–41 (1988).

an accounting in a trademark infringement case.[22] If the request for an accounting, however, is instead based on an attempt to approximate the actual damages done to the plaintiff, the same courts will not require a showing of willfulness.[23] Sometimes the request for an accounting looks like a request for punitive damages; sometimes it does not. Although this chapter does not ultimately argue for the enforcement of a willfulness requirement to support a patent injunction, it does advocate a willingness on the part of courts to identify when a request for an injunction looks like a request for punitive damages and when it does not. Trademark law shows that this distinction can be made.

Although one could simplistically require courts to make a finding of willful infringement before issuing an injunction in a patent royalty hold-up case, the law of punitive damages has never been as simple as identifying and sanctioning willfulness. As Steven Calandrillo noted, "[i]n the United States, there was some confusion over the purpose of punitive damages when they were initially introduced into our legal system. At times they were used as extra-compensatory damages to account for the trial fees incurred by successful litigants, whereas at other times they focused on the more traditional goals of punishment and deterrence."[24] And Alexandra Klass explains, "[t]oday's apparent unanimity regarding the purposes of punitive damages has not always existed. Historically, at least four other purposes have been identified, such as (1) preserving the peace; (2) inducing private law enforcement; (3) compensating victims of otherwise uncompensable losses; and (4) paying the plaintiff's attorney's fees."[25] According to Michael Trebilcock, the law has always embraced rationales beyond retribution, including deterrence and compensatory goals, in addition to providing relief for special dignitary harms.[26]

Most who have canvassed punitive damages decisions in the United States conclude that the most convincing explanation for extra-compensatory damages does not rest on a simple desire to punish willful behavior.[27] Although there are dissenters,[28]

[22] *See Lindy Pen*, 982 F.2d.

[23] *Id.*

[24] Steve P. Calandrillo, *Penalizing Punitive Damages: Why the Supreme Court Needs a Lesson in Law and Economics*, 78 GEO. WASH. L. REV. 774, 781 (2010).

[25] Alexandra Klass, *Punitive Damages and Valuing Harm*, 92 MINN. L. REV. 83, 92 (2007).

[26] Bruce Chapman & Michael Trebilcock, *Punitive Damages: Divergence in Search of a Rationale*, 40 ALA. L. REV. 741, 805–26 (1989). *See also* Anthony Sebok, *Punitive Damages: From Myth to Theory*, 92 IOWA L. REV. 957, 960 (2007) ("I argue that punitive damages are awarded to vindicate an interest in social dignity held by private citizens.").

[27] *See* Sergey Budylin, *Punitive Damages as a Social Harm Measure: An Economic Analysis Continues*, 31 OKLA. CITY L. REV. 457, 458 (2006) ("[T]here seems to be no clear-cut economic way to either define the notion of reprehensibility, or, most importantly, to calculate the optimal amount of punitive damages"); Calandrillo, *supra* note 24, at 779 ("[L]aw and economics movement provides a principled, workable solution by viewing punitive damages as a means of creating socially optimal deterrence and levels of care, rather than as a tool for imposing punishment for morally reprehensible actions.").

[28] *See* Sebok, *supra* note 26; Benjamin Zipursky, *A Theory of Punitive Damages*, 84 TEX. L. REV. 105, 107 (2005) ("The plaintiff's right to be punitive constitutes the core of a civil aspect of punitive damages, while the state's goal of inflicting punishment upon the defendant is the root of a criminal aspect.").

the most recent commentary assumes that punitive damages developed as a mechanism to attain socially optimal deterrence in situations where compensatory damages provided insufficient behavioral incentives,[29] including situations where the defendant's conduct was not necessarily morally reprehensible.[30] In this view, the role of extra-compensatory damages is purely instrumental – a tool used by courts to deter inefficient behavior when an award of compensatory damages is inadequate. Of course, even with this view, intent may be linked to punitive damages in at least two ways. First, an intentional wrongdoer may be more likely than a negligent one to hide its wrongdoing (remember the infringer of the process patent offered earlier). Punitive damages law may rationally be taking into account the higher rate of undetected harm in cases of intentional infringement.[31] Second, punitive damages may serve to encourage consensual transactions instead of forceful takings. If so, the threat of extraordinary compensation may often deter those who would otherwise intentionally or recklessly avoid negotiating.[32]

The modern thinking on punitive damages culminates with Polinsky and Shavell's 1998 article, *Punitive Damages: An Economic Analysis*,[33] where they argue that total damages awarded in tort cases should be equal to the harm suffered by the plaintiff, multiplied by the reciprocal of the chance of non-detection of the wrong.[34] In other words, if the secretive infringer of a process patent will be caught only one in ten times, then the patent owner's actual damages should be multiplied by a factor of ten. Judge Posner endorsed this view in Mathias v. Accor Economy Lodging (the

[29] *See* Budylin, *supra* note 27, at 459 ("[A] potential tortfeasor is motivated to maximize the total social utility, including that of himself, of potential victims, and of unassignable parties, society as a whole."); Calandrillo, *supra* note 24, at 779 ("The ultimate goal of modern tort law jurisprudence should be to make injurers internalize the full costs of all of their actions so that they will take the proper level of care – not too much, not too little, but just right."); Cooter, *supra* note 12, at 89 ("Conversely, imposing extra-compensatory damages measured relative to the baseline of perfect compensation or risk-equivalent damages, provides incentives for excessive self-monitoring. In other words, extra-compensatory damages create incentives for unreasonably costly vigilance."); Keith Hylton, *Punitive Damages and the Economic Theory of Penalties*, 87 GEO. L. J. 421, 423 (1998) ("In simplest terms, the rule that I propose is as follows: If the offender's gain is probably greater than the victim's loss, then the punitive award should aim to internalize victim losses; if the offender's gain is probably less than or equal to the victim's loss, then the punitive award should aim to eliminate the prospect of gain on the part of the offender."); Mitchell Polinsky & Steven Shavell, *Punitive Damages: An Economic Analysis*, 111 HARV. L. REV. 869, 873 (1998) ("[I]njurers should be made to pay for the harm their conduct generates, not less, not more. If injurers pay less than for the harm they cause, underdeterrence may result – that is, precautions may be inadequate, product prices may be too low, and risk-producing activities may be excessive.").

[30] For example, Klass suggests that courts should use punitive damages to account for non-monetary harm to the environment. *See* Klass, *supra* note 25, at 88.

[31] *See* Cooter, *supra* note 12, at 74 ("Deterring intentional wrongdoing, however, requires additional liability. In circumstances explained in Part V. B., optimal deterrence requires increasing compensatory damages by the reciprocal of the enforcement error.").

[32] *See* Polinsky & Shavell, *supra* note 29, at 945–47.

[33] *Id.*

[34] *See id.* at 874; *see also* Cooter, *supra* note 12, at 74 ("[O]ptimal deterrence requires increasing compensatory damages by the reciprocal of the enforcement error.").

famous "bed bug case"), stating "[i]f a tortfeasor is 'caught' only half the time he commits torts, then when he is caught, he should be punished twice as heavily in order to make up for the times he gets away."[35] Landes and Posner tie this insight to intent, concluding that an intentional tortfeasor "has a strong incentive to conceal his identity or . . . avoid his being sued . . . so optimal damages would be a multiple of the victim's injury."[36] Cooter concurs, although his view is somewhat idiosyncratic: he agrees with the multiplier approach, but ties the extra liability trigger to the defendant's intent on a theory of insufficient self-monitoring.[37]

Shortly after Polinsky and Shavell offered their prescription, Keith Hylton suggested that their scheme might be overgenerous where the offender's gains were smaller that the victim's losses.[38] In such a case, the multiplier, he argued should be applied to the offender's gain.[39] For example, imagine a victim's loss caused by misconduct is $1,000, whereas the wrongdoer only expected to benefit $600 and the chance of non-enforcement is 50 percent. In such a case, Hylton argued, an award of two times $600, or $1,200, (plus a nominal amount) would be enough to make the victim whole and, from an ex ante perspective, adequate to deter the wrongdoer in the future. He concluded that "[i]n simplest terms, the rule that I propose is as follows: If the offender's gain is probably greater than the victim's loss, then the punitive award should aim to internalize victim losses; if the offender's gain is probably less than or equal to the victim's loss, then the punitive award should aim to eliminate the prospect of gain on the part of the offender."[40] At a minimum, Polinsky, Shavell, and Hylton would agree that no punitive award would ever be justified in a case where the victim (for example, a patent owner) suffered no actual damages or where the infringement occurred in the open and was certain to be detected.

Economists, therefore, have a difficult time with the rare case such as Jacque v. Steenburg Homes, Inc.[41] In *Jacque*, the Wisconsin Supreme Court affirmed a punitive award of $100,000 in a case involving a mobile home being dragged in plain sight across a farmer's field without the farmer's permission. The jury awarded nominal compensatory damages because no harm was done to the property, but the court nonetheless justified the punitive damages awarded by the jury on several

35 *See* Mathias v. Accor Econ. Lodging, 347 F.3d 672, 677 (7th Cir. 2003).

36 *See* William M. Landes & Richard A. Posner, *An Economic Theory of Intentional Torts*, 1 INT'L REV. L. & ECON. 127, 135 (1981).

37 *See* Cooter, *supra* note 12, at 74 ("To compute the minimum, I distinguish between intentional and unintentional wrongdoing by a theory of rational self-monitoring. Imperfect self-monitoring results in lapses that cause unintentional violations of legal obligations. I show that liability for compensatory damages provides efficient incentives for self-monitoring. Deterring intentional wrongdoing, however, requires additional liability. In circumstances explained in Part V. B., optimal deterrence requires increasing compensatory damages by the reciprocal of the enforcement error.").

38 Hylton, *supra* note 29.

39 *Id.* at 423, 460. From an ex ante perspective, one might argue that the multiplier should be applied to the tortfeasor's expected gain at the time of the tort.

40 *Id.* at 423.

41 563 N.W.2d 154 (Wisc. 1997).

noneconomic grounds.[42] The court emphasized the special nature of interests in real property and the dignitary interests of the farmer who protested the trespass vehemently. Descriptive economic theories of common law punitive damages may dominate the commentary, but they clearly cannot explain all cases. Although we must acknowledge purely "proprietarian" justifications for punitive damages in real property cases,[43] our paradigmatic patent case is distinguishable on several grounds. The typical corporate victim of patent infringement does not hold the same sort of personal dignity interest as a small farmer; nor do property rights in patents involve the same visceral and natural rights foundation as rights in one's homestead.[44] Most importantly, cases such as *Jacque* do not usually involve the hold-up problem that is the focus of this chapter.[45]

Despite its lack of universal explanatory power, the deterrent-multiplier approach to punitive damages helps us understand the suggestion made by the concurring Justices in *eBay* that injunctions in patent cases may be inappropriate when the patent owner has suffered no actual damages due to the infringement.[46] This view is consistent with the notion that extra-compensatory damages should usually not be available in the absence of actual damage to the plaintiff.[47] The deterrent-multiplier discussion, however, does little to explain the absence of a rule, or even the hint of a rule, in patent cases that open and notorious infringers should be immune from injunctive relief. A significant class of infringers violate the patent owner's rights by openly selling commercial products that embody the infringed invention. Their chance of being caught is high, often close to 100 percent. A simplistic version of Polinsky, Shavell, Cooter, and Hylton's positions would suggest that, except for cases such as the infringement of a process patent going on behind closed doors,[48] the availability of injunctive relief in patent hold-up cases is rather mysterious.

42 *Id.* at 11. *See also* Restatement (Second) of Torts, § 163, cmts. c & e (1979) (noting that "outrageous" trespasses to land justify punitive damages, even in the absence of actual harm); W. Page Keeton et al., Prosser and Keeton on the Law of Torts § 2, at 14 (5th ed. 1984).

43 Richard Epstein also uses a proprietarian justification for awarding injunctions in real property cases and would extend that reasoning to mechanically awarding injunctions in patent infringement cases. See Richard A. Epstein, *The Property Rights Movement and Intellectual Property*, Regulation 58, 62 (Winter 2008).

44 Adam Mossoff has shown, however, that patents were considered property for purposes of the Takings Clause throughout the nineteenth century. *See* Adam Mossoff, *Patents as Constitutional Private Property: The Historical Protection of Patents under the Takings Clause*, 87 B.U. L. Rev. 689 (2007).

45 But a case might. *See* Epstein, *supra* note 43, at 62 ("For land, this demand could require encroachers to rip down expensive buildings unless they pay a king's ransom to purchase a license to maintain their structures. The severe sanctions are justified to preserve voluntary markets.").

46 *See* eBay Inc. v. MercExchange, LLC, 547 U.S. 388, 396 (2006) ("An industry has developed in which firms use patents not as a basis for producing and selling goods but, instead, primarily for obtaining licensing fees."). Those who do not produce and sell goods do not suffer lost profits when infringement occurs.

47 *See* sources cited *supra* note 42, which suggest an "outrageous" conduct exception.

48 Federal patent law creates a burden-shifting rule to benefit owners of process patents who believe they are the victims of unseen infringement. *See* 35 U.S.C. § 295.

One possible answer to the mystery might be found in Hylton's justification for his proposal: "social welfare is maximized by a scheme that does not deter those offenders whose gain exceeds the losses of their victims as long *as they are required to pay the full social costs of their conduct*."[49] In the context of patent infringement, the full social cost of the misconduct may go beyond the actual damages suffered by a patent owner in a particular case. Denying relief generally to patent owners who do not suffer lost profits might well dampen the incentive to invent. Only manufacturing owners could recover under such a restriction, and those hoping to invent and then license might lose the monetary incentive to continue their research. Those familiar with patent law already know how it addresses this negative externality: a successful patent owner is entitled to no less than a reasonable royalty from the infringer.[50] A reasonable royalty roughly maintains adequate incentives to invent and thereby approximates an internalization of the full social cost of infringement.

Of course, the reasonable royalty in patent law assumes that the infringer would have negotiated a license at a profitable rate. U.S. patent law does not force the infringer to disgorge its profit; an accounting is no longer a remedy. This rule is consistent with Hylton's assertion that a tortfeaser (patent infringer) should be allowed to profit as long as its profits exceed losses to the victim. As long as the reasonable royalty measure maintains adequate incentives to invent, then the full social cost of the infringement is internalized. Interestingly, a reasonable royalty is not available in the case of trademark infringement, where economics identifies no parallel threat to inventive incentives.[51]

Of course, if the reasonable royalty remedy maintains adequate incentives to invent, can economics explain the persistence of injunctive relief in hold-up cases where the victim of the infringement has been made whole and incentives to invent are not threatened? Neither the simplistic common law analogy nor the deterrence/multiplier approach seems to explain injunctions when (i) the infringer's conduct is not intentional, (ii) the victim of the infringement is made whole via a monetary remedy, or (iii) the infringer commits its wrongful acts in plain sight. These three situations surely cover the vast majority of patent infringements, and yet injunctive relief is still commonplace.[52]

Polinsky and Shavell, however, offer a second justification for punitive damages that is independent of their deterrence-multiplier rationale.[53] They suggest that even in cases where enforcement is certain, it may sometimes be "desirable to impose punitive damages in order to encourage market transactions."[54] Polinsky and Shavell

49 Hylton, *supra* note 29, at 433 (emphasis added).

50 *See* 35 U.S.C. § 284.

51 *See* Qualitex Co. v. Jacobson Prods., 514 U.S. 159, 164–65 (1995) (stating that trademark law is not concerned with creating incentives to develop new trademarks).

52 *See supra* note 9 (reporting 70–75% of patent cases grant permanent injunctions).

53 *See* Polinsky & Shavell, *supra* note 29, at 947 ("As we noted above, this rationale for punitive damages, when applicable, is independent of the escaping liability rationale.").

54 *Id.* at 946.

identify cases where a tort looks like a forced taking by the tortfeasor from the victim in a situation where an ex ante negotiation should have resulted in a consensual transfer. Theft is a species of their generic example, and one explanation for punishing theft criminally (surely an extra-compensatory remedy) is the need to provide adequate incentives for market transactions to take place, instead of surreptitious takings.[55] Polinsky and Shavell even offer copyright infringement as one possible example where punitive damages might be needed to incentivize consensual transfers.[56] In fact, the Russian Federation and Germany (but not the United States or the European Union) has criminalized some forms of patent infringement.[57]

In the class of cases that Polinsky and Shavell identify, extra-compensatory damages are merited in order to encourage a negotiation rather than a taking. Society should prefer a negotiation over a nonconsensual taking for several reasons. First, a private negotiation by the parties will result in a more accurate valuation of the property. Second, a private negotiation saves the public the costs of using the judicial system to perform the valuation function. As Landes and Posner note in their discussion of punitive damages, "[s]ociety is better off if the market is used, because the costs of the market are lower than the costs of a coercive transaction with compensation enforced by the legal system."[58] Third, to the extent consensual transfers are encouraged, property owners have to spend fewer resources fencing their property off from those who would take it or looking for those who have infringed their rights.[59] Finally, private litigation costs are also saved. All these rationales seem to apply with significant force to cases of patent infringement where the infringer knew or should have known its actions would infringe a valid patent.

In other words, even in situations where enforceability is not in doubt and no multiplier is needed to account for the chance the wrong will escape detection, Polinsky and Shavell, Landes and Posner, and perhaps Cooter too[60] recognize a separate rationale for imposing punitive damages based on the goal of promoting consensual transfers where possible. Clearly, the objective of encouraging consensual transfers has direct application to patent infringement cases where the infringer is using technology that the owner would be willing to license. The prevalence of the reasonable royalty as a remedy for patent infringement suggests the willingness to license can often be assumed, and even in cases where the patent owner and infringer are competitors, a consensual license that accounts for any sales lost to the

[55] *See* Richard A. Posner, Economic Analysis of Law 203 (3d ed. 1986).

[56] Polinsky & Shavell, *supra* note 29, at 945.

[57] Ugolovnyi Kodeks Rossiiskoi Federatsii (Criminal Code) 147 (provides for criminal penalties for patent infringement).

[58] *See* Landes & Posner, *supra* note 36, at 135.

[59] *See* Polinsky & Shavell, *supra* note 29, at 947 ("The foregoing problems – an excessive amount of harm and wasteful efforts to take and protect property – can be avoided if punitive damages are imposed.").

[60] *See* Cooter, *supra* note 12, at 74 ("Imperfect self-monitoring results in lapses that cause unintentional violations of legal obligations. I show that liability for compensatory damages provides efficient incentives for self-monitoring. Deterring intentional wrongdoing, however, requires additional liability.").

patent owner can be calculated. Indeed, the wrong in many cases is not a concerted assault on the business of the patent owner, but is rather a failure to negotiate. Here, the patent injunction/punitive damages analogy does a nice bit of work. The availability of injunctions in patent hold-up cases provides strong incentives for potential infringers to negotiate rather than take technology without permission, a function that Polinsky and Shavell also assign to punitive damages.

This explanation for the availability of injunctive relief in patent infringement cases also sits well with the sanction of willful conduct that one finds in punitive damages case law and the *Restatement (Second) of Torts*. Willfulness is key to the *Restatement* formulation of punitive damages and is also relevant to the incentive-to-negotiate justification for injunctive relief. After all, where the infringer knows that the patent owner has an enforceable property right and infringes anyway, he or she has deliberately foregone a consensual negotiation. In a world where mere compensation to the victim of infringement is the only remedy, the infringer has a diminished incentive to negotiate, but when an injunction functions punitively, the incentive to negotiate is increased. As a descriptive matter, therefore the punitive damages analogy helps explain some awards of injunctive relief in patent cases.

Other mysteries remain, however. For example, why do courts not expressly consider the intent of the infringer or whether the infringer had knowledge of the patent before awarding an injunction? Why do courts not expressly distinguish between patent hold-up situations and non–hold-up situations? Can courts be more precise in calibrating the incentive to negotiate? As a blunt policy tool, do injunctions in patent cases over-deter?

II. NORMATIVE ANALYSIS OF INJUNCTIONS AS PUNITIVE DAMAGES

Given that American patent law already has a treble damages provision for willful infringement,[61] the question naturally arises whether routinely awarded injunctive relief might not over-deter patent infringement. Given that many infringers are the most efficient exploiters of an invention (especially in situations where the patent owner is not exploiting the invention at all), one might expect the law to be fairly tolerant of innocent infringers, especially those who are improvers or independent inventors.[62] Most of those who write about punitive damages are acutely aware of the dangers of over-deterrence. Hylton argues for "'appropriate or optimal deterrence,' which implies deterring offensive conduct only up to the point at which society begins to lose more from deterrence efforts than from the offenses

[61] *See* 35 U.S.C. § 284.

[62] *See* Polinsky & Shavell, *supra* note 29, at 918 ("a policy of removing the defendant's gain may result in overdeterrence"); Hylton, *supra* note 29, at 433 at ("[S]ocial welfare is maximized by a scheme that does not deter those offenders whose gain exceeds the losses of their victims, as long as they are required to pay the full social costs of their conduct.")

it deters."[63] Calandrillo worries that too high punitive damages will "lead to over-deterrence, price increases beyond optimum, quantity of goods purchased far below optimum, and a significant reduction in overall social welfare . . . incentiviz[ing] companies to take excess care."[64] Cooter worries that "extra-compensatory damages create incentives for unreasonably costly vigilance."[65] Polinsky and Shavell add that "if injurers are made to pay more than for the harm they cause, wasteful precautions may be taken, product prices may be inappropriately high, and risky but socially beneficial activities may be undesirably curtailed."[66]

The import of their concerns is clear. Simply because one can justify some injunctions in patent cases under the punitive damages/incentive-to-negotiate rationale, this does not mean the remedy should be unthinkingly endorsed. The specter of excessive care is very real in the innovation context. As Bessen and Meurer have convincingly shown in their recent work, patents are difficult to find and often vague and unclear in scope when discovered.[67] Given the gross imperfections in the patent notice system, searching can easily become wasteful. More importantly, excessive remedies can dampen innovation. Think of the initial hypothetical. The provision of injunctive relief resulted in a net loss to Greensweep, which was ready to commercialize a socially valuable innovation. Deterring those who create value for society is by definition excessive remediation. Therefore, the attempt should be made to define the situations more narrowly when injunctive relief is appropriate and to fine-tune the extant test to fit the proper remedy. Again, this chapter only considers the patent hold-up situation. As noted earlier, in situations where the infringer's switching costs are lower than a reasonable royalty, it does not matter whether an injunction issues or not.

The first step is to identify the primary situations when the punitive damages analogy teaches that injunctive relief might be appropriate: (i) when enforceability is imperfect (e.g., when the infringer of a process patent covers his tracks); (ii) when an incentive is necessary to encourage a consensual negotiation; and (iii) when over-deterrence is not a worry (e.g., when the infringer is a blatant counterfeiter and not a follow-on innovator).

When considering imperfect enforceability, the problem can often be addressed solely under the treble damages provision of the Patent Act, which authorizes the

[63] *See* Hylton, *supra* note 29, at 421.

[64] *See* Calandrillo, *supra* note 24, at 780, 797. *See also id.* at 780, 799 ("[I]ndiscriminate punitive damages awards have the potential to create perverse second-order consequences [and] a decline in overall social welfare.")

[65] Cooter, *supra* note 12, at 89.

[66] Polinsky & Shavell, *supra* note 29, at 873. *See also id.* at 880 ("Although the notion of excessive spending on precautions might seem counterintuitive to the reader, it is quite real, and often recognized as such. For example, commentators frequently make reference to 'defensive medicine,' by which is meant physicians' wasteful use of tests and diagnostic procedures in response to the threat of liability.").

[67] *See* Michael J. Meurer & James Bessen, Patent Failure: How Judges, Lawyers, and Bureaucrats Put Inventors at Risk (2009).

court to "increase the damages up to three times the amount found or assessed."[68] As long as the chance that the infringement will be undetected is greater than one out of three, adequate deterrence can be calibrated under 35 U.S.C. § 284. If the chance of detection is lower, say only 20 percent, then treble damages will not be enough to deter, and the threat of an injunction may be necessary as an additional remedy. Note that an injunction is a blunt instrument. If switching costs are low enough, it may not provide additional deterrence, and if switching costs are very high, the remedy may be excessive. Courts can control the cost of complying with damage awards by adjusting damages, but they cannot control the cost of an injunction, because the courts cannot affect switching costs. Nonetheless, at least in the case of deliberate infringement and obfuscation by the infringer, over-deterrence should seldom be a worry. Stimulating excessive searching for the patent will not be a problem, because the infringer already has the knowledge. Additionally, the infringer is likely not innovating, but rather stealing, so the spirit of inventiveness should not be overly dampened.[69]

In addition to addressing the problem of imperfect enforceability, treble damages under § 284 can be used to provide incentives for potential users of technology to find and negotiate with patent holders. Extra-compensatory relief should be available when the patent could have been discovered by a reasonable search, and therefore the infringer saved the cost of searching for the patent and negotiating a license. Calculating saved search and negotiation costs is relatively straightforward for one experienced in the art, and adequate deterrence could be effected by augmenting the monetary remedy by a figure nominally higher than those saved costs. In line with Polinsky and Shavell, however, a court in some cases might want to multiply the amount of saved costs by the probability of non-detection. Such an augmentation performed under § 284 should normally be adequate to create incentives for infringers to negotiate rather than infringe. By the same token, conducting a reasonable search should always be a defense to extra-compensatory relief under this rationale, be it punitive damages under § 284 or injunctive relief.[70] By definition, an extra award in such a case would stimulate wasteful searching.

Therefore, the most fruitful and direct result of the patent injunction/punitive damages analogy suggests that injunctions should only issue in a very narrow band of cases where (i) the chance of enforcement against the infringer is less than one out of three; (ii) the infringer's intentionally or recklessly saved costs of searching and negotiating are so high that the treble damages provision of § 284 is inadequate to impose offsetting costs; or (iii) the risk of over-deterrence is minimal (e.g., the infringer is a blatant counterfeiter as opposed to a follow-on innovator). Under this standard, only a small fraction of patent owners should qualify for injunctive relief.

68 35 U.S.C. § 284.

69 Although the infringer might be making a valuable improvement to the invention.

70 *See* Paul J. Heald, *Optimal Remedies for Patent Infringement: A Transactional Approach*, 45 Houston L. Rev. 1165, 1200 (2008).

The final remaining normative question is whether the equitable framework presented by the Supreme Court in *eBay* can be adapted to serve the ends advocated earlier in the chapter. In *eBay* the court held that injunctions should issue in patent cases when the plaintiff demonstrates

> (1)that it has suffered an irreparable injury; (2) that remedies available at law, such as monetary damages, are inadequate to compensate for that injury; (3) that considering the balance of hardships between the plaintiff and defendant, a remedy in equity is warranted; and (4) that the public interest would not be disserved by a permanent injunction.[71]

The formulation focuses on the parties to the dispute as opposed to potential, similarly situated parties in a range of future similar disputes; nonetheless, a sufficient link to under-enforcement concerns and the incentive-to-negotiate rationale can be found in the *eBay* test.

First, the court must identify whether it is faced with a patent hold-up problem. On this issue, the defendant should bear the burden of presenting adequate evidence of his or her switching costs. If there is no hold up, then the injunction lacks a punitive aspect and whether an injunction issues or not is irrelevant from the standpoint of public welfare. As a general matter, if a hold up is likely, then it would seem that the balance of hardships swings firmly to the infringer's favor.[72] And, of course, to the extent that an injunction would stimulate excessive searching or dampen the spirit of independent invention improvement, the public interest would be disserved by the granting of equitable relief. However, in the context of under-enforcement or incentive-to-negotiate problems that cannot be solved through augmented monetary remedies under § 284, the balance of hardships would seem to swing to the patent owner (or at least to patent owners in general), while the public would have an interest in seeing the punitive function of the patent injunction realized.

Although the permanent injunction rationale (as justified by reference to the proper function of punitive damages) can be fit within the existing framework for injunctive relief in patent cases, an injunction is surely a blunt instrument to accomplish the goals described earlier. In cases of low switching costs, an injunction will do no work at all. In cases of hold up, an injunction might still lead to over-compensation and possibly over-deterrence. For this reason, my prior theoretical work on patent remedies[73] relied on the remedy of an accounting, or a partial accounting, of the infringer's profits to achieve a punitive effect when justified. Consider two examples where extra-compensatory relief should be awarded: (i) the

[71] eBay Inc. v. MercExchange, L.L.C., 547 U.S. 388, 391 (2006).

[72] Of course, switching costs might be very high in a situation where the patented technology is extremely valuable. In such a case, an award close to the size of the infringer's switching costs might be justified, because an ex ante arms-length negotiation might well have resulted in a massive licensing fee.

[73] *See* Heald, *Optimal Remedies*, *supra* note 70 (arguing that patent remedies should incentivize optimal levels of invention by incentivizing the optimal amount of transacting between firms that invent and firms that require inventions).

damage done to the patentee is $1,000 and the chance of detection is one out of four, or (ii) the damage done to the patentee is $1,000 and the search costs saved by the infringer are $4,000. In both cases, the treble damages provision in 35 U.S.C. § 284 will result in an award of no more than $3,000, when at least $4,000 is appropriate. It is difficult to calibrate an injunction so that the necessary extra $1,000 cost is surgically imposed on the infringer. A partial accounting, however, might be used to transfer more precisely the appropriate amount from the infringer to the plaintiff.

Unfortunately, an accounting of the patentee's profits is no longer a remedy authorized by the patent statute.[74] It disappeared in 1946,[75] and when treble damages do not suffice, we are left with the clumsy operation of injunctive relief to achieve the regulatory goals of punitive damages. Indeed, it may be that the elimination of an accounting led to the pre-*eBay* acceptance of permanent injunctive relief as the norm. The model that I advocate in *Optimal Remedies for Patent Infringement: A Transactional Approach*[76] is broadly consistent with the permanent injunction/punitive damages analogy explored here, but requires the resurrection of the accounting remedy. It also expressly considers patent quality as a variable that should in some cases diminish the multiplier effect discussed earlier.[77]

CONCLUSION

In the patent hold-up situation, injunctive relief is extra-compensatory and should be judged by the normal standards under which courts judge the appropriateness of such relief. Common law cases involving punitive damages (and economic analysis that tries to make sense of those cases) provide a helpful set of tools for judging when injunctive relief is appropriate. Of course, when the infringer's cost of switching to a substitute technology is lower than a reasonable royalty, injunctions may freely issue (or not), because they have no punitive character. However, in the case of patent hold up – when the infringer's switching costs are higher than a reasonable royalty – an injunction takes on a punitive aspect and can only be justified in three narrow situations. First, when the likelihood that the infringement will go unpunished is greater than one in three, the award of treble damages under § 284 will be inadequate to deter the infringer and injunctive relief may provide the necessary added deterrence. Second, in the rare case when the award of punitive damages

74 *See* Caprice Roberts, *The Case for Restitution and Unjust Enrichment in Patent Law*, 14 Lewis & Clark L. Rev. 653 (2010).

75 *Id.* at 660.

76 *See* Heald, *supra* note 73.

77 When a rational potential licensee considers negotiating a license, the potential invalidity of the patent will be considered. If a potential licensee rationally concludes that the patent will be held invalid 90 percent of the time, it will either negotiate a discounted fee or choose to risk an infringement suit. Remedies in patent infringement cases must be calibrated so that potential licensees are not incentivized to purchase licenses in situations where that is not the rational strategy.

under § 284 is inadequate to generate an award greater than the amount saved by the infringer's failure to search for the patent or negotiate a license, then an injunction will provide an additional incentive for a consensual transfer instead of a forced taking of the patented technology. Finally, injunctions should readily issue when the infringer is a counterfeiter or a pirate who deliberately and slavishly copied the patentee's protected goods in order to appropriate the patentee's custom. This final category comports with economic analysis, because the risk of over-deterrence is low; it also comports with the common law's requirements for punitive damages and noneconomic arguments offered by commentators advocating corrective justice rationales.[78]

[78] *See* Zipursky, *supra* note 28.

24

Sequential Injunctions in Patent Litigation

The Gratuitous Novelty of TiVo *v.* EchoStar

*Richard A. Epstein**

INTRODUCTION

On April 20, 2011, the Federal Circuit issued its long-awaited decision in *TiVo* v. *EchoStar*.[1] The case revolved around the scope of injunctive relief in patent cases – but with a twist. In the conventional patent case of this sort, the usual question is whether to issue an injunction once it is found that the defendant has marketed or used an infringing device. In *TiVo*, the discussion swirled around a somewhat neglected variation on the main theme, which asks the question of what should be done with *sequential* injunctions. More precisely, the case asks how the system of injunctive relief should be administered the *second* time around, when the defendant, who is bound by the initial injunction, seeks to design around the original patent.

Early in the case, the plaintiff TiVo obtained both an injunction and monetary damages against EchoStar for its breach of TiVo's patents. EchoStar then introduced into the market a workaround product, claiming it steered free of the TiVo patents; TiVo disagreed. The main issue in the *TiVo* case was whether the district court judge was correct in deciding to use a short-form trial, on the ground that there was a high probability that EchoStar's proposed workaround resulted in the creation of a second infringing device.

* The Laurence A. Tisch Professor of Law, New York University School of Law; The Peter and Kirsten Bedford Senior Fellow, The Hoover Institution; Senior Lecturer, The University of Chicago. I wrote an amicus brief on behalf of *TiVo*, which helped shape the arguments contained in this article. Brief for Distinguished Professors of Law and Economics as Amici Curiae Supporting Appellee, TiVo Inc. v. Echostar Corp., 646 F.3d 869 (Fed. Cir. 2011). I would like to thank Shyamkrishna Balganesh and F. Scott Kieff for valuable comments on earlier drafts of this paper. I would also like to thank Sean Childers, Chris Dodge and Chris Lang of NYU Law School class of 2013, and Samuel Eckman, University of Chicago Law School, class of 2013, for their valuable research assistance.

1 TiVo Inc. v. EchoStar Corp., 646 F.3d 869 (Fed. Cir. 2011) [hereinafter *TiVo, en banc*].

In my view, the answer to that question should have been in the affirmative, so long as two questions were, as the district court urged, resolved for the plaintiff. The first of these was whether a comparison between "the adjudged product" – the defendant's original device – and the modified product – the product made in order to evade the injunction – were "more than colorably different," at which point a full trial was required. Under *KSM*, answering this question lay within the sound discretion of the trial court. If the differences on the threshold question did not rise to that level, a contempt proceeding to enforce the injunction against the modified product was allowed if it could be shown that "the modified device has not been changed from the adjudged device in a way which affects an element of a claim."[2] Once that question was resolved, the plaintiff then had the burden to show by clear and convincing evidence that the second product still infringes the original patent, holding constant the construction of the original claim.[3]

On appeal, all twelve members of the en banc Federal Circuit rejected the *KSM* procedure. They all accepted a test more favorable to the defendant, only to disagree on how it was to be applied. To the entire court, proof of actual infringement at the second stage was insufficient to justify the use of the contempt proceeding to support the original injunction. In addition, once the proceedings were initiated, all the judges agreed that the plaintiff had to show by clear and convincing evidence that the modified patent did not differ significantly from the original design. The split in opinion within the Federal Circuit came only on the factual question, where the seven-member majority thought that the question was close enough to remand the case on this point, whereas the five-member minority thought that the issue so clearly favored EchoStar that it held that the contempt proceedings should be stopped then and there.

Exactly how profound the difference between the two groups was will never be known, because the two parties settled the case in the aftermath of the Federal Circuit's decision for the sum of $500 million, with various cross-licensing agreements.[4] It is very difficult to draw any inferences as to how the parties thought that they would fare on remand because the settlement also reflected the fact that the majority of the Court made favorable rulings on two others issues that I discuss only briefly. The first of these was that it held (wrongly, in my view) that, even if the contempt proceedings were not fully justified, EchoStar had waived any right to challenge that decision for overbreadth. The second ruling was that the majority allowed the plaintiff to keep some $90 million that it had been awarded in the earlier proceeding based on

[2] TiVo Inc. v. Dish Network Corp., 640 F. Supp. 2d 853, 861 (2009) (quoting KSM Fastening Sys., Inc. v. H.A. Jones Co., 776 F.2d 1522, 1528–32 (Fed. Cir. 1985) [hereinafter *KSM*]).

[3] *Id.* at 862 (quoting *KSM*, 776 F.2d 1522, 1529–30).

[4] For the details of the settlement, see Gene Quinn, *TiVo, DISH and EchoStar, The $500 Million Patent Settlement*, IPWATCHDOG (May 2, 2011), http://ipwatchdog.com/2011/05/02/tivo-dish-and-echostar-the-500-million-patent-settlement/id=16740/.

violation of the injunction that the majority had (by ordering remand) dissolved on appeal.[5]

In dealing with this remedial choice, it is clear that all members of the Federal Circuit sought to reduce the protection afforded to patent holders by injunctive relief. As such, the decision can be read as taking its cue from the watershed Supreme Court decision in *eBay* v. *MercExchange*.[6] There the Court appeared to break with a long-established position that awarded these injunctions as a matter of course once the infringement was established. In its place, *eBay* relied on a four-part test that looked both at adequacy of damages and the consequences of issuing or denying an injunction on various third-party interests.[7] As matters have shaken out, it appears that *eBay's* departure from past practice may not be, at ground level, quite as dramatic as many commentators expected.[8] Instead, the subsequent case law tends toward the position that the plaintiff is entitled to an injunction as a matter of course when it is engaged in practicing or licensing the patented technology for its own advantage.[9] Those cases therefore have tended to forestall any possibility that damages would become the preferred remedy, with injunctions used only in a few cases. In fact, although the percentage of injunctions did dip, the decline was least in those areas where the patent was practiced or where the defendant was in direct competition with the defendant.[10] The main offset to this rule arises in those cases where the

5 *TiVo, en banc*, at 14.

6 eBay v. MercExchange, 547 U.S. 388 (2006).

7 "A plaintiff must demonstrate: (1) that it has suffered an irreparable injury; (2) that remedies available at law, such as monetary damages, are inadequate to compensate for that injury; (3) that, considering the balance of hardships between the plaintiff and defendant, a remedy in equity is warranted; and (4) that the public interest would not be disserved by a permanent injunction." *Id.* at 391.

8 *Compare* Yikin H. Tang, *The Future of Patent Enforcement After* eBay *v.* MercExchange, 20 HARV. J.L. & TECH. 235, 244 (2006) ("*eBay* reduced the likelihood that patent rights will be enforced through the use of permanent injunctions, especially for patent holders who do not themselves practice the patented inventions."), *and* Miranda Jones, *Permanent Injunction, A Remedy by Any Other Name Is Patently Not the Same: How* eBay v. MercExchange *Affects the Patent Right of Non-Practicing Entities*, 14 GEO. MASON L. REV. 1035, 1059 (2007) (claiming, early on, that Justice Kennedy's concurring opinion in *eBay*, announcing the four-part test, is "prevailing" in district courts), *with* Jetti Gibson, *Almost Quiet on the Copyright Front: eBay's False Alarm*, 14 RICH. J.L. & TECH. 6 (2007) (arguing that for courts other than the Federal Circuit, *eBay* "did not seem to have much of a general effect" because equitable principles were practiced both before and after *eBay*).

9 For a brief discussion, see Richard A. Epstein & F. Scott Kieff, *Questioning the Frequency and Wisdom of Compulsory Licensing for Pharmaceutical Patents*, 78 U. CHI. L. REV. 71, 87–91 (2011).

10 For an early tabulation of results, see AILPA 2007 Patent Law Committee, Injunctive Relief after eBay, *available at* http://www.foley.com/files/tbl_s31Publications/FileUpload137/4541/Injunctive ReliefAftereBay.pdf. Practicing patentees still obtained injunctions 82% of the time. Injunctions were given against direct competitors close to 70% of the time. *See also* Ernest Grumbles III, Rachel C. Hughey, & Susan Perera, *The Three Year Anniversary of* eBay v. MercExchange: *A Statistical Analysis of Permanent Injunctions*, INTELLECTUAL PROPERTY TODAY, Nov. 2009 at 25–29 (describing a statistical analysis of cases and finding that although "patent holders can no longer rely on a presumptive entitlement to permanent injunctive relief after proving infringement," injunctive relief was nonetheless granted 72% of the time.). For a more extensive collection of post-*eBay* statistics, see PATSTATS.ORG, http://patstats.org/ (last visited Jan. 8, 2012). One commentator, reviewing that website on the fifth anniversary of *eBay*, argues that *eBay* represents a significant departure, because although it used to

infringing device contains components covered by multiple patents, such that the immediate injunction will disrupt the expectations of many other third persons.[11] More recently, in its decision in *Microsoft* v. *i4i Limited Partnership*,[12] the court reaffirmed the longstanding rule that the defense of patent invalidity had to be established by clear and convincing evidence, which reflected a change in direction from *eBay*.[13]

eBay itself played only a modest direct role in the *TiVo* en banc decision. But it seems that the decision to stiffen the requirements for injunctive relief in the follow-on case derives in large measure from some skepticism about the desirability of injunctive relief in general. In my view, this skepticism about injunctions is generally misplaced.[14] The routine injunction should be a key cornerstone of a sound system of patent law. Any alternative system that treats damages as the first line of defense makes it impossible for a given patentee to develop a coherent plan of commercialization for its patented technologies. Any organized effort to issue exclusive or nonexclusive licenses can easily be disrupted by a third person who, without a license, uses the technology to gain a short-term advantage at the expense of patent licensees who necessarily operate with a cost disadvantage. Damage suits against multiple infringers might take years to resolve, assuming, of course, that the patentee has the resources to mount a multiple-front war against a broad array of infringers. Injunctive relief helps forestall those risks by forcing people to enter into voluntary transactions whose completeness allows them to maximize the joint value of their property. The security of all patented technologies in turn has the desirable, if indirect, effect of curbing monopoly rents. It does this by encouraging firms with newer technologies to enter the same market niche, knowing their own technologies will be protected by a similar set of secure property rights.

The key issue presented in *TiVo* was how this preference for injunctive relief should play out in connection with TiVo's claim that EchoStar committed a second round of violations against TiVo's patents. To examine this issue, I proceed as follows. In Part I, I offer a brief account of the facts of the case. In Part II, I offer an analysis of what I believe to be the proper theoretical framework for evaluating the question of injunctive relief in these sequential cases. In Part III, I review and

be "virtually unheard of for a district court to deny a victorious plaintiff a permanent injunction in [a] patent infringement case," nonetheless, that denial only occurs in about 25% of cases and thus still represents the exception rather than the norm. Gene Quinn, *Happy 5th Anniversary: The Impact of* eBay v. MercExchange, IPWATCHDOG (May 15, 2011, 11:00 AM), http://www.ipwatchdog.com/2011/05/15/happy-5th-anniversary-ebay-v-mercexchange/id=16894/.

[11] *z4 Technologies, Inc. v Microsoft Corp.*, 434 F. Supp. 2d 437 (E.D. Tex. 2006) (denying injunction for a component, but awarding hefty damages).

[12] 131 S. Ct. 2238 (2011).

[13] See Ronald Mann, *Commentary: Tide Turns for Federal Circuit in Patent Cases*, SCOTUSBLOG (July 6, 2011), http://www.scotusblog.com/2011/07/ronald-mann-reviews-the-patent-cases-of-ot2010/.

[14] For a discussion of those views, see generally Richard A. Epstein, *The Disintegration of Intellectual Property? A Classical Liberal Response to Premature Obituary*, 62 STAN. L. REV. 455, 484–516 (2010).

defend the position on injunctive relief taken by the district court in reliance on the then-regnant *KSM* test. Part IV looks at the majority and minority en banc positions in *TiVo* and argues that the *KSM* test is superior to the new test announced there – regardless of which way it is applied. Part V then briefly examines two other issues that divided the en banc panel: the application of the injunction to the modified devices under all three (*KSM*, majority, and minority) approaches, and the soundness of the $90 million contempt payments (which were made conditional on the disobedience of the contempt order). I conclude that, because the injunction should cover both the original and modified device, both the injunction and contempt order were sound. Yet, if the views of the en banc panel were correct, then the enforcement of the injunction against the modified device and the payment of damages for noncompliance with the district court order were both incorrect. Strong remedies should follow only the disregard of valid injunctions, not questionable or invalid ones. A brief summary wraps up.

I. THE *TIVO* V. *ECHOSTAR* SAGA

The *TiVo* litigation focused on TiVo Inc. Patent No. 6,233,389 (hereafter, '389 patent), which covered its invention of the digital video recorder (DVR). That patent marked a major advance in broadcasting by introducing a technology that, for the first time, simultaneously performed multiple functions highly desired by consumers. Among its advances, TiVo's technology stores for future use any signals it receives from either a cable or satellite transmitter. At any future time chosen by the consumer, TiVo plays back these stored signals. In effect, the system allows for greatly increased flexibility in consumer behavior by severing any connection between the time a given program is broadcast and the time the consumer watches it. Within short order, the TiVo patent not only set a new industry standard but also converted "TiVo" into a recognized verb in the English language.[15]

TiVo was at all times prepared to license this technology to others. One party that chose not to acquire that license was the large media company EchoStar, which introduced its own variation with its "50X products" and "Broadcom Products." In 2004, TiVo brought suit against EchoStar in the United States District Court for the Eastern District of Texas on a variety of claims.[16] In March 2006 a jury found that EchoStar willfully infringed on TiVo's patents, for which it awarded TiVo close to $74 million in damages. The district court also issued an injunction that required EchoStar, in the words of the en banc Panel, "(1) to stop making, using, offering to sell, and selling" the receivers that had been found infringing by

[15] The difficulties of this lawsuit may well have contributed to this grammatical decline. Keith Hahn, *Even the Verb "TiVo" is Losing Valuable Predicate Share*, Dealbreaker (August 30, 2007), http://dealbreaker.com/2007/08/even-the-verb-tivo-is-losing-valuable-predicate-share/.

[16] For the full history of the case, see *TiVo, en banc*, at 7–9.

the jury (the "infringement" provision)[17] and (2) to disable the DVR functionality in existing receivers that had already been placed with EchoStar's customers and in new placements that were yet to be placed with EchoStar's customers (the "disablement" provision).[18]

EchoStar sought to invent around the TiVo patent and thus escape the injunction by outfitting its cable boxes with a new software download that incorporated a discrete set of design changes. EchoStar did not keep the district court apprised of its new efforts, even though the case was still actively in litigation. When the new EchoStar device eventually came to the court's attention, EchoStar claimed that its modified software fell outside of the four corners of the original patent. It also stressed that its effort to design around the original TiVo patent was no slapdash affair, but required the work of fifteen engineers for about 8,000 hours of work.[19]

EchoStar's decision to install its new device into machines already in the field (and to incorporate it in products yet to be marketed) sparked TiVo's motion for a contempt order against EchoStar for violating the original injunction. The key question was the kind of procedure needed to resolve this second-round dispute in the district court.

The district court opted for an approach that allowed both parties extensive discovery, after which it held a three-day bench trial, where both parties introduced documentary evidence and offered witness testimony subject to cross-examination. After an additional four-month delay, the district court issued its contempt order in June, 2009, which the Federal Circuit promptly stayed in July 2009. Thereafter, in March, 2010, a divided panel of the Federal Circuit denied EchoStar's claim for emergency relief. The entire case was then heard en banc on November 9, 2010, to determine whether the district court followed correct procedures in issuing its contempt decree.[20] The en banc proceeding produced a unanimous panel on setting the standard for issuing the contempt citation, but a sharp 7–5 division on how that standard should be applied.

[17] The infringement provision stated: "Each Defendant, its officers, agents, servants, employees, and attorneys, and those persons in active concert of participation with them who receive actual notice hereof, are hereby restrained and enjoined, pursuant to 35 U.S.C. 283 and Fed. R. Civ. P. 65(d), from making, using, offering to sell, selling, or importing in the United States, the Infringing Products, either alone or in combination with any other product and all other products that are only colorably different therefrom in the context of the Infringed Claims, whether individually or in combination with other products or as a part of another product, and from otherwise infringing or inducing others to infringe the Infringed Claims of the '389 patent." TiVo Inc. v. Dish Network Corp., 640 F. Supp. 2d 853, 858.

[18] "The disablement provision reads: Defendants are hereby FURTHER ORDERED to, within thirty (30) days of the issuance of this order, disable the DVR functionality (i.e., disable all storage to and playback from a hard disk drive of television data) in all but 192,708 units of the Infringing Products that have been placed with an end user or subscriber. The DVR functionality, i.e., disable all storage to and playback from hard disk drive of television data) [sic] shall not be enabled in any new placements of the Infringing Products." *Id.*

[19] *TiVo, en banc*, at 5.

[20] TiVo Inc. v. EchoStar Corp., 376 F.App'x 21 (Fed. Cir. 2010).

The heart of this dispute involves EchoStar's effort to work around two of the claim elements in TiVo's '389 patent. EchoStar's original product created an "index" of "start codes" that was found to infringe the TiVo patent. Its purported workaround replaced TiVo's start code mechanism with a "brute force" method that estimated the location of stored data by reference to average frame rate statistics collected during playback. The district court held that the elimination of start code detection and indexing did not take the new device out of the reach of TiVo's patent. TiVo's original claim contained the word "parsing," which the district court construed to mean "analyzing" data from outside sources, and which the modified EchoStar device continued to do, albeit in a manner different from its original design.

EchoStar's second challenged workaround involved the removal of the "record buffer" found in its original device. EchoStar's "transport buffer" had contained ten cells, each of which stored information separately until it could be transferred to the hard drive. The record buffer, in the first device, served as an eleventh intermediary cell that allowed information to be transferred from one transport buffer cell to the hard drive only after the contents of another cell had been completely transferred. EchoStar's removal of the record buffer allowed all information to travel directly from the transport buffer to the hard drive, but it did not change the operation of the ten transport buffers that were common elements in the two systems. The district court held that this change from eleven buffers to ten was "not more than colorably different from the original product," and thus remained covered by the '389 patent."[21] The en banc proceeding concerned the soundness of the district court's procedure to review the second case, which resulted in the contempt citation.

II. SEQUENTIAL INJUNCTIONS IN THEORETICAL PERSPECTIVE

The key theoretical issue in these sequential injunction cases is the extent to which the information that was gleaned in the first round of litigation should be put to use in resolving the second case. Here, as a matter of principle, the objective remains what it has always been in cases of injunctive relief. One wants to design the procedures in a fashion that will minimize two potential sources of error: granting an injunction where none should be allowed or denying an injunction where one should be allowed. In the usual first-round dispute, the burdens on any plaintiff to prove the case for an injunction start from ground zero, because there is no prior proceeding that sheds light on what should be done with the case before the court. In those circumstances, the usual rule is that the plaintiff has to prove from scratch the case for an injunction, with a presumption against so powerful a remedy. The rapid, pro-plaintiff procedural system creates the risk that plaintiffs with weak cases will take advantage of a lax regime on injunctions to leverage a favorable settlement from a non-infringing defendant. To guard against this risk, the Supreme Court in *Winter* v. *Natural Res. Def. Council, Inc.* reaffirmed the traditional rule that it was

[21] TiVo Inc. v. Dish Network Corp., 640 F. Supp. 2d 853, 871.

improper to issue a preliminary injunction just because there was a "possibility" that the defendant's conduct could lead to some threatened harm that would later justify the imposition of some sanctions.[22] Instead the Court held that the applicable standard required more: "A plaintiff seeking a preliminary injunction must establish that he is likely to succeed on the merits, that he is likely to suffer irreparable harm in the absence of preliminary relief, that the balance of equities tips in his favor, and that an injunction is in the public interest."[23]

No judicial strategy that seeks to balance risks in the face of uncertainty is bulletproof. There are always some cases in which the best ex ante guess will yield the wrong solution after the fact. So it goes with the reluctance to issue preliminary injunctions. Trials in these settings can take up a good deal of time, during which the defendant remains free to use the patented technology, so long as it is prepared to pay the damages that could result from an adverse decision. The plaintiff may get money from that litigation, but a defendant who establishes a business beachhead for the infringing technology may well garner gains from selling complementary products. The patentee, of course, necessarily loses the sale of its complementary products and the favorable publicity that goes with that increased presence in the marketplace.

TiVo's central claim is that, once the past infringement was established, the information generated in that first proceeding should be used in evaluating the claim for the second injunction. The question is how. At this point there are two scenarios that bear mention. In the first, the previous infringer starts up with a new device that performs the same storage and replay functions as the originally patented TiVo device, but does so by means of a design that is wholly its own. In this scenario, the key patent doctrine is that legal protection is never offered in ways that give one party the control over a particular type of function, wholly apart from the device that is used to embody it. It was for just this reason that Samuel Morse could not obtain a patent for harnessing electricity and magnetism for remote communications, even if he could get a patent for his own particular telegraphic device.[24] In essence, the independent creation of that new device has to stand or fall on its own, so that the holder of the previous device does not get a leg up in the second proceeding. At the extremes, this position has to be correct, but because issues dealing with differences always lie on some sort of continuum, some cases will of necessity be closer to the line.

At the other extreme lie those cases where the new device is made by nominal extensions of the earlier invention. In this situation, there is of necessity some free-riding off the information and skills that were acquired by the earlier patentee. That overlap would not be sufficient to condemn the new patent claim in and of itself, because much depends on the level of spacing that the second patent owner was able to create for itself. But the closer the resemblances, the more attractive the case

[22] 555 U.S. 7, 20 (2008).
[23] *Id.*
[24] *See O'Reilly v. Morse*, 56 U.S. 62, 112–13 (1854).

for an expedited proceeding. Indeed *TiVo* falls at this imitative end of the spectrum, because all sides agreed that EchoStar used the original TiVo device as the basis for its efforts to design around the patent. In effect, EchoStar's strategy was to keep some elements of that design and to strip out others. By design, the new device accomplished the same basic task as the original device, albeit in a *less* efficient way given (which no one would ever do for economic reasons) the elimination of some key desirable functionalities from TiVo's original patented device. At this point, it seems like a gross error in calculation to start the evaluation process on the assumption that this derivative device is an independent invention. It is, of course, not the case that the design-around in question necessarily establishes that the new device infringes TiVo's patent. Quite the opposite: one reason for requiring a complete set of patent disclosures is to facilitate entrance into the market of other inventors who design new devices that, although not imitations of the original device, are nonetheless inspired by that development.

At this point, therefore, the proper way to minimize error is to *update* the initial presumption in favor of the defendant to reflect the uncontroverted evidence that the defendant has misbehaved (especially because the infringement was willful) in the past and is now likely to misbehave a second time if not promptly checked. The case for using contempt procedures is even stronger if, as here, the defendant knows from the outset that it may well be left better off even if it does infringe, so long as it can delay or even avoid injunctive relief.

There is one substantial risk here: if the shortened contempt procedure is not permitted for the first modified device, it will be equally unavailable for the second or any subsequent modification. But, by the second time around, the skilled defendant will have a good idea of just how much daylight is needed between its device and the patent in order to force the plaintiff to start from scratch in its uncertain quest to obtain injunctive relief. Denying use of any abbreviated procedure thus opens the door to nonstop strategic behavior by defendants who are willing to pay damages to keep their own products on the market. In these circumstances, we can be quite confident that all large players are in a position to calculate their sums correctly. In this case, TiVo, although battered by the experience, had sufficient resources to push the case to a substantial settlement, albeit one that might not have restored it to the financial position that it would have enjoyed if EchoStar had never infringed. But one may ask whether smaller inventors with equally valuable patents could be able to withstand this repeated onslaught as they are forced to divert scarce resources to a litigation war against seasoned veterans with more resources at their disposal. The first time through, the patentee bears a heavy burden. But in subsequent cases where the two devices are closely related, it makes sense to shift that burden, as the older *KSM* rule provided.

In principle, nothing justifies the creation of a remedial rule that allows the defendant to profit, perhaps repeatedly, from its own wrong. The sensible approach, therefore, is to use an initial determination of resemblance to determine whether to expedite the hearing on whether the second device infringes the original patent.

The argument here is that, because the chances that the new device infringes on the old patent are better than they were the first time round, it becomes proper to make some adjustments in the trial procedures to take account of that fact. The question is what procedures should be used, and why. The answer to that question does not begin with the *KSM* case, but goes back to 1865, when the word "colorable" first made its appearance in patent law. Like so many key concepts in the law – of which the doctrine of *res ipsa loquitur* is perhaps the best example[25] – this term draws its content from a single remark in the course of a judicial trial. The parallel moment for "colorable" took place in *Liddle* v. *Cory*,[26] where the question was whether the design of the defendant's furnaces was sufficiently close both to that of the plaintiff's furnace and to that of a previously infringing furnace. Benedict, J., first observed,

> Now, it is shown, beyond dispute, in the affidavits before the court, and, indeed, is conceded by the plaintiff, that the Excelsior furnace, although it has a corrugated body, is without the plates on the inside or the outside, and without any contrivance in their place intended to produce the same result as that produced by the plates in the plaintiff's furnace, the body of the Excelsior furnace being a simple corrugated body, without tubes of any sort whatever upon it. It is conceded, also, that the ledges cast upon the bottom of the radiator of the plaintiff's furnace are omitted in the Excelsior furnace, leaving the radiator with a smooth bottom, not calculated to detain upon it ashes, dust or soot.

On the strength of these observations, he concluded, without argument that some form of expedited relief should be allowed in some patent cases, but not in this one. That concession on a matter of principle, however, provided no help for the instant plaintiff:

> I should make such an order [of contempt], without hesitation, if there was any reason to suppose that further proofs would show the changes made by the defendants in their furnace to be merely colorable alterations, introduced for the purpose of escaping the effect of the [prior] decree, or if there was any doubt as to what was the extent of the alterations made by the defendants; for, a defendant is not to be permitted to avoid a decree against him by making some slight changes in the article.

[25] *Byrne v. Boadle*, 159 Eng. Rep. (Ex. 1863), concerning the doctrine of *res ipsa loquitur*, in which the entire discussion went as follows:

> Pollock, C.B.: "The presumption is that the defendant's servants were engaged in removing the defendant's flour. If they were not it was competent to the defendant to prove it." Defendant's attorney replied that "Surmise ought not to be substituted for strict proof when it is thought to fix a defendant with serious liability. The plaintiff should establish his case by affirmative evidence. . . . The plaintiff was bound to give affirmative proof of negligence. But there was not a scintilla of evidence, unless the occurrence is of itself evidence of negligence." Pollock, C.B.: "There are certain cases of which it may be said res ipsa loquitur and this seems one of them. In some cases the Court had held that the mere fact of the accident having occurred is evidence of negligence, as, for instance, in the case of railway collisions."

[26] 15 F. Cas. 506 (C.C.S.D.N.Y. 1865).

In working through this analysis, it is clear that two elements matter. The first is the relationship between the defendant's second device and his first device. The second is the relationship between the plaintiff's patented device and the defendant's device. By using the term "colorable" in connection with the term "alteration," it is clear that it is the differences between the two generations of defendant devices that, under the orthodox view, triggered the case for the use of the abbreviated contempt proceedings. In just this manner the table was set for Judge Folsom's district court's decision in the instant case that relied on a direct descendant of *Liddle* v. *Cory*, which laid the intellectual foundations for the *KSM* decision handed down by the Federal Circuit in 1985.

III. THE TIVO CONTEMPT PROCEEDINGS IN THE DISTRICT COURT

Judge Folsom's opinion followed faithfully the two-part procedure adumbrated in *Liddle* and formalized in *KSM*[27]:

> An enjoined party is entitled to design around the claims of a patent without the threat of contempt proceedings with respect to every modified device although he bears the risk that the enjoining court may find changes to be too insubstantial to avoid contempt.
>
> Conversely, where an injunction is written narrowly against a particular infringing device, contempt may, nevertheless, be found on the basis of a modified infringing device. An enjoined party under a narrow decree will not be permitted to escape on a purely "in rem" theory that only a particular device is prohibited, where it is evident that the modifications do not avoid infringement and were made for the purpose of evasion of the court's order. Again, the standard is whether the differences between the two devices are merely colorable.[28]

These passages shape the analysis of the instant litigation. First, the aggrieved party will indeed prefer to invoke the power of the court that already controls the case rather than begin a new action. Because the district court already has personal jurisdiction over the defendants, the continued action is not subject to the variety of procedural hurdles that intrude when a new suit is brought with no presumption of validity in its favor. In addition, the contempt procedure cuts down on delay and cost by getting the case quickly before a judge who knows the record intimately and has the available tools to respond promptly to the peril. This speedy procedure serves not only the plaintiff's interest but also the social interest. Given that the flouting of patents undermines patent law's core mission to encourage innovation, an expedited procedure is needed to protect patent rights from systematic infringement.

[27] 776 F.2d 1522, 1530–32 (Fed. Cir. 1985).
[28] *Id.* at 1526 (citations omitted).

In this case, moreover, the contempt procedures were especially appropriate. There is ample evidence that the differences between EchoStar's two designs were not more than "colorable," given that EchoStar was consciously seeking to "escape" this narrowly written injunction by making small modifications to skirt the literal language of the decree. The district court found, in essence, that the new devices are best described as a knock-off and simplification of a device that had already been found to infringe the plaintiff's patent. EchoStar's effort had been to put just enough separation between its new and old devices to force TiVo to gear up for yet another round of expensive litigation beginning at square one.

At this point it is clear, as the en banc decision affirmed,[29] that the question is simply whether the infringement has taken place. It is not one of whether the defendant holds an honest or good-faith belief – even if attested to by the opinion of counsel – that the modification does not cover an infringing device.[30] The standard of liability here is strict. That standard should not be relaxed on a rehearing because there is a high likelihood that, if the infringement is found, it will also be held to be willful.

There is no magic test to decide just what changes are too substantial to allow for the use of the contempt proceeding; questions of degree never permit dogmatic answers.[31] As the issue developed in *KSM*, the full inquiry necessarily took place in two stages, briefly referred to earlier. In more detail, the first stage is to decide whether to believe that the similarity between the plaintiff's patented device and the defendant's new invention is close enough to warrant an expedited contempt proceeding. Because there is no final decision at this stage, the appropriate analogy is to some preliminary decision at arrest or even at arraignment on whether to hold a prisoner for bail. The standards for holding someone do not require proof beyond a reasonable doubt. Some lower standard of reasonable suspicion or probable cause, depending on the precise issue, is surely appropriate, precisely because the accused has a full chance to defend on the question of guilt or innocence when the burden of proof is thereafter shifted to the other party. In most instances, moreover, the question of similarity will be sufficiently obvious that the burden of proof does not matter.

EchoStar insisted that the district court had to establish the similarity between the defendant's original device and its modified device by clear and convincing evidence. But, as the district court found, nothing in *KSM* supports the imposition of this needless obstacle to speedy remedial action, given the more ample protections

[29] *See TiVo, en banc*, at *6–9.

[30] *See id.* at *6.

[31] For the argument that contempt proceedings should be used sparingly, see Brief for Erwin Chemerinsky, Rex R. Perschbacher, et al. as Amici Curiae Supporting Defendants-Appellants, TiVo Inc. v. EchoStar Corp., 98 U.S.P.Q.2d (BNA) 1413 (2011) (No. 2009–1374). This brief does not see any significant differences in how the contempt power is used by subject matter, although there is surely a difference between jailing a reporter for refusing to divulge a source and using that power to enforce an injunction in a commercial case where it is easy to comply.

afforded at the second, or contempt, stage of the proceedings. The district court properly held that *KSM* only requires the plaintiff make a minimal showing of similarity between the defendant's original and modified products.[32] As a matter of principle, the appropriate standard seems to be that which was in effect at the district court level: the burden of proof is only a preponderance of evidence, where the standard of review should be for abuse of discretion.[33]

That result is correct because this initial stage of the contempt proceeding has no binding consequences on the defendant. The *ultimate* issue is not whether EchoStar's two devices were in fact similar; it is whether its modified DVR also infringes the basic '389 patent. But the *preliminary* issue was whether the adjudged and accused devices are "colorably different," as specified in *KSM*.[34] That question of fact was correctly resolved by the district court given that the defendant had designed this new patent simply by stripping out elements from its former design in the hope of escaping liability. That situation is a far cry from a dispute in which the defendant engineered a new product design from scratch. Indeed, if the defendant is confident that it has a new device, it can just ask the court to provide it with clearance in advance and thus use the expedited device to its own advantage.

In this case, the second stage of the contempt proceedings is not all that difficult either. The close similarity between EchoStar's original and modified product only increased the odds that the modified product in fact infringed on the TiVo patent. The district court, moreover, properly treated the definition of key terms in the TiVo patent, such as "parsing" and "automatic flow control," as having been settled at the earlier stages of the litigation. The court's only remaining task, therefore, was to decide whether EchoStar's stripped-down device counted as a second violation of the TiVo '389 patent.[35] The translation from the one case to the other was relatively obvious. In light of this, yielding to the defendant's insistence on a new trial would have created a formidable obstacle to contempt proceedings because of the high threshold to any continued supervisory action. Let that rule control, and the astute defendant can unleash a parade of modified devices, knowing that it could keep first one and then the next on the market by resisting new lawsuits, perhaps for the entire life of the plaintiff's patent.

The *TiVo* case is, moreover, easily distinguishable from *KSM*, where the Federal Circuit found, as in *Liddle*, a contempt proceeding to be inappropriate.[36] Unlike the plaintiff in the present case, the plaintiff in *KSM* had shown the requisite similarity only between the plaintiff's original and defendant's modified device. But, as the court in *KSM* noted, that initial showing only allowed the district court judge to

[32] *See* TiVo Inc. v. Dish Network Corp., 640 F. Supp. 2d 853, 863.

[33] *See* TiVo, Inc. v. EchoStar Commc'ns Corp., 516 F.3d 1290, 1311 (Fed. Cir. 2008); *see also Additive Controls & Measurement Sys., Inc. v. Flowdata, Inc.*, 154 F.3d 1345, 1349–50 (Fed. Cir. 1998) ("We review the district court's decision to proceed via a contempt hearing for abuse of discretion.").

[34] *See TiVo*, 640 F. Supp. 2d at 861.

[35] *See id.* at 871.

[36] *KSM*, 776 F.2d at 1532.

proceed to the second question of actual infringement. What was missing in *KSM* was "the refusal of the district court to consider whether [the defendant's] devices infringed the claims of the [plaintiff's] '217 patent."[37] At this point, the Federal Circuit in *KSM* pinpointed the shortfall in substantive inquiry of the district court whose decision it reviewed:

> The difficulty is simply that the modified doctrine of equivalents [comparing the adjudged and modified devices] ... does not assure a proper finding that the modified device infringes the claims. It may not properly be assumed, as does the ... standard [adopted by the district court], that, because the [modified] devices, in a sense, are "equivalents" to the enjoined ... device, they are also equivalents of the patent claims.[38]

One way to think of this is by asking about resemblances, which is one image often evoked by the doctrine of equivalents. Just because A meets the test of equivalents with B, and B meets that same test with C, it need not follow, because A, B, and C are all different, that the doctrine of equivalents could be used to establish that A is equivalent to C. Resemblances are not logical identities and do not permit any necessary inference on grounds of transitivity.

Liddle and *KSM*, moreover, are not the only cases in which the use of contempt proceedings was inappropriate. The situation in *TiVo* was also markedly different from the Supreme Court's early decision in *California Artificial Stone Paving Co. v. Molitor*,[39] which also examined the limits on the use of the contempt power. In that case, the original plaintiff pioneered a technique for laying concrete in discrete blocks separated by either tar paper or sand, in ways that protected one block from cracking and breaking even if another block were damaged. The defendant then developed a new technique with that same purpose that avoided the separation of the block, but used small indentations in one long slab in the hopes of achieving the same result. Unlike the present situation, the defendant's new device lacked an essential element – separation – of the older patent. To make matters more complex, the entire case was governed by an 1802 statute that permitted expedited decisions only on pure questions of law, and not on mixed questions of law and fact.[40]

Within that framework, the Supreme Court held that the summary proceedings were not appropriate. Justice Bradley explained, "By the final decree in the case, made in 1881, the court decided that the pavements which the defendant had been theretofore making did infringe the patent. How those pavements were constructed we are not informed; and therefore we do not know what was the precise construction given by the court to the patent."[41] Owing to a division of opinion below, the

37 *Id.* at 1524.
38 *Id.* at 1528 (citations omitted).
39 113 U.S. 609, 618 (1885).
40 *Id.* at 615–16.
41 *Id.* at 617–18.

Court held that the plaintiff had to bring a separate action. The Court concluded its opinion by noting that "[p]rocess of contempt is a severe remedy, and should not be resorted to where there is fair ground of doubt as to the wrongfulness of the defendant's conduct."[42] Justice Bradley's concluding statement was addressed to the state of the evidence as it reached the Court; it did not rule out the use of contempt proceedings in appropriate cases. The case's reference to a "fair ground of doubt" arose because of the division of opinion between the two judges who heard the evidence in separate proceedings. There is no similar indefiniteness in the record in this case.

In light of *California Artificial Stone*, the district court was therefore correct to say that the heightened burden only came on the merits; it lay within the "discretion" of the trial court to initiate the inquiry in the first place. The protection for the defendant comes in the substantive standard on infringement that has to be met. In this instance, the district court was required under *KSM* to examine the mixed questions of fact and law raised by the asserted infringement even after the question of claim construction had been resolved. In reviewing the record in light of the district court's finding that the infringement by the modified device was supported by clear and convincing evidence, there could not have been "a fair ground of doubt" as to the state of the record below. There is little doubt in my view that the district court decision followed *KSM*. But more surprises were in store.

IV. TIVO IN THE FEDERAL CIRCUIT

The entire pattern of discourse changed once the case reached the Federal Circuit. All twelve sitting judges pulled a major surprise by rejecting *KSM's* two-stage process for handling contempt proceedings. The key passage reads as follows:

> We recognize now that that inquiry confuses the merits of the contempt with the propriety of initiating contempt proceedings. Moreover, as a practical matter, district courts do not separately determine the propriety of a contempt proceeding before proceeding to the merits of the contempt itself. As a result, we will telescope the current two-fold KSM inquiry into one, eliminating the separate determination whether contempt proceedings were properly initiated. That question, we hold, is left to the broad discretion of the trial court to be answered based on the facts presented. Additive Controls, 154 F.3d 1345 at 1349 (The district court "has broad discretion to determine how best to enforce its injunctive decrees."). What is required for a district court to hold a contempt proceeding is a detailed accusation from the injured party setting forth the alleged facts constituting the contempt. As with appeals from findings of civil contempt in other areas of law, we will only review whether the injunction at issue is both enforceable and violated, and whether the sanctions imposed were proper. Allegations that contempt proceedings were improper in the first instance do not state a defense to contempt. As to

[42] *Id.* at 618.

> the question whether an injunction against patent infringement has been violated, courts should continue to employ a "more than colorable differences" standard as discussed below.[43]

The passage indicates an obvious displeasure with the *KSM* rule, but offers no explanation as to why. The initial thrust is that "in practice" judges cannot keep the two stages of the contempt process separate. But that is precisely what the district court did when it held that the first stage of the process asks whether the defendant's modified product is sufficiently similar to the defendant's former device to move to the second stage, which asks the question whether the modified device infringed the plaintiff's patent. The separation mattered because a higher burden of proof attached to the second issue. If this two-part procedure had created administrative confusion in the present case, or in other cases during the twenty-five years since *KSM* came down, a reexamination of the basic question might have been needed to resolve the confusion. But the opinion of Judge Lourie (on this point for the entire court) refers to no such difficulties. What is even odder is that, after the dust settles, the new Federal Circuit test preserves, as it must, a two-part structure anyhow. Under the revised rule, the district court retains "broad discretion" to decide whether the new contempt proceedings should be initiated, so long as the plaintiff offers a "detailed accusation" setting forth the basis for the contempt hearing. Yet that step is one that plaintiffs will always undertake, because the new case necessarily involves evidence that compares the defendant's modified device first to the defendant's prior device, and ultimately, to the plaintiff's patented one.

The majority's reason for the remand necessarily lies in the way in which it treats the second, or substantive, part of the hearing, and there it is clear that the rules of the game have changed. Under the *KSM* test, a lower standard of proof applied to the question of colorable differences between the original and modified products. No more – now that question becomes the focal point for attention. Two key passages make the point for the unanimous Federal Circuit:

> Thus, the party seeking to enforce the injunction must prove both that the newly accused product is not more than colorably different from the product found to infringe and that the newly accused product actually infringes.[44]

> If those differences between the old and new elements are significant, the newly accused product as a whole shall be deemed more than colorably different from the adjudged infringing one, and the inquiry into whether the newly accused product actually infringes is irrelevant. Contempt is then inappropriate.[45]

The decision thus has the consequence that a finding in the abbreviated proceeding that the modified device infringes by clear and convincing evidence is no longer

[43] *TiVo, en banc*, at *6.

[44] *TiVo, en banc*, at *19.

[45] *TiVo, en banc*, at *20.

the ultimate issue in the case. Rather, the prior finding of substantial similarity between the original and modified device must be proved by the same high standard of proof. If there is failure on the first part of the test, the finding of infringement on the second part of the test is not sufficient to carry the day.

What is so striking about this reformulation of the original test is how it works at cross-purposes with the fundamental objective of error minimization in sequential injunction cases. The two-part test of *KSM* makes a real shot at this task by stressing the ultimate fact of infringement after a preliminary finding of similarity. The newer test goes the opposite way. It never explains why a finding of infringement, by clear and convincing evidence, should be rejected solely because the level of proof was insufficient at the earlier stage – which had the sole purpose of seeing whether the contempt proceeding was warranted in the first place. In putting forward the revised test, the Federal Circuit achieves an unfortunate double blunder by endorsing a process that invokes more expensive procedures to produce less reliable results.

Once the Federal Circuit rejected the district court's reliance on *KSM*, it had to rethink the judgment of the district court. For the entire court, the higher standard of proof on the similarity question necessitated revisiting the entire proceeding below. It was at this juncture that the unanimous coalition split in two. The majority of seven thought there was enough uncertainty on the question of colorable differences that it was prepared to remand the case for a new trial. The minority of five, in a much shorter and more emphatic statement, held that the issue of resemblance was too clear to require a retrial: the substitution of the brute statistical estimation process for the "parsing" feature of the original claim introduced a new element into the claim and thus negated any substantial similarity. "The statistical estimation feature, which replaced the start-code-detection feature, was not present in original software and was not earlier viewed by TiVo as being capable of performing the required function."[46] Because that statistical technique was not covered by any prior art, it followed that the new element was substantially different as a matter of law.[47]

The majority took a somewhat broader view of "parsing" and held that the chink in TiVo's armor took place prior to the contempt proceeding, given that TiVo had never taken the position that the PID filter satisfied the parsing element of the claim (even though the district court had held that EchoStar had "conceded" this point). But under the revised standard, the majority instructed the district court to decide on remand whether the statistical estimation feature was significantly different from the start code procedure of the patented TiVo device. In essence, the finding of infringement did not satisfy that requirement.

Both of these views take too narrow of an approach to the ultimate issue of infringement. In dealing with this issue, the now-discredited discussion in *KSM*

46 *TiVo, en banc*, at *23 (Dyk, J., concurring and dissenting in part).
47 *Id.* at *22.

alluded to the question of how the doctrine of equivalents should play into the contempt proceedings. It came up with the correct conclusion that a simple showing of equivalence between the original and modified devices did not show that either of them infringed, as was required under the second *KSM* step that requires proof of infringement by clear and convincing evidence. In this instance, it looks as though both steps of the equivalence analysis apply.

As is commonly understood, patent law is of two minds on the question of whether a given design-around should receive patent protection. On the one hand, proper design-arounds serve the essential function of allowing new products to enter into the market in competition with older ones. Indeed, the en banc minority is quite explicit in recognizing that "designing new and possibly better or cheaper functional equivalents" for existing products "is the stuff of which competition is made."[48] It does not stop to ask how this rationale should play out when the modified device is recognized on all sides to be inferior to the original patented product.

More importantly, neither the minority nor the majority opinion chooses to cite to any cases that deal with the doctrine of equivalents,[49] which has exactly the opposite message: excessive free-riding on the original invention dulls innovation by allowing the new entrant to reap where the other party has sown. As I understand matters, the doctrine of infringement serves a similar function to that of colorable differences in the context of contempt proceedings. Each is intended to police the line between market competition and unfair competition, between those cases where one party outthinks another and those cases where one party outmaneuvers the other. As Learned Hand once famously said, the purpose of the doctrine of equivalents is "to temper unsparing logic and prevent an infringer from stealing the benefit of the invention."[50] The same risk arises in *TiVo*. No matter how much sophistication is brought to this issue, the ultimate distinction between a welcome design-around and an improper equivalent involves matters of degree. In dealing with that question, moreover, the distance between the patented device and its imitation is one key factor. Similarly, the question of whether the new entrant started from scratch or used the first patented device as a template for its own work should be equally critical to the overall evaluation. The risks of impermissible free-riding are far greater when the use of the prior patented technology is a point-by-point substitution of one

[48] See *TiVo*, *en banc*, concurrence at *15, citing *State Indus. Inc. v. A.O. Smith Corp.*, 751 F.2d 1226, 1235–36 (Fed. Cir. 1985).

[49] The full statutory provision reads:

> An element in a claim for a combination may be expressed as a means or step for performing a specified function without the recital of structure, material, or acts in support thereof, and such claim shall be construed to cover the corresponding structure material, or acts described in the specification and the equivalents thereof.

35 U.S.C. § 112, ¶ 6 (2011).

[50] Royal Typewriter Co. v. Remington Rand, Inc., 168 F.2d 691, 692 (2d Cir. 1948).

mechanism for another and a different technique is used to achieve the identical result.

Justice Kennedy hinted at this point when, in *Festo Corp.* v. *Shoketsu Kinzoku Kogyo Kabushiki Co.*, he said of the doctrine of equivalents: "If patents were always interpreted by their literal terms, their value would be greatly diminished. Unimportant and insubstantial substitutes for certain elements could defeat the patent, and its value to inventors could be destroyed by simple acts of copying."[51] Thus in *Festo* the plaintiff's patent covered "an improved magnetic rodless cylinder, which was a piston-driven device that relied on magnets to move objects in a conveying system."[52] The defendant's device differed: "rather than using two one-way sealing rings, [it] employs a single sealing ring with a two-way lip. Furthermore, SMC's sleeve is made of a nonmagnetizable alloy."[53]

In *Festo* proper, one key issue was whether the patentee consciously reduced the scope of his patent to avoid invalidation by prior art. In effect, the Court held that the prosecution history created an estoppel in those cases where this process of conscious exclusion took place, but did not do so where amendments to the initial patent claims were done for other reasons.[54] In those circumstances, Justice Kennedy was correct to say that the doctrine of equivalents should be of no use to the patentee who has consciously avoided staking out the territory in which the defendant's new invention falls. Put otherwise, once the patentee beat a conscious retreat from some territory, he or she cannot protest the decision by the defendant to occupy that vacated territory. Nor could the patentee say that he or she was unable to articulate language that was precise enough to cover that abandoned terrain.

TiVo is devoid of any issues of prosecution estoppel, so that the only question that remains is just how far beyond literally copying should the doctrine of equivalents be allowed to run. On that question, at least, *Festo* provides some guidelines. Both of the changes in that case required some degree of reengineering. Yet nothing in the Supreme Court's decision suggests the precise role played in the analysis by findings directed to the extent and cost of reengineering. Nonetheless, the substitution of a nonmagnetic for a magnetic mechanism is likely to require some extensive reworking of other elements of the claim, which could be as extensive as those that are involved with the EchoStar workaround. Moreover, defining "parsing" to include all forms of "analysis" makes it credible to think that there is an element of literal infringement in the claim as well.

All in all, in the absence of some real showing that the defendant stands in a strong position to win the ultimate struggle, it seems unwise to let those modest changes block the expedited contempt procedures. Indeed, even the new hearing on the

51 535 U.S. 722, 731–32 (2002).
52 *Id.* at 728.
53 *Id.* at 729.
54 *Id.* at 733–37.

issue, which was awarded, seems to overestimate the amount of new information that this already heavily litigated case could have generated in another extended trial. The lax standard involved, moreover, carries with it the real risk that, were this change to provoke a full hearing, so too would virtually any other new wrinkle that EchoStar introduced so as to evade yet another claim element. The entire process, when so elongated, raises the real risk that drawn-out proceedings could convert a strong patent right into a compulsory license. In the end, it appears that *KSM* set the correct standard and that Judge Folsom in the district court reached the right result applying that standard. It is only the new movement away from strong property rights in intellectual property that seems to spur the shifts.

V. SCOPE OF INJUNCTION AND DAMAGES

One issue left untouched is how the treatment of sequential injunctions determines the scope of the injunction as applied both to disabling current devices and to prohibiting the marketing of identical ones in the future. The easiest way to start the analysis is to assume that the district court was correct to find that EchoStar's modified device infringed on TiVo's patent. At that point, the relevant calculations are easy. Quite simply, it does not matter whether EchoStar switched devices in the boxes that were already in the field. Both the new and the old devices infringed, so that the use of either of them violates the injunction and adds to the dollar tab.

The situation is less straightforward if one follows the position of the en banc majority and believes it is unclear whether the substitution of the modified design runs afoul of the TiVo patent. As a matter of first principle, it is not proper to grant an injunction against conduct whose legality is yet to be determined. Nor does Rule 65 of the Federal Rules of Civil Procedure leave any room for ambiguity in the order.[55] The correct response is to allow the units to be sold and then to let the award of possible damages abide the ultimate disposition of the case. If those units are found to infringe, then at that time additional damages can be assessed. If not, then nothing further remains to be done.

Unfortunately, on this issue the en banc majority took the position that the failure of EchoStar to challenge the scope of the injunction meant that they waived this objection, so that they were bound by the injunction even with respect to devices that could turn out to be non-infringing.[56] But it is dangerous to imply waivers of this sort when the usual rule is, as the en banc minority argued, that the burden lies on

[55] Fed. R. Civ. P. 65(d)(1): 1) Contents.
Every order granting an injunction and every restraining order must:

(A) state the reasons why it issued;
(B) state its terms specifically; and
(c) describe in reasonable detail – and not by referring to the complaint or other document – the act or acts restrained or required.

[56] *TiVo, en banc.*

the party that wishes to enforce the injunction to see that it applies. The situation, of course, looks still stranger if the en banc minority is in fact correct that the modified device does not infringe at all. Why then enjoin its use in any part?

The confusion is further compounded because the en banc majority took it on itself to uphold the $90 million in contempt against EchoStar for not complying with the injunction.[57] In its view, so long as EchoStar had to comply with both the injunctions on infringement and disablement, it was sufficient that it violated one of the commands even if it complied with the other. That result is quite unproblematic under the district court's view that both EchoStar's original and modified devices infringed. But it is, as the en banc minority pointed out, far more problematic to sustain that award in full when the underlying injunction was itself suspect.[58] There is, I think, little to be gained by going over these arguments in detail because their long-term impact pales in comparison to the key question of sequential injunctions. Once the issue has been vetted, well-advised lawyers will protest early and often the terms of any injunction to make sure that they are not trapped by a novel doctrine of waiver. At that point, procedural slips will be a thing of the past, so that all the attention will be focused where it ought to be: on the key question of sequential harms.

IV. BEYOND *TIVO V. ECHOSTAR*

Given the importance of the question of sequential damages, it should not be surprising that *TiVo* has already generated some subsequent litigation that speaks to the soundness of the decision of the Federal Circuit to jettison its *KSM* decision. Thus in many ways, *nCube Corporation* (now *ARRIS Group, Inc* v. *SeaChange International*) leads to the simple conclusion that the changes that *TiVo* introduced did little more than add yet another chapter to litigation that has been going on for a decade. The situation was in effect yet another rerun of *TiVo*. ARRIS is a firm that supplies technology to the video-on-demand market that uses network connections to reach its customer base. This abstract-sounding technology allows customers to download movies for a fee for display on their own screens. SeaChange International introduced its own technology a short time later, which was found to willfully infringe on the ARRIS patents. After it was hit by the injunction, SeaChange modified its devices in ways that it claimed took it out from under the ARRIS patents; however, ARRIS claimed that these changes were only minor modifications of the original infringing devices. There were nonstop disputes over the scope and significances of the various changes, giving rise to a protracted battle of the experts.

[57] *TiVo, en banc*, at *35.

[58] *TiVo, en banc*, at *24 (Dyk, J, concurring and dissenting in part). "Because it is clear that the sanctions award was based in large part on EchoStar's alleged violation of the infringement provision, the award cannot be sustained based on the alleged violation of the disablement provision alone."

The district court rightly rejected SeaChange's claim that the doctrine of res judicata blocked the ARRIS claims on the ground that the company sought to bring a new theory of liability that it did not present the first time round; the correct response to that claim was that in a single proceeding the plaintiff can redirect its fire when the defendant first concealed information and then altered the structure of its device.[59] It then went through a variety of narrow objections on the evidence, such that by the time all was over, it looked as though the plaintiffs had established a solid case that would have carried the day on the old *KSM* standards, given that there was credible evidence on the matter of colorable differences and strong evidence that the modified product still infringed. At this point, the district court concluded, "In short, based on the record developed to this point, the Court is inclined to find that there are no colorable differences between the infringing ITV system and SeaChange's modified IT product. At the same time, however, the Court recognizes SeaChange's observation at the March 1 hearing that it did not have a full opportunity to present all of the evidence it felt was necessary to provide the Court will [sic] a complete understanding of this issue." And thus the case was set up to hear more information. Perhaps the amount of time given to the initial hearing was insufficient for the purpose, at which point a modest change in the trial schedule could have finished the deal. But the overwhelming impression created by *nCube* is that the older *KSM* formula would have worked just fine in this situation, sparing the lower court from having to figure out what, if any, changes, were required by the reformulation of the rule. On balance, it looks as though not that much will change from the earlier regime, leading to the clear conclusion that longstanding rules should not be changed on the kind of flimsy arguments that persuaded the entire Federal Circuit to march off in a new and unwanted direction.

CONCLUSION

As has often been remarked, attitudes toward patent protection have ebbed and flowed over the past century. In the last decade or so the Supreme Court and those courts below it have taken a somewhat hostile attitude toward patent protection, resulting in limitations on both the ability to gain injunctive relief against strangers and the ability of patentees to enforce license agreements with their trading partners. The decision of the Federal Circuit in *TiVo* v. *EchoStar* is in harmony with those views. In earlier times, the high respect for patents was translated into a system that gave strong protection against infringement and encouraged the formation of licensing contracts that maximized gains from trade. The newer approach tends to put less weight on the use of strong property and contract rights to stimulate both innovation and commercialization, and far greater weight on the creation of a larger public domain to facilitate the use of those inventions and technologies that have

59 *Id.* at 20.

already been created. There is no question that any sensible system of patent law has to contain both a large private and a large public component, and the key question is what it always has been: how best to determine their relative sizes.

On this score I cast my lot with those who think that the balance should, in doubtful cases, be aligned with product development and commercialization,[60] as opposed to thinking that some self-referential deontological theory could do the job.[61] The latter types of theory give little indication of how to deal with error and uncertainty and thus have little or no role to play in dealing with remedial issues. But once the focus is on how to make the system work, it becomes clear that, for the mundane virtues of simplicity and clarity, the district court in *TiVo* was correct in applying the two-part test in *KSM* to those cases in which a defendant seeks to design-around a valid patent when hit with an injunction against further infringement. The issue here is a close one in many regards, which is why the initial presumption concerning the role of the relative sizes of the private and public domains plays so large a role in its resolution. That said, any effort to minimize the errors of over- or under-enforcement must in the end take into account the substantial risk that a defendant who has once infringed a patent may have strong incentives to do it a second time, if the law will permit it. It is for that reason that, in cases of colorable resemblances, the burden of proof should shift to the defendant to exonerate itself. In the end, therefore, the more pro-property approach of the district court offers sounder reconciliation of the relevant interests than either of the more pro-defendant positions set out by both the majority and minority positions in the Federal Circuit.

60 *See, e.g.*, F. Scott Kieff, *Coordination, Property, and Intellectual Property: An Unconventional Approach to Anticompetitive Effects and Downstream Access*, 56 EMORY L. REV. 327 (2006); F. Scott Kieff, *Property Rights and Property Rules for Commercializing Inventions*, 85 MINN. L. REV. 697 (2001) (comparative institutional analysis of patent-enforcing rules).

61 Margaret JANE RADIN, REINTERPRETING PROPERTY (1993) (championing a Hegelian theory of personhood); Jeremy Waldron, *From Authors to Copiers: Individual Rights and Social Values in Intellectual Property*, 68 CHI.-KENT L. REV. 841, 866 (1993). *See generally*, Justin Hughes, *The Philosophy of Intellectual Property*, 77 GEO. L.J. 287 (1988) (reviewing philosophical approaches). The great danger of these deontological theories is that they make light of the consideration of scarcity. They may explain why any individual may wish to use the property, but they do not explain why that person can exclude others, for which a more functional explanation is needed. For a recent reprise on this dispute, see Shyamkrishna Balganesh, *The Obligatory Structure of Copyright Law: Unbundling the Wrong of Copying*, 125 HARV. L. REV. 1664 (2012), to which I reply at Richard A. Epstein, *Unifying Copyright Law: An Instrumental's Response to Shyamkrishna Balganesh*, 125 HARV. L. REV. F. 120 (2012).

Index